Dear Student,

The current employment environment presents difficult, but not insurmountable, challenges. The good news is that you're already on the right path; you just need now to take full advantage of it.

To begin, what are the challenges? As of this writing, the U.S. unemployment rate hovers around 9.2 percent, with unemployment among people in their twenties closer to 20 percent. The employment situation will likely improve by the time you graduate, but not for everyone. According to the U.S. Bureau of Labor Statistics, job growth will be greatest for highly skilled workers holding jobs that require a 4-year degree and specialized training. Ironically, job growth will also be strong for very low-skill, low-paying jobs. These are not jobs, however, that you want.

Where did the midskill jobs go? Either they went overseas to cheaper labor sources or they were replaced by information systems. Bank lobbies that once held dozens of workers now have two or three tellers and account administrators. Robots replaced painters on the production line. And for every 100 painters that worked in the factory, one or two robot technicians are needed today.

When you entered the university, you started down a pathway toward one of those high-skilled jobs. However, it is unlikely that there will be jobs for every reasonably successful graduate of every 4-year school. You do not have the luxury of majoring in just anything. If you're reading this book, you are most likely a business student, which means, again, that you're on a promising pathway.

It is dangerous to assume, however, that there will be a job for every reasonably successful business school graduate. Instead, assume that when you graduate you will be competing with several others for the same job. You compete not only with the person sitting next to you in class, but also with students in business schools throughout the United States and beyond.

So, how do you best prepare for that competition? Chapter 1 discusses the recommendations of two highly regarded, well-respected sources. Their bottom line is that you need the skills to succeed as a nonroutine, symbolic worker. You need to excel at systems thinking, abstract thinking, collaboration, and experimentation. Chapter 1 explains these in more detail.

As you will learn, this course is one of the best in the business school for learning those skills. You may be surprised to learn that. In spite of what you may think, this is not a computer class. Instead, it is a class about how organizations use information systems (including, usually, a computer) to achieve their strategy. You will need to learn technology, but the deeper learning is how to use that technology to help your employer achieve its goals and objectives.

People who can do that will play key roles in solving healthcare problems, in increasing the efficiency of government, and in enabling organizations to compete on a global scale. And, they will have interesting, well-paying, and socially beneficial jobs.

Congratulations for the decisions you have made to place you on the pathway you're on. You're off to a good start; now double down and take advantage of every opportunity you can. Read the book; read the Guides, the two-page spreads with many hints about using your knowledge to get a job. When the exercises say, "formulate your answer to this question in a 1-minute statement you could use in a job interview," do it.

I wish you, as an emerging business professional, the very best success!

Sincerely,

David Kroenke

The Guides

Each chapter includes three unique **guides** that focus on current issues in information systems. In each chapter, one of the guides focuses on an ethical issue in business. The other two guides focus on the application of the chapter's contents to other business aspects. The content of each guide is designed to stimulate thought, discussion, and active participation to help YOU develop your problem-solving skills and become a better business professional.

Learning Aids for Students

We have structured this book so you can maximize the benefit from the time you spend reading it. As shown in the following table, each chapter includes various learning aids to help you succeed in this course.

Resource	Description	Benefit	Example
Guides	Each chapter includes three guides that focus on current issues in information systems. One of the three in each chapter addresses ethics.	Stimulate thought and discussion. Address ethics once per chapter. Help develop your problem-solving skills.	Social Recruiting, p. 290
Chapter-Introduction Business Example	Each chapter begins with a description of a business situation that motivates the need for the chapter's contents. Two businesses are used: GearUp and Fox Lake Country Club.	Understand the relevance of the chapter's content by applying it to a business situation.	Chapter 1, "Fired," p. 2; Chapter 8, "She said WHAT?" p. 257
Query-Based Chapter Format	Each chapter starts with a list of questions; each major heading is a question; the Active Review contains tasks for you to perform to demonstrate you are able to answer the questions.	Use the questions to manage your time, guide your study, and review for exams.	Chapter 2, starting on p. 32 with "Q1 What are the two key characteristics of collaboration?"
Using MIS InClass	Each chapter of this text includes an exercise called "Using MIS InClass." This feature contains exercises, projects, and questions for you and a group of your fellow students to perform in class. Some of those exercises can be done in a single class period; others span several class sections with out-of-class activities in-between.	Understand how the material in the chapter applies to everyday situations.	Using MIS InClass 1, "Information Systems and Online Dating," p. 12
2022?	Each chapter concludes with a discussion of how the concepts, technology, and systems described in that chapter might change by 2022.	Learn to anticipate changes in technology and recognize how those changes may impact the future business environment.	Chapter 5, NoSQL, p. 164; Chapter 7, Islands of Automation, Version 2.0, p. 244
Active Review	This review provides a set of activities for you to perform to demonstrate you are able to answer the primary questions addressed by the chapter.	After reading the chapter, use the Active Review to check your comprehension. Use for class and exam preparation.	Chapter 2, Active Review, p. 68
Using Your Knowledge	These exercises ask you to take your new knowledge one step further and apply it to a practice problem.	Test your critical-thinking skills.	Chapter 3, Questions 1–6, pp. 99–100

Resource	Description	Benefit	Example
Collaboration Exercises	These exercises and cases ask you to collaborate with a group of fellow students, using collaboration tools introduced in Chapter 2.	Practice working with colleagues toward a stated goal.	Chapter 5, pp. 172–173
Case Studies	Each chapter includes a case study at the end of the chapter.	Apply newly acquired knowledge to real-world situations.	Case Study 4, "The Apple of Your i," p. 137 Case Study 6, "Turbulent Air in Those Azure Clouds," p. 210
Application Exercises	These exercises ask you to solve situations using spreadsheet (Excel) or database (Access) applications.	Develop your computer skills.	Exercise 1-1, p. 468; Exercise 7-1, p. 477
International Dimension	Module at the end of the text that discusses international aspects of MIS. Includes the importance of international IS, the localization of system components, the roles of functional and cross-functional, international applications, supply chain management, and challenges of international systems development.	Understand the international implications and applications of the chapters' content.	Page 452
Videos	Fox Lake chapter-opening scenarios for Chapters 7–12 are depicted in a series of short dramatizations that emphasize the importance of the chapter content.	Videos increase interest and relevance of introductory cases.	Available in MyMISLab
MyMISLab™	MyMISLab contains a Microsoft Office 2010 simulation environment with tutorials, SharePoint collaboration tools and assignments, student assessments, and classroom videos.	Expands the classroom experience with valuable hands-on activities and tools.	www.mymislab.com

Using MIS

Fifth Edition

David M. Kroenke

PEARSON

Boston   Columbus   Indianapolis   New York   San Francisco   Upper Saddle River
Amsterdam   Cape Town   Dubai   London   Madrid   Milan   Munich   Paris   Montreal   Toronto
Delhi   Mexico City   Sao Paulo   Sydney   Hong Kong   Seoul   Singapore   Taipei   Tokyo

Dedicated to CJ, Carter, and Charlotte

Editorial Director: Sally Yagan
Executive Editor: Bob Horan
Director of Development: Steve Deitmer
Development Editor: Laura Town
Editorial Project Manager: Kelly Loftus
Editorial Assistant: Ashlee Bradbury
Director of Marketing: Maggie Moylan
Senior Marketing Manager: Anne Fahlgren
Senior Managing Editor: Judy Leale
Senior Operations Supervisor: Arnold Vila
Operations Specialist: Maura Zaldivar
Creative Director: Blair Brown
Sr. Art Director/Design Supervisor: Janet Slowik

Interior and Cover Designer: Karen Quigley
Interior Illustrations: Simon Alicea
Cover Icon Art: Simon Alicea
Cover iPad Photo: Nikada/iStock
Editorial Media Project Manager: Allison Longley
Production Media Project Manager: Lisa Rinaldi
Full-Service Project Management: Jennifer Welsch/Bookmasters
Composition: Integra Software Services Pvt. Ltd.
Printer/Binder: Courier/Kendallville
Cover Printer: Lehigh-Phoenix Color/Hagerstown
Text Font: 10/12 Utopia

Credits and acknowledgments borrowed from other sources and reproduced, with permission, in this textbook appear on the appropriate page within text.

Microsoft® and Windows® are registered trademarks of the Microsoft Corporation in the U.S.A. and other countries. Screen shots and icons reprinted with permission from the Microsoft Corporation. This book is not sponsored or endorsed by or affiliated with the Microsoft Corporation.

Library of Congress Cataloging-in-Publication Data
Kroenke, David.
    Using MIS / David M. Kroenke.—5th ed.
       p. cm.
    Includes bibliographical references and index.
    ISBN 978-0-13-266267-3 (pbk. : alk. paper)
1. Management information systems.   I. Title.
    HD30.213.K76 2013
    658.4'038011—dc23

                            2011045839

10 9 8 7 6 5 4 3 2 1

ISBN 10:   0-13-266267-1
ISBN 13: 978-0-13-266267-3

Brief Contents

Describes key skills for business professionals and how they relate to this course. Defines *MIS, information systems,* and *information.*

Describes characteristics, criteria for success, and the primary purposes of collaboration. Discusses components of collaboration IS and describes collaboration for communication and content sharing. Illustrates use of Office 365 and other collaboration tools.

Describes reasons why organizations create and use information systems: to gain competitive advantage, to solve problems, and to support decisions.

Describes the manager's essentials of hardware and software technology. Discusses mobile operating systems and the renewed importance of client-server architecture.

Explores database fundamentals, applications, modeling, and design. Discusses the entity-relationship model. Explains the role of Access and enterprise DBMS products. Describes NoSQL databases.

Defines essential data communication concepts and terms. Describes the Internet. Discusses technology used by Web servers and three-tier architecture.

Discusses workgroup, enterprise, and interenterprise IS. Describes problems of information silos and cross-functional solutions. Presents CRM, ERP, and EAI. Discusses ERP vendors and implementation challenges.

Describes components of social media IS (SMIS) and explains how SMIS can contribute to organizational strategy. Discusses the theory of social capital and the role of SMIS in the hyper-social organization. Explains Web 2.0 and ways organizations manage the risks of SMIS.

Describes business intelligence and knowledge management, including reporting systems, data mining, and knowledge management systems.

Discusses the need for BPM and BPM process. Introduces BPMN. Differentiates between processes and information systems. Presents SDLC stages. Explains keys to success for process and IS development.

Describes the role, structure, and function of the IS department; the role of the CIO and CTO; outsourcing; and related topics.

Describes organizational response to information security: security threats, policy, and safeguards.

Contents

PART 2: Information Technology   103

4: Hardware and Software   104

PART 3: Using IS for Competitive Advantage   213

7: Structured Processes and Information Systems   214

9: Business Intelligence Systems 296

PART 4: Information Systems Management   341

10: Business Process and Information Systems Development   342

12: Information Security Management 412

Preface to Instructors

Why This Fifth Edition, Now?

The past 12 months have been one of the most exciting years for MIS that I can recall. Consider these data points:

- Organizations lease servers from Rackspace for a penny an hour, programmatically configure 1,000 of them, and 3 hours later programmatically release them—for $30.
- Apple continued its string of innovations with iOS 5, Lion, and iCloud.
- Microsoft delivered Office 365, its hosted collaboration toolset.
- Facebook, Twitter, and others pushed NoSQL databases to new heights.
- Google bought Motorola Mobility with a third of its cash.
- The explosive growth of portable devices caused analysts to ask if the PC is dead.
- An organizational presence on Twitter, Facebook, and LinkedIn has become mandatory.

And meanwhile,

- On November, 29, 2010, Amazon.com customers ordered 13.7 million items, worldwide, an average of 158 items *per second.*

These developments, and the organizational responses to them, redouble my gratitude to Pearson for publishing this text as an annual edition. Even so, this pace reminds me of Carrie Fisher's statement, "The problem with instantaneous gratification is that it's just not fast enough."

Table 1 lists the changes in this Fifth Edition. Major changes include replacing the FlexTime case in Chapters 1–6 with a new case of a company named GearUp, an online event sales startup, which has a business model that better serves the discussion of recent MIS developments. Another substantial change is that 7 of the 12 end-of-chapter cases are new. In the past, I didn't emphasize the case studies because I believe they so quickly become outdated. However, now that we're publishing an annual edition, I decided to revamp them with what I hope is useful, informative, and always current content. I'll remove outdated material and cases each year.

Both Chapter 2 (Collaboration) and Chapter 8 (Social Media) are brand new, complete rewrites. Chapter 2 contains a new model of the roles for collaboration and includes a new section on the use of Office 365. Even if students do not employ Office 365 in their projects, I believe that it is important for them to know its features and functions because it is the future direction of Office.

Chapter 8 has been rewritten to focus entirely on fundamentals. Students do not need this text or our classes to learn how to use Facebook, Twitter, foursquare, or any other contemporary social media site. Rather, they need to know how organizations can use social media to accomplish their strategies. The new Chapter 8 discusses the components of social media IS (SMIS); the ways in which SMIS contribute to organizational strategy; an overview of social capital; a discussion of hyper-social organizations and the dynamic process organizations employ to become hyper-social; and, finally, a discussion of the ways that organizations manage the risks of social media, especially by developing a social media policy.

Table 1 lists other changes as well. A good many of them were required to incorporate the increasing importance of the cloud. Others were made to focus on the importance of process quality and process improvements. Chapter 4 has been

Table 1 Changes in the Fifth Edition

Chapter or Part	Change	Chapter or Part	Change
Parts 1 & 2	Replaced FlexTime with GearUp.	Chapter 7	New process orientation. Introduction of structured versus dynamic process types. Discussion of process quality and role of IS in improving process quality.
Chapter 1	Revised definition of *MIS* to focus on strategy. Refined definition of *data* and clarified data/information distinction. New Amazon.com case.	Chapter 8	Complete rewrite to modernize (after 1 year, **modernize!**). New discussions of SMIS, SMIS and organizational strategy, and hyper-social organizations. New analogy in 2022.
Chapter 2	Restructured for clarity and relevance in 2012. New criteria for collaboration success. Demonstrated how to use Office 365/Lync. New dogfooding case.	Chapter 9	New guided discussion of a BI reporting solution to GearUp's Chapter 5 problem. Rewritten to update and improve terminology.
Chapter 3	Revised strategy focus to fit revised definition of MIS.	Chapter 10	New discussion of process quality and impact of cloud servers on development by 2022.
Chapter 4	iPad development dilemma for GearUp. Mobile IS; reemergence of client/server. iOS and Lion. New Apple of Your i case.	Chapter 11	Shortened to make room for new content in other chapters. New iPad development case.
Chapter 5	Dynamo, Bigtable, Cassandra. NoSQL case.	Chapter 12	Rewritten to clean up terminology problems and to modernize. Removed discussion of digital signatures and digital certificates to make space. New security case.
Chapter 6	New discussion of why the cloud is inevitable (for most) and SaaS, PaaS, and IaaS. Microsoft's cloud problem case.	International Dimension	GearUp goes international.

updated to include mobile operating systems as well as the reemergence of client-server computing on mobile devices like iOS.

As you look at this list, do not panic. You will not need to revolutionize your course. The same 12 chapters appear in the same order, and although Chapters 2 and 8 are brand new, it will not be difficult to adapt to them. The remaining changes use the basic themes from prior editions, but those themes are dressed in the most contemporary settings and examples that I could find, as of August 2011.

To reiterate from the Preface from the fourth edition, I believe we need to make these annual adaptations because the delays associated with a 2-year revision cycle are too long for the students' benefit. Text materials that I develop starting in May of one year are published in January of the next year and are first used by students in September—a minimum 16-month delay. In its second year, by the time the students read the text, the materials are from 28 to 36 months old.

By the way, why wait for September? This content is perishable; like farmer's produce that was just picked today, why let all of this fresh, plump, content fade in the stall until next August? Why not use it in June? Just a thought from the farmer.

Importance of MIS

I continue to believe we can enter the classroom with confidence that we are teaching the single most important course in the business school.[1] The rationale for this bold statement is presented in Chapter 1, starting on page 4. In brief, the argument relies on two observations. First, because of nearly free data storage and data communications, businesses are increasingly finding and, more important, increasingly *required* to find innovative applications for information systems. The incorporation of Facebook and Twitter into marketing systems is an obvious example, but this example is only the tip of the iceberg. For at least the next 10 years, every business professional will, at the minimum, need to be able to assess the efficacy of proposed IS applications. To excel, business professionals will need not only to assess, but also to define innovative IS applications. Further, professionals who want to emerge from the middle ranks of management will, at some point, need to demonstrate the ability to manage projects that develop these innovative information systems.

Such skills will not be optional. Businesses that fail to create systems that take advantage of nearly free data storage and communication will fall prey to the competition that can create such systems. So, too, will business professionals.

The second premise for the singular importance of the MIS class relies on the work of Robert Reich, former Secretary of Labor for the Clinton administration. In *The Work of Nations*,[2] Reich identified four essential skills for knowledge workers in the twenty-first century:

- Abstract thinking
- Systems thinking
- Collaboration
- Experimentation

For reasons set out in Chapter 1, beginning on page 4, I believe the MIS course is the single best course in the curriculum for learning these four key skills.

Today's Role for Professors

When I first began teaching many years ago, I was the possessor of the knowledge, and my goal was to impart my knowledge to my students. I would give detailed, fact-filled, and sometimes long lectures; students would gratefully take notes. Class attendance was high because students needed class notes to succeed. I had no PowerPoints to share and no way to share them if I had. Library resources were limited and woefully dated.

Today, that environment is gone, and thankfully so. But this changed environment has, I believe, changed my role with the students. Students don't need me for definitions; they have the Web for that. They don't need me for detailed notes; they have the PowerPoints. Consequently, when I attempt to give long and detailed lectures, student attendance falls. And, this situation is even more dramatic for online courses.

So, what is my role? These circumstances have made me a coach. No longer the sole possessor of the knowledge, I am the person who helps the students apply MIS knowledge to their goals and objectives. I have become more like the track coach than the chemistry professor of the past. Accordingly, my class sessions have changed. I no longer attempt to give a 50- or 90-minute lecture. Instead, I present certain materials, or ask the students to do so, and then arrange projects and in-class activities to reinforce the material just discussed. Present a bit more. Rinse and repeat.

---

[1] The letter to the student on the back of the front cover has also been rewritten to reenforce this opinion, and I hope you will direct the students' attention to it. Our students are on the right path, but they need to take advantage of this course to take the next keys steps.

[2] Robert B. Reich, *The Work of Nations* (New York: Alfred A. Knopf, 1991), p. 229.

The structure of this edition of *Using MIS* facilitates that new role. In addition to Using MIS InClass, each chapter includes a collaboration exercise that students use for team projects both inside and outside of class. As with earlier editions, each chapter contains three guides that describe practical implications of the chapter contents that can be used for small in-class exercises. Finally, this edition contains 28 Office application exercises (see page 468).

GearUp and Fox Lake Country Club Cases

The chapters in this fifth edition are introduced by two running cases. Chapters 1 through 6 are introduced by problems and opportunities at GearUp, an online daily-sale site that features sporting goods. Chapters 7 through 12 are introduced by problems and opportunities at Fox Lake Country Club.

The goal of these cases is to increase student interest in the application of the concepts, technology, and systems of each chapter. GearUp is a hot new startup that sells limited numbers of sporting goods during 3-day, Internet sales events (similar to Woot). It needs to reduce its operational expenses and develop an iPad application, and its employees need the knowledge of Chapters 1 through 6 to do so.

Fox Lake Country Club decides to increase its revenue by starting a new wedding events business. It does so, however, without thinking through the consequences on enterprise processes, particularly processes that concern facilities use and maintenance. Fox Lake, like many small companies, does not properly manage its IS resources and suffers from the consequences.

According to Marilla Svinicki,[3] a leading researcher on student learning at the University of Texas, student retention increases when students are emotionally involved with the material. Thus, in these vignettes I attempt to bring out the human side of the story in a way that will capture the students' emotion. Chapter 1, in fact, begins with an employee being fired because she did not possess the four skills identified by Reich.

2022?

Every chapter concludes with a question labeled "2022?" This section presents my guesses about how the subject of that chapter is likely to change between now and 2022. Clearly, if I had a crystal ball that would give good answers to that question, I wouldn't be writing textbooks. . . . However, I make what I hope is a reasonable stab at an answer. I suspect you will have different ideas, and we can hope that our students will have different ideas as well. The goal is to cause the students to think, to wonder, to assess, and to project about future technology.

Why Might You Want Your Students to Use SharePoint?

When I began to teach collaboration, the next question was how to assess it. Collaboration assessment is not simply finding out which students did the bulk of the work. It also involves assessing feedback and iteration; that is, identifying who provided feedback, who benefitted from the feedback that was provided, and how well the work product evolved over time.

My students and I were experimenting with different collaborative tools when I stumbled into an unanticipated benefit. I discovered that Microsoft SharePoint automatically maintains detailed records of all changes that have been made to a SharePoint site. It tracks

---

[3] Marilla Svinicki, *Learning and Motivation in the Postsecondary Classroom* (Bolton, MA: Anker Publishing, 2004).

document versions, along with the date, time, and version author. It also maintains records of user activity—who visited the site, how often, what site features they visited, what work they did, what contributions they made, and so forth. That data made it easy to determine which students were making sincere efforts to collaborate by giving and receiving critical feedback throughout the project assignment and which students were making a single contribution 5 minutes before midnight the day before the project was due.

Additionally, SharePoint has built-in facilities for team surveys, team wikis, and member blogs, as well as document and list libraries. All of this capability is backed up by a rich and flexible security system. To be clear, I do not use SharePoint to run my class; we use Blackboard for that purpose. I am, however, requiring my students to use SharePoint for their collaborative projects. A side benefit is that they can claim, rightfully, experience and knowledge of using SharePoint in their job interviews.

You might want to use Office 365 as well because it includes SharePoint Online as well as Lync and hosted Exchange. However, Microsoft's intentions for Office 365 in education are unclear as of September 2011. Please see www.Office365InEducation.com for the current status and most up-to-date information.

Why Are the Chapters Organized by Questions?

The chapters of *Using MIS* are organized by questions. According to Professor Svinicki, we should not give reading assignments like, "Read pages 50 through 70." The reason is that today's students need help organizing their time. With such a reading assignment, they will fiddle with pages 50 through 70 while texting their friends, surfing the Internet, and listening to their iPod. After 30 or 45 minutes, they will conclude they have fiddled enough and will believe they have completed the assignment.

Instead, she states we should give the students a list of questions and tell them their job is to answer those questions, treating pages 50 through 70 as a resource for that purpose. When the students can answer the questions, they have finished the assignment.

Using that philosophy, every chapter in this text begins with a list of questions. Each major heading in the chapter is one of those questions, and the Active Review at the end of each chapter provides students a set of actions to take to demonstrate that they are able to answer the questions. Since learning this approach from Professor Svinicki, I have used it in my class and have found that it works exceedingly well.

What Are the Guides?

Each chapter of this text includes three two-page essays called "Guides." In each chapter, one of the guides addresses ethical aspects of the use of the chapter's content. The other two guides pertain to security, problem solving, managing contrarian employees ("opposing forces"), and reflecting on the implications of the chapter's content on industry or society.

Each chapter includes an ethics guide because I strongly believe it is important to address ethics repeatedly, and not just once in the "ethics chapter." With an ethics guide in each chapter, I address ethics every week, in repeated small doses. That repetition underlines the importance of ethical considerations and behavior in business.

I use the guides in class to break up my lecture. I have the students read the guide in class and then answer the questions in small groups of three or four students. I then ask some of the groups to report their conclusions to the rest of the class.

Ideas and suggestions for answers to the guides' discussion questions are included in the Teaching Guidelines in the Annotated Instructor's Edition and also at the Online Instructor Resource Center for this text. For more on the Teaching Guidelines, see the description on page xxxv of this preface.

How Does This Book Differ from *Experiencing MIS* and from *Processes, Systems, and Information*?

In addition to *Using MIS,* I've written an MIS text entitled *Experiencing MIS* and coauthored with Earl McKinney of Bowling Green State University a third MIS text entitled *Processes, Systems, and Information: An Introduction to MIS.* These three texts provide three different perspectives for teaching this class. I am committed to all three books and plan to revise them all for some time.

The principal difference between *Using MIS* and *Experiencing MIS* is that the latter is modular in design and has a more "in-your-face" attitude about MIS. Modularity has a role and place, but not every class needs or appreciates the flexibility and brevity that a modular text offers. In *Using MIS,* I have endeavored to take advantage of continuity and to build the discussion and knowledge gradually through the chapter sequence, in many places taking advantage of knowledge from prior chapters.

Processes, Systems, and Information (PSI) represents a third approach to this class. *PSI* is structured around business processes, has a strong ERP emphasis, and includes two chapters on SAP as well as two chapter tutorials for using the SAP Alliance Global Bikes simulation. My coauthor, Earl, has taught SAP for many years and has extensive experience in teaching others how to use the Global Bikes simulation.

My goal in writing these three books is to offer professors a choice of approach. I sincerely hope that one of these three books will fit your style and objectives for teaching this increasingly important class.

Supplements

For Students

CourseSmart. CourseSmart eTextbooks were developed for students looking to save on required or recommended textbooks. Students simply select their eText by title or author and purchase immediate access to the content for the duration of the course using any major credit card. With a CourseSmart eText, students can search for specific keywords or page numbers, take notes online, print out reading assignments that incorporate lecture notes, and bookmark important passages for later review. For more information or to purchase a CourseSmart eTextbook, visit *www.coursesmart.com.*

For Instructors

The following supplements are available to ease and improve your experience teaching the course:

- **Online Instructor's Resource Center.** The online resource center (accessible through *www.pearsonhighered.com/kroenke*) includes the following supplements: Instructor's Manual, Test Item File, TestGen, TestGen conversions in WebCT and Blackboard-ready files, PowerPoint Presentations, and Image Library (text art).
- **Instructor's Manual.** Prepared by Roberta Roth of the University of Northern Iowa, the manual includes answers to all review and discussion questions, exercises, and case questions, plus teaching tips and lecture notes. It is a convenient source of answers as well as material to enhance lectures and classroom teaching.
- **Test Item File.** This Test Item File, prepared by ANSR Source, Inc., contains approximately 1,500 questions, including multiple-choice, true/false, and essay. Each question is followed by the correct answer, the learning objective it ties to, page reference, AACSB category, and difficulty rating.

- **PowerPoint Presentations.** Prepared by Stephen Loy of Eastern Kentucky University, the PowerPoints highlight text learning objectives and key topics and serve as an excellent aid for classroom presentations and lectures.
- **Image Library.** This collection of the figures and tables from the text offers another aid for classroom presentations and PowerPoint slides.
- **TestGen.** Pearson Education's test-generating software is available from *www.pearsonhighered.com/irc*. The software is PC/MAC compatible and preloaded with all of the Test Item File questions. You can manually or randomly view test questions and drag and drop to create a test. You can add or modify test-bank questions as needed. Our TestGens are converted for use in Blackboard and WebCT. These conversions can be found on the Instructor's Resource Center. Conversions to Moodle, D2L, or Angel can be requested through your local Pearson sales representative.
- **SharePoint.** As part of MyMISLab, Pearson is pleased to host SharePoint sites for use by your students. At your request, we will create a site collection for your students. You will be given administrator privileges for that collection, and you can create subsites for sections, teams, and projects. Each collection will include templates for students to use when answering the collaboration exercises at the end of each chapter. Contact your sales representative to learn more about using SharePoint in your class.
- **MyMISLab™ (www.mymislab.com).** MyMISLab is an easy-to-use online tool that personalizes course content and provides robust assessment and reporting to measure individual and class performance. All of the resources you need for course success are in one place—flexible and easily adapted for your course experience. Students can purchase access to MyMISLab with a Pearson eText of all chapters or without a Pearson eText by visiting *www.mymislab.com*. They can also purchase an access card packaged with the text from *www.pearsonhighered.com* at a reduced price.

AACSB Learning Standards Tags

What Is the AACSB?

AACSB is a nonprofit corporation of educational institutions, corporations, and other organizations devoted to the promotion and improvement of higher education in business administration and accounting. A collegiate institution offering degrees in business administration or accounting may volunteer for AACSB accreditation review. The AACSB makes initial accreditation decisions and conducts periodic reviews to promote continuous quality improvement in management education. Pearson Education is a proud member of the AACSB and is pleased to provide advice to help you apply AACSB Learning Standards.

What Are AACSB Learning Standards?

One of the criteria for AACSB accreditation is the quality of the curricula. Although no specific courses are required, the AACSB expects a curriculum to include learning experiences in such areas as:

- Communication Abilities
- Ethical Understanding and Reasoning Abilities
- Analytic Skills
- Use of Information Technology
- Dynamics of the Global Economy
- Multicultural and Diversity Understanding
- Reflective Thinking Skills

These seven categories are AACSB Learning Standards. Questions that test skills relevant to these standards are tagged with the appropriate standard. For example, a question testing the moral questions associated with externalities would receive the Ethical Reasoning tag.

How Can I Use These Tags?

Tagged questions help you measure whether students are grasping the course content that aligns with AACSB guidelines. In addition, the tagged questions may help to identify potential applications of these skills. This, in turn, may suggest enrichment activities or other educational experiences to help students achieve these goals.

Acknowledgments

I wish to thank Carey Cole at James Madison University for serving as the community proctor for professors who are using our SharePoint program. Carey has helped dozens of universities and thousands of students to successful employ SharePoint in this MIS class. Thanks, too, to Carey and his Fall 2011 MIS classes for testing some of the material in this edition. I am especially grateful to Earl McKinney at Bowling Green State University for many interesting conversations on the role and interrelationship of processes, IS, and information. Earl also reviewed and tested several of the chapters in this edition.

Many thanks to Randy Boyle, author of *Applied Information Security*, coauthor, with Ray Panko, of *Corporate Computer Security*, and professor at the University of Utah for numerous conversations, ideas, and helpful hints for the new treatment of security in Chapter 12. Thanks to John Hupp of Columbus State University for fascinating discussions on the role of games for student learning and retention. Stay tuned for more from John! A special thanks to my friends and colleagues with whom I maintain active correspondence about this course, especially David Auer at Western Washington University, Jami Cotler at Siena University, Bob Grauer at the University of Miami, and Rick Mathieu at James Madison.

At Microsoft, I'm grateful for the continuing support from Steve Fox, who has provided invaluable insight and access to SharePoint, Office 365, and Azure. I also thank Rob Howard at Microsoft for many ideas and thoughts about the best uses of SharePoint and SharePoint workflows. All of us at Pearson are thankful, too, to Kent Foster, for the support he has given us over the years in making Microsoft products and technology available to professors. I thank Don Nilson, my coauthor on the text *Office 365 in Business* for many helpful discussions on cloud-based security as well as best practices on the use of Lync, hosted Exchange, and Outlook.

This book is produced through the collaborative effort of an incredible team of people without whose unflagging support this annual edition would be impossible. Bob Horan, my editor now for 10 years, has provided invaluable guidance, support, and encouragement for all of my MIS books. It has been my great good fortune to work with Bob this past decade! Laura Town is the development editor on all of my MIS books and I am deeply grateful for her support, and her ability to successfully and gracefully manage several complicated MIS projects at the same time. Kelly Loftus is the senior editorial project manager for MIS at Pearson, and Kelly's ability to manage hundreds of details involving many disparate team members and production groups is the key to bringing these several MIS books together on time! It is no overstatement to say that it would be impossible for us to publish this annual edition without the dedication, commitment (and long hours) of both Laura and Kelly.

Thanks as well to Janet Slowik, art director, and her team for the attention to details that makes this book interesting and attractive. Finally, I thank Jen Welsch of

Bookmasters for managing the production and printing of the book. I think Jen and Bookmasters must have done at least a dozen editions of my books by now and it's always been a pleasure to work with her and this dedicated and professional group.

No textbook makes its way into the hands of students without the active involvement of the dedicated and professional sales force. I thank the Pearson sales team, and especially Anne Fahlgren, the marketing manager for this text. Note: Anne is also the author of the Facebook entry that introduces Chapter 8.

Finally, thanks to my wife Lynda, for her untiring love and support.

David Kroenke
Seattle, Washington

Thanks to Our Reviewers

The following people deserve special recognition for their review work on this and previous editions of the book—for their careful reading, thoughtful and insightful comments, sensitive criticism, and for their willingness to follow up with email conversations, many lengthy, when necessary. Their collaboration on this project is truly appreciated.

Dennis Adams, *University of Houston, Main*

Heather Adams, *University of Colorado*

Hans-Joachim Adler, *University of Texas, Dallas*

Mark Alexander, *Indiana Wesleyan University*

Paul Ambrose, *University of Wisconsin, Whitewater*

Craig Anderson, *Augustana College*

Laura Atkins, *James Madison University*

Cynthia Barnes, *Lamar University*

Reneta Barneva, *SUNY Fredonia*

Michael Bartolacci, *Penn State Lehigh Valley*

Ozden Bayazit, *Central Washington University*

Jack Becker, *University of North Texas*

Paula Bell, *Lock Haven University*

Doug Bickerstaff, *Eastern Washington University*

Hossein Bidgoli, *California State University, Bakersfield*

James Borden, *Villanova University*

Mari Buche, *Michigan Technological University*

Thomas Case, *Georgia Southern University*

Thomas Cavaiani, *Boise State University*

Vera Cervantez, *Collin County Community College*

Siew Chan, *University of Massachusetts, Boston*

Andrea Chandler, *independent consultant*

Joey Cho, *Utah State University*

Jimmy Clark, *Austin Community College*

Tricia Clark, *Penn State University, Capital Campus*

Daniel Connolly, *University of Denver*

Jeff Corcoran, *Lasell College*

Jami Cotler, *Siena University*

Stephen Crandell, *Myers University*

Michael Cummins, *Georgia Institute of Technology*

Mel Damodaran, *University of Houston, Victoria*

Charles Davis, *University of St. Thomas*

Roy Dejoie, *Purdue University*

Carol DesJardins, *St. Claire Community College*

Dawna Dewire, *Babson College*

Michael Doherty, *Marian College of Fond du Lac*

Mike Doherty, *University of Wyoming*

Richard Dowell, *The Citadel*

Chuck Downing, *University of Northern Illinois*

Dave Dulany, *Aurora University*

Charlene Dykman, *University of St. Thomas*

William Eddins, *York College*

Lauren Eder, *Rider University*

Kevin Lee Elder, *Georgia Southern University*

Patrick Fan, *Virginia Polytechnic Institute and State University*

Badie Farah, *Eastern Michigan University*

M. Farkas, *Fairfield University*

Lawrence Feidelman, *Florida Atlantic University*

Daniel Fischmar, *Westminster College*

Robert W. Folden, *Texas A&M University*

Charles Bryan Foltz, *University of Tennessee at Martin*

Jonathan Frank, *Suffolk University*

Jonathan Frankel, *University of Massachusetts, Boston Harbor*

Linda Fried, *University of Colorado, Denver*

William H. Friedman, *University of Central Arkansas*

Sharyn Gallagher, *University of Massachusetts, Lowell*

Beena George, *University of St. Thomas*

Biswadip Ghosh, *Metropolitan State College of Denver*

Dawn Giannoni, *Nova Southeastern University*

Steven Gordon, *Babson College*

Donald Gray, *independent consultant*

George Griffin, *Regis University*

Randy Guthrie, *California Polytechnic State University, Pomona*

Tom Hankins, *Marshall University*

Bassam Hasan, *University of Toledo*

Richard Herschel, *St. Joseph's University*

Vicki Hightower, *Elon University*

Bogdan Hoanca, *University of Alaska Anchorage*

Richard Holowczak, *Baruch College*

Walter Horn, *Webster University*

Dennis Howard, *University of Alaska Anchorage*

James Hu, *Santa Clara University*

Adam Huarng, *California State University, Los Angeles*

John Hupp, *Columbus State University*

Brent Hussin, *University of Wisconsin*

Mark Hwang, *Central Michigan University*

James Isaak, *Southern New Hampshire University*

Wade Jackson, *University of Memphis*

Thaddeus Janicki, *Mount Olive College*

Chuck Johnston, *Midwestern State University*

Susan Jones, *Utah State University*

Iris Junglas, *University of Houston, Main*

George Kelley, *Erie Community College–City Campus*

Richard Kesner, *Northeastern University*

Jadon Klopson, *United States Coast Guard Academy*

Brian Kovar, *Kansas State University*

Andreas Knoefels, *Santa Clara University*

Chetan Kumar, *California State University, San Marcos*

Subodha Kumar, *University of Washington*

Jackie Lamoureux, *Central New Mexico Community College*

Yvonne Lederer-Antonucci, *Widener University*

Joo Eng Lee-Partridge, *Central Connecticut State University*

Diane Lending, *James Madison University*

David Lewis, *University of Massachusetts, Lowell*

Keith Lindsey, *Trinity University*

Stephen Loy, *Eastern Kentucky University*

Steven Lunce, *Midwestern State University*

Efrem Mallach, *University of Massachusetts*

Purnendu Mandal, *Marshall University*

Ronald Mashburn, *West Texas A&M University*

Richard Mathieu, *James Madison University*

Sathasivam Mathiyalakan, *University of Massachusetts, Boston*

Dan Matthews, *Trine University*

Ron McFarland, *Western New Mexico University*

Patricia McQuaid, *California Polytechnic State University, San Luis Obispo*

Stephanie Miserlis, *Hellenic College*

Wai Mok, *University of Alabama in Huntsville*

Janette Moody, *The Citadel*

Ata Nahouraii, *Indiana University of Pennsylvania*

Adriene Nawrocki, *John F. Kennedy University*

Anne Nelson, *Nova Southeastern University*

Irina Neuman, *McKendree College*

Margaret O'Hara, *East Carolina University*

Ravi Patnayakuni, *University of Alabama, Huntsville*

Ravi Paul, *East Carolina University*

Lowell Peck, *Central Connecticut State University*

Richard Peschke, *Minnesota State University, Mankato*

Doncho Petkov, *Eastern Connecticut State University*

Olga Petkova, *Central Connecticut State University*

Leonard Presby, *William Paterson University of New Jersey*

Terry Province, *North Central Texas College*

Adriane Randolph, *Kennesaw State University*

Harry Reif, *James Madison University*

Frances Roebuck, *Wilson Technical Community College*

Richard Roncone, *United States Coast Guard Academy*

Roberta Roth, *University of Northern Iowa*

Bruce Russell, *Northeastern University*

Ramesh Sankanarayanan, *University of Connecticut*

Eric Santanen, *Bucknell University*

Atul Saxena, *Mercer University*

Charles Saxon, *Eastern Michigan University*

David Scanlan, *California State University, Sacramento*

Herb Schuette, *Elon University*

Ken Sears, *University of Texas, Arlington*

Tom Seymour, *Minot State University*

Sherri Shade, *Kennesaw State University*

Geanesan Shankar, *Boston University*

Emily Shepard, *Central Carolina Community College*

David Smith, *Cameron University*

Glenn Smith, *James Madison University*

Stephen Solosky, *Nassau Community College*

Howard Sparks, *University of Alaska Fairbanks*

George Strouse, *York College*

Gladys Swindler, *Fort Hays State University*

Arta Szathmary, *Bucks County Community College*

Robert Szymanski, *University of Central Florida*

Albert Tay, *Idaho State University*

Winston Tellis, *Fairfield University*

Asela Thomason, *California State University, Long Beach*

Lou Thompson, *University of Texas, Dallas*

Anthony Townsend, *Iowa State University*

Goran Trajkovski, *Towson University*

Kim Troboy, *Arkansas Technical University*

Jonathan Trower, *Baylor University*

Ronald Trugman, *Cañada College*

Nancy Tsai, *California State University, Sacramento*

Betty Tucker, *Weber State University*

William Tucker, *Austin Community College*

David VanOver, *Sam Houston State University*

Therese Viscelli, *Georgia State University*

Linda Volonino, *Canisius University*

William Wagner, *Villanova University*

Rick Weible, *Marshall University*

Melody White, *University of North Texas*

Robert Wilson, *California State University, San Bernardino*

Elaine Winston, *Hofstra University*

Joe Wood, *Webster University*

Michael Workman, *Florida State University*

Kathie Wright, *Salisbury University*

James Yao, *Montclair State University*

Don Yates, *Louisiana State University*

Introduction to the Teaching Guidelines

The textbook you have in your hands is an annotated instructor's version of *Using MIS, 5th edition.* It differs from the student version in that it contains suggested teaching ideas for the introductory scenarios for each chapter and for each of the "Guides" in the chapters and chapter extensions. These suggestions are printed on pale yellow pages, easily identifiable from the regular text pages.

I wrote these annotations in the hope that they will provide you with useful background, save you time, and possibly make the class more fun to teach. Consider the material in the annotations as fodder for your class preparation, to be used in any way that meets your needs. You may decide to use them as is, or you might combine them with your own stories, or adapt them to companies in your local area, or use them as examples with which you disagree. Or, if they do not fit your teaching style, just ignore them. The text will work just fine without the annotations.

Notation

The teaching guidelines have two types of information: information for you, and also information for you to give to your students. Thus, we needed to introduce some notation to separate one category from the other. Comments and questions that you can address *directly to students* are typeset in boldface type and appear as follows:

- **What are some of the major limitations of data mining?**
- **If you are interested in learning more about data-mining techniques, you should take the department's database processing class. Drop me an e-mail if you want to know more.**

Because these statements are intended for the instructor's use, the me in the above statement refers to you, the professor (and not me, the author). These are just thoughts for statements you might want to make.

General statements and conceptual points *addressed to you*, the instructor, are set in regular type, as follows:

I like to start the class even before the class begins. I arrive 5 minutes or so early and talk with the students. I ask the students their names, where they are from, what their majors are, what they know about computers, etc., as a way of breaking the ice.

I hope at least some of this will be useful to you. Have fun!

David Kroenke

About the Author

David Kroenke has many years of teaching experience at Colorado State University, Seattle University, and the University of Washington. He has led dozens of seminars for college professors on the teaching of information systems and technology; in 1991 the International Association of Information Systems named him Computer Educator of the Year. In 2009, David was named Educator of the Year by the Association of Information Technology Professionals-Education Special Interest Group (AITP-EDSIG).

David worked for the U.S. Air Force and Boeing Computer Services. He was a principal in the start up of three companies. He also was vice president of product marketing and development for the Microrim Corporation and was chief of technologies for the database division of Wall Data, Inc. He is the father of the semantic object data model. David's consulting clients have included IBM, Microsoft, and Computer Sciences Corporations, as well as numerous smaller companies. Recently, David has focused on using information systems for teaching collaboration and teamwork.

His text *Database Processing* was first published in 1977 and is now in its 12th edition. He has authored and coauthored many other textbooks, including *Database Concepts,* 5th ed. (2011), *Experiencing MIS,* 3rd ed. (2012), *MIS Essentials,* 2nd ed. (2012), *SharePoint for Students* (2012), *Office 365 in Business* (2012), and *Processes, Systems, and Information: An Introduction to MIS* (2013). David lives in Seattle. He is married and has two children and three grandchildren. He enjoys woodworking and his wife tells him he enjoys gardening as well.

Part 1

Why MIS?

GearUp is a 3-year-old, privately owned company that sells quality brand-name athletic gear and clothing at deep discount over the Web. GearUp is a private buying club; before customers can purchase, they must first register.

Each day, GearUp sends emails to its customers announcing that day's sales event. Because events typically last 72 hours, GearUp normally has three events running simultaneously. Members buy until the sale ends or until the maximum quantity that GearUp can obtain has been sold. Because the total quantity is limited, customers are incentivized to buy early.

When the sale ends, GearUp buys the quantity it sold from its supplier, receives the goods in its inventory in Indianapolis, and then repackages the merchandise and ships orders to customers.

GearUp buyers negotiate with suppliers for maximum item quantities, sales prices, and costs. For example, a buyer might agree to purchase up to 5,000 soccer balls, sell them at a price of $22 each, and purchase them for $14 each. Buyers also negotiate shipping costs to the GearUp warehouse.

Once the terms are agreed upon, operations personnel contact the vendor for photos and descriptions of the goods, for creating attractive displays on computer browsers and phones.

Kelly Summers is GearUp's founder and CEO. During her twenties, Kelly played professional soccer, but after a serious knee injury she

retired and began working in sales for a national sports retailer. After three years, she moved to corporate marketing, where she worked two more years before leaving that position to start GearUp.

She took several key employees with her, including Lucas Massey, GearUp's director of IT services, who keeps the Web and sales sites running. Emily Johnson came over as CFO; Drew Mills as manager of event operations; and Addison Lee, who started as GearUp's first buyer, is now the lead buyer for the company.

"Every day is a new world for our customers," according to Kelly. "When you come to our site, you don't know whether you'll find a great deal on volleyballs and nets, hot fashions in ski wear, or premium golf clubs."

Sales revenue the first three years was $3 million, $11 million, $26 million. At present, sales are restricted to the United States. "We're just not ready to get into international shipping, pricing, currencies, etc."

According to Emily Johnson, "Our biggest problem is margins. We're selling more, but not seeing the economies of scale that we should. Our profit, as a percent of sales, has actually gone down. Not much, but a little, and it should be going up. I don't know why that is, but I told Kelly we've got to get on top of it."

Information systems are key to GearUp's success, as you are about to learn.

The Importance of MIS

"Fired? You're firing me?"

"Well, *fired* is a harsh word, but . . . well, GearUp has no further need for your services."

"But, Kelly, I don't get it. I really don't. I worked hard, and I did everything you told me to do."

"Jennifer, that's just it. You did everything *I* told you to do."

"I put in so many hours. How could you fire me????"

"Your job was to find ways we can reduce operational expenses without curtailing our effectiveness."

"Right! And I did that."

"No, you didn't. You followed up on ideas *that I gave you*. But we don't need someone who can follow up on my plans. We need someone who can figure out what we need to do, create her own plans, and bring them back to me. . . . And others."

"How could you expect me to do that? I've only been here 6 months!!!"

"It's called teamwork. Sure, you're just learning our business, but I made sure all of our senior staff would be available to you . . ."

"I didn't want to bother them."

"Well, you succeeded. I asked Drew what he thought of the plans you're working on. 'Who's Jennifer?' he asked."

"But, doesn't he work down at the warehouse?"

"Right. He's the operations manager . . . and it would seem to be worth talking to him."

"I'll go do that!"

"Jennifer, do you see what just happened? I gave you an idea and you said you'll do it. That's not what I need. I need you to find solutions on your own."

"I worked really hard. I put in a lot of hours. I've got all these reports written."

"Has anyone seen them?"

"I talked to you about some of them. But, I was waiting until I was satisfied with them."

"Right. That's not how we do things here. We develop ideas and then kick them around with each other. Nobody has all the smarts. Our plans get better when we comment and rework them . . . I think I told you that."

"Maybe you did. But I'm just not comfortable with that."

"Well, it's a key skill here."

"I know I can do this job."

"Jennifer, you've been here almost 6 months; you have a degree in business. Several weeks ago, I asked you for your first idea about how to identify problematic vendors. Do you remember what you said?"

"Yes, I wasn't sure how to proceed. I didn't want to just throw something out that might not work."

"But how would you find out if it would work?"

"I don't want to waste money . . ."

"No, you don't. So, when you didn't get very far with that task, I backed up and asked you to send me a diagram of the life cycle for one of our events . . . how we select the vendors, how we negotiate with them, how we create the web pages, run the events, ship the goods. Not details, just the overview."

"Yes, I sent you that diagram."

"Jennifer, it made no sense. Your diagram had vendors sending us sales materials before we finished negotiating with them."

"I know that process, I just couldn't put it down on paper. But, I'll try again!"

"Well, I appreciate that attitude, but times are tight. We don't have room for trainees. When the economy was strong, I'd have been able to look for a spot for you, see if we can bring you along. But, to get our margins up, we can't afford to do that now."

"What about my references?"

"I'll be happy to tell anyone that you're reliable, that you work 40 to 45 hours a week, and that you're honest and have integrity."

"Those are important!"

"Yes, they are. But today, they're not enough." ∎

Study Questions

Q1 Why is Introduction to MIS the most important class in the business school?

Q2 What is MIS?

Q3 How can you use the five-component model?

Q4 Why is the difference between information technology and information systems important?

Q5 What is information?

Q6 What are necessary data characteristics?

Q7 2022?

"But today, they're not enough."

Do you find that statement sobering? And if timely, hard work isn't enough, what is? We'll begin this book by discussing the key skills that Jennifer (and you) need and explain why this course is the single best course in all of the business school for teaching you those key skills.

You may find that last statement surprising. If you are like most students, you have no clear idea of what your MIS class will be about. If someone were to ask you, "What do you study in that class?" you might respond that the class has something to do with computers and maybe computer programming. Beyond that, you might be hard-pressed to say more. You might add, "Well, it has something to do with computers in business," or maybe, "We are going to learn to solve business problems with computers using spreadsheets and other programs." So, how could this course be the most important one in the business school?

We begin with that question. After you understand how important this class will be to your career, we will discuss fundamental concepts. We'll wrap up with some practice on one of the key skills you need to learn.

Q1 Why Is Introduction to MIS the Most Important Class in the Business School?

Introduction to MIS is the most important class in the business school. That statement was not true in 2005, and it may not be true in 2020. But it is true in 2012.

Why?

The ultimate reason lies in a principle known as **Moore's Law**. In 1965, Gordon Moore, cofounder of Intel Corporation, stated that because of technology improvements in electronic chip design and manufacturing, "The number of transistors per square inch on an integrated chip doubles every 18 months." His statement has been commonly misunderstood to be, "The speed of a computer doubles every 18 months," which is incorrect, but captures the sense of his principle.

Because of Moore's Law, the ratio of price to performance of computers has fallen from something like $4,000 for a standard computing device to something around a penny for that same computing device.[1] See Figure 1-1.

As a future business professional, however, you needn't care how fast a computer your company can buy for $100. That's not the point. Here's the point:

> **Because of Moore's Law, the cost of data communications and data storage is essentially zero.**

Think about that statement before you hurry to the next paragraph. What happens when those costs are essentially zero? Here are some consequences:

- YouTube
- Facebook
- Pandora
- LinkedIn
- iPad
- Woot
- Twitter
- Foursquare

None of these was prominent in 2005, and, in fact, most didn't exist in 2005.

---

[1] These figures represent the cost of 100,000 transistors, which can roughly be translated into a unit of a computing device. For our purposes, the details don't matter. If you doubt any of this, just look at your $199 iPhone and realize that you pay $40 a month to use it.

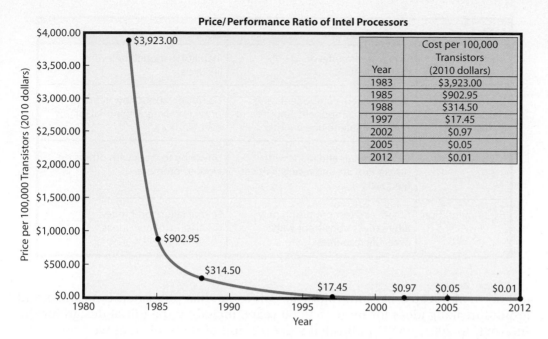

Price/Performance Ratio of Intel Processors

Year	Cost per 100,000 Transistors (2010 dollars)
1983	$3,923.00
1985	$902.95
1988	$314.50
1997	$17.45
2002	$0.97
2005	$0.05
2012	$0.01

Figure 1-1
Computer Price/Performance Ratio Decreases

Are There Cost-Effective Business Applications of Facebook and Twitter?

Of course. GearUp is profitably using them today. Event moderators post announcements via Twitter. GearUp collects those tweets and posts them on its Facebook page. Total cost to GearUp? Zero.

But ask another question: Are there wasteful, harmful, useless business applications of Facebook and Twitter? Of course. Do I care to follow the tweets of the mechanic who changes the oil in my car? I don't think so.

But there's the point. Maybe I'm not being creative enough. Maybe there are great reasons for the mechanic to tweet customers and I'm just not able to think of them. Also, Facebook and Twitter are old news now. What's new on the horizon that GearUp and the mechanic should be thinking about? All of this leads us to the first reason Introduction to MIS is the most important course in the business school today:

> **Future business professionals need to be able to assess, evaluate, and apply emerging information technology to business.**

You need the knowledge of this course to attain that skill.

How Can I Attain Job Security?

Many years ago I had a wise and experienced mentor. One day I asked him about job security, and he told me that the only job security that exists is "a marketable skill and the courage to use it." He continued, "There is no security in our company, there is no security in any government program, there is no security in your investments, and there is no security in Social Security." Alas, how right he turned out to be.

So what is a marketable skill? It used to be that one could name particular skills, such as computer programming, tax accounting, or marketing. But today, because of Moore's Law, because the cost of data storage and data communications is essentially zero, any routine skill can and will be outsourced to the lowest bidder. And if you live in the United States, Canada, Australia, Europe, or other advanced economy, that is unlikely to be you.

Numerous organizations and experts have studied the question of what skills will be marketable during your career. Consider two of them. First, the RAND Corporation,

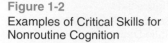

Figure 1-2
Examples of Critical Skills for
Nonroutine Cognition

Skill	Example	Jennifer's Problem at GearUp
Abstraction	Construct a model or representation.	Inability to model the event life cycle.
Systems thinking	Model system components and show how components' inputs and outputs relate to one another.	Confusion about how vendors provide collateral material for events.
Collaboration	Develop ideas and plans with others. Provide and receive critical feedback.	Unwilling to work with others on work-in-progress.
Experimentation	Create and test promising new alternatives, consistent with available resources.	Fear of failure prohibited discussion of new ideas.

a think tank located in Santa Monica, California, has published innovative and groundbreaking ideas for more than 60 years, including the initial design for the Internet. In 2004, RAND published a description of the skills that workers in the twenty-first century will need:

> Rapid technological change and increased international competition place the spotlight on the skills and preparation of the workforce, particularly the ability to adapt to changing technology and shifting demand. Shifts in the nature of organizations . . . favor strong nonroutine cognitive skills.[2]

Whether you're majoring in accounting or marketing or finance or information systems, you need to develop strong nonroutine cognitive skills.

What are such skills? Robert Reich, former Secretary of Labor, enumerates four components:[3]

- Abstract reasoning
- Systems thinking
- Collaboration
- Ability to experiment

Figure 1-2 shows an example of each. Reread the GearUp case that started this chapter, and you'll see that Jennifer lost her job because of her inability to practice these key skills.

How Can Intro to MIS Help You Learn Nonroutine Skills?

Introduction to MIS is the best course in the business school for learning these four key skills because every topic will require you to apply and practice them. Here's how.

Abstract Reasoning

Abstract reasoning is the ability to make and manipulate models. You will work with one or more models in every course topic and book chapter. For example, later in this chapter you will learn about a *model* of the five components of an information

---

[2] Lynn A. Kaoly and Constantijn W. A. Panis, *The 21st Century at Work* (Santa Monica, CA: RAND Corporation, 2004), p. xiv.
[3] Robert B. Reich, *The Work of Nations* (New York: Alfred A. Knopf, 1991), p. 229.

system. This chapter will describe how to use this model to assess the scope of any new information system project; other chapters will build upon this model.

In this course, you will not just manipulate models that your instructor or I have developed, you will also be asked to construct models of your own. In Chapter 5, for example, you'll learn how to create data models, and in Chapter 10 you'll learn to make process models.

Systems Thinking

Can you go down to a grocery store, look at a can of green beans, and connect that can to U.S. immigration policy? Can you watch tractors dig up a forest of pulp wood trees and connect that woody trash to Moore's Law? Do you know why Cisco Systems is one of the major beneficiaries of YouTube?

Answers to all of these questions require systems thinking. **Systems thinking** is the ability to model the components of the system, to connect the inputs and outputs among those components into a sensible whole that reflects the structure and dynamics of the phenomenon observed.

As you are about to learn, this class is about information *systems*. We will discuss and illustrate systems; you will be asked to critique systems; you will be asked to compare alternative systems; you will be asked to apply different systems to different situations. All of those tasks will prepare you for systems thinking as a professional.

Collaboration

Collaboration is the activity of two or more people working together to achieve a common goal, result, or work product. Chapter 2 will teach you collaboration skills and illustrate several sample collaboration information systems. Every chapter of this book includes collaboration exercises that you may be assigned in class or as homework.

Here's a fact that surprises many students: Effective collaboration isn't about being nice. In fact, surveys indicate the single most important skill for effective collaboration is to give and receive critical feedback. Advance a proposal in business that challenges the cherished program of the VP of marketing, and you'll quickly learn that effective collaboration skills differ from party manners at the neighborhood barbeque. So, how do you advance your idea in the face of the VP's resistance? And without losing your job? In this course, you can learn both skills and information systems for such collaboration. Even better, you will have many opportunities to practice them.

Ability to Experiment

"I've never done this before."
"I don't know how to do it."
"But will it work?"
"Is it too weird for the market?"

Fear of failure: the fear that paralyzes so many good people and so many good ideas. In the days when business was stable, when new ideas were just different verses of the same song, professionals could allow themselves to be limited by fear of failure.

But think again about the application of social networking to the oil change business. Is there a legitimate application of social networking there? If so, has anyone ever done it? Is there anyone in the world who can tell you what to do? How to proceed? No. As Reich says, professionals in the twenty-first century need to be able to experiment.

Successful experimentation is not throwing buckets of money at every crazy idea that enters your head. Instead, **experimentation** is making a reasoned analysis of an opportunity, envisioning potential solutions, evaluating those possibilities, and developing the most promising ones, consistent with the resources you have.

In this course, you will be asked to use products with which you have no familiarity. Those products might be Microsoft Excel or Access, or they might be features and functions of Blackboard that you've not used. Or, you may be asked to collaborate using Office 365 or SharePoint or Google Docs. Will your instructor explain and show every feature of those products that you'll need? You should hope not. You should hope your instructor will leave it up to you to experiment, to envision new possibilities on your own, and experiment with those possibilities, consistent with the time you have available.

The bottom line? This course is the most important course in the business school because

1. **It will give you the background you need to assess, evaluate, and apply emerging information systems technology to business.**
2. **It can give you the ultimate in job security—marketable skills—by helping you learn abstraction, systems thinking, collaboration, and experimentation.**

With that introduction, let's get started! Welcome aboard.

Q2 What Is MIS?

We've used the term *MIS* several times, and you may be wondering exactly what it is. **MIS** stands for **management information systems**, which we define as *the management and use of information systems that help businesses achieve their strategies*. This definition has three key elements: *management and use, information systems*, and *strategies*. Let's consider each, starting first with information systems and their components.

Components of an Information System

A **system** is a group of components that interact to achieve some purpose. As you might guess, an **information system (IS)** is a group of components that interact to produce information. That sentence, although true, raises another question: What are these components that interact to produce information?

Figure 1-3 shows the **five-component framework**—a model of the components of an information system: **computer hardware, software, data, procedures**, and **people**. These five components are present in every information system, from the simplest to the most complex. For example, when you use a computer to write a class report, you are using hardware (the computer, storage disk, keyboard, and monitor), software (Word, WordPerfect, or some other word-processing program), data (the words, sentences, and paragraphs in your report), procedures (the methods you use to start the program, enter your report, print it, and save and back up your file), and people (you).

Consider a more complex example, say an airline reservation system. It, too, consists of these five components, even though each one is far more complicated. The hardware consists of dozens or more computers linked together by data communications hardware. Further, hundreds of different programs coordinate communications among the computers, and still other programs perform the reservations and related services. Additionally, the system must store millions upon millions of characters of data about flights, customers, reservations, and other facts. Hundreds of different procedures are followed by airline personnel, travel agents, and customers. Finally, the information system includes people, not only the users of the system, but also

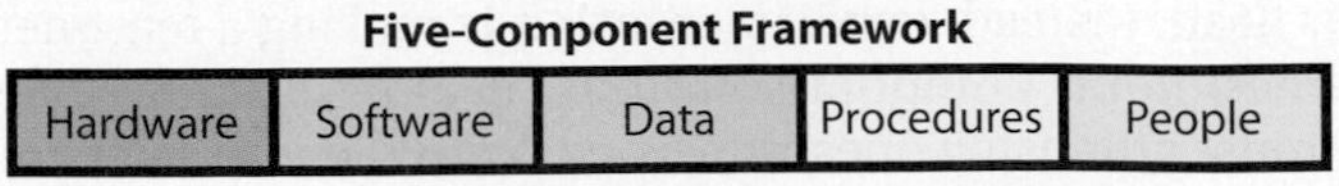

Figure 1-3
Five Components
of an Information System

Five-Component Framework

Hardware	Software	Data	Procedures	People

those who operate and service the computers, those who maintain the data, and those who support the networks of computers.

The important point here is that the five components in Figure 1-3 are common to all information systems, from the smallest to the largest. As you think about any information system, including a new one like social networking by mechanics, learn to look for these five components. Realize, too, that an information system is not just a computer and a program, but rather an assembly of computers, programs, data, procedures, and people.

As we will discuss later in this chapter, these five components also mean that many different skills are required besides those of hardware technicians or computer programmers when building or using an information system. People are needed who can design the databases that hold the data and who can develop procedures for people to follow. Managers are needed to train and staff the personnel for using and operating the system. We will return to this five-component framework later in this chapter, as well as many other times throughout this book.

Before we move forward, note that we have defined an information system to include a computer. Some people would say that such a system is a **computer-based information system**. They would note that there are information systems that do not include computers, such as a calendar hanging on the wall outside of a conference room that is used to schedule the room's use. Such systems have been used by businesses for centuries. Although this point is true, in this book we focus on computer-based information systems. To simplify and shorten the book, we will use the term *information system* as a synonym for *computer-based information system*.

Management and Use of Information Systems

The next element in our definition of MIS is the *management and use* of information systems. Here, we define management to mean develop, maintain, and adapt. Information systems do not pop up like mushrooms after a hard rain; they must be developed. They must also be maintained and, because business is dynamic, they must be adapted to new requirements.

You may be saying, "Wait a minute, I'm a finance (or accounting or management) major, not an information systems major. I don't need to know how to manage information systems." If you are saying that, you are like a lamb headed for fleecing. Throughout your career, in whatever field you choose, information systems will be built for your use, and sometimes under your direction. To create an information system that meets your needs, you need to take an *active role* in that system's development. Even if you are not a programmer or a database designer or some other IS professional, you must take an active role in specifying the system's requirements and in managing the system's development project. Without active involvement on your part, it will only be good luck that causes the new system to meet your needs.

As a business professional, you are the person who understands business needs and requirements. If you want to apply social networking to your products, you are the one who knows how best to obtain customer responses. The technical people who build networks, the database designers who create the database, the IT people who configure the computers—none of these people know what is needed and whether the system you have is sufficient or whether it needs to be adapted to new requirements. You do!

In addition to management tasks, you will also have important roles to play in the *use* of information systems. Of course, you will need to learn how to employ the system to accomplish your goals. But you will also have important ancillary functions as well. For example, when using an information system, you will have responsibilities for protecting the security of the system and its data. You may also have tasks for backing up data. When the system fails (most do, at some point), you will have tasks to perform while the system is down as well as tasks to accomplish to help recover the system correctly and quickly.

Security is critically important when using information systems today. You'll learn much more about it in Chapter 12. But, you need to know about strong passwords and their use now, before you get to that chapter. Read and follow the password Guide on pages 22–23.

Achieving Strategies

The last part of the definition of MIS is that information systems exist to help businesses achieve their *strategies*. First, realize that this statement hides an important fact: Businesses themselves do not "do" anything. A business is not alive, and it cannot act. It is the people within a business who sell, buy, design, produce, finance, market, account, and manage. So, information systems exist to help people who work in a business to achieve the strategies of that business.

Information systems are not created for the sheer joy of exploring technology. They are not created so that the company can be "modern" or so that the company can show it has a social networking presence on the Web. They are not created because the information systems department thinks it needs to be created or because the company is "falling behind the technology curve."

This point may seem so obvious that you might wonder why we mention it. Every day, however, some business somewhere is developing an information system for the wrong reasons. Right now, somewhere in the world, a company is deciding to create a Facebook presence for the sole reason that "every other business has one." This company is not asking questions such as:

- "What is the purpose of our Facebook page?"
- "What is it going to do for us?"
- "What is our policy for employees' contributions?"
- "What should we do about critical customer reviews?"
- "Are the costs of maintaining the page sufficiently offset by the benefits?"

But that company should ask those questions! Chapter 3 addresses the relationship between information systems and strategy in more depth. Chapter 8 addresses social media and strategy specifically.

Again, MIS is the development and use of information systems that help businesses achieve their strategies. Already you should be realizing that there is much more to this class than buying a computer, working with a spreadsheet, or creating a Web page.

Q3 How Can You Use the Five-Component Model?

The five-component model in Figure 1-3 can help guide your learning and thinking about IS, both now and in the future. To understand this framework better, first note in Figure 1-4 that these five components are symmetric. The outermost components, hardware and people, are both actors; they can take actions. The software and procedure components are both sets of instructions: Software is instructions for hardware, and procedures are instructions for people. Finally, data is the bridge between the computer side on the left and the human side on the right.

Figure 1-4
Characteristics of the Five Components

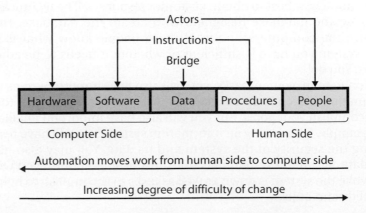

Now, when we automate a business task, we take work that people are doing by following procedures and move it so that computers will do that work, following instructions in software. Thus, the process of automation is a process of moving work from the right side of Figure 1-4 to the left.

The Most Important Component—YOU

You are part of every information system that you use. When you consider the five components of an information system, the last component, *people*, includes you. Your mind and your thinking are not merely *a* component of the information systems you use, they are *the most important* component.

Consider an example. Suppose you have the perfect information system, one that can predict the future. No such information system exists, but assume for this example that it does. Now suppose that on December 14, 1966, your perfect information system tells you that the next day, Walt Disney will die. Say you have $50,000 to invest; you can either buy Disney stock or you can short it (an investment technique that will net you a positive return if the stock value decreases). Given your perfect information system, how do you invest?

Before you read on, think about this question. If Walt Disney is going to die the next day, will the stock go up or down? Most students assume that the stock will go down, so they short it, on the theory that the loss of the founder will mean a dramatic drop in the share price.

In fact, the next day, the value of Disney stock increased substantially. Why? The market viewed Walt Disney as an artist; once he died, he would no longer be able to create more art. Thus, the value of the existing art would increase because of scarcity, and the value of the corporation that owned that art would increase as well.

Here's the point: Even if you have the perfect information system, if you do not know what to do with the data that it produces, you are wasting your time and money. The *quality of your thinking* is a large part of the quality of the information system. Substantial cognitive research has shown that although you cannot increase your basic IQ, you can dramatically increase the quality of your thinking. You cannot change the computer in your brain, so to speak, but you can change the way you have programmed your brain to work.

We discuss thinking skills in an MIS book, because improving your thinking improves the quality of every information system that you use. The Guide on pages 20–21 presents ideas from cognitive science and applies them to business situations.

High-Tech Versus Low-Tech Information Systems

Information systems differ in the amount of work that is moved from the human side (people and procedures) to the computer side (hardware and programs). For example, consider two different versions of a customer support information system: A system that consists only of a file of email addresses and an email program is a very low-tech system. Only a small amount of work has been moved from the human side to the computer side. Considerable human work is required to determine when to send which emails to which customers.

In contrast, a customer support system that keeps track of the equipment that customers have and the maintenance schedules for that equipment and then automatically generates email reminders to customers is a higher-tech system. This simply means that more work has been moved from the human side to the computer side. The computer is providing more services on behalf of the humans.

Often, when considering different information systems alternatives, it will be helpful to consider the low-tech versus high-tech alternatives in light of the amount of work that is being moved from people to computers.

Understanding the Scope of New Information Systems

The five-component framework can also be used when assessing the scope of new systems. When in the future some vendor pitches the need for a new technology to you, use the five components to assess how big of an investment that new technology

Using MIS InClass 1 *A Group Exercise*

Information Systems and Online Dating

"Why should I go to a bar and take the risk that nobody I'm interested in will be there during the 2 hours I'm there, when I can spend half an hour searching online for people that I *am* likely to be interested in? At worst, I've wasted half an hour. And at least I didn't have to blow-dry my hair."

■ **Lori Gottlieb,** *The Atlantic,* **February 7, 2006, www.theatlantic.com/doc/200602u/online-dating**

Some online dating services match couples using a proprietary algorithm (method) based on a theory of relationships:

Chemistry (*www.chemistry.com*). Matches are made on the basis of a personality test developed by Dr. Helen Fisher.

eHarmony (*www.eharmony.com*). Matches are made on the basis of a test called the "Compatibility Matching System" by Dr. Neil Clark Warren.

PerfectMatch (*www.perfectmatch.com*). Matches are made on the basis of a test based on Duet, a system developed by Dr. Pepper Schwartz.

Other sites match people by limiting members to particular groups or interests:

Political interests:

Conservative Dates (*www.republicanpeoplemeet.com*)— "Creating Relationships. Connecting Lives."

Liberal Hearts (*www.liberalhearts.com*)—"Uniting Democrats, Greens, animal lovers & environmentalists who are like in mind and liberal in love."

Common social/economic interests:

Good Genes (*www.goodgenes.com*)—"[Helping] Ivy Leaguers and similarly well-educated graduates and faculty find others with matching credentials."

MillionaireMatch (*www.millionairematch.com*)—"Where you can add a touch of romance to success and achievement!"

Common activity interests:

Golfmates (*www.golfmates.com*)—"The world's premier online dating service designed specifically for the golfing community."

EquestrianCupid (*www.equestriancupid.com*)—"The best dating site in the world for friends and singles who are horse lovers."

Single FireFighters (*www.singlefirefighters.com*)— "The ONLY place to meet firefighters without calling 911!"

Asexual Pals (*www.asexualpals.com*)—"Because there is so much more to life!"

InClass Group Exercise:

1. Visit one of the proprietary method sites and one of the common interest sites.

2. Summarize the matching process that is used by each site.

3. Describe the revenue model of each site.

4. Using general terms, describe the need these sites have for:
   - **a.** Hardware   **d.** Procedures
   - **b.** Software   **e.** People
   - **c.** Data

5. People sometimes stretch the truth, or even lie, on matching sites. Describe one innovative way that one of the two companies your team chose in step 1 could use information systems to reduce the impact of this tendency. As you prepare your team's answer, keep the availability of nearly free data communications and data storage in mind.

6. Suppose that the company in your answer to step 5 has requested your team to implement your idea on reducing the impact of lying. Explain how having strong personal skills for each of Reich's four abilities (i.e., abstract thinking, systems thinking, experimentation, and collaboration) would enable each of you to be a better contributor to that team.

7. Working as a team, prepare a 3-minute verbal description of your answers to steps 5 and 6 that all of you could use in a job interview. Structure your presentation to illustrate that you have the four skills in step 6.

8. Deliver your answer to step 7 to the rest of the class.

represents. What new hardware will you need? What programs will you need to license? What databases and other data must you create? What procedures will need to be developed for both use and administration of the information system? And, finally, what will be the impact of the new technology on people? Which jobs will change? Who will need training? How will the new technology affect morale? Will you need to hire new people? Will you need to reorganize?

Components Ordered by Difficulty and Disruption

Finally, as you consider the five components keep in mind that Figure 1-4 shows them in order of ease of change and the amount of organizational disruption. It is a simple matter to order additional hardware. Obtaining or developing new programs is more difficult. Creating new databases or changing the structure of existing databases is still more difficult. Changing procedures, requiring people to work in new ways, is even more difficult. Finally, changing personnel responsibilities and reporting relationships and hiring and terminating employees are both very difficult and very disruptive to the organization.

The Ethics Guide in each chapter of this book considers the ethics of information systems use. These guides challenge you to think deeply about ethical standards, and they provide for some interesting discussions with classmates. The Ethics Guide on pages 16–17 considers the ethics of using data that is not intended for you.

Q4 Why Is the Difference Between Information Technology and Information Systems Important?

Information technology and information systems are two closely related terms, but they are different. **Information technology (IT)** refers to the products, methods, inventions, and standards that are used for the purpose of producing information. IT pertains to the hardware, software, and data components. In contrast, an *information system (IS)* is an assembly of hardware, software, data, procedures, and people that produces information.

Information technology drives the development of new information systems. Advances in information technology have taken the organizations from the days of punched cards to e-commerce and social media, and such advances will continue to take the industry to the next stages and beyond.

Why does this difference matter to you? Knowing the difference between IT and IS can help you avoid a common mistake: You cannot buy an IS.

You can buy IT; you can buy or lease hardware, you can license programs and databases, and you can even obtain predesigned procedures. Ultimately, however, it is *your* people who execute those procedures to employ that new IT.

For any new system, you will always have training tasks (and costs), you will always have the need to overcome employees' resistance to change, and you will always need to manage the employees as they utilize the new system. Hence, you can buy IT, but you cannot buy IS.

Consider a simple example. Suppose your organization decides to develop a Facebook page. Facebook provides the hardware and programs, the database structures, and standard procedures. You, however, provide the data to fill your portion of their database, and you must extend their standard procedures with your own procedures for keeping that data current. Those procedures need to provide, for example, a means to review your page's content regularly and a means to remove content that is judged inappropriate. Furthermore, you need to train employees on how to follow those procedures and manage those employees to ensure that they do.

Managing your own Facebook page is as simple an IS as exists. Larger, more comprehensive IS that involve many, even dozens, of departments and thousands of employees require considerable work. Again, you can buy IT, but you can never buy an IS!

Q5 What Is Information?

Based on our earlier discussions, we can now define an information system as an assembly of hardware, software, data, procedures, and people that interact to produce information. The only term left undefined in that definition is *information*, and we turn to it next.

Definitions Vary

Information is one of those fundamental terms that we use every day but that turns out to be surprisingly difficult to define. Defining information is like defining words such as *alive* and *truth*. We know what those words mean, we use them with each other without confusion, but nonetheless, they are difficult to define.

In this text, we will avoid the technical issues of defining information and will use common, intuitive definitions instead. Probably the most common definition is that **information** is knowledge derived from data, whereas *data* is defined as recorded facts or figures. Thus, the facts that employee James Smith earns $17.50 per hour and that Mary Jones earns $25.00 per hour are *data*. The statement that the average hourly wage of all the aerobics instructors is $22.37 per hour is *information*. Average wage is knowledge that is derived from the data of individual wages.

Another common definition is that *information is data presented in a meaningful context*. The fact that Jeff Parks earns $10.00 per hour is data.[4] The statement that Jeff Parks earns less than half the average hourly wage of the aerobics instructors, however, is information. It is data presented in a meaningful context.

Another definition of information that you will hear is that *information is processed data,* or sometimes, *information is data processed by summing, ordering, averaging, grouping, comparing, or other similar operations*. The fundamental idea of this definition is that we do something to data to produce information.

There is yet a fourth definition of information, which is presented in the Guide on page 20. There, information is defined as *a difference that makes a difference*.

For the purposes of this text, any of these definitions of information will do. Choose the definition of information that makes sense to you. The important point is that you discriminate between data and information. You also may find that different definitions work better in different situations.

Where Is Information?

Suppose you create a graph of Amazon.com's stock price and net income over its history, like that shown in Figure 1-5. Does that graph contain information? Well, if it shows a difference that makes a difference or if it presents data in a meaningful context, then it fits two of the definitions of information, and it's tempting to say that the graph contains information.

Figure 1-5
Amazon.com Stock Price and Net Income

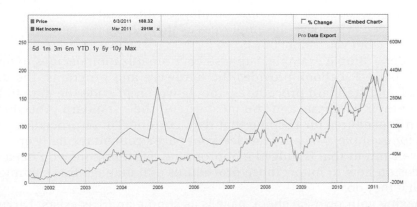

---

[4] Actually the word *data* is plural; to be correct we should use the singular form *datum* and say, "The fact that Jeff Parks earns $10 per hour is a datum." The word *datum* however, sounds pedantic and fussy, and we will avoid it in this text.

However, show that graph to your family dog. Does your dog find information in that graph? Well, nothing about Amazon.com, anyway. The dog might learn what you had for lunch, but it won't obtain any information about Amazon.com's stock price over time.

Reflect on this experiment and you will realize that the graph is not, itself, information. The graph is data that you and other humans perceive, and from that perception you conceive information. In short, if it's on a piece of paper or on a digital screen, it's data. If it's in the mind of a human, it's information.

Why, you're asking yourself, do I care? Well, for one, it further explains why you, as a human, are the most important part of any information system you use. The quality of your thinking, of your ability to conceive information from data, is determined by your cognitive skills. The data is the data, the information you conceive from it is the value that you add to the information system.

Furthermore, as the Guide on page 20 explores, people have different perceptions and points of view. Not surprisingly, then, they will conceive different information from the same data. You cannot say to someone, "Look, it's right there in front of you, in the data," because it's not right there in the data. Rather, it's in your head, and your job is to explain what you have conceived so that others can understand it.

Finally, once you understand this, you'll understand that all kinds of common sentences make no sense. "I sent you that information," cannot be true. "I sent you the data, from which you conceived the information," is the most we can say. During your business career, this observation will save you untold frustration if you remember and apply it.

Q6 What Are Necessary Data Characteristics?

You have just learned that humans conceive information from data. As stated, the quality of the information that you can create depends, in part, on your thinking skills. It also, depends, however, on the quality of the data that you are given. Figure 1-6 summarizes critical data characteristics.

Accurate

First, good information is conceived from accurate, correct, and complete data, and it has been processed correctly as expected. Accuracy is crucial; business professionals must be able to rely on the results of their information systems. The IS function can develop a bad reputation in the organization if a system is known to produce inaccurate data. In such a case, the information system becomes a waste of time and money as users develop work-arounds to avoid the inaccurate data.

A corollary to this discussion is that you, a future user of information systems, ought not to rely on data just because it appears in the context of a Web page, a well-formatted report, or a fancy query. It is sometimes hard to be skeptical of data delivered with beautiful, active graphics. Do not be misled. When you begin to use a new information system, be skeptical. Cross-check the data you are receiving. After weeks or months of using a system, you may relax. Begin, however, with skepticism. Again, you cannot conceive accurate information from inaccurate data.

- **Accurate**
- **Timely**
- **Relevant**
  - To context
  - To subject
- **Just sufficient**
- **Worth its cost**

Figure 1-6
Data Characteristics Required for Good Information

Ethics Guide

Ethics of Information from Misdirected Data

Consider the following situations:

Situation A: Suppose you are buying a condo and you know that at least one other party is bidding against you. While agonizing over your best strategy, you stop at a local Starbucks. As you sip your latte, you overhear a conversation at the table next to yours. Three people are talking loudly enough that it is difficult to ignore them, and you soon realize that they are the real estate agent and the couple who is competing for the condo you want. They are preparing their offer. Should you listen to their conversation? If you do, do you use the data you hear to your advantage?

Situation B: Consider the same situation from a different perspective—instead of overhearing the conversation, suppose you receive that same data in an email. Perhaps an administrative assistant at the agent's office

16

confuses you and the other customer and mistakenly sends you the terms of the other party's offer. Do you read that email? If so, do you use the information that you conceive to your advantage?

Situation C: Suppose that you sell computer software. In the midst of a sensitive price negotiation, your customer accidentally sends you an internal email that contains the maximum amount that the customer can pay for your software. Do you read that email? Do you use that data to guide your negotiating strategy? If your customer discovers that the email may have reached you and asks, "Did you read my email?" how do you answer?

Situation D: In this scenario, a friend mistakenly sends you an email that contains sensitive personal medical data. Further, suppose you read the email before you know what you're reading and you're embarrassed to learn something very personal that truly is none of your business. Your friend asks you, "Did you read that email?" How do you respond?

Situation E: Finally, suppose that you work as a network administrator and your position allows you unrestricted access to the mailing lists for your company. Assume that you have the skill to insert your email address into any company mailing list without anyone knowing about it. You insert your address into several lists and, consequently, begin to receive confidential emails that no one intended for you to see. One of those emails indicates that your best friend's department is about to be eliminated and all of its personnel fired. Do you forewarn your friend? ■

Discussion Questions

1. Answer the questions in situations A and B. Do your answers differ? Does the medium by which the data is obtained make a difference? Is it easier to avoid reading an email than it is to avoid hearing a conversation? If so, does that difference matter?

2. Answer the questions in situations B and C. Do your answers differ? In situation B, the data is for your personal gain; in C, the data is for both your personal and your organization's gain. Does this difference matter? How do you respond when asked if you have read the email?

3. Answer the questions in situations C and D. Do your answers differ? Would you lie in one case and not in the other? Why or why not?

4. Answer the question in situation E. What is the essential difference between situations A through D and situation E? Suppose you had to justify your behavior in situation E. How would you argue? Do you believe your own argument?

5. In situations A through D, if you access the data you have done nothing illegal. You were the passive recipient. Even for item E, although you undoubtedly violated your company's employment policies, you most likely did not violate the law. So, for this discussion, assume that all of these actions are legal.

    a. What is the difference between legal and ethical? Search the Internet for a definition of each and explain how they differ.

    b. Make the argument that business is competitive, and that if something is legal then it is acceptable if it helps to further your goals.

    c. Make the argument that it is never appropriate to do something unethical.

6. Summarize your beliefs about proper conduct when you receive misdirected data.

Timely

Good information requires that data be timely—available in time for its intended use. A monthly report that arrives six weeks late is most likely useless. The data arrives long after the decisions have been made that needed your information. An information system that sends you a poor customer credit report after you have shipped the goods is unhelpful and frustrating. Notice that timeliness can be measured against a calendar (6 weeks late) or against events (before we ship).

When you participate in the development of an IS, timeliness will be part of the requirements you specify. You need to give appropriate and realistic timeliness needs. In some cases, developing systems that provide data in near real time is much more difficult and expensive than producing data a few hours later. If you can get by with data that is a few hours old, say so during the requirements specification phase.

Consider an example. Suppose you work in marketing and you need to be able to assess the effectiveness of new online ad programs. You want an information system that not only will deliver ads over the Web, but that also will enable you to determine how frequently customers click on those ads. Determining click ratios in near real time will be very expensive; saving the data in a batch and processing it some hours later will be much easier and cheaper. If you can live with data that is a day or two old, the system will be easier and cheaper to implement.

Relevant

Data should be relevant both to the context and to the subject. Considering context, you, the CEO, need data that is summarized to an appropriate level for your job. A list of the hourly wage of every employee in the company is unlikely to be useful. More likely, you need average wage information by department or division. A list of all employee wages is irrelevant in your context.

Data should also be relevant to the subject at hand. If you want data about short-term interest rates for a possible line of credit, then a report that shows 15-year mortgage interest rates is irrelevant. Similarly, a report that buries the data you need in pages and pages of results is also irrelevant to your purposes.

Just Barely Sufficient

Data needs to be sufficient for the purpose for which it is generated, but just barely so. We are inundated with data; one of the critical decisions that each of us has to make each day is what data to ignore. The higher you rise into management, the more data you will be given, and, because there is only so much time, the more data you will need to ignore. So, data should be sufficient, but just barely.

Worth Its Cost

Data is not free. There are costs for developing an information system, costs of operating and maintaining that system, and costs of your time and salary for reading and processing the data the system produces. For data to be worth its cost, an appropriate relationship must exist between the cost of data and its value.

Consider an example. What is the value of a daily report of the names of the occupants of a full graveyard? Zero, unless grave robbery is a problem for the cemetery. The report is not worth the time required to read it. It is easy to see the importance of economics for this silly example. It will be more difficult, however, when someone proposes new technology to you. You need to be ready to ask, "What's the value of the information that I can conceive from this data?" "What is the cost?" "Is there an appropriate relationship between value and cost?" Information systems should be subject to the same financial analyses to which other assets are subjected.

Q7 2022?

In Q1, we said that future businesspeople need to be able to assess, evaluate, and apply emerging technology. What technology might that be? And how might it pertain to future business?

Let's take a guess at technology in the year 2022. Of course, we won't have perfect insight and, in fact, these guesses will probably seem ludicrous to the person who finds this book for sale for a dollar at a Goodwill Store in 2022. But, let's exercise our minds in that direction.

One reasonable guess is that most computers won't look like computers. Apple's iPad, for example, does not look like a traditional desktop or laptop, but you can use it to watch videos, listen to music, read books, store photos, surf the Internet, and network online. You can also buy apps for the iPad that are educational, such as ones designed to aid toddlers in learning their ABCs and others focused on helping high school students learn the periodic table.

Amazon.com's Kindle Fire, which is advertised as a media device, is a computer. It just doesn't look like one. What happens when you turn on that Kindle? You are connected, magically as it were, to the Amazon.com store. You can buy books and magazine subscriptions, and so on, with a single click.

Furthermore, everyday items now have computers in them. Tanita offers a scale that sends an electrical pulse through your body and then provides not only your weight, but also your body fat, bone mass, metabolism, and level of hydration. You can wear a watch that counts the calories you have burned and the number of miles you have walked or run and reports them back to a Web site. You could link this data with your fitness center's computers so it would be available to your personal coach.

We can expect that televisions and autos and parking meters will all be computers, or at least have a computer inside. We can further imagine some middle-aged, overweight man sitting at a Pizza Hut when the 911 staff arrives to carry him away.

"Why are you here?" he'll say, "I'm fine."

"Oh, no you're not. Your pacemaker called us because you're having a heart attack."

So it seems reasonable to assume that between now and 2022 you should be on the lookout for opportunities to include networked computers into whatever products you're making, marketing, or selling.

But let's apply systems thinking to a larger view. What will all of these **computers-in-a-product** mean to industry in general? Who will be the winners and who will be the losers? The U.S. Postal Service will continue to lose, but who else? What about Dell? If Dell continues to define itself as a maker of computers, then by 2022 Dell will be a shadow of its present self. Who else will be affected? Microsoft? Microsoft may be a loser, depending on how it responds to this change. The world wants a Windows slate, like the iPad, but can Microsoft deliver?

Who will be the big winners? Students. Publishers will sell innovative content over the Kindles-to-be. If they do so in a way that eliminates used books, students will pay $40 instead of $140 for a textbook. Book resellers will lose.

And what about classrooms? Why go to class if you have a classroom in a box? Let's phrase this differently, because the traditional classroom does have value, especially to those students who learn from comments and questions asked by more able students.[5] Put it this way: Suppose you can go to a traditional classroom for $25,000 a year or go to the classroom in a box for $3,500 per year. Either way, you earn a degree; maybe the box's degree is not as prestigious, but it is an accredited degree. Which would you choose?

We'll take a 2022 look at the end of each chapter. For now, think about it: Who are the winners and the losers in the computers-in-products era?

---

[5] Louise Nemanich, Michael Banks, and Dusya Vera, "Enhancing Knowledge Transfer in Classroom Versus OnLine Settings: The Interplay Among Instructor, Student, and Context," *Decision Sciences Journal of Innovative Education* 7, no. 1 (2009): 140.

Guide

Understanding Perspectives and Points of View

Every human being speaks and acts from the perspective of a personal point of view. Everything we say or do is based on—or equivalently, is biased by—that point of view. Thus, everything you read in any textbook, including this one, is biased by the author's point of view. The author may think that he is writing an unbiased account of neutral subject material. But no one can write an unbiased account of anything, because we all write from a perspective.

Similarly, your professors speak to you from their points of view. They have experience, goals, objectives, hopes, and fears, and, like all of us, those elements provide a framework from which they think and speak.

The statement in Q1 that this course is the single most important course in the business school is clearly an opinion. Other professors in other departments may disagree. Is one of us right and the other wrong? I think so, but do you?

Other opinions are less apparently opinions. Consider the following definition of information: "Information is a difference that makes a difference." By this definition, there are many differences, but only those that make a difference qualify as information.

This definition is not obviously an opinion, but it nevertheless was written from a biased perspective. The perspective is just less evident because the statement appears as a definition, not an opinion. But, in fact, it is the definition of information in the opinion of the well-known psychologist Gregory Bateson.

I find his definition informative and useful. It is imprecise, but it is a good guideline, and I have used it to advantage when designing reports and queries for end users. I ask myself, "Does this report show someone a difference that makes a difference to them?" So, I find it a useful and helpful definition.

My colleagues who specialize in quantitative methods, however, find Bateson's definition vapid and useless. They ask, "What does it say?" "How could I possibly use that definition to formalize anything?" or "A difference that makes a difference to what or whom?" Or they say, "I couldn't quantify anything about that definition; it's a waste of time."

And they are right, but so am I, and so was Gregory Bateson. The difference is a matter of perspective, and, surprisingly, conflicting perspectives can all be true at the same time.

One last point: Whether it is apparent or not, authors write and professors teach not

only from personal perspectives, but also with personal goals. I write this textbook in the hope that you will find the material useful and important and tell your professor that it is a great book so that he or she will use it again. Whether you (or I) are aware of that fact, it and my other hopes and goals bias every sentence in this book.

Similarly, your professors have hopes and goals that influence what and how they teach. Your professors may want to see light bulbs of recognition on your face, they may want to win the Professor of the Year award, or they may want to gain tenure status in order to be able to do some advanced research in the field. Whatever the case, they, too, have hopes and goals that bias everything they say.

So, as you read this book and as you listen to your professor, ask yourself, "What is her perspective?" and "What are her goals?" Then compare those perspectives and goals to yours. Learn to do this not just with your textbooks and your professors, but with your colleagues as well. When you enter the business world, being able to discern and adapt to the perspectives and goals of those with whom you work will make you much more effective. ■

Source: © Sharon Dominick/iStockphoto.com.

Discussion Questions

1. Consider the following statement: "The quality of your thinking is the most important component of an information system." Do you agree with this statement? Do you think it is even possible to say that one component is the most important one?

2. This text claims that although it is not possible to increase your IQ, it is possible to improve the quality of your thinking. Do you agree? Whether or not you agree, give three examples that illustrate differences in quality of thinking as it pertains to the creation of information. They can be all from one person or they can be examples from three different people.

3. Though it does not appear to be so, the statement, "There are five components of an information system: hardware, software, data, procedures, and people" is an opinion based on a perspective. Suppose you stated this opinion to a computer engineer who said, "Rubbish. That's not true at all. The only components that count are hardware and maybe software." Contrast the perspective of the engineer with that of your MIS professor. How do those perspectives influence their opinions about the five-component framework? Which is correct?

4. Consider Bateson's definition, "Information is a difference that makes a difference." How can this definition be used to advantage when designing a Web page? Explain why someone who specializes in quantitative methods might consider this definition to be useless. How can the same definition be both useful and useless?

5. Some students hate open-ended questions. They want questions that have one correct answer, like 7.3 miles per hour. When given a question like that in question 4, a question that has multiple, equally valid answers, some students get angry or frustrated. They want the book or the professor to give them the answer. How do you feel about this matter?

6. Questions like those in the 2022 section obviously have no correct answer. Or, they have a correct answer, but that answer won't be known until 2022. Because this is true, are such questions worthless? Are you wasting your time thinking about them? Why or why not? Because the answer cannot be known on a timely basis, is any answer as good as any other? Why or why not?

7. Do you think someone can improve the quality of his or her thinking by learning to hold multiple, contradictory ideas in mind at the same time? Or, do you think that doing so just leads to indecisive and ineffective thinking? Discuss this question with some of your friends. What do they think? What are their perspectives?

Guide
Passwords and Password Etiquette

All forms of computer security involve passwords. Most likely, you have a university account that you access with a user name and password. When you set up that account, you were probably advised to use a **"strong password."** That's good advice, but what is a strong password? Probably not "sesame," but what then? Microsoft, a company that has many reasons to promote effective security, provides a definition that is commonly used. Microsoft defines a strong password as one with the following characteristics:

- Has nine or more characters
- Does not contain your user name, real name, or company name
- Does not contain a complete dictionary word, in any language
- Is different from previous passwords you have used
- Contains both upper- and lowercase letters, numbers, and special characters (such as ~ ! @; # $ % ^ &; * ( ) _ +; - =; { } | [ ] \ : " ; ' <; >;? , ./)

Examples of good passwords are:

- Qw37^T1bb?at
- 3B47qq<3>5!7b

The problem with such passwords is that they are nearly impossible to remember. And the last thing you want to do is write your password on a piece of paper and keep it near the device where you use it. Never do that!

One technique for creating memorable, strong passwords is to base them on the first letter of the words in a phrase. The phrase could be the title of a song or the first line of a poem or one based on some fact about your life. For example, you might take the phrase, "I was born in Rome, New York, before 2000." Using the first letters from that phrase and substituting the character < for the word *before*, you create the password IwbiR, NY<2000. That's an acceptable password, but it would be better if all of the numbers were not placed on the end. So, you might try the phrase, "I was born at 3:00 A.M. in Rome, New York." That phrase yields the password Iwba3:00AMiR,NY which is a strong password that is easily remembered.

Once you have created a strong password, you need to protect it with proper behavior. Proper password etiquette is one of the marks of a business professional. Never write down your password, and do not share it with others. Never ask someone else for his password, and never give your password to someone else.

But, what if you need someone else's password? Suppose, for example, you ask someone to help you with a problem on your computer. You sign on to an information system, and for some reason, you need to enter that other person's password. In this case, say to the other person, "We need your password," and then get out of your chair, offer your keyboard to the other person, and look away while she enters the password. Among professionals working in organizations that take security seriously, this little "do-si-do" move—one person getting out of the way so that another person can enter her password—is common and accepted.

If someone asks for your password, do not give it out. Instead, get up, go over to that person's machine, and enter your own password, yourself. Stay present while your password is in use, and ensure that your account is logged out at the end of the activity. No one should mind or be offended in any way when you do this. It is the mark of a professional. ∎

Discussion Questions

1. Here are the first two lines of a famous poem by T. S. Eliot, "Let us go then, you and I, When the evening is spread out against the sky." Explain how to use these lines to create a password. How could you add numbers and special characters to the password in a way that you will be able to remember?

2. List two different phrases that you can use to create a strong password. Show the password created by each.

3. One of the problems of life in the cyber-world is that we all are required to have multiple passwords—one for work or school, one for bank accounts, another for eBay or other auction sites, and so forth. Of course, it is better to use different passwords for each. But in that case you have to remember three or four different passwords. Think of different phrases you can use to create a memorable, strong password for each of these different accounts. Relate the phrase to the purpose of the account. Show the passwords for each.

4. Explain proper behavior when you are using your computer and you need to enter, for some valid reason, another person's password.

5. Explain proper behavior when someone else is using her computer and that person needs to enter, for some valid reason, your password.

Active Review

Use this Active Review to verify that you understand the ideas and concepts that answer the chapter's study questions.

Q1 Why is Introduction to MIS the most important class in the business school?

Define *Moore's Law* and explain why its consequences are important to business professionals today. State how business professionals should relate to emerging information technology. Give the text's definition of *job security* and use Reich's list to explain how this course will help you attain that security.

Q2 What is MIS?

Identify the three important phrases in the definition of *MIS*. Name the five components of an information system. Explain why end users need to be involved in the management of information systems. Explain why it is a misconception to say that organizations do something.

Q3 How can you use the five-component model?

Name and define each of the five components. Explain the symmetry in the five-component model. Show how automation moves work from one side of the five-component structure to the other. Explain how the components are ordered according to difficulty of change and disruption. Name the most important component and state why it is the most important. Use the five-component model to describe the differences between high-tech and low-tech information systems. Explain why information can never be written on a piece of paper or shown on a display device.

Q4 Why is the difference between information technology and information systems important?

Using the five-component model, explain the difference between IT and IS. Explain why you can buy IT,

but you can never buy IS. What does that mean to you, as a potential future business manager?

Q5 What is information?

State four different definitions of information. Identify the one that is your favorite and explain why. State the difference between data and information. Explain why information can never be written on a piece of paper or shown on a display device.

Q6 What are necessary data characteristics?

Create a mnemonic device for remembering the characteristics of good data. Explain how these data characteristics relate to information quality.

Q7 2022?

Explain the term *computers-in-a-product*. Explain how Dell might be a loser in this new era. What must Dell do to respond to this movement? Under which circumstances will Microsoft lose in this environment? What must Microsoft do? Why is your college or university challenged by computers-in-a-box? Is it seriously challenged or is this just a passing fad? If your school is publicly funded, is it more at risk? Summarize how answering these questions contributes to your skill as a nonroutine thinker.

Using Your Knowledge at GearUp

Reread the GearUp vignette at the start of this chapter. Using the knowledge you've gained from this chapter, especially that in Q1, identify five mistakes that Jennifer made. For each, explain what you would do differently. Be specific.

Key Terms and Concepts

Abstract reasoning   6
Collaboration   7
Computer hardware   8
Computer-based information
   system   9
Computers-in-a-product   19
Data   8

Experimentation   7
Five-component framework   8
Information   14
Information system (IS)   8
Information technology (IT)   13
Management information
   systems (MIS)   8

Moore's Law   4
People   8
Procedures   8
Software   8
Strong password   22
System   8
Systems thinking   7

Using Your Knowledge

1. One of life's greatest gifts is to be employed doing work that you love. Reflect for a moment on a job that you would find so exciting that you could hardly wait to get to sleep on Sunday night so that you could wake up and go to work on Monday.

   a. Describe that job. Name the industry, the type of company or organization for whom you'd like to work, the products and services they produce, and your specific job duties.
   b. Explain what it is about that job that you find so compelling.
   c. In what ways will the skills of abstraction, systems thinking, collaboration, and experimentation facilitate your success in that job?
   d. Given your answers to parts a through c, define three to five personal goals for this class. None of these goals should include anything about your GPA. Be as specific as possible. Assume that you are going to evaluate yourself on these goals at the end of the quarter or semester. The more specific you make these goals, the easier it will be to perform the evaluation. Use Figure 1-2 for guidance.

2. Consider costs of a system in light of the five components: costs to buy and maintain the hardware; costs to develop or acquire licenses to the software programs and costs to maintain them; costs to design databases and fill them with data; costs of developing procedures and keeping them current; and finally, human costs both to develop and use the system.

   a. Over the lifetime of a system, many experts believe that the single most expensive component is people. Does this belief seem logical to you? Explain why you agree or disagree.
   b. Consider a poorly developed system that does not meet its defined requirements. The needs of the business do not go away, but they do not conform themselves to the characteristics of the poorly built system. Therefore, something must give. Which component picks up the slack when the hardware and software programs do not work correctly? What does this say about the cost of a poorly designed system? Consider both direct money costs as well as intangible personnel costs.
   c. What implications do you, as a future business manager, take from parts a and b? What does this say about the need for your involvement in requirements and other aspects of systems development? Who eventually will pay the costs of a poorly developed system? Against which budget will those costs accrue?

3. Consider the four definitions of information presented in this chapter. The problem with the first definition, "knowledge derived from data," is that it merely substitutes one word we don't know the meaning of (*information*) for a second word we don't know the meaning of (*knowledge*). The problem with the second definition, "data presented in a meaningful context," is that it is too subjective. Whose context? What makes a context meaningful? The third definition, "data processed by summing, ordering, averaging, etc.," is too mechanical. It tells us what to do, but it doesn't tell us what information is. The fourth definition, "a difference that makes a difference," is vague and unhelpful.

   Also, none of these definitions helps us to quantify the amount of information we receive. What is the information content of the statement that every human being has a navel? Zero—you already know that. In contrast, the statement that someone has just deposited $50,000 into your checking account is chock-full of information. So, good information has an element of surprise.

Considering all of these points, answer the following questions:

a. What is information made of?

b. If you have more information, do you weigh more? Why or why not?

c. When you give a copy of your transcript to a prospective employer, how is information produced? What part of that information production process do you control? What, if anything, can you do to improve the quality of information that the employer conceives?

d. Give your own best definition of information.

e. Explain how you think it is possible that we have an industry called the *information technology industry,* but we have great difficulty defining the word *information.*

4. The text states that data should be worth its cost. Both cost and value can be broken into tangible and intangible factors. *Tangible* factors can be directly measured; *intangible* ones arise indirectly and are difficult to measure. For example, a tangible cost is the cost of a computer monitor; an intangible cost is the lost productivity of a poorly trained employee.

Give five important tangible and five important intangible costs of an information system. Give five important tangible and five important intangible measures of the value of an information system. If it helps to focus your thinking, use the example of the class scheduling system at your university or some other university information system. When determining whether an information system is worth its cost, how do you think the tangible and intangible factors should be considered?

▬ Collaboration Exercise 1

With a team of your fellow students, develop an answer to the following questions. Use Google Docs, Google+, Windows Live SkyDrive, SharePoint, Office 365, or some other collaboration tool to conduct your meetings.

1. Abstract reasoning.

   a. Define *abstract reasoning,* and explain why it is an important skill for business professionals.

   b. Explain how a list of items in inventory and their quantity on hand is an abstraction of a physical inventory.

   c. Give three other examples of abstractions commonly used in business.

   d. Explain how Jennifer failed to demonstrate effective abstract-reasoning skills.

   e. Can people increase their abstract-reasoning skills? If so, how? If not, why not?

2. Systems thinking.

   a. Define *systems thinking,* and explain why it is an important skill for business professionals.

   b. Explain how you would use systems thinking to explain why Moore's Law caused a farmer to dig up a field of pulp wood trees. Name each of the elements in the system, and explain their relationships to each other.

   c. Give three other examples of the use of system thinking with regard to consequences of Moore's Law.

   d. Explain how Jennifer failed to demonstrate effective systems thinking skills.

   e. Can people improve their system thinking skills? If so, how? If not, why not?

3. Collaboration.

   a. Define *collaboration,* and explain why it is an important skill for business professionals.

   b. Explain how you are using collaboration to answer these questions. Describe what is working with regards to your group's process and what is not working.

   c. Is the work product of your team better than any one of you could have done separately? If not, your collaboration is ineffective. If that is the case, explain why.

   d. Does the fact that you cannot meet face to face hamper your ability to collaborate? If so, how?

   e. Explain how Jennifer failed to demonstrate effective collaboration skills.

f. Can people increase their collaboration skills? If so, how? If not, why not?

4. Experimentation.
   a. Define *experimentation,* and explain why it is an important skill for business professionals.
   b. Explain several creative ways you could use experimentation to answer this question.
   c. How does the fear of failure influence your willingness to engage in any of the ideas you identified in part b?
   d. Explain how Jennifer failed to demonstrate effective experimentation skills.
   e. Can people increase their willingness to take risks? If so, how? If not, why not?

5. Job security.
   a. State the text's definition of *job security*.
   b. Evaluate the text's definition of job security. Is it effective? If you think not, offer a better definition of job security.
   c. As a team, do you agree that improving your skills on the four dimensions in Collaboration Exercises 1–4 will increase your job security?
   d. Do you think technical skills (accounting proficiency, financial analysis proficiency, etc.) provide job security? Why or why not? Do you think you would have answered this question differently in 1980? Why or why not?

▆ Case Study 1

The Amazon of Innovation

On November 29, 2010, Amazon.com customers ordered 13.7 million items worldwide, an average of 158 items per second. On its peak order-fulfillment day, Amazon shipped over 9 million units, and over the entire 2010 holiday season it shipped to 178 countries.[6] Such performance is only possible because of Amazon's innovative use of information systems. Some of its major innovations are listed in Figure 1-7.

You may think of Amazon as simply an online retailer, and that is indeed where the company achieved most of its success. To do this, Amazon had to build enormous supporting infrastructure—just imagine the information systems and fulfillment facilities needed to ship 9 million items on a single day. That infrastructure, however, is only needed during the busy holiday season. Most of the year, Amazon is left with excess infrastructure capacity. Starting in 2000, Amazon began to lease some of that capacity to other companies. In the process, it played a key role in the creation of what are termed *cloud services,* which you will learn about in Chapter 4. For now, just think of cloud services as computer resources somewhere out in the Internet that are leased on flexible terms. Today,

Amazon's business lines can be grouped into three major categories:

- Online retailing
- Order fulfillment
- Cloud services

Consider each.

Amazon created the business model for online retailing. It began as an online bookstore, but every year since 1998 it has added new product categories. In 2011, the company sold goods in 29 product categories. Undoubtedly, there will be more by the time you read this.

Amazon is involved in all aspects of online retailing. It sells its own inventory. It incentivizes you, via the Associates program, to sell its inventory as well. Or, it will help you sell your inventory within its product pages or via one of its consignment venues. Online auctions are the major aspect of online sales in which Amazon does not participate. It tried auctions in 1999, but it could never make inroads against eBay.[7]

Today, it's hard to remember how much of what we take for granted was pioneered by Amazon. "Customers who bought this, also bought that;" online customer

[6] Amazon, "Third-Generation Kindle Now the Bestselling Product of All Time on Amazon Worldwide," News release, December 27, 2010. Available at http://phx.corporate-ir.net/phoenix.zhtml?c=176060&p=irol-newsArticle&ID=1510745&highlight= (accessed June 2011).
[7] For a fascinating glimpse of this story from someone inside the company, see "Early Amazon: Auctions" at http://glinden.blogspot.com/2006/04/early-Amazon.com-auctions.html (accessed June 2011).

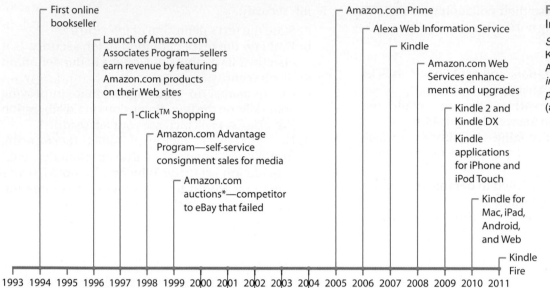

Figure 1-7
Innovation at Amazon

Source: Amazon.com, "Media Kit and History," February 2011. Available at *http://phx.corporate-ir. net/phoenix.zhtml?c=176060& p=irol-corporateTimeline* (accessed July 2011).

reviews; customer ranking of customer reviews; books lists; Look Inside the Book; automatic free shipping for certain orders or frequent customers; and Kindle books and devices were all novel concepts when Amazon introduced them.

Amazon's retailing business operates on very thin margins. Products are usually sold at a discount from the stated retail price, and 2-day shipping is free for Amazon Prime members (who pay an annual fee of $80). How do they do it? For one, Amazon drives its employees incredibly hard. Former employees claim the hours are long, the pressure is severe, and the workload is heavy. But what else? It comes down to Moore's Law and the innovative use of nearly free data processing, storage, and communication.

In addition to online retailing, Amazon also sells order fulfillment services. You can ship your inventory to an Amazon warehouse and access Amazon's information systems just as if they were yours. Using technology known as Web services (discussed in Chapter 6), your order processing information systems can directly integrate, over the Web, with Amazon's inventory, fulfillment, and shipping applications. Your customers need not know that Amazon played any role at all. You can also sell that same inventory using Amazon's retail sales applications.

Amazon Web Services (AWS) allows organizations to lease time on computer equipment in very flexible ways. Amazon's Elastic Cloud 2(EC2) enables organizations to expand and contract the computer resources they need within minutes. Amazon has a variety of payment plans, and it is possible to buy computer time for less than a penny an hour. Key to this capability is the ability for the leasing organization's computer programs to interface with Amazon's to automatically scale up and scale down the resources leased. For example, if a news site publishes a story that causes a rapid ramp-up of traffic, that news site can, programmatically, request, configure, and use more computing resources for an hour, a day, a month, whatever. Amazon.com also uses EC2 to support Silk, the innovative browser on the Kindle Fire. You will learn more about the cloud in Chapter 4.

Questions

1. In what ways does Amazon, as a company, evidence the willingness and ability to collaborate?

2. In what ways does Amazon, as a company, evidence the willingness and ability to experiment?

3. In what ways do you think the employees at Amazon must be able to perform systems and abstract thinking?

4. Describe, at a high level, the principal roles played by each of the five components of an information system that supports order fulfillment.

5. Choose any five of the innovations in Figure 1-7 and explain how you think Moore's Law facilitated that innovation.

6. Suppose you work for Amazon or a company that takes innovation as seriously as Amazon does. What do you suppose is the likely reaction to an employee who says to his or her boss, "But, I don't know how to do that!"?

7. Using your own words and your own experience, what skills and abilities do you think you need to have to thrive at an organization like Amazon?

TEACHING SUGGESTIONS

GearUp, Part 1 and Chapter 1

GOALS

Use GearUp to:

- Engage students' interest and emotions.

- Impart that Reich's four skills are not an academic theory; they are skills needed by business professionals today.

- Convey that people without Reich's four skills are at a disadvantage.

- Set up the GearUp case for use with Chapters 2–6.

BACKGROUND

1. GearUp is similar to private-buying clubs for high-end fashion and home goods such as MYHABIT (*www.myhabit.com*) and Zulily (*www.zulily.com*), but for sporting goods equipment and clothing. It negotiates specific maximum quantities of particular products and costs to be offered to GearUp customers at certain prices (vendors do not want GearUp to offer prices that are too low). GearUp runs the event and sells up to the maximum quantity. It then purchases the amount sold, takes delivery, and then reships the items to its customers.

2. Most of the time, this business model works. However, some vendors have been known to promise a higher quantity than they can deliver. Also, some vendors are less than careful about packaging, and damages become a problem. When shortages occur, GearUp must cancel some customer orders. Such cancellations cause both cost and reputation problems.

3. GearUp wants to compete on price; it strives to offer the lowest possible prices on quality sporting goods and apparel. Because it competes on price, it must do all it can to lower costs, as is indicated here.

4. The purpose of Jennifer's firing is to gain the students' attention. Jennifer was unable to perform any of Reich's four key skills. She worked hard, but ineffectively.

5. You can use this example if you are confronted with any students this term who tell you they should have earned a higher grade because they "worked really hard." Jennifer worked really hard, too; she also worked ineffectively.

HOW TO GET STUDENTS INVOLVED

1. In the chapter-opening scenario, why is Jennifer fired? Does this seem fair? Why or why not? And, even if unfair, does that matter?

2. Ask the class to compare the reasons she was fired to Reich's four key skills:

- **Abstract reasoning**
- **Systems thinking**
- **Experimentation**
- **Collaboration**

3. What should Jennifer have done differently?

4. Ask the students to what extent those four skills have been required in their education so far. How do the students feel about working with ambiguity? See also the guide on Questioning Your Questions.

VIDEO

We decided not to do videos for GearUp for this edition. However, the video for FlexTime (from the previous edition of this book) is close to this same scenario, and you can use it if you want to further gain the students' attention. If you do use it, consider the following.

In this video, we see Kelly fire Jennifer. The particular goal here is to cause the students to look back at Reich's four key skills and ask themselves, seriously, how well they themselves might do.

Another key goal is to cause the students to view this course as a chance to improve their abilities on those four skills.

Also, use this video to drive home the point that, difficult as it might be to get that first job, it is just the start. Serious students should use their school years to learn skills that will enable them to keep and excel at those jobs.

BOTTOM LINE

■ Every business needs IS.

■ Every businessperson needs a working knowledge of MIS.

■ Reich's four key skills are not just theory . . . people get fired for not having them.

■ Use this class to learn skills to excel as a professional.

■ You need these skills not only to obtain a professional job, but also to be able succeed and thrive in that job.

YOU BE THE GUIDE

Using the Ethics Guide: Ethics of Information from Misdirected Data (pages 16–17)

GOALS

- Teach students about the problem of unintentionally revealing sensitive data in public places.

- Explore ethical issues concerning the use of misdirected data.

- Differentiate between *unethical* and *illegal*.

BACKGROUND AND PRESENTATION STRATEGIES

I begin by asking the students what are the only two questions that a business professional can ask in an elevator. Usually someone will have worked in a law or CPA office and they'll know. The standard answer is:

■ **What floor?**

■ **How is the weather?**

That's it. *No other question is allowed in an elevator.* Airplanes and public places, like Starbucks in this story, are other places to avoid conversations about sensitive matters.

The first scenario happened to me. Fortunately, I was relieved of my ethical dilemma when a third party purchased the property from underneath all of us.

The people were loud and boorish. I wasn't sneaking around picking up newspapers by their table. I was passively sitting while they talked, very loudly. They were speaking loudly on cell phones to their inspector and their bank! I suppose I'm confounding my dislike for loud, public, cell phone users with my ethical principles. What difference does it make, ethically, if they were rude?

Did I have a responsibility to move to another table where I couldn't hear them? Or to warn them that I could hear them and that I was bidding on the same property? Or, did fate just drop something into my lap, like winning the lottery? I asked our agent about it, and she said by all means use the data. But do I want the realtor to be the guardian of my ethical principles? If so, I am avoiding my personal responsibility.

Usually, my students say they would use the data and never look back. I don't think I agree. When evaluating behavior in business, we can consider three sets of criteria: *Ethics, corporate policy,* and *laws.* Behaviors concerning the latter two categories are easy to define: Is the behavior against a law or corporate policy?

Ethical behavior is harder to define. Microsoft Encarta defines *ethical* as "conforming to accepted standards" or "consistent with agreed principles of correct moral conduct" and *ethics* as "a system of moral principles governing the appropriate conduct for an individual or group."

So, the question becomes, "What system of moral principles governs conduct for business professionals?" This is the core of the matter that we will address in all of the Ethics Guides in the text.

The legal community makes this issue clear, at least among lawyers and in the courts. Use of any misdirected data is unethical, and court judgments can be lost by a party that uses such data. Legal ethics state that if a lawyer mistakenly receives a document intended for the other side, the lawyer is forbidden to use the contents of that document and is supposed to direct the document to its proper source, or at least return it to the sender with an appropriate notice. Often, law firms place a notice reminding the receiver of that obligation at the bottom of every email or other correspondence. (You also will find it at the bottom of some corporate emails.)

■ **If we apply the lawyer's criteria to the scenarios in A–D, they are all unethical.**

■ **Should professional businesspeople have a lower standard than lawyers?**

SUGGESTED RESPONSES FOR DISCUSSION QUESTIONS

1. I don't think the medium should make a difference. Using the lawyer's criteria mentioned earlier, the use of data in either case is unethical. Also, there's a difference in that the email server at the real estate office has a record that it sent that email to you. In scenario A, no one could prove you heard. That difference doesn't change ethics—it just changes the chance that you might be discovered.

   Also, in scenario B there is another possibility: If you received the terms of their offer, there's a good chance the addresses were switched and they received the terms of your offer. From a practical perspective, setting aside the ethical issues, it's probably best to let your agent know what happened.

2. Scenario C is more complicated. For one, what if the customer wants you to have that data? Or, what if that data is false, the real number is higher, but the customer wants you to think that's their top number? This could be a mistake or a negotiating ploy. I think notifying the customer is not only ethical, it's also smart.

   ■ **Nothing is more serviceable than the truth. Maybe it's not the most convenient, but it's the easiest in the long run.**

   ■ **I don't think whether the data gives you or your company an advantage is relevant. By the way, your company may have a written ethical policy that governs your behavior here. You could lose your job by not following those guidelines.**

3. I think a person could make an argument that it is more ethical to lie to your friend about having received the email. The purpose of your lie would be to save your friend from embarrassment. However, lying to friends is not a great way to build relationships. It might be better to tell your friend that you did receive the email; that you're available to talk about it if he or she wants; and that, as a good friend, you can also forget all about it.

4. I think the actions of the person in scenario E are most unethical and undoubtedly against corporate policy. This is *"You're fired!"* territory. Were I that person's employer, I would not provide a reference. I don't think the person should have received the email, and I don't think the person should notify his or her friend. Anyone who abused his job authorities in this way is unlikely to care about the ethical principles of telling his or her friend, however. They'd probably tell. To me, the whole scenario stinks!

   ■ **By the way, this is mentioned in several places in the text, but it's worth reminding students that email is not secure, and email on the organization's network is subject to organizational scrutiny. Even if someone has not invaded the corporate system, as this person did, emails you send at work are not private.**

   a. For definitions, see "Background and Presentation Strategies."

   b. I suppose one could argue that business is competitive; it's dog eat dog, and you'll take any advantage that falls in your lap. (There is the possibility that the emails are setups, and you could be playing into someone's plan.) Or, it might be that in some industries, such behaviors are normal. If they are truly normal, if everyone accepts them, then according to the definition of ethical, these behaviors are ethical.

   c. One argument, a pragmatic one, centers on the idea that "nothing is more serviceable than the truth." Once you start taking advantage of data under the table, you've placed yourself in a spot to be manipulated (if, for example, the top number in scenario C is not really the top number). Another argument is a personal one: "I strive to act ethically, and I know I won't be happy engaging in unethical behavior. I want to work around people and industries in which ethical behavior is expected." A third argument takes the moral high ground. It doesn't matter if ethical behavior is pragmatic or personally preferred, unethical behavior is just wrong.

6. Answer is up to the students. See the Wrap Up.

WRAP UP

Some questions to summarize the discussion:

■ **How do you define the difference between legal and ethical?**

■ **Can something be against corporate policy and still be legal?**

■ **What is your personal policy about dealing with data that is misdirected to you?**

■ **Did your thoughts about this matter change as a result of this discussion? If so, how?**

Using the Guide: Understanding Perspectives and Points of View

(pages 20–21)

GOALS

- Reinforce the text's statement that, although none of us can change our IQ, we can improve the way we think, and thus improve our effective "smarts."

- Teach the importance of perspective in thinking and communication—everyone interprets the world in the context of their perspective.

- Encourage the students to think critically about the text, about your presentations, and about comments made by their fellow students.

BACKGROUND AND PRESENTATION STRATEGIES

I begin the discussion of this guide with the text's story (on page 11) about Walt Disney's death and the impact it had on Disney's stock price. (By the way, this story was told to me many years ago by a bond trader whose girlfriend worked at the hospital where they admitted Walt Disney. She told him she doubted that Disney would live through the night. He shorted Disney for the next day and lost his shirt. He told me, "That was the last time I traded on insider information. Not only is it illegal, it seldom works.")

Considerable academic research supports the notion that one can improve the quality of one's thinking. If the students search online under "critical-thinking skills" or "problem-solving skills," they will find hundreds of references.

If the students learn nothing else from this class except how to improve their thinking skills, even a little bit, it will be worth hundreds of hours of labor and thousands of dollars. (And, they're going to learn a lot more than that!) Here's an example of perspective:

■ If I say that our MIS class is more important than Intro to Accounting and if your accounting professor says that Intro to Accounting is more important than MIS, is either of us wrong?

■ Is one of us lying? Is one of us being insincere?

■ Is it possible to prove that one of us is right and one of us is wrong?

■ In fact, each of us is right. So, here's the million-dollar question:

■ What do you, as a student, do about that? Whom do you believe?

■ How does the concept of perspective—mine and the accounting prof's—relate to this?

No one can make any statement except from a perspective. Just as one must have a physical location (one has to be standing, sitting, or reclining somewhere), so, too, one's statements arise from a mental location, from a perspective. We cannot speak about anything except from some perspective. Usually, when two people disagree strongly, it is because they have different perspectives. Which leads to:

■ If I have a different perspective from someone, and if we're arguing about something, will any discussion about the facts of the matter have any impact on the outcome?

(No. We have to come to the same perspective.)

■ How likely is it that the other person will change his or her perspective?

(Not very.)

■ So what can I do?

(Understand what's going on and adapt.)

It's very difficult for people to change their perspective. Most people will resist, and strongly. However, successful businesspeople seem to have mastered the skill, or at least are better at it than most people.

There's a story about Bill Gates in the early days of the computer profession, when he was meeting with another company, and the meeting was going nowhere. Finally, Gates is supposed to have said, "Wait. I see the problem. We think we're the customer, and you think you're the customer. Actually, you're right—you are the customer. We need to go back and rethink our position. We'll get back to you in a couple of weeks." There are so many apocryphal stories about Bill Gates, but I think this one is true. It was told to me by someone who was in the meeting.

A key skill: Being able to perceive that difference in perspective is the root of a problem, and being able to alter one's perspective to achieve a solution, or to at least be able to communicate about a solution.

■ The key difference between animals and humans isn't that humans can think. Animals can think. The key difference is that humans can think about thinking. We can examine how we think, evaluate how our techniques are working for us, and choose to change how we think. Try it!

SUGGESTED RESPONSES FOR DISCUSSION QUESTIONS

1. I wrote that statement based on my perspective. I wrote it because I've watched end users misuse the outputs of well-designed information systems or not use them at all. But, another author, one with a different perspective, might say something else.

   The students don't have enough experience to know if they agree or not. They might decide provisionally to believe that statement until they know more. At this stage, the biggest impact on what they believe is you, their professor!

   From one perspective: If a system is like a chain, then every link is equally important. The third link is not more important than the fifth one. So all five components are the same. From a different perspective: How one thinks about the data people receive has the greatest impact on what they will do with that data. So, from that perspective, the statement is true.

2. There's a lot of research to back it up. Usually the students will agree, too, or at least they'll **want** to believe that it's true.

   The point of this question is to compel the students to think about different kinds and quality of thinking. Here are three examples of three different qualities:

   "I'm taking this class because it's required."

   "I'm not sure about this class. In fact, I'm not sure I'm in the right major. I always thought I'd be a business major, but that was because my Dad so loved accounting. I'm starting to wonder about my goals."

   "My expectations are modest. If I can get three or four useful skills or ideas out of a class, and if it's more or less interesting and enjoyable, then I'm content. I hope this will be one of those classes."

3. The engineer will have spent his or her career thinking about computer design. All the "interesting" problems will lie there. The MIS professor will have spent his or her career thinking about information systems; that is, what they are, how they are built, and how they do or do not facilitate the goals of organizations. The "important" problems arise when groups of people try to work together to accomplish something. Both are correct, from their own perspectives.

4. Design the Web page so that the critical data, the differences that are important to that person, are obvious and easily perceived. But, in quantitative methods, where's the equation? What can I compute? That definition is given from a perspective—it's useful for problems that are within the scope of its perspective.

5. Most classes have students who are at different levels of thinking. Some students will feel most comfortable when the answer is concrete. Others will have advanced to understand that thinking occurs within a particular context. I like to address this issue head on. Often students with higher cognitive skills can help those with less-developed skills. This exercise works well in groups—especially if the students have varying ages and life experiences. William Perry wrote several articles on this topic that had a profound impact on my teaching.[1]

6. Not worthless . . . for two good reasons, at least. First, by pondering where technology might go, one might learn something about unexpected relationships. The fall in the price/performance ratio of computing devices may have led to the wide variety of investment instruments, like accumulator stocks. That, in turn, could have led to instability in stock market prices. Knowledge of such relationships may lead to other unexpected relationships.

   Second, pondering the future can lead to strategies for future behavior. After identifying possible technology directions, one can develop responses to those directions. "If this happens, then we can do that." As in a chess game; you don't know what your opponent is going to do, but you can plan different responses for different possibilities.

   No, answers vary in quality; some are far superior to others. In both of the examples above, unrealistic or silly projections will be worthless and possibly misleading and dangerous.

7. The discussion, especially involving students of different levels of cognitive maturity, is the critical part of this exercise. Multifaceted thinking can seem (and be) indecisive. However, it can be wise. There is no answer. It depends. Some students will be squirming at this point, and that's OK. I just want to keep them talking about why they're squirming.

WRAP UP

- **The quality of your thinking can be improved.**

- **One way to improve your thinking is to consider perspectives—yours and others.**

- **Suppose you ask two people how far it is to the business school library. Suppose one of them is sitting next to you in class and the other is sitting at the nearest airport. Will they give different answers to the same question? Of course! Is either wrong? No. Are you surprised?**

- **Suppose you ask two people if college tuition is too high. Suppose one works two jobs to pay for school and the other is dying of cancer. Will they give different answers?**

- **Bottom line: Consider perspectives when understanding yourself and anyone else!**

[1]William A. Perry, "Different Worlds in the Same Classroom," *On Teaching and Learning,* Harvard Danforth Center (May 1985), pp. 1–17; and William A. Perry, "Cognitive and Ethical Growth," in Arthur W. Chickering (Ed.), *The Modern American College* (San Francisco: Jossey-Bass, 1981), pp. 76–115. The first is available at *www.bookcenter.harvard.edu/docs/perry.html.*

YOU BE THE GUIDE

Using the Guide: Passwords and Password Etiquette (pages 22–23)

GOALS

- Teach the students an easy way to create and remember strong passwords.
- Teach the students proper password etiquette.
- Underline the importance of passwords and password protection.

BACKGROUND AND PRESENTATION STRATEGIES

This Guide concerns passwords, because students need to start practicing good password techniques, now. Universities are, unfortunately, common targets of security attacks. Thus, early in the course we need to teach very important self-protection strategies. We will discuss passwords again in more detail in Chapter 12. However, the sooner students learn how to create and use strong passwords, the better.

Using the initial letters of a line of poetry or a phrase is a very easy way to remember strong passwords. In order to create and remember different passwords for different accounts (one for the university, one for Amazon.com, one for the student's ISP, etc.), it's useful to employ a phrase that's relevant to the account. "Last year, 2011, I spent more than 700 dollars on books" yields, Ly2011Is>700dob, which is an easily remembered strong password. See Discussion Question 3.

The only reason any of us should ever type a password is for authentication. **There is no other valid reason to type it**. I tell my students if they find themselves typing their password for any other reason, stop! Whatever they're doing is wrong. Don't type it in an email, don't type it on a piece of paper to remember, don't type it in response to some phisher's query. (Phishing is described in detail in Chapter 12.)

I think we need to teach that among IS professionals it is rude not to look away when someone is typing a password. Recently, I was giving a demo to a very senior database manager at Microsoft and I needed to enter my password. Even though he and I have known each other for years and have become personal friends, as soon as he saw what I was doing, he quite pointedly looked out the window.

- **Brush your teeth twice a day, don't talk with your mouth full, and look out the window when someone is typing their password.**

The same comment applies to never asking someone for their password. It is rude. Ask the person to come to your computer and enter his or her password.

- **If someone asks for your password, don't tell them they're rude. Just smile, get up, go to their keyboard, and enter it yourself. Then be sure to stay around until they log off.**

All of these behaviors simply indicate that the person takes security seriously and is a thoughtful and professional businessperson.

Students may not know this, but for many networks, when they log in using their password they gain access not only to the network to which they're connecting, but also to other networks. One network (the business school) may authenticate them to a second network (the library), which will authenticate them to a third (the state library system), and so on. Thus, loss of a password may cause much more damage than just to the local network. We'll briefly mention Kerberos in Chapter 12, but the point for now is that one password may authenticate the student to many networks, networks the student may not even know about. Protect those passwords!

You might want to review Question 2022 in Chapter 12 before discussing this guide. It has some thoughts on why smaller targets, like individuals, are becoming more desirable targets.

 ## SUGGESTED RESPONSES FOR DISCUSSION QUESTIONS

These questions require straightforward application of the material in the guide and of the points just made. I use them not to create a discussion, but to be certain that the students understand the techniques.

1. This phrase is the first line of "The Lovesong of J. Alfred Prufrock" by T. S. Eliot. Without the commas, it is: LugtyaIwteisoats. That's a little long. Maybe put in the comma and use "Let us go then, you and I, before 6 PM," which results in the password Lugt,yaI<6PM.

2. A practice exercise to make sure the students understand the principle. Answers depend on the students.

3. Make the phrase be related to the purpose or nature of the account. Examples:

Account	Phrase	Password
Work	"Back in the saddle at 8:00 AM."	Bitsa8:00AM
School	"I take IS300 before Sarah."	ItIS300<S
eBay	"I want to sell more than 1,000 dollars of goods."	Iwts>1000dog or Iwts>$1000og
Bank	"Is University Savings before 3rd Street?"	IUS<3rdS?

4. Tell the other person what you are doing and why you need their password. Ask them to log on to your computer. Get out of your chair and let them sit at your keyboard and enter the password. Look away.

Use their account to do what you need to do and log off (or offer to let them log off). Thank the person and tell them that you have logged off.

■ **These are professional manners in a cyber world!**

5. Get up, go over to their computer, and ask to log in. Stay in the neighborhood while they're using your account. Sign out or be certain that they sign out. It's not bad manners, by the way, to inquire, politely, why they need your password.

WRAP UP

Some statements I make in summary:

■ **Passwords are important. As a professional, you have a responsibility to take your passwords seriously and to protect them.**

■ **Passwords are the foundation of most organizational security systems. You have a responsibility to yourself and your fellow employees to create strong passwords, to protect them, and to change them frequently.**

Chapter 2

Collaboration Information Systems

"No, Felix! Not again! Over, and over, and over! We decide something one meeting and then go over it again the next meeting and again the next. What a waste!"

"What do you mean, Drew? I think it's important we get this right."

"Well, Felix, if that's the case, why don't you come to the meetings?"

"I just missed a couple."

"Right. Last week we met here for, oh, two, maybe three, hours and we decided to look for ways to reduce operational expenses."

"But Drew, if we could increase revenue, we wouldn't have to cut costs. I think I have a couple of good ideas on how to do that."

"Felix! Last week we discussed that and decided it didn't make sense. Increasing volume with our same processes will increase both revenue AND costs. Plus, that's not what Kelly asked us to do."

"Look, Drew, Kelly just wants the company to be profitable. Margins are down. If we increase volume we can get more efficient . . . better scale, you know?"

"Right. But how do you do it? And, specifically, are we going to become more efficient? That's the point! Come on, Felix, you're driving me nuts. We discussed this *ad nauseam* last week. Let's make some progress. Why don't some of you other guys help me! Addison, what do you think?"

"Felix, Drew is right. We did have a long discussion on what we're doing—and we did agree to focus on reducing operational expenses."

"Well, Addison, I think it's a mistake. Why didn't anyone tell me? I put a lot of time into developing my plan."

"Did you read the email?" Addison asks tentatively.

"What email?"

"The meeting summary email that I send out each week."

"I got the email but I couldn't download the attachment. Something weird about a virus checker couldn't access a gizmo or something like that. . . "

Drew can't stand that excuse, "Here, Felix, take a look at mine. I'll underline the part where we concluded that we'd focus on operational expenses so you can be sure to see it."

"Drew, there's no reason to get snippy about this. I thought I had a good idea."

"OK, so we're agreed—*again this week*—that we're going to look for ways of reducing costs. Now, we've wasted enough time covering old ground. Let's get some new thinking going."

Felix slumps back into his chair and looks down at his cell phone.

"Oh, no, I missed a call from Mapplethorpe. Ahhhh."

"Felix, what are you talking about?"

"Mapplethorpe, my contact at General Sports. Wants to change the maximum quantity on tomorrow's event. I'm sorry, but I've got to call him. I'll be back in a few minutes."

Felix leaves the room.

Drew looks at the three team members who are left.

"Now what?" he asks. "If we go forward we'll have to rediscuss everything we do when Felix comes back. Maybe we should just take a break?"

Addison shakes her head. "Drew, let's not. It's tough for me to get to these meetings. I don't have to work until tonight, so I drove down here just for this. I've got to pick up Simone from day care. We haven't done anything yet. Let's just ignore Felix."

"OK, Addison, but it isn't easy to ignore Felix."

The door opens and Kelly, GearUp's CEO, walks in.

"Hi everyone! How's it going? OK if I sit in on your meeting?" ∎

Study Questions

Q1 What are the two key characteristics of collaboration?

Q2 What are three criteria for successful collaboration?

Q3 What are the four primary purposes of collaboration?

Q4 What are the components and functions of a collaboration information system?

Q5 How can you use collaboration tools to improve team communication?

Q6 How can you use collaboration tools to share content?

Q7 How can you use Office 365 for student projects?

Q8 2022?

Business is a social activity. While we often say that organizations accomplish their strategy, they don't. *People* in organizations accomplish strategy by working with other people, almost always working in groups. People do business with people.

Over the years, technology has increasingly supported group work. In your grandfather's day, communication was done using letter, phone, and office visits. Those technologies were augmented in the 1980s and 1990s with fax and email, and more recently by texting, conference calls, and videoconferencing. Today, products such as Office 365 provide a wide array of tools to support collaborative work.

This chapter investigates ways that information systems can support collaboration. We begin by defining collaboration, discussing collaborative activities, and setting criteria for collaboration success. Next, we'll address the kinds of work that collaborative teams do. Then, we'll discuss the components of collaborative information systems and illustrate important collaborative tools for improving communication and sharing content. We'll next illustrate ways that you can use Office 365 to improve your student collaborations, and we'll wrap up with collaboration in 2022!

Q1 What Are the Two Key Characteristics of Collaboration?

To answer this question, we must first distinguish between the terms *cooperation* and *collaboration*. **Cooperation** is a group of people working together, all doing essentially the same type of work, to accomplish a job. A group of four painters, each painting a different wall in the same room, are working cooperatively. Similarly, a group of checkers at the grocery store or clerks at the post office are working cooperatively to service customers. A cooperative group can accomplish a given task faster than an individual working alone, but the cooperative result is usually not better in quality than the result of someone working alone.

In this text, we define **collaboration** as a group of people working together to achieve a common goal *via a process of feedback and iteration*. Using feedback and iteration, one person will produce something, say the draft of a document, and a second person will review that draft and provide critical feedback. Given the feedback, the original author or someone else will then revise the first draft to produce a second. The work proceeds in a series of stages, or *iterations*, in which something is produced, members criticize it, and then another version is produced. Using iteration and feedback, the group's result can be better than what any single individual can produce alone. This is possible because different group members provide different perspectives. "Oh, I never thought of it that way," is a typical signal of collaboration success.

Many, perhaps most, student groups incorrectly use cooperation rather than collaboration. Given an assignment, a group of five students will break it up into five pieces, work to accomplish their piece independently, and then merge their independent work for grading by the professor. Such a process will enable the project to be completed more quickly, with less work by any single individual, but it will not be better than the result obtained if the students were to work alone.

The Ethics Guide on pages 40–41 addresses some of the ethical challenges that arise when teams hold virtual meetings.

In contrast, when students work collaboratively, they set forth an initial idea or work product, provide feedback to one another on those ideas or products, and then revise in accordance with feedback. Such a process can produce a result far superior to that produced by any student working alone.

Importance of Effective Critical Feedback

Given this definition, for collaboration to be successful members must provide and receive *critical* feedback. A group in which everyone is too polite to say anything critical cannot collaborate. As Darwin John, the world's first chief information officer (CIO) (see Chapter 11) once said, "If two of you have the exact same idea, then we have no need for one of you." On the other hand, a group that is so critical and negative that members come to distrust, even hate, one another cannot effectively collaborate either. For most groups, success is achieved between these extremes.

To underline this point, consider the research of Ditkoff, Allen, Moore, and Pollard. They surveyed 108 business professionals to determine the qualities, attitudes, and skills that make a good collaborator.[1] Figure 2-1 lists the most and least important characteristics reported in the survey. Most students are surprised to learn that 5 of the top 12 characteristics involve disagreement (highlighted in orange in

Twelve Most Important Characteristics for an Effective Collaborator

1. Is enthusiastic about the subject of our collaboration.

2. Is open-minded and curious.

3. Speaks their mind even if it's an unpopular viewpoint.

4. Gets back to me and others in a timely way.

5. Is willing to enter into difficult conversations.

6. Is a perceptive listener.

7. Is skillful at giving/receiving negative feedback.

8. Is willing to put forward unpopular ideas.

9. Is self-managing and requires "low maintenance."

10. Is known for following through on commitments.

11. Is willing to dig into the topic with zeal.

12. Thinks differently than I do/brings different perspectives.

Nine Least Important Characteristics for an Effective Collaborator

31. Is well organized.

32. Is someone I immediately liked. The chemistry is good.

33. Has already earned my trust.

34. Has experience as a collaborator.

35. Is a skilled and persuasive presenter.

36. Is gregarious and dynamic.

37. Is someone I knew beforehand.

38. Has an established reputation in field of our collaboration.

39. Is an experienced businessperson.

Figure 2-1
Important and Not Important Characteristics of a Collaborator

Source: Based on Dave Pollard, "The Ideal Collaborative Team." Available at: http://blogs.salon.com/0002007/stories/2005/11/18/theIdealCollaborativeTeamAndAConversationOnTheCollaborativeProcess.html (accessed May, 2009).

---

[1] Dave Pollard, "The Ideal Collaborative Team." Available at: http://blogs.salon.com/0002007/stories/2005/11/18/theIdealCollaborativeTeamAndAConversationOnTheCollaborativeProcess.html (accessed June 2011).

Figure 2-1). Most students believe that "we should all get along" and more or less have the same idea and opinions about team matters. Although it is important for the team to be social enough to work together, this research indicates that it is also important for team members to have different ideas and opinions and to express them to each other.

When we think about collaboration as an iterative process in which team members give and receive feedback, these results are not surprising. During collaboration, team members learn from each other, and it will be difficult to learn if no one is willing to express different, or even unpopular, ideas. The respondents also seem to be saying, "You can be negative, as long as you care about what we're doing." These collaboration skills do not come naturally to people who have been taught to "play well with others," but that may be why they were so highly ranked in the survey.

The characteristics rated *not relevant* are also revealing. Experience as a collaborator or in business does not seem to matter. Being popular also is not important. A big surprise, however, is that being well organized was rated 31st out of 39 characteristics. Perhaps collaboration itself is not a very well-organized process?

Guidelines for Giving and Receiving Critical Feedback

Giving and receiving critical feedback is the single most important collaboration skill. So, before we discuss the role that information systems can play for improving collaboration, study the guidelines for giving and receiving critical feedback shown in Figure 2-2.

Many students have found that when they first form a collaborative group, it's useful to begin with a discussion of critical feedback guidelines like those in Figure 2-2. Begin with this list, and then, using feedback and iteration, develop your own list. Of course, if a group member does not follow the agreed-upon guidelines, someone will have to provide critical feedback to that effect as well.

Warning!

If you are like most undergraduate business students, especially freshmen or sophomores, your life experience is keeping you from understanding the need for collaboration. So far, almost everyone you know has the same experiences as you and, more or less, thinks like you. Your friends and associates have the same educational

Figure 2-2
Guidelines for Providing and Receiving Critical Feedback

Guideline	Example
Be specific.	"I was confused until I got to Section 2" rather than "The whole thing is a disorganized mess."
Offer suggestions.	"Consider moving Section 2 to the beginning of the document."
Avoid personal comments.	Never: "Only an idiot would miss that point … or write that document."
Strive for balance.	"I thought Section 2 was particularly good. What do you think about moving it to the start of the document?"
Question your emotions.	"Why do I feel so angry about the comment he just made? What's going on? Is my anger helping me?"
Do not dominate.	If there are five members of the group, unless you have special expertise, you are entitled to just 20 percent of the words/time.
Demonstrate a commitment to the group.	"I know this is painful, but if we can make these changes our result will be so much better." or "Ouch. I really didn't want to have to redo that section, but if you all think it's important, I'll do it."

background, scored more or less the same on standardized tests, and have the same orientation toward success. So, why collaborate? Most of you think the same way, anyway: "What does the professor want and what's the easiest, fastest way to get it to her?"

So, consider this thought experiment. Your company is planning to build a new facility that is critical for the success of a new product line and will create 300 new jobs. The county government won't issue a building permit because the site is prone to landslides. Your engineers believe your design overcomes that hazard, but your CFO is concerned about possible litigation in the event there is a problem. Your corporate counsel is investigating the best way to overcome the county's objections while limiting liability. Meanwhile, a local environmental group is protesting your site because they believe it is too close to an eagle's nest. Your public relations director is meeting with those local groups every week.

Do you proceed with the project?

To decide, you create a working team of the chief engineer, the chief financial officer (CFO), your legal counsel, and the PR director. Each of those people has different education and expertise, different life experience, and different values. In fact, the only thing they have in common is that they are paid by your company. That team will participate collaboratively in ways that are far different from your experience so far. Keep this example in mind as you read this chapter.

Bottom line: The two key characteristics of collaboration are iteration and feedback.

Q2 What Are Three Criteria for Successful Collaboration?

J. Richard Hackman studied teamwork for many years, and his book *Leading Teams* contains many useful concepts and tips for future managers.[2] According to Hackman, there are three primary criteria for judging team success:

- Successful outcome
- Growth in team capability
- Meaningful and satisfying experience

Successful Outcome

Most students are primarily concerned with the first criterion. They want to achieve a good outcome, measured by their grade, or they want to get the project done with an acceptable grade while minimizing the effort required. For business professionals, teams need to accomplish their goals: make a decision, solve a problem, or create a work product. Whatever the objective is, the first success criterion is, "Did we do it?"

Although not as apparent in student teams, most business teams also need to ask, "Did we do it within the time and budget allowed?" Teams that produce a work product too late or far over budget are not successful, even if they did achieve their goal.

Growth in Team Capability

The other two criteria are surprising to most students, probably because most student teams are short-lived. But, in business, where teams often last months or years, it makes sense to ask, "Did the team get better?" If you're a football fan, you've undoubtedly heard your college's coach say, "We really improved as the season progressed." (Of course, for the team with 2 wins and 12 losses, you didn't hear that.) Football teams last only a season. If the team is permanent, say a team of customer support personnel, the benefits of team growth are even greater. Over time, as the team gets better, it becomes more efficient; thus, over time the team provides more service for a given cost or the same service for less cost.

---

[2] J. Richard Hackman, *Leading Teams: Setting the Stage for Great Performances* (Boston: Harvard Business Press, 2002).

How does a team get better? For one, it develops better work processes. Activities are combined or eliminated. Linkages are established so that "the left hand knows what the right hand is doing," or needs, or can provide. Teams also get better as individuals improve at their tasks. Part of that improvement is the learning curve; as someone does something over and over, he or she gets better at it. But team members also teach task skills and give knowledge to one another. Team members also provide perspectives that other team members need. We will investigate several of these possibilities in Chapters 7 and 8.

Meaningful and Satisfying Experience

The third element of Hackman's definition of team success is that team members have a meaningful and satisfying experience. Of course, the nature of team goals is a major factor in making work meaningful. But few of us have the opportunity to develop a life-saving cancer vaccine or safely land a stricken airliner in the middle of the Hudson River in winter. For most of us, it's a matter of making the product, or creating the shipment, or accounting for the payment, or finding the prospects, and so on.

So, in the more mundane world of most business professionals, what makes work meaningful? Hackman cites numerous studies in his book, and one common thread is that the work is perceived as meaningful by the team. Keeping prices up-to-date in the product database may not be the most exciting work, but if that task is perceived by the team as important, it will become meaningful.

Furthermore, if an individual's work is not only perceived as important, but the person doing that work is also given credit for it, then the experience will be perceived as meaningful. So, recognition for work well done is vitally important for a meaningful work experience.

Another aspect of team satisfaction is camaraderie. Business professionals, just like students, are energized when they have the feeling that they are part of a group, each person doing his or her own job, and combining efforts to achieve something worthwhile that is better than any could have done alone.

Q3 What Are the Four Primary Purposes of Collaboration?

Collaborative teams accomplish four primary purposes:

- Become informed.
- Make decisions.
- Solve problems.
- Manage projects.

These four purposes build on each other. For example, making a decision requires that team members be informed. In turn, to solve a problem, the team must have the ability to make decisions (and become informed). Finally, to conduct a project, the team must be able to solve problems (and make decisions and become informed).

Before we continue, understand you can use the hierarchy of these four purposes to build your professional skills. You cannot make good decisions if you do not have the skills to inform yourself. You cannot solve problems if you are unable to make good decisions. And you cannot manage projects if you don't know how to solve problems!

In this question, we will consider the collaborative nature of these four purposes and describe requirements for information systems that support them, starting with the most basic, becoming informed.

Becoming Informed

Informing is the first and most fundamental collaboration purpose. Recall from Chapter 1 that two individuals can receive the same data but construct different interpretations or, as stated in the terms of Chapter 1, conceive different information.

The goal of the informing is to ensure, as much as possible, that team members are conceiving information in the same way.

For example, as you read in the opening scenario, the team at GearUp has been assigned the task of reducing operational expenses. One of the team's first tasks is to ensure that everyone understands that goal and, further, understands what constitutes an operational expense.

Informing, and hence all of the purposes of collaboration, presents several requirements for collaborative information systems. As you would expect, team members need to be able to share data and to communicate with one another to share interpretations. Furthermore, because memories are faulty and team membership can change, it is also necessary to document the team's understanding of the information conceived. To avoid having to go "over and over and over" a topic, a repository of information, such as a wiki, is needed. We will say more about this in Q5.

Decision Making

Collaboration is used for some types of decision making, but not all. Consequently, to understand the role for collaboration we must begin with an analysis of decision making. Decisions are made at three levels: *operational, managerial,* and *strategic.*

Operational Decisions

Operational decisions are those that support operational, day-to-day activities. Typical operational decisions are: How many widgets should we order from vendor A? Should we extend credit to vendor B? Which invoices should we pay today?

Managerial Decisions

Managerial decisions are decisions about the allocation and utilization of resources. Typical decisions are: How much should we budget for computer hardware and programs for department A next year? How many engineers should we assign to project B? How many square feet of warehouse space do we need for the coming year?

In general, if a managerial decision requires consideration of different perspectives, then it will benefit from collaboration. For example, consider the decision of whether to increase employee pay in the coming year. No single individual has the answer. The decision depends on an analysis of inflation, industry trends, the organization's profitability, the influence of unions, and other factors. Senior managers, accountants, human resources personnel, labor relationships managers, and others will each bring a different perspective to the decision. They will produce a work product for the decision, evaluate that product, and make revisions in an iterative fashion—the essence of collaboration.

Strategic Decisions

Strategic decisions are those that support broad-scope, organizational issues. Typical decisions at the strategic level are: Should we start a new product line? Should we open a centralized warehouse in Tennessee? Should we acquire company A?

Strategic decisions are almost always collaborative. Consider a decision about whether to move manufacturing operations to China. This decision affects every employee in the organization, the organization's suppliers, its customers, and its shareholders. Many factors and many perspectives on each of those factors must be considered.

The Decision Process

Information systems can be classified based on whether their decision processes are *structured* or *unstructured.* These terms refer to the method or process by which the decision is to be made, not to the nature of the underlying problem. A **structured decision** process is one for which there is an understood and accepted method for making the decision. A formula for computing the reorder quantity of an item in inventory is an example of a structured decision process. A standard method for allocating furniture and equipment to employees is another structured decision process. Structured decisions seldom require collaboration.

An **unstructured decision** process is one for which there is no agreed-on decision-making method. Predicting the future direction of the economy or the stock market is a classic example. The prediction method varies from person to person; it is neither standardized nor broadly accepted. Another example of an unstructured decision process is assessing how well suited an employee is for performing a particular job. Managers vary in the manner in which they make such assessments. Unstructured decisions are often collaborative.

The Relationship Between Decision Type and Decision Process

The decision type and decision process are loosely related. Decisions at the operational level tend to be structured, and decisions at the strategic level tend to be unstructured. Managerial decisions tend to be both structured and unstructured.

We use the words *tend to be*, because there are exceptions to the relationship. Some operational decisions are unstructured (e.g., "How many taxicab drivers do we need on the night before the homecoming game?"), and some strategic decisions can be structured (e.g., "How should we assign sales quotas for a new product?"). In general, however, the relationship holds.

Decision Making and Collaboration Systems

As stated, few structured decisions involve collaboration. Deciding, for example, how much of product A to order from vendor B does not require the feedback and iteration among members that typify collaboration. Although the process of generating the order might require the coordinated work of people in purchasing, accounting, and manufacturing, there is seldom a need for one person to comment on someone else's work. In fact, involving collaboration in routine, structured decisions are expensive, wasteful, and frustrating. "Do we have to have a meeting about everything?" is a common lament.

The situation is different for unstructured decisions, because feedback and iteration are crucial. Members bring different ideas and perspectives about what is to be decided, how the decision will be reached, what criteria are important, and how decision alternatives score against those criteria. The group may make tentative conclusions, discuss potential outcomes of those conclusions, and members will often revise their positions. Figure 2-3 illustrates the change in the need for collaboration as decision processes become less structured.

Problem Solving

Problem solving is the third primary reason for collaborating. A **problem** is a perceived difference between what is and what ought to be. Because it is a perception, different people can have different problem definitions.

Figure 2-3
Collaboration Needs for
Decision Making

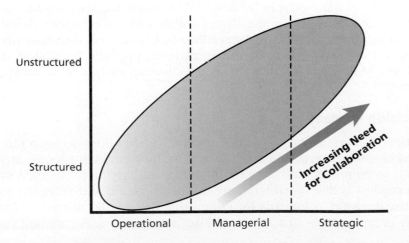

Figure 2-4
Problem-Solving Tasks

- Define the problem.
- Identify alternative solutions.
- Specify evaluation criteria.
- Evaluate alternatives.
- Select an alternative.
- Implement solution.

Figure 2-4
Problem-Solving Tasks

Therefore, the first and arguably the most important task for a problem-solving collaborative group is defining the problem. For example, the GearUp team has been assigned the problem of finding ways of reducing operational expenses. As stated as part of the informing purpose, the group needs first to ensure that the team members understand this goal and have a common definition of what an operational expense is.

However, because a problem is a difference between what is and what ought to be, the statement, "reduce operational expenses" does not go far enough. Is saving one dollar enough of a reduction? Is saving $100,000 enough? Does it take $1,000,000 for the reduction to be enough? A better problem definition would be to reduce operational expenses by 10 percent or by $100,000 or some other more specific statement of what is desired.

Figure 2-4 lists the principal problem-solving tasks. Because this text is about information systems and not about problem solving *per se*, we will not delve into those tasks here. Just note the work that needs to be done, and consider the role of feedback and iteration for each of these tasks.

Project Management

Project management is a rich and complicated subject, with many theories and methods and techniques.

Projects are formed to create or produce something. The end goal might be a marketing plan, the design of a new factory, or a new product, or it could be performing the annual audit. Because projects vary so much in nature and size, we will summarize generic project phases here. Figure 2-5 shows project management with four phases, the major tasks of each, and the kinds of data that collaborative teams need to share.

Phase	Tasks	Shared Data
Starting	Set team authority. Set project scope and initial budget. Form team. Establish team roles, responsibilities, and authorities. Establish team rules.	Team member personal data Start-up documents
Planning	Determine tasks and dependencies. Assign tasks. Determine schedule. Revise budget.	Project plan, budget, and other documents
Doing	Perform project tasks. Manage tasks and budget. Solve problems. Reschedule tasks, as necessary. Document and report progress.	Work in process Updated tasks Updated project schedule Updated project budget Project status documents
Finalizing	Determine completion. Prepare archival documents. Disband team.	Archival documents

Figure 2-5
Project Management Tasks and Data

Ethics Guide

Virtual Ethics?

The term *virtual* means something that appears to exist but does not exist in fact. A *virtual private network (VPN)* is an electronic network that appears to be private, but in fact operates on a public network (more on this in Chapter 6). The term *virtual meeting* describes a meeting in which everyone is present, but via an information system and not face-to-face.

However, and it is a big *however*, "Is everyone present?" Is the person who signed on as Lynda Rickey truly Lynda Rickey? Or is it someone else? Or is it Lynda Rickey with a staff of seven people, all of whom are anonymous to the rest of the group? What if Lynda (and her secret staff) are engaged in a chat session with Ashley and Bill but Bill isn't really there? Instead, Bill is being spoofed by his son Jordan, who is sitting in his organizational behavior

class at college, giving noncommittal answers, while Bill plays golf?

Suppose you run a consulting company and you want to send less experienced consultants out on jobs. During an initial meeting (held electronically, using text chat) with a potential client, you tell the client that he is meeting with Drew Suenas, a new and inexperienced employee. But, the meeting actually includes Drew and Eleanor Jackson, your most experienced and senior consultant. During the meeting, all of the remarks attributed to Drew were actually made by Eleanor. The client is most impressed with what it thinks are Drew's perceptive comments about its situation and agrees to hire Drew, even though he is inexperienced. You keep using Eleanor this way, spoofing several of your young associates to get jobs for them. You justify this by saying, "Well, if they get into trouble, we'll send Eleanor out to fix the problem."

Consider another possibility. Suppose you set up a virtual, synchronous meeting and you disagree with the position held by one of your team members, whose name is Bill. If you are setting up the meeting, what if you decide not to send Bill an invite? He does not know the meeting is scheduled, so he does not appear. Much to your joy, issues on which you disagree with him go unaddressed. During the meeting, you remain silent when people ask, "I wonder why Bill isn't here?"

Or, suppose you have an archrival, Ashley. You and Ashley compete for a future promotion, and you just cannot stand the idea of her moving ahead of you. So you set up a sequence of virtual meetings, but you never invite Ashley. Then, just before a crucial meeting, one that involves senior members of your organization, you invite Ashley to be your silent helper. You tell her you do not have the authority to invite her, but you want her to have a chance to express her thoughts. So you attend the meeting and you incorporate Ashley's thinking into your chat comments. People think you are the sole author of those ideas and are impressed. Ashley's work is never attributed to her.

Or, let's bring it closer to home. Suppose you take online tests as part of your class. What keeps you from taking the test with your brother, who happens to work for Google as a product manager for Google Docs? Suppose you take the test by yourself, but you believe others are taking their tests with silent helpers. Given that belief, are you justified in finding your own helper?

What do you think? Are your ethics virtual? ∎

Discussion Questions

1. Is it *illegal* to spoof someone? Does it matter whether you have that person's permission to spoof him or her?

2. Is it *ethical* to spoof someone? Does it matter whether you have that person's permission?

3. Under what circumstances do you believe it is ethical to spoof someone?

4. Consider the meeting of Lynda (and staff), Ashley, and Bill (spoofed by Jordan). What are the consequences to the organization of such a meeting? What happens when Bill meets Lynda in the hallway and Lynda asks, "What did you think of our meeting?" Who has the knowledge of the meeting? Who knows that they have that knowledge?

5. Considering Eleanor's spoofing of young associates, what is different between text chat and a speaker phone? Haven't we always had these problems, except Eleanor was passing notes and making comments while the phone was muted? What behavior should you follow when talking with someone who is on a speaker phone?

6. Is it ethical not to invite Bill to the meeting? Assume no one has asked you if you sent the invitation to him.

7. Is it ethical to take credit for Ashley's thinking? Suppose you are later heavily criticized for the quality of Ashley's ideas that you appropriated? Do you disclaim them? How?

8. Is it cheating to have a helper on an online test? Are you justified if everyone else is doing it? What control is possible for online tests? Should such tests be used at all?

Starting Phase

The fundamental purpose of the starting phase is to set the ground rules for the project and the team. In industry, teams need to determine or understand what authority they have. Is the project given to the team? Or, is part of the team's task to identify what the project is? Is the team free to determine team membership, or is membership given? Can the team devise its own methods for accomplishing the project, or is a particular method required? Student teams differ from those in industry because the team's authority and membership are set by the instructor. However, although student teams do not have the authority to define the project, they do have the authority to determine how that project will be accomplished.

Other tasks during the starting phase are to set the scope of the project and to establish an initial budget. Often this budget is preliminary and is revised after the project has been planned. An initial team is formed during this phase with the understanding that team membership may change as the project progresses. It is important to set team member expectations at the onset. What role will each team member play, and what responsibilities and authority will he or she have? Team rules are also established as discussed under decision making.

Planning Phase

The purpose of the planning phase is to determine "who will do what and by when." Work activities are defined, and resources such as personnel, budget, and equipment are assigned to them. As you'll learn when we discuss project management in Chapter 10, tasks can depend on one other. For example, you cannot evaluate alternatives until you have created a list of alternatives to evaluate. In this case, we say that there is a *task dependency* between the task *Evaluate alternatives* and the task *Create a list of alternatives*. The *Evaluate alternatives* task cannot begin until the completion of the *Create alternatives list* task.

Once tasks and resources have been assigned, it is possible to determine the project schedule. If the schedule is unacceptable, more resources can be added to the project or the project scope can be reduced. Risks and complications arise here, however, as will be discussed in Chapter 10. The project budget is usually revised at this point as well.

Doing Phase

Project tasks are accomplished during the doing phase. The key management challenge here is to ensure that tasks are accomplished on time, and, if not, to identify schedule problems as early as possible. As work progresses, it is often necessary to add or delete tasks, change task assignments, add or remove task labor or other resources, and so forth. Another important task is to document and report project progress.

Finalizing Phase

Are we done? This question is an important and sometimes difficult one to answer. If work is not finished, the team needs to define more tasks and continue the doing phase. If the answer is yes, then the team needs to document its results, document information for future teams, close down the project, and disband the team.

Review the third column of Figure 2-5. All of this project data needs to be stored in a location accessible to the team. Furthermore, all of this data is subject to feedback and iteration. That means that there will be hundreds, perhaps thousands, of versions of data items to be managed. We will consider ways that collaborative information systems can facilitate the management of such data in Q6.

Q4 What Are the Components and Functions of a Collaboration Information System?

As you would expect, a **collaboration information system** or, more simply, a **collaboration system**, is an information system that supports collaboration. Given our discussion in Q1, this means that the system needs to support iteration and feedback among team members. We will discuss specific system features in Q5 and Q6. For now, consider the components of a collaboration system as well as its basic functions.

The Five Collaboration System Components

As information systems, collaboration systems have the five components of every information system: hardware, software, data, procedures, and people. Concerning hardware, most collaboration systems are hosted on organizational servers or in what is called *the cloud*, which you will learn about in Chapters 4 and 5. We will ignore that component in the discussion in this chapter. Just know that the tools you're using and the data you're sharing are supported by computer hardware, somewhere. Collaboration programs are applications like email or text messaging that support collaborative work; we will discuss many such programs in Q5 and Q6.

Collaboration involves two types of data. **Project data** is data that is part of the collaboration's work product. For example, for a team that is designing a new product, design documents are examples of project data. A document that describes a recommended solution is project data for a problem-solving project. **Project metadata** is data that is used to manage the project. Schedules, tasks, budgets, and other managerial data are examples of project metadata. Both types of data, by the way, are subject to iteration and feedback.

Collaboration information systems procedures specify standards, policies, and techniques for conducting the team's work. An example is procedures for reviewing documents or other work products. To reduce confusion and increase control, the team might establish a procedure that specifies who will review documents and in what sequence. Rules about who can do what to which data are also codified in procedures.

The final component of a collaboration system is, of course, people. We discussed the importance of the ability to give and receive critical feedback in Q1. In addition, team members know how and when to use collaboration applications.

Primary Functions: Communication and Content Sharing

Figure 2-6 lists the five important collaboration activities discussed in Q1 and Q2 and summarizes the requirements those activities pose for collaboration systems. Notice these requirements fall into two categories: communication and the sharing of content. The second, fourth, and last of these activities concern communication, and the first and third concern tracking and require the storage and sharing of content. We will consider communication and content storage in the next two questions.

Figure 2-7 lists the five purposes of collaboration activities discussed in Q3 and summarizes IS requirements for collaboration systems for each purpose. Again, notice that these requirements fall into communication and content-sharing categories. As you think about your own collaboration projects in school, use Figures 2-6 and 2-7 as a guide for determining the tools you need for your own collaboration system.

Note the difference between the terms *collaboration system* and *collaboration tool*. A **collaboration tool** is the program component of a collaboration system. For the tool

See the Guide on pages 66–67 to learn one technique that business professionals use to obtain a common definition of a problem. That technique requires effective communication.

Figure 2-6
Collaboration System
Requirements

Collaborative Activity	Information Systems Requirements
Iteration.	Track many versions of many documents and other work product.
Feedback.	Provide easy-to-use and readily available multiparty communication.
Accomplish task within time and budget.	Track tasks, schedules, budgets, and other project metadata. Account for and report progress and status.
Promote team growth.	Provide for intrateam teaching.
Increase team satisfaction.	Provide for team and member recognition.

Figure 2-7
IS Requirements for Different
Collaboration Purposes

Purpose	IS Requirements
Become informed.	Share data. Support group communication. Store history.
Make decisions.	Share decision criteria, alternative descriptions, evaluation tools, evaluation results, and implementation plan. Support group communication during decision-making process. Publish decision, as needed. Store records of process and results.
Solve problems.	Share problem definitions, solution alternatives, costs and benefits, alternative evaluations, and solution implementation plan. Support group communication. Publish problem and solution, as needed. Store problem definition, alternatives, analysis, and plan.
Conduct projects.	Support starting, planning, doing, and finalizing project phases (Figure 2- 8).

Collaboration tools provide useful capabilities, but they also present some potential security risks. The Guide on pages 64–65 discusses those risks and how to avoid them.

to be useful, it must be surrounded by the other four components of an information system. With that understanding, consider the collaboration tools for communication and content sharing.

Q5 How Can You Use Collaboration Tools to Improve Team Communication?

Team communication is one of the two major functions of collaboration systems. The particular tools used depend on the ways that the team communicates as summarized in Figure 2-8. **Synchronous communication** occurs when all team members meet at the same time, such as with conference calls or face-to-face meetings. **Asynchronous communication** occurs when team members do not meet at the same time. Employees who work different shifts at the same location, or team members who work in different time zones around the world, must meet asynchronously.

Most student teams attempt to meet face-to-face, at least at first. Arranging such meetings is always difficult, however, because student schedules and responsibilities differ. If you are going to arrange such meetings, consider creating an online group calendar in which team members post their availability, week by week. Also, use the

Synchronous		Asynchronous
Shared calendars Invitation and attendance		
Single location	Multiple locations	Single or multiple locations
Office applications such as Word and PowerPoint Shared whiteboards	Conference calls Multiparty text chat Screen sharing Webinars Videoconferencing	Email Discussion forums Team surveys

Virtual meetings

Figure 2-8
Collaboration Tools
for Communication

meeting facilities in Microsoft Outlook to issue invitations and gather RSVPs. If you don't have Outlook, use an Internet site such as Evite (www.evite.com) for this purpose.

For most face-to-face meetings, you need little; the standard Office applications or their freeware lookalikes, such as Open Office will suffice. However, recent research indicates that face-to-face meetings can benefit from shared, online workspaces, such as that shown in Figure 2-9.[3] With such a whiteboard, team members can type, write, and draw simultaneously, which enables more ideas to be proposed in a given period of time than when team members must wait in sequence to express ideas verbally. If you have access to such a whiteboard, try it in your face-to-face meetings to see if it works for your team.

However, *given today's communication technology, most students should forgo face-to-face meetings.* They are too difficult to arrange and seldom worth the trouble. Instead, learn to use **virtual meetings** in which participants do not meet in the same place, and possibly not at the same time.

If your virtual meeting is synchronous (all meet at the same time), you can use conference calls, multiparty text chat, screen sharing, webinars, or videoconferencing. Some students find it weird to use text chat for school projects, but why not? You can

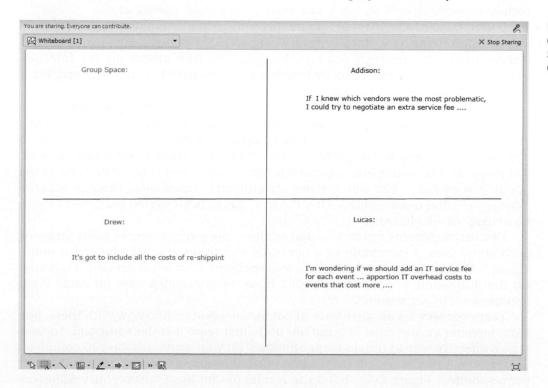

Figure 2-9
Office 365 Lync Whiteboard
Showing Simultaneous
Contributions

[3] Wouter van Diggelen, *Changing Face-to-Face Communication: Collaborative Tools to Support Small-group Discussions in the Classroom* (Groningen: University of Groningen, 2011).

Figure 2-10
Videoconferencing Example

Source: Zigy Kaluzny/Getty Images.

attend meetings wherever you are, without using your voice. Google Text supports multiparty text chat, as does Microsoft Lync. Google or Bing "multiparty text chat" to find other, similar products.

Screen-sharing applications enable users to view the same whiteboard, application, or other display. Figure 2-9 shows an example whiteboard for a GearUp meeting. This whiteboard, which is part of Office 365 Lync, allows multiple people to contribute simultaneously. To organize the simultaneous conversation, the whiteboard real estate is divided among the members of the group, as shown. Some groups save their whiteboards as minutes of the meeting.

A **webinar** is a virtual meeting in which attendees view one of the attendees' computer screens for a more formal and organized presentation. WebEx (www.webex.com) is a popular commercial webinar application used in virtual sales presentations.

If everyone on your team has a camera on his or her computer, you can also do **videoconferencing**, like that shown in Figure 2-10. Microsoft Lync, which we will discuss in Q7, is one such product, but you can find others on the Internet. Videoconferencing is more intrusive than text chat; you have to comb your hair, but it does have a more personal touch.

In some classes and situations, synchronous meetings, even virtual ones, are impossible to arrange. You just cannot get everyone together at the same time. In this circumstance, when the team must meet asynchronously, most students try to communicate via **email**. The problem with email is that there is too much freedom. Not everyone will participate, because it is easy to hide from email. (Did Felix, in the opening scenario, really not get the attachment?) Discussion threads become disorganized and disconnected. After the fact, it is difficult to find particular emails, comments, or attachments.

Discussion forums are an alternative. Here, one group member posts an entry, perhaps an idea, a comment, or a question, and other group members respond. Figure 2-11 shows an example. Such forums are better than email because it is harder for the discussion to get off track. Still, however, it remains easy for some team members not to participate.

Team surveys are another form of communication technology. With these, one team member creates a list of questions and other team members respond. Surveys are an effective way to obtain team opinions; they are generally easy to complete, so most team members will participate. Also, it is easy to determine who has not yet responded. Figure 2-12 shows the results of one team survey. SurveyMonkey (www. surveymonkey. com) is one common survey application program. You can find others on the Internet. Microsoft SharePoint has a built-in survey capability, as we discuss in Q7.

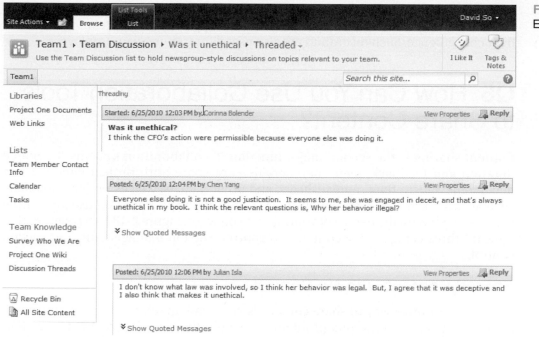

Figure 2-11
Example Discussion Forum

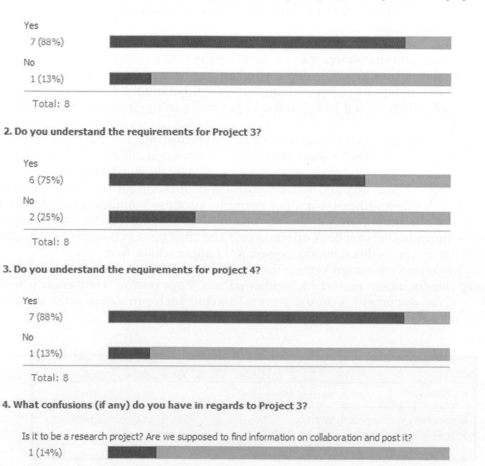

Figure 2-12
Example Survey Report

Video and audio recordings are also useful for asynchronous communication. Key presentations or discussions can be recorded and played back for team members at their convenience. Such recordings are also useful for training new employees.

Q6 How Can You Use Collaboration Tools to Share Content?

Content sharing is the second major function of collaboration systems. To enable iteration and feedback, team members need to share both project data, such as documents, illustrations, spreadsheets, and other data, as well as project metadata, such as tasks, schedules, and budgets. The information systems you use for sharing content depend on the degree of control that you want. Figure 2-13 lists collaboration tools for three categories of content: no control, version management, and version control.

Shared Content with No Control

The most primitive way to share content is via email attachments. However, email attachments have numerous problems. For one, there is always the danger that someone does not receive an email, does not notice it in his or her inbox, or does not bother to save the attachments. Then, too, if three users obtain the same document as an email attachment, each changes it, and each sends back the changed document via email, different, incompatible versions of that document will be floating around. So, although email is simple, easy, and readily available, it will not suffice for collaborations in which there are many document versions or for which there is a desire for content control.

Another way to share content is to place it on a shared **file server**, which is simply a computer that stores files . . . just like the disk in your local computer. If your team has access to a file server, you can put documents on the server and others can download them, make changes, and upload them back onto the server. Often a technology called **FTP** is used to get and put documents (discussed in Chapter 6).

Storing documents on servers is better than using email attachments because documents have a single storage location. They are not scattered in different team members' email boxes, and team members have a known location for finding documents.

However, without any additional control it is possible for team members to interfere with one another's work. For example, suppose team members A and B download a document and edit it, but without knowing about the other's edits. Person A stores his version back on the server and then person B stores her version back on the server. In this scenario, person A's changes will be lost.

Furthermore, without any version management it will be impossible to know who changed the document and when. Neither person A nor person B will know whose version of the document is on the server. To avoid such problems, some form of version management is recommended.

Figure 2-13
Collaboration Tools for Sharing Content

Alternatives for Sharing Content		
No Control	Version Management	Version Control
Email with attachments Shared files on a server	Wikis Google Docs Windows Live SkyDrive	Microsoft SharePoint

Increasing degree of content control

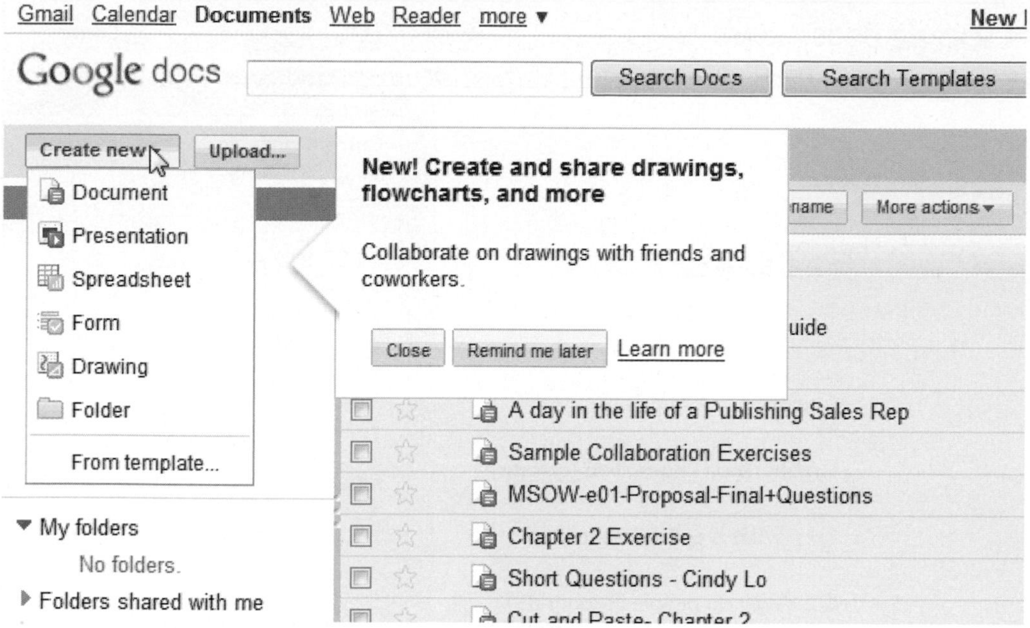

Figure 2-14
Available Types of Google Docs

Shared Content with Version Management

Systems that provide **version management** track changes to documents and provide features and functions to accommodate concurrent work. How this is done depends on the particular system used. In this section, we consider two free and readily available tools: Google Docs and Windows Live SkyDrive.

Google Docs

Google Docs is a free, thin-client application for sharing documents, spreadsheets, presentations, drawings, and other types of data, as shown in Figure 2-14. (Google Docs is evolving; by the time you read this, Google may have added additional file types or changed the system from what is described here. Google the name "Google Docs" to obtain the latest data.)

With Google Docs, anyone who edits a document must have a Google account, which is not the same as a Gmail account. You can establish a Google account using an email address from Hotmail, a university, or any other email service. Your Google account will be affiliated with whatever email account you enter.

To create a Google document, go to http://docs.google.com (note that there is no *www* in this address). Sign in with (or create) your Google account. From that point on, you can create, upload, process, save, and download documents. You can also save most of those documents to PDF and Microsoft Office formats, such as Word, Excel, and PowerPoint.

With Google Docs, you can make documents available to others by entering their email addresses or Google accounts. Those users are notified that the document exists and are given a link by which they can access it. If they have a Google account, they can edit the document; otherwise they can just view the document.

Documents are stored on a Google server. Users can access the documents from Google and simultaneously see and edit documents. In the background, Google merges the users' activities into a single document. You are notified that another user is editing a document at the same time as you are, and you can refresh the document to see their latest changes. Google tracks document revisions, with brief summaries of changes made. Figure 2-15 shows a sample revision for a sample document that has been shared among three users.

You can improve your collaboration activity even more by combining Google Docs with Google+.

Figure 2-15
Google Docs Sharing Example

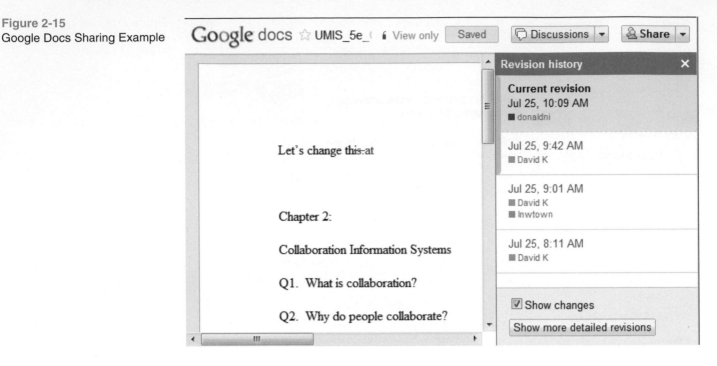

Windows Live SkyDrive

Windows Live SkyDrive is Microsoft's answer to Google Docs. It provides the ability to store and share Office documents and other files and offers free storage. Additionally, SkyDrive includes license-free Web application versions of Word, Excel, PowerPoint, and OneNote called **Office Web Apps**. These applications run in the browser and are quite easy to use. Figure 2-16 shows an instance of the Word Web App. These programs have less functionality than desktop Office programs, but they are free and readily accessed on the Web.

In addition to Office Web Apps, the desktop Office 2010 applications are tightly integrated with SkyDrive. You can open and save documents directly from and to SkyDrive from inside Microsoft Office products, as illustrated in Figure 2-17.

To set up a SkyDrive account, you need a Windows Live ID. If you have either a Hotmail or an MSN email account, that account is your Windows Live ID. If you do not have a Hotmail or an MSN email account, you can create a Windows Live ID with some other email account, or you can create a new Hotmail account, which is free.

Once you have a Windows Live ID, go to www.skydrive.com and sign in. You will be given 25GB of storage (if you don't know what that means, go to page 108). You can create file folders and files and use either Office or other Office Web Apps as well.

Figure 2-16
Example Use of
Word Web App

Microsoft Word Web App Figure 2-11 on SkyDrive

David Kroenke sign out

File Home Insert View

Paste Cut Copy Calibri (Body) 11 B I U abc x₂ x² A No Spacing Normal Heading 1 Heading 2 Heading 3 Spelling Open in Word

Clipboard Font Paragraph Styles Spelling Office

This document was created by the Word Web App. Notice it can include many features of rich text such as **bold** and *italics*, and highlighting.

You can have lists

- One
- Two
- Threee (note spell check)

And Headings
Give it a try.

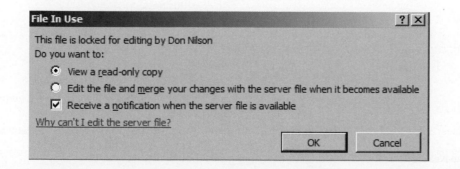

Figure 2-17
Saving a Word 2010 Document
in a SkyDrive Account

Similar to Google accounts, you can share folders with others by entering their Office Live IDs or their email accounts. Users who have an Office Live ID can view and edit documents; users who do not have an Office Live ID can only view documents.

Only one user at a time can open SkyDrive documents for editing. If you attempt to open a document that someone else is editing, you'll receive the message shown in Figure 2-18. As shown, you can open the document in read-only mode, you can have your changes merged with the document when it is available, or you can simply be notified when the document is available.

Both Google Docs and Windows Live SkyDrive are free and very easy to use. They are both far superior to exchanging documents via email or via a file server. If you are not using one of these two products, you should. Go to http://docs.google.com and www.skydrive.com and check them out. You'll find easy-to-understand demos if you need additional instruction.

Shared Content with Version Control

Version management systems improve the tracking of shared content and potentially eliminate problems caused by concurrent document access. They do not, however, provide **version control**, the process that occurs when the collaboration tool limits, and sometimes even directs, user activity. Version control involves one or more of the following capabilities:

- User activity limited by permissions
- Document checkout
- Version histories
- Workflow control

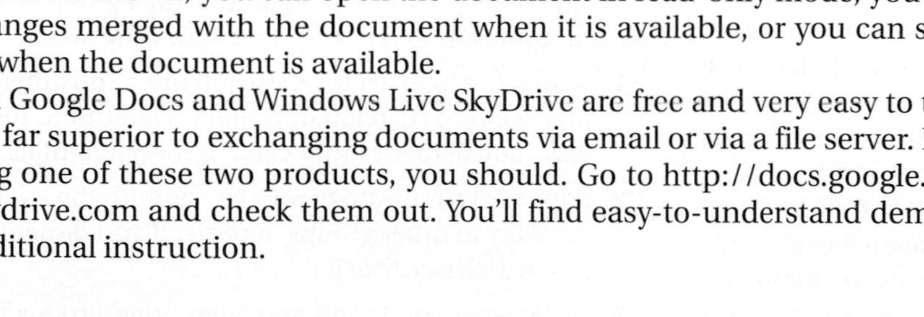

Figure 2-18
Opening a Document
Locked by Another User
in Word Web App

Using MIS InClass 2 *A Group Exercise*

Get a Job! Get a Good Job!

Source: Jirsak/Shutterstock.com.

In Chapter 1, Jennifer got fired because she couldn't perform four key skills, one of which is collaboration. You're learning those four skills now, but you can't leave it at that. To avoid being fired you first have to be HIRED. Thus, while in the business school, you also need to develop skills that add to your competitive advantage. (See the Guide on page 96–97.)

In these worrisome economic times, you have to be proactive in your job search. You cannot wait until you're a senior to discover that you've majored in something for which there are no jobs. You need to target careers that (a) interest you and (b) are likely to see job increases, not decreases.

Many career opportunities exist, but while you're taking this class, you should definitely consider those that involve MIS. With data processing, storage, and communication costs near zero, the business application of IT is one of hottest areas of innovation in business. According to a report from the Terradata Corporation, in 2011, 48 percent of job recruiters reported openings for IT analysts and 58 percent reported openings for business analysts who are knowledgeable about MIS.[4] The highly regarded consulting firm McKinsey & Company reported in May 2011 that the need for highly skilled business intelligence workers (see Chapter 9) will exceed the supply by 60 percent by 2018. By that same year, there will be a need for 1.5 million more data-savvy managers and analysts.[5]

Figure 1 shows several popular business-related job titles and the information system components to which they are aligned. Note that as you move from left to right with these components that the need and value of business knowledge combined with technology increases.

Using these job titles as a guide, form a group as instructed by your professor and perform the following tasks:

1. Search the Internet for these job titles and others you find that seem to be related to them. Determine the kinds of tasks and activities that each of these job titles performs.

2. Report your findings to the rest of the class. Listen carefully to other groups' reports. If you disagree, provide constructive critical feedback.

3. Using what you found and what other groups report, list three job titles that the members of your group find most appealing as possible careers. Provide feedback and

Figure 1

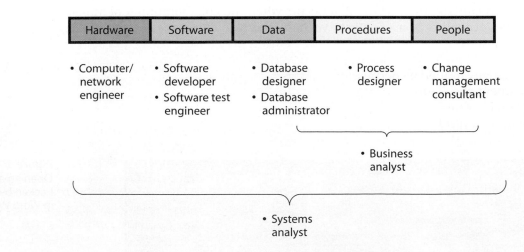

(*continued*)

---

[4] http://www.teradata.com/News-Releases/2011/Todays-College-Grads-are-Ill-prepared-to-Meet-Industrys-Needs-for-Data-Savvy-Workers/ (accessed August 2011).

[5] McKinsey Global Institute, "Big Data: The Next Frontier for Innovation, Competition and Productivity," May 2011.

iterate as you make this list. Consider how you can assess whether you would be good at those jobs. Prepare an explanation of your logic for choosing these three.

4. Report your findings in item 3 to the rest of the class. Listen carefully to other groups' reports. If you disagree, provide constructive critical feedback.

5. Based on what you have heard, adjust your list, if necessary.

6. For each of the three job titles in your list, search the Internet and use your own knowledge and intuition to determine the skills needed to perform these jobs.

7. Read the Thomas Friedman article at www.nytimes.com/2011/07/13/opinion/13friedman.html?_r=1. When Friedman quotes Hoffman—"professionals need an entirely new mind-set and skill set to compete"—what does he mean?

8. For each of the skills you listed in item 6, in light of the guidance provided in the article in item 7 describe classes to take and experiences that you can have as a student to prepare.

9. Report your findings in item 7 to the rest of the class.

Keep thinking about these issues, and don't wait to get started on your job search!

Permission-Limited Activity

With most version control tools, each team member is given an account with a set of permissions. Then, shared documents are placed into shared directories, sometimes called **libraries**. For example, on a shared site with four libraries, a particular user might be given read-only permission for library 1; read and edit permission for library 2; read, edit, and delete permission for library 3; and no permission even to see library 4.

Document Checkout

With version control applications, document directories can be set up so that users are required to check out documents before they can modify them. When a document is checked out, no other user can obtain it for the purpose of editing it. Once the document has been checked in, other users can obtain it for editing.

Figure 2-19 shows a screen for a user of Microsoft SharePoint 2010. The user, Allison Brown (shown in the upper right-hand corner of the screen), is checking out a document named Project One Assignment. Once she has it checked out, she can edit it and return it to this library. While she has the document checked out, no other user will be able to edit it, and her changes will not be visible to others.

Figure 2-19
Checking Out a Document

Version History

Because collaboration involves feedback and iteration, it is inevitable that dozens, or even hundreds, of documents will be created. Imagine, for example, the number of versions of a design document for the Boeing 787. In some cases, collaboration team members attempt to keep track of versions by appending suffixes to file names. The result for a student project is a file name like *Project1_lt_kl_092911_most_ recent_draft.docx*, or something similar. Not only are such names ugly and awkward, no team member can tell whether this is the most current version.

Collaboration tools that provide version control have the data to readily provide histories on behalf of the users. When a document is changed (or checked in), the collaboration tool records the name of the author and the date and time the document is stored. Users also have the option of recording notes about their version. You can see an example of a version history report produced by SharePoint 2010 later in the chapter in Figure 2-36.

Workflow Control

Collaboration tools that provide **workflow control** manage activities in a pre-defined process. If, for example, a group wants documents to be reviewed and approved by three people in a particular sequence, the group would define that workflow to the tool. Then, the workflow is started, and the workflow control will set tasks and send emails to manage that process. For example, Figure 2-20 shows a SharePoint workflow in which the group defined a document review process that involves a sequence of reviews by three people. Given this definition, when a document is submitted to a library, SharePoint assigns a task to the first person, Joseph Schumpeter, to approve the document and sends an email to him to that effect. Once he has completed his review (the green checkmark means that he has already done so), SharePoint assigns a task for and sends an email to Adam Smith to approve the document. When all three reviewers have completed their review, SharePoint marks the document as approved. If any disapprove, the document is marked accordingly and the workflow is terminated.

Workflows can be defined for complicated, multistage business processes. See *SharePoint for Students*[6] for more on how to create them.

Numerous version control applications exist. For general business use, SharePoint is the most popular; we will discuss it next. Other document control systems include MasterControl (www.mastercontrol.com) and Document Locator (www.documentlocator.com). Software development teams use applications such as CVS (www.nongnu.org/cvs) or Subversion (http://subversion.tigris.org) to control versions of software code, test plans, and product documentation.

Figure 2-20
Example Workflow

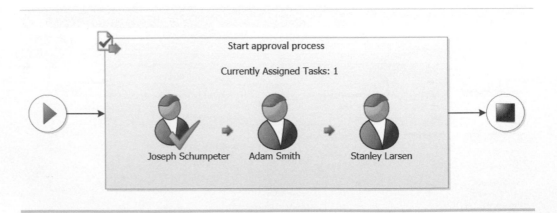

---

[6] Carey Cole, Steve Fox, and David Kroenke, *SharePoint for Students* (Upper Saddle River, NJ: Pearson Education, 2012), pp. 116–129.

Q7 How Can You Use Office 365 for Student Projects?

Office 365 is a suite of programs that offers the collaboration facilities shown in Figure 2-21. Office 365 was first released in June 2011, and it has seen rapid adoption and use since then. As shown in Figure 2-21, the Lync component supports collaboration communication with text, audio, and video communication. SharePoint Online supports the sharing of content with document libraries and lists, as well as other capabilities. Exchange is an email service that is integrated with Lync and SharePoint Online, as you will see. Office 2010 includes Word, Excel, PowerPoint, OneNote, and other Office programs.

The last row of Figure 2-21 uses the phrase *hosted integration*. The term *hosted* means that Microsoft provides these capabilities on computers and communication infrastructure that it provides—somewhere on the Internet. Hosted means that neither your university nor you needs to set up the infrastructure to access these services. Instead, after you install a few programs on your computer, you are up and running. As noted, these hosted components are closely integrated with easy access and transformation among them. You'll learn more about hosting when you learn about the cloud in Part 2 (Chapters 4 through 6).

You can obtain Office 365 in two ways. If your college or university adopts Office 365 as a standard, students can use it at no cost. Your university will have set up procedures and policies for you to follow. If Office 365 is not used by your institution, then your student groups can purchase an Office 365 for Small Business site for $6 per student per month. Thus, if you are working in a team of five, the five of you can purchase use of Office 365 for $30 a month. You can use it for as many months as you wish. Small Business sites are limited to 50 users. You can find more information and signup instructions at www.office365forstudents.com.

Microsoft Lync

Microsoft Lync supports collaboration communication. Figure 2-22 shows the Lync window from which all communications are started. To initiate communication with someone, click the person's name and then select the type of communication that you want to use. In Figure 2-22, the user David Kroenke is setting up a communication with another user, Earl McKinney. Clicking the icon buttons at the bottom of the pop-out window will initiate email, instant messaging, and audio/video calls, as shown by the figure labels. By default, audio/video calls use the Internet; no telephone is needed. We will discuss this use of the Internet further in Chapter 6.

Component	Features
Lync	Multiparty text chat Audio- and videoconferencing Online content sharing Webinars with PowerPoint
SharePoint Online	Content management and control using libraries and lists Discussion forums Surveys Wikis Blogs
Exchange	Email integrated with Lync and Share Point Online
Office 2010	Concurrent editing for Word, Excel, PowerPoint, and OneNote
Hosted integration	Infrastructure built, managed, and operated by Microsoft

Figure 2-21
Office 365 Components and Features

Figure 2-22
Starting a Lync Conversation

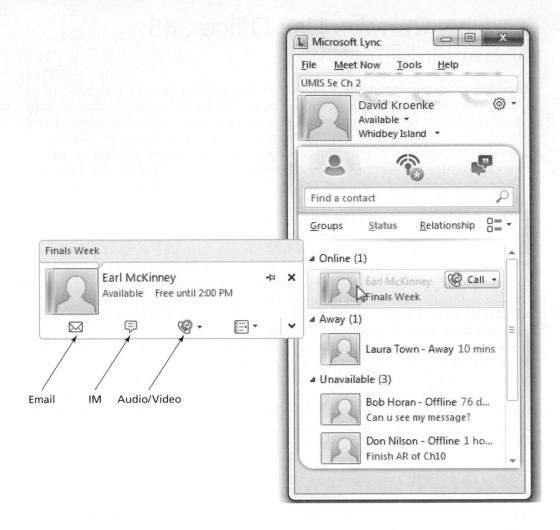

Notice the color coding next to the team members' names. Green means that person is available. Yellow means that the person has been away from the computer for some time but is still signed in to Lync. White/gray means that the person is not signed in to Lync. Red (not shown) indicates that the person is occupied in a different Lync meeting or is otherwise not available.

One of the major advantages of Lync is that group members can share their desktops and programs and write on a community whiteboard. They can also take online polls. Figure 2-23 shows a video meeting of three people (see the list of names under Presenters) in which the meeting members are sharing a whiteboard.

Figure 2-23
Shared Whiteboard

To indicate who typed what, this group has a policy that each person will type his or her name at the top of his or her entries. During the call, Lync determines who is speaking and places that person's picture in the main video window. In Figure 2-23, Earl is speaking, and his video appears. The small window shows the local participant (David) how he will appear to the rest of the group.

In a videoconference, participants control whether they appear on camera. If a user does not want his or her image to appear, he or she can close the video and still maintain voice contact with the group.

It is possible to conduct webinars via Lync. To do so, the group sends invitations to attendees via email; people need not have Lync installed to attend. Prior to the meeting, the meeting leader uploads a PowerPoint file to present. Attendees are classified as presenters and participants. Presenters can take control of the presentation and add to it. Attendees are only allowed to view (and speak). You and your team could use this facility to make presentations to your professor or to other groups in your class.

SharePoint Online

SharePoint Online is an industrial-strength product for content sharing. It has deep and rich features, and it can handle massive amounts of data and hundreds of users. You can use libraries and lists to manage and/or control content, you can gather team opinions with surveys and wikis, and you can share team members' opinions with blogs.

Figure 2-24 shows an example student SharePoint site for a group of students, called Team 3, that has been assigned a project involving GearUp. The team created this site and then customized its appearance to show a potential GearUp logo. As shown in the center of the pages, this team uses a library named Shared Documents, which contains three documents.

The left-hand side of this page is a list of links called the **Quick Launch,** which contains three groups of links: Libraries, Lists, and Discussions. Users can go to any of the resources in Quick Launch by clicking the item name. For example, clicking Tasks will open a page with a Tasks list.

Document Library

The Shared Documents library appears both in the center of the Home page as well as in Quick Launch. The Shared Documents library shows the type of document, its name, when it was modified, the name of the person who made the modification, and other data that is not shown here. Students can use all of the content management

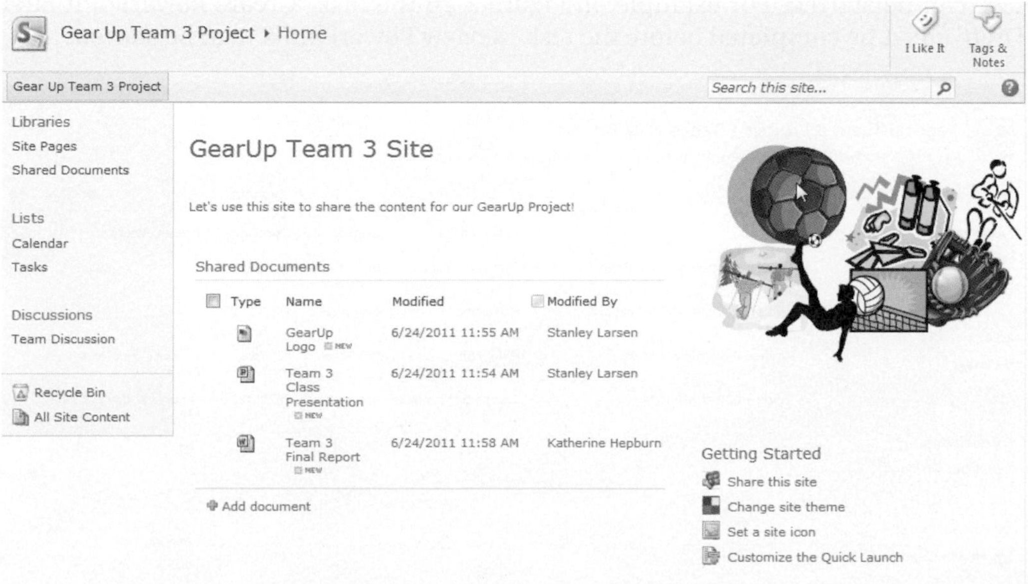

Figure 2-24
Example Student
SharePoint Site

Figure 2-25
Content Control Options
for Student Document

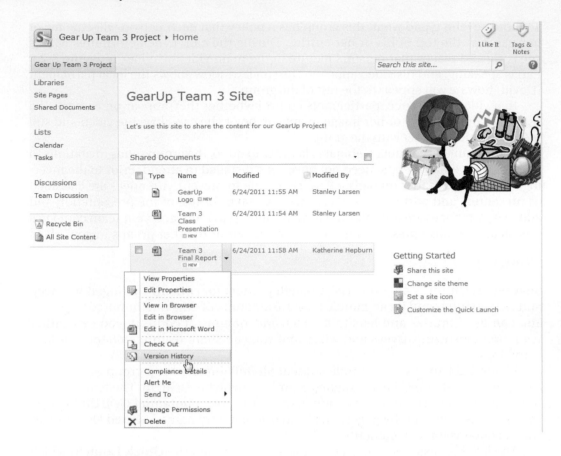

and control techniques described in Q6 as well as several others that are beyond the scope of this text. Figure 2-25 shows a user who is selecting the Version History report on a Word document named Team 3 Final Report. The result will be similar to that shown in Figure 2-36 (page 73).

Tasks List

When the user clicks Tasks in the Quick Launch, SharePoint will display the page shown in Figure 2-26. This group currently has four tasks in its Tasks list. This list displays the task title, the name of the person it is assigned to, the status of the task, the date it is due, and any predecessor tasks that need to be accomplished before this task can be started. For example, in Figure 2-26 the task "Create PowerPoint First Draft" must be completed before the task "Review PowerPoints" can be started.

Figure 2-26
Example Tasks List for Student
Project

Title	Assigned To	Status	Due Date	Predecessors
Create PowerPoint First Draft	Stanley Larsen	In Progress	2/2/2012	
Write first draft of Final report	Katherine Hepburn	Completed	1/15/2012	
Review PowerPoints	Kelly Loftus	Not Started	2/7/2012	Create PowerPoint First Draft
Review first draft	Joseph Schumpeter	Not Started	2/7/2012	Write first draft of Final report

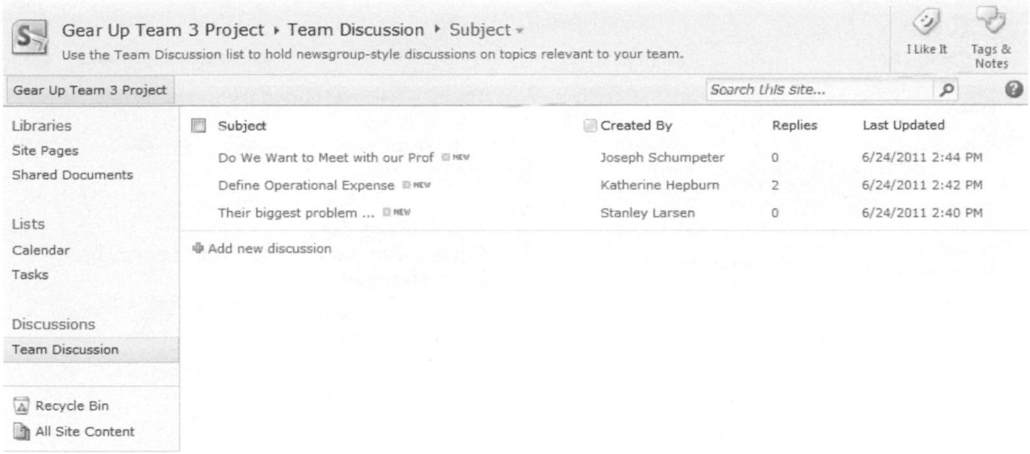

Figure 2-27
Example Student Team
Discussions

Discussion Forums

SharePoint supports discussion forums in which team members can conduct an asynchronous online discussion; such discussions are the asynchronous equivalent of a conversation thread in a face-to-face meeting.

In Figure 2-27, the user has clicked Team Discussion under Discussions in the Quick Launch. In response, SharePoint displays the three discussions underway for this team. A user can add a new topic by clicking +Add new discussion. Or, to contribute to an existing topic, the user can double-click the Subject of a topic.

Figure 2-28 shows the result when the user clicks Define Operational Expense. This view is called a *threaded view* because it shows the topic and responses in an indented format. Another view, flat, can be shown by clicking the word *Threaded* in the top right of the screen.

The advantage of a discussion board is that you have documentation of the discussion. In industry, this is useful as a memory aid and for training new team members. In school, such documentation can be used to demonstrate the work accomplished by your team.

Other SharePoint Facilities

SharePoint supports many features in addition to document libraries, lists, and discussion boards. You can easily create a team wiki and conduct team surveys; individual team members can also publish their own blogs.

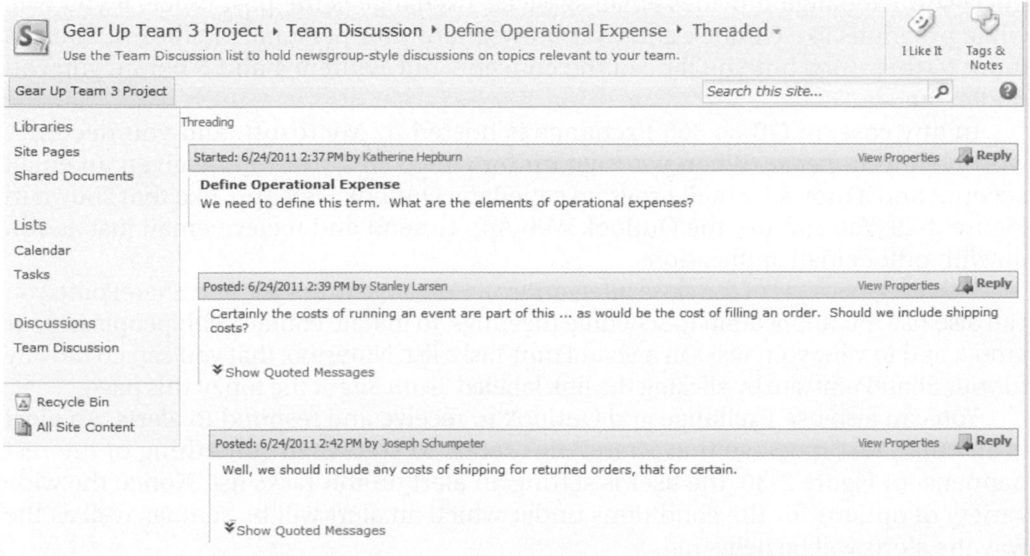

Figure 2-28
Threaded View of
Discussion Item

Figure 2-29
Outlook Web App Example

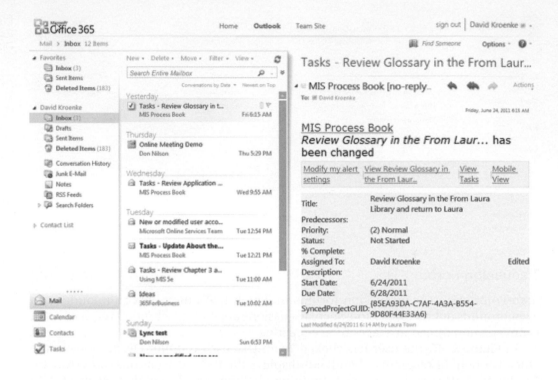

Microsoft designed SharePoint for large organizations to publish their content. Most organizations care a great deal about the modification of their content, and so the SharePoint designers created an elaborate system of user and group permissions. That system can become quite complicated, and is useful for large tasks like publishing the *Wall Street Journal.* For student use, the default, simpler security settings are recommended. Be aware, though, that you can limit what various team members can see and what they can do in very specific ways.

In addition to the permissions system, SharePoint also maintains metadata about who did what to which content and when. The version history report is an example of that metadata. The advantage of this data to you, as a student, is that SharePoint gives you documentation of who in your group did what work on your team site. This capability can be advantageous when it comes to assigning individual credit for group work.

Alerts and Presence with Exchange

Microsoft Exchange provides email services. Exchange is the post office, if you will, while programs like Outlook and your browser are your personal mailboxes. There is more to this story, but you'll need the concepts of Chapters 4 and 6 before you can understand it.

In any case, in Office 365 Exchange is hosted by Microsoft, and you need not worry about it, *per se.* When you sign up for Office 365, you will be given an email account and a browser email program called the Outlook Web App, like that shown in Figure 2-29. You can use the Outlook Web App to send and receive email just as you do with other email applications.

However, because of the close integration of Exchange with Lync and SharePoint, you can also use this application to schedule meetings, to initiate contact with people in your group, and to view your tasks in a SharePoint Tasks list. Note, too, that you can go directly to your SharePoint site by clicking the link labeled *Team Site* at the top of this page.

You can also use Exchange and Outlook to receive and respond to alerts. An **alert** is an email text message that SharePoint sends to you when something of interest happens. In Figure 2-30, the user is setting an alert on the Tasks list. Notice the wide variety of options for the conditions under which an alert will be sent, as well as the way the alerts will be delivered.

Figure 2-30
Setting an Alert

Change Type	Only send me alerts when:
Specify the type of changes that you want to be alerted to.	◉ All changes
	○ New items are added
	○ Existing items are modified
	○ Items are deleted
Send Alerts for These Changes	Send me an alert when:
Specify whether to filter alerts based on specific criteria. You may also restrict your alerts to only include items that show in a particular view.	◉ Anything changes
	○ A task is assigned to me
	○ A task becomes complete
	○ A high priority task changes
	○ Someone else changes a task assigned to me
	○ Someone else changes a task
	○ Someone else changes a task created by me
	○ Someone else changes a task last modified by me
	○ Someone changes an item that appears in the following view:
	[My Tasks ▼]
When to Send Alerts	
Specify how frequently you want to be alerted. (mobile alert is only available for immediately send)	◉ Send notification immediately
	○ Send a daily summary
	○ Send a weekly summary
	Time:
	[Saturday ▼] [9:00 AM ▼]

Figure 2-31 shows an alert that was sent to David Kroenke when the task "Review Glossary" was assigned to him into the Tasks list. This figure shows one other integration point between Exchange/Outlook and Lync. The little green box next to his name is called the **presence indicator**. This icon is colored according to any team members' availability, as described above for Lync, and if it is green it can be clicked to start a Lync conversation with that person, as shown by the Lync popup menu in Figure 2-31.

Figure 2-31
Using Presence in an Alert Message

MIS Process Book

Review Glossary in the From Laur... has been changed

Modify my alert settings | View Review Glossary in the From Laur... | View Tasks | Mobile View

Title:	Review Glossary in the From Laura Library and return to Laura	
Predecessors:		
Priority:	(2) Normal	
Status:	Not Started	
% Complete:		
Assigned To:	David Kroenke	Edited
Description:		
Start Date:	6/24/2011	
Due Date:	6/28/2011	

Office Web Apps and Office 2010

As stated, an Office Web App is a browser-based application that provides a subset of the capabilities of a desktop Office application. As of November, 2011, Office 365 includes four Office Web Apps: Word, Excel, PowerPoint, OneNote, and Outlook. These applications are free to all users, but they do not have the full capabilities of Office.

When you become a member of an Office 365 team, you are given a license to install and use most of the Office Desktop applications, such as Word, Excel, PowerPoint, and OneNote. These applications do not run in a browser and require that you install them on your computer. In addition to the full capability of these programs, they provide two benefits for teams. First, team members can do simultaneous editing of Word, Excel, PowerPoint, and OneNote documents. You and another team member can add, for example, paragraphs to the same document and Word will track what each of you is doing and merge your changes.

Second, the desktop Office applications are integrated with Lync presence. You can, for example, click File/Info to see the authors of a document. The presence indicator will precede the names of the authors, and you can click it to establish a Lync communication with them.

Learning More

In this short survey, we have just touched on the ways that you can use Office 365 for your student projects. To learn more about Office 365, go to either www.office365 forstudents.com or www.office365inbusiness.com. Also, if you want to know more about using SharePoint specifically, see *SharePoint for Students.*[7]

Q8 2022?

So, how will we collaborate in 2022? Where will the current trends take us? Clearly, free data communications and data storage will make collaboration systems cheaper and easier to use. One consequence is that by 2022 face-to-face (F2F) meetings will be rare.

F2F meetings require everyone to be in the same place at the same time, and both of those *sames* can be problematic. When employees work in different locations, bringing them together is expensive in travel cost and time. Employees standing in line in airport security or waiting in their cars in traffic are hardly productive. And, bringing everyone together is unfriendly to the environment.

Even when employees work at the same location, they may have schedule conflicts or they may not work at that location at the same time. And, unless employees are providing an in-person service, such as physical training, or surgery, or construction, why do they need to work in the same location?

Furthermore, what happens when you finally do get employees together? Say you bring the top managers into the home office for training. They no sooner sit down then their cell phones ring, and off they go to the lobby to handle some raging problem back home. Twenty minutes later, they're back for another 5 minutes before their phones ring again. Meanwhile, a good portion of the managers who stayed in the meeting are texting their offices throughout the training.

In 2022, employees whose services need not be provided in person will work at home, if not full time, then at least several days a week. Nearly all corporate training will be online. Most will be asynchronous. If fuel prices continue to increase, this trend will become even more pronounced.

A mining company (that chooses to remain anonymous) in Washington State provided an international example in 2011. The company is located in the United

---

[7] Carey Cole, Steve Fox, and David Kroenke, *SharePoint for Students* (Upper Saddle River, NJ: Pearson Education, 2012).

States, close to the Canadian border, but owns several mines in Canada. For its annual audit, the company needed the services of a Canadian-chartered accounting firm from Vancouver, British Columbia. During the audit period, the border crossing was crowded, and the auditors were billing dozens of hours of expensive time while sitting unproductively in their cars at the crossing. To reduce the audit expense, the company eliminated most of this travel by storing audit data in SharePoint libraries.

But, by 2022, why be unproductive in your car? By then you should be able to use the full capabilities of Office 365 or the collaboration tools that replace it on any portable device. So, as long as you're not driving, use your device in your car, or your golf cart, or your boat, to get work done.

Further, as the example provided shows, by 2022 collaboration systems will greatly ease international business. If teams meet virtually most of the time, and if it doesn't matter where team members are located, then projects can involve the best, or perhaps the most affordable, workers worldwide. Further, work can follow the sun. Workers in the United States can submit documents for feedback by team members in Asia. The Asian workers can contribute their feedback during their normal workday and pass the documents along to European team members for review during *their* normal workday. All the reviewed work will be available to the U.S. workers when their next day begins.

Business travel will be a shadow of its former self. The travel industry will reorganize for near-exclusive recreational travel. Even conventions will become, well, virtual.

Because of these trends, now is a great time for you to learn online, asynchronous, collaboration skills. It's also a good time for you, as a future knowledge worker, to prepare yourself for global opportunities . . . and global competition. And, finally, when you're buying commercial real estate, buy that hotel in Hawaii, not the one in Paramus, New Jersey (unless, of course, it has a water slide for kids, a spa, a nearby golf course, and a casino)!

Guide
Securing Collaboration

Source: iStockphoto.com.

The collaboration tools described in this chapter do indeed facilitate collaboration: They help groups improve the quality of their work, while reducing travel and other logistical expenses and facilitating international work. They can enable people to participate in meetings asynchronously. However, they also pose security risks—possibly serious ones.

Consider Office 365. All documents are stored on Microsoft servers, which are located, well, who knows where. Does Microsoft protect those computers appropriately? If those computers are located in, say, San Francisco, will they survive an earthquake? Microsoft is a responsible, rich, and knowledgeable company that understands the need for disaster preparedness. But, as outsiders, we do not know how they protect their sites. Natural disasters are not the only threat; computer crime, the actions of disgruntled employees, and computer viruses (computer programs that replicate themselves) must be considered as well.

But, chances are—even that phrase is revealing, do you really want to gamble with your data?—Microsoft knows what it is doing, and your data is more than reasonably protected. However, how does the data get to that

Microsoft site? All the traffic to and from Lync and SharePoint is protected by encryption (Chapter 12), but email is not. As you will learn in Chapter 6, most wireless traffic, including email, is unprotected from wireless snoopers. Are you processing that data at a local coffee shop? Do you care that anyone in that shop can copy your data? And, the situation is worse for tools that do not automatically encrypt data.

But, more likely, you pose a greater risk to data security than either Microsoft, Google, or a snooper. To see why, suppose you are the manager of a product line and you observe an odd pattern in sales for your products. That pattern might be related to differences in advertising among geographic regions, or it might have something to do with changes in consumer purchasing behavior. You decide to have a webinar with some of your staff, employees of your advertising agency, and a marketing guru who specializes in contemporary consumer behavior.

To prepare for the meeting, you access your corporate computer systems and obtain all of the sales for your products over the past 12 months. That data is highly confidential and is protected by your IS department in many ways. You can access it only because you have access authority as an employee. But, without thinking about security, you post that data in a Google Docs folder and share it with your employees, your advertising agency, and the marketing guru. You have just violated corporate security. That confidential data is now available to the agency and the consultant. Either party can download it, and you have no way of knowing that the download was made or what was done with it.

Source: iStockphoto.com.

Suppose the marketing guru makes a copy and uses it to improve her knowledge of consumer behavior. Unknown to you, she also consults for your chief rival. She has used your data to improve her knowledge and is now using that knowledge to benefit your competitor. (This sets aside the even uglier possibility that she gives or sells your data to that competitor.)

Office 365 has extensive security features, and, except for email, as long as you stay within its bounds, it should be well protected. But, of course, SharePoint makes it easy to download data, and if you share that data with others via Google Docs or SkyDrive . . . well, you get the picture.

Collaboration tools have many benefits, but they do open the door to loss of critical assets. Let the collaborator beware! ■

Source: iStockphoto.com.

Discussion Questions

1. In most circumstances, email or instant messages that you send over a wireless device are open. Anyone with some free software and a bit of knowledge can snoop on your communications. In class, your professor could read all of your email and instant messages, as could anyone else in the class. Does this knowledge change your behavior in class? Why or why not?

2. Unless you are so foolish as to reveal personal data, such as credit card numbers, a Social Security number, or a driver's license number in an email or instant message, the loss of privacy to you, as an individual, is small. Someone might learn that you were gossiping about someone else, and it might be embarrassing, but that loss is not critical. How does that situation change for business communications? Describe losses, other than those in this Guide, that could occur when using email or Google Docs or Windows Live SkyDrive.

3. In addition to Google Docs, Google offers Gmail, a free email service with an easy-to-use interface and that famous Google search capability. Using Gmail, searching through past emails is easy, fast, and accurate. In addition, because mail is hosted on Google computers, it is easy to access one's email, contacts, and other data from any computer at any location. Many employees prefer using Gmail to their corporate email system. What are the consequences to the organization of some employees doing most of their email via Gmail? What are the risks?

4. Summarize the risks of using SkyDrive in a business setting. How can organizations protect themselves from such risks? Is there any new risk here? After all, organizations have been sharing data in other formats with their business partners for years. Is this much ado about nothing? Why or why not?

5. Do you think the risks of using collaboration tools Google Docs, SkyDrive, or Office 365 can be so large that it makes sense for organizations to disallow their use? Why or why not? What are the costs of disallowing such use? How could an organization prevent an employee from uploading data using a corporate computer at work and then accessing that data from browsers on iPads or iPhones?

Guide
Egocentric Versus Empathetic Thinking

As stated earlier, a problem is a perceived difference between what is and what ought to be. When developing information systems, it is critical for the development team to have a common definition and understanding of the problem. This common understanding can be difficult to achieve, however.

Cognitive scientists distinguish between egocentric and empathetic thinking. Egocentric thinking centers on the self; someone who engages in egocentric thinking considers his or her view as "the real view" or "what really is." In contrast, those who engage in empathetic thinking consider their view as one possible interpretation of the situation and actively work to learn what other people are thinking.

Different experts recommend empathetic thinking for different reasons. Religious leaders say that such thinking is morally superior; psychologists say that empathetic thinking leads to richer, more fulfilling relationships. In business, empathetic thinking is recommended because it is smart. Business is a social endeavor, and those who can understand others' points of view are always more effective. Even if you do not agree with others' perspectives, you will be much better able to work with them if you understand their views.

Consider an example. Suppose you say to your MIS professor, "Professor Jones, I couldn't come to class last Monday. Did we do anything important?" Such a statement is a prime example of egocentric thinking. It takes no account of your professor's point of view and implies that your professor talked about nothing important. As a professor, it is tempting to say, "No, when I noticed you weren't there, I took out all the important material."

To engage in empathetic thinking, consider this situation from the professor's point of view. Students who do not come to class cause extra work for their professors. It does not matter how valid your reason for not attending class; you may actually have been contagious with a fever of 102. But, no matter what, your not coming to class is more work for your professor. He or she must do something extra to help you recover from the lost class time.

Using empathetic thinking, you would do all you can to minimize the impact of your absence on your professor. For example, you could say, "I couldn't come to class, but I got the class notes from Mary. I read through them, and I have a question about establishing alliances as competitive advantage. . . . Oh, by the way, I'm sorry to trouble you with my problem."

Before we go on, let's consider a corollary to this scenario: Never, ever, send an email to your boss that says, "I couldn't come to the staff meeting on Wednesday. Did we do anything important?" Avoid this for the same reasons as those for missing class. Instead, find a way to minimize the impact of your absence on your boss.

Source: Eric Isselee/Shutterstock.com.

Now, what does all of this have to do with MIS? Consider the GearUp team at the start of this chapter. What is the problem? Drew thinks a big problem is that Felix doesn't come to meetings. Felix thinks the team is focused on operational cost reductions and should focus on efficiencies of scale from increased sales. Addison thinks the problem the team should address is operational cost reductions. Kelly, once she understands what is going on, is likely to be focused on wasted employee time.

Now imagine yourself in that meeting. If everyone engages in egocentric thinking, what will happen? The meeting will be argumentative and acrimonious and likely will end with nothing accomplished.

Suppose, instead, that the attendees think empathetically. In this case, Drew may make an effort to find out why Felix is missing meetings. Felix would make an effort to understand why his behavior is a problem to the team. The team would make a concerted effort to address the different points of view, and the outcome will be much more positive—possibly a recognition that the team should be meeting virtually and asynchronously. Either way, the attendees have the same information; the difference in outcomes results from the thinking style of the attendees.

Empathetic thinking is an important skill in all business activities. Skilled negotiators always know what the other side wants; effective salespeople understand their customers' needs. Buyers who understand the problems of their vendors get better service. And students who understand the perspective of their professors get better . . . ■

Discussion Questions

1. In your own words, explain how egocentric and empathetic thinking differ.

2. Suppose you miss a staff meeting. Using empathetic thinking, explain how you can get needed information about what took place in the meeting.

3. How does empathetic thinking relate to problem definition?

4. Suppose you and another person differ substantially on a problem definition. Suppose she says to you, "No, the real problem is that . . ." followed by her definition of the problem. How do you respond?

5. Again, suppose you and another person differ substantially on a problem definition. Assume you understand his definition. How can you make that fact clear?

6. Explain the following statement: "In business, empathetic thinking is smart." Do you agree?

Active Review

Use this Active Review to verify that you understand the ideas and concepts that answer the chapter's study questions.

Q1 What are two key characteristics of collaboration?

In your own words, explain the difference between cooperation and collaboration. Name the two key characteristics of collaboration and explain how they improve group work. Name the key component of a collaboration IS and explain why the text claims this is so. Summarize important skills for collaborators and list what you believe are the best ways to give and receive critical feedback.

Q2 What are three criteria for successful collaboration?

Name and describe three criteria for collaboration success. Summarize how these criteria differ between student and professional teams.

Q3 What are the four primary purposes of collaboration?

Name and describe four primary purposes of collaboration. Explain their relationship. Describe ways that collaboration systems can contribute to each purpose.

Q4 What are the components and functions of a collaboration information system?

Name and describe the five components of a collaboration information system. Name and describe two key collaboration IS functions.

Q5 How can you use collaboration tools to improve team communication?

Explain why communication is important to collaboration. Define *synchronous* and *asynchronous communication* and explain when each is used. Name two collaboration tools that can be used to help set up synchronous meetings. Describe collaboration tools that can be used for face-to-face meetings. Describe tools that can be used for virtual, synchronous meetings. Describe tools that can be used for virtual, asynchronous meetings.

Q6 How can you use collaboration tools to share content?

Describe two ways that content is shared with no control and explain the problems that can occur. Explain how control is provided by Google Docs and Windows Live SkyDrive. Explain the difference between version management and version control. Describe how user accounts, passwords, and libraries are used to control user activity. Explain how check-in/checkout works. Describe workflows and give an example.

Q7 How can you use Office 365 for student projects?

List the four major components of Office 365. Using Figure 2-21 as a guide, summarize the ways that Office 365 can help you with your group work in school. Explain what the term *hosted* means. Reread the Guide on pages 64–65 and summarize risks of using hosted systems.

Q8 2022?

Describe the impact that free data storage and data communications have on collaboration systems. Explain why F2F meetings are expensive in both cost and time. Explain why meetings such as F2F training sessions can be ineffective. Summarize the ways collaboration systems reduce the costs and difficulties of international business. Explain how collaboration systems are changing the scope of workers with whom you will compete. Describe consequences of all this to the travel industry. If you disagree with any of the conclusions in this 2022, explain how and why.

Using Your Knowledge at GearUp

Reread the GearUp scenario at the start of this chapter. Using the knowledge you've gained from this chapter, explain how this team could use collaboration tools to be more effective. Describe how such tools can solve Felix's problems as well as result in better communication and higher quality results for the team.

Key Terms and Concepts

Using Your Knowledge

1. Reread about 2022 in Q8. Do you agree with the conclusions? Why or why not? If F2F meetings become rare, what additional impacts do you see on the travel industry? In light of this change, describe travel industry investments that make sense and those that do not. What are promising investments in training? What are promising investments in other industries?

2. This exercise requires you to experiment with Google Docs. You will need two Google accounts to complete this exercise. If you have two different email addresses, then set up two Google accounts using those addresses. Otherwise, use your school email address and set up a Google Gmail account. A Gmail account will automatically give you a Google account.

    a. Using Microsoft Word, write a memo to yourself. In the memo, explain the nature of the communication collaboration driver. Go to http://docs. google.com and sign in with one of your Google accounts. Upload your memo using Google Docs. Save your uploaded document and share your document with the email in your second Google account. Sign out of your first Google account.

       (If you have access to two computers situated close to each other, use both of them for this exercise. You will see more of the Google Docs functionality by using two computers. If you have two computers, do not sign out of your Google account. Perform step b and all actions for the second account on that second computer. If you are using two computers, ignore the instructions

    in the following steps to sign out of the Google accounts.)

    b. Open a new window in your browser. Access http://docs.google.com from that second window and sign in using your second Google account. Open the document that you shared in step a.

    c. Change the memo by adding a brief description of content management. Save the document from your second account. If you are using just one computer, sign out from your second account.

    d. Sign in on your first account. Open the most recent version of the memo and add a description of the role of version histories. Save the document. (If you are using two computers, notice how Google warns you that another user is editing the document at the same time. Click *Refresh* to see what happens.) If you are using just one computer, sign out from your first account.

    e. Sign in on your second account. Re-open the shared document. From the *File* menu, save the document as a Word document. Describe how Google processed the changes to your document.

3. This exercise requires you to experiment with Windows Live SkyDrive. You will need two Office Live IDs to complete this exercise. The easiest way to do it is to work with a classmate. If that is not possible, set up two Office Live accounts using two different Hotmail addresses.

    a. Go to www.skydrive.com and sign in with one of your accounts. Create a memo about collaboration tools using the Word Web App. Save your memo. Share your document with the email in your second Office Live account. Sign out of your first account.

(If you have access to two computers situated close to each other, use both of them for this exercise. If you have two computers, do not sign out of your Office Live account. Perform step b and all actions for the second account on that second computer. If you are using two computers, ignore the instructions in the following steps to sign out of the Office Live accounts.)

b. Open a new window in your browser. Access www.skydrive.com from that second window and sign in using your second Office Live account. Open the document that you shared in step a.

c. Change the memo by adding a brief description of content management. Do not save the document yet. If you are using just one computer, sign out from your second account.

d. Sign in on your first account. Attempt to open the memo and note what occurs. Sign out of your first account and sign back in with your second account. Save the document. Now, sign out of your second account and sign back in with the first account. Now attempt to open the memo.

(If you are using two computers, perform these same actions on the two different computers.)

e. Sign in on your second account. Re-open the shared document. From the File menu, save the document as a Word document. Describe how SkyDrive processed the changes to your document.

4. If you have access to Office 365, Lync, and SharePoint, go to www.pearsonhighered.com/ kroenke and find the file *Chapter 2 Office 365 Exercises*. Perform the exercises shown there.

5. Reflect on your experience working on teams in previous classes as well as on collaborative teams in other settings, such as a campus committee. To what extent was your team collaborative? Did it involve feedback and iteration? If so, how? How did you use collaborative information systems, if at all? If you did not use collaborative information systems, describe how you think such systems might have improved your work methods and results. If you did use collaborative information systems, explain how you could improve on that use, given the knowledge you have gained from this chapter.

▬ Collaboration Exercise 2

With a team of your fellow students, develop an answer to the following questions. Use Google Docs, Google+, Windows Live SkyDrive, SharePoint, Office 365, or some other collaboration tool to conduct your meetings.

a. What is collaboration? Reread Q1 in this chapter, but do not confine yourselves to that discussion. Consider your own experience working in collaborative teams, and search the Web to identify other ideas about collaboration. Dave Pollard, one of the authors of the survey that Figure 2-1 is based on, is a font of ideas on collaboration.

b. What characteristics make for an effective team member? Review the survey of effective collaboration skills in Figure 2-1 and the guidelines for giving and receiving critical feedback and discuss them as a group. Do you agree with them? What skills or feedback techniques would you add to

this list? What conclusions can you, as a team, take from this survey? Would you change the rankings in Figure 2-1?

c. What would you do with an ineffective team member? First, define an *ineffective team member*. Specify five or so characteristics of an ineffective team member. If your group has such a member, what action do you, as a group, believe should be taken?

d. How do you know if you are collaborating well? When working with a group, how do you know whether you are working well or poorly? Specify five or so characteristics that indicate collaborative success. How can you measure those characteristics?

Deliver your answers to these four questions to your instructor in the format required—on paper as a SharePoint site, or some other innovative format.

Case Study 2

Eating Our Own Dog Food

Dogfooding is the process of using a product or idea that you develop or promote. The term arose in the 1980s in the software industry when someone observed that their company wasn't using the product they developed. Or, "they weren't eating their own dog food." Wikipedia attributes the term to Brian Valentine, test manager for Microsoft LAN Manager in 1988, but I recall using the term before that date. Whatever its origin, if, of their own accord, employees choose to dogfood their own product or idea, many believe that product or idea is likely to succeed.

You may be asking, "So what?" Well, this text was developed by a collaborative team, using Office 365 and many of the techniques described in this chapter. We dogfooded the ideas and products in this chapter.

Figure 2-32 shows a diagram of the process that transforms a draft chapter in Word, PowerPoint, and PNG image format into PDF pages. You will learn more about process diagrams like this in Chapters 7 and 10. For now, just realize that each column represents the activities taken by a role, which in this case is a particular person. The process starts with the thin-lined circle in the top left and ends with the thick-lined circle near the bottom right. The dashed lines represent the flow of data from one activity to another.

As shown in this diagram, the author works closely with the developmental editor, who ensures that the text is complete and complies with the market requirements, as specified by the acquisitions editor. We need not delve into this process in detail here; just observe that many different versions of chapter text and chapter art are created as people playing the various roles edit and approve and adjust edits.

Face-to-face meetings are impossible because the people fulfilling the roles in Figure 2-32 live in different geographic locations. In the past, the developmental process was conducted using the phone, email, and an FTP server. As you can imagine, considerable confusion can ensue with the hundreds of documents, art exhibits, and multiple reviewed copies of each. Furthermore, task requests that are delivered via email are easily lost. Dropped tasks and incorrect versions of documents and art are not common, but they do occur.

For this text, the development team decided to eat its own dogfood and use Office 365 for the production of this text. During this process, the author, the developmental editor Laura Town, and the production editor Kelly Loftus met frequently on Lync. Figure 2-33 shows a typical Lync meeting. Notice that the three actors in this process are sharing a common whiteboard. Each can write or draw on that whiteboard. At the end of the meeting, the

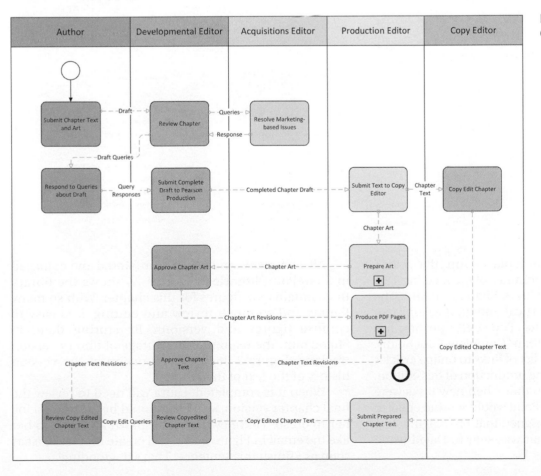

Figure 2-32
Chapter Development Process

Figure 2-33
SharePoint Group
Conversation

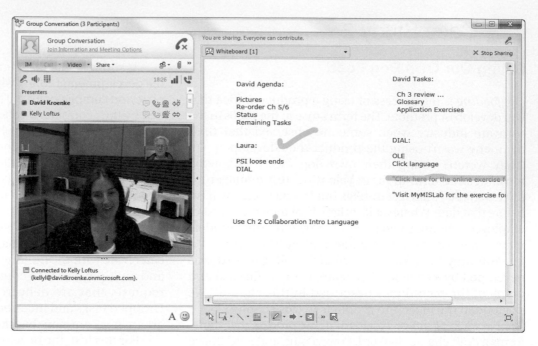

Figure 2-34
Using MIS, 5th Edition
SharePoint Development Site

whiteboards were saved and placed on the team's SharePoint site to be used as minutes of the meeting.

Figure 2-34 shows the team's SharePoint site. The Quick Launch (left-side vertical menu) has links to important content on the site. The center portion has tasks that have a value other than "Completed" for Status. The right-hand section has a list of links to online articles of particular importance to the production of this edition.

The team set up alerts so that when new tasks were created in the Tasks list, SharePoint would send an email to the person who had been assigned that task. Figure 2-31 (page 61) shows an email that was sent to David when Laura added a task to the Tasks list.

All documents and figures were stored and managed in SharePoint libraries. Figure 2-35 shows the library that contains the figures for this chapter. With so many figures and so much review and editing, it is easy to confuse figures and versions. By storing them in SharePoint, the team took advantage of library version tracking. Figure 2-36 shows a portion of the version history of the text of this chapter.

When it is completed, Laura will need to review the final chapter version, so a task should be created asking her to do so. That new task will spawn an email to her like the email in Figure 2-29. I will create that task just as soon as I finish this sentence! That's dogfooding!

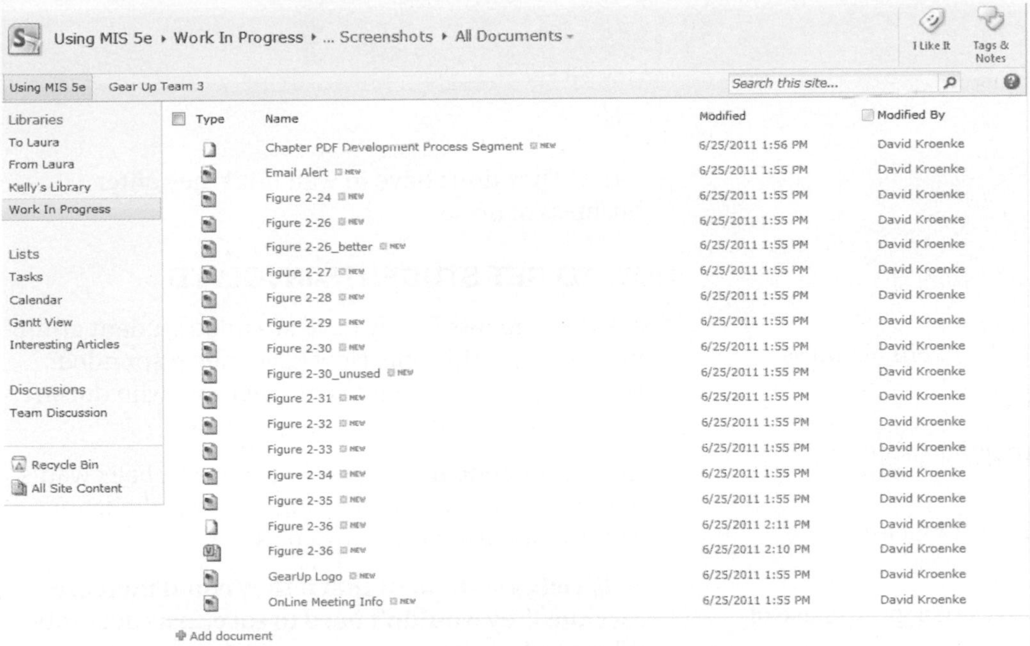

Type	Name	Modified	Modified By
	Chapter PDF Development Process Segment NEW	6/25/2011 1:56 PM	David Kroenke
	Email Alert NEW	6/25/2011 1:55 PM	David Kroenke
	Figure 2-24 NEW	6/25/2011 1:55 PM	David Kroenke
	Figure 2-26 NEW	6/25/2011 1:55 PM	David Kroenke
	Figure 2-26_better NEW	6/25/2011 1:55 PM	David Kroenke
	Figure 2-27 NEW	6/25/2011 1:55 PM	David Kroenke
	Figure 2-28 NEW	6/25/2011 1:55 PM	David Kroenke
	Figure 2-29 NEW	6/25/2011 1:55 PM	David Kroenke
	Figure 2-30 NEW	6/25/2011 1:55 PM	David Kroenke
	Figure 2-30_unused NEW	6/25/2011 1:55 PM	David Kroenke
	Figure 2-31 NEW	6/25/2011 1:55 PM	David Kroenke
	Figure 2-32 NEW	6/25/2011 1:55 PM	David Kroenke
	Figure 2-33 NEW	6/25/2011 1:55 PM	David Kroenke
	Figure 2-34 NEW	6/25/2011 1:55 PM	David Kroenke
	Figure 2-35 NEW	6/25/2011 1:55 PM	David Kroenke
	Figure 2-36 NEW	6/25/2011 2:11 PM	David Kroenke
	Figure 2-36 NEW	6/25/2011 2:10 PM	David Kroenke
	GearUp Logo NEW	6/25/2011 1:55 PM	David Kroenke
	OnLine Meeting Info NEW	6/25/2011 1:55 PM	David Kroenke

Figure 2-35
Document Library Used to Track Chapter 2 Figures

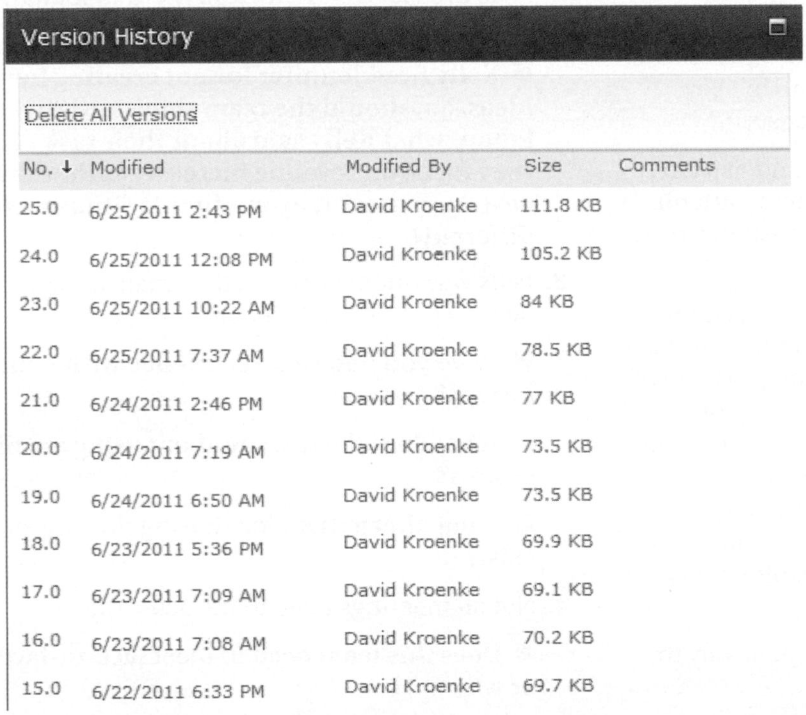

No. ↓	Modified	Modified By	Size	Comments
25.0	6/25/2011 2:43 PM	David Kroenke	111.8 KB	
24.0	6/25/2011 12:08 PM	David Kroenke	105.2 KB	
23.0	6/25/2011 10:22 AM	David Kroenke	84 KB	
22.0	6/25/2011 7:37 AM	David Kroenke	78.5 KB	
21.0	6/24/2011 2:46 PM	David Kroenke	77 KB	
20.0	6/24/2011 7:19 AM	David Kroenke	73.5 KB	
19.0	6/24/2011 6:50 AM	David Kroenke	73.5 KB	
18.0	6/23/2011 5:36 PM	David Kroenke	69.9 KB	
17.0	6/23/2011 7:09 AM	David Kroenke	69.1 KB	
16.0	6/23/2011 7:08 AM	David Kroenke	70.2 KB	
15.0	6/22/2011 6:33 PM	David Kroenke	69.7 KB	

Figure 2-36
Chapter 2 Version History

Questions

1. In your own words, define *dogfooding*. Do you think dogfooding is likely to predict product success? Why or why not? When would dogfooding not predict product success?

2. Explain how this team uses the shared whiteboard to generate minutes. What are the advantages of this technique?

3. Explain how this team uses alerts. Summarize the advantages to this team of using alerts.

4. Summarize the advantages to this team of using Lync.

5. Summarize the advantages to this team of using SharePoint.

6. Explain how you think Office 365 contributes to the efficiency of the development team. How might it contribute to the quality of this text?

7. Which aspects of Office 365 described here could have value to you when accomplishing student team projects? Explain why they add value compared to what you are currently doing.

TEACHING SUGGESTIONS

GearUp, Chapter 2

GOALS

Use GearUp to:

- Show a typical collaboration project in business.

- Illustrate a dysfunctional meeting.

- Demonstrate problems of irregular meeting attendance.

- Show some of the disadvantages of face-to-face meetings.

- Show some of the disadvantages of a group's use of email.

BACKGROUND

1. GearUp needs to find ways to reduce its operational expenses. Kelly has asked some of GearUp's key employees to identify ways of saving costs.

2. Felix has his own way of doing things and, if it isn't convenient to attend a meeting, he doesn't attend. That puts him behind the group's discussion, which aggravates the rest of the team.

3. This face-to-face meeting illustrates the need for collaboration IS . . . they need not meet face-to-face, nor even at the same time. An associate at Microsoft tells me that Microsoft has almost given up on face-to-face training for its employees. "It's not the expense. It's the fact that as soon as the training starts, someone's cell phone buzzes and that person leaves the room. They come back for 10 minutes and then it rings again." The scenario here illustrates that problem.

4. As discussed in the chapter, email is a poor way to share group results.

5. If they want, students can start gaining benefit from using collaboration IS with their teams in school,

today! They don't have to wait until they enter business to do so.

HOW TO GET STUDENTS INVOLVED

1. Ask the students if they have attended student group meetings like this one. How have they responded? What do they do about a team member who doesn't attend the meetings?

2. Gross profit equals revenue minus costs. Felix wants to increase profit by increasing revenue; the team wants to focus on reducing costs.

   ■ **Is Felix's statement that if they could increase revenue they wouldn't need to save costs accurate? Why or why not?**

   ■ **Is the fact that Kelly told them to focus on costs persuasive?**

   ■ **Kelly fired Jennifer for not creating her own ideas. So, should the team show initiative and ignore what Kelly said about their task . . . should they focus on revenue increases rather than cost decreases? Why might this situation be different?**

3. Felix was unable to open the email attachment (if, in fact, he even read the email).

   ■ **Have you had this experience with your groups?**

   ■ **What does the text say about using email for groups?**

   ■ **What alternatives for sharing documents exist?**

4. Not all meetings need to be face-to-face.

   ■ **Does this team need to meet face-to-face? Why or why not?**

   ■ **Under what conditions are face-to-face meetings required?**

- Do your team meetings need to be face-to-face? Why or why not?

- What IS can you use for your student teams?

BOTTOM LINE

- Face-to-face meetings have serious costs. Requiring everyone to be at the same place at the same time is expensive and aggravating.

- IS can greatly facilitate virtual meetings.

- Possibly, your default should be that all meetings are virtual . . . only special meetings need to be face-to-face.

YOU BE THE GUIDE

Using the Ethics Guide: Virtual Ethics? (pages 40–41)

GOALS

- Raise students' awareness to the possibilities of virtual-meeting spoofing.

- Ask students to assess their ethics about virtual-meeting spoofing.

- Address, as a class, the issue of cheating on online tests.

BACKGROUND AND PRESENTATION STRATEGIES

Virtual meetings are convenient, and they can be efficient. With virtual meetings, however, it is impossible to know that only authorized people are attending the meetings and that people are who they say they are. In most meetings, there is no deception, but the possibility exists.

I believe that any deception is a violation of a commonly accepted business code and is therefore unethical. I once had a professor perform a review of a text manuscript by giving the manuscript to his college-age daughter to read and comment upon. He made no indication that he did this. However, my editor followed up for clarification on several points, and the professor admitted that he had not read the manuscript. All of us felt deceived and cheated. Even though his daughter had made interesting and useful comments, the editorial team felt tricked and betrayed.

One could make the argument, however, that as long as the parties are better off, then spoofing is ethical. For example, if someone sends a better-qualified coworker to a virtual meeting, then one could argue everyone is better off because the team gains the expertise of the better-qualified worker. To me, though, the deception makes the action unethical.

Students should be aware that in virtual meetings everyone may not be who they say they are. Although I think actual spoofing is rare, I think it is common for people to silently attend meetings. On any conference call or multi-party chat session, students should learn to expect that there are unannounced people in the meeting.

■ **Never criticize anyone in a conference call or chat session. For all you know, that person may be in the meeting. Never give confidential information in such a call either. You have no way of knowing who is actually in the virtual room.**

On the topic of online testing: Having "helpers" during online testing is cheating and unethical. It does not matter if "everyone else is doing it." Most likely, everyone else is *not* doing it. And, if in fact a student truly believes that, then the matter should be brought to the attention of the professor. If everyone has a helper, then having helpers should be stated as the accepted practice, or groups should be officially allowed to take tests as a group.

People sometimes argue that if you allow someone else to take your test you are "only cheating yourself." That is true as far as the gain of knowledge is concerned. However, because grades are used for competitive purposes, then those who use test helpers are gaining an unethical competitive advantage. Unless group test-taking is the accepted practice, having a helper is always cheating and is unethical.

SUGGESTED RESPONSES FOR DISCUSSION QUESTIONS

1. It is illegal to spoof policemen, firemen, and military personnel. It is probably illegal to spoof certain professionals such as doctors, nurses, architects, and licensed engineers. In general, however, it is not illegal to spoof someone. If the person who is being spoofed gives permission for the act, then he or she is culpable if the behavior is illegal.

2. Spoofing is unethical. Almost every businessperson would define deception as unacceptable. Consequently, because ethical behavior is defined as adhering to a group norm, deception in the form of spoofing is always unethical. If the person being spoofed is aware of the deception, then he or she is culpable in the unethical act.

3. None, for the reasons described in 2.

4. Communication among members of the group who were supposed to be in the meeting will be surreal. Everyone will think that others know something that they do not know. The people who were at the meeting will know what transpired. They will not be *expected* to know anything about the meeting, yet will be the only ones who do know.

   This example is so overdrawn that it is almost silly. It points, however, to the communication problems that develop in organizations where deception is practiced.

5. The only difference between text chat and speaker phones or conference calls is that it is easier to spoof

with text chat. Yes, we have always had these problems, and yes, they have always been unethical. Text chat makes it easier and therefore possibly more prevalent. For any virtual meeting, whether via voice or text chat, always assume that unknown, unannounced people may be on the call or in the meeting.

6. I think this gets into a gray area. If you are setting up the meeting and if you know that Bill has an interest in the outcome, you probably do have an ethical responsibility to invite him. However, if you have no particular responsibility to invite Bill, if Bill would not feel betrayed by you for not inviting him, then your action may not be unethical. You do not, after all, have an ethical responsibility to bring trouble into your business life.

7. No, not ethical. This sort of behavior has a way of coming back at the perpetrator. "What goes around, comes around." Being criticized for her thinking that you advanced as your own is the universe getting even. You can't disclaim those ideas; and if you try, you'll look even worse.

8. It is always cheating and unethical to have a helper on an online test. You are not justified in having a helper even if you believe "everyone else is doing it." If you believe that is the case, raise the issue with your professor. Whether such tests should be used at all depends on the importance of the grade of the test. If the test largely determines a course grade, I believe that their use should be avoided.

WRAP UP

■ **In any conference call, speaker-phone call, or multiparty chat session, assume that unannounced guests may be on the line. Govern your comments as if you do not know who is in the room, because, indeed, you do not know.**

■ **Spoofing someone is always unethical and it may be illegal, depending on whom you are spoofing. If you know that someone is spoofing you, you share responsibility for the unethical behavior.**

■ **Having helpers on online tests is cheating and is always unethical.**

Using the Guide: Securing Collaboration (pages 64–65)

GOALS

- Raise students' awareness of security risks and potential problems when using collaboration software.

- Understand the risks to organizational data when data is shared with nonemployee personnel.

- Learn differences in security capabilities of Google Docs, Windows Live SkyDrive, and Office 365.

BACKGROUND AND PRESENTATION STRATEGIES

Collaboration tools enhance collaboration but introduce serious security risks. The more people who have access to data, the greater the likelihood of data loss. For example, if the probability that any single person uses data in only authorized ways is 0.99, if the group has three people, the probability that everyone in the group uses data only in authorized ways falls to 0.97 (assuming equal probability and independent events). However, if the group has 50 people, the probability that everyone in the group uses data in authorized ways falls to 0.61. This change occurs simply because with more people there is more chance that someone will use the data inappropriately.

Now, there is always risk in sharing data. If I attach a document with confidential data to an email and send it to a large group of people, I am exposing that confidential data to considerable risk. However, it is just one document. Suppose, instead, that I place numerous documents, schedules, tasks, and sketches on a Windows Live SkyDrive site and open that site to a large number of people. I am exposing that semantically linked group of documents to considerable risk. In some ways, the risk of sharing a SkyDrive site is greater than sharing a file server. Most file servers have so many documents that it can be difficult to find everything about some topic. All of the documents on a team site, however, contain data of interest to the purpose of the team. Critical documents have been centralized in one spot.

The problem of sharing confidential data with outsiders is not new. However, the problem of sharing an entire team's document set with outsiders is new. Again, the consequences may be higher because there are many documents, all with a similar purpose.

Of the three collaboration tools presented in this chapter, SharePoint has the potential for the most security. It has only the *potential* for the most security because the features and functions for excellent security are in the product, but it is incumbent on those who set up the SharePoint server and sites to create and implement security.

However, the adage "A chain is only as strong as its weakest link" pertains to document security. Documents can be highly protected on a SharePoint site, but if legitimate SharePoint users download that data to a Windows Live SkyDrive site, or to a Google Docs site, then the security enforced by SharePoint may have been overcome.

Digital rights management is a means of restricting the use of Microsoft Office documents. With it, the content of documents can be restricted to viewing by particular people or for particular periods of time and in other ways. This technology, however, is seldom used and has numerous holes.

The bottom line: Sharing confidential documents in team sites exposes those documents to increased security risks. This risk increases dramatically with employee's use of personal mobile devices. The IS Department has little to no control over their use and it is presently unclear how organizations can deal with security breaches via personal devices.

SUGGESTED RESPONSES FOR DISCUSSION QUESTIONS

1. When using a public wireless network, you should assume that any email you send or any IM message you write can be published on the front page of your campus newspaper tomorrow. Write only what you are willing to have published.

2. The financial exposure is much higher for businesses than for individuals. Again, any email or IM sent over a public wireless network is open and can be read by anyone. If you are using, say, Google Docs, to share accounting data with one of your clients over a public wireless network, you are exposing that data to snooping. Do not transmit sensitive data over a public wireless network.

3. Employees who process work emails on Gmail are exposing the content of those emails over the public Internet. Even if the employee is working inside the corporate network, and even if that

network is secure, as soon as the email goes on to the public Internet, it is vulnerable to snooping. If no public wireless network is used, then the snooper would have to physically tap into a wired network, which is much harder than wireless snooping, but it is still a possibility.

More important, Gmail is free software, and Google severely limits its liability for the quality of the product or service. Of course, Google would suffer an enormous public relations loss were its email servers to be compromised or lost, but, even still, any employee who stores company email on a Gmail server (and you cannot use Gmail without doing so) is exposing the company's data to the security policy established by Google. The company may or may not determine that to be an acceptable risk, but when employees do this on their own, their companies do not even know. It is a messy issue with no clear solution (nor barrier).

4. Organizations have no control over the ways that SharePoint Online (part of Office 365) sites are shared. An employee could store sensitive data on a SharePoint Online site and inadvertently share that site publicly, or share it inappropriately. An employee might give update permission to someone who has no authority to make updates. Partners could copy sensitive data from a SharePoint Online site and send it to competitors. Furthermore, the organization has no control over how Microsoft treats the data on its site. Microsoft could be hacked and lose data and, absent gross carelessness, the organization that lost the data would have no recourse. Ironically, ease of use is the culprit here. Both Google Docs and SharePoint Online are readily accessible and quite easy to use. This means that employees with less knowledge of the risks of sharing can readily use these services. Consider, too, that employees can be accessing Google Docs or SharePoint Online using their own iPhones or iPads, using network access that is paid for by the employee. The organization has no control over such use. **It is not much ado about nothing.** Organizations today have serious challenges to security in these services.

5. The risks of using SharePoint Online or Google Docs are no greater than the risks of using any file server. Few organizations today would disallow file servers, and thus few would be likely to disallow SharePoint Online or Google Docs on this same basis. In general, it is very difficult to enforce the prohibition of using particular programs. Even if the employees cannot install software on their work computers, they can install it on their own computers and copy data from the work computer to their home computer.

Chapter 12 discusses these issues in more detail. In general, it is cheaper and easier to perform security background checks on employees in sensitive positions, and to train those employees on security policy, than it is to prohibit employees from using certain software. With the numerous computing alternatives available today, employees can usually find a way around some prohibition if they are sufficiently motivated.

WRAP UP

■ **Collaboration software opens the door to security risks. Always think about security when you set up a team site. Realize that team members can always remove data to other locations and process it or transmit it elsewhere without your knowledge.**

■ **Sharing data with nonemployees is risky. Sharing Google Docs, or SharePoint Online sites with outsiders is even more risky because many related files and documents are consolidated at a single location.**

■ **Organizations have a serious security vulnerability from employees' use of personal, mobile devices such as iPhones, iPads, Android phones, and the like. Education and training of employees is crucial!**

YOU BE THE GUIDE

Using the Guide: Egocentric Versus Empathetic Thinking

(pages 66–67)

GOALS

- Raise the level of professionalism in the class.
- Explore empathetic thinking and discuss why it's smart.
- Discuss two applications of empathetic thinking.
- Emphasize that a problem is a perception and that perceptions differ among people.
- Discuss that different problem perceptions require different information systems.

BACKGROUND AND PRESENTATION STRATEGIES

How many times have we all been asked, "I couldn't come to class. Did we do anything important?" I'm always tempted to say, "No, when I saw you weren't here, I took all the important material out." Another rejoinder, more mature on my part is, "Well, first tell me what you think important material is." If they say, "Is it going to be on the test . . . ?" then we have some talking to do.

You might want to underline the corollary about not asking your boss, when you've missed a meeting, "Did we do anything important?"

Part of the reason for this guide is to raise the level of professionalism in the class. I find students' maturity rises to meet expectations. By asking them to engage in empathetic thinking with regard to not coming to class, I'm also asking them to step up in their maturity:

■ **If you choose not to come to class, that's your choice. But, realize there's a cost to me and our teaching assistants, and do what you can to minimize that cost.**

Empathetic thinking does result in better relationships, but this guide says that businesspeople should engage in it because it's smart. Negotiators, for example, need to know what the other side wants, what's important to it, what issues they can give on, and what ones are nonnegotiable.

Here's a simple example:

■ **Suppose you have an employee who wants more recognition in the group. You know the employee is doing a good job, and you want to reward her. Not** engaging in empathic thinking, you give her a pay raise. What have you done?

■ **How could empathetic thinking have helped you in this situation?**

So, using this example, just what is empathetic thinking?

■ **Understanding the other person's perspective (See the Guide "Understanding Perspectives and Points of View" in Chapter 1)**

■ **Realizing that people who hold a perspective different from yours are not necessarily WRONG (but you don't have to be wrong, either)**

■ **Not attempting to convince the other person that his or her perspective should be changed to match yours**

■ **Adapting your behavior in accordance with the other person's perspective**

■ **Does thinking empathically mean that you change your way of thinking to match the other person's?**

(No.)

■ **Does it mean always giving the other person what he or she wants?**

(No.)

■ **What are different ways you could adapt your behavior in accordance with another person's perspective?**

All of us have been in meetings that are going nowhere. Whenever we find ourselves in such a meeting, is the problem due to different perspectives? If so, one can sometimes find the root cause by engaging in empathetic thinking.

The scenario at the end of the guide is right on point. If three factions hold three different problem definitions, and if they don't realize they hold those different definitions, then the meeting will go nowhere. And it doesn't matter what the "facts" are. The facts aren't the problem; the different problem definitions are.

SUGGESTED RESPONSES FOR DISCUSSION QUESTIONS

1. Considering the other person's perspective:

   ■ **What are some examples of egocentric thinking?**

   ■ **What are some examples of empathetic thinking?**

2. Read the minutes, if any. Ask others who were at the meeting. Prior to the meeting, ask someone else to take notes or make a recording. If possible, let your boss know ahead of time that you'll be absent, and why. Otherwise, apologize for your absence, explain why, and say that you have the information. Minimize the burden on your boss!

3. A problem is a perception. Different people perceive in different ways. So, different people can have different problems, *even though they may give the same name to the problem.*

4. First, based on her words, the *real problem* is that you know she is not engaged in empathetic thinking. Notice that you are in a much stronger position than she is. You know that there are two (yours and hers), and possibly more, different problem definitions. Unlike her, your thinking is broad and flexible enough to understand that multiple perceptions, and hence multiple problem definitions, can exist at the same time.

   You have at least four different strategies: (1) Change your definition to match hers. (2) Try to teach her about empathetic thinking. (3) Without saying anything about her thinking skills, and without needlessly repeating your understanding of the problem, use your understanding of her and her definition to arrive at a solution that is mutually acceptable. (4) Say something polite and close the conversation because you're just wasting your time.

   ■ **Under what circumstances would you use each of these strategies?**

5. Restate his position to him. "You perceive the problem as . . . ," and do the best possible job of restating his position. This does not mean you agree with his position, but it will let him know that you understand his words. He'll know, if you continue to disagree with him, that it's not because you don't understand him.

   Having convinced him that you understand his position, you should attempt to express your view of the problem. His knowing that you understand his position may allow him to be able to understand yours. However, he may not be able to, in which case there may be no possibility of good communication with him on this issue.

6. It comes down to power. You are in a much more powerful position if you understand other people's perceptions and your own, but they understand only their own. You can imagine solutions and possibilities that they cannot. Also, as countless books on negotiating skills imply, understanding someone else's point of view enables you to manipulate them, if you are so inclined.

   Finally, empathetic thinking results in better relationships, and in the final analysis, business is nothing but relationships. Businesses themselves do nothing. Business is people working together in relationships. Better relationships equate to better business.

WRAP UP

Sometimes I end with a little practice:

■ **Anybody learn anything today? What?**

■ **All right, let's practice. Using empathetic thinking, tell me why you think I included this exercise in today's presentation.**

Strategy and Information Systems

"**Drew**, what's your hurry?" Addison Lee jumps out of the way as Drew comes barreling out of his office.

"Workload, Addison, workload. They've given me the operations responsibility for ALL the soccer sales. I've got events coming out of my ears!" Drew sounds exhausted.

"All the soccer sales events? Why?" Addison looks closely at him and realizes that he really is exhausted.

"All part of getting our operations costs down. You know, like Kelly's always saying, 'we've got to have the lowest prices on the Net.'"

"So . . ."

"So, to make any money at those low prices, we've got to get costs down. We can negotiate better deals with the vendors, but that only goes so far. After that, we take it out of our hide."

"Ouch."

"Yeah, and these people at General Sports are driving me nuts!"

"General Sports? They're always a problem. I can't tell you how much time I've wasted with them. I had an event completely negotiated, and they pulled the plug at the last minute." Addison has fire in her voice.

"You did? How come nobody told me?" Drew's surprised.

"I don't know. Why didn't you ask me?"

"Well, I didn't know you'd been working with them. I wonder who else has . . ."

"Sarah had much the same experience as I did. Check with her."

"I will. But, really, even if I knew ahead of time about your problems, I doubt it would help."

"No?"

"No. Nobody ever asks operations before they start negotiating their deal. They think that if they can buy soccer balls for $14 and sell them for $30, we've made 16 bucks."

"Haven't we?"

"Yes and no. I mean we've made 16 bucks a ball on the surface, but having to deal with General is twice as expensive for operations as dealing, with, say, San Diego Sports."

"Yeah, they're great to work with, aren't they?"

"I'm telling you, any deal with General is not making us the money Kelly thinks it is. Not by the time you factor in all the operational expenses of dealing with those jerks."

"I never thought of it like that, but I guess you're right."

"You buyers ought to change the way you pick these vendors. Sure, the products and their prices matter, but you should think about our costs, too."

"How would we do that? Where's the data?" Addison sounds intrigued, but skeptical.

"I don't know, and I've got to run. I don't have time to think about this, but somebody should." ∎

Study Questions

Q1 How does organizational strategy determine information systems structure?

Q2 What five forces determine industry structure?

Q3 How does analysis of industry structure determine competitive strategy?

Q4 How does competitive strategy determine value chain structure?

Q5 How do business processes generate value?

Q6 How does competitive strategy determine business processes and the structure of information systems?

Q7 How do information systems provide competitive advantages?

Q8 2022?

Recall from Chapter 1 that MIS is the development and use of information systems that enable organizations to achieve their strategies. In Chapter 2, you learned how information systems can help people collaborate. This chapter focuses on how information systems support competitive strategy and how IS can create competitive advantages. As you will learn in your organizational behavior classes, a body of knowledge exists to help organizations analyze their industry, select a competitive strategy, and develop business processes. In the first part of this chapter, we will survey that knowledge and show how to use it, via several steps, to structure information systems. Then, in the last section, we will discuss how companies use information systems to gain a competitive advantage.

GearUp provides a good example. Its strategy is to provide the lowest priced items on the Web. To do so, it needs to keep its costs as low as possible. An information system that tracks the expense of working with vendors would help it select better vendors, but, as of yet, it doesn't have one. Thus, GearUp's information systems are not supporting its strategy as well as they could.

Q1 How Does Organizational Strategy Determine Information Systems Structure?

According to the definition of MIS, information systems exist to help organizations achieve their strategies. As you will learn in your business strategy class, an organization's goals and objectives are determined by its *competitive strategy*. Thus, ultimately, competitive strategy determines the structure, features, and functions of every information system.

Figure 3-1 summarizes this situation. In short, organizations examine the structure of their industry and determine a competitive strategy. That strategy determines value chains, which, in turn, determine business processes. The structure of business processes determines the design of supporting information systems.

Michael Porter, one of the key researchers and thinkers in competitive analysis, developed three different models that can help you understand the elements of Figure 3-1. We begin with his five forces model.

Figure 3-1
Organizational Strategy Determines Information Systems

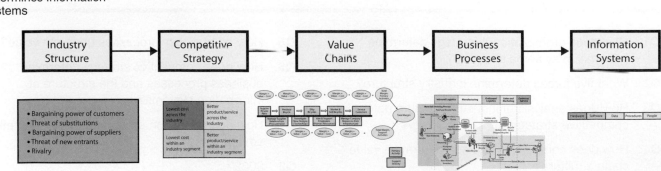

• Bargaining power of customers
• Threat of substitutions
• Bargaining power of suppliers
• Threat of new entrants
• Rivalry

Figure 3-2
Porter's Five Forces Model of
Industry Structure

Source: Based on Michael E. Porter,
*Competitive Advantage: Creating and
Sustaining Superior Performance*
(The Free Press, a Division of Simon &
Schuster Adult Publishing Group). Copyright ©
1985, 1998 by Michael E. Porter.

Q2 What Five Forces Determine Industry Structure?

Organizational strategy begins with an assessment of the fundamental characteristics and structure of an industry. One model used to assess an industry structure is Porter's **five forces model**,[1] summarized in Figure 3-2. According to this model, five competitive forces determine industry profitability: bargaining power of customers, threat of substitutions, bargaining power of suppliers, threat of new entrants, and rivalry among existing firms. The intensity of each of the five forces determines the characteristics of the industry, how profitable it is, and how sustainable that profitability will be.

To understand this model, consider the strong and weak examples for each of the forces in Figure 3-3. A good check on your understanding is to see if you can think of different forces of each category in Figure 3-3. Also, take a particular industry—say, auto repair—and consider how these five forces determine the competitive landscape of that industry.

Figure 3-4 illustrates GearUp's analysis of these five forces. The two strongest forces are from customers and rivalry. GearUp's response to the customer force is to provide the lowest prices for goods to be found, anywhere. Its response to the rivalry threat is to keep its customers' attention focused on GearUp via compelling emails.

Like GearUp, organizations examine these five forces and determine how they intend to respond to them. That examination leads to competitive strategy.

Force	Example of Strong Force	Example of Weak Force
Bargaining power of customers	Toyota's purchase of auto paint	Your power over the procedures and policies of your university
Threat of substitutions	Frequent-traveler's choice of auto rental	Patients using the only drug effective for their type of cancer
Bargaining power of suppliers	Students purchasing gasoline	Grain farmers in a surplus year
Threat of new entrants	Corner latte stand	Professional football team
Rivalry	Used car dealers	Internal Revenue Service

Figure 3-3
Examples of Five Forces

---

[1] Michael Porter, *Competitive Strategy: Techniques for Analyzing Industries and Competitors* (New York: Free Press, 1980).

Figure 3-4
Five Forces at GearUp

Force	GearUp Example	Force Strength	GearUp's Response
Bargaining power of customers	"I won't buy unless it's cheap."	Strong	Lowest possible prices
Threat of substitutions	"I can buy it at a sporting goods shop."	Weak	Web advertising
Bargaining power of suppliers	"You'll have to pay more."	Weak	Find other suppliers
Threat of new entrants	"There's a hot new site."	Medium	Lower prices, better products
Rivalry	"I shop the Internet for the lowest price."	Strong	Compelling emails to bring customers back, every day

See the Ethics Guide on pages 80–81 to learn how a change in strategy can greatly affect a company's culture.

Q3 How Does Analysis of Industry Structure Determine Competitive Strategy?

An organization responds to the structure of its industry by choosing a **competitive strategy**. Porter followed his five forces model with the model of four competitive strategies, shown in Figure 3-5.[2] According to Porter, firms engage in one of these four strategies. An organization can focus on being the cost leader, or it can focus on differentiating its products or services from those of the competition. Further, the organization can employ the cost or differentiation strategy across an industry, or it can focus its strategy on a particular industry segment.

Consider the car rental industry, for example. According to the first column of Figure 3-5, a car rental company can strive to provide the lowest-cost car rentals across the industry, or it can seek to provide the lowest-cost car rentals to an industry segment—say, U.S. domestic business travelers.

As shown in the second column, a car rental company can seek to differentiate its products from the competition. It can do so in various ways—for example, by providing a wide range of high-quality cars, by providing the best reservation system, by having the cleanest cars or the fastest check-in, or by some other means. The company can strive to provide product differentiation across the industry or within particular segments of the industry, such as U.S. domestic business travelers.

According to Porter, to be effective, the organization's goals, objectives, culture, and activities must be consistent with the organization's strategy. To those in the MIS field, this means that all information systems in the organization must reflect and facilitate the organization's competitive strategy.

Figure 3-5
Porter's Four Competitive Strategies

	Cost	Differentiation
Industry-wide	Lowest cost across the industry	Better product/service across the industry
Focus	Lowest cost within an industry segment	Better product/service within an industry segment

---

[2] Based on Michael Porter, *Competitive Strategy* (New York: Free Press, 1985).

GearUp has chosen a low-cost strategy focused within the sporting goods category, further focused within the segment of buyers who are interested in special, short-term sales. As the vignette at the start of this chapter indicates, it needs to do everything it can to keep costs down.

Q4 How Does Competitive Strategy Determine Value Chain Structure?

Organizations analyze the structure of their industry, and, using that analysis, they formulate a competitive strategy. They then need to organize and structure the organization to implement that strategy. If, for example, the competitive strategy is to be *cost leader*, like GearUp, then business activities need to be developed to provide essential functions at the lowest possible cost.

A business that selects a *differentiation* strategy would not necessarily structure itself around least-cost activities. Instead, such a business might choose to develop more costly processes, but it would do so only if those processes provided benefits that outweighed their costs. Porter defined **value** as the amount of money that a customer is willing to pay for a resource, product, or service. The difference between the value that an activity generates and the cost of the activity is called the **margin.** A business with a differentiation strategy will add cost to an activity only as long as the activity has a positive margin.

A **value chain** is a network of value-creating activities. That generic chain consists of five **primary activities** and four **support activities.**

Primary Activities in the Value Chain

To understand the essence of the value chain, consider a small manufacturer—say, a bicycle maker (see Figure 3-6). First, the manufacturer acquires raw materials using the inbound logistics activity. This activity concerns the receiving and handling of raw materials and other inputs. The accumulation of those materials adds value in the sense that even a pile of unassembled parts is worth something to some customer. A collection of the parts needed to build a bicycle is worth more than an empty space on a shelf. The value is not only the parts themselves, but also the time required to

Figure 3-6
Bicycle Maker's Value Chain

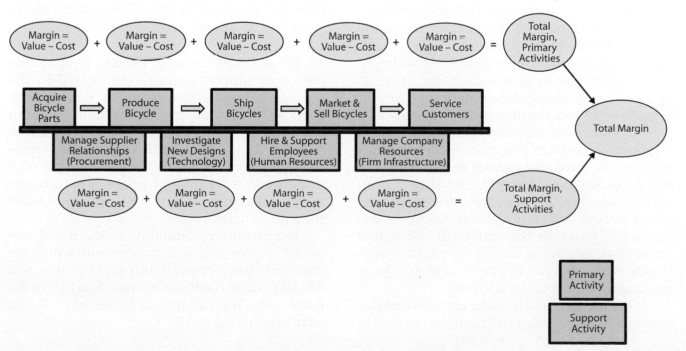

Ethics Guide

Yikes! Bikes

Suppose you are an operations manager for Yikes! Bikes, a manufacturer of high-end mountain bicycles with $20 million in annual sales. Yikes! has been in business over 25 years, and the founder and sole owner recently sold the business to an investment group, Major Capital. You know nothing about the sale until your boss introduces you to Andrea Parks, a partner at Major Capital, who is in charge of the acquisition. Parks explains to you that Yikes! has been sold to Major Capital and that she will be the temporary general manager. She explains that the new owners see great potential in you, and they want to enlist your cooperation during the transition. She hints that if your potential is what she thinks it is, you will be made general manager of Yikes!

Parks explains that the new owners decided there are too many players in the high-end mountain bike business, and they plan to change the competitive strategy of Yikes! from high-end differentiation to lowest-cost vendor. Accordingly, they will eliminate local manufacturing, fire most of the manufacturing department, and import bikes from China. Further, Major Capital sees a need to reduce expenses and plans a 10 percent across-the-board staff reduction and a cut of two-thirds of the customer support department. The new bikes will be of lesser quality than current Yikes! bikes, but the price will be substantially less. The new ownership group believes it will take a few years for the market to realize that Yikes! bikes are not the same quality as they were. Finally, Parks asks you to attend an all-employee meeting with the founder and her.

At the meeting, the founder explains that due to his age and personal situation, he decided to sell Yikes! to Major Capital and that starting today Andrea Parks is the general manager. He thanks the employees for their many years of service, wishes them well, and leaves the building. Parks introduces herself to the employees and states that Major Capital is very excited to own such a great company with a strong, quality brand. She says she will take a few weeks to orient herself to the business and its environment and plans no major changes to the company.

You are reeling from all this news when Parks calls you into her office and explains that she needs you to prepare two reports. In one, she wants a list of all the employees in the manufacturing department, sorted by their salary (or wage for hourly employees). She explains that she intends to cut the most costly employees first. "I don't want to be inflexible about this, though," she says. "If there is someone whom you think we should keep, let me know, and we can talk about it."

She also wants a list of the employees in the customer support department, sorted by the average amount of time each support rep spends with customers. She explains, "I'm not so concerned with payroll expense in customer support. It's not how much we're paying someone; it's how much time they're wasting with customers. We're going to have a bare-bones support department, and we want to get rid of the gabby chatters first."

You are, understandably, shocked and surprised . . . not only at the speed with which the transition has occurred, but also because you wouldn't think the founder would do this to the employees. You call him at home and tell him what is going on.

Source: Petr Nad/Shutterstock.com.

Source: Steve Beer/Shutterstock.com.

"Look," he explains, "when I sold the company, I asked them to be sure to take care of the employees. They said they would. I'll call Andrea, but there's really nothing I can do at this point; they own the show."

In a black mood of depression, you realize you don't want to work for Yikes! anymore, but your wife is 6 months' pregnant with your first child. You need medical insurance for her at least until the baby is born. But what miserable tasks are you going to be asked to do before then? And you suspect that if you balk at any task, Parks won't hesitate to fire you, too.

As you leave that night you run into Lori, the most popular customer support representative and one of your favorite employees. "Hey," Lori asks you, "what did you think of that meeting? Do you believe Andrea? Do you think they'll let us continue to make great bikes?" ∎

Discussion Questions

1. In your opinion, did the new owners take any illegal action? Is there evidence of a crime in this scenario?

2. Was the statement that Parks made to all of the employees unethical? Why or why not? If you questioned her about the ethics of her statement, how do you think she would justify herself?

3. What do you think Parks will tell the founder if he calls as a result of your conversation with him? Does he have any legal recourse? Is Major Capital's behavior toward him unethical? Why or why not?

4. Parks is going to use information to perform staff cuts. What do you think about her rationale? Ethically, should she consider other factors, such as number of years of service, past employee reviews, or other criteria?

5. How do you respond to Lori? What are the consequences if you tell her what you know? What are the consequences of lying to her? What are the consequences of saying something noncommittal?

6. If you actually were in this situation, would you leave the company? Why or why not?

7. In business school, we talk of principles like competitive strategy as interesting academic topics. But, as you can see from the Yikes! case, competitive strategy decisions have human consequences. How do you plan to resolve conflicts between human needs and tough business decisions?

8. How do you define *job security*?

Figure 3-7
Task Descriptions for Primary
Activities of the Value Chain

Source: Based on Michael E. Porter,
*Competitive Advantage: Creating and
Sustaining Superior Performance*
(The Free Press, a Division of Simon &
Schuster Adult Publishing Group) Copyright ©
1985, 1998 by Michael E. Porter.

Primary Activity	Description
Inbound Logistics	Receiving, storing, and disseminating inputs to the products
Operations/Manufacturing	Transforming inputs into the final products
Outbound Logistics	Collecting, storing, and physically distributing the products to buyers
Sales and Marketing	Inducing buyers to purchase the products and providing a means for them to do so
Customer Service	Assisting customers' use of the products and thus maintaining and enhancing the products' value

contact vendors for those parts, to maintain business relationships with those vendors, to order the parts, to receive the shipment, and so forth.

In the operations activity, the bicycle maker transforms raw materials into a finished bicycle, a process that adds more value. Next, the company uses the outbound logistics activity to deliver the finished bicycle to a customer. Of course, there is no customer to send the bicycle to without the marketing and sales value activity. Finally, the service activity provides customer support to the bicycle users.

Each stage of this generic chain accumulates costs and adds value to the product. The net result is the total margin of the chain, which is the difference between the total value added and the total costs incurred. Figure 3-7 summarizes the primary activities of the value chain.

Support Activities in the Value Chain

The support activities in the generic value chain contribute indirectly to the production, sale, and service of the product. They include procurement, which consists of the processes of finding vendors, setting up contractual arrangements, and negotiating prices. (This differs from inbound logistics, which is concerned with ordering and receiving in accordance with agreements set up by procurement.)

By the way, procurement is a support function for most businesses, but probably not for GearUp. Because GearUp has a new event, possibly with a different vendor, every day, procurement is more of a primary operations function. It still has a support procurement function for items like office desks and chairs, but procurement for items for events is part of its operations.

Porter defined technology broadly. It includes research and development, but it also includes other activities within the firm for developing new techniques, methods, and procedures. He defined human resources as recruiting, compensation, evaluation, and training of full-time and part-time employees. Finally, firm infrastructure includes general management, finance, accounting, legal, and government affairs.

Supporting functions add value, albeit indirectly, and they also have costs. Hence, as shown in Figure 3-6, supporting activities contribute to a margin. In the case of supporting activities, it would be difficult to calculate the margin because the specific value added of, say, the manufacturer's lobbyists in Washington, D.C., is difficult to know. But there is a value added, there are costs, and there is a margin, even if it is only in concept.

Value Chain Linkages

Porter's model of business activities includes **linkages,** which are interactions across value activities. For example, manufacturing systems use linkages to reduce inventory costs. Such a system uses sales forecasts to plan production; it then uses the production plan to determine raw materials needs and then uses the material needs to schedule purchases. The end result is just-in-time inventory, which reduces inventory sizes and costs.

By describing value chains and their linkages, Porter started a movement to create integrated, cross-departmental business systems. Over time, Porter's work led to the

Using MIS InClass 3 *A Group Exercise*

Industry Structure → Competitive Strategy → Value Chains → Business Processes → Information Systems

Source: © Corbis/SuperStock.

Source: © Image Source/SuperStock.

As shown in Figure 3-1, information systems are a logical consequence of an organization's analysis of industry structure via the chain of models shown in the title of this feature. Consequently, you should be able to combine your knowledge of an organization's market, together with observations of the structure and content of its Web storefront, to infer the organization's competitive strategy and possibly make inferences about its value chains and business processes. The process you use here can be useful in preparing for job interviews, as well.

Form a three-person team (or as directed by your professor) and perform the following exercises. Divide work as appropriate, but create common answers for the team.

1. The following pairs of Web storefronts have market segments that overlap in some way. Briefly visit each site of each pair:
   - *www.sportsauthority.com* vs. *www.soccer.com*
   - *www.target.com* vs. *www.sephora.com*
   - *www.woot.com* vs. *www.amazon.com*
   - *www.petco.com* vs. *www.healthyfoodforpets.com*
   - *www.llbean.com* vs. *www.rei.com*

2. Select two pairs from the list. For each pair of companies, answer the following questions:
   a. How do the companies' market segments differ?
   b. How do their competitive pressures differ?
   c. How do their competitive strategies differ?
   d. How is the "feel" of the content of their Web sites different?
   e. How is the "feel" of the user interface of their Web sites different?
   f. How could either company change its Web site to better accomplish its competitive strategy?
   g. Would the change you recommended in item f necessitate a change in one or more of the company's value chains? Explain.

3. Use your answers in step 2 to explain the following statement: "The structure of an organization's information system (here a Web storefront) is determined by its competitive strategy." Structure your answer so that you could use it in a job interview to demonstrate your overall knowledge of business planning.

4. Present your team's answers to the rest of the class.

creation of a new discipline called *business process design*. The central idea is that organizations should not automate or improve existing functional systems. Rather, they should create new, more efficient business processes that integrate the activities of all departments involved in a value chain. You will see an example of a linkage in the next section.

Value chain analysis has a direct application to manufacturing businesses like the bicycle manufacturer. However, value chains also exist in service-oriented companies like medical clinics. The difference is that most of the value in a service company is generated by the operations, marketing and sales, and service activities. Inbound and outbound logistics are not typically as important. You will have a chance to reflect on these differences in Using Your Knowledge Question 1, page 99.

Q5 How Do Business Processes Generate Value?

A **business process** is a network of activities that generate value by transforming inputs into outputs. The **cost** of the business process is the cost of the inputs plus the cost of the activities. The margin of the business process is the value of the outputs minus the cost.

A business process is a network of activities. Each **activity** is a business function that receives inputs and produces outputs. An activity can be performed by a human, by a computer system, or by both. The inputs and outputs can be physical, like bicycle parts, or they can be data, such as a Purchase Order. A **repository** is a collection of something; a database is a repository of data and a raw material repository is an inventory of raw materials. We will refine and extend these definitions in Chapter 7 and again in Chapter 10, but these basic terms will get us started.

Consider the three business processes for a bicycle manufacturer shown in Figure 3-8. The materials ordering process transforms cash[3] into a raw materials inventory. The manufacturing process transforms raw materials into finished goods. The sales process transforms finished goods into cash. Notice that the business processes span the value chain activities. The sales process involves sales and marketing as well as outbound logistics activities, as you would expect. Note, too, that while none of these three processes involve a customer-service activity, customer service plays a role in other business processes.

Figure 3-8
Three Examples of Business Processes

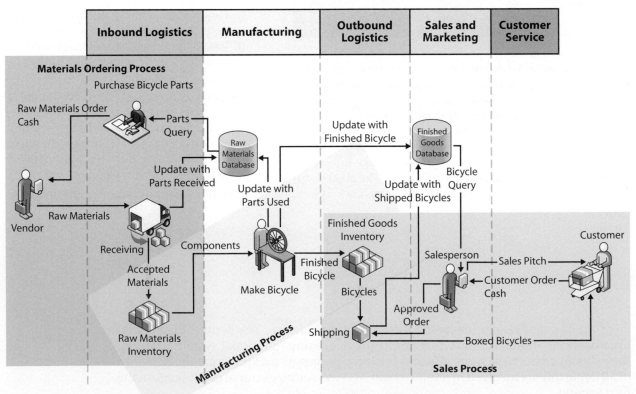

---

[3] For simplicity, the flow of cash is abbreviated in this diagram. Business processes for authorizing, controlling, making payments, and receiving revenue are, of course, vital.

Also notice that activities get and put data resources from and to databases. For example, the purchase-bicycle-parts activity queries the raw materials database to determine the materials to order. The receiving activity updates the raw materials database to indicate the arrival of materials. The make-bicycle activity updates the raw materials database to indicate the consumption of materials. Similar actions are taken in the sales process against the finished goods database.

Business processes vary in cost and effectiveness. In fact, the streamlining of business processes to increase margin (add value, reduce costs, or both) is key to competitive advantage. You will learn about process design when we discuss **business process management** in Chapter 10. To get a flavor of process design, however, consider Figure 3-9, which shows an alternate process for the bicycle manufacturer. Here, the purchase-bicycle-parts activity not only queries the raw materials inventory database, it also queries the finished goods inventory database. Querying both databases allows the purchasing department to make decisions not just on raw materials quantities, but also on customer demand. By using this data, purchasing can reduce the size of raw materials inventory, reducing production costs and thus adding margin to the value chain. This is an example of using a linkage across business processes to improve process margin.

As you will learn, however, changing business processes is not easy to do. Most process design requires people to work in new ways, to follow different procedures, and employees often resist such change. In Figure 3-9, the employees who perform the purchase-bicycle-parts activity need to learn to adjust their ordering processes to use customer purchase patterns. Another complication is that data stored in the finished goods database likely will need to be redesigned to keep track of customer demand data. As you will learn in Chapter 10, that redesign effort will require that some application programs be changed as well.

Figure 3-9
Improved Material Ordering Process

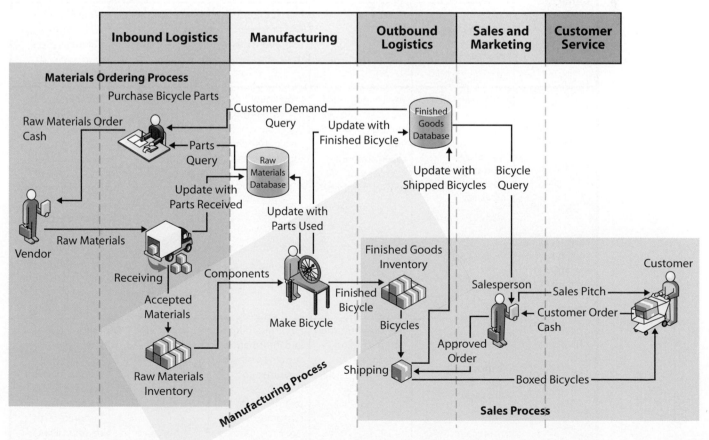

Q6 How Does Competitive Strategy Determine Business Processes and the Structure of Information Systems?

Figure 3-10 shows a business process for renting bicycles. The value-generating activities are shown in the top of the table and the implementation of those activities for two companies with different competitive strategies is shown in the rows below.

   The first company has chosen a competitive strategy of low-cost rentals to students. Accordingly, this business implements business processes to minimize costs. The second company has chosen a differentiation strategy. It provides "best-of-breed" rentals to executives at a high-end conference resort. Notice that this business has designed its business processes to ensure superb service. To achieve a positive margin, it must ensure that the value added will exceed the costs of providing the service.

Figure 3-10
Operations Value Chains for
Bicycle Rental Companies

	Value-Generating Activity	Greet Customer	Determine Needs	Rent Bike	Return Bike & Pay
Low-cost rental to students	Message that implements competitive strategy	"You wanna bike?"	"Bikes are over there. Help yourself."	"Fill out this form, and bring it to me over here when you're done."	"Show me the bike." "OK, you owe $23.50. Pay up."
	Supporting business process	None.	Physical controls and procedures to prevent bike theft.	Printed forms and a shoe box to store them in.	Shoe box with rental form. Minimal credit card and cash receipt system.
High-service rental to business executives at conference resort	Message that implements competitive strategy	"Hello, Ms. Henry. Wonderful to see you again. Would you like to rent the WonderBike 4.5 that you rented last time?"	"You know, I think the WonderBike Supreme would be a better choice for you. It has ..."	"Let me just scan the bike's number into our system, and then I'll adjust the seat for you."	"How was your ride?" "Here, let me help you. I'll just scan the bike's tag again and have your paperwork in just a second." "Would you like a beverage?" "Would you like me to put this on your hotel bill, or would you prefer to pay now?"
	Supporting business process	Customer tracking and past sales activity system.	Employee training and information system to match customer and bikes, biased to "up-sell" customer.	Automated inventory system to check bike out of inventory.	Automated inventory system to place bike back in inventory. Prepare payment documents. Integrate with resort's billing system.

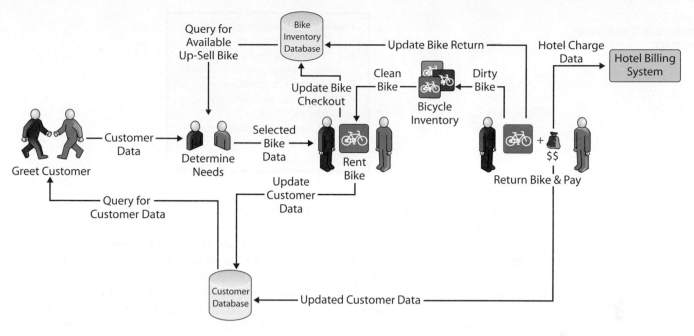

Figure 3-11
Business Process and
Information Systems for
High-Service Bike Rental

Now, consider the information systems required for these business processes. The student rental business uses a shoe box for its data facility. The only computer/software/data component in its business is the machine provided by its bank for processing credit card transactions.

The high-service business, however, makes extensive use of information systems, as shown in Figure 3-11. It has a sales tracking database that tracks past customer rental activity, and an inventory database that is used to select and up-sell bicycle rentals as well as to control bicycle inventory with a minimum of fuss to its high-end customers.

So the bottom line is this: Organizations analyze their industry and choose a competitive strategy. Given that strategy, they design business processes that span value-generating activities. Those processes determine the scope and requirements of each organization's information systems. Given this background, we will now examine how information systems generate a competitive advantage.

Q7 How Do Information Systems Provide Competitive Advantages?

In your business strategy class, you will study the Porter models in greater detail than we have discussed here. When you do so, you will learn numerous ways that organizations respond to the five competitive forces. For our purposes, we can distill those ways into the list of principles shown in Figure 3-12. Keep in mind that we are applying these principles in the context of the organization's competitive strategy.

Some of these competitive techniques are created via products and services, and some are created via the development of business processes. Consider each.

You can also apply these principles to your personal competitive advantage, as discussed in the Guide on pages 96–97.

Competitive Advantage via Products

The first three principles in Figure 3-12 concern products or services. Organizations gain a competitive advantage by creating *new* products or services, by *enhancing* existing products or services, and by *differentiating* their products and services

Figure 3-12
Principles of Competitive
Advantage

> **Product Implementations**
> 1. Create a new product or service
> 2. Enhance products or services
> 3. Differentiate products or services
>
> **Process Implementations**
> 4. Lock in customers and buyers
> 5. Lock in suppliers
> 6. Raise barriers to market entry
> 7. Establish alliances
> 8. Reduce costs

from those of their competitors. FlexTime differentiates on the basis of quality of workout.

Information systems create competitive advantages either as part of a product or by providing support to a product. Consider, for example, a car rental agency like Hertz or Avis. An information system that produces information about the car's location and provides driving instructions to destinations is part of the car rental and thus is part of the product itself (see Figure 3-13a). In contrast, an information system that schedules car maintenance is not part of the product, but instead supports the product (see Figure 3-13b). Either way, information systems can help achieve the first three principles in Figure 3-12.

The remaining five principles in Figure 3-12 concern competitive advantage created by the implementation of business processes.

Competitive Advantage via Business Processes

Organizations can *lock in customers* by making it difficult or expensive for customers to switch to another product. This strategy is sometimes called establishing high **switching costs**. Organizations can *lock in suppliers* by making it difficult to switch to another organization, or, stated positively, by making it easy to connect to

Figure 3-13
Two Roles for Information
Systems Regarding Products

a. Information System as Part of a Car Rental Product

Daily Service Schedule -- November 17, 2011

StationID	22
StationName	Lubrication

ServiceDate	ServiceTime	VehicleID	Make	Model	Mileage	ServiceDescription
11/17/2011	12:00 AM	155890	Ford	Explorer	2244	Std. Lube
11/17/2011	11:00 AM	12448	Toyota	Tacoma	7558	Std. Lube

StationID	26
StationName	Alignment

ServiceDate	ServiceTime	VehicleID	Make	Model	Mileage	ServiceDescription
11/17/2011	9:00 AM	12448	Toyota	Tacoma	7558	Front end alignment inspect

StationID	28
StationName	Transmission

ServiceDate	ServiceTime	VehicleID	Make	Model	Mileage	ServiceDescription
11/17/2011	11:00 AM	155890	Ford	Explorer	2244	Transmission oil change

b. Information System That Supports a Car Rental Product

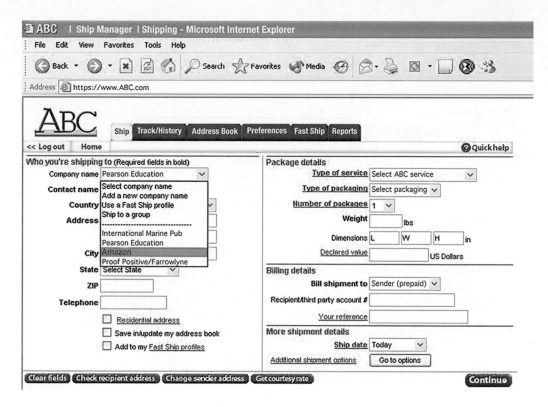

Figure 3-14
ABC, Inc., Web Page to
Select a Recipient from the
Customer's Records

and work with the organization. Finally, competitive advantage can be gained by *creating entry barriers* that make it difficult and expensive for new competition to enter the market.

Another means to gain competitive advantage is to *establish alliances* with other organizations. Such alliances establish standards, promote product awareness and needs, develop market size, reduce purchasing costs, and provide other benefits. Finally, organizations can gain competitive advantage by *reducing costs*. Such reductions enable the organization to reduce prices and/or to increase profitability. Increased profitability means not just greater shareholder value, but also more cash, which can fund further infrastructure development for even greater competitive advantage.

All of these principles of competitive advantage make sense, but the question you may be asking is, "How do information systems help to create competitive advantage?" To answer that question, consider a sample information system.

How Does an Actual Company Use IS to Create Competitive Advantages?

ABC, Inc.,[4] is a worldwide shipper with sales well in excess of $1 billion. From its inception, ABC invested heavily in information technology and led the shipping industry in the application of information systems for competitive advantage. Here we consider one example of an information system that illustrates how ABC successfully uses information technology to gain competitive advantage.

ABC maintains customer account data that include not only the customer's name, address, and billing information, but also data about the people, organizations, and locations to which the customer ships. Figure 3-14 shows a Web form that an ABC customer is using to schedule a shipment. When the ABC system creates the

---

[4] The information system described here is used by a major transportation company that did not want its name published in this textbook.

form, it fills the Company name drop-down list with the names of companies that the customer has shipped to in the past. Here, the user is selecting Pearson Education.

When the user clicks the Company name, the underlying ABC information system reads the customer's contact data from a database. The data consist of names, addresses, and phone numbers of recipients from past shipments. The user then selects a Contact name, and the system inserts that contact's address and other data into the form using data from the database, as shown in Figure 3-15. Thus, the system saves customers from having to reenter data for people to whom they have shipped in the past. Providing the data in this way also reduces data-entry errors.

Figure 3-16 shows another feature of this system. On the right-hand side of this form, the customer can request that ABC send email messages to the sender (the customer), the recipient, and others as well. The customer can choose for ABC to send an email when the shipment is created and when it has been delivered. In Figure 3-16, the user has provided three email addresses. The customer wants all three addresses to receive delivery notification, but only the sender will receive shipment notification. The customer can add a personal message as well. By adding this capability to the shipment scheduling system, ABC has extended its product from a package-delivery service to a package- *and* information-delivery service.

Figure 3-17 shows one other capability of this information system. It has generated a shipping label, complete with bar code, for the user to print. By doing this, the company not only reduces errors in the preparation of shipping labels, but it also causes the customer to provide the paper and ink for document printing! Millions of such documents are printed every day, resulting in a considerable savings to the company.

How Does This System Create a Competitive Advantage?

Now consider the ABC shipping information system in light of the competitive advantage factors in Figure 3-12. This information system *enhances* an existing service because it eases the effort of creating a shipment to the customer while reducing

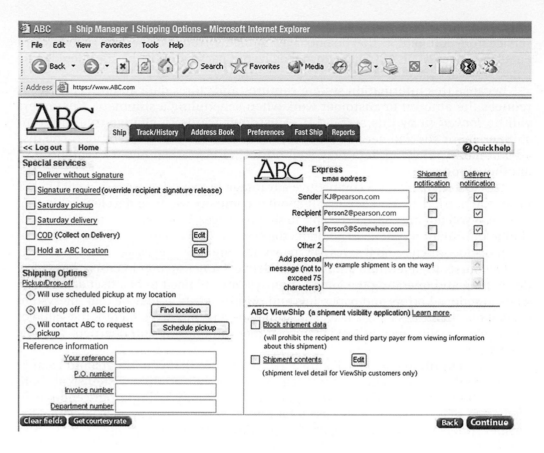

Figure 3-16
ABC, Inc., Web Page to Specify Email Notification

Figure 3-17
ABC, Inc., Web Page to Print a Shipping Label

Only customers who have access to the Internet can use this shipping system. Do organizations have an ethical obligation to provide equivalent services to those who do not have access? The Guide on pages 94–95 explores this question.

errors. The information system also helps to *differentiate* the ABC package delivery service from competitors that do not have a similar system. Further, the generation of email messages when ABC picks up and delivers a package could be considered to be a *new* service.

Because this information system captures and stores data about recipients, it reduces the amount of customer work when scheduling a shipment. Customers will be *locked in* by this system: If a customer wants to change to a different shipper, he or she will need to rekey recipient data for that new shipper. The disadvantage of rekeying data may well outweigh any advantage of switching to another shipper.

This system achieves a competitive advantage in two other ways as well: First, it raises the barriers to market entry. If another company wants to develop a shipping service, it will not only have to be able to ship packages, but it will also need to have a similar information system. In addition, the system reduces costs. It reduces errors in shipping documents, and it saves ABC paper, ink, and printing costs.

Of course, to determine if this system delivers a *net savings* in costs, the cost of developing and operating the information system will need to be offset against the gains in reduced errors and paper, ink, and printing costs. It may be that the system costs more than the savings. Even still, it may be a sound investment if the value of intangible benefits, such as locking in customers and raising entry barriers, exceeds the net cost.

Before continuing, review Figure 3-12. Make sure that you understand each of the principles of competitive advantage and how information systems can help achieve them. In fact, the list in Figure 3-12 probably is important enough to memorize, because you can also use it for non-IS applications. You can consider any business project or initiative in light of competitive advantage.

Q8 2022?

It's unlikely that GearUp will exist by 2022. Like most startups, it will likely go bankrupt before then, but, if not, GearUp will probably be purchased by a large retailer. Or perhaps it will merge with other personal shopping sites to form a supersite. Or, possibly, but the odds are against this, it will grow into a bigger and bigger company, serving more industry segments, and it will become a supersite of its own. This has been Amazon.com's trajectory over the past 20 years (See Case 1, page 27); however, this path has been successfully trodden by very few.

This doesn't mean that all the opportunities for startups based on innovative information technology are gone. In the early 1990s, industry pundits said that Microsoft and Oracle had swept the market and that all the good opportunities were gone; "There will never be another Microsoft, etc." Since then, Amazon, Google, YouTube, Facebook, Twitter, and dozens of others have proved those pundits wrong. So, it's worth considering what new opportunities for IT-based organizations might arise by 2022.

In 2012, the United States faces a daunting fiscal challenge. A major factor is that the Baby Boomers are retiring and will make exponentially increasing financial demands on Medicare and medical services. Just as information technology provides ways for companies like GearUp to reduce costs, so, too, it can provide ways to reduce medical costs. However, no government, including the U.S. government, has ever been a leader in implementing innovative systems. The risk/reward ratio does not favor risk-taking by government employees. However, the situation is quite different for companies that support government functions like Medicare and related programs.

So, if you're looking for growth opportunities involving technology in the next 10 years, one place to look is companies that support health and the government's management of health care. Such companies might be consulting companies; they're always popular for the government. But to make a stronger contribution, consider companies that find innovative ways of providing information systems services to health care and government organizations or that solve consumer problems created by such organizations.

If you're looking for an opportunity for a startup, talk to your parents or grandparents about their data needs. Many retired Baby Boomers complain that they can't keep up with what medical bills they've received, which ones have been paid by Medicare, which ones have been paid by supplemental insurance, or which ones haven't been paid at all. A startup could offer a Web-based service to track those expenses. That sort of business is likely to be thriving by 2022. See Using Your Knowledge Exercise 1, page 99, for more ideas.

Guide

Limiting Access to Those Who Have Access

An adage of investing is that it's easier for the rich to get richer. Someone who has $10 million invested at 5 percent earns $500,000 per year. Another investor with $10,000 invested at that same 5 percent earns $500 per year. Every year, the disparity increases as the first investor pulls farther and farther ahead of the second.

This same adage applies to intellectual wealth as well. It's easier for those with considerable knowledge and expertise to gain even more knowledge and expertise. Someone who knows how to search the Internet can learn more readily than someone who does not. And every year, the person with greater knowledge pulls farther and farther ahead. Intellectual capital grows in just the same way that financial capital grows.

Searching the Internet is not just a matter of knowledge, however. It's also a matter of access. The increasing reliance on the Web for information and commerce has created a **digital divide** between those who have Internet access and those who do not. This divide continues to deepen as those who are connected pull farther ahead of those who are not.

Various groups have addressed this problem by making Internet access available in public places, such as libraries, community centers, and retirement homes. The Bill and Melinda Gates Foundation has given hundreds of millions of dollars to libraries in the United States and 10 other countries to provide computers, infrastructure, and training to libraries and librarians. The Foundation continues to expand this program, particularly with matching funds to support computer maintenance and faster Internet connectivity (see www.gates foundation.org/topics/Pages/libraries.aspx#).

Such gifts help, but not everyone can be served this way, and even with such access, there's a big convenience difference between going to the library and walking across your bedroom to access the Internet—and you don't have to stand in line.

As smartphones become cheaper, more available, and more powerful, phone access to the Web's intellectual capital may replace computer-based access. Even still, it will only do so for those who can afford such a phone and its monthly charges and know how to use it to search the Web.

All of this intellectual capital resides on the Internet because businesses benefit by putting it there. It's much cheaper to provide product support information over the Internet than on printed documents. The savings include not only the costs of printing, but also the costs of warehousing and mailing. Further, when product specifications change, the organization just changes the Web site. There is no obsolete material to dispose of and no costs for printing and distributing the revised material. Those who have Internet access gain current information faster than those who do not.

What happens to those who do not have Internet access? They fall farther and farther behind. The digital divide segregates the haves from the have-nots, creating new class structures. Such segregation is subtle, but it is segregation, nonetheless.

Do organizations have a responsibility to address this matter? If 98 percent of a company's market segment has Internet access, does the company have a responsibility to provide non-Internet materials to that other 2 percent? On what basis does that responsibility lie? Does a government agency have a responsibility to provide equal information to those who have Internet access and those who do not? When those who are connected can obtain information nearly instantaneously, 24/7, is it even possible to provide equal information to the connected and the unconnected?

It's a worldwide problem. Connected societies and countries pull farther and farther ahead. How can any economy that relies on traditional mail compete with an Internet-based economy?

If you're taking MIS, you're already connected; you're already one of the haves, and you're already pulling ahead of the have-nots. The more you learn about information systems and their use in commerce, the faster you'll pull ahead. The digital divide increases. ∎

Discussion Questions

1. Do you see evidence of a digital divide on your campus? In your hometown? Among your relatives? In countries you've visited? Describe personal experiences you've had regarding the digital divide.

2. Some students have access to the Internet from iPads and other easy-to-use devices. Does that create another type of digital divide? Why or why not?

3. Do organizations have a legal responsibility to provide the same information for nonconnected customers that they do for connected customers? If not, should laws be passed requiring organizations to do so?

4. Even if there is no current legal requirement for organizations to provide equal information to nonconnected customers, do they have an ethical responsibility to do so?

5. Are your answers to questions 3 and 4 different for government agencies than they are for commercial organizations?

6. Because it may be impossible to provide equal information, another approach for reducing the digital divide is for the government to enable nonconnected citizens to acquire Internet access via subsidies and tax incentives. Do you favor such a program? Why or why not?

7. Suppose that nothing is done to reduce the digital divide and that it is allowed to grow wider and wider. What are the consequences? How will society change? Are these consequences acceptable?

Guide
Your Personal Competitive Advantage

Consider the following possibility: You work hard, earning your degree in business, and you graduate, only to discover that you cannot find a job in your area of study. You look for 6 weeks or so, but then you run out of money. In desperation, you take a job waiting tables at a local restaurant. Two years go by, the economy picks up, and the jobs you had been looking for become available. Unfortunately, your degree is now 2 years old; you are competing with students who have just graduated with fresh degrees (and fresh knowledge). Two years of waiting tables, good as you are at it, does not appear to be good experience for the job you want. You're stuck in a nightmare—one that will be hard to get out of, and **one that you cannot allow to happen**.

Examine Figure 3-12 again, but this time consider those elements of competitive advantage as they apply to you personally. As an employee, the skills and abilities you offer are your personal product. Examine the first three items in the list, and ask yourself, "How can I use my time in school—and in this MIS class, in particular—to create new skills, to enhance those I already have, and to differentiate my skills from the competition?" (By the way, you will enter a national/international market. Your competition is not just the students in your class; it's also students in classes in Ohio, California, British Columbia, Florida, New York, and every place else they're teaching MIS today.)

Suppose you are interested in professional sales. Perhaps you want to sell in the pharmaceutical industry. What skills can you learn from your MIS class that will make you more competitive as a future salesperson? Ask yourself, "How does the pharmaceutical industry use MIS to gain competitive advantage?" Get on the Internet and find examples of the use of information systems in the pharmaceutical industry. How does Pfizer, for example, use a customer information system to sell to doctors? How can your knowledge of such systems differentiate you from your competition for a job there? How does Pfizer use a knowledge management system? How does the firm keep track of drugs that have an adverse effect on each other?

The fourth and fifth items in Figure 3-12 concern locking in customers, buyers, and suppliers. How can you interpret those elements in terms of your personal competitive advantage? Well, to lock in, you first have to have a relationship to lock. So do you have an internship? If not, can you get one? And once you have an internship, how can you use your knowledge of MIS to lock in your job so that you get a job offer? Does the company you are interning for have a sales tracking system (or any other information system that is important to the company)? If users are happy with the system, what characteristics make it worthwhile? Can you lock in a job by becoming an expert user of this system? Becoming an expert user not only locks you into your job, but it also raises barriers to entry for others who might be competing for the job. Also, can you suggest ways to improve the system, thus using your knowledge of the company and the system to lock in an extension of your job?

Human resources personnel say that networking is one of the most effective ways of finding a job. How can you use this class to establish alliances with other students? Is there an email list server for the students in your class? What about Facebook? LinkedIn? Twitter? How can you use those facilities to develop job-seeking alliances with other students? Who in your class already has a job or an internship? Can any of those people provide hints or opportunities for finding a job?

Don't restrict your job search to your local area. Are there regions of your country where jobs are more plentiful? How can you find out about student organizations in those regions? Search the Web for MIS classes in other cities, and make contact with students there. Find out what the hot opportunities are in other cities.

Finally, as you study MIS, think about how the knowledge you gain can help you save costs for your employers. Even more, see if you can build a case that an employer would actually save money by hiring you. The line of reasoning might be that because of your knowledge of IS you will be able to facilitate cost savings that more than compensate for your salary.

In truth, few of the ideas that you generate for a potential employer will be feasible or pragmatically useful. The fact that you are thinking creatively, however, will indicate to a potential employer that you have initiative and are grappling with the problems that real businesses have. As this course progresses, keep thinking about competitive advantage, and strive to understand how the topics you study can help you to accomplish, personally, one or more of the principles in Figure 3-12. ■

Discussion Questions

1. Summarize the efforts you have taken thus far to build an employment record that will lead to job offers after graduation.

2. Considering the first three principles in Figure 3-12, describe one way in which you have a competitive advantage over your classmates. If you do not have such competitive advantage, describe actions you can take to obtain one.

3. In order to build your network, you can use your status as a student to approach business professionals. Namely, you can contact them for help with an assignment or for career guidance. For example, suppose you want to work in banking and you know that your local bank has a customer information system. You could call the manager of that bank and ask him or her how that system creates a competitive advantage for the bank. You also could ask to interview other employees and go armed with the list in Figure 3-12. Describe two specific ways in which you can use your status as a student and the list in Figure 3-12 to build your network in this way.

4. Describe two ways that you can use student alliances to obtain a job. How can you use information systems to build, maintain, and operate such alliances?

Active Review

Use this Active Review to verify that you understand the ideas and concepts that answer the chapter's study questions.

Q1 How does organizational strategy determine information systems structure?

Diagram and explain the relationship of industry structure, competitive strategy, value chains, business processes, and information systems. Working from industry structure to IS, explain how the knowledge you've gained in these first three chapters pertains to that diagram.

Q2 What five forces determine industry structure?

Name and briefly describe the five forces. Give your own examples of both strong and weak forces of each type, similar to those in Figure 3-3.

Q3 How does analysis of industry structure determine competitive strategy?

Describe four different strategies as defined by Porter. Give an example of four different companies that have implemented each of the strategies.

Q4 How does competitive strategy determine value chain structure?

Define the terms *value*, *margin*, and *value chain*. Explain why organizations that choose a differentiation strategy can use value to determine a limit on the amount of extra cost to pay for differentiation. Name the primary and support activities in the value chain and explain the purpose of each. Explain the concept of linkages.

Q5 How do business processes generate value?

Define *business process*, *cost*, and *margin* as they pertain to business processes. Explain the purpose of an activity and describe types of repository. Explain the importance of business process redesign and describe the difference between the business processes in Figure 3-8 and those in Figure 3-9.

Q6 How does competitive strategy determine business processes and the structure of information systems?

In your own words, explain how competitive strategy determines the structure of business processes. Use the examples of a clothing store that caters to struggling students and a clothing store that caters to professional businesspeople in a high-end neighborhood. List the activities in the business process for the two companies and create a chart like that in Figure 3-9. Explain how the information systems requirements differ between the two stores.

Q7 How do information systems provide competitive advantages?

List and briefly describe eight principles of competitive advantage. Consider your college bookstore. List one application of each of the eight principles. Strive to include examples that involve information systems.

Q8 2022?

Describe possible outcomes for GearUp. Describe one potential industry for creating an IT-based startup in 2022. Summarize the opportunity presented.

Using Your Knowledge at GearUp

Explain in your own words how GearUp's focused cost strategy dictates the kinds of information systems that it needs. Use the example of Drew's idea for using vendor cost data as part of vendor selection to illustrate your answer.

Key Terms and Concepts

Using Your Knowledge

1. Reread Q8 on page 92. Consider the opportunity of providing a Web-based service to help Baby Boomers track medical bills and payments. Using that business:

   a. Describe what you think is the best way for this business to earn revenue. Justify your decision.

   b. Give an example of each of the five types of competitive threats shown in Figure 3-2. Classify each threat as weak, medium, or strong. Justify your classification.

   c. Select a competitive strategy and justify your selection.

   d. Give one example of each of the primary value chain activities.

   e. Describe one important business process for this new company.

   f. Describe the basic features and functions of an information system to support the business process you identified in part e.

   g. Give an example of one way you can attain each of the competitive advantages in Figure 3-12.

   h. Develop an explanation of your work on this exercise that you can give in 2 to 3 minutes during a job interview.

2. Apply the value chain model to a mail-order company such as L.L.Bean (www.llbean.com). What is its competitive strategy? Describe the tasks L.L.Bean must accomplish for each of the primary value chain activities. How does L.L.Bean's competitive strategy and the nature of its business influence the general characteristics of its information systems?

3. Suppose you decide to start a business that recruits students for summer jobs. You will match available students with available jobs. You need to learn what positions are available and what students are available for filling those positions. In starting your business, you know you will be competing with local newspapers, Craigslist (www.craigslist.org), and with your college. You will probably have other local competitors as well.

   a. Analyze the structure of this industry according to Porter's five forces model.

   b. Given your analysis in part a, recommend a competitive strategy.

   c. Describe the primary value chain activities as they apply to this business.

   d. Describe a business process for recruiting students.

   e. Describe information systems that could be used to support the business process in part d.

   f. Explain how the process you describe in part d and the system you describe in part e reflect your competitive strategy.

4. Consider the two different bike rental companies in Figure 3-10. Think about the bikes that they rent. Clearly, the student bikes will be just about anything that can be ridden out of the shop. The bikes for the business executives, however, must be new, shiny, clean, and in tip-top shape.

   a. Compare and contrast the operations value chains of these two businesses as they pertain to the management of bicycles.

   b. Describe a business process for maintaining bicycles for both businesses.

   c. Describe a business process for acquiring bicycles for both businesses.

   d. Describe a business process for disposing of bicycles for both businesses.

   e. What roles do you see for information systems in your answers to the earlier questions? The information systems can be those you develop within your company or they can be those developed by others, such as Craigslist.

5. Samantha Green owns and operates Twigs Tree Trimming Service. Samantha graduated from the forestry program of a nearby university and worked for a large landscape design firm, performing tree trimming and removal. After several years of experience, she bought her own truck, stump grinder, and other equipment and opened her own business in St. Louis, Missouri.

Although many of her jobs are one-time operations to remove a tree or stump, others are recurring, such as trimming a tree or groups of trees every year or every other year. When business is slow, she calls former clients to remind them of her services and of the need to trim their trees on a regular basis.

Samantha has never heard of Michael Porter or any of his theories. She operates her business "by the seat of her pants."

a. Explain how an analysis of the five competitive forces could help Samantha.

b. Do you think Samantha has a competitive strategy? What competitive strategy would seem to make sense for her?

c. How would knowledge of her competitive strategy help her sales and marketing efforts?

d. Describe, in general terms, the kind of information system that she needs to support sales and marketing efforts.

6. Camplite, Inc., is a small business owned by Curt and Julie Robards. Based in Brisbane, Australia, Camplite manufactures and sells a lightweight camping stove called the Fired Now. Curt, who previously worked as an aerospace engineer, invented and patented a burning nozzle that enables the stove to stay lit in very high winds—up to 90 miles per hour. Julie, an industrial designer by training, developed an elegant folding design that is small, lightweight, easy to set up, and very stable. Curt and Julie manufacture the stove in their garage, and they sell it directly to their customers over the Internet and via phone.

a. Explain how an analysis of the five competitive forces could help Camplite.

b. What does Camplite's competitive strategy seem to be?

c. Briefly summarize how the primary value chain activities pertain to Camplite. How should the company design these value chains to conform to its competitive strategy?

d. Describe business processes that Camplite needs in order to implement its marketing and sales and also its service value chain activities.

e. Describe, in general terms, information systems to support your answer to part d.

Collaboration Exercise 3

With a team of your fellow students, develop an answer to the following questions. Use Google Docs, Google+, Windows Live SkyDrive, SharePoint, Office 365, or some other collaboration tool to conduct your meetings.

Singing Valley Resort is a top-end 50-unit resort located high in the Colorado mountains. Rooms rent for $400 to $4,500 per night, depending on the season and the type of accommodations. Singing Valley's clientele are well-to-do; many are famous entertainers, sports figures, and business executives. They are accustomed to, and demand, superior service.

Singing Valley resides in a gorgeous mountain valley and is situated a few hundred yards from a serene mountain lake. It prides itself on superior accommodations; tip-top service; delicious, healthful, organic meals; and exceptional wines. Because it has been so successful, Singing Valley is 90 percent occupied except during the "shoulder seasons" (November, after the leaves change and before the snow arrives, and late April, when winter sports are finished but the snow is still on the ground).

Singing Valley's owners want to increase revenue, but because the resort is nearly always full and because its rates are already at the top of the scale it cannot do so via occupancy revenue. Thus, over the past several years it has focused on up-selling to its clientele activities such as fly-fishing, river rafting, cross-country skiing, snowshoeing, art lessons, yoga and other exercise classes, spa services, and the like.

To increase the sales of these optional activities, Singing Valley prepared in-room marketing materials to advertise their availability. Additionally, it trained all registration personnel on techniques of casually and appropriately suggesting such activities to guests on arrival.

The response to these promotions was only mediocre, so Singing Valley's management stepped up its promotions. The first step was to send email to its clientele advising them of the activities available during their stay. An automated system produced emails personalized with names and personal data.

Unfortunately, the automated email system backfired. Immediately upon its execution, Singing Valley management received numerous complaints. One long-term customer objected that she had been coming to Singing Valley for 7 years and asked if they had yet noticed that she was confined to a wheelchair. If they had noticed, she said, why did they send her a personalized invitation for a hiking trip? The agent of another famous client complained that the personalized email was sent to her client and her husband, when anyone who had turned on a TV in the past 6 months knew the two of them were involved in an exceedingly acrimonious divorce. Yet another customer complained that, indeed, he and his wife had vacationed at Singing Valley 3 years ago, but he had not been there since. To his knowledge, his wife had not been there, either, so he was puzzled as to why the email referred to their visit last winter. He wanted to know if, indeed, his wife had recently been to the resort, without him. Of course, Singing Valley had no way of knowing about customers it had insulted who never complained.

During the time the automated email system was operational sales of extra activities were up 15 percent. However, the strong customer complaints conflicted with its competitive strategy so, in spite of the extra revenue, Singing Valley stopped the automated email system, sacked the vendor who had developed it, and demoted the Singing Valley employee who had brokered the system. Singing Valley was left with the problem of how to increase its revenue.

Your team's task is to develop two innovative ideas for solving Singing Valley's problem. At the minimum, include the following in your response:

a. An analysis of the five forces of the Singing Valley market. Make and justify any necessary assumptions about their market.

b. A statement of Singing Valley's competitive strategy.

c. A statement of the problem. Recall from Chapter 2 that a problem is a perceived difference between what is and what ought to be. If the members of your group have different perceptions of the problem, all the better. Use a collaborative process to obtain the best possible problem description to which all can agree.

d. Document in a general way (like the top row of Figure 3-10), the process of up-selling an activity.

e. Develop two innovative ideas for solving the Singing Valley problem. For each idea, provide:
   - A brief description of the idea
   - A process diagram (like Figure 3-11) of the idea. Figure 3-11 was produced using Microsoft Visio; if you have access to that product, you'll save time and have a better result if you also use it.
   - A description of the information system needed to implement the idea

f. Compare the advantages and disadvantages of your alternatives in part e and recommend one of them for implementation.

Case Study 3

Bosu Balance Trainer

The Bosu Balance Trainer is a device for developing balance, strength, and aerobic conditioning. Invented in 1999, Bosu has become popular in leading health clubs, in athletic departments, and in homes. Bosu stands for "both sides up," because either side of the equipment can be used for training. Figure 3-18 shows a Bosu in use.

Bosu is not only a new training device, but it also reflects a new philosophy in athletic conditioning that focuses on balance. According to the Bosu inventor, David Weck, "The Bosu Balance Trainer was born of passion to improve my balance. In my lifelong pursuit of enhanced athleticism, I have come to understand that balance is the foundation on which all other performance components are built." In order to obtain broad market acceptance, both for his philosophy as well as for the Bosu product, Weck licensed the sales and marketing of Bosu to Fitness Quest in 2001.

Bosu devices have been very successful and that success attracted copycat products. Fitness Quest successfully defeated such products using a number of techniques, but primarily by leveraging its alliances with professional trainers.

According to Dustin Schnabel, Bosu product manager,

"We have developed strong and effective relationships with more than 10,000 professional trainers. We do all we can to make sure those trainers succeed with Bosu and they in turn encourage their clients to purchase our product rather than some cheap imitation.

"It's all about quality. We build a quality product, we create quality relationships with the trainers, and we make sure those trainers have everything they need from us to provide a quality experience to their clients."

That strategy worked well. In the fall of 2004, Fitness Quest had a serious challenge to Bosu from a large sports equipment vendor who had preexisting alliances with major chains such as Target and Wal-Mart. The competitor introduced a Bosu copycat at a slightly lower price. Within a few months, in an effort to gain sales, they reduced their price, eventually several times, until it was less than half the price of the Bosu. Today, that copycat product is not to be seen. According to Schnabel, "They couldn't give that product away. Why? Because customers were coming in the store to buy the Bosu product that their trainers recommended."

Fitness Quest maintains a database of trainer data. It uses that database for email and postal correspondence, as well as for other marketing purposes. For example, after a marketing message has been sent, Schnabel and others watch the database for changes in trainer registration. Registrations increase after a well-received message, and they fall off when messages are off-target.

Fitness Quest and Schnabel are in the process of introducing a new piece of cardio training equipment

Figure 3-18

Figure 3-19

called Indo-Row (shown in Figure 3-19), for which they intend to use the same marketing strategy. First, they will leverage their relationships with trainers to obtain trainer buy-in for the new concept. Then, when that buy-in occurs, they will use it to sell Indo-Row to individuals.

Go to www.indorow.com and watch the video. As you'll see, IndoRow competes directly with other equipment-based forms of group exercise like Spinning®. Schnabel states that many clubs and workout studios are looking for a new, fun, and innovative group training medium, and Indo-Row offers a solution to that need.

You can learn more about Bosu devices at www.bosu.com, more about IndoRow at www.indorow.com, and more about Fitness Quest at www.fitnessquest.com.

Sources: Bosu, www.bosu.com (accessed June 2009); IndoRow, www.indorow.com (accessed June 2009); and Conversation with Dustin Schnabel, July 2009. Used with permission of Fitness Quest, Inc.

Questions

1. Review the principles of competitive advantage in Figure 3-12. Which types of competitive advantage has Bosu used to defeat copycat products?

2. What role did information systems play in your answer to question 1?

3. What additional information systems could Fitness Quest develop to create barriers to entry to the competition and to lock in customers?

4. In 2004, Fitness Quest had alliances with trainers and its competitor had alliances with major retailers. Thus, both companies were competing on the basis of their alliances. Why do you think Fitness Quest won this competition? To what extent did its success leveraging relationships with trainers depend on information systems? On other factors?

5. The case does not state all of the uses that Fitness Quest makes of its trainer database. List five applications of that database that would increase Fitness Quest competitive position.

6. Describe major differences between the Bosu product and the IndoRow product. Consider product use, product price, customer resistance, competition, competitive threats, and other factors related to market acceptance.

7. Describe information systems that Fitness Quest could use to strengthen its strategy for bringing IndoRow to market. Consider the factors you identified in your answer to question 6 in your response.

TEACHING SUGGESTIONS

GearUp, Chapter 3

GOALS

Use GearUp to:

- Practice using Porter's Five Forces Model.
- Understand the application of competitive strategy.
- Consider the risks of changes in operations to competitive strategy.
- Understand how information and IS can help inform a decision.

BACKGROUND

1. GearUp wants to have the lowest prices on the "net," so it definitely has a low-cost strategy.

2. Addison may have a general idea that some vendors are harder to deal with than others, but she doesn't know how significant the problem is. Actually, no one at GearUp knows how significant that problem is.

3. As Drew says, someone ought to look at the data. We'll visit this again in Chapter 5, and Chapter 9 shows specific examples of reports that GearUp will generate to determine which vendors present such problems and to what extent. You might choose to show one or two of the reports that Drew and Addison will generate. The specifics of how they deal with those reports are too advanced at this point, however.

4. In my experience, in a small, startup organization like GearUp it's not uncommon for people to be working so hard solving problems that they don't have time to look up, consider the bigger picture, and find a way to prevent problems. Or, as the old adage goes, "We're so busy fighting alligators that we don't have time to drain the swamp." That's what's happening at GearUp. A key element of reducing costs is to eliminate vendors that are causing it to cancel customer orders because of short-shipment or quality problems.

HOW TO GET STUDENTS INVOLVED

One way to use GearUp is to work your way across Figure 3-1 in class.

1. Ask the students to analyze the five forces.

   ■ **Using your knowledge of vendors like MYHABIT (or even Woot), comment on the forces listed in Figure 3-2. Do you agree with the forces shown there?**

   ■ **Identify at least one additional force for each of the five forces. Classify the force's strength. Justify your classification.**

2. Competitive strategy:

   ■ **Using the facts of this case, place GearUp's competitive strategy into one of the four quadrants in Figure 3-5.**

   ■ **Briefly state GearUp's competitive strategy.**

3. Cost-saving measures:

   ■ **Given the facts in this case, describe potential sources of cost savings at GearUp.**

   ■ **If GearUp does identify particular vendors that are causing shortage and shipping-damage problems, what actions, other than not working with that vendor, might it take?**

   ■ **Do you think it's possible to say that working at a company with a low-cost strategy will be less enjoyable than working at one with a differentiation strategy? Why or why not?**

   When addressing this question, consider the Yikes! Bikes guide as well.

4. Value chains:

   ■ **Summarize the major primary value chain activities at GearUp.**

   ■ **Besides reducing costs due to problematic vendors, what other activities at GearUp might be ripe for cost savings? Read the Yikes Bikes! Guide for potential ideas.**

5. Business processes:

- **Using the data we have, sketch the process of conducting a sales event at GearUp.**

- **Could GearUp save costs by having goods delivered directly from the vendor to its customers? What do you think keeps it from doing so?**

- **Using your own knowledge of business, sketch the process for dealing with product shortages. Consider both quantity shortages as well as shortages due to damaged goods.**

6. Information systems:

- **Describe, in general terms, the information systems needed to conduct an event at GearUp.**

- **Describe, in general terms, the information systems needed to respond to product shortages.**

BOTTOM LINE

- **GearUp's business model requires information systems.**

- **Information systems must be a logical consequence (via strategy to value chains to business processes) of the organization's analysis of its industry structure.**

- **As a professional, understand how critical it is for you to know your organization's competitive strategy and to align all of your work, including any work you do for information systems, with that strategy.**

- **An analysis of data in GearUp's database is critical to reducing costs!**

- **Database to the rescue!**

Using the Ethics Guide: Yikes! Bikes (pages 80–81)

GOALS

- Sensitize the students to the fact that a competitive strategy is not just an academic topic. Changing competitive strategy has dramatic impacts on personnel and company culture.

- Understand practical applications of business reports.

- Explore ethical questions concerning communication about sensitive topics.

BACKGROUND AND PRESENTATION STRATEGIES

Ownership changes are always traumatic. In my experience, new management always says, "We're going to make few significant changes" (unless the company has been in dire straits), but invariably major changes are on the way.

This guide illustrates the uncomfortable position that many managers face when they possess knowledge that cannot be communicated to everyone in the company.

■ **As a manager, you will sometimes have data that you are not supposed to communicate to employees. If an employee asks you directly about that data, you can either divulge it or lie. Which would you choose? What are the consequences of either choice?**

■ **Is there an alternative between inappropriately divulging data and lying? What is it? What disadvantages does that alternative have?**

■ **In general what are the consequences on the organization's culture of moving from a differentiation strategy to a low-cost strategy?**

■ **In general what are the consequences on the organization's culture of moving from a low-cost strategy to a differentiation strategy?**

SUGGESTED RESPONSES FOR DISCUSSION QUESTIONS

1. No. No evidence of crime. They own the company and can change the competitive strategy and culture as they see fit.

2. She's lying. If you believe that any lie is unethical, then her behavior is unethical. But, what should she do? If she announces that they plan an across-the-board staff reduction, work and productivity will cease for that day . . . and maybe much longer. Plus, she can make no specific statement about who will be cut, so being more forthright would just raise employee anxiety, and unnecessarily for 90 percent of the employees. Ask the students how they might change her opening remarks to make them more honest without causing panic.

3. Depends on her mood, I think. She could tell him that he no longer owns the company and to keep his thoughts to himself. Or, she could listen, make some empty statement, and then do what she plans to do anyway. Unless there was something specific about no staff reductions in the purchase agreement (unlikely), he has no legal recourse. I see no ethical lapse with regard to him.

   He asked them to take care of the employees and their change doesn't allow them to meet his request. You had better hope, however, that he didn't tell Ms. Parks that you called him. She might be vindictive.

4. Major Capital is implementing a change in competitive strategy. The company wants to be a low-cost vendor; so it needs to cut costs. Parks' plan may not be the most effective in terms of minimizing employee stress, but she and Major Capital have every right to implement their strategy however they want. They own the show.

5. Lori is the most popular support rep because she spends a lot of time with the customer. She's likely to be one of the first employees fired. Knowing that, you have to be very careful lest you end up as part of a wrongful termination lawsuit. Sad to say, but that's the reality. To respect your chain of command, you cannot tell her she's about to be fired. But, you don't want to lie, either, lest Lori sue you when she does get fired (setting aside any moral or ethical issues). You have to say something noncommittal. It has to be true, but noninformative. Perhaps something like, "Well, this is their first day. Let's wait and see what develops." You might even say something like, "I suspect change is in the air," but if you do that, you encourage further conversation.

6. Answer has to be personal. It is worth asking the students to think about how they might behave if they were stuck in a job that they hated for some reason.

7. This is a complex and difficult question. It really depends on how one views the responsibility that an organization has to its employees.

8. Recall the definition of job security in Chapter 1: "Possess a marketable skill and the courage to use it." Companies are legal entities, nothing more. No such entity will give you security.

WRAP UP

Has the discussion of this guide changed student thinking in any way? In particular,

- What does a change in competitive strategy mean to employees?

- When a company changes ownership, what is a good posture for thinking employees to take?

- How will you behave when you possess knowledge that you cannot disclose and someone asks you directly about it? How will you deal with that situation when you cannot say that you know something but cannot reveal it?

- What is job security, for you?

YOU BE THE GUIDE

Using the Guide: Limiting Access to Those Who Have Access

(pages 94–95)

GOALS

- Teach students that knowledge grows exponentially—just like capital.
- Sensitize students to the social problem of the digital divide.
- Explore the responsibilities for business and government with respect to the digital divide.

BACKGROUND AND PRESENTATION STRATEGIES

The more money you have, the easier it is to make more money. **And the more knowledge you have, the easier it is to acquire more knowledge.** Knowledge and capital both grow exponentially.

Thus, learning the *strategies for learning* is critical. Learning how to learn efficiently using the Web and other contemporary resources should be one of the students' primary goals while in college.

Being connected, by the way, means being able to send emails, use FTP, engage in instant messaging and texting, etc. All of these are also important ways of learning. (IM as a tool for learning? Of course.)

But what about those who are on the nonconnected side of the digital divide? What happens to them? They fall farther and farther behind. Actually, they stay right where they are, and the rest of the world moves farther and farther ahead, accelerating. The gap grows exponentially.

The Gates Foundation donated hundreds of millions of dollars for libraries to buy computers to provide Internet access for the public. See *www.gatesfoundation.org/libraries* for more information about the Foundation's library program, including a state map that describes library donations.

To the surprise of many (including, I believe, the Gates Foundation), the most popular activity on those library computers was finding a job!

The Gates' donation was a generous and appropriate action for the world's richest couple. But what about businesses? What about government?

- **Today, in the United States, what groups of people are not connected to the Internet? (Examples include** those living in poverty, the elderly, the poorly educated, and those who've stuck their heads in the sand.)

- **Does it make sense for benefactors or government agencies to provide access to those in poverty?**

- **What keeps the elderly from accessing the Internet?**

- **Should the government help the elderly?**

- **What could be done to provide Internet access for the poorly educated? Does government have a role?**

Most MIS classes have a number of foreign students. If yours does, you might want to consider this guide from a world perspective.

- **Some of you are from outside the United States. What is the connectivity situation in your country?**

- **Is there a digital divide?**

- **Are some countries more behind the connectivity trend than others?**

- **What does this mean for those countries' ability to compete? For the citizens of those countries?**

Today, two trends are underway that complicate the situation: ubiquitous high-speed data communications and the merger of computers and entertainment devices.

- **How do these changes alter the situation for the nonconnected?**

I think these questions lead to an optimistic note. Once televisions are merged with Internet access devices, then anyone who can afford and operate a TV will have some kind of computer. And, with cheaper and cheaper data communications, they will have at least some access to the Internet.

SUGGESTED RESPONSES FOR DISCUSSION QUESTIONS

1. Answers will depend on students' experiences. Are there students on campus who are disadvantaged by a lack of computer equipment? How do they cope? Do they have access at home or through relatives?

   What about foreign students? Is their situation different from students in the United States? See comments in the Background section about bringing in the perspective of different countries.

2. It does, but maybe not as much of a digital divide. Intelligent cell phones and other mobile devices are cheaper and more ubiquitous than PCs. It is more likely that more people will have them. So, on balance, such devices may serve to reduce, but not eliminate, the digital divide.

3. No, there is no law that requires organizations to provide equal access to the nonconnected. *Should there be?*

   Laws imply enforcement, and enforcement implies lawsuits. This all gets very expensive for society. Some would say it would be better to focus resources on programs like the Gates' library donation.

   Another argument uses the Declaration of Independence. Citizens have equal rights to life, liberty, and the pursuit of happiness. If being non-connected threatens any of these, then laws should be passed to protect the disconnected.

   But, is going to a movie one aspect of the pursuit of happiness? So, if movie theaters have a Web site, do they have a responsibility to provide access for the nonconnected? This seems silly.

4. Whether organizations have an ethical obligation to provide equal access depends on the organization. A religious organization would seem to have an ethical responsibility to ensure equal access to information for its members. What about a yacht club? What about an athletic league?

5. I think most would agree that government agencies have greater responsibilities than do commercial entities. Public health information, for example, should be equally available to the connected and the nonconnected. But, how is this possible? With instantaneous 24/7 connectivity, there is no way that a nonconnected person can have the same access to late-breaking disease information as the connected person. However, what government will buy computers for its citizens just for that reason?

6. What groups are nonconnected? Would those groups be helped by subsidies or tax incentives? Is the answer in education? Or, is the problem of Internet access so low on the list of priorities of these groups that any available tax dollars should be spent on other programs? Obviously, there is no clear answer.

7. The following are several questions to explore this:

   ■ **Is the gap between the connected and the nonconnected the same gap as that between the educated and the noneducated?**

   ■ **In the future, will there be just three kinds of employees: techies, flunkies, and managers?**

   ■ **What sort of world will that be? Will it be stable?**

   ■ **Those of us on an academic campus will have opportunities that those on the wrong side of the digital divide will not have. What responsibilities do we have to help those nonconnected people?**

WRAP UP

■ **Knowledge grows exponentially. Those with more knowledge will be able to obtain new knowledge at a faster rate. Not being connected reduces the rate at which people can obtain knowledge.**

■ **In school, it is important to focus on ways to use the Web and other resources to learn, and to do so efficiently.**

■ **People who are not connected are at a serious disadvantage. It's not an easy disadvantage to fix. Equal access through traditional means is impossible. A brochure cannot provide the latest information, 24/7.**

■ **Possibly the best hope, the great equalizer, will be the blending of television and Internet devices. Then, everyone with a TV (almost every person) can have Internet access. Cheap data communications will make it easy to connect as well.**

Using the Guide: Your Personal Competitive Advantage

(pages 96–97)

GOALS

- Raise students' awareness that they should be engaged in job planning/searching right now.
- Show the application of the principles of competitive advantage to career planning.
- Suggest innovative tasks for job searching.

BACKGROUND AND PRESENTATION STRATEGIES

Students seldom understand how their status as students gives them access to businesspeople that they will lose after they graduate. Ask the students if they understand the difference in the response they will receive to the following two statements:

■ **Hi, my name is XXX, and I'm a student at YYY University. We're studying information systems and competitive advantage. I see that your company, ZZZ, is using a CRM application. I'm wondering if you would have a few minutes to talk with me about how your CRM system gives ZZZ a competitive advantage.**

■ **Hi, my name is XXX, and I'm looking for a job. I see that your company, ZZZ, is using a CRM application. I'm wondering if you would have a few minutes to talk with me about how your CRM system gives you a competitive advantage.**

What will be the difference in response? Huge. In the first, the person will feel like they're helping some bright, ambitious person. Most will say, sure, and maybe offer to buy the student a cup of coffee. In the second, the person will feel like they're being manipulated to find a job. Most will say, "Contact our HR department."

Why should students talk with businesspeople, and now? To build their networks.

■ **Have the conversation. Make a list of great questions to ask; be appreciative that the businessperson took the time. Then, toward the end of the interview, ask if the person has any advice for finding a job in that industry. Not, *do they have a job*, but rather, *do they have any advice for finding a job*. If they have a job, they'll tell you. If not, they may give you some good advice. Even if**

you get no good advice, you have another point in your network. Take Figure 3-12 along and ask the person how you can use it to gain a competitive advantage.

See question 3.

Why do students not use their special student status in this way? I don't know, but I try to ensure that they at least know about these strategies.

Some students may be too shy. If this is the case, sometimes I make it an assignment, possibly an extra credit assignment.

Similarly, students should be availing themselves of every resource the university provides for outreach to businesspeople.

■ **If there is a mentor program, get a mentor. If there is a chance to visit a business, go visit the business. If someone from industry speaks on a topic of interest, by all means go. Talk to the speaker afterward, make one or two positive comments, and ask a good question. Ask for the person's business card. In a day or two, send them an email thanking them. See if you can get an interview to discuss some topic of mutual interest.**

Sometimes I lead them carefully through the disaster scenario. I tell them I had this horrible dream last night. And my dream was that they graduated, couldn't get a job, took a dead-end job for 2 years, and then couldn't get out of that track. To avoid this nightmare, they have to start thinking about their jobs, now! (And unfortunately, this is not just a dream. It's happening everyday; they need to do something to avoid this trap, starting now!)

SUGGESTED RESPONSES FOR DISCUSSION QUESTIONS

1. Answer depends on the student. Sometimes I say, "If your list is short, tell me what you plan to do in the next quarter."

2. Again, the answer depends on the student. I also encourage them to realize that they aren't competing just with the students they see on our campus. They're competing with students all over the world.

3. There are many ways to build networks. Here are two types of answers:

   - Read trade magazines, relevant Web sites (e.g., *www.cio.com*), and other sources. Find an article on a topic of interest and think of ways the ideas in that article apply to you and one or more items in the list in Figure 3-1. Contact the author of the article. Make a few complimentary comments; ask questions that pertain to the article, you, and the list.

- Approach businesspeople working in your major field of study and ask them how you can use knowledge of information systems to gain a competitive advantage in that field. Tell them of your interest in both your major and in IS. Use this situation to generate further introductions, perhaps to specialists in your field.

4. Get active. Join clubs. Meet with lots of students. Participate in campus life both in and beyond the business school. As we'll discuss in the guide in Chapter 6 (pages 206–207), you add more connections to your network by meeting students who are outside of your major or even outside of the business school. As you meet people, tell them of your career interests. Ask if they know anyone working in that field. Ask if they know someone you could meet with, as described in question 3.

Join a business-specific club, for example, the Accounting Club or the Marketing Club. Get involved, especially with activities that engage local businesspeople. Arrange for speakers and host speakers on campus. As you meet businesspeople on campus, query them about their careers. How did they get where they are?

Use an IS to keep track of the people whom you've met. Put contacts in a spreadsheet or database. Keep track of contacts you've had, emails you've sent, meetings you've attended. At an interview, when appropriate, show off your database. Use the Web and email to contact people who are doing interesting things.

Join LinkedIn if you have not yet done so. Clean up and organize your Facebook site so that you don't harm your employment prospects. See also the Social Recruiting Guide in Chapter 8.

WRAP UP

■ **You don't want to find just any job. You want to find a *great* job! You want to find one with appropriate responsibilities, with a growing company, with job growth potential, and where you work with interesting people. You also want one that pays well.**

■ **Finding that great job may not be easy. Start now! Start thinking about what kind of job you want, and start preparing yourself to find that job. The last semester of your senior year will be too late.**

■ **If you're not an IS major, combining IS knowledge with your other major can make for a great combination. Think about taking some more IS classes.**

Part 2

Information Technology

The next three chapters address the technology that underlies information systems. You may think that such technology is unimportant to you as a business professional. However, as you will see, today's managers and business professionals work with information technology all the time, as consumers, if not in a more involved way.

Chapter 4 discusses hardware and software and defines basic terms and fundamental computing concepts. You will see that GearUp has important decisions to make about a critical software development project.

Chapter 5 addresses the data component of information technology by describing database processing. You will learn essential database terminology and be introduced to techniques for processing databases. We will also introduce data modeling, because you may be required to evaluate data models for databases that others develop for you.

Chapter 6 continues the discussion of computing devices begun in Chapter 4 and describes data communications and Internet technologies. GearUp needs to make decisions about building its infrastructure for the next stage of its growth. To make those decisions, it needs to understand the advantages and disadvantages of cloud-based computing.

The purpose of these three chapters is to teach you technology sufficient for you to be an effective IT consumer, like Addison, Drew, and Emily at GearUp. You will learn basic terms, fundamental concepts, and useful frameworks so that you will have the knowledge to ask good questions and make appropriate requests of the information systems professionals who will serve you. Those concepts and frameworks will be far more useful to you than the latest technology trend, which may be outdated by the time you graduate!

Hardware and Software

Emily Johnson, GearUp's CFO; Lucas Massey, IT director; and Drew Mills, events operations manager, are having an impromptu meeting in the company's lunchroom. Drew continues to text while they talk.

"We don't have the resources," Lucas says in response to a question from Drew. Lucas is looking at the top of Drew's head.

"What do you mean?" Drew looks up . . . his short response sounds angry.

"As in money, you know. *Dinero*. Budget. Don't have it."

"Emily, is that right?" Drew looks at Emily while he texts.

"Well, this sounds important. We might be able to. . . ." She can't finish her sentence before Lucas jumps back in.

"Wait a minute; weren't we talking about *reducing* expenses last week?" Lucas' face is turning red.

"Lucas, I don't know about budget, but what I'm telling you is that if we don't have an iPad app, we don't have a business." Drew furiously texts on his phone . . .

"OK, let's talk about it for a second. You want an iPhone app, too?"

"Yes."

"Which version of iOS do you want?"

"You're not listening. I don't want iOS . . . I don't even know what that is. I want an iPad app."

"iOS . . . it's the iPad's operating system, you nitwit."

"Hold it, guys, hold it. Let's all calm down." Emily's thinking about their voices carrying down the hall.

"OK, sorry," Drew actually sounds contrite. "Are there different versions? Why does it matter?"

"Well, iOS 5 has features and functions that earlier versions don't. So, you need to tell me if we need those new features."

"Can we build for both . . . new and old?"

"Sure, it just comes down to . . ." Lucas is trying to stay calm.

"Resources." Drew finishes his sentence for him.

"Yup."

"Look, it's not just me. I was just texting Addison, and she says she's having a hard time with San Diego Sports."

"No! Not San Diego!" Emily jumps in, "We need them. What's going on?" Emily knows they're a key supplier in this year's revenue plan.

"Addison says they brought up the iPad issue in her negotiations for the golf clubs. They said they didn't think we were competitive . . . because we don't have an iPad app."

"Well, customers can order on Safari." Lucas offers this lamely, by now he knows this issue isn't going away.

"Yeah, they can, Lucas. But they don't want to! They want to use their iPads and iPhones."

There's a pause in the conversation. Then Emily continues, "Lucas, have you looked into international development?" Emily's realizing they have to do something about this, too.

"You mean India?"

"Yeah, or some Asian company somewhere. Jerome over at Pickins.com told me that's what they did."

"We know nothing about it. What are we gonna do, run an ad in a New Delhi newspaper?" Lucas stares at the ceiling.

"No, but I can find out what Jerome did." Emily ignores his sarcasm.

Lucas realizes he needs to chill out. "I was looking into Indian developers last week, Emily . . . for something else. It's pretty scary."

"Why?"

"Like I said, we don't know what we're doing. We could waste a lot of money and time."

"Well . . ."

"One site had bad grammar and misspelled words," but as he says this, he's getting more interested.

"Does that matter?"

"Maybe not. It doesn't inspire confidence, though. I wonder about open source . . . . Nah," Lucas muses.

Emily interrupts him, "I've heard about it, but what exactly is open source?"

"It's when a bunch of amateurs get together over beer and munchies and write computer programs for a hobby." Drew sounds irritated as he puts his phone away. That's more than Lucas can stand.

"Drew, you know that's ludicrous. What about Linux? Huh? Seems to work pretty well for us. But I don't think open source will work here . . ."

"Linux, Schmenix. I've got to go. I'm setting up tomorrow's golf club event . . . assuming we get the deal. I'm telling you two, you want to stay in business, get us an iPad app . . . like this week."

Drew strides out of the room, leaving Lucas and Emily staring at one another.

"Lucas, I think we better do something."

"OK, I'll look into it. How much money you got?"

"Nice try. Send me a proposal and we'll see." Emily didn't get to be a CFO by falling for that question.

"OK, give me a week to look around. Meanwhile, would you find out what Pickens.com did?"

"Sure." ■

Study Questions

Q1 What do business professionals need to know about computer hardware?

Q2 What do business professionals need to know about software?

Q3 Is open source software a viable alternative?

Q4 How can you use this knowledge?

Q5 2022?

What would you do if you were Drew? Or Emily? How hard is it to build an iPad application? How much should it cost? How should they proceed? Is Lucas too conservative? What is open source, and is it a viable alternative here? If you're wondering why, as a future business professional, you need to know about hardware and software, think about those questions. Those and others of greater complexity—most likely ones involving technology that will be invented between now and the time you graduate—will come your way.

You don't need to be an expert. You don't need to be a hardware engineer or a computer programmer. You do need to know enough, however, to be an effective consumer. You need the knowledge and skills to ask important, relevant questions and understand the answers. We begin with basic hardware and software concepts. Next we will discuss open source software development and then ways you can use this chapter's knowledge for buying, budgeting, and specifying requirements. We wrap up by forecasting trends in hardware and software in 2022.

Q1 What Do Business Professionals Need to Know About Computer Hardware?

As discussed in the five-component framework, **hardware** consists of electronic components and related gadgetry that input, process, output, and store data according to instructions encoded in computer programs or software. Figure 4-1 shows the components of a generic computer. Notice that the basic hardware categories are input, process, output, and storage.

Basic Components

As shown in Figure 4-1, typical **input hardware** devices are the keyboard, mouse, document scanners, and bar-code (Universal Product Code) scanners like those used in grocery stores. Microphones also are input devices; with tablet PCs, human handwriting can be input as well. Older input devices include magnetic ink readers (used for reading the ink on the bottom of checks) and scanners such as the Scantron test scanner.

Figure 4-1
Input, Process, Output, and Storage Hardware

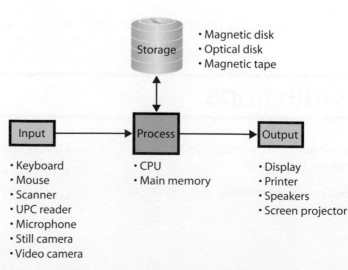

Processing devices include the **central processing unit (CPU)**, which is sometimes called "the brain" of the computer. Although the design of the CPU has nothing in common with the anatomy of animal brains, this description is helpful, because the CPU does have the "smarts" of the machine. The CPU selects instructions, processes them, performs arithmetic and logical comparisons, and stores results of operations in memory. Some computers have two or more CPUs. A computer with two CPUs is called a **dual-processor** computer. **Quad-processor** computers have four CPUs. Some high-end computers have 16 or more CPUs.

CPUs vary in speed, function, and cost. Hardware vendors such as Intel, Advanced Micro Devices, and National Semiconductor continually improve CPU speed and capabilities while reducing CPU costs (as discussed under Moore's Law in Chapter 1). Whether you or your department needs the latest, greatest CPU depends on the nature of your work, as you will learn.

The CPU works in conjunction with **main memory**. The CPU reads data and instructions from memory, and it stores results of computations in main memory. We will describe the relationship between the CPU and main memory later in the chapter. Main memory is sometimes called **RAM**, for random access memory.

Output hardware consists of video displays, printers, audio speakers, overhead projectors, and other special-purpose devices, such as large flatbed plotters.

Storage hardware saves data and programs. Magnetic disk is by far the most common storage device, although optical disks such as CDs and DVDs also are popular. Thumb drives are small, portable magnetic storage devices that can be used to back up data and to transfer it from one computer to another. In large corporate data centers, data is sometimes stored on magnetic tape.

In the past, many different plug receptacles were required to connect keyboards, mice, printers, cameras, and so on. Starting in 2000, all of these were replaced with **Universal Serial Bus (USB)** connectors like that shown in Figure 4-2. USB connectors simplified the connection of peripheral gear to computers for both manufacturers and users and are widely used.

Computer Data

Before we can further describe hardware, we need to define several important terms. We begin with binary digits.

Binary Digits

Computers represent data using **binary digits**, called **bits**. A bit is either a zero or a one. Bits are used for computer data because they are easy to represent electronically, as illustrated in Figure 4-3. A switch can be either closed or open. A computer can be designed so that an open switch represents zero and a closed switch represents one. Or the orientation of a magnetic field can represent a bit; magnetism in one direction

Figure 4-2
USB Connector

Source: alekup/Shutterstock.com.

Figure 4-3
Bits Are Easy to Represent
Physically

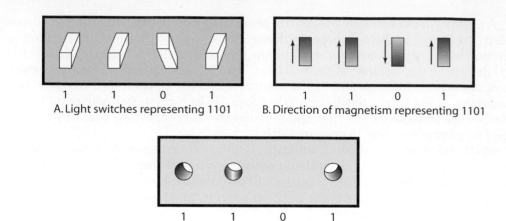

A. Light switches representing 1101

B. Direction of magnetism representing 1101

C. Reflection/no reflection representing 1101

represents a zero, magnetism in the opposite direction represents a one. Or, for optical media, small pits are burned onto the surface of the disk so that they will reflect light. In a given spot, a reflection means a one; no reflection means a zero.

Sizing Computer Data

All computer data are represented by bits. The data can be numbers, characters, currency amounts, photos, recordings, or whatever. All are simply a string of bits.

For reasons that interest many but are irrelevant for future managers, bits are grouped into 8-bit chunks called **bytes**. For character data, such as the letters in a person's name, one character will fit into one byte. Thus, when you read a specification that a computing device has 100 million bytes of memory, you know that the device can hold up to 100 million characters.

Bytes are used to measure sizes of noncharacter data as well. Someone might say, for example, that a given picture is 100,000 bytes in size. This statement means the length of the bit string that represents the picture is 100,000 bytes or 800,000 bits (because there are 8 bits per byte).

The specifications for the size of main memory, disk, and other computer devices are expressed in bytes. Figure 4-4 shows the set of abbreviations that are used to represent data-storage capacity. A **kilobyte**, abbreviated **K**, is a collection of 1,024 bytes. A **megabyte**, or **MB**, is 1,024 kilobytes. A **gigabyte**, or **GB**, is 1,024 megabytes, a **terabyte**, or **TB**, is 1,024 gigabytes, a **petabyte**, or **PB**, is 1,024 terabytes, and an **exabyte**, or **EB**, is 1,024 petabytes.

Sometimes you will see these definitions simplified as 1K equals 1,000 bytes and 1MB equals 1,000K. Such simplifications are incorrect, but they do ease the math. Also, disk and computer manufacturers have an incentive to propagate this misconception. If a disk maker defines 1MB to be 1 million bytes—and not the correct 1,024K—the manufacturer can use its own definition of MB when specifying drive capacities.

Figure 4-4
Important Storage-Capacity
Terminology

Term	Definition	Abbreviation
Byte	Number of bits to represent one character	
Kilobyte	1,024 bytes	K
Megabyte	1,024 K = 1,048,576 bytes	MB
Gigabyte	1,024 MB = 1,073,741,824 bytes	GB
Terabyte	1,024 GB = 1,099,511,627,776 bytes	TB
Petabyte	1,024 TB = 1,125,899,906,842,624 bytes	PB
Exabyte	1,024 PB = 1,152,921,504,606,846,976 bytes	EB

A buyer may think that a disk advertised as 100MB has space for $100 \times 1,024K$ bytes, but in truth the drive will have space for only $100 \times 1,000,000$ bytes. Normally, the distinction is not too important, but be aware of the two possible interpretations of these abbreviations.

In Fewer Than 300 Words, How Does a Computer Work?

Figure 4-5 shows a snapshot of a computer in use. The CPU is the major actor. To run a program or process data, the computer first transfers the program or data from disk to *main memory*. Then, to execute an instruction, it moves the instruction from main memory into the CPU via the **data channel** or **bus**. The CPU has a small amount of very fast memory called a **cache**. The CPU keeps frequently used instructions in the cache. Having a large cache makes the computer faster, but cache is expensive.

Main memory of the computer in Figure 4-5 contains program instructions for Microsoft Excel, Adobe Acrobat, and a browser (Microsoft Internet Explorer or Mozilla Firefox). It also contains a block of data and instructions for the **operating system (OS)**, which is a program that controls the computer's resources.

Main memory is too small to hold all of the programs and data that a user might want to process. For example, no personal computer has enough memory to hold all of the code in Microsoft Word, Excel, and Access. Consequently, the CPU loads programs into memory in chunks. In Figure 4-5, one portion of Excel was loaded into memory. When the user requested additional processing (say, to sort the spreadsheet), the CPU loaded another piece of Excel.

If the user opens another program (say, Word) or needs to load more data (say, a picture), the operating system will direct the CPU to attempt to place the new program or data into unused memory. If there is not enough memory, it will remove something, perhaps the block of memory labeled More Excel, and then it will place the just-requested program or data into the vacated space. This process is called **memory swapping**.

Why Does a Manager Care How a Computer Works?

You can order computers with varying sizes of main memory. An employee who runs only one program at a time and who processes small amounts of data requires very little memory—1GB will be adequate. However, an employee who processes many programs at the same time (say, Word, Excel, Firefox, Access, Acrobat, and other programs) or an employee who processes very large files (pictures, movies, or sound files) needs lots of main memory, perhaps 3GB or more. If that employee's computer

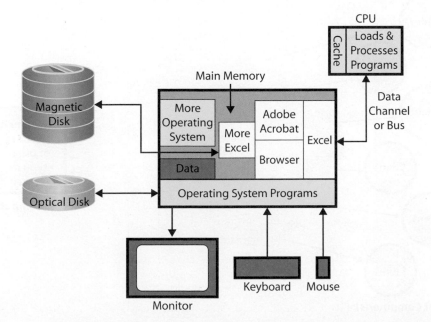

Figure 4-5
Computer Components, in Use

The Ethics Guide on pages 112–113 poses questions about computer hardware and software that offer more than most users need.

has too little memory, then the computer will constantly be swapping memory, and it will be slow. (This means, by the way, that if your computer is slow and if you have many programs open, you likely can improve performance by closing one or more programs. Depending on your computer and the amount of memory it has, you might also improve performance by adding more memory.)

You can also order computers with CPUs of different speeds. CPU speed is expressed in cycles called *hertz*. In 2011, a slow personal computer has a speed of 1.5 Gigahertz. A fast personal computer has a speed of 3+ Gigahertz, with dual processors. As predicted by Moore's Law, CPU speeds continually increase.

Additionally, CPUs today are classified as **32-bit** or **64-bit**. Without delving into the particulars, a 32-bit is less capable and cheaper than a 64-bit CPU. The latter can address more main memory; you need a 64-bit processor to effectively utilize more than 4GB of memory. 64-bit processors have other advantages as well, but they are more expensive than 32-bit processors.

An employee who does only simple tasks such as word processing does not need a fast CPU; a 32-bit, 1.5 Gigahertz CPU will be fine. However, an employee who processes large, complicated spreadsheets or who manipulates large database files or edits large picture, sound, or movie files needs a fast computer like a 64-bit, dual processor with 3.5 Gigahertz or more.

One last comment: The cache and main memory are **volatile**, meaning their contents are lost when power is off. Magnetic and optical disks are **nonvolatile**, meaning their contents survive when power is off. If you suddenly lose power, the contents of unsaved memory—say, documents that have been altered—will be lost. Therefore, get into the habit of frequently (every few minutes or so) saving documents or files that you are changing. Save your documents before your roommate trips over the power cord.

What Is the Difference Between a Client and a Server?

Before we can discuss computer software, you need to understand the difference between a client and a server. Figure 4-6 shows the computing environment of the typical user. Users employ **client** computers for word processing, spreadsheets, database access, and so forth. Most client computers also have software that enables them to connect to a network. It could be a private network at their company or school, or it could be the Internet, which is a public network. (We will discuss networks and related topics in Chapter 6. Just wait!)

Figure 4-6
Client and Server Computers

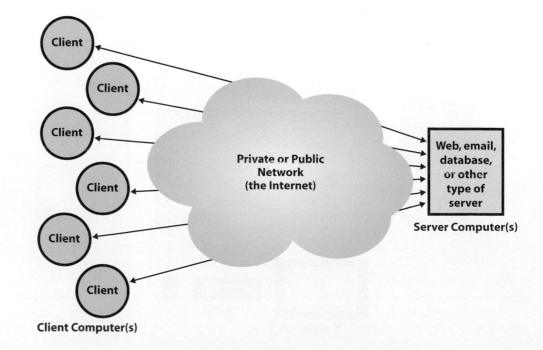

Figure 4-7
A Server Farm

Source: Amy Walters/Shutterstock.

Servers, as their name implies, provide some service. Some servers process email; others process Web sites; others process large, shared databases; and some provide all of these functions or other, similar functions.

A server is just a computer, but, as you might expect, server computers must be fast and they usually have multiple CPUs. They need lots of main memory, at least 4GB, and they require very large disks—often a terabyte or more. Because servers are almost always accessed from another computer via a network, they have limited video displays, or even no display at all. For the same reason, many have no keyboard.

For sites with large numbers of users (e.g., Amazon.com), servers are organized into a collection of servers called a **server farm** like the one shown in Figure 4-7. Servers in a farm coordinate their activities in an incredibly sophisticated and fascinating technology dance. They receive and process hundreds, possibly thousands, of service requests per minute. For example, as you learned in Case 1, on November 29, 2010, Amazon.com processed an average of 158 items per second for 24 hours. In this dance, computers hand off partially processed requests to each other while keeping track of the current status of each request. They can pick up the pieces when a computer in the farm fails. All of this is done in the blink of an eye, with the user never knowing any part of the miracle underway. It is absolutely gorgeous engineering!

Increasingly, server infrastructure is delivered as a service in what is termed *the cloud*. We will discuss cloud computing in Chapter 6, after you have some knowledge of data communications.

Q2 What Do Business Professionals Need to Know About Software?

As a future manager or business professional, you need to know the essential terminology and software concepts that will enable you to be an intelligent software consumer. To begin, consider the basic categories of software shown in Figure 4-8.

Every computer has an operating system, which is a program that controls that computer's resources. Some of the functions of an operating system are to read and write data, allocate main memory, perform memory swapping, start and stop programs, respond to error conditions, and facilitate backup and recovery. In addition, the operating system creates and manages the user interface, including the display, keyboard, mouse, and other devices.

Ethics
Guide   Churn and Burn

An anonymous source, whom we'll call Janet, made the following statements about computing devices:

"I never upgrade my system. At least, I try not to. Look, I don't do anything at work but write memos and access email. I use Microsoft Word, but I don't use any features that weren't available in Word 3.0, 25 years ago. This whole industry is based on 'churn and burn': They churn their products so we'll burn our cash.

"All this hype about 64-bit processors and 500GB disks—who needs them? I'm sure I don't. And if Microsoft hadn't put so much junk into Windows, we could all be happy on an Intel 486 processor like the one I had in 1993. We're suckers for falling into the 'you gotta have this' trap.

"Frankly, I think there's a conspiracy between hardware and software vendors. They both want to sell new products, so the hardware people come up with these incredibly fast and huge computers. Then, given all that power, the software types develop monster products bloated with features and functions that nobody uses. It would take me months to learn all of the features in Word, only to find out that I don't need those features.

"To see what I mean, open Microsoft Word, click on View, then select Toolbars. In my version of Word, there are 19 toolbars to select, plus one more to customize my own toolbar. Now what in the world do I need with 19 toolbars? I write all the time, and I have two selected: Standard and Formatting. Two out of 19! Could I pay Microsoft 2/19 of the price of Word, because that's all I want or use?

"Here's how they get you, though. Because we live in a connected world, they don't have to get all of us to use those 19 toolbars, just one of us.

Take Bridgette, over in Legal, for example. Bridgette likes to use the redlining features, and she likes me to use them when I change draft contracts she sends me. So if I want to work on her documents, I have to turn on the Reviewing toolbar. You get the idea; just get someone to use a feature and, because it is a connected world, then all of us have to have that feature.

"Viruses are one of their best ploys. They say you better buy the latest and greatest in software— and then apply all the patches that follow so that you'll be protected from the latest zinger from the computer 'bad guys.' Think about that for a minute. If vendors had built the products correctly the first time, then there would be no holes for the baddies to find, would there? So they have a defect in their products that they turn into a sales advantage. You see, they get us to focus on the virus and not on the hole in their product. In truth, they should be saying, 'Buy our latest product to protect yourself from the defective junk we sold you last year.' But truth in advertising hasn't come that far.

"Besides that, users are their own worst enemies as far as viruses are concerned. If I'm down on 17th Street at 4 in the morning, half drunk and with a bundle of cash hanging out of my pocket, what's likely to happen to me? I'm gonna get mugged. So if I'm out in some weirdo chat room—you know, out where you get pictures of weird sex acts and whatnot—and download and run a file, then of course I'm gonna get a virus. Viruses are brought on by user stupidity, that's all.

"One of these days, users are going to rise up and say, 'That's enough. I don't need any more. I'll stay with what I have, thank you very much.' In fact, maybe that's happening right now. Maybe that's why Microsoft has to push Office 365 down our throats. Maybe people have finally said, 'No more toolbars!'" ■

Discussion Questions

1. Summarize Janet's view of the computer industry. Is there merit to her argument? Why or why not?

2. What holes do you see in the logic of her argument?

3. Someone could take the position that these statements are just empty rantings—that Janet can say all she wants, but the computer industry is going to keep on doing as it has been. Is there any point in Janet sharing her criticisms?

4. Comment on Janet's statement—"Viruses are brought on by user stupidity, that's all."

5. All software products ship with known problems. Microsoft, Adobe, and Apple all ship software that they know has failures. Is it unethical for them to do so? Do software vendors have an ethical responsibility to openly publish the problems in their software? How do these organizations protect themselves from lawsuits for damages caused by known problems in software?

6. Suppose a vendor licenses and ships a software product that has both known and unknown failures. As the vendor learns of the unknown failures, does it have an ethical responsibility to inform the users about them? Does the vendor have an ethical responsibility to fix the problems? Is it ethical for the vendor to require users to pay an upgrade fee for a new version of software that fixes problems in an existing version?

Figure 4-8
Categories of Computer
Software

	Operating System	**Application Programs**
Client	Programs that control the client computer's resources	Applications that are processed on client computers
Server	Programs that control the server computer's resources	Applications that are processed on server computers

Although the operating system makes the computer usable, it does little application-specific work. If you want to check the weather or access a database, you need application programs such as an iPad weather application or Oracle's customer relationship management (CRM) software.

Both client and server computers need an operating system, though they need not be the same. Further, both clients and servers can process application programs. The application's design determines whether the client, the server, or both, process it.

You need to understand two important software constraints. First, a particular version of an operating system is written for a particular type of hardware. For example, Microsoft Windows works only on processors from Intel and companies that make processors that conform to the Intel instruction set (the commands that a CPU can process). Furthermore, the 32-bit version of Windows runs only on Intel computers with 32-bit CPUs, and the 64-bit version of Windows runs only on Intel computers with 64-bit CPUs. With other operating systems, such as Linux, many versions exist for many different instruction sets and for both 32- and 64-bit computers.

Second, application programs are written to use a particular operating system. Microsoft Access, for example, will only run on the Windows operating system. Some applications come in multiple versions. For example, there are Windows and Macintosh versions of Microsoft Word. But unless informed otherwise, assume that a particular application runs on just one operating system.

We will next consider the operating system and application program categories of software.

What Are the Major Operating Systems?

The major operating systems are listed in Figure 4-9. Consider each.

Nonmobile Client Operating Systems

Nonmobile client operating systems are used on desktops and portable computers. Here we consider the four most popular.

For nonmobile business use, the most important operating system is **Microsoft Windows**. Some version of Windows resides on more than 85 percent of the world's desktops, and, if we consider just business users, the figure is more than 95 percent. That percentage is declining, however, as Windows loses market share to the Macintosh. Three client versions of Windows are available today: Windows 7, Windows Vista, and Windows XP.

Apple Computer, Inc., developed its own operating system for the Macintosh, **Mac OS**. The current version is Mac OS X Lion. Apple touts it as the world's most advanced desktop operating system, and it is. Until recently, Macintosh computers were used primarily by graphic artists and workers in the arts community. But for many reasons, the Mac has made recent headway into the traditional Windows market. According to Apple, Mac sales have increased 28 percent in the past year while sales of Windows personal computers have fallen 1 percent.[1]

Mac OS X Lion includes many of the features that Apple made popular on the iPhone and iPad. Many believe that in terms of ease of use Mac OS X Lion far surpasses Windows.

---

[1] Steve Jobs presentation in June 2011.

Category	Operating System	Used for	Remarks
Nonmobile Clients	Windows	Personal computer clients	Most widely used operating system in business. Current version is Windows 7.
	Mac OS X	Macintosh clients	Used by graphic artists and others in arts community.
	Unix	Workstation clients	Popular on powerful client computers used in engineering, computer-assisted design, architecture. Difficult for the nontechnical user.
	Linux	Just about anything	Open source variant of Unix. Adapted to almost every type of computing device. On a PC, used with Open Office application software.
Mobile Clients	Symbian	Nokia, Samsung, and other phones	Popular worldwide, but less so in North America.
	BlackBerry OS	Research In Motion BlackBerries	Device and OS developed for use by business. Very popular in beginning, but strongly challenged by iPhone and others.
	iOS	iPhone, iPod Touch, iPads	Rapidly increasing installed base with success of the iPhone and iPad. Based on Mac OS X.
	Android	T-Mobile and other phones and devices	Linux-based phone operating system from Google. Rapidly increasing market share.
Servers	Windows Server	Servers	Businesses with a strong commitment to Microsoft.
	Unix	Servers	Fading from use. Replaced by Linux.
	Linux	Servers	Very popular. Aggressively pushed by IBM.

Figure 4-9
Major Operating Systems

Mac OS was designed originally to run the line of CPU processors from Motorola. In 1994, Mac switched to the PowerPC processor line from IBM. As of 2006, Macintosh computers are available for both PowerPC and Intel CPUs. A Macintosh with an Intel processor is able to run both Windows and the Mac OS.

Unix is an operating system that was developed at Bell Labs in the 1970s. It has been the workhorse of the scientific and engineering communities since then. Unix is generally regarded as being more difficult to use than either Windows or the Mac. Many Unix users know and employ an arcane language for manipulating files and data. However, once they surmount the rather steep learning curve, most Unix users become fanatic supporters of the system. Sun Microsystems and other vendors of computers for scientific and engineering applications are the major proponents of Unix. In general, Unix is not for the business user.

Linux is a version of Unix that was developed by the open source community (discussed on page 116). This community is a loosely coupled group of programmers who mostly volunteer their time to contribute code to develop and maintain Linux. The open source community owns Linux, and there is no fee to use it. Linux can run on client computers, but usually only when budget is of paramount concern. Linux is by far most popular as a server OS.

Mobile Client Operating Systems

Figure 4-9 lists four principal mobile operating systems. **Symbian** is popular on phones in Europe and the Far East, but less so in North America. **BlackBerry OS** was one of the most successful early mobile operating systems and was used primarily by business users on BlackBerry devices. It is now losing market share to iOS and Android.

iOS is the operating system used on the iPhone, iPod Touch, and iPad. When first released, it broke new ground with its ease of use and compelling display, features that are now being copied by the BlackBerry OS and Android. With the popularity of the iPhone and iPad, Apple has been increasing its market share of iOS and now claims that it is used on 44 percent of all mobile devices.

Android is a mobile operating system licensed by Google. Android devices have a very loyal following, especially among technical users. Recently, Android has been gaining market share over the BlackBerry OS.

Most industry observers would agree that Apple has led the way, both with the Mac OS and the iOS, in creating easy-to-use interfaces. Certainly, many innovative ideas have first appeared in a Macintosh or iSomething and then later been added, in one form or another, to Windows or one of the mobile operating systems.

Server Operating Systems

The last three rows of Figure 4-9 show the three most popular server operating systems. **Windows Server** is a version of Windows that has been specially designed and configured for server use. It has much more stringent and restrictive security procedures than other versions of Windows and is popular on servers in organizations that have made a strong commitment to Microsoft.

Unix can also be used on servers, but it is gradually being replaced by Linux.

Linux is frequently used on servers by organizations that want, for whatever reason, to avoid a server commitment to Microsoft. IBM is the primary proponent of Linux and in the past has used it as a means to better compete against Microsoft. Although IBM does not own Linux, IBM has developed many business systems solutions that use Linux. By using Linux, neither IBM nor its customers have to pay a license fee to Microsoft.

Own Versus License

When you buy a computer program, you are not actually buying that program. Instead, you are buying a **license** to use that program. For example, when you buy a Windows license, Microsoft is selling you the right to use Windows. Microsoft continues to own the Windows program. Large organizations do not buy a license for each computer user. Instead, they negotiate a **site license**, which is a flat fee that authorizes the company to install the product (operating system or application) on all of that company's computers or on all of the computers at a specific site.

In the case of Linux, no company can sell you a license to use it. It is owned by the open source community, which states that Linux has no license fee (with certain reasonable restrictions). Large companies such as IBM and smaller companies such as RedHat can make money by supporting Linux, but no company makes money selling Linux licenses.

Virtualization

Virtualization is the process by which one computer hosts the appearance of many computers. One operating system, called the **host operating system**, runs one or more operating systems as applications. Those hosted operating systems are called **virtual machines (vm)**. Each virtual machine has disk space and other resources allocated to it. The host operating system controls the activities of the virtual machines it hosts to prevent them from interfering with one another. With virtualization, each vm is able to operate exactly the same as it would if it were operating in a stand-alone, non-virtual environment.

Three types of virtualization exist:

- PC virtualization
- Server virtualization
- Desktop virtualization

With **PC virtualization**, a personal computer, such as a desktop or portable computer, hosts several different operating systems. Say a user needs, for some

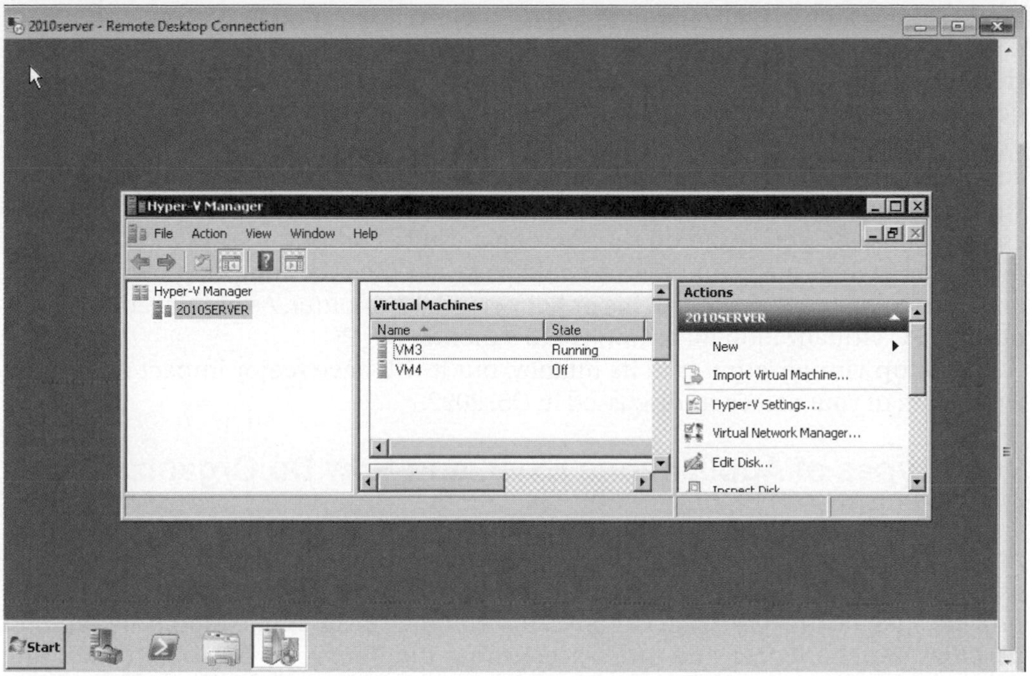

Figure 4-10
Windows Server Computer
Hosting Two Virtual Machines

reason, to have both Windows Vista and Windows 7 running on his or her computer. In that circumstance, the user can install a virtual host operating system and then both Vista and Windows 7 on top of it. In that way, the user can have both systems on the same hardware. VMWare Workstation is a popular PC virtualization product that can run both Windows and Linux operating systems.

With **server virtualization**, a server computer hosts one or more, other server computers. In Figure 4-10, a Windows Server computer is hosting two virtual machines. Users can log onto either of those virtual machines and they will appear as normal servers. Figure 4-11 shows how virtual machine VM3 appears to a user of that server. Notice that a user of VM3 is running a browser that is accessing SharePoint. In fact, this virtual machine was used to generate many of the SharePoint figures in Chapter 2. Server virtualization plays a key role for cloud vendors, as you'll learn in Chapter 6.

Figure 4-11
Virtual Machine

PC and server virtualization are important and interesting, but it is possible that desktop virtualization will revolutionize desktop processing. With **desktop virtualization**, a server hosts many versions of desktop operating systems. Each of those desktops has a complete user environment and appears to the user to be just another PC. However, the desktop can be accessed from any computer to which the user has access. Thus, you could be at an airport and go to an airport computer and access your virtualized desktop. To you, it appears as if that airport computer is your own personal computer. Later, you could do the same to a utility computer sitting in your hotel room. Meanwhile, many other users could have accessed the computer in the airport, and each thought he or she had his or her personal computer. As of June 2011, IBM is offering PC virtualization for as low as $12 a month, per PC.

Desktop virtualization is in its infancy, but it will have major impact during the early years of your career, as discussed in Q5, 2022.

What Types of Applications Exist, and How Do Organizations Obtain Them?

Application software performs a service or function. Some application programs are general purpose, such as Microsoft Excel or Word. Other application programs provide specific functions. QuickBooks, for example, is an application program that provides general ledger and other accounting functions. We begin by describing categories of application programs and then describe sources for them.

What Categories of Application Programs Exist?

Horizontal-market application software provides capabilities common across all organizations and industries. Word processors, graphics programs, spreadsheets, and presentation programs are all horizontal-market application software.

Examples of such software are Microsoft Word, Excel, and PowerPoint. Examples from other vendors are Adobe's Acrobat, Photoshop, and PageMaker and Jasc Corporation's Paint Shop Pro. These applications are used in a wide variety of businesses, across all industries. They are purchased off-the-shelf, and little customization of features is necessary (or possible).

Vertical-market application software serves the needs of a specific industry. Examples of such programs are those used by dental offices to schedule appointments and bill patients, those used by auto mechanics to keep track of customer data and customers' automobile repairs, and those used by parts warehouses to track inventory, purchases, and sales.

Vertical applications usually can be altered or customized. Typically, the company that sold the application software will provide such services or offer referrals to qualified consultants who can provide this service.

One-of-a-kind application software is developed for a specific, unique need. The IRS develops such software, for example, because it has needs that no other organization has.

How Do Thin Clients Compare to Thick Clients?

When you use an application such as Adobe Photoshop, it runs only on your computer and does not need to connect to any server to run. Such programs are called *desktop programs* and are not considered clients.

Applications that process code on both the client and the server are called **client-server applications**. A **thick-client application** is an application program that must be preinstalled on the client. A **thin-client application** is one that runs within a browser and does not need to be preinstalled. When the user of a thin-client application starts that application, if any code is needed, the browser loads that code dynamically from the server. The client code does not need to be preinstalled.

For example, the Office Web Applications that come with Windows Live SkyDrive and Office 365 are thin clients, whereas the Office 2010 versions are thick clients. Thus, the Word Web Application is thin; the full version of Office 2010 Word is thick. The latter application needs to be installed, as you learned if you acquired a license to Office 365.

To summarize, the relationship of application types is as follows:

- Desktop application
- Client-server application
  - Thick client
  - Thin client

Thick and thin clients each have their own advantages and disadvantages. Because thick clients can be larger (they don't have to be downloaded while the user waits), they can have more features and functions. However, they do have to be installed, as when you buy a new application for your iPhone or other mobile device. Periodically, you update to new versions when you synch your phone or otherwise connect to the source of the application. To you, as an individual, this isn't much of a problem. However, in a large organization, where it is important that everyone use the same version of the same application, such installation and version management is an expensive administrative burden.

Thin-client applications are preferred to thick-client applications because they require only a browser; no special client software needs to be installed. This also means that when a new version of a thin-client application is created, the browser automatically downloads that new code. However, because the code is downloaded during use, thin clients need to be smaller.

Today, organizations use a wide mixture of applications and operating systems. Figure 4-12 shows a typical situation. Two clients are running Windows; one is running the Mac OS, and the other is running iOS on an iPhone. Two thin clients are running only a browser, like Google Chrome. The thick clients each have a thick-client email application installed; one is running Microsoft Office Outlook, and the other is running Apple's iPhone email application and other thick applications.

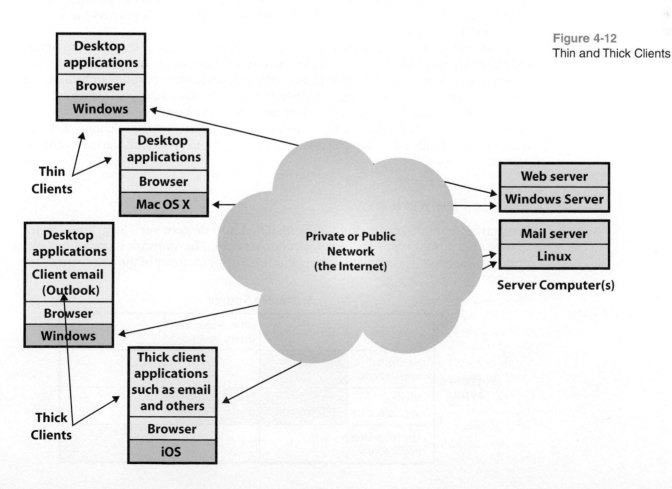

Figure 4-12
Thin and Thick Clients

Figure 4-12 also shows two servers; the Windows Server computer is supporting a Web server, and the Linux server is supporting email.

How Do Organizations Acquire Application Software?

You can acquire application software in exactly the same ways that you can buy a new suit. The quickest and least risky option is to buy your suit off-the-rack. With this method, you get your suit immediately, and you know exactly what it will cost. You may not, however, get a good fit. Alternately, you can buy your suit off-the-rack and have it altered. This will take more time, it may cost more, and there's some possibility that the alteration will result in a poor fit. Most likely, however, an altered suit will fit better than an off-the-rack one.

Finally, you can hire a tailor to make a custom suit. In this case, you will have to describe what you want, be available for multiple fittings, and be willing to pay considerably more. Although there is an excellent chance of a great fit, there is also the possibility of a disaster. Still, if you want a yellow and orange polka-dot silk suit with a hissing rattlesnake on the back, tailor-made is the only way to go. You can buy computer software in exactly the same ways: **off-the-shelf software**, **off-the-shelf with alterations software**, or tailor-made. Tailor-made software is called **custom-developed software**.

Organizations develop custom application software themselves or hire a development vendor. Like buying the yellow and orange polka-dot suit, such development is done in situations in which the needs of the organization are so unique that no horizontal or vertical applications are available. By developing custom software, the organization can tailor its application to fit its requirements.

Custom development is difficult and risky. Staffing and managing teams of software developers is challenging. Managing software projects can be daunting. Many organizations have embarked on application development projects only to find that the projects take twice as long—or longer—to finish as planned. Cost overruns of 200 and 300 percent are not uncommon. We will discuss such risks further in Chapter 10.

In addition, every application program needs to be adapted to changing needs and changing technologies. The adaptation costs of horizontal and vertical software are amortized over all of the users of that software, perhaps thousands or millions of customers. For custom-developed software, however, the using organization must pay all of the adaptation costs itself. Over time, this cost burden is heavy.

Because of the risk and expense, custom-development is the last-choice alternative and is used only when there is no other option. Figure 4-13 summarizes software sources and types.

What Is Firmware?

Firmware is computer software that is installed into devices such as printers, print servers, and various types of communication devices. The software is coded just like other software, but it is installed into special, read-only memory of the printer or other

Figure 4-13
Software Sources and Types

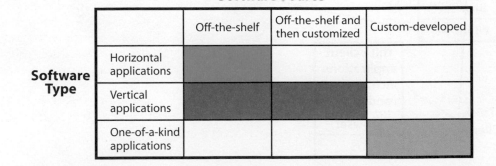

		Software Source		
		Off-the-shelf	Off-the-shelf and then customized	Custom-developed
Software Type	Horizontal applications			
	Vertical applications			
	One-of-a-kind applications			

device. In this way, the program becomes part of the device's memory; it is as if the program's logic is designed into the device's circuitry. Users do not need to load firmware into the device's memory.

Firmware can be changed or upgraded, but this is normally a task for IS professionals. The task is easy, but it requires knowledge of special programs and techniques that most business users choose not to learn.

Q3 Is Open Source Software a Viable Alternative?

To answer this question, you first need to know a bit about the open source movement and process. Most computer historians would agree that Richard Matthew Stallman is the father of the movement. In 1983, he developed a set of tools called **GNU** (a self-referential acronym meaning *GNU Not Unix*) for creating a free Unix-like operating system. Stallman made many other contributions to open source, including the **GNU general public license (GPL) agreement**, one of the standard license agreements for open source software. Stallman was unable to attract enough developers to finish the free Unix system, but continued making other contributions to the open source movement.

In 1991, Linus Torvalds, working in Helsinki, began work on another version of Unix, using some of Stallman's tools. That version eventually became Linux, the high-quality and very popular operating system discussed previously.

The Internet proved to be a great asset for open source, and many open source projects became successful, including:

- Open Office (a Microsoft Office look-alike)
- Firefox (a browser)
- MySQL (a DBMS, see Chapter 5)
- Apache (a Web server, see Chapter 8)
- Ubuntu (a Windows-like desktop operating system)
- Android (a mobile-device operating system)

Why Do Programmers Volunteer Their Services?

To anyone who has never enjoyed writing computer programs, it is difficult to understand why anyone would donate their time and skills to contribute to open source projects. Programming is, however, an intense combination of art and logic, and designing and writing a complicated computer program is exceedingly pleasurable (and addictive). Like many programmers, at times in my life I have gleefully devoted 16 hours a day to writing computer programs—day after day—and the days would fly by. If you have an artistic and logical mind, you ought to try it.

Anyway, the first reason that people contribute to open source is that it is great fun! Additionally, some people contribute to open source because it gives them the freedom to choose the projects upon which they work. They may have a programming day job that is not terribly interesting, say, writing a program to manage a computer printer. Their job pays the bills, but it's not fulfilling.

In the 1950s, Hollywood studio musicians suffered as they recorded the same style of music over and over for a long string of uninteresting movies. To keep their sanity, those musicians would gather on Sundays to play jazz, and a number of high-quality jazz clubs resulted. That's what open source is to programmers. A place where they can exercise their creativity while working on projects they find interesting and fulfilling.

Another reason for contributing to open source is to exhibit one's skill, both for pride as well as to find a job or consulting employment. A final reason is to start a business selling services to support an open source product.

Using MIS InClass 4 *A Group Exercise*

Google Mobility?

Source: James M Phelps, Jr/Shutterstock.com.

Source: 1000 Words/Shutterstock.com.

Source: Annette Shaff/Shutterstock.com.

On August 15, 2011, Google announced its intention to buy Motorola Mobility for $12.5 billion in cash. Google is a wealthy company, but this is a substantial amount, about one-third of Google's $39 billion valuation.[2] The deal has yet to clear antitrust departments in the United States and the EU, but it is likely that it will do so.

In August 2011, about 150 million Android phones were in use, which is the largest market share of any mobile phone operating system. However, these 150 million Android phones were manufactured by 39 different vendors; no single Android phone matched the iPhone in popularity.

By buying a phone manufacturer, Google confounds its channel; the other 38 Android phone manufacturers may fear that this acquisition gives Google phones an unfair advantage. And, even though Larry Page, Google's CEO, has said Android will remain open, that decision could always be reversed. Consequently, the purchase may send some Android phone manufacturers into the arms of Microsoft, which has been struggling to make headway with its Windows 7 Phone.

Motorola Mobility's value is not just in handset sales, however. At the time of the offer, Motorola Mobility had an enormous patent portfolio of 17,000 patents, with 7,000 more in the pipeline. Paige has stated that these patents will help protect Google from patent infringement lawsuits from Microsoft, Apple, and others.

(By the way, Google won't just acquire patents that concern what it wants to do with mobile phones; it also will acquire a large portfolio of patents that relate to what Microsoft, Apple, and others want to do with their products. At this level, companies engage in a patent battle of mutually assured destruction: "You sue me using your patent about X, technology that I care about, and I'll sue you using my patent about Y, which I don't use, but which you need.")

In a blog post, Larry Page stated, "Motorola is also a market leader in the home devices and video solutions business."[3] What does that mean?

Form a group of three or as otherwise directed by your professor. In your group, discuss and formulate answers to the following questions. Strive to practice iteration and feedback in your conversation.

1. Microsoft has avoided PC manufacturing. It licenses its software to as many different PC vendors as can compete. Apple, in contrast, has been a hardware/software company that manufactures its own computers and devices and does not allow others to do so. Google is proposing to operate as a hybrid; both manufacturing its own devices as well as licensing software to others.
   a. Can this hybrid work?
   b. What steps does Google need to take to ensure that it does work?
   c. If Google is able to obtain substantial market share with its own phone, does it need to make this model work?

2. In what ways does this purchase help Microsoft's Series 7 phone? What must Microsoft do to turn these potential advantages into real advantages?

3. If you were advising a midlevel (not the most popular nor the least) Android phone manufacturer, how would you advise it to proceed? In your answer, consider your responses to items 1 and 2.

4. Investing one-third of your cash is a substantial commitment. Summarize the benefits to Google of this purchase. Does this purchase make you more or less willing to invest in Google stock? Why or why not?

5. Most of Google's success is due to Internet ad sales. This purchase could signal that (a) Google intends to expand its business model to include the sale of phones and mobile devices; (b) Google sees mobile devices as key for expanding its ad revenue; or (c) both a and b. Consider Page's statement that "Motorola is also a market leader in the home devices and video solutions business." Which of these three do you think is likely? Does your answer to this question change your answer to item 3? Why or why not?

---

[2] Erick Schonfeld, "Google Goes Soup-to-Nuts on Android with Bid for Motorola," TechCrunch, August 15, 2011. http://techcrunch.com/2011/08/15/google-android-motorola/.

[3] Larry Page, "Supercharging Android: Google to Acquire Motorola Mobility," August 15, 2011. http://googleblog.blogspot.com/2011/08/supercharging-android-google-to-acquire.html (accessed September 12, 2012).

How Does Open Source Work?

The term *open source* means that the source code of the program is available to the public. **Source code** is computer code as written by humans and that is understandable by humans. Figure 4-14 shows a portion of the computer code that I wrote for the Web site www.LearningMIS.com. Source code is compiled into **machine code** that is processed by a computer. Machine code is, in general, not understandable by humans and cannot be modified. When you access www.LearningMIS.com, the machine code version of the program in Figure 4-14 runs on your computer. We do not show machine code in a figure because it would look like this:

11010010100101111110011101111001000111000001111110111101111100111 . . .

In a **closed source** project, say Microsoft Office, the source code is highly protected and only available to trusted employees and carefully vetted contractors. The source code is protected like gold in a vault. Only those trusted programmers can make changes to a closed source project.

With open source, anyone can obtain the source code from the open source project's Web site. Programmers alter or add to this code depending on their interests and goals. In most cases, programmers can incorporate code they find into their own projects. They may be able to resell those projects depending on the type of license agreement the project uses.

Open source succeeds because of collaboration. A programmer examines the source code and identifies a need or project that seems interesting. He or she then creates a new feature, redesigns or reprograms an existing feature, or fixes a known problem. That code is then sent to others in the open source project who then evaluate the quality and merits of the work and add it to the product, if appropriate.

Typically, there is a lot of give and take. Or, as described in Chapter 2, there are many cycles of iteration and feedback. Because of this iteration, a well-managed project with strong peer reviews can result in very high-quality code, like that in Linux.

So, Is Open Source Viable?

The answer depends on to whom and for what. Open source has certainly become legitimate. According to *The Economist,* "It is now generally accepted that the future

```
#region Dependency Properties

public static readonly DependencyProperty
    LessonIDProperty = DependencyProperty.Register(
        "LessonID",
        typeof(int),
        typeof(Lesson),
        new PropertyMetadata(new PropertyChangedCallback(Lesson.OnLessonDataChanged)));

public int LessonID
{
    get { return (int)GetValue(LessonIDProperty); }
    set { SetValue(LessonIDProperty, value); }
}

private static void OnLessonDataChanged(DependencyObject d, DependencyPropertyChangedEventArgs e)
{

    // reload the stage for the new TopicID property
    Lesson thisLesson = d as Lesson;

    lessonObject = thisLesson; // there is only one lesson object ... this is a static ref to it

    thisLesson.LoadLessonData(); // get data from xml file on server
    //call to thisLesson.CreateLessonForm(); must be done after load b/c of asynchronous read
}

#endregion
```

Figure 4-14
Source Code Sample

will involve a blend of both proprietary and open-source software."[4] During your career, open source will likely take a greater and greater role in software. However, whether open source works for a particular situation depends on the requirements and constraints of that situation. You will learn more about matching requirements and programs in Chapter 10.

In some cases, companies choose open source software because it is "free." It turns out that this advantage may be less important than you'd think, because in many cases support and operational costs swamp the initial licensing fee.

Q4 How Can You Use This Knowledge?

Over the course of your career, application software, hardware, and firmware will change, sometimes rapidly. The Guide on pages 130–131 challenges you to choose a strategy for addressing this change.

As a future business professional, you will need basic knowledge of hardware and software for several reasons. For one, you will need it to make some decisions about which products you use. Second, as a manager, you will be involved in creating or approving hardware budgets. Third, you may someday be in a position like Emily's at GearUp. You may need to help your organization decide how to create applications such as iPad apps. Consider each.

What Buying Decisions Do You Make?

In general, most business professionals have some role in the specification of the client hardware and software they use. Business managers also play a role in the specification of client hardware and software for employees whom they manage. The particular role depends on the policy of the manager's organization. Large organizations will have an IS department that is likely to set standards for client hardware and software. You will learn more about such standards in Chapter 11.

In medium to small organizations, policies are often less formal, and managers will need to take an active role in setting the specifications for their own and their employees' computers. Figure 4-15 summarizes sources of costs and Figure 4-16 lists the major criteria for selecting both hardware and software. The goal, of course, is to select the hardware and software that will meet requirements at the minimum total system cost.

Except in rare circumstances, medium to small organizations will usually standardize on a single client operating system because the costs of supporting more than one are unjustifiable. Most organizations choose Microsoft Windows clients. Some arts and design businesses standardize on the Macintosh, and some engineering firms standardize on Unix. Organizations that have limited budgets might choose to use Linux with Ubuntu and Open Office on the clients, but this is rare.

Figure 4-15
Sources of System Costs

	Development	Operational
Hardware	Hardware purchases	Hardware maintenance fees
Software	Software licenses Project costs for custom software	Software maintenance and support fees and costs
Data	Data conversion costs	Data acquisition costs
Procedures	Design, development, and documentation	Procedure maintenance costs
People	Initial training costs	Labor costs of using system

---

[4] "Unlocking the Cloud," *The Economist*, May 28, 2009. Available at www.economist.com/opinion/displaystory.cfm?story_id=13740181 (accessed June 2009).

Category	Hardware	Software
Client	Specify: • CPU speed • Size of main memory • Size of magnetic disk • CD or DVD and type • Monitor type and size	Specify: • Windows, Mac, or Linux OS. May be dictated by organizational standard. • PC applications such as Microsoft Office, Adobe Acrobat, Photoshop, Paint Shop Pro. May be dictated by organizational standard. • Browser such as Internet Explorer, Safari, or Netscape Navigator. • Requirements for the client side of client-server applications. • Need for thin or thick client.
Server	In most cases, a business manager has no role in the specification of server hardware (except possibly a budgetary one).	• Specify requirements for the server side of client-server applications. • Work with technical personnel to test and accept software.

Figure 4-16
A Business Manager's Role in Hardware and Software Specifications

Managers and their employees might have a role in specifying horizontal application software, such as Microsoft Office, or other software appropriate for their operating systems. They will also have an important role in specifying requirements for vertical market or custom applications. We will say more about this role in Chapter 10.

Concerning the server, a business manager typically has no role in the specification of server hardware, other than possibly approving the budget. Instead, technical personnel make such decisions. A business manager and those who will be the clients of a client-server application specify the requirements for vertical and custom-server software. They will also work with technical personnel to test and accept that software.

What Process Should You Use to Establish a Computer Budget?

The steps for preparing a departmental hardware budget are summarized in Figure 4-17. You need first to determine the base requirements. This involves assessing the work your employees perform, creating job categories, and determining the computer workload requirements for each category.

In accounts payable, for example, you might determine that you have three categories of workers: administrators, accounts payable specialists, and managers. You further determine that the administrators need hardware and software to access the company's Web portal, to email, and to perform minimal word processing. The accounts payable specialists need the same capabilities as the administrators, but they also need access to the organization's accounts payable system. Finally, you and other managers need to be able to perform the same work as the specialists, plus you need to process large spreadsheets for preparing budgets. You also need to access the company's payroll and human resources systems.

Once you have identified the job categories and the computer workload requirements for each, you can apply the knowledge from this chapter to determine hardware and software requirements for each type. You can also use past departmental experience as a guide. If employees complain about computer performance with the equipment they have, you can determine if more is needed. If there are no bottlenecks or performance problems, you know the current equipment will do.

Given the base requirements, the next step is to forecast changes. Will you be adding or losing employees during the year? Will the workload change? Will your department be given new tasks that will necessitate additional hardware or software? Finally, during the year will your organization mandate changes in hardware or software? Will you be required to upgrade your operating system or applications software? If so, will your budget be charged for those upgrades?

Establishing a computer budget involves knowing the right questions to ask. The Guide on pages 132–133 discusses the importance of improving your ability to ask intelligent questions.

Figure 4-17
A Process for Preparing a
Departmental IT Budget

Determine base requirements:
• The types of workload your employees perform
• The hardware requirements for each type
• The software requirements for each type

Forecast requirement changes during the budget period:
• Changes in the number of employees
• Changes in workload—new job tasks or information systems
• Mandatory changes in hardware or software

Prepare the budget:
• Using guidance from the IT department and accounting,
  price the hardware and software
• Determine if your department will be charged for networks,
  servers, communications, or other overhead expenses
• Add overhead charges as necessary

Assess results:
• Consider budget in context of competitive strategy
• If substantial increases in budget size, prepare justification
• Consider budget in context of prior year's budget
• Determine sources of significant difference and explain
• Modify budget as appropriate

Document results:
• Prepare for justification
• Save documents and notes for preparation of next year's IT budget

Once you have the base requirements and your change forecasts, you can prepare the budget. The first task is to price the hardware and software. As you will learn in Chapter 11, your IT department will most likely have established standards for hardware and software from which you will select. They will probably have negotiated prices on your behalf. If not, the accounting department can probably help you estimate costs based on their prior experience. You can also learn from the past experience of your own department.

Your organization may have a policy of charging the department's overhead fees for networks, servers, and communications. If so, you will need to add those charges to the budget as well.

When you have finished the preparation of the budget, you should assess it for feasibility and reasonableness. First, consider your organization's competitive strategy. If your organization is a cost leader, any increases in your budget will be carefully scrutinized, and you should be prepared with strong justifications. If your organization uses a differentiation strategy, then be certain that any increases in your budget relate directly to the ways in which your company differentiates. Before submitting your budget, prepare justifications for any such increases.

You can expect that your budget will be reviewed in the context of prior years' budgets. If you are proposing substantial changes to your budget, anticipate that you will be asked to justify them. Reasons that you may need more equipment include:

• Substantial change in your departmental head count
• Important new departmental functions or responsibilities
• Upgrading to major new versions of operating system or other software
• Implementation of new systems that require additional hardware
• Change in the way overhead expenses are allocated to your department

If you find it difficult to justify budgetary increases, you may need to review and revise your budget. Perhaps you can do with refurbished equipment, or maybe you can delay the upgrade of all of your computers to the new operating system, or maybe you can find ways of reallocating hardware among the employees in your department that will save costs. Even if none of these options are workable, you can demonstrate that you investigated them in your budget justification or mention them in any budgetary review meetings.

Finally, document your results. You can use such documentation not only to justify your budget this year but also to help you prepare next year's budget. Keep any spreadsheets as well as notes and documents used to prepare and justify your budget.

What Are Your Business Requirements?

GearUp provides a third reason that you, as a future business professional, need the knowledge of this chapter. You don't want to be like Drew; you don't want to say you want an iPad app, but you don't want an iOS application. Statements like that do make you sound like a "nitwit," even though that isn't a professional term.

As a knowledge worker, you need to be thinking about how to improve marketing or accounting or manufacturing or whatever it is you do with innovative applications of emerging technology. By the time you read this, the iPad will be old news, and by the time you graduate something not yet announced will offer great value to you in your new professional job. To develop your ideas, you'll need to work with MIS professionals, and to do that you need to be able to collaborate. Your Lucas (the IT professional at GearUp) doesn't know about marketing or accounting or manufacturing, and he or she can't envision how to use emerging products and technology in your field. Nor is it your Lucas' job to do so. That's your job.

So, you need the knowledge of this chapter first to be able to know what's available and second to know the vocabulary and concepts so that you can effectively work with your Lucas. You need to provide the requirements, the features, and the functions of whatever innovation you imagine. This chapter provided you a hardware/software foundation. The next two expand that foundation for databases and networking. You need the knowledge of all of them, so keep reading!

Q5 2022?

The year 2011 was an interesting one for the computer industry. Apple continued to dominate and enrich itself based on its mobile computing success (See Case 4, The Apple of Your i, on page 137), while Google's Android emerged as a serious competitor. Microsoft, which has fumbled every mobile opportunity it has had, bought Skype. Will it fumble Skype as well? We will see.

Microsoft also dominates, at least today, in the office worker, nonmobile, personal computer market. Even though Mac OS X Lion makes Windows 7 look like a clunker, Windows is installed on most office computers. Between now and 2022, what happens to Microsoft? The Office 365 bundle of hosted Exchange, Lync, and SharePoint is innovative and provides huge value to collaborating groups. Can Microsoft take Office 365 into the mobile market via its Skype acquisition and new phone? We will see.

And what about the others? Google employs thousands of creative workers and has plenty of money. IBM turned 100 years old in 2011, and the venerable company, which once dominated the computer industry, shows signs of innovation with inexpensive desktop virtualization.

It's easy to understand where these trends take entertainment and recreational gaming, but where does it take the business computer user? Today, everyone takes

Figure 4-18
A PC Mule at the Airport

Source: Pedro Coll/Photolibrary.com.

their PC or other device wherever they go. Every day, business professionals, working like **PC mules**, work their way through airport security, unpacking and packing their computer loads. (See Figure 4-18.)

By 2022, PC mules will be rarer than pack mules. Users will carry their phones, their iPads, and whatever iSomethings come along. They'll do so because they're small and powerful.

But what about large-screen access? Maybe some PC mules will survive, but more likely is that large-screen computing/connectivity devices will be available everywhere, like pay telephones once were. Instead of carrying your computer, you'll simply use a public device and connect to your data in the cloud. You won't need your desktop Office applications because you'll be using Web apps in your browser. You won't need your local data files because all those files will be in the cloud.

This trend will accelerate with thin-client versions of all applications. If any computer will provide access to those applications and your data, why carry a computer? We PC mules will be the first to agree.

But there is a limitation. My personal computer provides more than just data and thick-client applications. It has my personal organization. It has my screensaver, it has my desktop picture and icons, it has my files arranged just the way I want them. I need my computer to provide my personal world in a familiar way.

Enter desktop virtualization. By 2022, any cost performance issues of desktop virtualization will be gone, and you will access any public computer, connect to your personal virtual desktop, and, voilá, be running what you now think to be your computer. In fact, it is your computer, except that it is running on a public machine that is connected to your virtual desktop somewhere "out there."

If that is the case, why haul any hardware anywhere? At least why haul any hardware that weighs more than a few ounces? In this world, your hotel room comes with a computer; your airplane seat comes with a computer, your bus seat comes with a computer, your convention center is full of computers. With all of these devices, you need only access your virtual client, somewhere in the cloud, and you are up and running on "your machine."

This mode of access solves another aggravating problem. Many professionals use several different computers and have different sets of data on each. This situation creates data synchronization problems. If you work on your computer at home, when you get to work you have to synchronize (or **synch**) your computer at work with any changes you've made on the computer you took home. But, if your machine is a virtual client in the cloud, everything is always synchronized, because there's only one version.

So, where does that leave Microsoft? Or Google? Or Apple? It's the Wild West all over again. Who knows? Everything depends on how those companies respond, which ultimately comes down to you and your classmates. The next decade will bring enormous change in hardware/software technologies, companies, industries, and users. You will be in the vanguard of consumers who decide. And a small percentage of you will have the great good fortune to work in the IT industry during this raucous time, cowboy hats and all!

Guide

Keeping Up to Speed

Have you ever been to a cafeteria where you put your lunch tray on a conveyor belt that carries the dirty dishes into the kitchen? That conveyor belt reminds me of technology. Like the conveyor, technology just moves along, and all of us run on top of the technology conveyor, trying to keep up. We hope to keep up with the relentless change of technology for an entire career without ending up in the techno-trash.

Technology change is a fact, and the only appropriate question is, "What am I going to do about it?" One strategy you can take is to bury your head in the sand: "Look, I'm not a technology person. I'll leave it to the pros. As long as I can send email and use the Internet, I'm happy. If I have a problem, I'll call someone to fix it."

That strategy is fine, as far as it goes, and many businesspeople have used it. Following that strategy won't give you a competitive advantage over anyone, and it will give someone else a competitive advantage over you, but as long as you develop your advantage elsewhere, you'll be OK—at least for yourself.

What about your department, though? If an expert says, "Every computer needs a 500GB disk," are you going to nod your head and say, "Great. Sell 'em to me!" Or are you going to know enough to realize that's a big disk (by 2012 standards, anyway) and ask why everyone needs such a large amount of storage? Maybe then you'll be told, "Well, it's only another $50 per machine from the 120GB disk." At that point, you can make a decision, using your own decision-making skills, and not rely solely on the IS expert. Thus, the prudent business professional in the twenty-first century has a number of reasons not to bury his or her head in the technology sand.

At the other end of the spectrum are those who love technology. You'll find them everywhere—they may be accountants, marketing professionals, or production-line supervisors who not only know their field, but also enjoy information technology. Maybe they were IS majors or had double majors that combined IS with another area of expertise (e.g., IS with accounting). These people read CNET News and ZDNet most days, and they can tell you the latest on desktop virtualization. Those people are sprinting along the technology conveyor belt; they will never end up in the techno-trash, and they will use their knowledge of IT to gain competitive advantage throughout their careers.

Many business professionals fall in between these extremes. They don't want to bury their heads, but they don't have the desire or interest to become technophiles (lovers of technology) either. What to do? There are a couple of strategies. For one, don't allow yourself to ignore technology. When you see a technology article in the *Wall Street Journal*, read it. Don't just skip it because it's about technology. Read the technology ads, too. Many vendors invest heavily in ads that instruct without seeming to. Another option is to take a seminar or pay attention to professional events that combine your specialty with technology. For example, when you go to the banker's convention, attend a session or two on "Technology Trends for Bankers." There are always sessions like that, and you might make a contact with similar problems and concerns in another company.

Probably the best option, if you have the time for it, is to get involved as a user representative in technology committees in your organization. At a company like GearUp, get involved in the specifications for the iOS app. Or, if your company is doing a review of its CRM system, see if you can get on the review committee. When there's a need for a representative from your department to discuss needs for the next-generation help-line system, sign up. Or, later in your career, become a member of the business practice technology committee, or whatever they call it at your organization.

Just working with such groups will add to your knowledge of technology. Presentations made to such groups, discussions about uses of technology, and ideas about using IT for competitive advantage will all add to your IT knowledge. You'll gain important contacts and exposure to leaders in your organization as well.

It's up to you. You get to choose how you relate to technology. But be sure you choose; don't let your head fall into the sand without thinking about it. ■

Discussion Questions

1. Do you agree that the change of technology is relentless? What do you think that means to most business professionals? To most organizations?

2. Think about the three postures toward technology presented here. Which camp will you join? Why?

3. Write a two-paragraph memo to yourself justifying your choice in question 2. If you chose to ignore technology, explain how you will compensate for the loss of competitive advantage. If you're going to join one of the other two groups, explain why, and describe how you're going to accomplish your goal.

4. Given your answer to question 2, assume that you're in a job interview and the interviewer asks about your knowledge of technology. Write a three-sentence response to the interviewer's question.

Guide
Questioning Your Questions

Many school experiences mislead you to believe that answering a question is the important part of learning. In fact, answering a question is the easy part. For most problems in the business world, the difficult and creative acts are generating the questions—and formulating a strategy for getting the answers. Once the questions and strategy are set, the rest is simply legwork.

As a future consumer of information technology and services, you will benefit from being able to ask good questions and effectively obtain answers to them. It is probably the single most important behavior you can learn. Because of the rapid change of technology, you will constantly be required to learn about new IS alternatives and how you can apply them in your business.

Perhaps you've heard that "there is no such thing as a bad question." This statement is nonsense. There are billions of bad questions, and you will be better off if you learn not to ask them.

Questions can be bad in three ways: They can be irrelevant, dead, or asked of the wrong source. Consider the first way. If you know the subject and if you're paying attention, you can avoid asking irrelevant questions. One of the goals of this text is to teach you about IT and IS so that you can avoid asking irrelevant technology questions.

A dead question is one that leads to nowhere—it provides no insight into the subject. Here's an example of a dead question: "Is the material on How a Computer Works going to be on the test?" The answer will tell you whether you need to study that topic for the exam, but it won't tell you why. The answer will help you in school, but it won't help you use MIS on the job.

Instead, ask questions like, "What is the purpose of the section on how a computer works?" "Why are we studying it?" or "How will it help me use MIS in my career?" These are good questions because they go somewhere. Your professor may respond, "From that discussion you'll learn how to save money because you'll know whether to buy your staff more memory or a faster CPU." Possibly, you won't understand that answer; in that case, you can ask more questions that will lead you to understand how it pertains to your use of MIS.

Or, your professor may say, "Well, I think that section is a waste of time, and I told the author that in a recent email." From there, you can ask your professor why she thinks it's a waste of time, and you can wonder why the author would write something that is a waste of time. Maybe the author and your professor have different points of view. Such musings are excellent because they lead you to more learning.

The third way questions can be bad is that they are asked of the wrong source. Information technology questions fall into three types: "What is it?" "How can I use it?" and "Is it the best

> *It is not possible to become a good thinker and be a poor questioner. Thinking is not driven by answers, but rather, by questions.*[5]

---

[5] Richard Paul and Linda Elder, *Critical Thinking* (Upper Saddle River, NJ: Prentice Hall, 2001), p. 113.

choice?" The first type asks for a simple definition. You can easily Google or Bing the answers to such questions. Hence, you ought not to ask "What is it?" questions of valuable or expensive sources; you are wasting your money and their time if you do. And, when you ask such a question, you appear unprepared because you didn't take the time to find the easy answer.

The next type of question, "How can I use it?" is harder. Answering that question requires knowledge of both technology and your business. Although you can research that question over the Internet, you need knowledge to relate it to your present circumstance. In a few years, this is the sort of question that you will be expected to answer for your organization. It's also the type of question you might ask an expert.

Finally, the most difficult type of question is, "Is it the best choice for our company or situation?" Answering this type of question requires the ability to judge among alternatives according to appropriate criteria. These are the kinds of questions you probably do want to ask an expensive source.

Notice, too, that only "What is it?" questions have a verifiably correct answer. The next two types are questions of judgment. No answer can be shown to be correct, but some answers are better than others. As you progress in your educational career, you should be learning how to discern the quality of judgment and evaluative answers. Learn to question your questions. ■

Discussion Questions

Suppose you are interviewing an expert about how she thinks Microsoft will respond to the challenge of OS X Lion. Using that as an example, answer questions 1 through 7.

1. Using your own words, what is the difference between a good question and a bad one?

2. What types of questions waste time?

3. What types of questions are appropriate to ask your professor?

4. How do you know when you have a good answer to a question? Consider the three types of questions described here in your answer.

5. Under what circumstances would you ask a question to which you already know the answer?

6. Suppose you have 15 minutes with your boss's boss's boss. What kinds of questions are appropriate in such an interview? Even though you don't pay money to meet with this person, explain how this is an expensive source.

7. Evaluate the quality of questions 1 through 5. Which are the best questions? What makes one better than the other? If you can, think of better ways of asking these questions, or even better questions.

Active Review

Use this Active Review to verify that you understand the ideas and concepts that answer the chapter's study questions.

Q1   What do business professionals need to know about computer hardware?

List categories of hardware and explain the purpose of each. Define *bit* and *byte*. Explain why bits are used to represent computer data. Define the units of bytes used to size memory. In general terms, explain how a computer works. Explain how a manager can use this knowledge. Explain why you should save your work from time to time while you are using your computer. Define *server farm* and summarize the technology dance that occurs on a server farm.

Q2   What do business professionals need to know about software?

Review Figure 4-9 and explain the meaning of each cell in this table. Describe three kinds of virtualization, and explain the use of each. Explain the difference between software ownership and software licenses. Compare thin and thick clients and give an example of each on an iPhone. Explain the differences among horizontal-market, vertical-market, and one-of-a-kind applications. Describe the three ways that organizations can acquire software.

Q3   Is open source software a viable alternative?

Define *GNU* and *GPL*. Name three successful open source projects. Describe four reasons programmers contribute to open source projects. Define *open source, closed source, source code,* and *machine code.* In your own words, explain why open source is a legitimate alternative but may or may not be appropriate for a given application.

Q4   How can you use this knowledge?

Describe the three major reasons you need the knowledge of this chapter. Review Figure 4-16 and explain each cell of this table. Summarize the process you should use to develop a computer budget. Explain how the knowledge of this chapter can help you as an innovator.

Q5   2022?

Summarize the important events of 2011 described in this question. Explain how this trend in computing devices will eliminate PC mules. Describe the role and value of desktop virtualization. Explain how you will access your computer in 2022 and why you will not need to synch. Summarize what we can say about the impact of these trends on Microsoft, Google, Apple, IBM, and you.

Using Your Knowledge at GearUp

Suppose you are Drew. Explain how the knowledge of this chapter would help you be better able to converse with Lucas and Emily. How would your ability impact GearUp?

▬ Key Terms and Concepts

Using Your Knowledge

1. Suppose that your roommate, a political science major, asks you to help her purchase a new laptop computer. She wants to use the computer for email, Internet access, and for note-taking in class. She wants to spend less than $1,000.

   a. What CPU, memory, and disk specifications would you recommend?

   b. What software does she need?

   c. Shop www.dell.com, www.hp.com, and www.lenovo.com for the best computer deal.

   d. Which computer would you recommend, and why?

2. Suppose that your father asks you to help him purchase a new computer. He wants to use his computer for email, Internet access, downloading pictures from his digital camera, uploading those pictures to a shared photo service, and writing documents to members of his antique auto club.

   a. What CPU, memory, and disk specifications would you recommend?

   b. What software does he need?

   c. Shop www.dell.com, www.hp.com, and www.lenovo.com for the best computer deal.

   d. Which computer would you recommend, and why?

3. Microsoft offers free licenses of certain software products to students at colleges and universities that participate in the Microsoft Developer Network (MSDN) Academic Alliance (AA). If your college or university participates in this program, you have the opportunity to obtain hundreds of dollars of software, for free. Here is a partial list of the software you can obtain:

   - Microsoft Access 2010
   - OneNote 2010
   - Expression Studio 4
   - Windows 2008 Server
   - Microsoft Project 2010
   - Visual Studio Developer
   - SQL Server 2008
   - Visio 2010

   a. Search www.microsoft.com, www.google.com, or www.bing.com and determine the function of each of these software products.

   b. Which of these software products are operating systems and which are application programs?

   c. Which of these programs are DBMS products (the subject of the next chapter)?

   d. Which of these programs should you download and install tonight?

   e. Either (1) download and install the programs in your answer to part d, or (2) explain why you would not choose to do so.

   f. Does the MSDN AA provide an unfair advantage to Microsoft? Why or why not?

4. Suppose you work at GearUp and Emily asks you to create a list of the top five features needed by the GearUp iOS application. Visit a company similar to GearUp, say Woot (www.woot.com), to get a sense of the requirements. If you have access to an iPhone or an iPad, download Woot's iOS application and study it. List what you think are the application's top five features and functions and briefly describe each.

5. Visit www.apple.com, www.microsoft.com, and www.ibm.com. Summarize differences in the look and feel of each of these sites. Do you think one of these sites is superior to the others? If not, say why. If so, do you think the look and feel of the superior site should be copied by the other companies? Why or why not?

Collaboration Exercise 4

With a team of your fellow students, develop an answer to the following questions. Use Google Docs, Google +, Windows Live SkyDrive, SharePoint, Office 365, or some other collaboration tool to conduct your meetings.

Suppose you manage the sales and marketing department at a company that generates $100 million in sales—say, a manufacturer of fireplace inserts and related equipment. Assume you just started the job and that at the end of your second day the corporate operations officer (COO) sticks her head into your office and announces, "I'm in a rush and have to go, but I wanted to let you know that I put $80,000 in the budget for computers for your department next year. Is that OK? Unfortunately, I've got to know by the day after tomorrow. Thanks."

How do you respond? You have 2 days to decide. If you agree to the $80,000 and it turns out to be insufficient, then sometime next year your department will lack computing resources and you'll have a management problem. If that happens, you may have to spend over your budget. You know that cost control is important to your new employer, so you dread overspending. However, if you ask for more than $80,000, you need to justify why you need it. You will need to document the computer equipment and software your department needs, explain why you need it, and estimate how much it will cost.

Given the short time frame, and given that as a new employee you probably have already scheduled the next 2 days full of meetings, you will need to delegate at least part of this problem to someone. You might delegate it to a computer salesperson, but that is akin to inviting the fox to babysit the chickens. Or, you could delegate it to some of your employees, but as a new employee you do not yet know who has the capability to answer this question. You could also ask the IS department at your organization to help you.

In any case, whether you find the time to answer this question yourself, assign it to your employees, or ask for help from the IS department, you will need knowledge of computer hardware and software capabilities and costs in order to assess the quality of the answer you have.

To respond to this request, assume you have been given the following list of data about the department and its information needs:

- You will upgrade all of your department's computers to Windows 7 and Office 2010 in the next year. Your

company has negotiated a site license for these products, and the IS department allocates that license cost to each computer. For your department, you will pay $100 for each computer that uses Office 2010 and another $75 for each computer that uses Windows 7. You are not required nor allowed to buy any software for new computers. If the computer comes with software, that software will be destroyed by the IS department's standard installation process.

- You have identified three classes of computer users in your department. The main memory, RAM, and disk storage requirements for each class of user are shown in Figure 4-19. This figure shows the specifications of existing computers as well as the hardware requirements for each class after the upgrade.

- Figure 4-20 shows the job titles of employees in your department, the number of employees of each type, the class of computer they require, and whether they use a desktop or a laptop. (You are a new employee, do not yet have a computer, and can specify your own requirements.)

- A computer can be reassigned to other employees as long as the computer meets the minimum processing requirements. A laptop can substitute for a desktop if a display, keyboard, and mouse are purchased to go with it.

- The IS department assesses each computer an annual $1,200 fee for network, server, and other overhead costs.

- Assume that telesales personnel will grow by 10 percent in the next year but there will be no other changes in the number of personnel in your department.

- Ten of the existing class B computers have a maximum main memory of 1GB. The rest of the class B computers have a maximum main memory of 512MB. All of the existing class C computers have a maximum main memory of 4GB.

a. Given this data, is $80,000 enough? If not, how much money should be allocated in your department?
b. Explain how you will meet the computer needs of the employees in your department. Assume you are required to buy new computers and equipment from Dell, HP, or Lenovo.

Class of Computer	Current Hardware Specification (Main Memory, Processor, Disk)	Hardware Required After Upgrade (Main Memory, Processor, Disk)
A	256MB, 0.5GHz, 30GB	1GB, 1GHz, 80GB
B	512MB, 1GHz, 80GB	2GB, 2GHz, 150GB
C	1GB, 2GHz, 2 × 125GB	4GB, 2GHz—dual, 2 × 250GB

Figure 4-19
Hardware Specifications for Three Classes of Computers

Figure 4-20
Department Employees and
Computer Requirements

Job Title	Number of Employees	Computer System Required	Computer Type
Product manager	8	B	Laptop
Telesales	12	A	Desktop
Department administrator	2	A	Desktop
Marketing communications manager	4	B	Laptop
Marketing analyst	4	C (desktop) B (laptop)	Both, a desktop and laptop for each analyst
Marketing programs manager	6	B	Desktop
You	1	???	???

c. Describe how you will modify and reallocate existing computers (e.g., upgrading an existing class B computer and assigning it to an employee who next year needs a class A computer). You may wish to develop the spreadsheet in Application Exercise 4–1 on page 471 to facilitate your analysis.

Case Study 4

The Apple of Your i

A quick glance at Apple's stock history in Figure 4-21 will tell you that Apple, Inc., is a very successful company. You might be surprised to learn, however, just *how* successful. In roughly 3 years, Apple has tripled its market capitalization (the number of outstanding shares times the stock price) to more than $300 billion, making Apple the second largest public company in the world (Exxon Mobil is the largest). To put that number in perspective, Microsoft—for years the market capitalization leader of software companies—has a market

Figure 4-21
Growth in Apple Stock Price

Source: Yahoo! Finance.

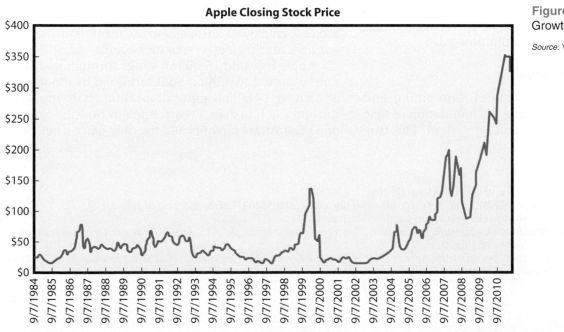

Apple Closing Stock Price

capitalization of $212.5 billion, and Google has a market capitalization of $155.58 billion.[6]

In late June 2011, numerous market analysts were predicting that the $332 stock would increase another $100 within 6 months. In fact, within a month, it was trading over $400. Apple has been so successful that the Nasdaq stock exchange concluded that it was over-influential in the computation of the Nasdaq-100 Index and reduced Apple's weight in that index from 20 to 12 percent. That's success!

Alas, it wasn't always that way.

Early Success and Downfall

At the dawn of the personal computer age, in the early 1980s, Apple pioneered well-engineered home computers and innovative interfaces with its Apple II PC for the home and its Macintosh computer for students and knowledge workers. At one point, Apple owned more than 20 percent of the PC market, competing against many other PC vendors, most of which are no longer relevant (or in business).

However, Apple lost its way. In 1985, Steve Jobs, Apple's chief innovator lost a fight with the Apple board and was forced out. He founded another PC company, NeXT, which developed and sold a groundbreaking PC product that was too groundbreaking to sell well in that era. Meanwhile, Apple employed a succession of CEOs, starting with John Sculley, who was hired away from Pepsi-Cola where he'd enjoyed considerable success. Sculley's knowledge and experience did not transfer well to the PC business, however, and the company went downhill so fast that CNBC named him the 14th worst American CEO of all time.[7] Two other CEOs followed in Sculley's footsteps.

During this period, Apple made numerous mistakes, among them not rewarding innovative engineering, creating too many products for too many market segments, and losing the respect of the retail computer stores. Apple's market PC share plummeted.

Steve Jobs, Second Verse

In 1996, Apple bought Jobs' NeXT Computing and gained technology that became the foundation of Mac OS X, today's Macintosh operating system. The true asset it acquired, however, was Steve Jobs. Even he, however, couldn't create an overnight miracle. It is exceedingly difficult to regain lost market share and even more difficult to regain the respect of the retail channel that had come to view Apple's products with disdain. Even by 2011, Apple's market PC market share was in the range of 10 to 12 percent, down from a high of 20 percent in the 1980s.

In response to these problems, Apple broke away from the PC and created new markets with its iPod, iPhone, and iPad. It also countered retailer problems by opening its own stores. In the process, it pioneered the sale of music and applications over the Internet.

iPod, iPhone, and iPad devices are a marvel of creativity and engineering. They exude not only ease of use, but also now/wow/fun coolness. By selling hot music for the iPod, Apple established a connection with a dynamic segment of the market that was willing to spend lots of money on bright, shiny objects. The ability to turn the iPhone on its side to rotate images probably sold more iPhones than anything else. With the iPad, portable devices became readable, and the market responded by awarding Apple a 44 percent (and growing) share of the mobile market.[8]

All of this success propelled Apple's stores not only beyond vanilla retailers like Best Buy, but also beyond the lofty heights of Tiffany & Co. In 2011, Apple stores were grossing more than $4,000 per square foot, compared to $3,000 for Tiffany and a mere $880 for Best Buy. As of 2011, Apple operates over 300 such retail outlets and has welcomed over 1 billion customer visits.[9]

Apple encourages customer visits and loyalty with its open and inviting sales floor, its Genius Bar help desk, and its incredibly well-trained and disciplined sales force. Salespeople, who are not commissioned, are taught to be consultants who help customers solve problems. Even some vocabulary is standardized. When an employee cannot solve a customer's problem, the word *unfortunately* is to be avoided; employees are taught to use the phrase *as it turns out,* instead.[10] Try that on your next exam!

Apple has sold 15 billion songs through its iTunes online store, 130 million books through its iBookstore, and a mere 14 billion applications through its App Store, the latter in less than 3 years. Apple is now the number one PC software channel and the only place a customer

[6] http://finance.yahoo.com, accessed and date as of June 27, 2011.

[7] "Portfolio's Worst CEOs of All Time," CNBC.com. Available at www.cnbc.com/id/30502091?slide=8 (accessed July 2011).

[8] Apple presentation at the Apple Worldwide Developers Conference, June 6, 2011.

[9] Carl Howe, "Apple Reboots Retail with Connected Experiences," Yankee Group, March 23, 2011. Available at www.yankeegroup.com/ResearchDocument.do?id=56472 (accessed July 2011).

[10] Yukari Iwatani Kane and Ian Sherr, "Secret's from Apple's Genius Bar: Full Loyalty, No Negativity," *Wall Street Journal,* June 15, 2011. Available at http://online.wsj.com/article/SB10001424052702304563104576364071955678908.html (accessed June 2011).

can buy the Mac X Lion, which sells for $30 instead of the $130 for the earlier OS X that sold through the software channel.[11]

To encourage the development of iPhone and iPad apps, Apple shares its revenue with application developers. That would be $2.5 billion paid to developers in less than 3 years! Developers responded by creating 445,000 iOS applications, and an army of developers are at work building thousands more while you read this.

By the way, if you want to build an iOS application, what's the first thing you need to do? Buy a Macintosh. Apple closed its development to any other development method. Adobe Flash? No way. Apple claims that Flash has too many bugs, and perhaps so. Thus, Flash developers are excluded. Microsoft Silverlight? Nope. Microsoft developers are out in the cold, too. The non-Apple development community was furious, and Apple's response was, in essence, "Fine, we'll pay our $2.5 billion to someone else."

The bottom line? Every sales success feeds every other sales success. Hot music fed the iPod. The iPod fed iTunes and created a growing customer base that was ripe for the iPhone. Sales of the iPhone fed the stores, whose success fed the developer community, which fed more applications, which fed the iPhone and set the stage for the iPad, which fed the App Store, which enabled the $30 price on the OS X Lion, which led to more loyal customers, and, of course, to more developers. No wonder some shareholders want Steve Ballmer to resign as CEO over at Microsoft![12]

Questions

1. Which of Porter's four competitive strategies does Apple engage in? Explain.

2. What do you think are the three most important factors in Apple's incredible success? Justify your answer.

3. Steve Jobs passed away in the Fall of 2011. Until his death, he had been the heart and soul of Apple's innovation. Today, 35,000 Apple employees continue onward in his absence. A huge question to many investors is whether the company can be successful without him. What is your opinion? What role did he play? How can Apple respond to his loss? Would you be willing to invest in Apple without his leadership? Why or why not?

4. Microsoft took an early lead in the development of slate devices (like the iPad), and it had the world's leading operating system and applications for over 20 years. Provide five reasons why Microsoft was not able to achieve the same success that Apple has. Most industry analysts would agree that the skills and abilities of Microsoft's 88,000 employees are as good, on average, as Apple's.

5. Considering your answers to the four questions above, if you had a spare $5,000 in your portfolio and wanted to buy an equity stock with it, would you buy AAPL (Apple)? Why or why not?

[11] Apple presentation at the Apple Worldwide Developers Conference, June 6, 2011.
[12] Sharon Pian Chan, "Steve Ballmer Pre-Announces 2011 Earnings for Microsoft," *Seattle Times*, June 30, 2011. Available at http://seattletimes.nwsource.com/html/businesstechnology/2015465692_microsoftballmer30.html (accessed July 2011).

TEACHING SUGGESTIONS

GearUp, Part 2 and Chapter 4

GOALS

Use GearUp to:

- Illustrate the need for business professionals' knowledge of basic technology and terminology.

- Learn a practical application for the difference between hardware (iPad) and software (iOS).

- Set up the need for business managers (like Emily and Drew) to know something about sources of software.

- Show how competitive pressures can force technology development.

BACKGROUND

1. Drew illustrates his ignorance (that's a harsh term, but it's exactly how people like Lucas will view Drew) when he doesn't know that iOS is an operating system. His lack of knowledge reduces his negotiating strength in the meeting in front of Emily. He's insisting on something but he doesn't quite know what it is he's insisting upon.

2. Competitive pressures are requiring GearUp to do something about an iPad application. Based on the scenario, it seems like GearUp is about to rush into something. It doesn't sound like the staff will do a careful analysis of what GearUp's customers want (we don't know that, but it sounds like they are going to rush to an offshore developer). This may turn out OK, but, given the staff's lack of knowledge, it would appear more likely that the result will be a poor application obtained at a high cost.

3. A knowledge of IS would enable Drew to better explain what he wants and Emily to be better able to make decisions on how to proceed.

4. Case Study 11, page 410, discusses outsourcing alternatives for this situation. You might have the students read that case now.

HOW TO GET STUDENTS INVOLVED

1. Ask the students if any of them have any experience developing iOS or Android applications. If not, do any of them know anyone who has such experience? If so, ask the students to share their experiences.

2. According to Case Study 4, Apple paid $2.5 billion dollars to iOS developers in the first 3 years.

   ■ **Should GearUp charge for its application? If not, why not. If so, how much should it charge?**

   ■ **How much should GearUp be willing to pay for its application? How can Kelly make that determination?**

   ■ **It's tempting to say that we have no idea how much she should pay. However, Kelly must decide. What can you conclude from this situation?**

3. What sort of application does GearUp need? Ask the students to visit Woot, MYHABIT, or a similar site. Based on that experience:

   ■ **Describe five key features of an iOS application for GearUp.**

   ■ **What features of such an application would cause it to become popular?**

   ■ **As long as customers can use the application to order items, does it matter how "cool" that application is? Explain.**

4. How many applications does GearUp need?

   ■ **If GearUp has an iOS application, does it need an Android one as well?**

   ■ **Does GearUp need a Windows Series 7 phone application?**

   ■ **What criteria should GearUp use when deciding how many applications to have?**

5. Open source:

   ■ **What is open source?**

   ■ **Is open source appropriate for GearUp's iOS application? Why or why not?**

BOTTOM LINE

■ Modern business forces businesspeople to make technology management decisions, whether they want to or not.

■ Decision makers often need to make decisions under a high degree of uncertainty.

■ By the time you have a decision-making position, the issue will no longer be iOS applications; it will be something else.

■ Get ready! This could happen to you! And it certainly will if you become a manager.

YOU BE THE GUIDE

Using the Ethics Guide: Churn and Burn (pages 112–113)

GOALS

● Think critically about software products.

● Assess the responsibilities of users and software vendors.

● Be a better consumer of software products by learning when to hold software vendors accountable.

● Consider ways of managing an employee like Janet.

BACKGROUND AND PRESENTATION STRATEGIES

You can use this guide not only to engage the students via the opinions of the contrarian, but also to extend the discussion beyond basic definitions to consider software as a product, the nature of the software industry, and the financial needs of software vendors. Questions 5 and 7 work well for this purpose.

Products like Microsoft Office are developed from market feedback. Microsoft and others convene hundreds of focus groups that tell them what features to add. They invite groups of typical users, show them various possibilities, and ask for opinions. They also ask typical users what else they want. The favorite feature of every one of these focus groups gets put "into the pot," for possible inclusion in the product. This is feature design by committee—and it leads to bloated products with little conceptual integrity.

Taking items out of the pot is the job of product managers. But it's difficult for product managers to say, "No, that's just too much, we won't add that feature." The design strategy has been to hide the extra complexity behind not-visible toolbars. As long as the semiconductor industry keeps churning out faster computers with bigger memories, this strategy will probably continue to work.

Software vendors should be *held accountable for security holes* in their products. They allowed the problem to be there in the first place, and they should bear some consequences. In some ways, computer users are too polite; they should object more to security holes than they do. To avoid continuing PR problems, vendors like Microsoft and Adobe are making it easier and easier to obtain and install updates to their products. This easy installation *hides the fact that they are fixing glitches* in their products. With Office 365, Microsoft is now making such installations automatic, as Google and other Web 2.0 vendors have done for years.

Google and other Web 2.0 companies (see Chapter 8) are changing the playing field. Web 2.0 programs are paid for by advertising. You might ask the students what this means for the "churn and burn" strategy.

Also, you might discuss with the class ways in which SaaS cloud offerings like Office 365 change this situation. (Recall some licenses for Office 365 include constant updates to Office 2010.) Vendors can make changes and improvements to software and the user will never know it.

SUGGESTED RESPONSES FOR DISCUSSION QUESTIONS

These questions are all open-ended and subject to judgment and interpretation. Thus, this section provides questions to ask the students to stimulate the conversation.

1. One way to answer this question is to ask:

■ **What can we learn from Janet's contrarian position? Describe some of the points she makes.**

Write the list on the board and then ask the class to rank the items in order of importance. At each point, ask the class if they agree with the point, and how important it is. You might also ask them what the software vendors could do differently to eliminate the problem.

■ **Do you agree with Janet's point about software patches and security holes?**

Vendors want to manage this patch process so as to make it as invisible as possible and avoid close scrutiny and the attendant bad PR. In truth, the vendors did leave the holes in the product in the first place, and they did leave their customers vulnerable to attack. They should be accountable in some way. However, read the license agreements—according to the agreements, the vendors are liable for the cost of the CD, at most $1.50. They may not be liable even for that much, if the product was shipped electronically.

Another line of questions relates to the analogy of being mugged in a bad neighborhood. You might ask:

■ **Are viruses brought on by user stupidity?**

■ **Is the analogy of being mugged in a bad neighborhood a good one?**

- How can a student find out which cyber-neighborhoods are bad?

2. You may have answered this question if you asked the students to prioritize the list in question 1. If not, here are some questions to ask to stimulate the discussion:

- **Are software products bloated?**

- **Isn't it an advantage to have features that you don't need now, but might need in the future?**

- **Would Janet really be happy with her old computer? It might take her hours just to read her email.**

- **What is the relationship between hardware and software vendors? How do they depend on one another? What will happen to software if Moore's Law stops?**

3. This is a fun question that we can ask for many of the contrarians in the guides.

- **Is there any point in Janet sharing her opinions?**

- **Does it do any good for her to say what she says?**

- **Is there a way that Janet could change her questions and behavior to accomplish more good?**

4. Some viruses are brought on by user stupidity, but not all.

- **What are instances of viruses that are not caused by user stupidity?**

5. It's always been done that way, so it fits the general expectations of the industry, so, it's ethical in that strict sense. Vendors might do more to make customers aware of this fact, but they are unlikely to do so. Vendors protect themselves with limitations of liability on their license agreements (which nearly no one reads).

6. Again, using the definition of ethical in that it meets general expectations, it is not unethical for vendors not to publish flaws in their products. It is also not illegal because their license agreements protect them from unknown defects. Vendors have a business reason to fix serious, but not all, failures. It's certainly ethical to charge for new versions that fix problems. It may or may not be a smart business decision to do so.

WRAP UP

Most students will agree that people like Janet do exist. I tell the class:

- **Contrarians are like hot-pepper flakes: They make a great contribution to the stew, but too much ruins the dinner. The question is how to manage someone like Janet without letting her ruin the group.**

Chances are there's a Janet in the class. It's very interesting to see how such students respond to some of the guides. Often, their responses are insightful.

YOU BE THE GUIDE

Using the Guide: Keeping Up to Speed (pages 130–131)

GOALS

- Raise students' awareness of the unrelenting change of technology.

- Encourage students to take a stand about how they will react to technological change—in the words of the guide, to "choose a posture."

- Emphasize that this issue is inescapable in modern business. If students ignore it, they are unknowingly and by default choosing a personal competitive *disadvantage*.

- Teach the students the benefits of this class and of IS education, in general.

BACKGROUND AND PRESENTATION STRATEGIES

Technological change is a factor in every business-person's life. Many of the hardware facts described in this chapter are susceptible to change. It's *perishable content:* Just like produce at the market, it has a short shelf life.

So what's a professional to do? One response is to recognize the problem and to *choose a response*. Business professionals must decide how to respond. They may choose to stick their heads in the sand, but, if so, they'd better find other ways to gain a competitive advantage over their peers.

I tell my students:

■ **Please, after taking the MIS class, don't let random happenstance determine your technology posture. Instead, consciously choose a posture.**

Students who don't want to stick their heads in the sand and ignore technology need to learn coping strategies. First, *they need to learn how to learn about technology*, and they need to learn *how to learn it efficiently*.

The best strategy, I think, is to combine learning about technology with some other activity. This guide recommends volunteering to sit on technology review committees, volunteering to work with systems development professionals as user representatives, going to conferences, and sitting in on at least one or two technology sessions.

The advantage of such a strategy is that it's a "three-fer":

1. As a business professional, you are serving the business, while at the same time making a deposit in your knowledge bank.

2. You also are networking, so the next time you need an answer to a difficult technology question, you'll know whom to ask. (Note: In terms of the "Questioning Your Questions" guide, networking allows the student to obtain the opinion of an expensive source for a cheap price.)

3. It's also a way of being noticed in a positive way while learning and extending—a great way to obtain a competitive advantage.

Encourage students who are currently employed to *volunteer for projects* now, even as interns. I had a student who, as an intern, volunteered to sit on a CRM review committee to provide end-user feedback. He made his section of the report, and the manager of the review committee was impressed and asked him why he volunteered for the committee. He said he learned about it in his MIS class. The manager said, "Be sure our company picks up the cost of that class."

All this is just creating strategies to turn a problem—the rapid change of technology—into a *competitive advantage*. If you are comfortable confronting your class, ask them to look around and see who is bored and not paying attention and who isn't. Those who are actively participating are creating a competitive advantage. I ask my students just to think about it. This is also a good time to promote additional IS classes—maybe a database class or a systems development class—for the non-IS major.

All of the related collaboration exercises deal with the use of some new technology, but it is likely that most of these examples will be outdated by the time today's students are into their careers. You can encourage your students to think about even-newer technologies, though:

■ **Most of the examples in the exercises will be outdated by the time you are well into your business careers. That means that new innovation opportunities will involve technology that is just now emerging or will emerge in the next few years. Don't stop thinking about new technologies. If you choose to avoid technology, you will be unable to take advantage of many opportunities.**

SUGGESTED RESPONSES FOR DISCUSSION QUESTIONS

1. Technology change is a good news/bad news situation.

   ■ **How does technology change impact you in positive ways?**
   - It continuously creates new opportunities.
   - You'll never get bored; there will always be something new to learn and do.
   - Technology change will relevel the playing field frequently. People who have dominant expertise in some technology domain will lose that expertise—creating an opportunity for you.

   ■ **How does technology change impact you in negative ways?**
   - You constantly need to learn.
   - Your expertise is perishable. Without renewal or without knowledge of new technology, you'll fall behind.

   ■ **How does technology change impact organizations in positive ways?**
   - It continuously creates new opportunities for competitive advantage.
   - It will relevel the playing field frequently. Organizations that have dominant expertise in some technology domain will lose that expertise—creating an opportunity for your organization.

   ■ **How does technology change impact organizations in negative ways?**
   - The cost of adapting to new technology can be high.
   - Competitive advantages may not be sustainable.

2. The three choices are:

   a. Head-in-the-sand

   b. Technophile

   c. Technology-informed professional

   Ask sample students:

   ■ **Which posture do you choose? Why?**

If students choose head-in-the-sand, they'd better develop a competitive advantage in another field or discipline.

   ■ **Does choosing technophile or technology-informed mean writing computer programs or designing electronic circuits?**

   No, definitely not! It means knowing about *technology and how to use it* to solve business problems in innovative ways.

3. The purpose of this question is to *compel* the students to choose a posture. They must not kid themselves—which posture will they choose and why? You might ask the students to read their memos to the class.

4. This is another question to *compel* the students to choose a posture. There can be good reasons for the head-in-the-sand posture, but again, does the student truly want to choose that posture? But rather than focus on that posture, I like to ask:

   ■ **For those of you who have chosen to be IS technology-informed professionals, how do you respond?**

   Then I help them hone and improve their answers. I know, all this discussion is advertising for IS education, but, hey, this is an IS class!

WRAP UP

   ■ **Wake up to the opportunities that the conveyor belt of technology change offers.**

   ■ **Because you cannot ignore this issue, choose a strategy. Otherwise, fate will choose a strategy for you.**

   ■ **Learning about IS does not mean, necessarily, becoming a computer programmer or a communications technician. It means helping businesses to use information technology and information systems to accomplish and manage their strategies. (This is the definition of MIS given in Chapter 1.)**

   ■ **If you want to know about other IS classes we offer that you should be taking, drop me an email or come by my office.**

YOU BE THE GUIDE

Using the Guide: Questioning Your Questions (pages 132–133)

GOALS

- Teach the difference between formulating questions and answering questions.

- Emphasize the importance of question formulation.

- Describe and illustrate questions of varying quality.

BACKGROUND AND PRESENTATION STRATEGIES

Eleanore Baxendale, a seasoned and successful business commerce trial attorney, gave me the idea for this guide. She told me that she'd learned over the years that the key to winning judgments lay in *determining what questions to ask*. Once she had the right list of questions, she could delegate to others the task of obtaining the answers. Her role, and a major reason for her success, was being able to think of the right questions to ask. "The rest is just legwork," she said.

The Paul and Elder quote at the start of this guide provides another perspective. *Questions guide thinking.* As the students sit in the class, the questions they are asking themselves are guiding their thoughts. If they're asking themselves, "When is the class going to be over?" that leads them down one path. If they're asking, "How does this knowledge relate to the $80,000 question?" that leads them down another. Which path do they want to be on? On which path are the students against whom they're competing?

Students may be threatened by all of this discussion regarding bad questions. They may feel inhibited about asking questions in class. My goal here is to *challenge the students to do their best work*—to endeavor not to ask irrelevant or dead questions—but *to do so in a nonthreatening way*. I let them know that although I expect good questions, bad questions will not be disastrous for them.

Every question requires taking a calculated risk. And *this class can help them* to ask effective questions of IT and IS professionals.

Very important: Only simple, unimportant questions have a single, demonstrably correct answer. Every other kind of question depends on perspective and can have multiple, correct answers. Depending on their cognitive development, some students will not be comfortable with the idea of multiple correct answers.

Some students are so grounded in the "Professor, you are the font of all knowledge, just give me the answer" mind-set that they will resist this notion. In fact, some feel angry because they *don't want to deal with the anxiety* of a world in which there are multiple correct answers. Some will say that I'm an incompetent teacher, or that I don't prepare for classes, or that I'm not as good a professor as Dr. ABC who always gives good answers.

I think I have a professional responsibility to stand up to that criticism. To me, a major purpose of college education is to help those students advance themselves past this immature way of viewing the world. And this advancement in thinking is especially important in business. Consider, for example, questions like, "Should IBM have sold its personal computer business?" There is no single, demonstrably correct answer.

(By the way, I'm easily trapped by my own ego into the students' expectations. There's a part of me that *wants to be the font* of all knowledge. It makes me feel powerful. Alas, it's all illusion.)

A great source on this phenomenon, by the way, is the work of William Perry.[1]

SUGGESTED RESPONSES FOR DISCUSSION QUESTIONS

Note: The questions in this guide vary in quality. Some, like question 2, are intentionally not as good as others, in order to set up question 7.

1. According to the guide, bad questions fall into three types: *irrelevant, dead,* or *asked of the wrong source.* Good questions are *questions that lead somewhere* and that are *asked of an appropriate source.* Good questions are also those beyond "What is it?" questions, such as "How can I use it?" and "Is it the best choice?"

   ■ **What are examples of irrelevant, dead, and asked-of-the-wrong-source questions?**

   ■ **Using the $80,000 question, give examples of good questions.**

   ■ **Do you agree with the definition of bad question in the guide?**

[1]William A. Perry, "Different Worlds in the Same Classroom," *On Teaching and Learning,* Harvard Danforth Center (May 1985), pp. 1–17; and William A. Perry, "Cognitive and Ethical Growth," in Arthur W. Chickering (ed.), *The Modern American College* (San Francisco: Jossey-Bass, 1981), pp. 76–115.

- **Are there other kinds of bad questions?**

- **Have you ever been embarrassed by a question you or someone else has asked? What was it? Why were you embarrassed?**

- **Are you intimidated by this discussion? Does it make you reluctant to ask a question?**

   (If so, what's to be done? See comments in the Background and Presentation Strategies.)

   Application: It is very common for a naïve and inexperienced manager to ask technical people a question that is so irrelevant that it is embarrassing. When that happens, the techies lose respect for that manager. This is never desirable, but it may be OK if the manager has little interaction with the techies. However, if he or she is managing the techies, it's a start toward a miserable existence. This class can help avoid that situation!

2. This question, as stated, isn't a very good question. It's almost a dead question. The following are questions that waste time: bad questions (see previous discussion); questions that aren't really questions (i.e., I want to show off my ability to ask a question); questions that were just asked by someone else; questions that we all know the answer to.

   - **What do you think of this question?**

   - **How could this question be made stronger?**
      (Change it to also ask, "What can we learn from this?")

3. A professor is an expensive source of information, so don't ask "What is it?" questions. Instead ask questions like, "How can I use it?" "Is it the best choice?" and other questions that lead somewhere. Like all such sources, think about the questions you ask. You only get so many.

   - **When have you been in a position of authority? As a camp counselor, maybe? As a manager in an office or factory? In some other setting?**

   - **What did you think when you were asked bad questions? What were the consequences?**

4. This is a very difficult, interesting question that goes somewhere, so I would rank it as a good question. The answer can be judged correct or not. Answers to "How can I use it?" questions depend on how creative one is. Answers to "Is it the best choice?" depend on one's ability to make analyses as well as one's creativity in thinking of alternatives. The latter two questions are created for collaboration (meaning iteration and feedback).

5. You might ask a question to which you already know the answer when you want to test another person's knowledge. It's been reported that former U.S. president Franklin Roosevelt seldom asked a question for which he did not already know the answer. He was always testing the person. Keep this in mind.

   - **Your boss may already know the answer and may just be testing your knowledge. It could be dangerous to blather on.**

6. This person is an expensive source. Given this, this is a dead question, because it's nothing more than a thinly veiled attempt at making the same point as question 3.

   - **How good is this question?**

   - **How could this question be made better?**

   - **Given question 3, should this question even be in the list?**

7. On a scale of 1 (poor) to 5 (excellent): Question 1 is a 3, it asks for more than regurgitation; Question 2 is a 1, simple answer that goes nowhere; Question 3 is a 2 because it requires an application of material; question 4 is a 5 because it requires careful thought and leads to important insights; question 5 is a 4 because it requires some thinking of principles and may lead to insight about the nature of questioning.

WRAP UP

- **What did you learn? Did you change your perspective about questions?**

- **If so, how? If not, why not?**

- **How would you apply this knowledge to the $80,000 question?**

- **How can you apply this knowledge to this course? Other courses? Your life?**

- **By the way, asking bad questions does happen. When it does, what should one do?**

- **Everyone, usually because of inadequate meeting preparation, does ask a stupid question from time to time (but, one hopes, only rarely). Here's what to do: Make a very brief apology, shut up, and sit down. Don't make the situation worse by attempting to justify the question. You'll just be digging the hole deeper and deeper. Change the subject and move on.**

Database Processing

Kelly Summers, CEO of GearUp, assigned

Drew Mills and Addison Lee the task of finding ways to reduce operational costs. Drew and Addison know that one source of inefficiency is order cancellations that happen when suppliers don't ship the inventory they say they will. Even though Drew and Addison know this is a problem, they don't know how big of a problem, and they can't convince Kelly on the basis of a hunch.

Accordingly, Drew and Addison set up a meeting with Lucas Massey, the director of GearUp's IT department, to request a report that they need.

"This looks like trouble! The two of you at once, I mean." Lucas is only partly kidding as he looks at the two of them.

"Oh, come on, Lucas, you can handle us just fine," Drew responds as he sits down. "Besides, if you have

trouble, it's sitting right over there," he says, nodding at Addison.

"OK, here's the deal," Addison doesn't have patience for this small talk. "We're trying to get our operational costs down and we know some vendors are causing us a ton of extra expense."

"For example," Drew jumps in, "we know that General Sports routinely tells us they have inventory they don't have."

"So what happens?" Lucas knows the answer, but he wants to hear how Drew or Addison understands it.

"We have to cancel any of the customer orders that depended on that inventory, which I think you know . . ." Drew's in mid-sentence when Addison finishes his thought.

"Or, make a partial shipment of what we do have, but even that's got problems. You know, if you buy a kayak and a paddle from us, and we only send you the paddle . . . well, you get the picture."

"And no matter what," continues Drew, "even if the cancellation is clean, we have extra costs as well as lost customer goodwill."

"So where do I come in?" asks Lucas.

"We need data. We know that General causes us problems, but we don't know how much. So we want a report of all the cancellations caused by General's short shipments." Addison is pleased to finally get to the point.

"Actually, it's not just General. We know other vendors ship shortages that cause cancellations as well. But we really don't know which ones and how much," Drew adds.

"So," Lucas pauses while he ponders his response, "you want a report of all the cancelled orders?"

"No, not all the cancelled orders, just all those that were cancelled because we didn't get the inventory from the supplier."

"Hmmm. We'll have to combine data from our customer order and shipping system with data from accounts payable. It can be done. How soon do you need it?"

"Today." Addison's in a hurry.

"No way. I can't do that. How about I give you a data extract and you create the report. I could do that by Monday."

"We don't know anything about . . ." Drew starts to object when Addison jumps in.

"Can you put the data into Access?"

"Sure."

"Alright. We'll take you up on that. What time Monday?"

"Noon?"

"OK."

After the meeting, Addison and Drew are talking quietly on their way back to Drew's cubicle.

"Addison, what are you doing? We don't know anything about creating reports . . . ," Drew whispers.

"No, Drew, YOU don't know anything about report writing. This isn't hard. If he gives me the data, I can munge around in Access to make the report. It's just for us; we're not gonna post it on the Web site."

"Seems hard to me, but I'll go along. I hope that's not a mistake."

"It won't be. Just watch." ■

Study Questions

Q1 What is the purpose of a database?

Q2 What is a database?

Q3 What are the components of a database application system?

Q4 How do database applications make databases more useful?

Q5 How are data models used for database development?

Q6 How is a data model transformed into a database design?

Q7 What is the users' role in the development of databases?

Q8 2022?

Businesses of every size organize data records into collections called *databases*. At one extreme, small businesses use databases to keep track of customers; at the other extreme, huge corporations such as Dell and Microsoft use databases to support complex sales, marketing, and operations activities. In between are businesses like GearUp that use databases as a crucial part of their operations. Such businesses have a small staff of professionals and can't always support special needs, like those of Addison and Drew at GearUp. To obtain the one-of-a-kind reports they need, Addison and Drew need to be creative and adaptable.

This chapter discusses the why, what, and how of database processing. We begin by describing the purpose of databases and then explain the important components of database systems. We then overview the process of creating a database system and summarize your role as a future user of such systems.

Users have a crucial role in the development of database applications. Specifically, the structure and content of the database depends entirely on how users view their business activity. To build the database, the developers will create a model of that view using a tool called the entity-relationship model. You need to understand how to interpret such models, because the development team might ask you to validate the correctness of such a model when building a system for your use. Finally, we describe the various database administration tasks.

This chapter focuses on database technology. Here we consider the basic components of a database and the functions of database applications. You will learn how Addison used database reporting to solve the GearUp problem in Chapter 9.

Q1 What Is the Purpose of a Database?

The purpose of a database is to keep track of things. When most students learn that, they wonder why we need a special technology for such a simple task. Why not just use a list? If the list is long, put it into a spreadsheet.

In fact, many professionals do keep track of things using spreadsheets. If the structure of the list is simple enough, there is no need to use database technology. The list of student grades in Figure 5-1, for example, works perfectly well in a spreadsheet.

Suppose, however, that the professor wants to track more than just grades. Say that the professor wants to record email messages as well. Or, perhaps the professor wants to record both email messages and office visits. There is no place in Figure 5-1

Figure 5-1
A List of Student Grades, Presented in a Spreadsheet

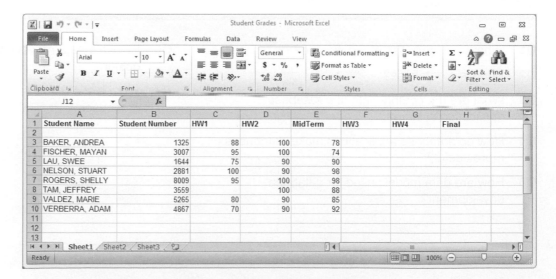

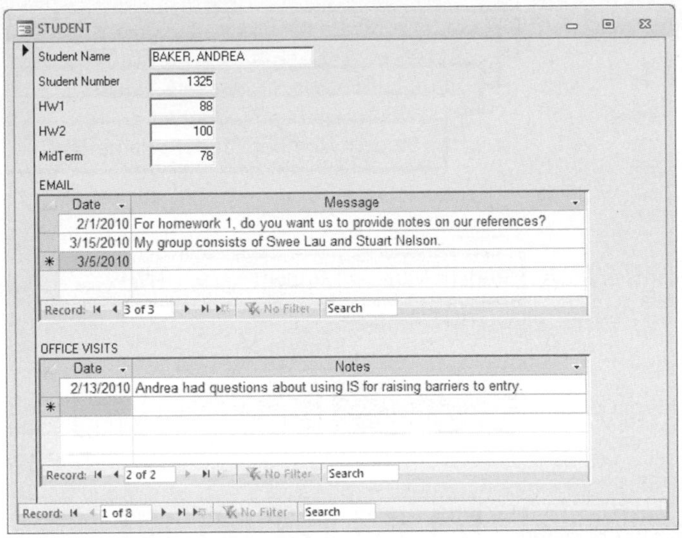

Figure 5-2
Student Data Shown in a Form, from a Database

to record that additional data. Of course, the professor could set up a separate spreadsheet for email messages and another one for office visits, but that awkward solution would be difficult to use because it does not provide all of the data in one place.

Instead, the professor wants a form like that in Figure 5-2. With it, the professor can record student grades, emails, and office visits all in one place. A form like the one in Figure 5-2 is difficult, if not impossible, to produce from a spreadsheet. Such a form is easily produced, however, from a database.

The key distinction between Figures 5-1 and 5-2 is that the data in Figure 5-1 is about a single theme or concept. It is about student grades only. The data in Figure 5-2 has multiple themes; it shows student grades, student emails, and student office visits. We can make a general rule from these examples: Lists of data involving a single theme can be stored in a spreadsheet; lists that involve data with multiple themes require a database. We will say more about this general rule as this chapter proceeds.

As you will see, databases can be more difficult to develop than spreadsheets; this difficulty causes some people to prefer to work with spreadsheets—or at least pretend to—as described in the Guide on pages 166–167.

Q2 What Is a Database?

A **database** is a self-describing collection of integrated records. To understand the terms in this definition, you first need to understand the terms illustrated in Figure 5-3. As you learned in Chapter 4, a **byte** is a character of data. In databases, bytes are grouped into **columns**, such as *Student Number* and *Student Name*. Columns are also

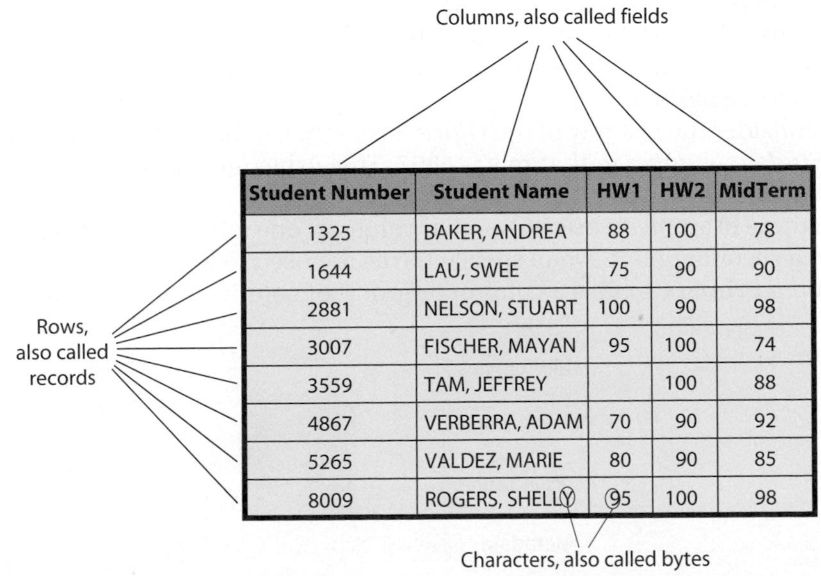

Columns, also called fields

Figure 5-3
Student Table (also called a file)

Student Number	Student Name	HW1	HW2	MidTerm
1325	BAKER, ANDREA	88	100	78
1644	LAU, SWEE	75	90	90
2881	NELSON, STUART	100	90	98
3007	FISCHER, MAYAN	95	100	74
3559	TAM, JEFFREY		100	88
4867	VERBERRA, ADAM	70	90	92
5265	VALDEZ, MARIE	80	90	85
8009	ROGERS, SHELLY	95	100	98

Rows, also called records

Characters, also called bytes

Figure 5-4
Hierarchy of Data Elements

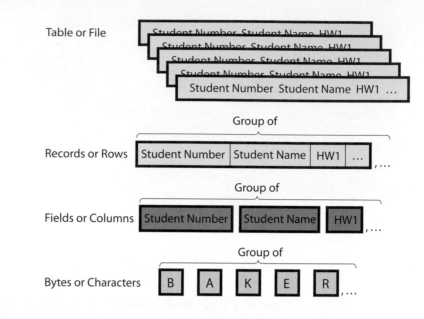

Figure 5-4
Hierarchy of Data Elements

called **fields**. Columns or fields, in turn, are grouped into **rows**, which are also called **records**. In Figure 5-3, the collection of data for all columns (*Student Number, Student Name, HW1, HW2,* and *MidTerm*) is called a *row* or a *record*. Finally, a group of similar rows or records is called a **table** or a **file**. From these definitions, you can see that there is a hierarchy of data elements, as shown in Figure 5-4.

It is tempting to continue this grouping process by saying that a database is a group of tables or files. This statement, although true, does not go far enough. As shown in Figure 5-5, a database is a collection of tables *plus* relationships among the rows in those tables, *plus* special data, called *metadata*, that describes the structure of the database. By the way, the cylindrical symbol 🛢 labeled "database" in Figure 5-5 represents a computer disk drive. It is used like this because databases are normally stored on magnetic disks.

What Are Relationships Among Rows?

Consider the terms on the left-hand side of Figure 5-5. You know what tables are. To understand what is meant by *relationships among rows in tables*, examine Figure 5-6. It shows sample data from the three tables *Email, Student,* and *Office_Visit*. Notice the column named *Student Number* in the *Email* table. That column indicates the row in *Student* to which a row of *Email* is connected. In the first row of *Email*, the *Student Number* value is 1325. This indicates that this particular email was received from the student whose *Student Number* is 1325. If you examine the *Student* table, you will see that the row for Andrea Baker has this value. Thus, the first row of the *Email* table is related to Andrea Baker.

Now consider the last row of the *Office_Visit* table at the bottom of the figure. The value of *Student Number* in that row is 4867. This value indicates that the last row in *Office_Visit* belongs to Adam Verberra.

From these examples, you can see that values in one table relate rows of that table to rows in a second table. Several special terms are used to express these ideas. A **key** (also called a **Primary Key**) is a column or group of columns that identifies a unique

Figure 5-5
Components of a Database

Tables or Files
+
Relationships
Among
Rows in Tables
+
Metadata
} = Database

Email Table

EmailNum	Date	Message	Student Number
1	2/1/2012	For homework 1, do you want us to provide notes on our references?	1325
2	3/15/2012	My group consists of Swee Lau and Stuart Nelson.	1325
3	3/15/2012	Could you please assign me to a group?	1644

Student Table

Student Number	Student Name	HW1	HW2	MidTerm
1325	BAKER, ANDREA	88	100	78
1644	LAU, SWEE	75	90	90
2881	NELSON, STUART	100	90	98
3007	FISCHER, MAYAN	95	100	74
3559	TAM, JEFFREY		100	88
4867	VERBERRA, ADAM	70	90	92
5265	VALDEZ, MARIE	80	90	85
8009	ROGERS, SHELLY	95	100	98

Office_Visit Table

VisitID	Date	Notes	Student Number
2	2/13/2012	Andrea had questions about using IS for raising barriers to entry.	1325
3	2/17/2012	Jeffrey is considering an IS major. Wanted to talk about career opportunities.	3559
4	2/17/2012	Will miss class Friday due to job conflict.	4867

Figure 5-6
Example of Relationships Among Rows

row in a table. *Student Number* is the key of the *Student* table. Given a value of *Student Number*, you can determine one and only one row in *Student*. Only one student has the number 1325, for example.

Every table must have a key. The key of the *Email* table is *EmailNum*, and the key of the *Office_Visit* table is *VisitID*. Sometimes more than one column is needed to form a unique identifier. In a table called *City*, for example, the key would consist of the combination of columns (*City, State*), because a given city name can appear in more than one state.

Student Number is not the key of the *Email* or the *Office_Visit* tables. We know that about *Email* because there are two rows in *Email* that have the *Student Number* value 1325. The value 1325 does not identify a unique row, therefore *Student Number* cannot be the key of *Email*.

Nor is *Student Number* a key of *Office_Visit*, although you cannot tell that from the data in Figure 5-6. If you think about it, however, there is nothing to prevent a student from visiting a professor more than once. If that were to happen, there would be two rows in *Office_Visit* with the same value of *Student Number*. It just happens that no student has visited twice in the limited data in Figure 5-6.

In both Email and Office_Visit, *Student Number* is a key, but it is a key of a different table, namely *Student*. Hence, the columns that fulfill a role like that of *Student Number* in the *Email* and *Office_Visit* tables are called **foreign keys**. This term is used because such columns are keys, but they are keys of a different (foreign) table than the one in which they reside.

Before we go on, databases that carry their data in the form of tables and that represent relationships using foreign keys are called **relational databases**. (The term *relational* is used because another, more formal name for a table like those we're discussing is **relation**.) You'll learn about another kind of database, or data store, in Q8 and in Case Study 5.

Metadata

Recall the definition of database: A database is a self-describing collection of integrated records. The records are integrated because, as you just learned, rows can be tied together by their key/foreign key relationship. Relationships among rows are represented in the database. But what does *self-describing* mean?

It means that a database contains, within itself, a description of its contents. Think of a library. A library is a self-describing collection of books and other materials. It is self-describing because the library contains a catalog that describes the library's contents. The same idea also pertains to a database. Databases are self-describing because they contain not only data, but also data about the data in the database.

Metadata are data that describe data. Figure 5-7 shows metadata for the *Email* table. The format of metadata depends on the software product that is processing the database. Figure 5-7 shows the metadata as they appear in Microsoft Access. Each row of the top part of this form describes a column of the *Email* table. The columns of these descriptions are *Field Name*, *Data Type*, and *Description*. *Field Name* contains the name of the column, *Data Type* shows the type of data the column may hold, and *Description* contains notes that explain the source or use of the column. As you can see, there is one row of metadata for each of the four columns of the *Email* table: *EmailNum*, *Date*, *Message*, and *Student Number*.

Metadata makes databases easy to use, for both authorized and unauthorized purposes, as described in the Ethics Guide on pages 150–151.

The bottom part of this form provides more metadata, which Access calls *Field Properties*, for each column. In Figure 5-7, the focus is on the *Date* column (note the light rectangle drawn around the *Date* row). Because the focus is on *Date* in the top pane, the details in the bottom pane pertain to the *Date* column. The Field Properties describe formats, a default value for Access to supply when a new row is created, and the constraint that a value is required for this column. It is not important for you to remember these details. Instead, just understand that metadata are data about data and that such metadata are always a part of a database.

The presence of metadata makes databases much more useful. Because of metadata, no one needs to guess, remember, or even record what is in the database. To find out what a database contains, we just look at the metadata inside the database.

Figure 5-7
Sample Metadata (in Access)

Field Name	Data Type	Description
EmailNum	AutoNumber	Primary key -- values provided by Access
Date	Date/Time	Date and time the message is recorded
Message	Memo	Text of the email
Student Number	Number	Foreign key to row in the Student Table

Field Properties

General	Lookup	
Format	Short Date	
Input Mask	99/99/0000;0;#	
Caption		
Default Value	=Now()	
Validation Rule		
Validation Text		
Required	Yes	
Indexed	No	
IME Mode	No Control	
IME Sentence Mode	None	
Smart Tags		
Text Align	General	
Show Date Picker	For dates	

A field name can be up to 64 characters long, including spaces. Press F1 for help on field names.

Q3 What Are the Components of a Database Application System?

A database, all by itself, is not very useful. The tables in Figure 5-6 have all of the data the professor wants, but the format is unwieldy. The professor wants to see the data in a form like that in Figure 5-2 and also as a formatted report. Pure database data are correct, but in raw form they are not pertinent or useful.

Figure 5-8 shows the components of a **database application system**. Such applications make database data more accessible and useful. Users employ a database application that consists of forms (like that in Figure 5-2), formatted reports, queries, and application programs. Each of these, in turn, calls on the database management system (DBMS) to process the database tables. We will first describe DBMSs and then discuss database application components.

What Is a Database Management System?

A **database management system (DBMS)** is a program used to create, process, and administer a database. As with operating systems, almost no organization develops its own DBMS. Instead, companies license DBMS products from vendors such as IBM, Microsoft, Oracle, and others. Popular DBMS products are **DB2** from IBM, **Access** and **SQL Server** from Microsoft, and **Oracle Database** from the Oracle Corporation. Another popular DBMS is **MySQL**, an open source DBMS product that is license-free for most applications.[1] Other DBMS products are available, but these five process the great bulk of databases today.

Note that a DBMS and a database are two different things. For some reason, the trade press and even some books confuse the two. A DBMS is a software program; a database is a collection of tables, relationships, and metadata. The two are very different concepts.

Creating the Database and Its Structures

Database developers use the DBMS to create tables, relationships, and other structures in the database. The form in Figure 5-7 can be used to define a new table or to modify an existing one. To create a new table, the developer just fills the new table's metadata into the form.

To modify an existing table—say, to add a new column—the developer opens the metadata form for that table and adds a new row of metadata. For example, in Figure 5-9 the developer has added a new column called *Response?*. This new column has the data type *Yes/No*, which means that the column can contain only one value—*Yes* or *No*. The professor will use this column to indicate whether he has responded to the student's email. A column can be removed by deleting its row in this table, though doing so will lose any existing data.

Processing the Database

The second function of the DBMS is to process the database. Such processing can be quite complex, but, fundamentally, the DBMS provides applications for four processing

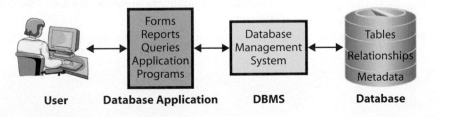

User   Database Application   DBMS   Database

Figure 5-8
Components of a Database Application System

---

[1] MySQL was supported by the MySQL company. In 2008, that company was acquired by Sun Microsystems, which was, in turn, acquired by Oracle later that year. Because MySQL is open source, Oracle does not own the source code, however.

Using MIS InClass 5   *A Group Exercise*

How Much Is a Database Worth?

Sources: © ryasick/iStockphoto.com; © dlbrova/iStockphoto.com; © Exactostock/SuperStock

FlexTime, a workout studio, realizes over 15,000 person-visits, an average of 500 visits per day. Neil, one of the two business partners, believes that the database is FlexTime's single most important asset. According to Neil:

> Take away anything else—the building, the equipment, the inventory—anything else, and we'd be back in business 6 months or less. Take away our customer database, however, and we'd have to start all over. It would take us another 8 years to get back where we are.

Why is the database so crucial? It records everything the company's customers do.

If FlexTime decides to offer an early morning kickboxing class featuring a particular trainer, it can use its database to offer that class to everyone who ever took an early morning class, a kickboxing class, or a class by that trainer. Customers receive targeted solicitations for offerings they care about

and, maybe equally important, they don't receive solicitations for those they don't care about. Clearly, the FlexTime database has value and, if it wanted to, FlexTime could sell that data.

In this exercise, you and a group of your fellow students will be asked to consider the value of a database to organizations other than FlexTime.

1. Many small business owners have found it financially advantageous to purchase their own building. As one owner remarked upon his retirement, "We did well with the business, but we made our real money by buying the building." Explain why this might be so.

2. To what extent does the dynamic you identified in your answer to item 1 pertain to databases? Do you think it likely that, in 2050, some small businesspeople will retire and make statements like, "We did well with the business, but we made our real money from the database we generated?" Why or why not? In what ways is real estate different from database data? Are these differences significant to your answer?

3. Suppose you had a national database of student data. Assume your database includes the name, email address, university, grade level, and major for each student. Name five companies that would find that data valuable, and explain how they might use it. (For example, Pizza Hut could solicit orders from students during finals week.)

4. Describe a product or service that you could develop that would induce students to provide the data in item 3.

5. Considering your answers to items 1 through 4, identify two organizations in your community that could generate a database that would potentially be more valuable than the organization itself. Consider businesses, but also think about social organizations and government offices.

   For each organization, describe the content of the database and how you could entice customers or clients to provide that data. Also, explain why the data would be valuable and who might use it.

6. Prepare a 1-minute statement of what you have learned from this exercise that you could use in a job interview to illustrate your ability to innovate the use of technology in business.

7. Present your answers to items 1–6 to the rest of the class.

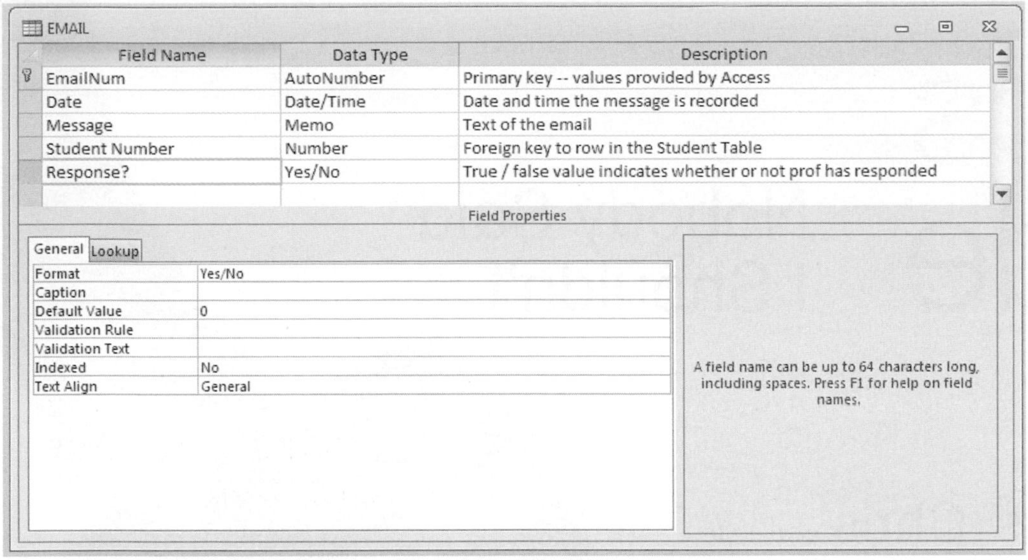

Figure 5-9
Adding a New Column
to a Table (in Access)

operations: to read, insert, modify, or delete data. These operations are requested in application calls upon the DBMS. From a form, when the user enters new or changed data, a computer program behind the form calls the DBMS to make the necessary database changes. From a Web application, a program on the client or on the server application program calls the DBMS directly to make the change.

Structured Query Language (SQL) is an international standard language for processing a database. All five of the DBMS products mentioned earlier accept and process SQL (pronounced "see-quell") statements. As an example, the following SQL statement inserts a new row into the *Student* table:

```
INSERT INTO Student
([Student Number], [Student Name], HW1, HW2, MidTerm)
VALUES
(1000, 'Franklin, Benjamin', 90, 95, 100);
```

As stated, statements like this one are issued "behind the scenes" by programs that process forms. Alternatively, they can be issued directly to the DBMS by an application program.

You do not need to understand or remember SQL language syntax. Instead, just realize that SQL is an international standard for processing a database. SQL can also be used to create databases and database structures. You will learn more about SQL if you take a database management class.

Administering the Database

A third DBMS function is to provide tools to assist in the administration of the database. Database administration involves a wide variety of activities. For example, the DBMS can be used to set up a security system involving user accounts, passwords, permissions, and limits for processing the database. To provide database security, a user must sign on using a valid user account before she can process the database.

Permissions can be limited in very specific ways. In the Student database example, it is possible to limit a particular user to reading only *Student Name* from the *Student* table. A different user could be given permission to read the entire *Student* table, but limited to update only the *HW1*, *HW2*, and *MidTerm* columns. Other users can be given still other permissions.

In addition to security, DBMS administrative functions include backing up database data, adding structures to improve the performance of database applications, removing data that are no longer wanted or needed, and similar tasks.

Ethics Guide

Nobody Said I Shouldn't

"**My name is Chris** and I do systems support for our group. I configure the new computers, set up the network, make sure the servers are operating, and so forth. I also do all of the database backups. I've always liked computers. After high school, I worked odd jobs to make some money, then I got an associate degree in information technology from our local community college.

"Anyway, as I said, I make backup copies of our databases. One weekend, I didn't have much going on, so I copied one of the database backups to a DVD and took it home. I had taken a class on database processing as part of my associate degree, and we used SQL Server (our database management system) in my class. In fact, I suppose that's part of the reason I got the job. Anyway, it was easy to restore the database on my computer at home, and I did.

"Of course, as they'll tell you in your database class, one of the big advantages of database processing is that databases have metadata, or data that describe the content of the database. So, although I didn't know what tables were in our database, I did know how to access the SQL Server metadata. I just queried a table called *sysTables* to learn the names of our tables. From there it was easy to find out what columns each table had.

"I found tables with data about orders, customers, salespeople, and so forth, and, just to amuse myself, and to see how much of the query language SQL that I could remember, I started playing around with the data. I was curious to know which order entry clerk was the best, so I started querying each clerk's order data, the total number of orders, total order amounts, things like that. It was easy to do and fun.

"I know one of the order entry clerks, Jason, pretty well, so I started looking at the data for his orders. I was just curious, and it was very simple SQL. I was just playing around with the data when I noticed something odd. All of his biggest orders were with one company, Valley Appliances, and even stranger, every one of its orders had a huge discount. I thought, well, maybe that's typical. Out of curiosity, I started looking at data for the other clerks, and very few of them had an order with Valley Appliances. But, when they did, Valley didn't get a big discount. Then I looked at the rest of Jason's orders, and none of them had much in the way of discounts, either.

"The next Friday, a bunch of us went out for a beer after work. I happened to see Jason, so I asked him about Valley Appliances and made a joke about the discounts. He asked me what I meant, and then I told him that I'd been looking at the data for fun and that I saw this odd pattern. He just laughed, said he just 'did his job,' and then changed the subject.

"Well, to make a long story short, when I got to work on Monday morning, my office was cleaned out. There was nothing there except a note telling me to go see my boss. The bottom line was, I was fired. The company also threatened that if I didn't return all of its data, I'd be in court for the next 5 years . . . things like that. I was so mad I didn't even tell them about Jason. Now my problem is that I'm out of a job, and I can't exactly use my last company for a reference." ■

Discussion Questions

1. Where did Chris go wrong?

2. Do you think it was illegal, unethical, or neither for Chris to take the database home and query the data?

3. Does the company share culpability with Chris?

4. What do you think Chris should have done upon discovering the odd pattern in Jason's orders?

5. What should the company have done before firing Chris?

6. Is it possible that someone other than Jason is involved in the arrangement with Valley Appliances? What should Chris have done in light of that possibility?

7. What should Chris do now?

8. "Metadata make databases easy to use, for both authorized and unauthorized purposes." Explain what organizations should do in light of this fact.

Category	Database Administration Task	Description
Development	Create and staff DBA function	Size of DBA group depends on size and complexity of database. Groups range from one part-time person to small group.
	Form steering committee	Consists of representatives of all user groups. Forum for community-wide discussions and decisions.
	Specify requirements	Ensure that all appropriate user input is considered.
	Validate data model	Check data model for accuracy and completeness.
	Evaluate application design	Verify that all necessary forms, reports, queries, and applications are developed. Validate design and usability of application components.
Operation	Manage processing rights and responsibilities	Determine processing rights/restrictions on each table and column.
	Manage security	Add and delete users and user groups as necessary; ensure that security system works.
	Track problems and manage resolution	Develop system to record and manage resolution of problems.
	Monitor database performance	Provide expertise/solutions for performance improvements.
	Manage DBMS	Evaluate new features and functions.
Backup and Recovery	Monitor backup procedures	Verify that database backup procedures are followed.
	Conduct training	Ensure that users and operations personnel know and understand recovery procedures.
	Manage recovery	Manage recovery process.
Adaptation	Set up request tracking system	Develop system to record and prioritize requests for change.
	Manage configuration change	Manage impact of database structure changes on applications and users.

For important databases, most organizations dedicate one or more employees to the role of **database administration**. Figure 5-10 summarizes the major responsibilities for this function. You will learn more about this topic if you take a database management course.

Q4 How Do Database Applications Make Databases More Useful?

A **database application** is a collection of forms, reports, queries, and application programs that process a database. A database may have one or more applications, and each application may have one or more users. Figure 5-11 shows three applications used at GearUp. Buyers use the first one to schedule events; operations personnel use the second to set up the graphics and auction terms and screens; and accounting personnel use the third to process event financial results. These applications have different purposes, features, and functions, but they all process the same GearUp event database.

What Are Forms, Reports, and Queries?

Figure 5-2 shows a typical database application data entry **form**, and Figure 5-12 shows a typical **report**. Data entry forms are used to read, insert, modify, and delete data. Reports show data in a structured context.

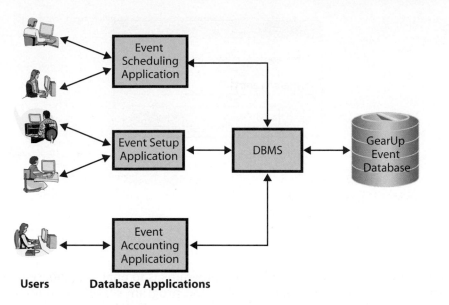

Figure 5-11
Users of Multiple Database
Applications

Recall from Chapter 1 that one of the definitions of information is "data presented in a meaningful context." The professor can create information from this report because it shows the student data in a context that will be meaningful to the professor. Some reports, like the one in Figure 5-12, also compute values as they present the data. An example is the computation of *Mid Term Total* in Figure 5-12.

DBMS programs provide comprehensive and robust features for querying database data. For example, suppose the professor who uses the Student database remembers that one of the students referred to the topic *barriers to entry* in an office visit, but cannot remember which student or when. If there are hundreds of students and visits recorded in the database, it will take some effort and time for the professor to search through all office visit records to find that event. The DBMS, however, can find any such record quickly. Figure 5-13 (a) (on the next page) shows a **query** form in which the professor types in the keyword for which she is looking. Figure 5-13 (b) shows the results of the query.

Why Are Database Application Programs Needed?

Forms, reports, and queries work well for standard functions. However, most applications have unique requirements that a simple form, report, or query cannot meet. For example, in an order-entry application what should be done if only a portion of a customer's request can be met? If someone wants 10 widgets and we only have 3 in stock, should a backorder for 7 more be generated automatically? Or, should some other action be taken?

Application programs process logic that is specific to a given business need. In the Student database, an example application is one that assigns grades at the end of the term. If the professor grades on a curve, the application reads the breakpoints for each grade from a form, and then processes each row in the *Student* table, allocating a grade based on the break points and the total number of points earned.

Student Name	Student Number	HW1	HW2	MidTerm	Mid Term Total	Date	Message
BAKER, ANDREA	1325	88	100	78	266		
						2/1/2010	For homework 1, do you want us to provide notes on our references?
						3/15/2010	My group consists of Swee Lau and Stuart Nelson.
LAU, SWEE	1644	75	90	90	255		
						3/15/2010	Could you please assign me to a group?

Student Report with Emails

Student Report with Emails

Friday, March 05, 2010   Page 1 of 1

Figure 5-12
Example of a Student Report

Figure 5-13a
Sample Query Form Used
to Enter Phrase for Search

Enter Parameter Value

Enter words or phrase for search:

barriers to entry|

OK   Cancel

Figure 5-13b
Sample Query Results
of Query Operation

Office Visits Keyword Query

Student Name	Date	Notes
BAKER, ANDREA	2/13/2012	Andrea had questions about using IS for raising barriers to entry.

Record: 1 of 1   No Filter   Search

Another important use of application programs is to enable database processing over the Internet. For this use, the application program serves as an intermediary between the Web server and the database. The application program responds to events, such as when a user presses a submit button; it also reads, inserts, modifies, and deletes database data.

For example, Figure 5-14 shows four different database application programs running on a Web server computer. Users with browsers connect to the Web server via the Internet. The Web server directs user requests to the appropriate application program. Each program then processes the database as necessary. You will learn more about Web-enabled databases in the next chapter.

Multi-User Processing

Figures 5-11 and 5-14 show multiple users processing the database. Such **multi-user processing** is common, but it does pose unique problems that you, as a future manager, should know about. To understand the nature of those problems, consider the following scenario.

Two GearUp customers, Andrea and Jeffrey, are both attempting to buy the last 500 soccer balls available for a particular event. Andrea uses her browser to access the GearUp Web site and finds that 500 are available. She places all of them in her shopping cart. She doesn't know it, but when she opened the event form she invoked an application on GearUp's server that read the database to find that 500 soccer balls are available. Before she checks out, she takes a moment to verify with her supervisor that she should buy all 500.

Meanwhile, Jeffrey uses his browser and also finds that 500 soccer balls are available because his browser activates that same application that reads the database and finds (because Andrea has not yet checked out) that 500 are available. He places 500 in his cart and checks out.

Figure 5-14
Four Application Programs
on a Web Server Computer

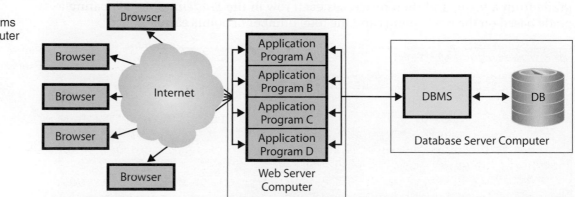

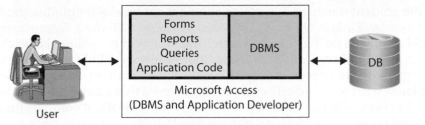

Figure 5-15
Personal Database System

Meanwhile, Andrea learns that she should buy all 500, so she checks out. Clearly, we have a problem. Both Andrea and Jeffrey have purchased the same 500 soccer balls. One of them is going to be disappointed.

This problem, known as the **lost-update problem**, exemplifies one of the special characteristics of multi-user database processing. To prevent this problem, some type of locking must be used to coordinate the activities of users who know nothing about one another. Locking brings its own set of problems, however, and those problems must be addressed as well. We will not delve further into this topic here, however.

Realize from this example that converting a single-user database to a multi-user database requires more than simply connecting another computer. The logic of the underlying application processing needs to be adjusted as well.

Be aware of possible data conflicts when you manage business activities that involve multi-user processing. If you find inaccurate results that seem not to have a cause, you may be experiencing multi-user data conflicts. Contact your IS department for assistance.

Enterprise DBMS Versus Personal DBMS

DBMS products fall into two broad categories. **Enterprise DBMS** products process large organizational and workgroup databases. These products support many, possibly thousands, of users and many different database applications. Such DBMS products support 24/7 operations and can manage databases that span dozens of different magnetic disks with hundreds of gigabytes or more of data. IBM's DB2, Microsoft's SQL Server, and Oracle's Oracle Database are examples of enterprise DBMS products.

Personal DBMS products are designed for smaller, simpler database applications. Such products are used for personal or small workgroup applications that involve fewer than 100 users, and normally fewer than 15. In fact, the great bulk of databases in this category have only a single user. The professor's Student database is an example of a database that is processed by a personal DBMS product.

In the past, there were many personal DBMS products—Paradox, dBase, R:base, and FoxPro. Microsoft put these products out of business when they developed Access and included it in the Microsoft Office suite. Today, about the only remaining personal DBMS is Microsoft Access.

To avoid one point of confusion for you in the future, the separation of application programs and the DBMS shown in Figure 5-11 is true only for enterprise DBMS products. Microsoft Access includes features and functions for application processing along with the DBMS itself. For example, Access has a form generator and a report generator. Thus, as shown in Figure 5-15, Access is both a DBMS *and* an application development product.

Q5 How Are Data Models Used for Database Development?

In Chapter 10, we will describe the process for developing information systems in detail. However, business professionals have such a critical role in the development of database applications that we need to anticipate part of that discussion here by introducing two topics—data modeling and database design.

Because the design of the database depends entirely on how users view their business environment, user involvement is critical for database development. Think about the Student database. What data should it contain? Possibilities are: *Students, Classes, Grades, Emails, Office_Visits, Majors, Advisers, Student_Organizations*—the list could go on and on. Further, how much detail should be included in each? Should the database include campus addresses? Home addresses? Billing addresses?

In fact, there are dozens of possibilities, and the database developers do not and cannot know what to include. They do know, however, that a database must include all the data necessary for the users to perform their jobs. Ideally, it contains that amount of data and no more. So, during database development the developers must rely on the users to tell them what to include in the database.

Database structures can be complex, in some cases very complex. So, before building the database the developers construct a logical representation of database data called a **data model**. It describes the data and relationships that will be stored in the database. It is akin to a blueprint. Just as building architects create a blueprint before they start building, so, too, database developers create a data model before they start designing the database.

Figure 5-16 summarizes the database development process. Interviews with users lead to database requirements, which are summarized in a data model. Once the users have approved (validated) the data model, it is transformed into a database design. That design is then implemented into database structures. We will consider data modeling and database design briefly in the next two sections. Again, your goal should be to learn the process so that you can be an effective user representative for a development effort.

For a philosophical perspective on data models, see the Guide on pages 168–169.

What Is the Entity-Relationship Data Model?

The **entity-relationship (E-R) data model** is a tool for constructing data models. Developers use it to describe the content of a data model by defining the things (*entities*) that will be stored in the database and the *relationships* among those entities. A second, less popular, tool for data modeling is the **Unified Modeling Language (UML)**. We will not describe that tool here. However, if you learn how to interpret E-R models, with a bit of study you will be able to understand UML models as well.

Entities

An **entity** is some thing that the users want to track. Examples of entities are *Order, Customer, Salesperson,* and *Item*. Some entities represent a physical object, such as *Item* or *Salesperson*; others represent a logical construct or transaction, such as *Order* or *Contract*. For reasons beyond this discussion, entity names are always singular. We use *Order*, not *Orders*; *Salesperson*, not *Salespersons*.

Entities have **attributes** that describe characteristics of the entity. Example attributes of *Order* are *OrderNumber, OrderDate, SubTotal, Tax, Total,* and so forth. Example attributes of *Salesperson* are *SalespersonName, Email, Phone,* and so forth.

Entities have an **identifier**, which is an attribute (or group of attributes) whose value is associated with one and only one entity instance. For example, *OrderNumber* is an identifier of *Order*, because only one *Order* instance has a given value of *OrderNumber*. For the same reason, *CustomerNumber* is an identifier of *Customer*. If each member of the sales staff has a unique name, then *SalespersonName* is an identifier of *Salesperson*.

Figure 5-16
Database Development
Process

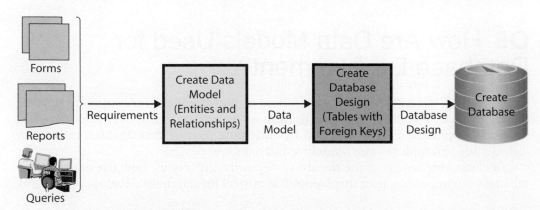

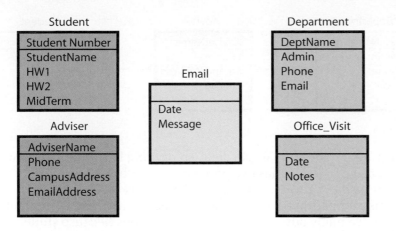

Figure 5-17
Student Data Model Entities

Before we continue, consider that last sentence. Is the salesperson's name unique among the sales staff? Both now and in the future? Who decides the answer to such a question? Only the users know whether this is true; the database developers cannot know. This example underlines why it is important for you to be able to interpret data models, because only users like you will know for sure.

Figure 5-17 shows examples of entities for the Student database. Each entity is shown in a rectangle. The name of the entity is just above the rectangle, and the identifier is shown in a section at the top of the entity. Entity attributes are shown in the remainder of the rectangle. In Figure 5-17, the *Adviser* entity has an identifier called *AdviserName* and the attributes *Phone*, *CampusAddress*, and *EmailAddress*.

Observe that the entities *Email* and *Office_Visit* do not have an identifier. Unlike *Student* or *Adviser*, the users do not have an attribute that identifies a particular email. We *could* make one up. For example, we could say that the identifier of *Email* is *EmailNumber*, but if we do so we are not modeling how the users view their world. Instead, we are forcing something onto the users. Be aware of this possibility when you review data models about your business. Do not allow the database developers to create something in the data model that is not part of your business world.

Relationships

Entities have **relationships** to each other. An *Order*, for example, has a relationship to a *Customer* entity and also to a *Salesperson* entity. In the Student database, a *Student* has a relationship to an *Adviser*, and an *Adviser* has a relationship to a *Department*.

Figure 5-18 shows sample *Department*, *Adviser*, and *Student* entities and their relationships. For simplicity, this figure shows just the identifier of the entities and not

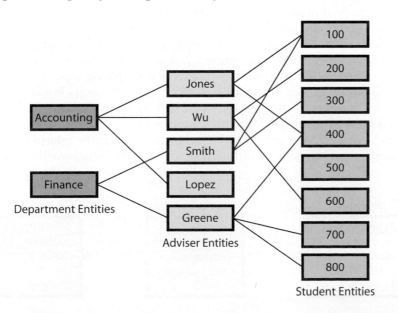

Figure 5-18
Example of Department, Adviser, and Student Entities and Relationships

Figure 5-19
Sample Relationships
Version 1

the other attributes. For this sample data, *Accounting* has three professors—Jones, Wu, and Lopez—and *Finance* has two professors—Smith and Greene.

The relationship between *Advisers* and *Students* is a bit more complicated, because in this example an adviser is allowed to advise many students, and a student is allowed to have many advisers. Perhaps this happens because students can have multiple majors. In any case, note that Professor Jones advises students 100 and 400 and that student 100 is advised by both Professors Jones and Smith.

Diagrams like the one in Figure 5-18 are too cumbersome for use in database design discussions. Instead, database designers use diagrams called **entity-relationship (E-R) diagrams**. Figure 5-19 shows an E-R diagram for the data in Figure 5-18. In this figure, all of the entities of one type are represented by a single rectangle. Thus, there are rectangles for the *Department*, *Adviser*, and *Student* entities. Attributes are shown as before in Figure 5-17.

Additionally, a line is used to represent a relationship between two entities. Notice the line between *Department* and *Adviser*, for example. The forked lines on the right side of that line signify that a department may have more than one adviser. The little lines, which are referred to as **crow's feet**, are shorthand for the multiple lines between *Department* and *Adviser* in Figure 5-18. Relationships like this one are called **1:N**, or **one-to-many relationships**, because one department can have many advisers, but an adviser has at most one department.

Now examine the line between *Adviser* and *Student*. Notice the short lines that appear at each end of the line. These lines are the crow's feet, and this notation signifies that an adviser can be related to many students and that a student can be related to many advisers, which is the situation in Figure 5-18. Relationships like this one are called **N:M**, or **many-to-many relationships**, because one adviser can have many students and one student can have many advisers.

Students sometimes find the notation N:M confusing. Interpret the N and M to mean that a variable number, greater than one, is allowed on each side of the relationship. Such a relationship is not written *N:N*, because that notation would imply that there are the same number of entities on each side of the relationship, which is not necessarily true. *N:M* means that more than one entity is allowed on each side of the relationship and that the number of entities on each side can be different.

Figure 5-20 shows the same entities with different assumptions. Here, advisers may advise in more than one department, but a student may have only one adviser, representing a policy that students may not have multiple majors.

Which, if either, of these versions is correct? Only the users know. These alternatives illustrate the kinds of questions you will need to answer when a database designer asks you to check a data model for correctness.

Figures 5-19 and 5-20 are typical examples of an entity-relationship diagram. Unfortunately, there are several different styles of entity-relationship diagrams. This

Figure 5-20
Sample Relationships
Version 2

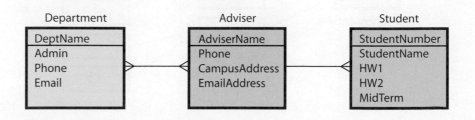

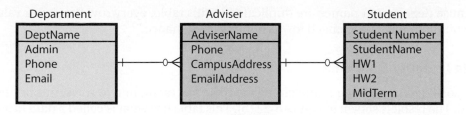

one is called, not surprisingly, a **crow's-foot diagram** version. You may learn other versions if you take a database management class.

The crow's-foot notation shows the maximum number of entities that can be involved in a relationship. Accordingly, they are called the relationship's **maximum cardinality**. Common examples of maximum cardinality are 1:N, N:M, and 1:1 (not shown).

Another important question is, "What is the minimum number of entities required in the relationship?" Must an adviser have a student to advise, and must a student have an adviser? Constraints on minimum requirements are called **minimum cardinalities**.

Figure 5-21 presents a third version of this E-R diagram that shows both maximum and minimum cardinalities. The vertical bar on a line means that at least one entity of that type is required. The small oval means that the entity is optional; the relationship *need not* have an entity of that type.

Thus, in Figure 5-21 a department is not required to have a relationship to any adviser, but an adviser is required to belong to a department. Similarly, an adviser is not required to have a relationship to a student, but a student is required to have a relationship to an adviser. Note, also, that the maximum cardinalities in Figure 5-21 have been changed so that both are 1:N.

Is the model in Figure 5-21 a good one? It depends on the policy of the university. Again, only the users know for sure.

Q6 How Is a Data Model Transformed into a Database Design?

Database design is the process of converting a data model into tables, relationships, and data constraints. The database design team transforms entities into tables and expresses relationships by defining foreign keys. Database design is a complicated subject; as with data modeling, it occupies weeks in a database management class. In this section, however, we will introduce two important database design concepts: normalization and the representation of two kinds of relationships. The first concept is a foundation of database design, and the second will help you understand important design considerations.

Normalization

Normalization is the process of converting a poorly structured table into two or more well-structured tables. A table is such a simple construct that you may wonder how one could possibly be poorly structured. In truth, there are many ways that tables can be malformed—so many, in fact, that researchers have published hundreds of papers on this topic alone.

Consider the *Employee* table in Figure 5-22 (a) on the next page. It lists employee names, hire dates, email addresses, and the name and number of the department in which the employee works. This table seems innocent enough. But consider what happens when the Accounting department changes its name to Accounting and Finance.

Because department names are duplicated in this table, every row that has a value of "Accounting" must be changed to "Accounting and Finance."

Data Integrity Problems

Suppose the Accounting name change is correctly made in two rows, but not in the third. The result is shown in Figure 5-22 (b). This table has what is called a **data integrity problem**: Some rows indicate that the name of Department 100 is "Accounting and Finance," and another row indicates that the name of Department 100 is "Accounting."

This problem is easy to spot in this small table. But consider a table like the *Customer* table in the Amazon.com database or the eBay database. Those databases may have millions of rows. Once a table that large develops serious data integrity problems, months of labor will be required to remove them.

Data integrity problems are serious. A table that has data integrity problems will produce incorrect and inconsistent information. Users will lose confidence in the data, and the system will develop a poor reputation. Information systems with poor reputations become serious burdens to the organizations that use them.

Normalizing for Data Integrity

The data integrity problem can occur only if data are duplicated. Because of this, one easy way to eliminate the problem is to eliminate the duplicated data. We can do this by transforming the table in Figure 5-22 into two tables, as shown in Figure 5-23. Here, the name of the department is stored just once; therefore no data inconsistencies can occur.

Of course, to produce an employee report that includes the department name, the two tables in Figure 5-23 will need to be joined back together. Because such joining of tables is common, DBMS products have been programmed to perform it efficiently, but it still requires work. From this example, you can see a trade-off in database design: Normalized tables eliminate data duplication, but they can be slower to process. Dealing with such trade-offs is an important consideration in database design.

The general goal of normalization is to construct tables such that every table has a *single* topic or theme. In good writing, every paragraph should have a single theme. This is true of databases as well; every table should have a single theme. The problem with the table in Figure 5-22 is that it has two independent themes: employees and departments. The way to correct the problem is to split the table into two tables, each

Figure 5-22
A Poorly Designed
Employee Table

Employee

Name	HireDate	Email	DeptNo	DeptName
Jones	Feb 1, 2010	Jones@ourcompany.com	100	Accounting
Smith	Dec 3, 2012	Smith@ourcompany.com	200	Marketing
Chau	March 7, 2012	Chau@ourcompany.com	100	Accounting
Greene	July 17, 2011	Greene@ourcompany.com	100	Accounting

(a) Table Before Update

Employee

Name	HireDate	Email	DeptNo	DeptName
Jones	Feb 1, 2010	Jones@ourcompany.com	100	Accounting and Finance
Smith	Dec 3, 2012	Smith@ourcompany.com	200	Marketing
Chau	March 7, 2012	Chau@ourcompany.com	100	Accounting and Finance
Greene	July 17, 2011	Greene@ourcompany.com	100	Accounting

(b) Table with Incomplete Update

Employee

Name	HireDate	Email	DeptNo
Jones	Feb 1, 2010	Jones@ourcompany.com	100
Smith	Dec 3, 2012	Smith@ourcompany.com	200
Chau	March 7, 2012	Chau@ourcompany.com	100
Greene	July 17, 2011	Greene@ourcompany.com	100

Department

DeptNo	DeptName
100	Accounting
200	Marketing
300	Information Systems

Figure 5-23
Two Normalized Tables

with its own theme. In this case, we create an *Employee* table and a *Department* table, as shown in Figure 5-23.

As mentioned, there are dozens of ways that tables can be poorly formed. Database practitioners classify tables into various **normal forms** according to the kinds of problems they have. Transforming a table into a normal form to remove duplicated data and other problems is called *normalizing* the table.[2] Thus, when you hear a database designer say, "Those tables are not normalized," she does not mean that the tables have irregular, not-normal data. Instead, she means that the tables have a format that could cause data integrity problems.

Summary of Normalization

As a future user of databases, you do not need to know the details of normalization. Instead, understand the general principle that every normalized (well-formed) table has one and only one theme. Further, tables that are not normalized are subject to data integrity problems.

Be aware, too, that normalization is just one criterion for evaluating database designs. Because normalized designs can be slower to process, database designers sometimes choose to accept non-normalized tables. The best design depends on the users' processing requirements.

Representing Relationships

Figure 5-24 shows the steps involved in transforming a data model into a relational database design. First, the database designer creates a table for each entity. The identifier of the entity becomes the key of the table. Each attribute of the entity becomes a column of the table. Next, the resulting tables are normalized so that each table has a single theme. Once that has been done, the next step is to represent relationship among those tables.

- Represent each entity with a table
  - Entity identifier becomes table key
  - Entity attributes become table columns
- Normalize tables as necessary
- Represent relationships
  - Use foreign keys
  - Add additional tables for N:M relationships

Figure 5-24
Transforming a Data Model into a Database Design

---

[2] See David Kroenke and David Auer, *Database Processing*, 12th ed. (Upper Saddle River, NJ: Prentice Hall, 2012) for more information.

For example, consider the E-R diagram in Figure 5-25 (a). The *Adviser* entity has a 1:N relationship to the *Student* entity. To create the database design, we construct a table for *Adviser* and a second table for *Student*, as shown in Figure 5-25 (b). The key of the *Adviser* table is *AdviserName*, and the key of the *Student* table is *StudentNumber*.

Further, the *EmailAddress* attribute of the *Adviser* entity becomes the *EmailAddress* column of the *Adviser* table, and the *StudentName* and *MidTerm* attributes of the *Student* entity become the *StudentName* and *MidTerm* columns of the *Student* table.

The next task is to represent the relationship. Because we are using the relational model, we know that we must add a foreign key to one of the two tables. The possibilities are: (1) place the foreign key *StudentNumber* in the *Adviser* table or (2) place the foreign key *AdviserName* in the *Student* table.

The correct choice is to place *AdviserName* in the *Student* table, as shown in Figure 5-25 (c). To determine a student's adviser, we just look into the *AdviserName* column of that student's row. To determine the adviser's students, we search the *AdviserName* column in the *Student* table to determine which rows have that adviser's

Figure 5-25
Representing a
1:N Relationship

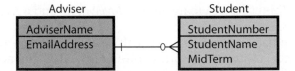

(a) 1:N Relationship Between Adviser and Student Entities

Adviser Table—Key is AdviserName

AdviserName	EmailAddress
Jones	Jones@myuniv.edu
Choi	Choi@myuniv.edu
Jackson	Jackson@myuniv.edu

Student Table—Key is StudentNumber

StudentNumber	StudentName	MidTerm
100	Lisa	90
200	Jennie	85
300	Jason	82
400	Terry	95

(b) Creating a Table for Each Entity

Adviser Table—Key is AdviserName

AdviserName	EmailAddress
Jones	Jones@myuniv.edu
Choi	Choi@myuniv.edu
Jackson	Jackson@myuniv.edu

Foreign Key
Column
Represents
Relationship

Student—Key is StudentNumber

StudentNumber	StudentName	MidTerm	AdviserName
100	Lisa	90	Jackson
200	Jennie	85	Jackson
300	Jason	82	Choi
400	Terry	95	Jackson

(c) Using the *AdviserName* Foreign Key to Represent the 1:N Relationship

name. If a student changes advisers, we simply change the value in the *AdviserName* column. Changing *Jackson* to *Jones* in the first row, for example, will assign student 100 to Professor Jones.

For this data model, placing *StudentNumber* in *Adviser* would be incorrect. If we were to do that, we could assign only one student to an adviser. There is no place to assign a second adviser.

This strategy for placing foreign keys will not work for N:M relationships, however. Consider the data model in Figure 5-26 (a); here advisers and students have a many-to-many relationship. An adviser may have many students, and a student may have multiple advisers (for multiple majors).

The foreign key strategy we used for the 1:N data model will not work here. To see why, examine Figure 5-26 (b). If student 100 has more than one adviser, there is no place to record second or subsequent advisers.

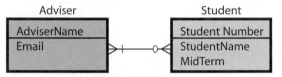

(a) N:M Relationship Between Adviser and Student

Figure 5-26
Representing an N:M
Relationship

Adviser—Key is AdviserName

AdviserName	Email
Jones	Jones@myuniv.edu
Choi	Choi@myuniv.edu
Jackson	Jackson@myuniv.edu

No room to place
second or third
AdviserName

Student—Key is StudentNumber

StudentNumber	StudentName	MidTerm	AdviserName
100	Lisa	90	Jackson
200	Jennie	85	Jackson
300	Jason	82	Choi
400	Terry	95	Jackson

(b) Incorrect Representation of N:M Relationship

Adviser—Key is AdviserName

AdviserName	Email
Jones	Jones@myuniv.edu
Choi	Choi@myuniv.edu
Jackson	Jackson@myuniv.edu

Student—Key is StudentNumber

StudentNumber	StudentName	MidTerm
100	Lisa	90
200	Jennie	85
300	Jason	82
400	Terry	95

Adviser_Student_Intersection

AdviserName	StudentNumber
Jackson	100
Jackson	200
Choi	300
Jackson	400
Choi	100
Jones	100

Student 100 has
three advisers.

(c) Adviser_Student_Intersection Table Represents the N:M Relationship

To represent an N:M relationship, we need to create a third table, as shown in Figure 5-26 (c). The third table has two columns, *AdviserName* and *StudentNumber*. Each row of the table means that the given adviser advises the student with the given number.

As you can imagine, there is a great deal more to database design than we have presented here. Still, this section should give you an idea of the tasks that need to be accomplished to create a database. You should also realize that the database design is a direct consequence of decisions made in the data model. If the data model is wrong, the database design will be wrong as well.

Q7 What Is the Users' Role in the Development of Databases?

As stated, a database is a model of how the users view their business world. This means that the users are the final judges as to what data the database should contain and how the records in that database should be related to one another.

The easiest time to change the database structure is during the data modeling stage. Changing a relationship from one-to-many to many-to-many in a data model is simply a matter of changing the 1:N notation to N:M. However, once the database has been constructed, loaded with data, and application forms, reports, queries, and application programs have been created, changing a one-to-many relationship to many-to-many means weeks of work.

You can glean some idea of why this might be true by contrasting Figure 5-25 (c) with Figure 5-26 (c). Suppose that instead of having just a few rows, each table has thousands of rows; in that case, transforming the database from one format to the other involves considerable work. Even worse, however, is that someone must change application components as well. For example, if students have at most one adviser, then a single text box can be used to enter *AdviserName*. If students can have multiple advisers, then a multiple-row table will need to be used to enter *AdviserName* and a program will need to be written to store the values of *AdviserName* into the *Adviser_Student_Intersection* table. There are dozens of other consequences, consequences that will translate into wasted labor and wasted expense.

Thus, *user review of the data model is crucial.* When a database is developed for your use, you must carefully review the data model. If you do not understand any aspect of it, you should ask for clarification until you do. *Entities must contain all of the data you and your employees need to do your jobs, and relationships must accurately reflect your view of the business.* If the data model is wrong, the database will be designed incorrectly, and the applications will be difficult to use, if not worthless. Do not proceed unless the data model is accurate.

As a corollary, when asked to review a data model, take that review seriously. Devote the time necessary to perform a thorough review. Any mistakes you miss will come back to haunt you, and by then the cost of correction may be very high with regard to both time and expense. This brief introduction to data modeling shows why databases can be more difficult to develop than spreadsheets.

Q8 2022?

With ever cheaper data storage and data communications, we can be sure that the volume of database data will continue to grow, probably exponentially, through 2022. All that data contains patterns that can be used to conceive information to help businesses and organizations achieve their strategies, as you'll learn when you study business intelligence in Chapter 9. Furthermore, as databases become bigger and bigger, they're more attractive as targets for theft or mischief, a subject you'll consider in Chapter 12.

Setting these ideas aside, what else can we imagine for database technology by 2022? Something most unusual has occurred over the past 5 years that may portend a major change. Amazon.com determined that relational database technology wouldn't meet its needs, and it developed a nonrelational data store called **Dynamo**.[3] Meanwhile, for many of the same reasons, Google developed a nonrelational data store called **Bigtable**.[4] Facebook took concepts from both of these systems and developed a third nonrelational data store called **Cassandra**.[5] In 2008, Facebook turned Cassandra over to the open source community, and now Apache has dubbed it a Top-level Product (TLP), which is the height of respectability among open source projects. Such nonrelational databases have come to be called **NoSQL databases**, where NoSQL means nonrelational databases that support very high transaction rates processing relatively simple data structures, replicated on many servers in the cloud. NoSQL is not the best term; *NotRelationalDatabases* would have been better, but the die has been cast. You can learn more about the rationale for NoSQL products and some of their most intriguing features in Case Study 5, page 174.

Consider these developments in light of the software industry. None of these NoSQL systems were developed by a software vendor such as Microsoft or Oracle. They were developed by hugely successful companies that had business requirements unmet by relational DBMS products. Most companies would not be able to afford the costs and risks of such development, but these very rich companies employed highly skilled technical personnel, and they could and did build them. And, having done so, they turned that software over to the open source community, or at least Facebook did in the case of Cassandra.

Will this become a trend for the server software business? Will Microsoft and Oracle and other DBMS vendors lose their market to open source products? Will they follow IBM's path? Become less of a vendor of software and more a seller of services supporting open source software like Cassandra?

What about inside Microsoft? SharePoint uses SQL Server to store its data, but should it? Wouldn't SharePoint run better, especially in the cloud, if it used a NoSQL product?

The relational model and its products have been the workhorse of the computer industry more than 30 years. Something important is afoot; by 2022, the database world will look much different. Let the DBMS vendors beware!

---

[3] Werner Vogel, "Amazon's Dynamo," All Things Distributed blog, October 2, 2007. Available at www.allthingsdistributed.com/2007/10/amazons_dynamo.html (accessed June 2011).
[4] Fay Chang, Jeffrey Dean, Sanjay Ghemawat, Wilson C. Hsieh, Deborah A. Wallach, Mike Burrows, Tushar Chandra, Andrew Fikes, and Robert E. Gruber, "Bigtable: A Distributed Storage System for Structured Data," OSDI 2006, Seventh Symposium on Operating System Design and Implementation, Seattle, WA, November 2006. Available at http://labs.google.com/papers/bigtable.html (accessed June 2011).
[5] Jonathan Ellis, "Cassandra: Open Source Bigtable + Dynamo." Available at www.slideshare.net/jbellis/cassandra-open-source-bigtable-dynamo (accessed June 2011).

Guide

No, Thanks, I'll Use a Spreadsheet

"**I'm not buying** all this stuff about databases. I've tried them and they're a pain—way too complicated to set up, and most of the time, a spreadsheet works just as well. We had one project at the car dealership that seemed pretty simple to me: We wanted to keep track of customers and the models of used cars they were interested in. Then, when we got a car on the lot, we could query the database to see who wanted a car of that type and generate a letter to them.

"It took forever to build that system, and it never did work right. We hired three different consultants, and the last one finally did get it to work. But it was so complicated to produce the letters. You had to query the data in Access to generate some kind of file, then open Word, then go through some mumbo jumbo using mail/merge to cause Word to find the letter and put all the Access data in the right spot. I once printed over two hundred letters and had the name in the address spot and the address in the name spot and no date. And it took me over an hour to do even that. I just wanted to do the query and push a button to get my letters generated. I gave up. Some of the salespeople are still trying to use it, but not me.

"No, unless you are getting billions in government bailouts, I wouldn't mess with a database. You have to have professional IS people to create it and keep it running. Besides, I don't really want to share my data with anyone. I work pretty hard to develop my client list. Why would I want to give it away?

"My motto is, 'Keep it simple.' I use an Excel spreadsheet with four columns: Name, Phone Number, Car Interests, and Notes. When I get a new customer, I enter the name and phone number, and then I put the make and model of cars they like in the Car Interests column. Anything else that I think is important I put in the Notes column—extra phone numbers, address data if I have it, email addresses, spouse names, last time I called them, etc. The system isn't fancy, but it works fine.

"When I want to find something, I use Excel's Data Filter. I can usually get what I need. Of course, I still can't send form letters, but it really doesn't matter. I get most of my sales using the phone, anyway." ■

Discussion Questions

1. To what extent do you agree with the opinions presented here? To what extent are the concerns expressed here justified? To what extent might they be due to other factors?

2. What problems do you see with the way that the car salesperson stores address data? What will he have to do if he ever does want to send a letter or an email to all of his customers?

3. From his comments, how many different themes are there in his data? What does this imply about his ability to keep his data in a spreadsheet?

4. Does the concern about not sharing data relate to whether or not he uses a database?

5. Apparently, management at the car dealership allows the salespeople to keep their contact data in whatever format they want. If you were management, how would you justify this policy? What disadvantages are there to this policy?

6. Suppose you manage the sales representatives, and you decide to require all of them to use a database to keep track of customers and customer car interest data. How would you sell your decision to this salesperson?

7. Given the limited information in this scenario, do you think a database or a spreadsheet is a better solution?

Source: © Exactostock/SuperStock.

Guide
Immanuel Kant, Data Modeler

Only the users can say whether a data model accurately reflects their business environment. What happens when the users disagree among themselves? What if one user says orders have a single salesperson but another says that sales teams produce some orders? Who is correct?

It's tempting to say, "The correct model is the one that better represents the real world." The problem with this statement is that data models do not model "the real world." A data model is simply a model of what the data modeler perceives. This very important point can be difficult to understand; but if you do understand it, you will save many hours in data model validation meetings and be a much better data modeling team member.

The German philosopher Immanuel Kant reasoned that what we perceive as reality is based on our perceptive apparatus. That which we perceive he called phenomena. Our perceptions, such as of light and sound, are processed by our brains and made meaningful. But we do not and cannot know whether the images we create from the perceptions have anything to do with what might or might not really be.

Kant used the term *noumenal world* to refer to the essence of "things in themselves"—to whatever it is out there that gives rise to our perceptions and images. He used the term *phenomenal world* to refer to what we humans perceive and construct.

It is easy to confuse the noumenal world with the phenomenal world, because we share the phenomenal world with other humans. All of us have the same mental apparatus, and we all make the same constructions. If you ask your roommate to hand you the toothpaste, she hands you the toothpaste, not a hairbrush. But the fact that we share this mutual view does not mean that the mutual view describes in any way what is truly out there. Dogs construct a world based on smells, and orca whales construct a world based on sounds. What the "real world" is to a dog, a whale, and a human are completely different. All of this means that we cannot ever justify a data model as a "better representation of the real world." Nothing that humans can do represents the real, noumenal world. A data model, therefore, is a model of a human's model of what appears to be "out there." For example, a model of a salesperson is a model of the model that humans make of salespeople.

To return to the question that we started with, what do we do when people disagree about what should be in a data model? First, realize that anyone attempting to justify her data model as a better representation of the real world is saying, quite arrogantly, "The way I think of the world is the way that counts." Second, in times of disagreement we must ask the question, "How well does the data model fit the mental models of the people who are going to use the system?" The person who is constructing the data model may think the model under construction is a weird way of viewing the world, but that is not the point. The only valid point is whether it reflects how the users view their world. Will it enable the users to do their jobs? ∎

Discussion Questions

1. What does a data model represent?

2. Explain why it is easy for humans to confuse the phenomenal world with the noumenal world.

3. If someone were to say to you, "My model is a better model of the real world," how would you respond?

4. In your own words, how should you proceed when two people disagree on what is to be included in a data model?

Active Review

Use this Active Review to verify that you understand the ideas and concepts that answer the chapter's study questions.

Q1 What is the purpose of a database?

State the purpose of a database. Explain the circumstances in which a database is preferred to a spreadsheet. Describe the key difference between Figures 5-1 and 5-2.

Q2 What is a database?

Define the term *database*. Explain the hierarchy of data and name three elements of a database. Define *metadata*. Using the example of *Student* and *Office_Visit* tables, show how relationships among rows are represented in a database. Define the terms *primary key*, *foreign key*, and *relational database*.

Q3 What are the components of a database application system?

Explain why a database, by itself, is not very useful to business users. Name the components of a database application system and sketch their relationship. Explain the acronym DBMS and name its functions. List five popular DBMS products. Explain the difference between a DBMS and a database. Summarize the functions of a DBMS. Define *SQL*. Describe the major functions of database administration.

Q4 How do database applications make databases more useful?

Name and describe the components of a database application. Explain the need for application programs. For multi-user processing, describe one way in which one user's work can interfere with another's. Explain why multi-user database processing involves more than just connecting another computer to the network. Define two broad categories of DBMS and explain their differences.

Q5 How are data models used for database development?

Explain why user involvement is critical during database development. Describe the function of a data model. Sketch the database development process. Define *E-R model, entity, relationship, attribute,* and *identifier*. Give an example, other than one in this text, of an E-R diagram. Define *maximum cardinality* and *minimum cardinality*. Give an example of three maximum cardinalities and two minimum cardinalities. Explain the notation in Figures 5-18 and 5-19.

Q6 How is a data model transformed into a database design?

Name the three components of a database design. Define *normalization* and explain why it is important. Define *data integrity problem* and describe its consequences. Give an example of a table with data integrity problems and show how it can be normalized into two or more tables that do not have such problems. Describe two steps in transforming a data model into a database design. Using an example not in this chapter, show how 1:N and N:M relationships are represented in a relational database.

Q7 What is the users' role in the development of databases?

Describe the users' role in the database development. Explain why it is easier and cheaper to change a data model than to change an existing database. Use the examples of Figures 5-25 (c) and 5-26(c) in your answer. Describe two criteria for judging a data model. Explain why it is important to devote time to understanding a data model.

Q8 2022?

Define *NoSQL data store* and give three examples. Explain what is unusual about the development of these systems. Describe one possible consequence of this trend on existing software vendors.

Using Your Knowledge at GearUp

Lucas is going to provide Addison with two tables of data. She will need to combine them using keys and foreign keys to create the report she wants. You will see how she does this in Chapter 9 and have a chance to do some of her work in Application Exercise 9-3.

Key Terms and Concepts

Access   147
Attributes   156
Bigtable   165
Byte   143
Cassandra   165
Columns   143
Crow's feet   158
Crow's-foot diagram   159
Data integrity problem   160
Data model   156
Database   143
Database administration   152
Database application   152
Database application system   147
Database management system (DBMS)   147
DB2   147
Durability   175
Dynamo   165
Elastic   175

Enterprise DBMS   155
Entity   156
Entity-relationship (E-R) data model   156
Entity-relationship (E-R) diagrams   158
Fields   144
File   144
Foreign keys   145
Form   152
Identifier   156
Key   144
Lost-update problem   155
Many-to-many (N:M) relationships   158
Maximum cardinality   159
Metadata   146
Minimum cardinality   159
Multi-user processing   154
MySQL   147

Normal forms   161
Normalization   159
NoSQL databases   165
One-to-many (1:N) relationships   158
Oracle Database   147
Personal DBMS   155
Primary Key   144
Query   153
Records   144
Relation   145
Relational databases   145
Relationships   157
Report   152
Rows   144
SQL Server   147
Structured Query Language (SQL)   149
Table   144
Unified Modeling Language (UML)   156

Using Your Knowledge

1. Draw an entity-relationship diagram that shows the relationships among a database, database applications, and users.

2. Consider the relationship between *Adviser* and *Student* in Figure 5-20. Explain what it means if the maximum cardinality of this relationship is:

   a. N:1
   b. 1:1
   c. 5:1
   d. 1:5

3. Identify two entities in the data entry form in Figure 5-27. What attributes are shown for each? What do you think are the identifiers?

4. Using your answer to question 3, draw an E-R diagram for the data entry form in Figure 5-27. Specify cardinalities. State your assumptions.

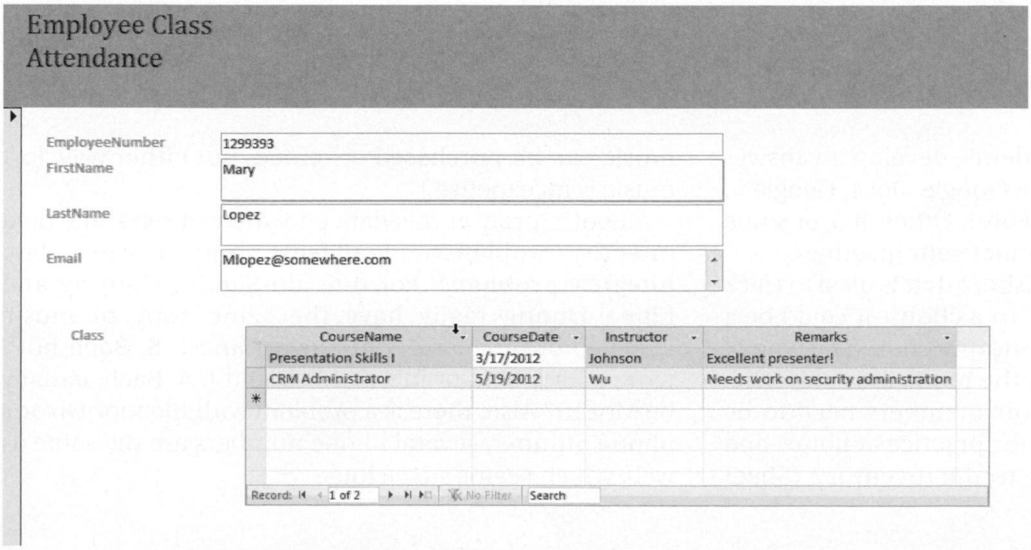

Figure 5-27
Sample Data Entry Form

Employee Class Attendance

EmployeeNumber	1299393
FirstName	Mary
LastName	Lopez
Email	Mlopez@somewhere.com

Class

CourseName	CourseDate	Instructor	Remarks
Presentation Skills I	3/17/2012	Johnson	Excellent presenter!
CRM Administrator	5/19/2012	Wu	Needs work on security administration

Record: 1 of 2   No Filter   Search

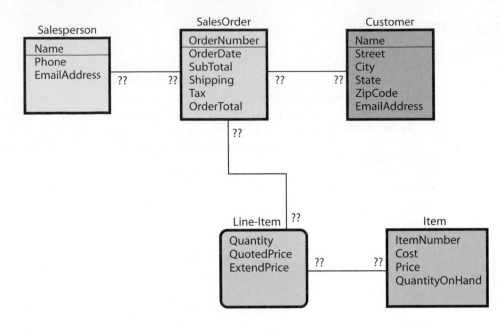

Figure 5-28
Partial E-R Diagram for
SalesOrder

5. The partial E-R diagram in Figure 5-28 is for a sales order. Assume there is only one *Salesperson* per *SalesOrder*.

   a. Specify the maximum cardinalities for each relationship. State your assumptions, if necessary.

   b. Specify the minimum cardinalities for each relationship. State your assumptions, if necessary.

6. Visit www.acxiom.com Navigate the site to answer the following questions.

   a. According to the Web site, what is Acxiom's privacy policy? Are you reassured by its policy? Why or why not?

   b. Navigate the Acxiom site and make a list of 10 different products that Acxiom provides.

   c. Describe Acxiom's top customers.

   d. Examine your answers in parts b and c and describe, in general terms, the kinds of data that Acxiom must be collecting to be able to provide those products to those customers.

   e. What is the function of InfoBase?

   f. What is the function of PersonicX?

   g. In what ways might companies like Acxiom need to limit their marketing so as to avoid a privacy outcry from the public?

   h. Should there be laws that govern companies like Acxiom? Why or why not?

   i. Should there be laws that govern the types of data services that governmental agencies can buy from companies like Acxiom? Why or why not?

▬▬ Collaboration Exercise 5

With a team of your fellow students, develop an answer to the following questions. Use Google Docs, Google+, Windows Live SkyDrive, SharePoint, Office 365, or some other collaboration tool to conduct your meetings.

Figure 5-29 shows a spreadsheet that is used to track the assignment of sheet music to a choir—it could be a church choir or school or community choir. The type of choir does not matter, because the problem is universal. Sheet music is expensive, choir members need to be able to take sheet music away for practice at home, and not all of the music gets back to the inventory. (Sheet

music can be purchased or rented, but either way, lost music is an expense.)

Look closely at this data and you will see some data integrity problems—or at least some possible data integrity problems. For one, do Sandra Corning and Linda Duong really have the same copy of music checked out? Second, did Mozart and J. S. Bach both write a Requiem, or in row 15 should J. S. Bach actually be Mozart? Also, there is a problem with Eleanor Dixon's phone number; several phone numbers are the same as well, which seems suspicious.

	A	B	C	D	E
1	**Last Name**	**First Name**	Email	**Phone**	**Part**
2	Ashley	Jane	JA@somewhere.com	703.555.1234	Soprano
3	Davidson	Kaye	KD@somewhere.com	703.555.2236	Soprano
4	Ching	Kam Hoong	KHC@overhere.com	703.555.2236	Soprano
5	Menstell	Lori Lee	LLM@somewhere.com	703.555.1237	Soprano
6	Corning	Sandra	SC2@overhere.com	703.555.1234	Soprano
7		B-minor mass	J.S. Bach	Soprano Copy 7	
8		Requiem	Mozart	Soprano Copy 17	
9		9th Symphony Chorus	Beethoven	Soprano Copy 9	
10	Wei	Guang	GW1@somewhere.com	703.555.9936	Soprano
11	Dixon	Eleanor	ED@thisplace.com	703.555.12379	Soprano
12		B-minor mass	J.S. Bach	Soprano Copy 11	
13	Duong	Linda	LD2@overhere.com	703.555.8736	Soprano
14		B-minor mass	J.S. Bach	Soprano Copy 7	
15		Requiem	J.S. Bach	Soprano Copy 19	
16	Lunden	Haley	HL@somewhere.com	703.555.0836	Soprano
17	Utran	Diem Thi	DTU@somewhere.com	703.555.1089	Soprano

Figure 5-29
Spreadsheet Used for Assignment of Sheet Music

Additionally, this spreadsheet is confusing and hard to use. The column labeled *First Name* includes both people names and the names of choruses. *Email* has both email addresses and composer names, and *Phone* has both phone numbers and copy identifiers. Furthermore, to record a checkout of music the user must first add a new row and then reenter the name of the work, the composer's name, and the copy to be checked out. Finally, consider what happens when the user wants to find all copies of a particular work: The user will have to examine the rows in each of four spreadsheets for the four voice parts.

In fact, a spreadsheet is ill-suited for this application. A database would be a far better tool, and situations like this are obvious candidates for innovation.

a. Analyze the spreadsheet shown in Figure 5-29 and list all of the problems that occur when trying to track the assignment of sheet music using this spreadsheet.

b. Figure 5-30 (a) shows a two-entity data model for the sheet-music-tracking problem.

   (1) Select identifiers for the *ChoirMember* and *Work* entities. Justify your selection.

   (2) This design does not eliminate the potential for data integrity problems that occur in the spreadsheet. Explain why not.

   (3) Design a database for this data model. Specify key and foreign key columns.

c. Figure 5-30 (b) shows a second alternative data model for the sheet-music-tracking problem. This alternative shows two variations on the *Work* entity. In the second variation, an attribute named *WorkID*

has been added to *Work_Version3*. This attribute is a unique identifier for the work; the DBMS will assign a unique value to *WorkID* when a new row is added to the *Work* table.

   (1) Select identifiers for *ChoirMember*, *Work_Version2*, *Work_Version3*, and *Copy_Assignment*. Justify your selection.

   (2) Does this design eliminate the potential for data integrity problems that occur in the spreadsheet? Why or why not?

   (3) Design a database for the data model that uses *Work_Version2*. Specify key and foreign key columns.

   (4) Design a database for the data models that uses *Work_Version3*. Specify key and foreign key columns.

   (5) Is the design with *Work_Version2* better than the design for *Work_Version3*? Why or why not?

d. Figure 5-30 (c) shows a third alternative data model for the sheet-music-tracking problem. In this data model, use either *Work_Version2* or *Work_Version3*, whichever you think is better.

   (1) Select identifiers for each entity in your data model. Justify your selection.

   (2) Summarize the differences between this data model and that in Figure 5-30 (b). Which data model is better? Why?

   (3) Design a database for this data model. Specify key and foreign key columns.

e. Which of the three data models is the best? Justify your answer.

Figure 5-30
Data-Model Alternatives for the
Assignment of Sheet Music

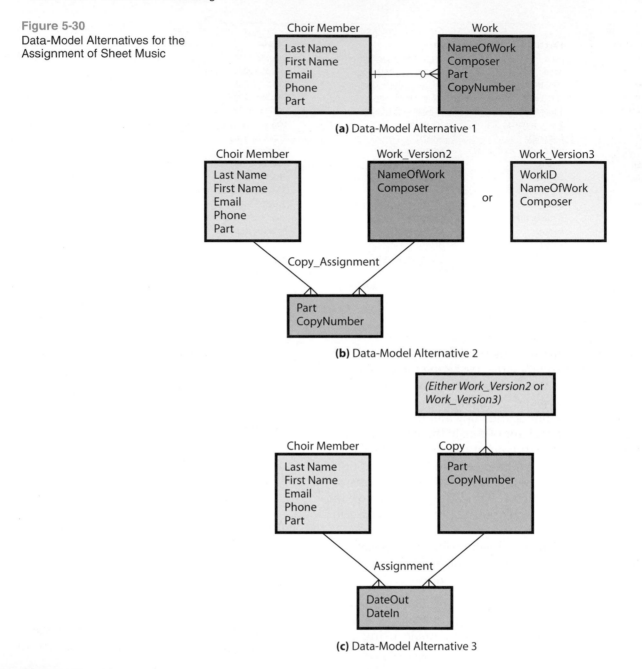

Figure 5-30
Data-Model Alternatives for the
Assignment of Sheet Music

(a) Data-Model Alternative 1

(b) Data-Model Alternative 2

(c) Data-Model Alternative 3

■ Case Study 5

Fail Away with Dynamo, Bigtable, and Cassandra

As you learned in Case Study 1, Amazon.com processed more than 158 order items per second on its peak day of the 2010 holiday sales season. To do that, it processed customer transactions on tens of thousands of servers. With that many computers, failure is inevitable. Even if the probability of any one server failing is .0001, the likelihood that not one out of 10,000 of them fails is .9999 raised to the 10,000 power, which is about .37. Thus, for these assumptions the likelihood of at least one failure is 63 percent. For reasons that go beyond the scope of this discussion, the likelihood of failure is actually much greater.

Amazon.com must be able to thrive, even in the presence of such constant failure. Or, as Amazon.com engineers stated: "Customers should be able to view and add items to their shopping cart even if disks are failing, network routes are flapping, or data centers are being destroyed by tornados."[6]

[6] Giuseppe DeCandia, Deniz Hastorun, Madan Jampani, Gunavardhan Kakulapati, Avinash Lakshman, Alex Pilchin, Swami Sivasubramanian, Peter Vosshall, and Werner Vogels, "Dynamo: Amazon's Highly Available Key-Value Store," *Proceedings of the 21st ACM Symposium on Operating Systems Principles*, Stevenson, WA, October 2007.

The only way to deal with such failure is to replicate the data on multiple servers. When a customer stores a Wish List, for example, that Wish List needs to be stored on different, geographically separated servers. Then, when (notice *when*, not *if*) a server with one copy of the Wish List fails, Amazon.com applications obtain it from another server.

Such data replication solves one problem, but introduces another. Suppose that the customer's Wish List is stored on servers A, B, and C and server A fails. While server A is down, server B or C can provide a copy of the Wish List, but if the customer changes it, that Wish List can only be rewritten to servers B and C. It cannot be written to A, because A is not running. When server A comes back into service, it will have the old copy of the Wish List. The next day, when the customer reopens his or her Wish List, two different versions exist: the most recent one on servers B and C and an older one on server A. The customer wants the most current one. How can Amazon.com ensure that it will be delivered? Keep in mind that 9 million orders are being shipped while this goes on.

None of the current relational DBMS products was designed for problems like this. Consequently, Amazon.com engineers developed Dynamo, a specialized data store for reliably processing massive amounts of data on tens of thousands of servers. Dynamo provides an always-open experience for Amazon.com's retail customers; Amazon.com also sells Dynamo store services to others via its S3 Web Services product offering.

Meanwhile, Google was encountering similar problems that could not be met by commercially available relational DBMS products. In response, Google created Bigtable, a data store for processing petabytes of data on hundreds of thousands of servers.[7] Bigtable supports a richer data model than Dynamo, which means that it can store a greater variety of data structures.

Both Dynamo and Bigtable are designed to be **elastic**; this term means that the number of servers can dynamically increase and decrease without disrupting performance.

In 2007, Facebook encountered similar data storage problems: Massive amounts of data, the need to be elastically scalable, tens of thousands of servers, and high volumes of traffic. In response to this need, Facebook began development on Cassandra, a data store that provides storage capabilities like Dynamo with a richer data model like Bigtable.[8,9] Initially, Facebook used Cassandra to power its Inbox Search. By 2008, Facebook realized that it had a bigger project on its hands than it wanted and gave the source code to the open source community. As of 2011, Cassandra is used by Facebook, Twitter, Digg, Reddit, Cisco, and many others.

Cassandra, by the way, is a fascinating name for a data store. In Greek mythology, Cassandra was so beautiful that Apollo fell in love with her and gave her the power to see the future. Alas, Apollo's love was unrequited and he cursed her so that no one would ever believe her predictions. The name was apparently a slam at Oracle.

Cassandra is elastic and fault-tolerant; it supports massive amounts of data on thousands of servers and provides **durability**, meaning that once data is committed to the data store, it won't be lost, even in the presence of failure. One of the most interesting characteristics of Cassandra is that clients (meaning the programs that run Facebook, Twitter, etc.) can select the level of consistency that they need. If a client requests that all servers always be current, Cassandra will ensure that that happens, but performance will be slow. At the other end of the trade-off spectrum, clients can require no consistency, whereby performance is maximized. In between, clients can require that a majority of the servers that store a data item be consistent.

Cassandra performance is vastly superior to relational DBMS products. In one comparison, Cassandra was found to be 2,500 times faster than MySQL for write operations and 23 times faster for read operations[10] on massive amounts of data on hundreds of thousands of possibly failing computers!

Questions

1. Clearly, Dynamo, Bigtable, and Cassandra are critical technology to the companies that create them. Why did they allow their employees to publish academic papers about them? Why did they not keep them as proprietary secrets?

2. What do you think this movement means to the existing DBMS vendors? How serious is the NoSQL threat? Justify your answer. What responses by existing DBMS vendors would be sensible?

3. Is it a waste of your time to learn about the relational model and Microsoft Access? Why or why not?

4. Given what you know about GearUp, should it use a relational DBMS, such as Oracle Database or MySQL, or should it use Cassandra?

5. Suppose that GearUp decides to use a NoSQL solution, but a battle emerges among the employees in the IT department. One faction wants to use Cassandra, but another faction wants to use a different NoSQL data store, named MongoDB (www.mongodb.org). Assume that you're Kelly, and Lucas asks for your opinion about how he should proceed. How do you respond?

---

[7] Fay Chang, Jeffrey Dean, Sanjay Ghemawat, Wilson C. Hsieh, Deborah A. Wallach, Mike Burrows, Tushar Chandra, Andrew Fikes, and Robert E. Gruber, "Bigtable: A Distributed Storage System for Structured Data," *OSDI 2006: Seventh Symposium on Operating System Design and Implementation*, Seattle, WA, November 2006. Available at http://labs.google.com/papers/bigtable.html (accessed June 2011).

[8] "Welcome to Apache Cassandra," The Apache Software Foundation. Available at http://cassandra.apache.org (accessed June 2011).

[9] www.parleys.com/#st=5&id=1866&sl=20 (accessed June 2011).

[10] Slide 21, www.parleys.com/#st=5&id=1866&sl=20 (accessed June 2011).

GearUp, Chapter 5

GOALS

Use GearUp to:

- Illustrate the utility of processing operational data.

- Demonstrate a realistic example of why students might want to become proficient using both Access and Excel.

BACKGROUND

1. The GearUp database provides data for determining which vendors are causing problems and the seriousness of those problems.

2. If Addison and Drew are dependent on Lucas (or the IT department) to produce the reports they need, they will (a) wait a long time and (b) probably not get what they want

3. Once they get the data, assuming that Addison does know how to create queries and reports, they can iterate on their own, without help from Lucas. They can: produce reports, see the results, produce more reports, and so forth. Relying on their own skills will give them much more freedom and better results.

4. One solution (or at least a good part of one solution) is illustrated in Chapter 9. You might choose to jump ahead and show that solution now.

HOW TO GET STUDENTS INVOLVED

1. Ask the students to describe, in words, the data they need to determine which vendors are not delivering the quantities they agreed to deliver.

   - Assume you have been asked to specify the data you need to determine which vendors are delivering insufficient quantities. Sketch the report that you need.

   - Describe, in words, how GearUp would process its operational database to obtain that report.

   - Does the processing required seem feasible? Why or why not?

2. Repeat the exercise in item 1, but for vendors that are not causing quality problems.

3. Show students a few easy queries in Access. Create the following two tables in Access:

   Goods_Received (OrderNumber, VendorNumber, QuantityOrdered, QuantityReceived)

   Vendor (VendorNumber, VendorName, ContactPerson)

   In class, create queries to:

   - Compute the quantity not received for each row in *Goods_Received.*

   - Compute the total quantity not received for every order (assume that some orders are received in multiple shipments).

   - Compute the total quantity not received for each vendor. For greater clarity, join vendor name from the *Vendor* table to the results.

4. These results are useful!

   - Consider how much stronger such reports would make Drew and Addison's position in discussions with Kelly.

   - Consider how much stronger such reports would give GearUp when negotiating with vendors.

BOTTOM LINE

■ Operational data often can be used to give precision to problems.

■ Knowing how to use Access to create relatively simple queries and reports is a valuable skill for business professionals. Here, it reduced the time that they needed to wait and will enable them to iterate as they examine the data.

■ Such queries and reports aren't difficult to produce.

■ Reports like these can be quite valuable.

YOU BE THE GUIDE

Using the Ethics Guide: Nobody Said I Shouldn't (pages 150–151)

GOALS

- Illustrate the utility of metadata and SQL, even for nonauthorized purposes.
- Discuss the ethics of unauthorized data access.
- Consider the need for organizational data policies.

BACKGROUND AND PRESENTATION STRATEGIES

SQL was designed to be powerful and easy to use. Here's an SQL statement Chris used to display the average order total and average discount for each combination of company and salesperson:

```
SELECT AVG(Total), AVG(Discount),
CompanyName, SPName
FROM SALES_ORDER
GROUP BY CompanyName, SPName;
```

That's all Chris needed! No programs, no special interfaces, just those few lines of SQL entered into the DBMS. It could be done in 5 minutes or less.

■ As a future business manager or owner, what does the ease with which this can be done tell you?

In order for Chris to write the SQL statement, he needed to know the names of the tables and columns to query. The names were easy for him to obtain because every database contains metadata that describes its content. Chris used the DBMS to query the metadata to learn there was a table named Sales_Order that contained the columns *Total, Discount, CompanyName*, and *SPName*.

Nothing that Chris did was illegal; it's even questionable that what he did was unethical. Suppose he stumbled upon an internal criminal conspiracy, one unknown to the company's management or ownership. By discovering it, he would be a hero, if the discovery was reported to someone not involved in the conspiracy.

If the company has a policy that no employee is to remove company data from the company premises, then he violated that policy. Can any company enforce such a policy today? If a sales manager sends an email with proprietary company product data to a salesperson working at a customer site, that action would be a violation of the policy not to remove data from company premises. But if the salesperson needs the data to support a crucial sale, who would want to prohibit that data access? Still, removing an entire database is on a different scale from sending an attachment in an email.

Data is an asset. Data is just as much an asset as buildings, trucks, and equipment. It has value and needs to be protected.

■ What is a reasonable policy for an organization to have regarding employees taking data home?

This question is not easy to answer. The policy needs to be loose enough to allow employees to do their work, while providing appropriate protection to data assets.

Most employment contracts use statements like "protect the company's data assets as directed by management" or other general language.

Bottom line: Companies need to have policies with regard to the data asset. We'll discuss this further when we discuss security management in Chapter 12.

We could view Chris as the victim of bad luck: His curiosity, knowledge of database technology, ambition, and friendships caused him to lose his job.

Chris probably should hire an attorney who might advise him to contact law enforcement as well. He may not get his job back, he may not want his job back, but he's probably entitled to some compensation. He also deserves a decent job referral—assuming he was otherwise a desirable employee.

SUGGESTED RESPONSES FOR DISCUSSION QUESTIONS

1. Chris went wrong by taking the data home. Had he processed the data at work, it would be hard to fault him.

■ Was he in error about mentioning to his friend what he'd found?

■ Once he saw the odd pattern, what should he have done?

This is a tough one. Either forget about it or do a careful analysis and then take the results to the most senior manager he can meet. But what if this is an innocuous coincidence? Then he'll look like he betrayed his friend. Maybe Chris hasn't done anything wrong, yet. *Maybe the story isn't over.* One possible continuation of the story is that he goes to an attorney who advises him to contact senior management and law enforcement.

2. It was not illegal. Taking the data home may have been against corporate policy. He may have been overly curious, but is that unethical? I think taking the data home might be construed as poor judgment on the part of a smart and ambitious employee, but I wouldn't say it was unethical. Recall Encarta's definition of *ethical:* "Consistent with agreed principles of correct moral conduct."

■ **Do his intentions matter? If he had gone home with the intention of using the customer data to sell his own home-care products, would your answer be different?**

■ **If he had gone home with the hope of gathering dirt on fellow employees, would your answer be different?**

■ **Why should his intentions matter?**

It goes back to "agreed principles." Most would find it hard to fault improving one's job skills, even if there is an element of unbridled curiosity.

3. Culpability for what? For allowing him to take home the data? If there is no clear company policy, if he had not been instructed not to remove data, then the company probably does share culpability. If he violated a clearly stated company policy of which he had been made aware, then probably not. Culpability for firing him? It depends on how high up the organization the conspiracy reaches. If it goes all the way to the top, then they do. If not, then firing him was the protective action of guilty employees. Company culpability depends on what happens next.

4. First, I ask the class to vote:

■ **How many of you think that Chris should:**
  • **Ignore the whole thing?**
  • **Confirm his analysis, gather even stronger evidence, if possible, and then take the data he has to the CFO?**
  • **Never have learned SQL? (This is a joke!)**
  • **Done what he did, and now go see an attorney?**

Now ask the students why they voted the way they did.

My vote: probably go to the CFO. If he then is fired, definitely go to the attorney.

5. If there is no criminal conspiracy, then I believe the company's actions were precipitous. He ought not to be fired for his ambition and knowledge, even if he did show poor judgment in taking the data home.

First, the company should determine if the data he created reveals employee wrongdoing. If not, then he should be instructed not to take data home, or maybe put on probation, but firing him seems overly harsh. This also depends on whether he violated a clear corporate policy on which he had been trained.

If there is a criminal conspiracy, then the company has major problems. They need to consult their attorneys and law enforcement. They also might want to hire investigators to identify members of the conspiracy and then clean up the organization.

6. I think there's little doubt that someone else is involved. Jason is not in a position to force Chris's firing. In that case, he should have not spoken with Jason. He should have gone as high in the organization as he could. But, see question 4.

7. Say nothing to anyone. Hire an attorney with expertise in labor law.

■ **Do you think he should "sue the pants off" this company?**

8. Understand their vulnerability. Treat organizational data as an important asset. Establish data safeguards and train employees on those safeguards. (More on this in Chapter 12.)

WRAP UP

■ **This is a rather weird case. Should we conclude:**
  • **A little knowledge is a dangerous thing?**
  • **Curiosity got the cat?**
  • **Don't stick your nose in other people's business?**
  • **Don't socialize with fellow employees after work?**

■ **Two sure conclusions:**
  • **Data is an important asset that needs to be protected.**
  • **Metadata and SQL are powerful.**

■ **We're in the middle of the story. What happened next? Did he hire an attorney? Or, did he slink off and take an entry-level job in another industry?**

■ **Assume he hired an attorney, and you finish the story. Think about it tonight and next class, after which two or three of you can tell us how the story ends.**

YOU BE THE GUIDE

Using the Guide: No, Thanks, I'll Use a Spreadsheet (pages 166–167)

GOALS

● Explore the differences between a spreadsheet and a database.

● Understand one way that users respond to technology challenges.

BACKGROUND AND PRESENTATION STRATEGIES

The story of the failed database project is, unfortunately, quite common. Often it involves small businesses or workgroups that have attempted to develop a database on their own. On the basis of my experience, the cause of such failures is usually either incompetent database developers or underfunding of the project. (This, by the way, differs from the causes of failure for information systems in general. As we will see in Chapter 10, based on a review of all systems development projects and not just database projects at small businesses, the most likely causes of failure are poor communication between users and systems developers, a lack of clear requirements, and an inability to manage requirements.)

It took this company three consultants to obtain a database that works. *But the one that "works" doesn't meet the requirements*—or at least it doesn't meet the requirements of this salesperson.

Organizations smaller than General Motors or Toyota can develop their own databases, but developing a database and its applications in-house does take time, money, and management attention. You, as a future manager, need to know what should be happening.

■ **We'll talk about systems development techniques in Chapter 10, but to build a database correctly, here's a quick summary of the work that needs to be done:**
  - **Determine and document requirements.**
  - **Construct a data model and have users validate it.**
  - **Design the database.**
  - **Implement the database and fill it with data (imported from other sources?).**
  - **Design, build, and test database applications.**
  - **Write procedures.**
  - **Train the users.**
  - **Maintain the system.**

■ **Developing a database requires *management attention*. Suppose you manage the dealership. What role do you see for yourself when a customer database is being developed for your sales staff?**

In light of the amount of work, the dealership might be better off to look for appropriate off-the-shelf software, such as Act! or GoldMine. These products, which do use databases, already exist and have interfaces that are built just for sales. Many small business salespeople use and recommend such products.

The issue of whether salespeople should share data is independent of the technology that the salesperson uses. Sharing data is a management policy. If management decides that salespersons' data should be private, there are ways to implement that policy with a database just as well as with a spreadsheet.

It's possible this person is using the failure of the database application to avoid sharing his data. He can hide his spreadsheet from management; they don't know that he's got his own customer data. It could be that he wants to keep his customer data private so that he can take it with him if he decides to work for another dealership. He might be using his disgust with the database project to cover his intentions.

Or, maybe not, but something doesn't fit: He doesn't want to use the database because it's difficult for him to send form letters or email. Yet, he says that he can't send them with his spreadsheet either and that sending letters is not that important to his sales activity.

Another possibility: His data are actually not his. He may have been stealing customers from other salespeople, and he doesn't want them to know that. Putting his data in a centralized database will reveal his actions.

Scrambling all of his data into the *Car Interests* and *Notes* columns will cause enormous problems if he ever wants to import his data to a database. Those problems will also be expensive to fix, because the work of separating the data into proper columns must be done manually. See Application Exercise 5-2 (pages 474–475) for a project that forces the students to deal with such issues. The Excel file that is given to the students is quite a mess! For more on this problem, see pages 148, 149 in *Database Processing, 12th Edition*.[1]

"Keep it simple" is a great motto, but it shouldn't be simpler than it needs to be. What happens when his customers stop answering their phones because they

[1]David Kroenke and David Auer, *Database Processing*, 12 ed. (Upper Saddle River, NJ: Pearson Education, 2012).

prefer email? He can still send emails one at a time, but without some kind of database application, it will be impossible to send bulk emails announcing the arrival of new cars, and so on. This person is condemning himself to the old-world style of business.

SUGGESTED RESPONSES FOR DISCUSSION QUESTIONS

1. Ask the students their opinions. I believe users have a right to information systems that allow them to do their jobs. Something doesn't fit here, though. He objects to the database application because it's difficult to send form letters, but then he says they're not that important to the way he sells. What else is going on? (See earlier comments.)

2. He's creating a nightmare for himself. How will he ever disentangle the addresses from the *Notes* column? What a mess!

3. I think some likely themes are *Customer, Auto_Interest, Contact*, and possibly others. *Multiple themes mean: Use a database!*

4. I suspect the concern does relate to using a database, but it ought not. Databases can be private and secure; accounts and roles can be set up so that salespeople do not share each other's data. However, I think he's hiding his desire not to share his data by complaining about the database. He's using frustration with technology to hide from the management policy of sharing data.

■ **If you were a manager, how would you deal with this possibility?**

5. First, management may be allowing each salesperson to have his or her own format. They may be trying to discourage it by building the shared database. The question is, who owns the contact data—the salespeople or the dealership? If the salespeople own it, then they can do what they want with it. If the dealership owns the data, then they can specify whatever format they want. The disadvantages to allowing different ways of keeping the data are inconsistent quality, missing data, difficulty of accessing common data, duplicated data, and so on.

6. Well, there's the soft approach and there's the tough one. The soft approach is to explain the need for the database—how it will make everyone more efficient, and how it will help salespeople not lose control of their customers to other salespeople. Also, explain that the database offers better security and control, including better protection, because it will be backed up and stored off-premises. Finally, explain that the database can integrate customer sales data with customer service data, and so forth.

   The tough approach is to mandate it: "We need centralized customer data to beat the competition and, ultimately, to survive. This may require you to make some changes, and it may be difficult for a while, but it's the way we're going to go. Get with it!" Then, provide support to ease the conversion efforts.

   ■ **Or, as I once heard between a partner in a law firm and a reluctant junior associate: "What possible incentive do I have to use this new system?" asked the junior associate. "Continued employment," responded the partner.**

7. A database is a better solution. Whether it's a database developed in-house or one that is embedded in a product like Act! or GoldMine is another question. But this type of problem begs for a database solution.

WRAP UP

■ **No doubt about it, databases can involve a lot of work and involve management challenges. That's one reason you should read this chapter carefully.**

■ **Given that databases can be expensive to develop in-house (not to mention expensive to maintain, which we'll discuss in Chapter 10), for a common need like customer management for sales, look first to off-the-shelf applications.**

■ **Sometimes people are frustrated with new systems and technology for justifiable reasons. Other times, they use that frustration for a cover for some other reason. That may have happened here. As a manager, keep that possibility in mind.**

Using the Guide: Immanuel Kant, Data Modeler (pages 168–169)

GOALS

- Understand why the statement, "My data model is a better model of reality than your data model" is nonsense—and arrogant!

- Realize that a data model is a model of users' mental models, *not* a model of reality.

- Stimulate students' curiosity about the philosophical foundations of information systems.

BACKGROUND AND PRESENTATION STRATEGIES

This guide presents two points: one practical and pragmatic, the other deep and philosophical. I have fun with this material; students are surprised to be discussing Immanuel Kant in this class.

This guide works best as a class discussion. I recommend either assigning it as reading ahead of time or having the students read it in class. I ask the students to discuss it among themselves, but if they're going nowhere, I lead the discussion along the following lines.

Humans have a brain, an instruction set. That brain has a built-in mental apparatus, or set of instincts if you will. That instruction set or instinctive structure enables us to process our perceptions and create what we refer to as "the real world." We think that world is real because we share the same mental apparatus with other humans. All of our interactions with other people reinforce the idea of the "real world," but it's a shared mutual hallucination. We have no idea of the nature of the correspondence between what we think and what is "out there." All we can say is that so far, our mental apparatus has enabled the human species to survive and flourish.

For background on the science of our mental apparatus, see Steven Pinker, *The Blank Slate* (Viking Adult, 2002).

For Kant, the *noumenal world* is that which exists—that which is "out there." He and others who followed (Karl Popper for one) believed that humans can know absolutely nothing about that world. We can know only what we can perceive, process, and construct. That world, the one we perceive and construct, is the *phenomenal world*.

For some students, understanding this difference leads to a fundamental existential awareness, one that can be uncomfortable: What we've always thought is "out there" is really "in here," inside my brain. The reality I know is in my head; I'm trapped by my perceptions and my mental apparatus. That's all I can ever know.

Now, why talk about this in an MIS class? In particular, why talk about it in the database lecture? A data model (and later, a database) is a model of the phenomenal world, not of the noumenal world. *It is not a model of reality because we cannot know what reality is.* Instead, it is a *model of users' models* of reality. It is a model of human models.

"What's the bottom line?" some students will ask. It is this: *No one can ever say, sensibly, "My model is a better model of the real world than your model."* The only accurate statement is "My model is a better model of the users' model than your model is."

I have wasted literally hundreds of hours of my life in meetings in which someone said that his or her model was a better model of reality. Then, everyone argues that, no, their model is a better model of reality. Those statements are arrogant: In essence, they are saying, "The way I see the world is the one that counts."

A data model is a model of how the users construct their world. Period. No more and no less. *If you want to know whose model is better, ask the users.* Database developers must rely on users' feedback in a collaborative project. Ask the students how the ideas of this guide pertain to such collaborative projects.

This is where our students come in. *As future businesspeople only they can determine which data model fits their world.* Hence, students need to learn how to interpret a data model. This is why I have included the material in this chapter on the entity-relationship model.

I hope you have as much fun with this guide as I do!

SUGGESTED RESPONSES FOR DISCUSSION QUESTIONS

1. A data model is a representation of the users' world. To illustrate this point, construct an E-R model in class about some aspect of the students' lives. Maybe one involving the entities: STUDENT, AUTO, PARKING_PERMIT, VIOLATION, and PAYMENT.

   ■ **What is the relationship between STUDENT and AUTO?**

   ■ **How many AUTOs does a STUDENT relate to? How many STUDENTs does an AUTO relate to?**

- I think one can justify that the relationship is 1:1. In this case, university policy dictates that a student may have a permit for one auto only. The university parking department doesn't care that the student has an auto collection at home. Also, that auto is owned by one student.

- Equally possible, I think one could say the relationship is 1:N. In this case, a student is allowed permits for each auto he or she owns. But each auto is owned by at most one student.

- Equally possible, I think one could say the relationship is N:1. In this case, the university allows a permit for only one auto per student, but it allows multiple students to be affiliated with an auto, say, for a group parking permit.

- Equally possible, I think one could say the relationship is N:M. In this case, the university allows multiple autos per permit, and it recognizes multiple students to be affiliated with a particular auto for a group parking permit.

- Pick one (it doesn't matter which), *and say, "My model is a better model of reality than your model."*

    Have fun. And, this is just one relationship! We've got several more to go.

    Now consider a business data model that has 100 entities. How long will it take to build the data model? And who pays for the data modeling meetings? Ugh.

2. Humans confuse the two worlds because we share a mutual hallucination that the phenomenal world is real. When I say (to a student), please pass me your book, the student passes me the book and not her purse.

3. You could respond with a lecture about Immanuel Kant and his epistemological theories. Or, and probably far preferable, you could tailor your response to who is making the statement. If it was made by a data modeler (shame on them!), you could say, "Well, that might be. But we're building this information system for the users, so let's ask them." If the person making this statement is a user, and if that person speaks for all the other users, then you say, "Thanks for the correction," and you change the data model to that view. If that person is just one user, then you say, "Great. Let's see how your model works for the other users."

4. The answer is really the same as question 3, but let the students respond. Let them paraphrase what you've said and summarize what they've learned.

WRAP UP

Some possible concluding remarks:

- I'll bet you never thought you'd be hearing about Immanuel Kant in this class! We've just seen one of the reasons why this field is so interesting: The study of the human uses of information systems takes you to so many interesting fields!

- The bottom line: A data model is a model of the users' world.

- Thus, and this is very important, the only people who can verify that the data model is accurate is *you*, the future users!

- Hence, *learn how to interpret a data model.* It's not that hard, and it will be a useful skill. You can also use data modeling skills to clarify your own thinking (e.g., to clarify your thinking about organizational relationships in a supply chain).

Data Communication and the Cloud

"**What's** your plan, Lucas?" Kelly Summers, CEO of GearUp, is meeting with Lucas Massey, IT director, and Emily Johnson, CFO, to discuss GearUp's Web hosting costs.

"Right now, Kelly, we're fine. Our hosting service processes our transactions on time and we've had no real outages, but . . ."

Emily can't stand this. "Well, we're fine until you look at the bills we're running up. Our hosting costs have increased 350 percent IN A YEAR."

"Yes, Emily, they have, but our volume's gone up 400 percent."

"True enough, but . . ."

Kelly has had enough and interrupts. "We've been over this before. No need to rehash it. We all agree that our hosting costs are too high. Lucas, I'd asked you to look into alternatives. What have you got?"

"The cloud."

"The WHAT???" Emily hopes he's not losing it.

"The cloud. We move our Web servers and databases to the cloud."

Kelly is curious. "OK, Lucas, I'll bite. What's the cloud?"

"It's a movement—I'd call it a fad, except I think it's here to stay."

"So how does it help us?"

"We lease server capability from a third party."

Emily's confused. "But, we're already doing that from our hosting vendor."

"Well, it's different. We can lease on very, very flexible, pay-as-you-go terms. If we have a popular item, like the golf clubs, we can acquire more resources—they use the term *provision*—we can provision more resources."

"You mean each day? We can change the terms of our lease on a daily basis?" Emily thinks that's not possible because she knows the terms of GearUp's contract with its current hosting vendor.

"No, I mean each hour. We can provision or release server resources by the hour." Lucas is enjoying this.

Emily is surprised. "No way. How do they do that? We have to give our hosting vendor at least a week's notice."

"Yeah, we do. But that's not how the cloud works, at least not how some cloud vendors work."

Emily persists. "I still don't get it."

"They use what's called *virtualization*. They don't actually provision new hardware; they provision new instances of servers on existing hardware."

"So one server is actually many?" Emily's read about this somewhere.

"No one server is virtually many." Lucas is having fun.

"Whatever." Emily does NOT like to be corrected.

"The point is they can do this programmatically, no humans involved. Our programs can tell their programs to give us another 10 servers; we can use them a few hours, and then give them back." Lucas gets serious again.

"OK, so how much does it cost? This can't be cheap." Emily's skeptical.

"How about a quarter an hour."

Kelly's puzzled at that. "You mean a quarter of an hour? 15 minutes?"

"No, I mean 25 cents an hour." Lucas grins as he says this.

"WHAT???" Emily's dumbfounded.

"Yeah, that's it. That's for processing. For databases, we have to commit to a monthly charge. Fifty dollars a month for what we'd need." Lucas isn't quite sure, because these are preliminary prices. He thinks the actual costs could be less.

"Lucas, you've got to be kidding. We can knock thousands out of our hosting fees. This is HUGE." As Emily says this, in the back of her mind she's thinking, "If it's true."

"Well, it's good, I don't know about huge. We still have development costs on our end. And we need to create the procedures, train people, the whole system thing . . ."

"Lucas, give me a plan. I want a plan." Kelly's thinking what these savings could mean to their next two quarters . . . and beyond.

"I'll give you something next week."

"I want it by Monday, Lucas."

"OK," he says, leaving the room thinking, "There went the weekend."

Kelly stays seated, pondering. Emily starts to get up.

"Emily, we need to find out if this is real."

"Seems too good to be true."

"It does. But let's find out. Someone else will be doing it, if it's real. What about Blue Nile, what are they doing? They'd talk to me. Find one or two of our friends and let's talk to them. Anyway, I want to know what the downside is."

"You want to go see them?"

"I will if I have to. First, let's talk. Set up a videoconference."

"Will do." ∎

Study Questions

Q1 What is a computer network?

Q2 What are the components of a LAN?

Q3 What are the fundamental concepts you should know about the Internet?

Q4 What processing occurs on a typical Web server?

Q5 Why is the cloud the future for most organizations?

Q6 How can organizations use the cloud?

Q7 2022?

If you go into business for yourself, there's an excellent chance you'll have a problem just like GearUp's. What is the best way to support your Web site or other information systems? Should you use the cloud? If so, for which applications, and how? Or maybe you just need to discuss with your vendor what kind of network infrastructure your business needs. In either case, you'll need the knowledge of this chapter to participate in the conversations you'll have. Of course, you could just rely on outside experts, but that doesn't work in the twenty-first century. Many of your competitors will be able to ask and understand those questions—and use the money their knowledge saves them for other purposes, such as reducing operations costs, as GearUp needs to do.

Or, what if you work in product management for a large company? Does your product "talk" to some network? If not, could it? Should it? Does it require a LAN or a WAN? Will some cloud offering make sense? How will you know without some knowledge of what the cloud is? In this chapter, we will define essential data communications terms and explain basic concepts. We'll discuss local area networks, the fundamentals of the Internet, how Web servers function, and the purpose of basic Web technologies. Finally, we'll discuss why the cloud is the future for most organizations and how they can use it.

Q1 What Is a Computer Network?

A computer **network** is a collection of computers that communicate with one another over transmission lines or wirelessly. As shown in Figure 6-1, the three basic types of networks are local area networks, wide area networks, and internets.

A **local area network (LAN)** connects computers that reside in a single geographic location on the premises of the company that operates the LAN. The number of connected computers can range from two to several hundred. The distinguishing characteristic of a LAN is *a single location*. A **wide area network (WAN)** connects computers at different geographic locations. The computers in two separated company sites must be connected using a WAN. To illustrate, the computers for a College of Business located on a single campus can be connected via a LAN. The computers for a College of Business located on multiple campuses must be connected via a WAN.

The single- versus multiple-site distinction is important. With a LAN, an organization can place communications lines wherever it wants, because all lines reside on its premises. The same is not true for a WAN. A company with offices in Chicago and Atlanta cannot run a wire down the freeway to connect computers in the two cities. Instead, the company contracts with a communications vendor that is licensed by the government and that already has lines or has the authority to run new lines between the two cities.

Many employees use their employer's computers and networks for personal email, Facebook, Twitter, and other personal and social applications. Is such usage ethical? We consider that question in the Ethics Guide on pages 196–197.

Figure 6-1
Major Network Types

Type	Characteristic
Local area network (LAN)	Computers connected at a single physical site
Wide area network (WAN)	Computers connected between two or more separated sites
The Internet and internets	Networks of networks

An **internet** is a network of networks. Internets connect LANs, WANs, and other internets. The most famous internet is **"the Internet"** (with an uppercase letter *I*), the collection of networks that you use when you send email or access a Web site. In addition to the Internet, private networks of networks, called *internets,* also exist. A private internet that is used exclusively within an organization is sometimes called an **intranet**.

Social networking relies on the Internet. For information on social network theory and how it can benefit you, see the Guide on pages 206–207. We discuss social networking in greater detail in Chapter 8.

The networks that comprise an internet use a large variety of communication methods and conventions, and data must flow seamlessly across them. To provide seamless flow, an elaborate scheme called a *layered protocol* is used. The details of protocols are beyond the scope of this text. Just understand that a **protocol** is a set of rules that programs on two communicating devices follow. There are many different protocols; some are used for LANs, some are used for WANs, some are used for internets and the Internet, and some are used for all of these. We will identify several common protocols in this chapter.

Q2 What Are the Components of a LAN?

As stated, a LAN is a group of computers connected together on a single site. Usually the computers are located within a half mile or so of each other. The key distinction, however, is that all of the computers are located on property controlled by the organization that operates the LAN. This means that the organization can run cables wherever needed to connect the computers.

A Typical SOHO LAN

Figure 6-2 shows a LAN that is typical of those in a **small office or a home office (SOHO)**. Typically such LANs have fewer than a dozen or so computers and printers. Many businesses, of course, operate LANs that are much larger than this one. The principles are the same for a larger LAN, but the additional complexity is beyond the scope of this text.

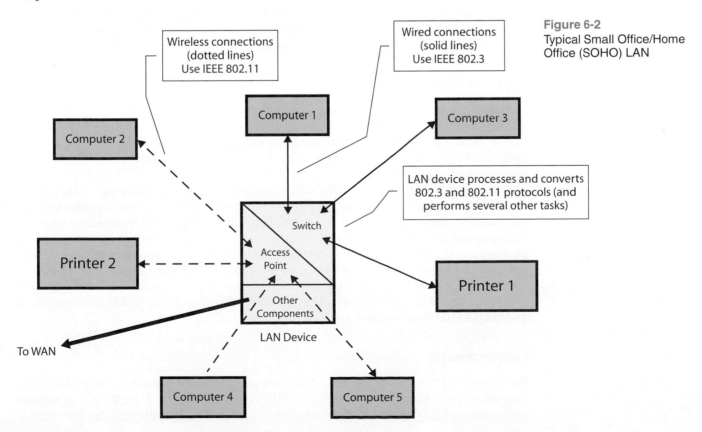

Figure 6-2
Typical Small Office/Home Office (SOHO) LAN

The computers and printers in Figure 6-2 communicate via a mixture of wired and wireless connections. Computers 1 and 3 and printer 1 use wired connections; computers 2, 4, and 5 as well as printer 2 use wireless connections. The devices and protocols used differ for wired and wireless connectivity.

Wired Connectivity

Computers 1 and 3 and printer 1 are wired to a **switch**, which is a special-purpose computer that receives and transmits wired traffic on the LAN. In Figure 6-2, the switch is contained within the box labeled "LAN Device." When either of these two computers communicates with each other or with printer 1, it does so by sending the traffic over wires to the switch, which redirects the traffic to the other computer or printer 1.

The **LAN device** is a small computer that contains the following networking components. It has a switch, as just described; it also has a device for wireless communication, as you are about to learn. In most cases, it has devices for connecting to a WAN and via the WAN to the Internet. For SOHO applications, LAN devices are usually provided by the phone or cable vendor. They have many different names, depending on the brand.

Each wired computer or printer on the LAN has a **network interface card (NIC)**, which is a device that connects the computer's or printer's circuitry to the network wires. The NIC works with programs in each device to implement the protocols necessary for communication. Most computers today ship from the factory with an **onboard NIC**, which is a NIC built into the computer's circuitry.

The computers, printers, and the switches on a wired LAN are connected using one of two wired media. Most LAN connections are made using **unshielded twisted pair (UTP) cable**. This cable contains sets of wires that are twisted together to improve signal quality. However, if the connection carries a lot of traffic, the UTP cable may be replaced by **optical fiber cables**. The signals on such cables are light rays, and they are reflected inside the glass core of the optical fiber cable.

LANs that are larger than the one in Figure 6-2 use more than one switch. Typically, in a building with several floors a switch is placed on each floor, and the computers on that floor are connected to the switch with UTP cable. The switches on each floor are connected to each other via the faster-speed optical fiber cable.

Wireless Connections

In Figure 6-2, three of the computers and one printer are connected to the LAN using wireless technology. The wireless computers and printer have a **wireless NIC (WNIC)** instead of a NIC. Today, nearly all personal computers ship from the factory with an onboard WNIC. (By the way, in almost all cases a NIC or WNIC can be added to a computer that does not have one.)

As shown in Figure 6-2, the WNIC devices connect to an **access point**, which is the component of the LAN device that processes wireless traffic and communicates with the wired switch. Thus, with this design every device on the LAN, whether wired or wireless, can communicate with every other device. Wireless devices communicate to each other via the access point. If wireless devices need to connect to a wired device, they do so via the access point, then to the switch, and then to the wired devices. Similarly, wired devices communicate to each other via the switch. If the wired devices need to connect to wireless ones, they do so via the switch, then to the access point, and then to the wireless devices.

LAN Protocols

For two devices to communicate, they must use the same protocol. The Institute for Electrical and Electronics Engineers (IEEE, pronounced "I triple E") sponsors committees that create and publish protocol and other standards. The committee that addresses LAN standards is called the *IEEE 802 Committee.* Thus, IEEE LAN protocols always start with the numbers 802.

The **IEEE 802.3 protocol** is used for wired LAN connections. This protocol standard, also called **Ethernet**, specifies hardware characteristics, such as which wire carries which signals. It also describes how messages are to be packaged and processed for wired transmission over the LAN.

The NICs in most personal computers today support what is called **10/100/1000 Ethernet**. These products conform to the 802.3 specification and allow for transmission at a rate of 10, 100, or 1,000 Mbps (megabits per second). Switches detect the speed that a given device can handle and communicate with it at that speed. If you check computer listings at Dell, Lenovo, and other manufacturers, you will see PCs advertised as having 10/100/1000 Ethernet. Today, speeds of up to 1 Gbps are possible on wired LANs.

By the way, the abbreviations used for communications speeds differ from those used for computer memory. For communications equipment, k stands for 1,000, not 1,024 as it does for memory. Similarly, M stands for 1,000,000, not $1,024 \times 1,024$; G stands for 1,000,000,000, not $1,024 \times 1,024 \times 1,024$. Thus, 100 Mbps is 100,000,000 bits per second. Also, communications speeds are expressed in *bits*, whereas memory sizes are expressed in *bytes.*

Wireless LAN connections use the **IEEE 802.11 protocol**. Several versions of 802.11 exist, and as of 2012 the most current one is IEEE 802.11n. The differences among these versions are beyond the scope of this discussion. Just note that the current standard, 802.11n, allows speeds of up to 600 Mbps.

Observe that the LAN in Figure 6-2 uses both the 802.3 and 802.11 protocols. The NICs operate according to the 802.3 protocol and connect directly to the switch, which also operates on the 802.3 standard. The WNICs operate according to the 802.11 protocol and connect to the wireless access point. The access point must process messages using both the 802.3 and 802.11 standards; it sends and receives wireless traffic using the 802.11 protocol and then communicates with the switch using the 802.3 protocol. Characteristics of LANs are summarized in the top two rows of Figure 6-3.

Technology enables cost-effective communicating appliances . . . maybe next year they'll be tweeting one another. But, do you care? See the Guide on pages 204–205 for a discussion of the planning of exponential phenomena.

Figure 6-3
Network Technology
Summary

Type	Topology	Transmission Line	Transmission Speed	Equipment Used	Protocol Commonly Used	Remarks
Local area network	Local area network	UTP or optical fiber	Common: 10/100/1000 Mbps Possible: 1 Gbps	Switch NIC UTP or optical	IEEE 802.3 (Ethernet)	Switches connect devices, multiple switches on all but small LANs.
	Local area network with wireless	UTP or optical for non-wireless connections	Up to 600 Mbps	Wireless access point Wireless NIC	IEEE 802.11n	Access point transforms wired LAN (802.3) to wireless LAN (802.11).
Connections to the Internet	DSL modem to ISP	DSL telephone	Personal: Upstream to 1 Mbps, downstream to 40 Mbps (max 10 likely in most areas)	DSL modem DSL-capable telephone line	DSL	Can have computer and phone use simultaneously. Always connected.
	Cable modem to ISP	Cable TV lines to optical cable	Upstream to 1 Mbps Downstream 300 Kbps to 10 Mbps	Cable modem Cable TV cable	Cable	Capacity is shared with other sites; performance varies depending on other's use.
	WAN wireless	Wireless connection to WAN	500 K to 1.7 Mbps	Wireless WAN modem	One of several wireless standards.	Sophisticated protocol enables several devices to use the same wireless frequency.

Bluetooth is another common wireless protocol. It is designed for transmitting data over short distances, replacing cables. Some devices, such as wireless mice and keyboards, use Bluetooth to connect to the computer. Smartphones use Bluetooth to connect to automobile entertainment systems.

Connecting to the Internet

Although you may not have realized it, when you connect your SOHO LAN, phone, iPad, or Kindle to the Internet, you are connecting to a WAN. You must do so because you are connecting to computers that are not physically located on your premises. You cannot start running wires down the street to plug in somewhere.

When you connect to the Internet, you are actually connecting to an **Internet service provider (ISP)**. An ISP has three important functions. First, it provides you with a legitimate Internet address. Second, it serves as your gateway to the Internet. The ISP receives the communications from your computer and passes them on to the Internet, and it receives communications from the Internet and passes them on to you. Finally, ISPs pay for the Internet. They collect money from their customers and pay access fees and other charges on your behalf.

Figure 6-3 shows the three common alternatives for connecting to the Internet. Notice that we are discussing how your computer connects to the Internet via a WAN; we are not discussing the structure of the WAN itself. WAN architectures and their protocols are beyond the scope of this discussion. Search the Web for "leased lines" or "PSDN" if you want to learn more about WAN architectures.

SOHO LANs (like that in Figure 6-2) and individual home and office computers are commonly connected to an ISP in one of three ways: a special telephone line called a DSL line, a cable TV line, or a wireless-phone-like connection. All three of these alternatives require that the *digital data* in the computer be converted to a wavy signal, or an **analog signal**. A device called a **modem**, or modulator/demodulator, performs this conversion. Figure 6-4 shows one way of converting the digital byte 01000001 to an analog signal.

(By the way, because LAN devices almost always contain a modem, they are sometimes called *modems*. As you have learned, however, they contain much more than just a modem, so we do not call them modems in this text.)

As shown in Figure 6-5, once the modem converts your computer's digital data to analog, that analog signal is then sent over the telephone line, TV cable, or air. If sent by telephone line, the first telephone switch that your signal reaches converts the signal into the form used by the international telephone system.

Figure 6-4
Analog Versus Digital Signals

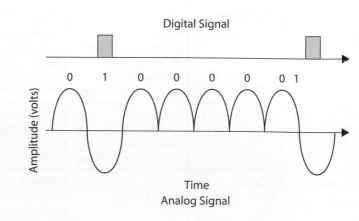

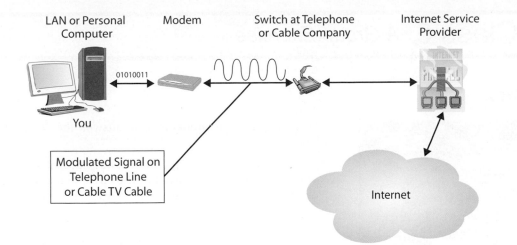

Figure 6-5
Personal Computer (PC)
Internet Access

DSL Modems

A **DSL modem** is the first modem type. DSL stands for **digital subscriber line**. DSL modems operate on the same lines as voice telephones, but they operate so that their signals do not interfere with voice telephone service. Because DSL signals do not interfere with telephone signals, DSL data transmission and telephone conversations can occur simultaneously. A device at the telephone company separates the phone signals from the computer signals and sends the latter signal to the ISP. DSL modems use their own protocols for data transmission.

Cable Modems

A cable modem is a second modem type. **Cable modems** provide high-speed data transmission using cable television lines. The cable company installs a fast, high-capacity optical fiber cable to a distribution center in each neighborhood that it serves. At the distribution center, the optical fiber cable connects to regular cable-television cables that run to subscribers' homes or businesses. Cable modems modulate in such a way that their signals do not interfere with TV signals.

Because up to 500 user sites can share these facilities, performance varies depending on how many other users are sending and receiving data. At the maximum, users can download data up to 50 Mbps and can upload data at 512 Kbps. Typically, performance is much lower than this. In most cases, the download speed of cable modems and DSL modems is about the same. Cable modems use their own protocols.

WAN Wireless Connection

A third way that you can connect your computer, iPhone, iPad, Kindle, or other communicating device is via a **WAN wireless** connection. Amazon.com's Kindle, for example, uses a Sprint wireless network to provide wireless data connections. The iPhone uses a LAN-based wireless network if one is available and a WAN wireless network if one is not. The LAN-based network is preferred because performance is considerably higher. As of 2012, WAN wireless provides average performance of 500 Kbps, with peaks of up to 1.7 Mbps, as opposed to the typical 50 Mbps for LAN wireless.

Before we leave the topic of network connections, you should learn the meaning of two other terms used to classify network speed. **Narrowband** lines typically have transmission speeds less than 56 Kbps. **Broadband** lines have speeds in excess of 256 Kbps. Today, all popular communication technologies provide broadband capability, and so these terms are likely to fade from use.

Using MIS InClass 6 *A Group Exercise*

Opening Pandora's Box

Source: Superstock.

Nearly free data communications and data storage have created unprecedented opportunities for businesses, as we have described numerous times. Inevitably, such technology will have a revolutionary impact in the home as well. The Guide on page 204 discusses why you should be wary of toasters and microwaves that talk to each other, but home entertainment is another matter.

Sonos is a good example. Sonos has leveraged emerging technologies, especially wireless technology, to develop easy-to-install, high-quality wireless audio systems. Customers hook up one of several different Sonos devices into their home LAN device using a wired Ethernet connection. That device then connects wirelessly to up to 32 other Sonos audio devices around the home. Each device can play its own music or other audio, some can play the same audio, or all can be forced to play the same audio.

Some Sonos devices provide wireless stereo to existing stereo systems; other devices include the wireless receiver and an amplifier, with the customer providing the speakers. Still other devices provide the wireless receiver, amplifier, and speakers in one unit.

Each Sonos device includes a computer running Linux. Those computers communicate wirelessly using a proprietary Sonos protocol. Because every device communicates with every other device, Sonos refers to its network of equipment as a *wireless mesh*. The benefit of this mesh to the consumer is flexibility and ease of installation. The devices find each other and determine their own data communications pathways (akin to, but different from, IP routing on the Internet).

Sonos works with any Internet radio source and with music services such as Pandora. With Pandora (and similar services), you establish a personal radio station by selecting a favorite song or musical work. Pandora then plays music based on your selection. You can vote thumbs up or thumbs down on music that is played. Based on your ratings, Pandora selects similar music based on proprietary algorithms.

Form a group of students and answer the following questions:

1. Imagine that you have graduated, have the job of your dreams, and want to install a wireless stereo system in your new condo. Assume that you have a spare bedroom you use as an office that has a LAN device connected to the Internet. You have an existing stereo system in your living room, a pair of unused speakers, but no other stereo equipment. Assume that you want to play audio and music in your office, your living room, and your bedroom.
   a. Visit the Sonos Web site at *www.sonos.com* and select and price the equipment you will need.
   b. Go to the Web sites of Sonos' competitors at http://www.logitech.com/en-us/speakers-audio or http://soundbridge.roku.com/soundbridge/index.php and select and price equipment you will need.
   c. Recommend one of the selections you identified in your answers to items a and b and justify your selection.
   d. Report your findings to the rest of the class.

2. Visit the Pandora Web site at *www.pandora.com*. Using the free trial membership, build a radio station for your group. Base your station on whatever song or music your group chooses.

3. The Sonos equipment has no on-off switch. Apparently, it is designed to be permanently on, like your LAN device. You can mute each station, but to turn a station off you must unplug it, an action few people take. Suppose you have tuned a Sonos device to a Pandora station, and you mute that device. Because the Sonos equipment is still on, it will continue downloading packets over the Internet to a device that no one is listening to.
   a. Describe the consequences of this situation on the Internet.
   b. You pay a flat fee for your Internet connection. In what ways does such a fee arrangement discourage efficiency?

4. Using your group's imagination and curiosity, describe the consequences of Internet-based audio on each of the following:
   a. Existing radio stations
   b. Vendors of traditional audio receivers
   c. Audio entertainment
   d. Cisco (a vendor of Internet routers)
   e. Your local ISP
   f. Any other companies or entities you believe will be impacted by wireless audio systems
   Report your conclusions to the rest of the class

(Continued)

5. Using history as a guide, we can image that audio leads the way for video.
  a. Explain how you could use a wireless video system in your new condo.
  b. In the opinion of your group, is having multiple wireless video players in your condo more or less desirable than wireless audio? Explain.
  c. Answer a–f in item 4, but use wireless video rather than audio as the driving factor.
  d. Report your answers to the rest of the class.
6. Considering all of your answers to items 1–5:

  a. What industries are the winners and losers?
  b. What companies are the winners and losers?
  c. How does your answer to parts a and b guide your job search?

7. Use the knowledge you have gained in answering items 1–6 to prepare a 1-minute statement that you could make in a job interview about emerging opportunities in Internet-based audio and video. Assume that with this statement you wish to demonstrate your ability to think innovatively. Deliver your statement to the rest of the class.

Q3 What Are the Fundamental Concepts You Should Know About the Internet?

As discussed in Q1, the Internet is an *internet*, meaning that it is a network of networks. As you might guess, the technology that underlies the Internet is complicated and beyond the scope of this text. However, because of the popularity of the Internet, certain terms have become ubiquitous in twenty-first-century business society. In this question, we will define and explain terms that you need to know to be an informed business professional and consumer of Internet services.

An Internet Example

Figure 6-6 illustrates one use of the Internet. Suppose that you are sitting in snowbound Minneapolis and you want to communicate with a hotel in sunny, tropical, northern

Figure 6-6
Using the Internet for a Hotel Reservation

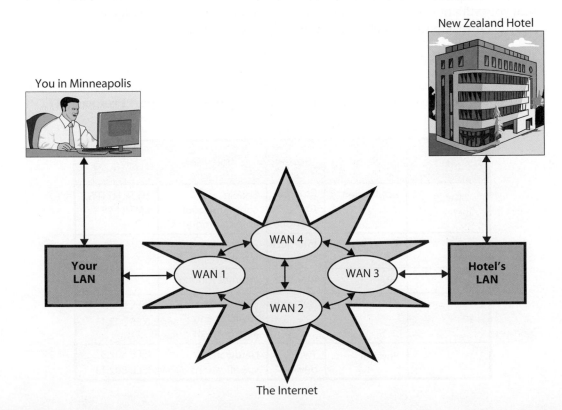

New Zealand. Maybe you are making a reservation using the hotel's Web site, or maybe you are sending an email to a reservations clerk inquiring about facilities or services.

To begin, note that this example is an internet because it is a network of networks. It consists of two LANs (yours and the hotel's) and four WANs. (In truth, the real Internet consists of tens of thousands of WANs and LANs, but to conserve paper we don't show all of them here.)

Your communication to the hotel involves nearly unimaginable complexity. Somehow, your computer communicates with a server in the New Zealand hotel, a computer that it has never "met" before and knows nothing about. Further, your transmission, which is too big to travel in one piece, is broken up into parts and each part passed along from WAN to WAN in such a way that it arrives intact. Then your original message is re-assembled, any parts that were lost or damaged (this happens) are resent, and the reconstructed message delivered to the server for processing. All of this is accomplished by computers and data communications devices that most likely have not interacted before.

What all these devices do know, however, is that they process the same set of protocols. Thus, we need to begin with Internet protocols.

The TCP/IP Protocol Architecture

The protocols used on the Internet are arranged according to a structure known as the **TCP/IP Protocol (TCP/IP) architecture**, which is a scheme of five protocol types arranged in layers. As shown in Figure 6-7, the top layer concerns protocols for applications like browsers and Web servers. The next two layers concern protocols about data communications across any internet (note the small *i*; this means any network of networks), including the Internet. The bottom two layers involve protocols that concern data transmission within a network. For example, the IEEE 802.3 and 802.11 LAN protocols operate at the bottom two layers.

As stated, a protocol is a set of rules and data structures for organizing communication. One or more protocols are defined at each layer. Data communications and software vendors write computer programs that implement the rules of a particular protocol. (For protocols at the bottom layer, the physical layer, they build hardware devices that implement the protocol.)

You are probably wondering, "Why should I know about this?" The reason is so that you will understand the terms you will hear and the products you will use, buy, or possibly invest in that relate to each other via this architecture.

Application-Layer Protocols

You will directly encounter at least three application-layer protocols in your professional life. (In fact, you have used two of them already). **Hypertext Transport Protocol (HTTP)**

Figure 6-7
TCP/IP Protocol Architecture

Layer	Name	Scope	Purpose	Example Protocol
5	Application	Program to program	Enable communication among programs	HTTP, HTTPS, SMTP, FTP
4	Transport	Internets	Reliable internet transport	TCP
3	Internet	Internets	Internet routing	IP
2	Data Link	Network	Flow among switches and access points	IEEE 802.3 IEEE 802.11
1	Physical	Two devices	Hardware specifications	IEEE 802.3 IEEE 802.11

is the protocol used between browsers and Web servers. When you use a browser such as Internet Explorer, Safari, or Chrome, you are using a program that implements the HTTP protocol. At the other end, at the New Zealand Hotel for example, there is a server that also processes HTTP, as you will learn in Q4. Even though your browser and the server at the hotel have never "met" before, they can communicate with one another because they both follow the rules of HTTP. Your browser sends requests for service encoded in a predefined HTTP *request format*; the server receives that request, does something, and formats a response in a predefined HTTP *response format*.

As you will learn in Chapter 12, there is secure version of HTTP called **HTTPS**. Whenever you see *https* in your browser's address bar, you have a secure transmission, and you can safely send sensitive data like credit card numbers. When you are on the Internet, if you do not see *https*, then you should assume that all of your communication is open and could be published on the front page of your campus newspaper tomorrow morning. Hence, when you are using HTTP, email, text messaging, chat, videoconferencing, or anything other than HTTPS, know that whatever you are typing or saying could be known by anyone else. Thus, in your classroom, when you send a text message to a fellow student, that message can be intercepted and read by anyone in your class, including your professor. The same is true of people at a coffee shop, an airport, or anywhere.

Two additional TCP/IP application-layer protocols are common. **SMTP**, or **Simple Mail Transfer Protocol**, is used for email transmissions (along with other protocols as well). **FTP**, or **File Transfer Protocol**, is used to move files over the Internet. One very common use for FTP is to maintain Web sites. When a Web site administrator wishes to post a new picture or story on a Web server, the administrator will often use FTP to move the picture or other item to the server. Like HTTP, FTP has a secure version as well, but do not assume you are using it.

With this knowledge, we can clear up one common misconception. You are using the Internet when you use any of these protocols. However, you are using the Web only when you use either HTTP or HTTPS. Thus, the **Web** is the Internet-based network of browsers and servers that process HTTP or HTTPS. When you send a file using FTP, you are using the Internet, but not the Web. It is incorrect to say you are using the Web to FTP files.

TCP and IP Protocols

You have some idea of the protocols used at the application (top) layer in Figure 6-7, and from the discussion in Q2 you have some idea of the LAN protocols used at the bottom two layers. But what is the purpose of the layers in between, the transport and internet layers? You know these two layers must be important because the architecture is named after their protocols.

These protocols manage traffic as it passes across an internet (including the Internet) from one network to another. The most important protocol in the transport layer is **TCP**, or the **Transmission Control Protocol**. As a transport protocol, TCP has many functions, most of which are beyond the scope of our discussion. One easily understood function, however, is that TCP programs break your traffic up into pieces and send each piece along its way. It then works with TCP programs on other devices in the internet to ensure that all of the pieces arrive at their destination. If one or more pieces are lost or damaged, TCP programs detect that condition and cause retransmission of that piece. Hence, the TCP layer is said to provide *reliable internet transport*.

The primary protocol of the Internet layer is called **IP (Internet Protocol)**, which is a protocol that specifies the routing of the pieces of your message through the networks that comprise any internet (including the Internet). In Figure 6-6, programs on devices at each of the networks (the two LANs and the four WANs) receive a portion of your message and route it to another computer in its network, or to another network altogether. A **packet** is a piece of a message that is handled by programs that implement IP. A **router** is a special-purpose computer that moves packet traffic according to the rules of the IP protocol.

Your message is broken into packets (for simplicity we're leaving a LOT out here) and each packet is sent out onto the Internet. The packet contains the address of where it is supposed to go. Routers along the way receive the packet, examine the destination IP address, and send it either to the desired destination, or to another router that is closer to the desired destination.

When your message starts on its way to the New Zealand hotel, no device knows what route the pieces will take. Until the last hop, a router just sends the packet to another router that it determines to be closer to the final destination. In fact, the packets that make up your message may take different pathways through the Internet (this is rare, but it does occur). Because of this routing scheme, the Internet is very robust. For example, in Figure 6-6, either WAN 2 or WAN 4 could fail and your packets will still get to the hotel.

To summarize, TCP provides reliable internet transport and IP provides internet routing.

IP Addressing

An **IP address** is a number that identifies a particular device. **Public IP addresses** identify a particular device on the public Internet. Because public IP addresses must be unique, worldwide, their assignment is controlled by a public agency known as **ICANN (Internet Corporation for Assigned Names and Numbers)**.

Private IP addresses identify a particular device on a private network, usually on a LAN. Their assignment is controlled within the LAN, usually by the LAN device shown in Figure 6-2. When you sign onto a LAN at a coffee shop, for example, the LAN device loans you a private IP address to use while you are connected to the LAN. When you leave the LAN, it reuses that address.

Use of Private IP Addresses

When your computer uses TCP/IP within a LAN, say to access a private Web server within the LAN, it uses a private IP address. However, and this is far more common, when you access a public site, say www.office365forstudents.com, from within the LAN, your traffic uses your internal IP address until it gets to the LAN device. At that point, the LAN device substitutes your private IP address for its public IP address and sends your traffic out onto the Internet.

This private/public IP address scheme has two major benefits. First, public IP addresses are conserved. All of the computers on the LAN use only one public IP address. Second, by using private IP addresses, you need not register a public IP address for your computer with ICANN-approved agencies. Furthermore, if you had a public IP address for your computer, every time you moved it, say from home to school, the Internet would have to update its addressing mechanisms to route traffic to your new location. Such updating would be a massive burden (and a mess)!

Functions of the LAN Device

Before we continue with IP addressing, note all of the functions of the LAN device. A lot is happening in that little box shown in Figure 6-2:

- Switch processing IEEE 802.3 wired LAN traffic
- Access-point processing IEEE 802.11 wireless LAN traffic
- Translation between IEEE 802.3 and IEEE 802.11
- Modem converting between Analog and Digital
- Server that assigns private IP addresses
- Private/public IP address translation converting between private and public IP addresses
- Internet router routing packets
- (And more that is beyond the scope of this discussion . . .)

Figure 6-8
Go Daddy Screenshot

Source: Copyright © 2010 GoDaddy.com, Inc.
All rights reserved.

Public IP Addresses and Domain Names

IP addresses have two formats. The most common form, called **IPv4**, has a four-decimal dotted notation like 165.193.123.253; the second, called **IPv6**, has a longer format and will not concern us here. In your browser, if you enter http://165.193.123.253, your browser will connect with the device on the public Internet that has been assigned to this address. Try it to find out who has this address.

Nobody wants to type IP addresses like http://165.193.123.253 to find a particular site. Instead, we want to enter names like www.pandora.com or www.woot.com or www.office365forstudents.com. To facilitate that desire, ICANN administers a system for assigning names to IP addresses. First, a **domain name** is a worldwide-unique name that is affiliated with a public IP address. When an organization or individual wants to register a domain name, it goes to a company that applies to an ICANN-approved agency to do so. Go Daddy (www.godaddy.com) is an example of such a company (Figure 6-8).

Go Daddy, or a similar agency, will first determine if the desired name is unique, worldwide. If so, then it will apply to register that name to the applicant. Once the registration is completed, the applicant can affiliate a public IP address with the domain name. From that point onward, traffic for the new domain name will be routed to the affiliated IP address.

Note two important points: First, several (or many) domain names can point to the same IP address. Second, the affiliation of domain names with IP addresses is dynamic. The owner of the domain name can change the affiliated IP addresses at its discretion.

Before we leave the Internet, you need to know one more term. A **URL (Uniform Resource Locator)** is an address on the Internet. Commonly, it consists of a protocol (like http:// or ftp://) followed by a domain name or public IP address. A URL is actually quite a bit more complicated than this description, but that detailed knowledge is beyond the scope of this text, so we'll hurry along. The preferred pronunciation of URL is to say the letters U, R, L.

Virtual Private Network

A **virtual private network (VPN)** uses the Internet to create the appearance of private point-to-point connections. In the IT world, the term *virtual* means something that appears to exist but in fact does not. Here, a VPN uses the public Internet to create the appearance of a private connection.

Figure 6-9
Remote Access
Using VPN; Actual
Connections

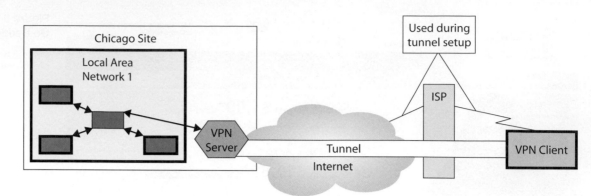

A Typical VPN

Figure 6-9 shows one way to create a VPN to connect a remote computer, perhaps an employee working at a hotel in Miami, to a LAN at a Chicago site. The remote user is the VPN client. That client first establishes a connection to the Internet. The connection can be obtained by accessing a local ISP, as shown in the figure, or, in some hotels, the hotel itself provides a direct Internet connection.

In either case, once the Internet connection is made, VPN software on the remote user's computer establishes a connection with the VPN server in Chicago. The VPN client and VPN server then have a point-to-point connection. That connection, called a **tunnel**, is a virtual, private pathway over a public or shared network from the VPN client to the VPN server. Figure 6-10 illustrates the connection as it appears to the remote user.

VPN communications are secure, even though they are transmitted over the public Internet. To ensure security, VPN client software *encrypts*, or codes (see Chapter 12, page 429), the original message so that its contents are protected from snooping. Then the VPN client appends the Internet address of the VPN server to the message and sends that package over the Internet to the VPN server. When the VPN server receives the message, it strips its address off the front of the message, *decrypts* the coded message, and sends the plain text message to the original address on the LAN. In this way, secure private messages are delivered over the public Internet.

VPNs offer the benefit of point-to-point leased lines, and they enable remote access, both by employees and by any others who have been registered with the VPN server. For example, if customers or vendors are registered with the VPN server, they can use the VPN from their own sites. Figure 6-11 shows three tunnels: one supports a point-to-point connection between the Atlanta and Chicago sites and the other two support remote connections.

Microsoft has fostered the popularity of VPNs by including VPN support in Windows. All versions of Microsoft Windows have the capability of working as VPN clients. Computers running Windows Server can operate as VPN servers.

Figure 6-10
Remote Access Using VPN:
Apparent Connection

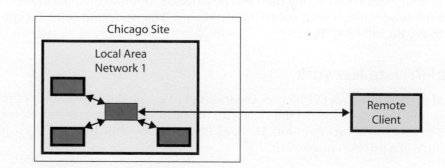

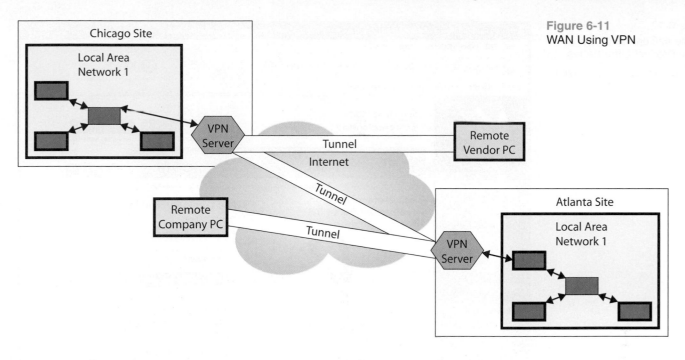

Figure 6-11
WAN Using VPN

Q4 What Processing Occurs on a Typical Web Server?

At this point, you know basic networking terms and have a high-level view of how internets and the Internet work. To complete this chapter's high-level survey of data communications, you need to know a bit about the processing that occurs on a Web server. For this discussion, we will use the example of a Web storefront, which is a server on the Web from which you can buy products.

Suppose you want to buy climbing equipment from REI, a co-op that sells outdoor clothing and equipment. To do so, you go to www.rei.com and navigate to the product(s) that you want to buy (see Figure 6-12). When you find something you want, you add it to your shopping cart and keep shopping. At some point, you check out by supplying credit card data.

In Q3, we discussed how your traffic crosses over the Internet to arrive at the REI server. The next question is: What happens at that server when it arrives? Or, from another perspective, if you want to set up a Web storefront for your company, what facilities do you need?

Three-Tier Architecture

Almost all e-commerce applications use the **three-tier architecture**, which is an arrangement of user computers and servers into three categories, or tiers, as shown in Figure 6-13. The **user tier** consists of computers, phones, and other devices that have browsers that request and process Web pages. The **server tier** consists of computers that run Web servers and process application programs. The **database tier** consists of computers that run a DBMS that processes requests to retrieve and store data. Figure 6-13 shows only one computer at the database tier. Some sites have multicomputer database tiers as well.

When you enter http://www.rei.com in your browser, the browser sends a request that travels over the Internet to a computer in the server tier at the REI site. That request is formatted and processed according to the rules of HTTP. (Notice, by the way, that if you just type www.rei.com, your browser will add the http:// to signify that it is using HTTP.) In response to your request, a server-tier computer sends back a **Web page**, which is a document that is coded in one of the standard page markup

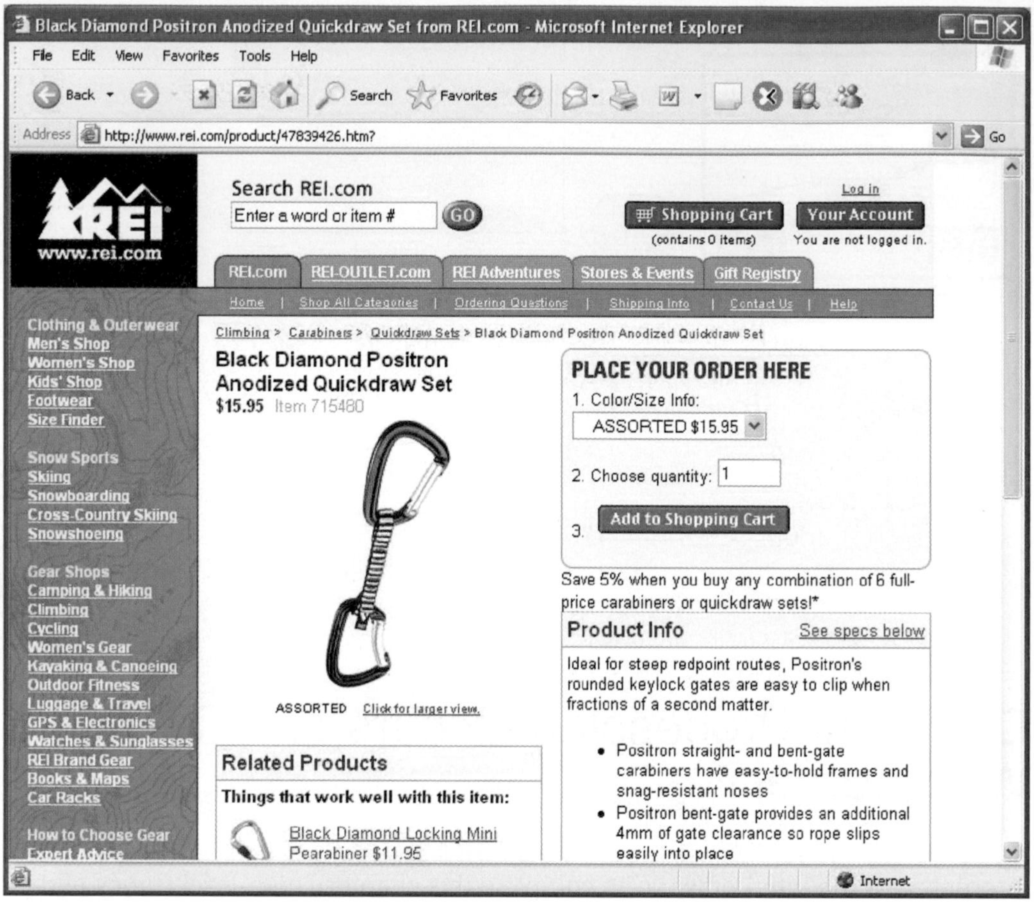

Figure 6-12
Sample of Commerce Server
Pages; Product Offer Pages

Source: Used with permission of REI and Black
Diamond.

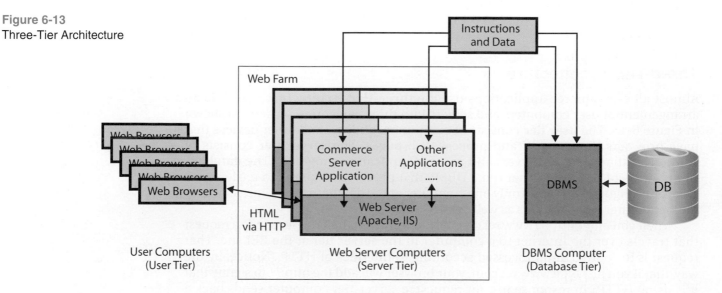

languages. The most popular page markup language is the *Hypertext Markup Language (HTML)*, which is described later in this section.

Web servers are programs that run on a server-tier computer and that manage HTTP traffic by sending and receiving Web pages to and from clients. A **commerce server** is an application program that runs on a server-tier computer. A commerce server receives requests from users via the Web server, takes some action, and returns a response to the users via the Web server. Typical commerce server

Figure 6-13
Three-Tier Architecture

functions are to obtain product data from a database, manage the items in a shopping cart, and coordinate the checkout process. In Figure 6-13, the server-tier computers are running a Web server program, a commerce server application, and other applications having an unspecified purpose.

To ensure acceptable performance, commercial Web sites usually are supported by several or even many Web server computers in a facility called a **Web farm**. Work is distributed among the computers in a Web farm so as to minimize customer delays. The coordination among multiple Web server computers is a fantastic dance, but, alas, we do not have space to tell that story here. Just imagine the coordination that must occur as you add items to an online order when, to improve performance, different Web server computers receive and process each addition to your order.

Watch the Three Tiers in Action!

To see a three-tier example in action, go to your favorite Web storefront site, place something in a shopping cart, and consider Figure 6-13 as you do so. When you enter an address into your browser, the browser sends a request for the default page to a server computer at that address. A Web server, and possibly a commerce server, process your request and send back the default page.

As you click Web pages to find products you want, the commerce server accesses the database to retrieve data about those products. It creates pages according to your selections and sends the results back to your browser via the Web server. Again, different computers on the server tier may process your series of requests and must constantly communicate about your activities. You can follow this process in Figure 6-13.

In Figure 6-12 the user has navigated through climbing equipment at REI.com to find a particular item. To produce this page, the commerce server accessed a database to obtain the product picture, price, special terms (a 5 percent discount for buying six or more), product information, and related products.

The user placed six items in her basket, and you can see the response in Figure 6-14 on the next page. Again, trace the action in Figure 6-13 and imagine what occurred to produce the second page. Notice that the discount was applied correctly.

When the customer checks out, the commerce server program will be called to process payment, schedule inventory processing, and arrange for shipping. Most likely the commerce server interfaces with enterprise applications like those you will learn about in Chapter 7. Truly this is an amazing capability!

Hypertext Markup Language (HTML)

Hypertext Markup Language (HTML) is the most common language for defining the structure and layout of Web pages. An HTML **tag** is a notation used to define a data element for display or other purposes. The following HTML is a typical heading tag:

<h2>Price of Item</h2>

Notice that tags are enclosed in < > (called *angle brackets*) and that they occur in pairs. The start of this tag is indicated by <h2>, and the end of the tag is indicated by </h2>. The words between the tags are the value of the tag. This HTML tag means to place the words "Price of Item" on a Web page in the style of a level-two heading. The creator of the Web page will define the style (font size, color, and so forth) for h2 headings and the other tags to be used.

Web pages include **hyperlinks**, which are pointers to other Web pages. A hyperlink contains the URL of the Web page to find when the user clicks the hyperlink.

Figure 6-14
Shopping-Cart Page

Source: Used with permission of REI.

The URL can reference a page on the server that generated the page containing the hyperlink or it can reference a page on another server.

Figure 6-15 (a) shows a sample HTML document. The document has a heading that provides metadata about the page and a body that contains the content. The tag <h1> means to format the indicated text as a level-one heading; <h2> means a level-two heading. The tag <a> defines a hyperlink. This tag has an **attribute**, which is a variable used to provide properties about a tag. Not all tags have attributes, but many do. Each attribute has a standard name. The attribute for a hyperlink is **href**, and its value indicates which Web page is to be displayed when the user clicks the link. Here, the page www.pearsonhighered.com/kroenke is to be returned when the user clicks the hyperlink. Figure 6-15 (b) shows this page as rendered by Internet Explorer.

XML, Flash, Silverlight, and HTML 5

HTML has been the workhorse of the Web for more than 15 years. However, it has problems and limitations that have been overcome by newer technologies. **XML (eXtensible Markup Language)** is a markup language that fixes several HTML deficiencies and is commonly used for program-to-program interaction over the Web. See the discussion of *service-oriented architecture* in Chapter 7 for more about this. **Flash** is an add-on to browsers that was developed by Adobe and is useful for providing animation, movies, and other advanced graphics inside a browser. **Silverlight** is a browser add-on that was developed by Microsoft for the same purposes as Flash. Silverlight has newer technology than Flash and greater functionality, but is less frequently used. Finally, HTML 5.0 is a new version of HTML that also supports animation, movies, and graphics.

```
<!DOCTYPE html PUBLIC "-//W3C//DTD XHTML 1.0 Transitional//EN" "http://www.w3.org/TR/xhtml1/DTD/xhtml1-transition
<html xmlns="http://www.w3.org/1999/xhtml">

<head>
<meta content="en-us" http-equiv="Content-Language" />
<meta content="text/html; charset=utf-8" http-equiv="Content-Type" />
<title>UMIS Example HTML</title>
<style type="text/css">
.style1 {
    font-size: xx-large;
    text-align: center;
    font-family: Arial, Helvetica, sans-serif;
}
.style2 {
    color: #FF00FF;
}
.style3 {
    font-size: medium;
    text-align: center;
    font-family: Arial, Helvetica, sans-serif;
}
.style5 {
    font-size: medium;
    text-align: left;
    font-family: Arial, Helvetica, sans-serif;
}
</style>
</head>

<body>

<p class="style1">
    <span class="style2"><strong>Using</strong></span>
    <strong>MIS</strong></p>
<p class="style1"> </p>
<p class="style3"><em>Fifth Edition</em></p>
<p class="style3"> </p>
<p class="style5">Example HTML Document</p>
<p class="style5"> </p>
<p class="style5"> </p>
<p class="style5">Click <a href="http://www.PearsonHigherEd.com/kroenke">here</a>
for the textbook&#39;s web site at Pearson Education.</p>

</body>

</html>
```

Figure 6-15a
Sample HTML Code Snippet

Almost all experts agree that XML will continue to be most important for interprogram communication on the Web. Given the success of iOS (see Case Study 4, page 137), most people believe that HTML 5.0 will replace standard HTML, Flash, and Silverlight.

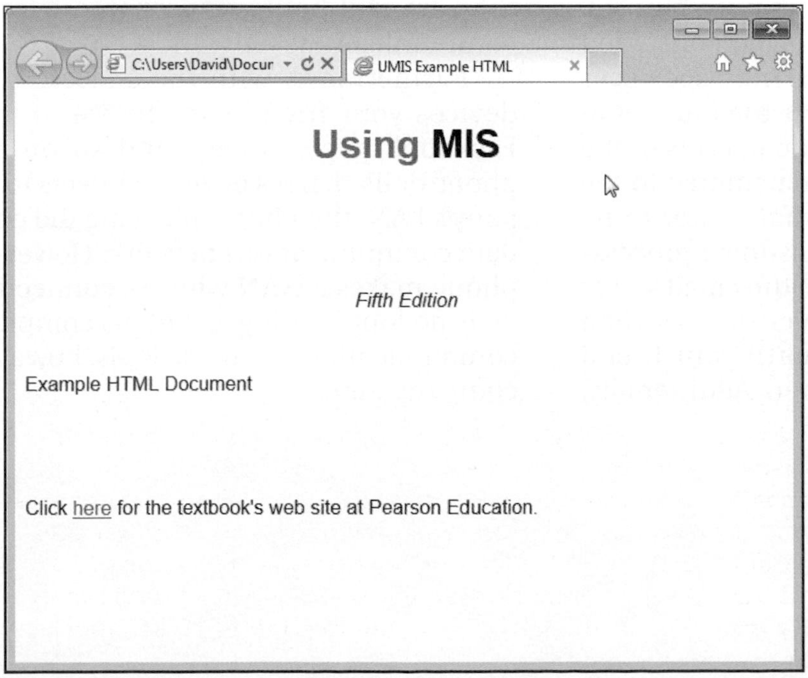

Figure 6-15b
Document Created from HTML Code in Figure 6-15a

Ethics Guide

Personal Work at Work?

Let's suppose you go on a vacation to New Zealand and you decide to email pictures of your amazing surfing skills to a friend who works at, say, some company in Ohio. Your email does not concern your friend's work or his company's business. It is not an emergency email, nor is it even a request for a ride to your house from the airport. Your email concerns your surfing skills! Even worse, your email is not just a few sentences that would consume a little file space. Rather, your email contains a dozen pictures, and, without noticing it, you sent very high-quality pictures that were 6.2 megabytes in size, each.

"Come on," you're saying, "give me a break! What's the matter with an email and some pictures? It's me surfing, it's not some weird pornographic material."

Maybe you're right; maybe it's not a big deal. But consider the resources you've consumed by sending that email: Your message, over 60 megabytes of it, traveled over the Internet to your friend's company's ISP. The packets of the email and picture were then transmitted to the company's router and from that router to its email server. Your message consumed processing cycles on the router and on the email server computer. A copy of your picture was then stored on that email server until your friend deleted it, perhaps weeks later. Additionally,

your friend will use his computer and the company LAN to download the pictures to his desktop computer, where they will be stored. In fact, the entire computing infrastructure, from the ISP to your friend's desk, is owned, operated, and paid for by your friend's employer. Finally, if your friend reads his email during his working hours, he will be consuming company resources—his time and attention, which the company has paid for while he is at work.

Of course, email is not the most time-consuming possibility. In addition to emailing pictures, you're likely to be updating your Facebook page with the photos, and your friend is likely using his computer to view those photos and to comment on your page and to update his. Now, the pictures are no longer stored on the company's servers, but they are still being transmitted over its data communications network.

Furthermore, with the success of mobile devices your friend can choose to read your Facebook page, tweets, and so on from his phone or iPad. If his device connects to his company's LAN, then he is still using the company's data communications network. However, if that phone makes a WAN wireless connection, then he is no longer using any of his company's data communications network. He is, however, using company time. ■

Discussion Questions

1. Is it ethical for you to send the email and picture to your friend at work?

2. Does your answer to question 1 change depending on the size of the pictures? Does your answer change if you send 100 pictures? If you send 1,000 pictures? If your answer does change, where do you draw the line?

3. Once the pictures are stored on the company's email server, who owns the pictures? Who controls those pictures? Does the company have the right to inspect the contents of its employees' mailboxes? If so, what should managers do when they find your picture that has absolutely nothing to do with the company's business?

4. What do you think is the greater cost to your friend's company: the cost of the infrastructure to transmit and store the email or the cost of the time your friend takes at work to read and view your pictures? Does this consideration change any of your answers above?

5. How does the use of Facebook and Twitter change the ethics of the situation? Is it ethical for your friend to read and update Facebook or tweets using the company's computers?

6. How do mobile devices like the iPad change the ethics of the situation? Is it any of the company's business what your friend does with his mobile device at work?

7. Describe a reasonable policy for computer/phone/communicating device use at work. Consider email, Facebook, and Twitter, as well as the use of mobile devices. Try to develop a policy that will be robust in the face of likely future data communications and mobile device developments.

Q5 Why Is the Cloud the Future for Most Organizations?

Until 2010 or so, most organizations constructed and maintained their own computing infrastructure. Organizations purchased or leased hardware, installed it on their premises, and used it to support organizational email, Web sites, e-commerce sites, and in-house applications, such as accounting and operations systems (you'll learn about them in the next chapter). After about 2010, however, organizations began to move their computing infrastructure to the cloud, and it is likely that in the future all, or nearly all, computing infrastructure will be leased from the cloud. So, just what is the cloud, and why is it the future?

We define the **cloud** as the *elastic* leasing of *pooled* computer resources over the *Internet*. The term *cloud* is used because most early diagrams of three-tier and other Internet-based systems used a cloud symbol to represent the Internet (see Figure 6-6 for an example), and organizations came to view their infrastructure as being "somewhere in the cloud."

Consider each of the italicized terms in the definition. The term **elastic**, which was first used this way by Amazon.com, means that the amount of resources leased can be increased or decreased dynamically, programmatically, in a short span of time and that organizations pay for just the resources that they use. The resources are **pooled**, because many different organizations use the same physical hardware; they share that hardware through virtualization. Cloud vendors dynamically allocate virtual machines to physical hardware as customer needs increase or decrease. Finally, the resources are accessed via **Internet protocols and standards**, which are additions to TCP/IP that enable cloud-hosting vendors to provide processing capabilities in flexible, yet standardized, ways.

An easy way to understand the essence of this development is to consider electrical power. In the very earliest days of electric power generation, organizations operated their own generators to create power for their company's needs. Over time, as the power grid expanded, it became possible to centralize power generation so that organizations could purchase just the electricity they needed from an electric utility.

Both cloud vendors and electrical utilities benefit from economies of scale. According to this principle, the average cost of production decreases as the size of the operation increases. Major cloud vendors operate enormous Web farms. Figure 6-16

Figure 6-16
Apple Data Center in Maiden, North Carolina

Source: Google Earth.

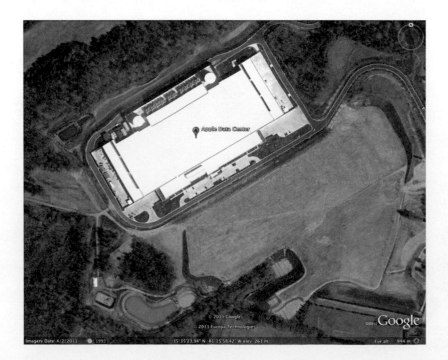

shows the building that contains the computers in the Web farm that Apple constructed in 2011 to support its iCloud offering (discussed in Q6). This billion-dollar facility contains more than 500,000 square feet.[1] IBM, Google, Amazon.com, Microsoft, Oracle, and other large companies each operate several or many similar farms as well.

Why Is the Cloud Preferred to In-House Hosting?

Figure 6-17 compares and contrasts cloud-based and in-house hosting. As you can see, the positives are heavily tilted toward cloud-based computing. The cloud vendor Rackspace will lease you one medium server for as little as 1.5 cents per hour. You can obtain and access that server today, actually within a few minutes. Tomorrow, if you need thousands of servers, you can readily scale up to obtain them. Furthermore, you know the cost structure; although you might have a surprise with regards to how many customers want to access your Web site, you won't have any surprises as to how much it will cost.

Figure 6-17
Comparison of Cloud and On-Site Alternatives

Cloud	On Site
Positive:	
Small capital requirements	Control of data location
Speedy development	In-depth visibility of security and disaster preparedness
Superior flexibility and adaptability to growing or fluctuating demand	
Known cost structure	
Possibly best-of-breed security/disaster preparedness	
No obsolesce	
Industry-wide economies of scale, hence cheaper	
Negative:	
Dependency on vendor	Significant capital required
Loss of control over data location	Significant development effort
Little visibility into true security and disaster preparedness capabilities	Annual maintenance costs
	Ongoing support costs
	Staff and train personnel
	Increased management requirements
	Difficult (impossible?) to accommodate fluctuating demand
	Cost uncertainties
	Obsolescence

[1] Patrick Thibodeau, "Apple, Google, Facebook Turn N.C. into Data Center Hub," *Computerworld*, June 3, 2011. Available at www.computerworld.com/s/article/9217259/Apple_Google_Facebook_turn_N.C._into_data_center_hub (accessed July 2011).

Another positive is that as long as you're dealing with large, reputable organizations, you'll be receiving best-of-breed security and disaster recovery (discussed in Chapter 12). In addition, you need not worry that you're investing in technology that will soon be obsolete; the cloud vendor is taking that risk. All of this is possible because the cloud vendor is gaining economies of scale by selling to an entire industry, not just to you.

The negatives of cloud computing involve loss of control. You're dependent on a vendor; changes in the vendor's management, policy, and prices are beyond your control. Further, you don't know where your data—which may be a large part of your organization's value—is located. Nor do you know how many copies of your data there are, or even if they're located in the same country as you are. Finally, you have no visibility into the security and disaster preparedness that is actually in place.

The positives and negatives of in-house hosting are shown in the second column of Figure 6-17. For the most part, they are the opposite of those for cloud-based computing; note, however, the need for personnel and management. With in-house hosting, not only will you have to construct your own data center, you'll also need to acquire and train the personnel to run it and then manage those personnel and your facility.

Why Now?

A skeptic responds to Figure 6-17 by saying "If it's so great, why hasn't cloud-based hosting been used for years?" Why now?

In fact cloud-based hosting (or a version of it under a different name) has been around since the 1960s. Long before the creation of the personal computer and networks, time-sharing vendors provided slices of computer time on a use-fee basis. However, the technology of that time, continuing up until the first decade of this century, did not favor the construction and use of enormous data centers.

Three factors have made cloud-based hosting advantageous today. First, processors, data communication, and data storage are so cheap as to be nearly free. At the scale of a Web farm of hundreds of thousands of processors, providing a virtual machine for an hour costs essentially nothing, as the 1.5 cent price per hour indicates. Because data communication is so cheap, getting the data to and from that processor is also nearly free.

Second, virtualization technology enables the near instantaneous creation of a new virtual machine. The customer provides (or creates in the cloud) a disk image of the data and programs of the machine it wants to provision. Virtualization software takes it from there.

Finally, new Internet-based protocols and standards have enabled cloud-hosting vendors to provide processing capabilities in flexible, yet standardized, ways. Chief among them are the **Web service standards** that sit on top of HTTP and are used to specify how computers interoperate. The provider of a Web service, such as a cloud-hosting organization, uses these standards to specify the work that it will perform and how it will provide it. Consumers of that service use those standards to request and receive service. The bottom line: Web service standards provide a vocabulary and grammar for programs on different computers to communicate.

When Does the Cloud Not Make Sense?

Cloud-based hosting makes sense for most organizations. The only organizations for which it may not make sense are those that are required by law or by industry standard practice to have physical control over their data. Such organizations might be forced to create and maintain their own hosting infrastructure. A financial institution, for example, might be legally required to maintain physical control over its data.

Even where physical control is a requirement, it is possible for organizations to obtain some of the benefits of cloud computing in what is termed the **private cloud**, which is in-house hosting, delivered via Web service standards, that can be configured dynamically. Some say that there is no such thing as a private cloud, however, because the infrastructure is owned by the using organization and the economies of scale cannot be shared with others.

In the final analysis, the cloud is the future for most organizations.

Q6 How Can Organizations Use the Cloud?

Cloud-based service offerings can be organized into the three categories shown in Figure 6-18. An organization that provides **software as a service (SaaS)** provides not only hardware infrastructure, but also an operating system and application programs on top of that hardware. For example, Salesforce.com provides programs for customer and sales tracking as a service. Similarly, Microsoft provides Office 365 as a service. Exchange, Lync, and SharePoint applications are provided as a service "in the cloud."

Apple's iCloud is probably the most exciting recent SaaS offering. Using iCloud, Apple will automatically sync all of its customers' iOS devices. As of 2011, Apple provides nine free applications in the iCloud. Calendar is a good example. When a customer enters an appointment in her iPhone, Apple will automatically push that appointment into the calendars on all of that customer's iOS devices. Further, customers can share calendars with others that will be synchronized as well. Mail, pictures, applications, and other resources are also synched via iCloud.

An organization can move to SaaS simply by signing up and learning how to use it. In Apple's case, there's nothing to learn. To quote the late Steve Jobs, "It just works."

The second category of cloud hosting is **platform as a service (PaaS)**, whereby vendors provide hosted computers, an operating system, and possibly a DBMS. Microsoft Windows Azure, for example, provides servers installed with Windows Server. Customers of Windows Azure then add their own applications on top of the hosted platform. Microsoft SQL Azure provides a host with Windows Server and SQL Server. Oracle on Demand provides a hosted server with Oracle Database. Again, for PaaS, organizations add their own applications to the host.

The most basic cloud offering is **infrastructure as a service (IaaS)**, which is the cloud hosting of a bare server computer or disk drive. The Amazon EC2 provides bare servers, and its Simple Storage Server provides, in essence, an unlimited, reliable disk drive in the cloud. Rackspace provides similar capabilities.

Organizations choose the cloud service they need. Lucas, for example, wants to host GearUp's e-commerce server in the cloud. In terms of Figure 6-11, GearUp needs to put its Web servers and its database server in the cloud using PaaS. To do so, GearUp could use, say, Windows Azure for the Web servers and SQL Azure for the database server. Lucas was thinking of that option when he cited the 25 cents per hour price.

If GearUp wanted to, it could also obtain bare servers from an IaaS vendor like Amazon.com or Rackspace. Were it to do so, GearUp would need to provision an operating system and DBMS on top of the server. Most likely, a small organization like GearUp would use PaaS.

Cloud Category	Examples
SaaS (software as a service)	Salesforce.com iCloud Office 365
PaaS (platform as a service)	Microsoft Azure Oracle on Demand
IaaS (infrastructure as a service)	Amazon EC2 (Elastic Cloud 2) Amazon S3 (Simple Storage Service)

Figure 6-18
Three Fundamental Cloud Types

Q7 2022?

The cloud brings both good and bad news. The good news is that organizations can readily obtain elastic resources at very low cost. This trend will benefit everyone from individuals on the iCloud to small groups using Office 365, startups like GearUp using PaaS, and huge organizations like Facebook using IaaS.

So, what's the bad news? That 500,000 square foot Apple Web farm in Figure 6-16? Note the size of the parking lot. That tiny lot accommodates the entire operations staff. According to *Computerworld,* that building will employ an operations staff of 50 people, which, spread over three shifts, 24/7, means that not many more than 8 people will be running that center at any one time. Seems impossible, but is it? Again look at the size of the parking lot.

Where are the jobs? In 2011, every city of almost any size supports small companies that install and maintain in-house Exchange and other servers. If SaaS products like Office 365 replace those servers, what happens to those local jobs? See Case Study 6, page 210 for more.

Perhaps the cloud will foster new categories of work. By 2022, everything will be connected to everything else, with most data stored in the cloud. New categories of products and services will emerge that should create jobs.

For example, **remote access systems** will provide computer-based activity or action at a distance. By enabling action at a distance, remote access systems save time and travel expense and make the skills and abilities of an expert available in places where he or she is not physically located. They also enable experts to scale their expertise. Consider a few examples:

Today, remote access systems include **telediagnosis**, which health care professionals can use to provide expertise in rural or remote areas. **Telesurgery** uses telecommunications to link surgeons to robotic equipment at distant locations. In 2001, Dr. Jacques Marescaux, located in New York City, performed the first trans-Atlantic surgery when he successfully operated on a patient in Strasbourg, France. Those examples, which are rare today, will become common by 2022.

Other uses for remote systems include **telelaw enforcement**, such as the RedFlex system that uses cameras and motion-sensing equipment to issue tickets for red-light and speeding violations. The RedFlex Group, headquartered in South Melbourne, Victoria, Australia, earns 87 percent of its revenue from traffic violations in the United States. It offers a turn-key traffic-citation information system that includes all five components.

Many remote systems are designed to provide services in dangerous locations, such as robots that clean nuclear reactors or biologically contaminated sites. Drones and other unoccupied military equipment are examples of remote systems used in war zones.

By 2022, with everything hosted and everything connected, teleaction can afford to move beyond high-value industries like medicine to lower-value services. Why does the world's best figure skating coach need to be physically present at a skater's practice? Why can't the world's best ski instructor provide high-value instruction to skiers on mountains all over the world?

Teleaction also reduces the value of local mediocrity. The claim "Well, I'm not the best, but at least I'm here" loses value in a teleaction world. In 1990, when former Secretary of Labor Robert Reich wrote *The Work of Nations,*[2] he could sensibly claim that those who provide routine face-to-face services are exempt from the dangers of offshoring. That claim loses validity in the teleaction world.

---

[2] Reich, Robert, *Work of Nations: Preparing Ourselves for Twenty-first Century Capitalism* (Vintage Books: New York, 1992), p. 176.

However, the need for local support staff increases with teleaction. The remote hospital may not need its own mediocre heart surgeon, but it will need staff who can prepare the patient for surgery; it will need a local anesthesiologist, and it will need local nurses. This is also true of a remote figure skating coach. Someone needs to be on-scene.

Finally, teleaction increases the value of robotics. Someone needs to design, build, market, sell, and support the machines that are on the other end of the expert's action. If the value of the expert increases, so, too, does the value of the robot.

All of this seems likely, and positive, but it does beg the question, where are the jobs? A famous surgeon or skating coach can reach a bigger market, faster and better, and, as stated, there is a need for some local support, but what about the rest of us? Better become an expert, in something. If you're not an expert, then find a way to be indispensable to someone who is. At the Apple Web farm, 500,000 square feet divided by 50 people is 10,000 square feet per person—managing some of the world's most sophisticated computing equipment. You've got to find a way to be an expert in the products that those 500,000 square feet of gear support. They next six chapters will show you some ways. Keep reading!

Guide

Thinking Exponentially Is Not Possible, but . . .

Nathan Myhrvold, the chief scientist at Microsoft Corporation during the 1990s, once said that humans are incapable of thinking exponentially. Instead, when something changes exponentially, we think of the fastest linear change we can imagine and extrapolate from there, as illustrated in the figure on the next page. Myhrvold was writing about the exponential growth of magnetic storage. His point was that no one could then imagine how much growth there would be in magnetic storage and what we would do with it.

This limitation pertains equally well to the growth of computer network phenomena. We have witnessed exponential growth in a number of areas: the number of Internet connections, the number of Web pages, and the amount of data accessible on the Internet. And, all signs are that this exponential growth isn't over.

You might wonder how this will affect you. Well, suppose you are a product manager for home appliances. Because most homes have a wireless network, it would be cheap and easy for appliances to talk to one another. How does that fact impact your existing product line? Will the competition's talking appliances take away your market share? However, talking appliances may not satisfy a real need. If a toaster and a coffee pot have nothing to say to each other, you'll be wasting money to create them.

Every business, every organization, needs to be thinking about the ubiquitous and cheap connectivity that is growing exponentially. What are the new opportunities? What are the new threats? How will our competition react? How should we position ourselves? How should we respond? As you consider these questions, keep in mind that because humans cannot think exponentially, we're all just guessing.

So what can we do to better anticipate changes brought by exponential phenomena? For one, understand that technology does not drive people to do things they've never done before, no matter how much the technologists suggest it might. (Just because we *can do* something does not mean anyone will *want to do* that something.)

Social progress occurs in small, evolutionary, adaptive steps. Right now, for example, if you want to watch a movie with someone, you both need to be in the same room. It needn't be that way. Using data communications, several people can watch the same movie, at the same time, together, but not in the same location. They can have an open audio line to make comments to each other during the movie or even have a Web cam so they can see each other watching the same movie. That sounds like something people might want to do—it's an outgrowth of what people are already doing.

However, emerging network technology enables my dry cleaner to notify me the minute my clothes are ready. Do I want to know? How much do I care to know that my clothes are ready Monday at 1:45 rather than sometime after 4:00 on Tuesday? In truth, I don't care. Such technology does not solve a problem that I have.

So, even if technology enables a capability, that possibility doesn't mean that anyone wants that capability. People want to do what they're already doing, but more easily; they want to solve problems that they already have.

Another response to exponential growth is to hedge your bets. If you can't know the outcome of an exponential phenomenon, don't commit to one direction. Position yourself to move as soon as the direction is clear. Develop a few talking appliances, position your organization to develop more, but wait for a clear sign of market acceptance before going all out.

Finally, notice in the exponential curve that the larger the distance between Now and The Future, the larger the error. In fact, the error increases exponentially with the length of the prediction. So, if you hear that the market for talking kitchen appliances will reach $1 billion in 1 year, assign that statement a certain level of doubt. However, if you hear that it will reach $1 billion in 5 years, assign that statement an exponentially greater level of doubt. ■

Discussion Questions

1. In your own words, explain the meaning of the claim that no one can think exponentially. Do you agree with this claim?

2. Describe a phenomenon besides connectivity or magnetic memory that you believe is increasing exponentially. Explain why it is difficult to predict the consequences of this phenomenon in 3 years.

3. To what extent do you think technology is responsible for the growth in the number of news sources? On balance, do you think having many news sources of varying quality is better than having just a few high-quality ones?

4. List three products or services, such as remote group movie viewing, that could dramatically change because of increased connectivity. Do not include movie viewing.

5. Rate your answers to question 4 in terms of how closely they fit with problems that people have today.

Source: Maxx-Studio/Shutterstock.com.

● Actual growth

● Growth we can imagine

Now   Future

Guide

Human Networks Matter More

In case you missed it, *Six Degrees of Separation* is a play by John Guare that was made into a movie starring Stockard Channing and Donald Sutherland. The title is related to the idea, originated by the Hungarian writer Frigyes Karinthy, that everyone on earth is connected to everyone else by five (Karinthy) or six (Guare) people.[3] For example, according to the theory, you are connected to Lady Gaga by no more than five or six people, because you know someone who knows someone, who knows someone, and so on. By the same theory, you are also connected to a Siberian seal hunter. Today, in fact, with the Internet, the number may be closer to three people than to five or six, but, in any case, the theory points out the importance of human networks.

Suppose you want to meet your university's president. The president has a secretary who acts as a gatekeeper. If you walk up to that secretary and say, "I'd like a half an hour with President Jones," you're likely to be palmed off to some other university administrator. What else can you do?

If you are connected to everyone on the planet by no more than six degrees, then surely you are connected to your president in fewer steps. Perhaps you play on the tennis team, and you know that the president plays tennis. In that case, it is likely that the tennis coach knows the president. So, arrange a tennis match with your coach and the president. Voilà! You have your meeting. It may even be better to have the meeting on the tennis court than in the president's office.

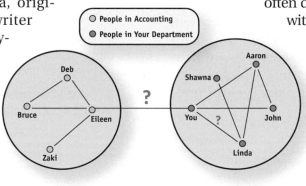

The problem with the six-degree theory, as Stockard Channing said so eloquently, is that even though those six people do exist, we don't know who they are. Even worse, we often don't know who the person is with whom we want to connect. For example, there is someone, right now who knows someone who has a job for which you are perfectly suited. Unfortunately, you don't know the name of that person.

It doesn't stop when you get your job, either. When you have a problem at work, like the need to understand how TCP/IP relates to the outlook for Cisco Systems (CSCO), there is someone who knows exactly how to help you. You, however, don't know who that is.

Accordingly, most successful professionals consistently build personal human networks. They use Facebook and LinkedIn to build and maintain their networks because they know that somewhere there is someone whom they need to know or will need to know. They also meet people at professional and social situations, collect and pass out cards, and engage in pleasant conversation (all part of a social protocol) to expand their networks.

You are undoubtedly using Facebook right now. You may even be using LinkedIn. But you can use these applications more effectively if you think about the power of weak ties. To understand weak ties, consider the network diagram above. Assume that each line represents a relationship between two people. Notice that the people in your

[3] See "The Third Link" in Albert Laszlo Barabasi's book *Linked* (New York: Perseus Publishing, 2002) for background on this theory.

department tend to know each other, and the people in the accounting department also tend to know each other. That's typical.

Now suppose you are at the weekly employee after-hours party and you have an opportunity to introduce yourself either to Linda or Eileen. Setting aside personal considerations, thinking just about network building, which person should you meet?

If you introduce yourself to Linda, you shorten your pathway to her from two steps to one and your pathway to Shawna from three to two. You do not open up any new channels because you already have them to the people in your department.

However, if you introduce yourself to Eileen, you open up an entirely new network of acquaintances. So, considering just network building, you use your time better by meeting Eileen and other people who are not part of your current circle. It opens up many more possibilities.

The connection from you to Eileen is called a weak tie in social network theory,[4] and such links are crucial in connecting you to everyone in six degrees. *In general, the people you know the least contribute the most to your network.* This phenomenon is true whether your network is face-to-face or virtual, like LinkedIn.

This concept is simple, but you'd be surprised by how few people pay attention to it. At most company events, everyone talks with the people they know, and, if the purpose of the function is to have fun, then that behavior makes sense. In truth, however, no business social function exists for having fun, regardless of what people say. Business functions exist for business reasons, and you can use them to create and expand networks. Given that time is always limited, you may as well use such functions efficiently. ■

Discussion Questions

1. Determine the shortest path from you to your university's president. How many links does it have?

2. Give an example of a network to which you belong that is like your department in the figure on the preceding page. Sketch a diagram of who knows whom for six or so members of that group.

3. Recall a recent social situation and identify two people, one of whom could have played the role of Linda (someone in your group whom you do not know) and one of whom could have played the role of Eileen (someone in a different group whom you do not know). Describe the advantages to your social network of introducing yourself to Eileen.

4. Does it seem too contrived and calculating to think about your social relationships in this way? Even if you do not approach relationships like this, are you surprised to think that others do? Under what circumstances does this kind of analysis seem appropriate, and when does it seem inappropriate?

5. Consider the phrase, "It's not what you know, it's whom you know that matters." Relate this phrase to the diagram. Under what circumstances is this likely to be true? When is it false?

6. Describe how you can apply the principle "The people you know the least contribute the most to your network" to your use of Facebook or LinkedIn during a search for a job.

---

[4] Albert Laszlo Barabasi, *Linked* (New York: Perseus Publishing, 2002).

Active Review

Use this Active Review to verify that you understand the ideas and concepts that answer the chapter's study questions.

Q1 What is a computer network?

Define *computer network*. Explain the differences among LANs, WANs, internets, and the Internet. Describe the purpose of a protocol.

Q2 What are the components of a LAN?

Explain the key distinction of a LAN. Describe the purpose of each component in Figure 6-2. Describe the placement of switches in a multistory building. Explain when optical fiber cables are used for a LAN. Define *IEEE 802.3* and *802.11* and explain how they differ. List three ways of connecting a LAN or computer to the Internet. Explain the nature of each.

Q3 What are the fundamental concepts you should know about the Internet?

Explain the statement, "The Internet is an internet." Define *TCP/IP* and name its layers. Explain, in general terms, the purpose of each layer. Explain the purpose of HTTP, HTTPS, SMTP, and FTP. Explain why TCP is said to provide *reliable internet transport*. Define *IP, packet,* and *router*. Explain why IP is said to provide internet routing. Describe the advantages of private and public IP addresses. List the purposes of the LAN device. Explain, in general terms, how you would obtain a domain name. Describe the relationship between domain names and public IP addresses. Define *URL*. Explain the purpose of a VPN and describe, in broad terms, how a VPN works.

Q4 What processing occurs on a typical Web server?

Explain what a Web storefront is. Define *three-tier architecture* and name and describe each tier. Explain the function of a Web page, a Web server, and a commerce server. Explain the purpose of a Web farm. Explain the function of each tier in Figure 6-13 as the pages in Figures 6-12 and 6-14 are processed. Define *HTML* and explain its purpose. Define *href* and *attribute*. Explain the purpose of XML, Flash, Silverlight, and HTML 5.

Q5 Why is the cloud the future for most organizations?

Define *cloud* and explain the three key terms in your definition. Using Figure 6-17 as a guide, compare and contrast cloud-based and in-house hosting. Explain three factors that make cloud computing possible today. When does it not make sense to use a cloud-based infrastructure?

Q6 How can organizations use the cloud?

Define *SaaS, PaaS,* and *IaaS*. Provide an example of each. For each, describe the requirements for when it would be the most appropriate option.

Q7 2022?

Summarize the good and the bad news that the cloud brings. Explain why the photo in Figure 6-16 is disturbing. Describe three categories of remote access systems. Explain how the low cost of the cloud is likely to bring remote access systems to lower-value applications. Summarize how this 2022 discussion pertains to you.

Using Your Knowledge at GearUp

Name the principal advantage of the cloud to GearUp. For hosting its Web site, which cloud offering—SaaS, PaaS, or IaaS—makes the most sense, given the size and nature of GearUp's business? If GearUp were larger and employed a more sophisticated IT staff, name another alternative that could make sense. Explain why.

Key Terms and Concepts

Using Your Knowledge

1. Suppose you manage a group of seven employees in a small business. Each of your employees wants to be connected to the Internet. Consider two alternatives:
Alternative A: Each employee has his or her own modem and connects individually to the Internet.
Alternative B: The employees' computers are connected using a LAN, and the network uses a single modem to connect to the Internet.
   a. Sketch the equipment and lines required for each alternative.
   b. Explain the actions you need to take to create each alternative.
   c. Compare the alternatives using the criteria in Figure 6-11.
   d. Which of these two alternatives do you recommend?

2. Suppose that you have a consulting practice implementing LANs for fraternities and sororities on your campus.
   a. Consider a fraternity house. Explain how a LAN could be used to connect all of the computers in the house. Would you recommend an Ethernet LAN, an 802.11 LAN, or a combination? Justify your answer.
   b. This chapter did not provide enough information for you to determine how many switches the fraternity house might need. However, in general terms, describe how the fraternity could use a multiple-switch system.
   c. Considering the connection to the Internet, would you recommend that the fraternity house use a DSL modem, a cable modem, or WAN wireless? Although you can rule out at least one of

these alternatives with the knowledge you already have, what additional information do you need in order to make a specific recommendation?

d. Should you develop a standard package solution for each of your customers? What advantages accrue from a standard solution? What are the disadvantages?

3. Define *cloud* and explain the three key terms in your definition. Using Figure 6-17 as a guide, compare and contrast cloud-based and in-house hosting.

In your opinion, explain the three most important factors that make cloud-based hosting preferable to on-site hosting.

4. Apple invested more than $1 billion in the North Carolina center that will host the iCloud. For Apple to spend such a sum, it must perceive the iCloud as being a key component of its future. Using the principles listed in Figure 3-12 (page 88), explain all the ways that you believe the iCloud will give Apple a competitive advantage over other mobile device vendors.

Collaboration Exercise 6

With a team of your fellow students, develop an answer to the following questions. Use Google Docs, Google +, Windows Live SkyDrive, SharePoint, Office 365, or some other collaboration tool to conduct your meetings.

The cloud is causing monumental changes in the information systems services industry. Giants like Microsoft need to change, the business model of small companies that support local networking solutions are being turned upside down, and opportunities for new companies and services are emerging. Investigate these changes and identify a potential opportunity by answering the following questions:

1. Read Case Study 6 and answer the questions at the end, paying particular attention to your answers to questions 6 and 7.

2. Suppose you are an ISV that is being displaced by Azure and the cloud and you decide to offer consulting services on the use of Office 365.

Reread Q7 of Chapter 2 (beginning on page 55).

List the four major components of Office 365 and describe three services that you could provide for each.

3. Identify a market of particular interest to your group (e.g., accounting firms, government offices, medical practices, etc.). For that market, list and describe four consulting services that you could provide.

4. Considering your answer to question 3, and keeping in mind that up until now you have provided consulting services for the installation and support of Exchange and similar servers, describe the ways that you will need to change your business, in particular personnel.

Case Study 6

Turbulent Air in Those Azure Clouds

"For the Cloud, we're all in."

—Steve Ballmer, Microsoft CEO, March 9, 2010[5]

What exactly does Ballmer mean? When the CEO for Microsoft, the world's leading software vendor, says they're all in for the cloud, what can he mean? How does Microsoft move its $15 billion server business into the cloud?

We can't peek behind the corporate curtain to view what the cloud really means to Microsoft's revenue, nor can we know with any degree of certainty what its strategy is and how it intends to achieve it. We also don't know

how much revenue Microsoft earns from particular products in particular channels, so we can't know if we're even in the right ballpark. Nonetheless, let's ponder.

Clearly, Microsoft has a huge problem. Change is in the air, the cloud is real, Apple has the momentum with young and hip customers, and however much they might want to turn back the clock to 1995, when they dominated everything except their U.S. antitrust lawsuit, they cannot. Here's Ballmer again, in mid-2011:

The cloud is essentially a buzzword that refers to using the Internet to connect you even more seamlessly to the people and information that's important to you. Those

---

[5] "Ballmer on the Cloud: We're All In," Microsoft.com, March 9, 2010. Available at www.microsoft.com/showcase/en/us/details/9c8601a 5-a82a-4452-965d-e4a04f38efb6 (accessed July 2011).

phenomena, in the large, will be the source of so many new companies . . . that it will be a really exciting time over the next 5, 10 years.[6]

If Ballmer were a venture capitalist, we could understand his enthusiasm for so many new companies, but he's the CEO of a company that has to grow and thrive through these turbulent times by outcompeting new, and old, companies.

Essentially, Microsoft has to find a profitable way to put a big part of its business out of business. During the quarterly earnings announcement in April 2011, Peter Klein, Microsoft's CFO, offered this:

We delivered strong financial results despite a mixed PC environment, which demonstrates the strength and breadth of our businesses. Consumers are purchasing Office 2010, Xbox, and Kinect at tremendous rates, and businesses of all sizes are purchasing Microsoft platforms and applications.[7]

Parse that statement carefully: "Customers are purchasing Office 2010, the Xbox, and Kinect *at tremendous*

rates" (emphasis added). However, businesses are just "*purchasing . . . platforms.*" Where's the *tremendous* in that last sentence? Now, this could mistakenly be overemphasizing a few words, but it may not. Run the numbers for a simple example.

Consider a small business that has, say, 20 employees, and suppose that business switches to Office 365 for Small Businesses. The basic version includes Exchange (Microsoft's email server), Lync, SharePoint Online, and Office Web Apps (browser-based, limited functionality versions of Office 2010). Office 365 costs $6 per month, per employee, which for 20 people, is $120 a month, or $1,440 per year.

First, can Microsoft earn profit at that price? Figure 6-19 lists prices for Microsoft Azure, Microsoft's primary cloud offering. As shown, if you're an outsider, you can purchase an hour of a mid-range server for 24 cents. Let's assume the cost of running that server is a little less than half, say, 10 cents. Because Rackspace can sell an hour on a bare server for a penny and a half, it's likely that a big part of that 24 cents is a license for Windows Server, and the

Figure 6-19
Azure Standard Rates

Windows Azure
- Compute
  - Extra small instance: $0.05 per hour
  - Small instance (default): $0.12 per hour
  - Medium instance: $0.24 per hour
  - Large instance: $0.48 per hour
  - Extra large instance: $0.96 per hour
- Storage
  - $0.15 per GB stored per month
  - $0.01 per 10,000 storage transactions
- Content Delivery Network (CDN)
  - $0.15 per GB for data transfers from European and North American locations
  - $0.01 per 10,000 transactions

SQL Azure
- Web Edition
  - $9.99 per database up to 1GB per month
  - $49.95 per database up to 5GB per month
- Business Edition
  - $9.99 per database up to 10GB per month
  - $199.98 per database up to 20GB per month
  - $299.97 per database up to 30GB per month
  - $399.96 per database up to 40GB per month
  - $499.95 per database up to 50GB per month

[6] Sharon Pian Chan, "Steve Ballmer Pre-Announces 2011 Earnings for Microsoft," *Seattle Times,* June 29, 2011. Available at http://seattletimes.nwsource.com/html/businesstechnology/2015465692_microsoftballmer30.html (accessed July 2011).
[7] "Microsoft Reports Record Third-Quarter Results," Microsoft Press Release, April 28, 2011. Available at www.microsoft.com/investor/EarningsAndFinancials/Earnings/PressReleaseAndWebcast/FY11/Q3/default.aspx (accessed July 2011).

true marginal cost to Microsoft is probably much less than 10 cents, but let's assume high.

Each year has 365 times 24 hours, or 8,760 hours. Thus the cost of running that mid-sized server for a year is 10 cents times 8,760, or $876. There are storage costs as well, but they're miniscule. Can Microsoft support 20 people on that one server? Based on typical resource use it's likely that it can support 200 people, maybe even 2,000 people, on that one server. But certainly it can support 20, so Microsoft's margin equals revenue of $1,440 minus costs of $876, or $564. So, yes, it can make money on Office 365.

EXCEPT, if that customer is typical, Office 365 is replacing an Exchange server. Based on similar situations, the typical installation cost for an Exchange server in a business of 20 people is about $12,000: $3,000 for the hardware, $4,000 for Exchange licenses to Microsoft, and $5,000 to the independent software vendor (ISV) that installs and supports that server.[8]

Office 365 replaces them all. Certainly that's bad news for Dell, as well as for the independent software vendors that install and maintain servers, who'd better find a way to make money supporting Office 365 or they'll be out of business.

But what about Microsoft? It has traded $4,000 in Exchange license fees for $564 in Office 365 profit. Why would it do that?

According to Microsoft's 2010 Annual Report, the server and tools business, which includes Windows Server, SQL Server, Exchange, and Azure, accounted for $15 billion in revenue, which was 24 percent of its total revenue. Azure, if it's successful, will replace Windows Server and SQL Server. Office 365 will replace Exchange.

The bottom line? Microsoft better sell a lot of Azure and Office 365! As in $15 billion worth. No wonder Ballmer says they're "all in for the cloud."

Questions

1. In your own words, summarize Microsoft's problem.

2. Explain the meaning of the following: ". . . you can purchase an hour of a mid-range server for 24 cents. Let's assume the cost of running that server is a little less than half, say, 10 cents. Because Rackspace can sell an hour on a bare server for a penny and a half, it's likely that a big part of that 24 cents is a license for Windows Server, and the true marginal cost to Microsoft is probably much less than 10 cents."

3. How does the example Office 365 marginal revenue analysis change if the cost of running that server is 1 cent, not 10?

4. How does the example Office 365 marginal revenue analysis change if that server supports 2,000 users, not 20?

5. As of this writing, Microsoft had just purchased Skype. Its reasons for doing so are unclear at present (November 2011), but most likely involve the problems addressed in this case study. By the time you read this, Microsoft's Skype strategy should be clear. Describe what it is and how it changes this analysis.

6. Over the years, Microsoft has devoted considerable resources and time to building a network of loyal ISVs. It provides training, sales support, conferences, and awards and even has categories of gold-, silver-, and bronze-level partners. From this case study, it appears to be throwing these ISVs under the bus. Do you think that it is? Why or why not? If you were an ISV, what would you do?

7. If you were Microsoft and you had a $15 billion server business that was threatened by the cloud, what would you do?

---

[8] Phil Wainewright, "How Much Does Exchange Really Cost? ZDNet, November 15, 2008. Available at www.zdnet.com/blog/saas/how-much-does-exchange-really-cost/609 (accessed July 2011).

TEACHING SUGGESTIONS

GearUp, Chapter 6

GOALS

Use GearUp to:

- Illustrate the importance (and promise) of the cloud.

- Show nontechnical business managers (Kelly and Emily) needing to engage in conversations and make decisions about information technology.

- See firsthand the benefits of the cloud to business . . . in this case, a small startup that needs to conserve its cash.

BACKGROUND

1. GearUp has been using a traditional, third-party hosting organization. It pays for a monthly plan for certain servers. Those servers may or may not be virtual (GearUp doesn't know how they're managed within the vendor), but they are most certainly not elastic.

2. It is likely that by the time you use this vignette in class the cost of servers will be less than 25 cents an hour. For this vignette, I used the June 2011 Azure pricing for a Windows server. Rackspace is offering IaaS servers for 1 cent an hour.

3. The benefits of the cloud are substantial to a business like GearUp. Some sales of very popular items will require many servers, but sales of less popular items or sales during slow periods of the year will require very few. Elastic servers are perfect for this situation.

4. However, GearUp will need to invest in applications programs to provision and release servers programmatically. This may or may not be within its skill set. Kelly needs to make that call; she might, for example, suggest to Lucas that he investigate outsourcing that work to an outsource vendor that has more experience with elastic cloud provisioning.

HOW TO GET STUDENTS INVOLVED

1. Ask the students to take the role of Kelly or Emily:

   - **Do you think this scenario is real? Can you imagine it happening today?**

   - **What knowledge and skills do Kelly and Emily need for this situation?**

   - **How can Kelly and Emily decide if what Lucas is proposing is real?**

   - **Both know that nothing can be quite as easy as this sounds. How do they find out what the downside is?**

   - **By the time you reach their level, the cloud will be old news. Some other technology will be hot. How can you prepare for that eventuality?**

2. Now consider Lucas' perspective:

   - **Two years ago, Lucas had never heard of the cloud. Today, he's read and heard of the low cost of cloud-based computing and the incredible flexibility of elasticity. What can he do to inform himself?**

   - **What support does Lucas need from Kelly? Budget, of course, but what else?**

   - **If you were Kelly, how can you best help Lucas?**

3. Today, organizations can obtain cloud servers from Amazon.com, IBM, Microsoft, Oracle, Rackspace, and many others.

   - **What criteria should GearUp use when choosing among these alternatives?**

   - **How can GearUp obtain data about its choices?**

   - **If you are Kelly, how will you evaluate Lucas' recommendations?**

BOTTOM LINE

■ Cloud computing is real and offers substantial benefits.

■ Moving to the cloud involves risk and some development work . . . at least moving to the elastic cloud.

■ As a business manager like Kelly or Emily, you will have responsibilities for participating in the discussion, for providing guidance, and for approving or rejecting recommendations.

■ Pay attention!

YOU BE THE GUIDE

Using the Ethics Guide: Personal Work at Work? (pages 196–197)

GOALS

- Alert students to the need to learn organizational policies regarding personal computer and network use at work.

- Stimulate thinking about professional and ethical responsibilities for sending email to people who are at work.

BACKGROUND AND PRESENTATION STRATEGIES

I wrote the email example using the example of someone sending a picture of herself surfing in New Zealand so as to capture the students' attention. But, as I wrote it, I realized that somewhere along the line, we need to question the ethics of this action. I didn't want to leave the student thinking that such behavior shouldn't at least be *examined for appropriateness.*

This situation is complicated because the woman sending the email has no relationship to the company in Ohio. Her friend, who is an employee of that company, is the passive recipient. This makes the ethics a bit difficult to untangle, but leads to a better discussion, I think.

First, there is no law that prohibits a person from sending or receiving personal emails at work, so the *action is certainly legal.*

If we fall back on the definition of *ethical* as "consistent with agreed principles of correct moral conduct," then we need to ask, "What are the agreed principles that pertain?" Most likely the Ohio company *has a corporate policy about personal use of computers and networks at work.* If so, that policy stipulates what the "agreed principles" are—at least from the company's standpoint—and the company's standpoint should be paramount, it seems to me, because it pays for the computers and networks.

So, at their first jobs, students *should learn the corporate policy for personal use of computers at work.* If they are not informed about that policy when they are hired, they should ask the human resources department about it. Asking their boss about such a policy at work may not set the right impression—maybe they can wait a week or so before asking that question.

This still leaves two possible ethical dilemmas:

■ **What if her friend's company has no such policy? Does that mean the company doesn't care, and employees should feel free to use the computers and networks without restriction?**

I think not; I think a sense of business professionalism should limit personal computer use at work, even in the absence of a policy.

■ **The second dilemma occurs if the company has such a policy, but employees disregard or ignore it. In that case the agreed principles, at least among the employees, are that such use is OK. Do you agree?**

I think it depends. If the employer knows about such use and doesn't take any action or issue any advisories about the policy, it would be hard to claim that such use is unethical. If, however, the company regularly asks employees not to use computers and networks for personal business at work and employees ignore that policy, then I think the action is unethical.

This leads to an important consideration for students as they join their employer:

■ **When you take your first job, you might want to restrict the people to whom you give your work email address to a few close friends and relatives. Use a private email account for most friends.**

■ **Of course, if you generate an email at work and send it to someone, they will automatically obtain your work email address.**

Nearer to home, you might also address computer-use policies on your campus.

■ **What are the policies for computer use at our campus?**

■ **Where do we go to find out?**

■ **Are the policies different for students than for professors?**

■ *Should* **they be different? Professors are employees, and students are clients.**

SUGGESTED RESPONSES FOR DISCUSSION QUESTIONS

Warning: These questions ask about the ethical responsibility of the woman sending the email, who is not an employee of the company in Ohio. If the person at work was sending the emails, the answers would be more clear.

I find it useful to consider the ethical situation from the standpoint of both parties, as described in the comments for each question.

1. First, consider the wording of the question:

   ■ **This question is asking whether it is ethical for you to send email to your friend at work,** *not* **whether it is ethical for you, at work, to receive your friend's email.**

   Unless your friend has asked you not to send email to him at work, I think you have no ethical problem, but see further considerations in subsequent questions.

   ■ **What if the question were, "Is it ethical for you to send personal email from work"?**

   In that case, I think the answer depends on organizational policy.

2. Your answer *might* change depending on the size of the picture. Even though it is your friend who is at work and not you, and even though you have no relationship to your friend's employer, a sense of business professionalism might cause you to pause before sending a large picture file to your friend's work email address. A very large file may attract unwanted attention to your friend's email account. A better course of action might be to send the picture to your friend's personal email account and a short email to your friend at work telling him that you did so.

   What about your friend? Do the ethics change for him depending on the size of the picture? Probably, depending on the company's policy.

3. The company both owns and controls the pictures that are stored on its computer. Of course companies have the right and do inspect employees' mailboxes. The manager should do whatever is stipulated by the company's computer-use policy.

4. The lost employee time is certainly the greater cost. Your friend has to alert you as to how he feels about using company time to view your pictures. He can always view them after work, too.

5. Facebook and Twitter don't change the ethics, they are just greater time sinks. Many companies would like to prohibit their use, but then again, social media sites have legitimate business purposes as well. Possibly only certain employees, those with a need to do social media work for the organization, can be allowed access. But see question 6.

6. The issue is your time. Are you being paid for your time, for putting in a set number of hours at work? Or, are you being paid for results? In the former case, it probably is unethical to spend any more than a few moments each day on personal work at work. That statement extends to any personal work, whether done on your iPad, the organization's computer, the telephone, or any other medium. If the latter, then as long as your personal work does not interfere with accomplishing your assigned tasks, then it is most likely not problematic. However, a certain modesty and decorum is appropriate. You don't want to flaunt your personal work in front of other workers, your boss, or customers. Such flaunting isn't unethical; it's impolite and unwise.

7. It is impossible to be precise in this statement without a knowledge of the organization and its culture. That said, a reasonable policy would prohibit any personal work that interferes with the functioning of the organization. This means personal work that interferes with accomplishing assigned tasks and any use of organizational resources that interferes with their performance of official work. Most organizations say something like "limited amounts of personal work using organizational resources are permitted as long as they do not interfere with the organization's functioning."

WRAP UP

■ **At work, you have a responsibility to learn your organization's policy for personal computer and network use. It is always unwise and probably unethical not to follow that policy.**

■ **You have a professional, and maybe an ethical, responsibility not to embarrass your friends by sending too much email to them at work. At least ask your friends if they would prefer you use their private accounts.**

YOU BE THE GUIDE

Using the Guide: Thinking Exponentially Is Not Possible, but . . . (pages 204–205)

GOALS

- Sensitize students to the difficulty (impossibility?) of thinking exponentially.

- Describe strategies that students can use to deal with exponential phenomena in their professional lives.

BACKGROUND AND PRESENTATION STRATEGIES

When Nathan Myhrvold was the chief technology officer at Microsoft, he wrote a paper entitled "Road Kill on the Information Superhighway," a classic that contained the statement, "No one can think exponentially." He was a graduate student of Stephen Hawking, later started his own company, and became a Microsoft employee when his company was acquired by Microsoft. Working at a very senior level at Microsoft during its glory years of the 1990s, he amassed vast wealth (and no longer works for Microsoft).

The graph in this guide shows it all. When told something grows exponentially, we think fast growth, but we do so *linearly*. We just cannot imagine the changes posed by exponential growth; it is even more difficult to understand the consequences. The exponential growth in the number of Internet users is a case in point. Who would have imagined the changes in politics and the news media that the bloggers have brought forward? Or who could have known about the incredible growth of YouTube?

I emphasize the words of caution regarding the talking appliances. Although we have the technology for the alarm clock to signal the coffee pot and for the coffee pot to signal the toaster, does anybody really want that capability?

I find it helps to discuss a contemporary example of a possibly exponential phenomenon. RFID could be one example. Another one that has begun to emerge since the text was written is *podcasting*, which is the preparation and distribution of MP3 audio files for playback on iPods and similar devices. Podcasts can be registered with aggregators like Podcasting.net for inclusion in podcast directories.

The following sequences of questions use foursquare as the example. They could use some other, new social media site just as well.

- **What is foursquare?**

- **What are potential commercial uses of foursquare? In public relations? In advertising? For employee education and training? Other?**

- **Could a company use podcasting to increase the productivity of its sales force while traveling on the road? If so, how?**

- **How can we apply the principles of this guide to the use of foursquare?**

- **The guide recommends hedging one's bets when addressing new technology. Put a little money on one or more possibilities; be positioned to move in the direction that the market takes. Watch and wait; move when the direction is clear.**

- **How could we hedge our bets with regard to commercial use of foursquare?**

Notice the impact of time on the size of the disparity between linear and exponential thinking. What will podcasting do in one year? Five years? Ten years?

- **Learn to read technology articles critically. Where exponential phenomena are concerned, any statement that begins, "XXX (the phenomenon) will double in 5 years," is so full of uncertainty as to be nearly meaningless.**

Here are two cases in point in our business: RFID and IPv6. For the first, organizations are still trying to figure out how to use it. Everyone seems to say that it will be important, but many suspect the best uses, those involving GIS, are just being developed. The impetus for IPv6 was that the world was going to run out of IP addresses. With DHCP and NAT, however, the utility of the existing IPv4 address space has expanded dramatically. IPv6 still has advantages over IPv4, but the pressure to convert is much less than most would have thought just 3 years ago.

SUGGESTED RESPONSES FOR DISCUSSION QUESTIONS

1. I think it's hard to disagree with this statement, but it will be interesting to see what the students think. The goal of the question is to make sure the students understand the point of the remark.

2. Examples of the rise of private sale sites are Woot.com, MYHABIT, and though fictitious, GearUp. Any of the newer social media sites are additional examples. We don't know where the consuming public will respond to new opportunities, or even if they will.

3. It's having a huge impact. Not just the 500 channels of TV, but the blogs and podcasters. Also consider video podcasting (by whatever name it will have). Look at how blogs have changed the political arena.

    Quality is interesting; a debate is underway right now. At one point, mainstream media (MSM) claimed that political blogs are of poor quality. The bloggers responded, "No, way—if I publish junk, other bloggers will be all over it in a matter of hours. It's much easier to publish rubbish in a newspaper than in a blog." The news reading public agreed. MSM, especially newspapers, are in considerable financial trouble.

4. Three possibilities are:
   - The IRS could replace its voluminous and confusing tax instructions with video clips. (*www.FineWoodworking.com* is doing this now.)
   - Parents could use GPS and embedded-under-the-skin RFID chips to keep track of their children.
   - Courts could use onboard auto video recordings to determine who did what during an accident.

5. These examples all fit closely with problems that people have today. We know that how-to magazines are meeting a market need because they currently sell well. Parents always need to know where their kids are, and insurance companies could use the video to reduce litigation and other accident expenses. In terms of *closeness to real problems*, I'd rank the three ideas as 2, 1, and 3. Child-embedded RFID is probably socially infeasible, however.

WRAP UP

■ **The terrific news in this guide is that technology constantly creates new opportunities for products and services. Your future career can be just as exciting as Steve Jobs' was. The opportunities will be there.**

■ **Don't automatically suppose people will want to do what technology enables them to do. People want to do what they are already doing, but better, faster, or cheaper.**

■ **Be careful with exponential phenomena. We don't *know* what all the ubiquitous, nearly free, ever-faster connectivity means. It will mean something—it will mean substantial change—but we don't know what.**

■ **Stay tuned!!! Lots of opportunities will come your way during your career!**

YOU BE THE GUIDE

Using the Guide: Human Networks Matter More (pages 206–207)

GOALS

- Teach students the importance of networking.
- Emphasize that business social functions are always business functions.

BACKGROUND AND PRESENTATION STRATEGIES

Successful businesspeople are constantly networking. They constantly add to their set of acquaintances. This is true even at the highest levels: Every summer Microsoft has a meeting of the CEOs of the world's 100 largest corporations. Almost all attend, not so much because of the presentations, but because they have so few opportunities to meet each other informally. When the CEO of 3M bumps into the CEO of Citibank at the coffee pot, who knows what transpires? The start of a new board seat for someone?

Business is nothing but relationships. People do business *with people.* Meeting the right people in an informal context makes it possible to better accomplish work in formal contexts. At the weekly softball game, when Brenda makes (or doesn't make) a double play with Don and Bill, a bond is formed that makes it more likely that Brenda and Bill will come to Don's network requirements meeting. It may not make sense, but that's just the way people are. In business, relationships are everything.

So, even though it may seem contrived and awkward, students should learn to attend business social events and to use those events for network building. Sometimes people go to events because they want to meet someone in particular, and sometimes they go just to expand their networks.

■ **Go to business social events and don't spend all your time talking to people you already know. Make a point of meeting new people who work in other departments.**

Warning: Business social events are business events. There is a difference between a softball game with your friends and one at work. There is a difference between a holiday party with your friends and one at work. The goal of all business social events is to expand networks and to enable people to relate to one another informally. A holiday party is not an opportunity for the company to reward its employees with unlimited free alcohol.

■ **Party with your friends, but network at business social functions.**

I once managed an exceedingly capable C++ developer who got drunk at the holiday party and made a fool of himself. The next Monday, our business unit manager wanted me to fire him. He was critical to our project, and I was able to help him keep his job. Our relationship, however, was never the same, and his stature at the company fell dramatically.

■ **Business social functions are business events.**

It is important, too, for students to use social organizations outside of their company for network building. The local chapter of professional accountants or marketers or software entrepreneurs or financial executives is an important source of professional relationships. The best way to build a network is not just to go to a meeting; rather, get involved with the group. Help run a meeting, become an officer, work on the membership committee.

■ **As the guide points out, there is someone out there who knows someone or something that you need to know. Because you don't and can't know who that person is, your only alternative is to meet as many interesting people as you can.**

 **SUGGESTED RESPONSES FOR DISCUSSION QUESTIONS**

1. The answer depends on the student and your local situation.

2. Use a fraternity or sorority, a student club, a church community, a dorm, a professional group, a job.

3. It's easier to meet Linda because she's in your group. You and she have many acquaintances in common. You also have your department's business in common, so you'll likely have much to say. It's more awkward to meet Eileen. You have no acquaintances in common; you may not know what group she works in or what she does. You may have little to say to one another, but she contributes more links to your social network than does Linda.

■ **It may be awkward to meet strangers, but it is important. Try it. Practice while you're in school.**

Get used to meeting people and talking with them. Learn to be better at it. If you're shy, force yourself to do it.

4. Business social events are business events. Period.

   ■ **You wouldn't go into an important meeting without having an agenda of what you want to accomplish. So, too, don't go to a business social function without having an objective; for example, "Today I'm going to meet two people from manufacturing and ask about the new MRP system." Having an idea about what you want to know will make it easier to meet people. Just don't turn an informal event into a formal meeting.**

   ■ **You probably don't want to treat parties with your friends this way, but a business social function is not a party. It's a business function.**

5. First, regarding the phrase, professionals need to know their profession. Accountants need to know accounting, financial analysts need to know finance, and network administrators need to know TCP/IP–OSI. That said, however, what differentiates two people with about the same level of knowledge? Their relationships!

   When you're designing a computer network, knowledge of data communications technology is critical; but when you're an accounts payable manager who's been asked to prepare a high-level management statement of networking alternatives, then knowing who to call for help is more important than your particular knowledge of data communications.

   ■ **Knowledge of data communications at the basic level of this chapter will help you better talk with experts in the field. It will help you build your network.**

6. Get out and meet people. Go to every possible business speaker event. Talk with the speaker afterward. Ask interesting questions about his or her talk. Get that person's business card. Follow up with an email thanking them and asking another pertinent question or two. Join relevant business clubs on campus. Get involved. When businesspeople come to campus, volunteer to greet them and buy them a cup of coffee before or afterward. Do everything you can to expand your network. All these actions increase the likelihood that you'll meet that person who knows about the job that would be ideal for you. And, by the way, your life on campus will be more enjoyable and interesting, too.

WRAP UP

One way to wrap up is to challenge the students to keep thinking about it:

■ **Networking is important—very important. In some ways, for the purposes of getting a job, developing a good network is more important than your GPA. Look how much time you put into your GPA. Just put some of that time into building your network.**

■ **Network building is, by the way, a lifelong activity. It may be that some relationships you build here on campus will pay dividends many years down the road.**

■ **Think seriously about these ideas. Discuss them with your friends. Determine what you believe about the relative importance of knowledge and networks. When is one more important than the other?**

■ **Again, it's your life, your career. I'm just trying to coach you into behaviors that will help you become a successful business professional. Give it some thought!**

Part 3

Using IS for Competitive Advantage

Fox Lake Country Club is a private golf and tennis club located in the suburbs of Hartford, Connecticut. Founded in 1982, the club includes two 18-hole golf courses, 14 tennis courts, a swimming pool, a restaurant, meeting rooms, and a pro shop that sells golf and tennis gear and clothing. The golf courses, designed by a leading golf professional, are beautiful and challenging. Indeed, all of the Fox Lake grounds are picturesque and meticulously maintained by the groundskeeping staff.

All of this beauty is not cheap; memberships cost $75,000, and the monthly fee is $425. The club's bylaws allow for up to 1,500 club memberships. Like most such organizations, member initiation fees are invested, and the proceeds pay mortgages on the club's facilities as well as maintenance expenses on capital equipment. Monthly membership charges pay operational expenses, including salaries for Fox Lake's 35 full-time employees and hourly wages for about 100 seasonal workers. The restaurant and pro shop are intended to be profit-generating centers for the club.

Fox Lake employs golf and tennis professionals as subcontractors. These professionals staff the pro shop and activity centers for a few hours each week. They spend the bulk of their time giving private lessons to club members.

The recent recession hit Fox Lake hard. For the first time in 30 years, in December 2008 the club had open memberships. As of 2012, all the memberships have been sold, but the waiting list is months long, rather than years long, as it was before 2008. Further, both the pro shop and the restaurant have been operating at a loss since 2009.

In response to these financial challenges, the club's board of directors asked the club's general manager, Jeff Lloyd, to seek additional sources of revenue. Because of the beauty of its grounds,

Fox Lake had been used as the site of several weddings, and Jeff developed a business plan to expand these occasional events into a wedding-hosting business. Fox Lake is gorgeous in the summer, of course, but even in the winter, when the grounds are covered with snow, the scene is lovely, and he reasoned that weddings and receptions could provide year-round revenue.

With the board's approval, Jeff hired Anne Foster to develop this new business. At the time, Foster was working as a successful independent wedding planner, and she wanted an opportunity to expand her business. It seemed to be a good match; Fox Lake provided her a beautiful venue and greater opportunity for more events, and her knowledge of the industry as well as her contacts with vendors and potential clients jump-started Fox Lake into the wedding events business.

To avoid unnecessary complication, we will ignore Fox Lake's tennis and swimming activities, as well as the pro shop. The golf, wedding events, restaurant, and facility business units will provide more than enough fodder for our investigation into organizational processes and information systems.

We will use Fox Lake Country Club as an illustrative example for Chapters 7 through 12. Part 3 consists of Chapters 7, 8, and 9. Chapter 7 discusses structured business processes and the ways that information systems can improve their quality. Chapter 8 addresses social media information systems. It discusses how such systems contribute to organizational strategy and add to organizational social capital. Finally, Chapter 9 discusses business intelligence and related information systems.

Structured Processes and Information Systems

"**Mike,** what are you telling me?"

Anne Foster struggles to keep her voice down as she talks with Mike Stone, the facilities manager.

"I'm saying that we've got to do the earthquake retrofit on the Oak Room."

"That's fine, Mike. Do it next winter. I'll work around it."

"Anne, that won't work. It's got to be done by November 1. The insurance company said so."

"Look, I'm a wedding planner—I plan weddings, in fact I've already got four of them for the first two weeks of October. The good news is that I only need the Oak Room for one."

"I'm sorry, Anne. I really am. I thought you knew."

"Knew? Would I plan a wedding that we can't do? What am I supposed to do, go back to the bride and say,

'Hey, change of plans, you'll have to do your wedding reception elsewhere!'"

"Sorry, but that's the way it is."

"Oh, no, Mike. You might be a good facilities manager; but you don't know anything about brides!" Anger and desperation fill her voice.

"Well, we can get 150 people into the Maple Suite, if we open the walls and set tables outside."

"Oh, great!!! Wonderful!!!! I've got two problems with that, Mike: One, what if the weather is bad? What if it's too cold to open the walls? But that's nothing compared to my second problem."

"Let's hear it."

"How old is your daughter, Mike?"

"Three."

"OK, I'll accept that you just don't get it. Our bride is having her special day. She and her betrothed sent out their save-the-date cards. In fact, they've even sent out their invitations. To 185 people, Mike! That's 185, not 150 if the weather is good."

"Anne, I scheduled this REQUIRED maintenance 6 months ago."

"Maybe so, Mike, but nobody told ME."

"OK, Anne. Imagine this: Let's say we put off this maintenance and, God forbid, we have an earthquake. You know what the lawyers would say if we knew we needed the work but didn't do it just for the revenue of another 35 people?"

"Lawyers!!!" Anne shouts, "You want to see lawyers???? Not only is the bride's father a partner in the biggest firm in Hartford, he is also a founding member of Fox Lake Country Club and a past president of the board."

"Then I'm sure he'll understand."

"Mike, you're an idiot."

"Let's go talk to Jeff . . ." ■

Study Questions

Q1 What are the basic types of structured processes?

Q2 How can information systems improve process quality?

Q3 How do enterprise systems eliminate the problem of information silos?

Q4 How do CRM, ERP, and EAI support structured enterprise processes?

Q5 What are the elements of an ERP system?

Q6 What are the challenges of implementing new enterprise information systems?

Q7 How will service-oriented architecture (SOA) impact enterprise information systems?

Q8 2022?

This chapter explores structured processes and their information systems within an organization. We will extend the business process discussion from Chapter 3 to investigate three types of processes and the scope of information systems that they use. We will also investigate the concept of process quality and explain how information systems can be used to increase it. Then, we will discuss information silos that occur with departmental information systems, explain why such silos can be problematic, and show how three types of enterprise systems can eliminate those problems. Enterprise resource planning (ERP) systems play a particularly important role in organizations today, and we will discuss their purpose and components and the major ERP vendors. Next, we survey the major challenges that occur when implementing enterprise systems. We'll wrap up the chapter by showing how service-oriented architecture (SOA) can benefit enterprise systems and discussing the implications (2022) of SOA-oriented enterprise systems in the cloud.

Q1 What Are the Basic Types of Structured Processes?

As you learned in Chapter 3, a business process is a network of activities that generate value by transforming inputs into outputs. Activities are subparts of processes that receive inputs and produce outputs. Activities can be performed by humans, only; by humans augmented by computer systems; and by computer systems, only.

Figure 7-1 shows a simplified view of a three-activity process for approving customer orders. Each of these activities is, itself, a subprocess of this overall process. You can see that each step—check inventory, check credit, and approve special terms—receives inputs and transforms them into outputs. You will learn how to better diagram such processes in Chapter 10; for now, just view Figure 7-1 as showing the gist of a typical business process.

How Do Structured Processes Differ from Dynamic Processes?

Businesses have dozens, hundreds, even thousands of different processes. Some processes are stable, almost fixed, in the flow among their activities. For example, the process of a salesclerk accepting a return at Nordstrom, or other quality retail

Figure 7-1
Business Process with Three Activities

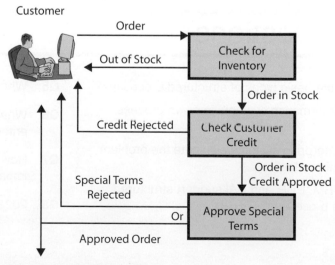

To Order Fulfillment Process

store, is fixed. If the customer has a receipt, take these steps . . . If the customer has no receipt, take these other steps . . . That process needs to be standardized so that customers are treated correctly, so that returned goods are accounted for appropriately, and so that sales commissions are reduced in a way that is fair to the sales staff.

Other processes are less structured, less rigid, and sometimes creative. For example, how does Nordstrom's management decide what women's clothes to carry next spring? They can look at past sales, consider current economic conditions, and make assessments about women's acceptance of new styles at recent fashion shows, but the process for combining all those factors into orders of specific garments in specific quantities and colors is not nearly as structured as that for accepting returns.

In this text, we divide processes into two broad categories. **Structured processes** are formally defined, standardized processes that involve day-to-day operations: accepting a return, placing an order, purchasing raw materials, and so forth. They have the characteristics summarized in the left-hand column of Figure 7-2.

Dynamic processes are flexible, informal, and adaptive processes that normally involve strategic and less specific managerial decisions and activities. Deciding whether to open a new store location or how best to solve the problem of excessive product returns are examples, as is using Twitter to generate buzz about next season's product line. The right hand column of Figure 7-2 shows examples of each.

We will discuss structured processes and information systems that support them in this chapter. We have already discussed one dynamic process, collaboration, in Chapter 2, and we will discuss another, social media, in Chapter 8. Some aspects of business intelligence, in Chapter 9, are also dynamic processes.

How Do Structured Processes Vary by Scope?

The character of structured business processes varies widely depending on the scope of the process. Processes that support a single function, say accounts payable, are simpler and easier to manage than those that support a network of independent organizations, such as a supply chain. Consider the nature of structured departmental, enterprise, and interenterprise processes.

Structured Departmental Processes

A **structured departmental process** is a structured process that exists to enable departmental employees to fulfill the charter, purpose, and goals of a particular organizational unit. At Fox Lake, the groundskeepers (personnel who maintain the golf courses and club lawns and gardens) use a departmental process for scheduling employees and tasks. The wedding events department has a structured departmental process for planning and scheduling events.

Structured	Dynamic
Support operational and structured managerial decisions and activities	Support strategic and less structured managerial decision and activities
Standardized	Less specific, fluid
Usually formally defined and documented	Usually informal
Exceptions rare and not (well) tolerated	Exceptions frequent and expected
Process structure changes slowly and with organizational agony	Adaptive processes that change structure rapidly and readily
Example: Customer returns, order entry, purchasing, payroll, etc.	**Example:** Collaboration, social networking, ill-defined, ambiguous situations

Figure 7-2
Structured Versus Dynamic Processes

Figure 7-3
Common Departmental
Information Systems

Department	Example Information Systems
Sales and marketing	• Lead generation • Lead tracking • Customer management • Sales forecasting • Product and brand management
Operations	• Order entry • Order management • Finished-goods inventory management
Manufacturing	• Inventory (raw materials, goods-in-process) • Planning • Scheduling • Operations
Customer service	• Order tracking • Account tracking • Customer support and training
Human resources	• Recruiting • Compensation • Assessment • HR planning
Accounting	• General ledger • Financial reporting • Cost accounting • Accounts receivable • Accounts payable • Cash management • Budgeting • Treasury management

Figure 7-3 lists common departmental processes. Notice that each of these processes is largely contained within a given department. These processes may receive inputs from other departments, and they may produce outputs that are used by other departments, but all, or at least the bulk of, the processes' activities lay within a single department.

A **departmental information system** is an information system that exists to support a departmental process. Characteristics of departmental information systems are summarized in the top row of Figure 7-4. Typical departmental information systems support 10 to 100 users. The procedures for using them must be understood by all members of the group. Often, procedures are formalized in documentation, and users frequently receive formal training in the use of those procedures.

Figure 7-4
Scope of Structured Processes

Scope	Fox Lake Example	Characteristics
Departmental	Scheduling of groundskeeping	10 to 100 of users; procedures understood within group; problem solutions within group; data duplication among departments; somewhat difficult to change
Enterprise	Charging of membership fees	100 to 1000s of users; procedures formalized; problem solutions affect enterprise; data duplication minimized; very difficult to change
Interenterprise	Ordering of restaurant supplies from suppliers	1000s of users; procedures formalized; problem solutions affect multiple organizations; controlled data duplication; difficult to change; interorganization IS required

When problems occur, they almost always can be solved within the group. If accounts payable duplicates the record for a particular supplier, the accounts payable group can make the fix. If the Web storefront has the wrong number of widgets in the inventory database, that count can be fixed within the storefront group.

(Notice, by the way, that the consequences of a problem are not isolated to the group. Because the departmental information system exists to provide a service to the rest of the organization, its problems have consequences throughout the organization. The fix to the problem can usually be obtained within the group, however.)

Two or more departments within an organization can duplicate data, and such duplication can be very problematic to the organization, as we discuss in Q2. Finally, because departmental information systems involve many users, changing them can be problematic. But, again, when problems do occur, they can be resolved within the department.

Structured Enterprise Processes

Structured enterprise processes are structured processes that span an organization and support activities in multiple departments. At Fox Lake, all customer charges are recorded against membership accounts; no cash or credit card transactions are allowed. The restaurant, the golf course, the pro shop, and the wedding events departments all use the same enterprise process to record sales. At a manufacturer, a process that determines raw materials order quantities based on current product sales crosses the boundaries of the sales, manufacturing, and purchasing departments, and thus is an enterprise process.

Enterprise information systems are information systems that support enterprise processes. As shown in the second row of Figure 7-4, they typically have hundreds to thousands of users. Procedures are formalized and extensively documented; users undergo formal procedure training. Sometimes enterprise systems include categories of procedures, and users are defined according to levels of expertise with the system as well as by level of authority.

The solutions to problems in an enterprise system usually involve more than one department. As you will learn in this chapter, a major advantage of enterprise systems is that data duplication is either eliminated altogether or, if it is allowed to exist, changes to duplicated data are carefully managed to maintain consistency.

Because enterprise systems span many departments and involve potentially thousands of users, they are very difficult to change. Changes must be carefully planned, cautiously implemented, and users given considerable training. Sometimes users are given incentives and other inducements to motivate them to change.

CRM, ERP, and EAI are three enterprise information systems that we will define and discuss in Q4.

Structured Interenterprise Processes

Structured interenterprise processes are structured processes that span two or more independent organizations. At Fox Lake, the process that the restaurant uses to order supplies and ingredients from its suppliers is an interenterprise process. The process by which an organization increases or decreases the resources provided by its cloud vendor is another interorganizational process. Because such processes involve many employees of different organizations, procedures are formalized and user training is mandatory.

Structured interenterprise information systems are information systems that support interenterprise processes. Such systems typically involve thousands of users, and solutions to problems require cooperation among different, usually independently owned, organizations. Problems are resolved by meeting, by contract, and sometimes by litigation.

Data are often duplicated between organizations, but such duplication is carefully managed. Because of their wide span, complexity, and use by multiple companies, such systems can be exceedingly difficult to change. Supply chain management (discussed in the International Dimension, pages 458–460) is the classic example of an interenterprise information system.

The Ethics Guide on pages 238–239 demonstrates how one person's actions can affect an entire company.

Q2 How Can Information Systems Improve Process Quality?

Processes are the fabric of organizations; they are the means by which people organize their activities to achieve the organization's goals. As such, process quality is an important, possibly the most important, determinant of organizational success.[1]

The two dimensions of process quality are efficiency and effectiveness. **Process efficiency** is a measure of the ratio process outputs to inputs. If an alternative to the process in Figure 7-1 can produce the same order approvals/rejections (output) for less cost or produce more approvals/rejections for the same cost, it is more efficient. In Chapter 2, GearUp is trying to find a more efficient way of conducting its online sales.

Process effectiveness is a measure of how well a process achieves organizational strategy. If an organization differentiates itself on quality customer service, and if the process in Figure 7-1 requires 5 days to respond to an order, then that process is ineffective. Fox Lake wants to use the revenue of its wedding events business to achieve its revenue goals. The processes that have led to conflict over the use of shared resources is ineffective because it does not support that strategy.

How Can Processes Be Improved?

Organizations can improve the quality (efficiency and/or effectiveness) of a process in one of three ways:

- Change the process structure.
- Change the process resources.
- Change both.

Change the Process Structure

In some cases, process quality can be changed just by reorganizing the process. The order approval process in Figure 7-1 might be made more efficient if customer credit was done first and inventory was checked second. This change might be more efficient because it would save the cost of checking inventory for customers whose credit will be denied. However, that change would also mean that the organization would pay for a credit check on customers for which it did not have appropriate inventory. We will investigate such changes further in Chapter 10. For now, just note that process structure has a strong bearing on process efficiency.

Changing process structure can also increase process effectiveness. If an organization chooses a cost-leader strategy, then that strategy might mean that no special terms should ever be approved. If the process in Figure 7-1 results in the authorization of orders with special terms, then eliminating the third activity will make it more effective (most likely it will save on cost as well).

Change Process Resources

Business process activities are accomplished by humans and information systems. One way to improve process quality is to change the allocation of those resources. For example, if the process in Figure 7-1 is not effective because it takes too long, one way to make it more effective is to identify the source of delays and then to add more resources. If delays are caused by the check customer credit activity, one way to increase process effectiveness is to add more people to that activity. Adding people should decrease delays, but it will also add cost, so the organization needs to find the appropriate balance between effectiveness and efficiency.

---

[1] The subject of this chapter is structured processes, and we will discuss process quality in terms of them. Note, however, that all of the concepts in this question pertain equally well to dynamic processes, as you'll see in Chapter 8.

Another way to shorten the credit check process would be to use an information system to perform the customer credit checks. Depending on the development and operational costs of the new system, that change might also be less costly and therefore more efficient.

Change Both Process Structure and Resources

Of course, it is possible to improve process quality by changing both the process's structure and resources. In fact, unless a structure change is only a simple reordering of tasks, changing the structure of a process almost always involves a change in resources as well.

How Can Information Systems Improve Process Quality?

Information systems can be used to improve process quality by:

- Performing an activity
- Augmenting a human who is performing an activity
- Controlling process flow

Performing an Activity

Information systems can perform the entirety of a process activity. In Figure 7-1, for example, the check credit activity could be entirely automated. When you purchase from Amazon.com or another major online retailer, information systems check your credit while your transaction is being processed. At GearUp, operations costs could be reduced by developing an information system that computes a surcharge for events when the goods are to be obtained from a problematic vendor. That surcharge could be computed and automatically added to the event's planning documents.

We have defined information systems as having five components, the last of which is people. So, if the activity is entirely automated, you might wonder if it would be more accurate to say that the activity is being performed by a *computer program* rather than by an *information system*. In fact, in most business situations neither term is accurate when describing a completely automated activity. The terminology is not particularly important, as long as you understand the problem with each term. (See Collaboration Exercise, page 252.)

Augmenting a Human Performing an Activity

A second way that information systems can improve process quality is by augmenting the actions of a human who is performing that activity. At Fox Lake, if all departments were to use a common facility reservation information system, then Anne could use that system when planning a wedding to ensure that the facilities she needs are available on the dates that she needs them. In this example, the reservation system augments one of the activities in the wedding planning process.

Controlling Process Flow

A third way that information systems can improve process quality is by controlling process flow. Consider the order approval process in Figure 7-1. If this process is controlled manually, then someone, say a salesperson, will obtain the order data from the customer and take whatever actions are needed to push that order through the three steps in the order process. If the salesperson gets busy or is distracted or away from work for a few days, or if there are unexpected delays in one of the activities, it is possible for an order to be lost or the approval unnecessarily delayed.

If, however, an information system is controlling the order approval process, then it can ensure that steps are performed in accordance with an established schedule. The information system can also be relied upon to make correct process-routing decisions for processes that are more complicated than that in Figure 7-1. SharePoint workflows, discussed in the context of collaboration in Chapter 2, can be used to automate structured processes.

Q3 How Do Enterprise Systems Eliminate the Problem of Information Silos?

An **information silo** is a condition that exists when data are isolated in separated information systems. For example, if an organization uses one information system for order processing and a second information system for customer service, the customer data are isolated in two separate systems. As a result, the customer service department might provide thousands of dollars of customer support to a customer who has only ordered a few hundred dollars of product.

How Do Information System Silos Arise?

No organization plans to create information silos. They arise as a consequence of information systems that support departmental rather than enterprise-level processes.

Consider the example of Fox Lake in Figure 7-5. The wedding events department is new, and Anne, the manager, has been given incentives to grow the business. At the same time, both she and Fox Lake have a reputation to protect, so she wants to grow the business so that Fox Lake weddings and receptions have a superior reputation.

Golf operations has a very different set of goals. Golfing is the primary concern of club members, and the club must provide golfers with accurate tee times (starting times) and with a pleasant golfing experience. The club contracts with professional golfers to teach golf lessons. The pros make most of their income from lessons, and in order to attract and keep quality pros the course needs to give them plenty of business. Other concerns of golf course operations are listed in Figure 7-5.

The goals of the facilities department are completely different from the other two groups. Facilities is concerned with maintenance for top-level appearance, protection of club assets, solving equipment problems, and so forth. Unlike wedding events or golf operations, facilities generates no revenue; it is all cost. So, the facilities manager is given incentives to carefully manage the facilities budget.

Each of these departments will develop business processes to achieve its particular goals. Wedding events will focus on processes for selling and accomplishing weddings, which are one-time events. Golf operations will develop processes for satisfying repeat customers and for selling those customers lessons on a continuing basis. Facilities will focus on processes for maintenance and problem solving within budget.

Because of these different processes, each group will develop information systems of a different character, as shown in Figure 7-6. Because these systems have nearly nothing to do with each other, they can operate as isolated entities for a long time, without problem. In fact, **islands of automation** is another term for information silo; it just means groups of information systems that operate in isolation from one other.

Figure 7-5
Fox Lake Country Club
Departmental Goals

Wedding Events	Golf Operations	Facilities

• Increase business	• Satisfy golfers	• Maintain top-level club appearance
• Develop high-quality reputation	• Keep golf pros busy	• Protect and conserve club physical assets
• Manage complicated details	• Extend season	• Resolve problems quickly
• One-off customers	• Manage pro shop profitably	• Stay within budget
	• Repeat customers	

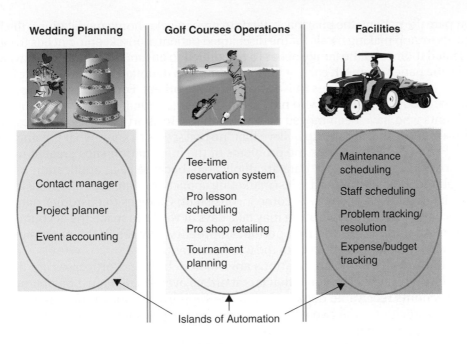

Figure 7-6
Fox Lake Country Club
Departmental Information
Systems

Information silos (or, equivalently, islands of automation) are not a problem until processes begin to use and store data about the same entities. Or, stated differently, until they duplicate data. At that point, they can become quite problematic, as Fox Lake learned when the wedding events department maintained its own copy of room reservation data that duplicated that same data in the facilities department.

What Problems Do Information Silos Cause?

We have seen one problem of information silos at Fox Lake. Because wedding events, facilities, and golf operations use the same physical structures, they duplicate data about those facilities in their isolated processes and systems. By storing isolated data, their activities can conflict, as they did.

Consider, however, the more complex example in Figure 7-7. Every day, patients are discharged from hospitals. Think about the numerous departments that need to be notified when that occurs. Doctors issue the discharge order. In response, nurses need to

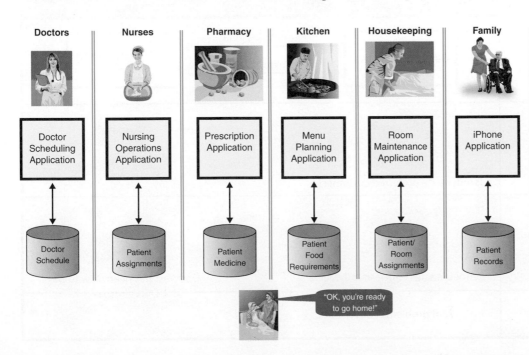

Figure 7-7
Examples of Islands of
Automation at a Hospital

prepare the patient, the pharmacy needs to prepare take-home medications, the kitchen needs to stop making meals for the discharged patient, housekeeping needs to clean the vacated room, and the family needs to be notified to ensure that someone is available to take the patient home. If each of these departments maintains its own island of automation, it will make decisions in isolation from the others. For example, the kitchen will prepare food for patients who have been discharged. Or, families will attempt to visit patients who have been moved to new locations. In short, patients, families, doctors, nurses, and staff will come to believe that "no one seems to know what is going on."

Figure 7-8 summarizes the problems of the information silos created by isolated information systems. First, data are duplicated, because each application has its own database. If accounting and sales/marketing applications are separated, customer data will be duplicated and may become inconsistent. Changes to customer data made in the sales/marketing application may take days or weeks to reach the accounting application's database. During that period, shipments may reach the customer without delay, but invoices will be sent to the wrong address.

Additionally, when applications are isolated, business processes are disjointed. Suppose a business has a rule that credit orders over $20,000 must be preapproved by the accounts receivable department. If the supporting applications are separated, it will be difficult for the two activities to reconcile their data, and the approval will be slow-to-grant and possibly erroneous.

In the second row of Figure 7-8, sales and marketing wants to approve a $20,000 order with Ajax. According to the sales and marketing database, Ajax has a current balance of $17,800, so sales requests a total credit amount of $37,800. The accounting database, however, shows Ajax with a balance of $12,300, because the accounts receivable application has credited Ajax for a return of $5,500. According to accounting's records, a total of $32,300 will be needed to approve the new $20,000 order, so that is all they grant. Sales and marketing doesn't understand what to do with a credit approval of $32,300. Was only $14,500 of the order approved? And why that amount?

Figure 7-8
Problems Created by Information Silos

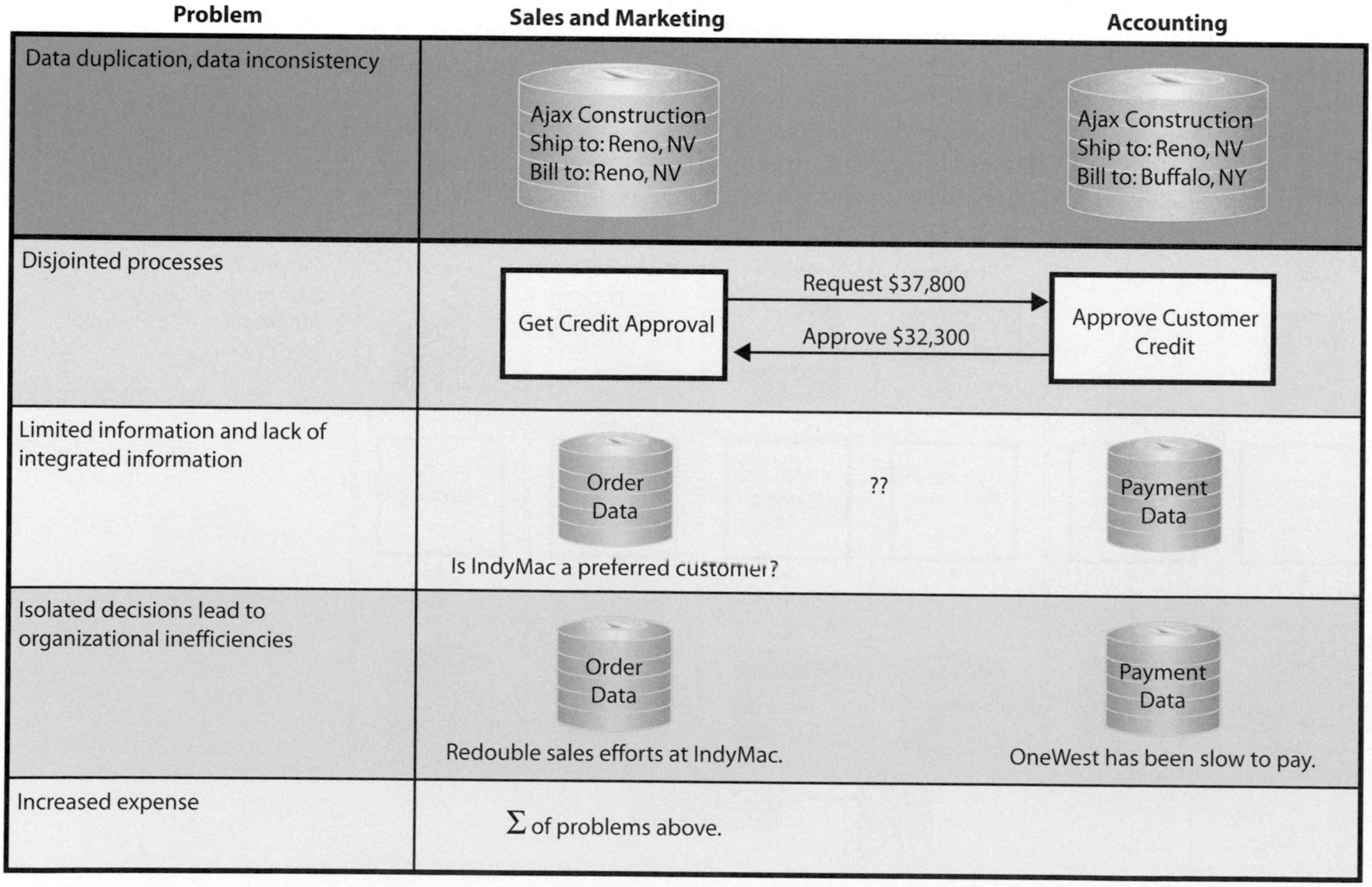

Problem	Sales and Marketing		Accounting
Data duplication, data inconsistency	Ajax Construction Ship to: Reno, NV Bill to: Reno, NV		Ajax Construction Ship to: Reno, NV Bill to: Buffalo, NY
Disjointed processes	Get Credit Approval	Request $37,800 → ← Approve $32,300	Approve Customer Credit
Limited information and lack of integrated information	Order Data Is IndyMac a preferred customer?	??	Payment Data
Isolated decisions lead to organizational inefficiencies	Order Data Redouble sales efforts at IndyMac.		Payment Data OneWest has been slow to pay.
Increased expense	Σ of problems above.		

Both departments want to approve the order. It will take numerous emails and phone calls, however, to sort this out. The interacting business processes are disjointed.

A consequence of such disjointed systems is the lack of integrated enterprise data. For example, suppose sales and marketing wants to know if IndyMac is still a preferred customer. Assume that determining a customer's status requires a comparison of order history and payment history data. However, with information silos, that data will reside in two different databases, and, in one of them, IndyMac is known by the name of the company that acquired it, OneWest bank. Data integration will be difficult. Making the determination will require manual processes and days, when it should be readily answered in seconds.

This leads to the fourth consequence: inefficiency. When using isolated functional applications, decisions are made in isolation. As shown in the fourth row of Figure 7-8, sales and marketing decided to redouble its sales effort with IndyMac. However, accounting knows that IndyMac was foreclosed by the FDIC and sold to OneWest and that there are far better prospects for increased sales attention. Without integration, the left hand of the organization doesn't know what the right hand is doing.

Finally, information silos can result in increased costs for the organization. Duplicated data, disjointed systems, limited information, and inefficiencies all mean higher costs.

These problems are solved by information systems that support enterprise-wide processes, and we consider them for the rest of this chapter.

How Information Systems Eliminate Silos

The fundamental problem of information silos is that data are duplicated in isolated systems. The most obvious fix is to eliminate that duplicated data by storing a single copy of data in a shared database and revising business processes (and applications) to use that database. Another remedy is to allow the duplication, but to manage it to avoid problems. We will discuss both techniques in this chapter.

An Enterprise System at Fox Lake

Figure 7-9 shows how the first remedy is applied at Fox Lake. First, a database is created that contains reservations for club facilities. Each department then alters its business processes (and applications) to use the shared database. In this simple example, the only change needed is to develop procedures to check availability before scheduling activities and to record any intended use for shared resources in the database. One or more database applications may need to be developed to enable availability checking.

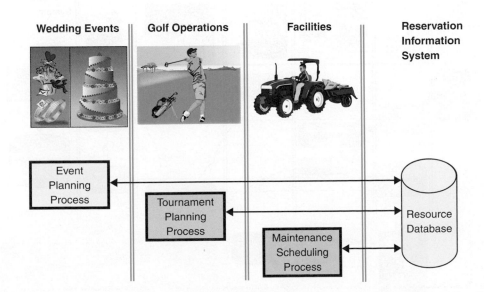

Figure 7-9
Fox Lake Country Club
Enterprise Reservation System

However, with this solution, each department must be mindful that it is processing a shared resource. For example, prior to the shared database, the facilities department would block out weeks of time on its calendar for building maintenance, much more time than it actually needed. It would then work in maintenance activities during that block in accordance with its own tasks and priorities. If facilities continues this practice, it will needlessly block out wedding events and reduce potential club revenue. With the shared database, facilities needs to schedule specific activities against specific buildings for the minimum necessary blocks of time.

Before we go on, this simple example illustrates a phenomenon that creates difficult management challenges. When the enterprise system is implemented, all the departments that use it must change their business processes. People do not like to change; in fact, unless the benefit of the change is easily recognized, people resist change. However, in some cases, new enterprise systems require departments to change without any obvious benefit *to that department*. In the Fox Lake example, when moving to the system in Figure 7-9, facilities will need to change its processes for the benefit of wedding events (and for Fox Lake as an enterprise), but for no benefit to itself. Facilities personnel may perceive the new system as a lot of trouble for nothing.

The system in Figure 7-9 is an enterprise information system in that different departments share data. However, notice that the business processes do not overlap departments; they are still isolated. This is not the case in most organizations. Usually, enterprise business processes span departments. When they do so, the development of enterprise systems is considerably more difficult but potentially more beneficial. Consider the hospital example previously introduced.

An Enterprise System for Patient Discharge

Figure 7-10 shows some of the hospital departments and processes involved in discharging a patient from a hospital. A doctor initiates the process by issuing a discharge patient order. That order is delivered to the appropriate nursing staff member, who initiates activities at the pharmacy, the patient's family, and housekeeping. Some of those activities initiate activities back at the nursing staff. The hospital will use an enterprise-wide information system to support this process (orange arrow). That information system will provide data entry forms, reports, and notifications to the human actors in this process. It will also control the flow of process activity, as shown by the dotted red line.

Prior to the enterprise system, the hospital had developed procedures for using a paper-based system and informal messaging via the telephone. Each department

Figure 7-10
Example Enterprise Process and Information System

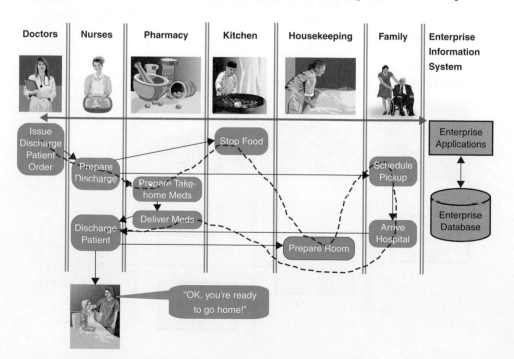

kept its own records. When the new enterprise information system was implemented, not only was the data integrated into a database, but new computer-based forms and reports were created. To use the new system, the staff needed to transition from the paper-based system to the computer-based one. They also needed to stop making phone calls and let the new information system make notifications across departments. These measures involved substantial change, and most organizations experience considerable anguish when undergoing such transitions.

Q4 How Do CRM, ERP, and EAI Support Structured Enterprise Processes?

Enterprise systems like the one in Figure 7-10 were not feasible until network, data communication, and database technologies reached a sufficient level of capability and maturity in the late 1980s and early 1990s. At that point, many organizations began to develop enterprise systems.

The Need for Business Process Engineering

As they did so, organizations realized that their existing business processes needed to change. In part, they needed to change to utilize the shared databases and to utilize new computer-based forms and reports. However, an even more important reason for changing business processes was that integrated data and enterprise systems offered the potential of substantial improvements in process quality. It became possible to do things that had been impossible before. Using Porter's language (Chapter 3, page 82), enterprise systems enabled the creation of stronger, faster, more effective *linkages* among value chains.

For example, when the hospital used a paper-based system, the kitchen would prepare meals for everyone who was a patient at the hospital as of midnight the night before. It was not possible to obtain data about discharges until the next midnight. Consequently, considerable food was wasted at substantial cost.

With the enterprise system, the kitchen can be notified about patient discharges as they occur throughout the day, resulting in substantial reductions in wasted food. But when should the kitchen be notified? Immediately? And what if the discharge is cancelled before completion? Notify the kitchen of the cancelled discharge? Many possibilities and alternatives exist. So, to design its new enterprise system, the hospital needed to determine how best to change its processes to take advantage of the new capability. Such projects came to be known as **business process reengineering**, which is the activity of altering and designing business processes to take advantage of new information systems.

Unfortunately, business process reengineering is difficult, slow, and exceedingly expensive. Business analysts need to interview key personnel throughout the organization to determine how best to use the new technology. Because of the complexity involved, such projects require high-level and expensive skills and considerable time. Many early projects stalled when the enormity of the project became apparent. This left some organizations with partially implemented systems, which had disastrous consequences. Personnel didn't know if they were using the new system, the old system, or some hacked-up version of both.

The stage was set for the emergence of enterprise application solutions, which we discuss next.

Emergence of Enterprise Application Solutions

When the process quality benefits of enterprise-wide systems became apparent, most organizations were still developing their applications in-house. At the time, organizations perceived their needs as being "too unique" to be satisfied by off-the-shelf or altered applications. However, as applications became more and more complex, in-house development costs became infeasible. As stated in Chapter 4, systems built in-house are expensive not only because of their high initial development costs, but also because of the continuing need to adapt those systems to changing requirements.

In the early 1990s, as the costs of business process reengineering were coupled to the costs of in-house development, organizations began to look more favorably on the idea of licensing pre-existing applications. "Maybe we're not so unique, after all."

Some of the vendors who took advantage of this change in attitude were People-Soft, which licensed payroll and limited-capability human resources systems; Siebel, which licensed a sales lead tracking and management system, and SAP, which licensed something new, a system called *enterprise resource management.*

These three companies, and ultimately dozens of others like them, offered not just software and database designs. They also offered standardized business processes. These **inherent processes**, which are predesigned procedures for using the software products, saved organizations from the expense, delays, and risks of business process reengineering. Instead, organizations could license the software and obtain, as part of the deal, prebuilt procedures, which the vendors assured them were based on "industry best practices."

Despite the clear benefits of inherent processes and ERP, there can be an unintended consequence. See the Guide on pages 248–249 and consider that risk.

Some parts of that deal were too good to be true because, as you'll learn in Q6, inherent processes are almost never a perfect fit. But, the offer was too much for many organizations to resist. Over time, three categories of enterprise applications emerged: customer relationship management, enterprise resource planning, and enterprise application integration. Consider each.

Customer Relationship Management (CRM)

A **customer relationship management (CRM) system** is a suite of applications, a database, and a set of inherent processes for managing all the interactions with the customer, from lead generation to customer service. Every contact and transaction with the customer is recorded in the CRM database. Vendors of CRM systems claim that using their products makes the organization *customer-centric.* Though that term reeks of sales hyperbole, it does indicate the nature and intent of CRM packages.

Figure 7-11 shows four phases of the **customer life cycle**: marketing, customer acquisition, relationship management, and loss/churn. Marketing sends messages to the target market to attract customer prospects. When prospects order, they become customers who need to be supported. Additionally, relationship management processes

Figure 7-11
The Customer Life Cycle

Source: Used with permission of Professor Douglas MacLachlan, Michael G. Foster School of Business, University of Washington.

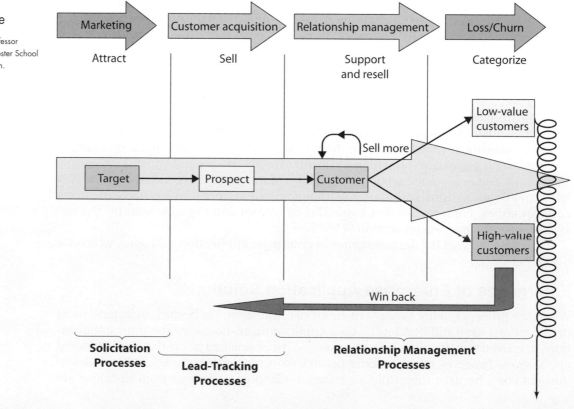

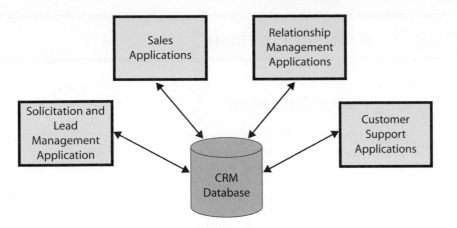

Figure 7-12
CRM Applications

increase the value of existing customers by selling them more product. Inevitably, over time the organization loses customers. When this occurs, win-back processes categorize customers according to value and attempt to win back high-value customers.

Figure 7-12 illustrates the major components of a CRM application. Notice that components exist for each stage of the customer life cycle. As shown, all applications process a common customer database. This design eliminates duplicated customer data and removes the possibility of inconsistent data. It also means that each department knows what has been happening with the customer at other departments. Customer support, for example, will know not to provide $1,000 worth of support labor to a customer that has generated $300 worth of business over time. However, they'll know to bend over backwards for the customers that have generated hundreds of thousands of dollars of business. The result to the customer is that he or she feels like they are dealing with one entity and not many.

CRM systems vary in the degree of functionality they provide. One of the primary tasks when selecting a CRM package is to determine the features you need and to find a package that meets that set of needs. You might be involved in just such a project during your career.

Enterprise Resource Planning (ERP)

Enterprise resource planning (ERP) is a suite of applications called **modules**, a database, and a set of inherent processes for consolidating business operations into a single, consistent, computing platform. An **ERP system** is an information system based on ERP technology. As shown in Figure 7-13, ERP systems include the functions

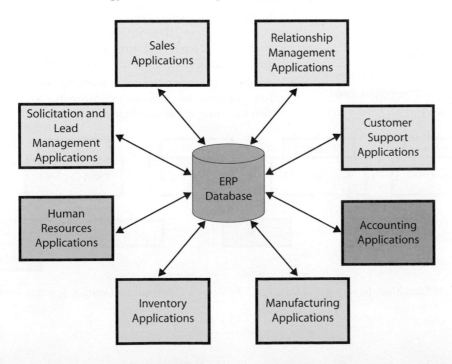

Figure 7-13
ERP Applications

Using MIS InClass 7 *A Group Exercise*

Improving the Process of Making Paper Airplanes[2]

Source: Benis Arapovic/Shutterstock.com.

The purpose of this exercise is to demonstrate process concepts. In this exercise, students will form assembly lines to create paper airplanes. Each assembly line will have the same four activities, each called a Work Center (WC), as shown in Figure 7-14. Raw material is a stack of plain paper, finished goods are the folded airplanes, and WIP is "Work in Progress," which is the output of the WC prior to the next WC.

One student is assigned to each of the four WCs in the assembly line. Student 1 (in WC 1) creates the first fold, as shown at the top of Figure 7-15. Student 2, at WC 2, folds the corners, also shown in Figure 7-15. The location and assembly instructions for Students 3 and 4 are also shown in Figure 7-15. In addition to the four students who fold the planes, seven other students observe, time, and record each assembly line, as listed below, using the three forms in Figure 7-16:

Observer 1: Use Form 1, record WC 1 task times.

Observer 2: Use Form 1, record WC 2 task times.

Observer 3: Use Form 1, record WC 3 task times.

Observer 4: Use Form 1, record WC 4 task times.

Observer 5: Use Form 2, record cycle time at the end of the line.

Observer 6: Use Form 3, record colored sheet throughput time.

Observer 7: Count WIP at the end of each run.

Each assembly line is run to construct 20 airplanes. Prior to beginning the process, each line will run a practice session of four or five planes. Then, clear the line, start the clock, and make the 20 airplanes. Each WC continues to work until the 20th plane is finished, which means that more than 20 will be started because there will be WIP when the 20th is finished. About halfway through the run, the instructor will insert a colored piece of paper as raw material. Each student assembler works at his or her own pace. As workers build planes, they should work at a comfortable pace and not speed. This is not a contest for maximum output, but for quality.

After the first run is completed, make a second run of 20 planes with all the same roles. However, each student can work only when there is an airplane in the inbox (WIP) and no airplane in the outbox (WIP). Again, midway through the run the instructor will insert a colored sheet of paper.

After the runs:

1. In teams, diagram the process using BPMN symbols such as roles, swimlanes, activities, and decisions. Name resources assigned to roles.

2. Apply the OMIS model to improve this process. Discuss the objectives of the assembly line. If you were in charge of an assembly line like this one, do you think your objectives would be efficiency or effectiveness? Specify the measures used to monitor progress toward your objective(s).

3. Assume that the WC folding is done by four machines. In that scenario, the second run uses different software than the first run. Does this new IS improve an activity, linkage, or control?

4. Are any data in an information silo on the first or second runs?

5. Which measure changed most significantly from the first to the second run? Did you anticipate this? Are other processes with other measures just as subject to change with a similar minor change in information?

6. Were there any controls on the assembly process? Could an IS improve the process by improving control? On which measure(s) will this improvement appear?

Figure 7-14
Classroom Assembly Line Setup

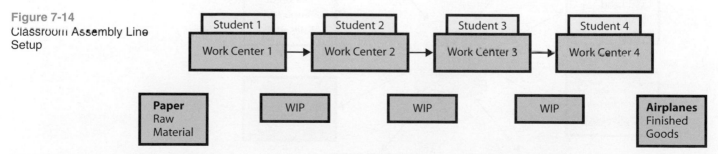

[2] Based on "A Classroom Exercise to Illustrate Lean Manufacturing Pull Concepts," by Peter J. Billington, in *Decision Sciences Journal of Innovative Education, 2*(1), 2004, pp. 71–77.

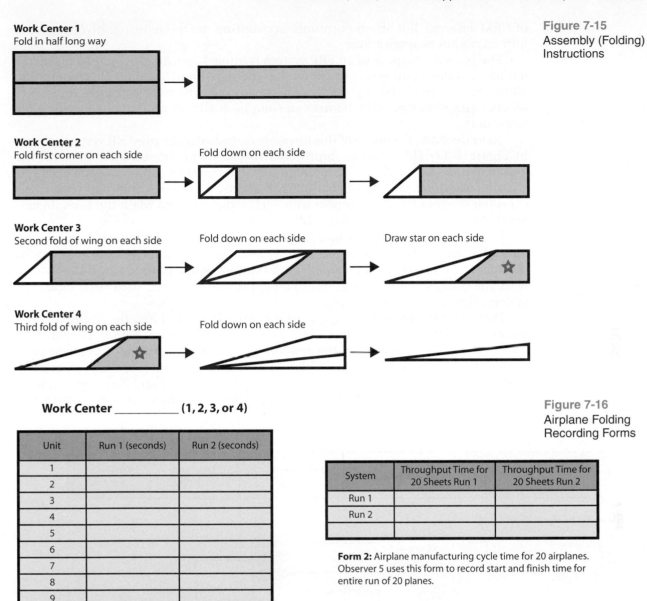

Figure 7-15
Assembly (Folding)
Instructions

Work Center 1
Fold in half long way

Work Center 2
Fold first corner on each side   Fold down on each side

Work Center 3
Second fold of wing on each side   Fold down on each side   Draw star on each side

Work Center 4
Third fold of wing on each side   Fold down on each side

Work Center _____ (1, 2, 3, or 4)

Figure 7-16
Airplane Folding
Recording Forms

Unit	Run 1 (seconds)	Run 2 (seconds)
1		
2		
3		
4		
5		
6		
7		
8		
9		
10		
11		
12		
13		
14		
15		
16		
17		
18		
19		
20		
Sum		
Average		

System	Throughput Time for 20 Sheets Run 1	Throughput Time for 20 Sheets Run 2
Run 1		
Run 2		

Form 2: Airplane manufacturing cycle time for 20 airplanes. Observer 5 uses this form to record start and finish time for entire run of 20 planes.

System	Throughput Time for Colored Sheets Run 1	Throughput Time for Colored Sheets Run 2
Run 1		
Run 2		

Form 3: Paper airplane manufacturing color sheet throughput time. Observer 6 uses this form to record start and finish time for colored sheet.

Form 1: Airplane manufacturing task time. Observers 1, 2, 3, and 4 use this form to record assembly times for each Work Center.

of CRM systems, but also incorporate accounting, manufacturing, inventory, and human resources applications.

The primary purpose of an ERP system is integration; an ERP system allows the left hand of the organization to know what the right hand is doing. This integration allows real-time updates globally, whenever and wherever a transaction takes place. Critical business decisions can then be made on a timely basis using the latest data.

To understand the utility of this integration, consider the pre-ERP systems shown in Figure 7-17. This diagram represents the same processes used by a bicycle manufacturer that we discussed in Chapter 3. It includes five different databases, one each for vendors, raw materials, finished goods, manufacturing plan, and CRM. Consider the problems that appear with such separated data when the sales department closes a large order, say, for 1,000 bicycles.

First, should the company take the order? Can it meet the schedule requirements for such a large order? Suppose one of the primary parts vendors recently lost capacity due to an earthquake, and the manufacturer cannot obtain parts for the order in time. If so, the order schedule ought not to be approved. However, with such separated systems this situation is unknown.

Even if parts can be obtained, until the order is entered into the finished goods database, purchasing is unaware of the need to buy new parts. The same comment applies to manufacturing. Until the new order is entered into the manufacturing plan, the production department doesn't know that it needs to increase manufacturing. And, as with parts, does the company have sufficient machine and floor capacity to fill the order on a timely basis? Does it have sufficient personnel with the correct skill

Figure 7-17
Pre-ERP Information Systems

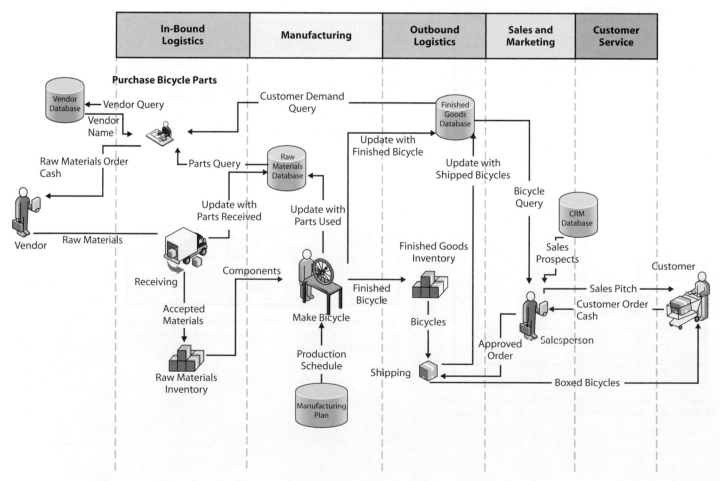

sets? Should it be hiring? Can production meet the order schedule? No one knows before the order is approved.

Figure 7-17 does not show accounting. We can assume, however, that the company has a separate accounting system that is similarly isolated. Eventually, records of business activity find their way to the accounting department and will be posted into the general ledger. With such a pre-ERP system, financial statements are always outdated, available several weeks after the close of the quarter or other accounting period.

Contrast this situation with the ERP system in Figure 7-18. Here, all activity is processed by ERP application programs and consolidated data are stored in a centralized ERP database. When sales is confronted with the opportunity to sell 1,000 bicycles, the information that it needs to confirm that the order, schedule, and terms are possible can be obtained from the ERP system immediately. Once the order is accepted, all departments, including purchasing, manufacturing, human resources, and accounting, are notified. Further, transactions are posted to the ERP database as they occur; the result is that financial statements are available quickly, in most cases correct financial statements can be produced in real time. With such integration, ERP systems can display the current status of critical business factors to managers and executives, as shown in the sales dashboard in Figure 7-19 on the next page.

Of course, the devil is in the details. It's one thing to draw a rectangle on a chart, label it "ERP Application Programs," and assume that data integration takes all the problems away. It is far more difficult to write those application programs and to design the database to store that integrated data. Even more problematic, what procedures should employees and others use to process those application programs?

Figure 7-18
ERP Information Systems

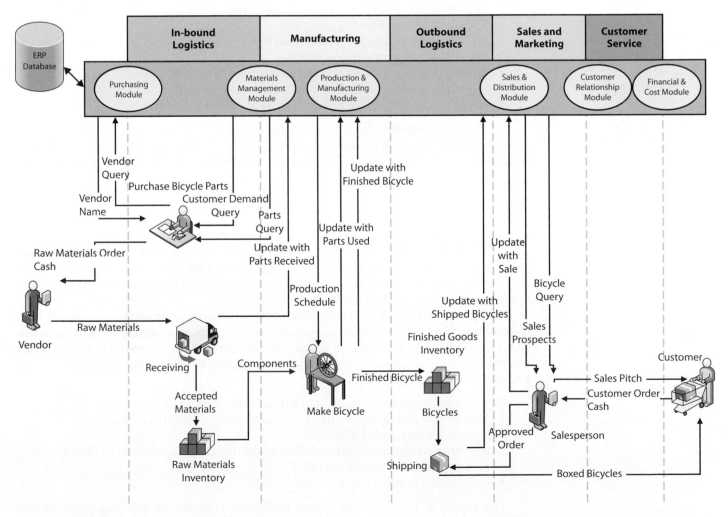

Figure 7-19
Sales Dashboard

Source: Microsoft Corporation.

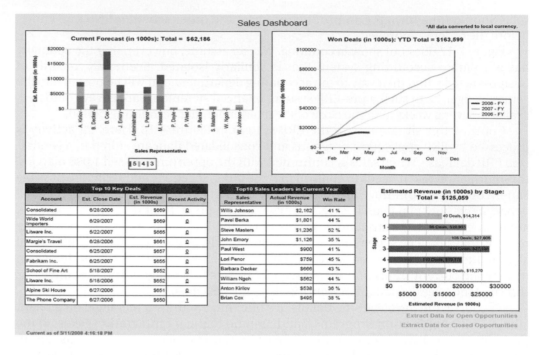

Specifically, for example, what actions should salespeople take before they approve a large order? Here are some of the questions that need to be answered or resolved:

- How does the sales department determine that an order is considered large? By dollars? By volume?
- Who approves customer credit (and how)?
- Who approves production capacity (and how)?
- Who approves schedule and terms (and how)?
- What actions need to be taken if the customer modifies the order?
- How does management obtain oversight on sales activity?

As you can imagine, many other questions must be answered as well. Because of its importance to organizations today, we will discuss ERP in further detail in question Q5. Before we do so, however, consider the third type of enterprise system: EAI.

Enterprise Application Integration (EAI)

ERP systems are not for every organization. For example, some nonmanufacturing companies find the manufacturing orientation of ERP inappropriate. Even for manufacturing companies, some find the process of converting from their current system to an ERP system too daunting. Others are quite satisfied with their manufacturing application systems and do not wish to change them.

Companies for which ERP is inappropriate still have the problems associated with information silos, however, and some choose to use **enterprise application integration (EAI)** to solve those problems. EAI is a suite of software applications that integrates existing systems by providing layers of software that connect applications together. EAI does the following:

- It connects system "islands" via a new layer of software/system.
- It enables existing applications to communicate and share data.
- It provides integrated information.
- It leverages existing systems—leaving functional applications as is, but providing an integration layer over the top.
- It enables a gradual move to ERP.

The layers of EAI software shown in Figure 7-20 enable existing applications to communicate with each other and to share data. For example, EAI software can

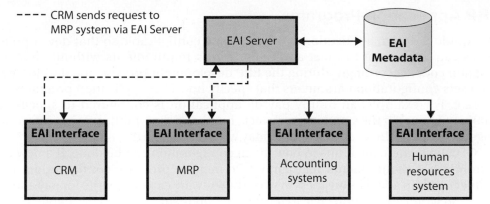

Figure 7-20
Design and Implementation
for the Five Components

be configured to automatically make the data conversion required to make data conversions among different systems. When the CRM applications send data to the manufacturing application system, for example, the CRM system sends its data to an EAI software program. That EAI program makes the conversion and then sends the converted data to the ERP system. The reverse action is taken to send data back from the ERP to the CRM.

Although there is no centralized EAI database, the EAI software keeps files of metadata that describe data formats and locations. Users can access the EAI system to find the data they need. In some cases, the EAI system provides services that provide a "virtual integrated database" for the user to process.

The major benefit of EAI is that it enables organizations to use existing applications while eliminating many of the serious problems of isolated systems. Converting to an EAI system is not nearly as disruptive as converting to an ERP system, and it provides many of the benefits of ERP. Some organizations develop EAI applications as a stepping-stone to complete ERP systems.

Q5 What Are the Elements of an ERP System?

Because of its importance to organizations today, we will consider ERP in more depth than CRM or EAI. To begin, the term *ERP* has been applied to a wide array of application solutions, in some cases erroneously. Some vendors attempted to catch the buzz for ERP by misapplying the term to applications that provided only one or two integrated functional applications.

The organization ERPsoftware360 publishes a wealth of information about ERP vendors, products, solutions, and applications. According to its Web site (www.erpsoftware360.com/erp-101.htm), for a product to be considered a true ERP product it must include applications that integrate:

- Supply chain (procurement, sales order processing, inventory management, supplier management, and related activities)
- Manufacturing (scheduling, capacity planning, quality control, bill of materials, and related activities)
- CRM (sales prospecting, customer management, marketing, customer support, call center support)
- Human resources (payroll, time and attendance, HR management, commission calculations, benefits administration, and related activities)
- Accounting (general ledger, accounts receivable, accounts payable, cash management, fixed asset accounting)

An ERP solution consists of application programs, databases, business process procedures, and training and consulting. We consider each, in turn.

ERP Application Programs

ERP vendors design application programs to be configurable so that development teams can alter them to meet an organization's requirements without changing program code. Accordingly, during the ERP development process, the development team sets configuration parameters that specify how ERP application programs will operate. For example, an hourly payroll application is configured to specify the number of hours in the standard workweek, hourly wages for different job categories, wage adjustments for overtime and holiday work, and so forth.

Of course, there are limits to how much configuration can be done. If a new ERP customer has requirements that cannot be met via program configuration, then it either needs to adapt its business to what the software can do or write (or pay another vendor to write) application code to meet its requirement. As stated in Chapter 4, such custom programming is expensive, both initially and in long-term maintenance costs. Thus, choosing an ERP solution that has applications that function close to the organization's requirements is critical to its successful implementation.

ERP Databases

An ERP solution includes a database design as well as initial configuration data. It does not, of course, contain the company's operational data. During development, the team must enter the initial values for that data as part of the development effort.

If your only experience with databases is creating a few tables in Microsoft Access, then you probably underestimate the value and importance of ERP database designs. SAP, the leading vendor of ERP solutions, provides ERP databases that contain over 15,000 tables. The design includes the metadata for those tables, as well as their relationships to each other, and rules and constraints about how the data in some tables must relate to data in other tables. The ERP solution also contains tables filled with initial configuration data.

Reflect on the difficulty of creating and validating data models (as discussed in Chapter 5), and you will have some idea of the amount of intellectual capital invested in a database design of 15,000 tables. Also, consider the magnitude of the task of filling such a database with users' data!

Although we did not discuss this database feature in Chapter 5, large organizational databases contain two types of program code. The first, called a **trigger**, is a computer program stored within the database that runs to keep the database consistent when certain conditions arise. The second, called a **stored procedure**, is a computer program stored in the database that is used to enforce business rules. An example of such a rule would be never to sell certain items at a discount. Triggers and stored procedures are also part of the ERP solution. Much of this program code needs to be configured during the ERP implementation as well.

Business Process Procedures

The third component of an ERP solution is a set of inherent procedures that implement standard business processes. ERP vendors develop hundreds, or even thousands, of procedures that enable the ERP customer organization to accomplish its work using the applications provided by the vendor. Figure 7-21 shows a part of the SAP ordering business process; this process implements a portion of the inbound logistics activities. Some ERP vendors call the inherent processes that are defined in the ERP solution **process blueprints**.

Without delving into the details, you should be able to understand the flow of work outlined in this process. Every function (rounded rectangles in Figure 7-21) consists of a set of procedures for accomplishing that function. Typically, these procedures require an ERP user to use application menus, screens, and reports to accomplish the activity.

As with application programs, ERP users must either adapt to the predefined, inherent processes and procedures or design new ones. In the latter case, the design of new procedures may necessitate changes to application programs and to database structures as well. Perhaps you can begin to understand why organizations attempt to conform to vendor standards.

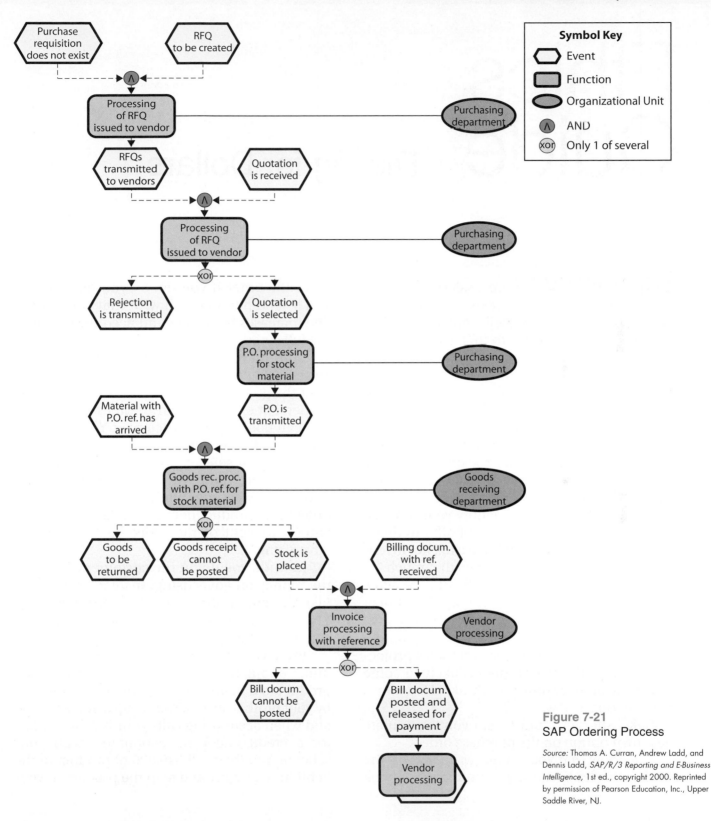

Figure 7-21
SAP Ordering Process

Source: Thomas A. Curran, Andrew Ladd, and Dennis Ladd, *SAP/R/3 Reporting and E-Business Intelligence,* 1st ed., copyright 2000. Reprinted by permission of Pearson Education, Inc., Upper Saddle River, NJ.

Training and Consulting

Because of the complexity and difficulty of implementing and using ERP solutions, ERP vendors have developed training curricula and classes. SAP operates universities, in which customers and potential customers receive training both before and after the ERP implementation. In addition, ERP vendors typically conduct classes on site. To reduce expenses, the vendors sometimes train the organization's employees, called Super Users, to become in-house trainers in training sessions called **train the trainer**.

Ethics Guide

Dialing for Dollars

Suppose you are a salesperson, and your company's CRM forecasts that your quarterly sales will be substantially under quota. You call your best customers to increase sales, but no one is willing to buy more.

Your boss says that it has been a bad quarter for all of the salespeople. It's so bad, in fact, that the vice president of sales has authorized a 20-percent discount on new orders. The only stipulation is that customers must take delivery prior to the end of the quarter so that accounting can book the order. "Start dialing for dollars," she says, "and get what you can. Be creative."

Using your CRM, you identify your top customers and present the discount offer to them. The first customer balks at increasing her inventory, "I just don't think we can sell that much."

"Well," you respond, "how about if we agree to take back any inventory you don't sell next quarter?" (By doing this, you increase your current sales and commission, and you also help your company make its quarterly sales projections. The additional product is likely to come back next quarter, but you think, "Hey, that's then and this is now.")

"OK," she says, "but I want you to stipulate the return option on the purchase order."

You know that you cannot write that on the purchase order because accounting won't book all of the order if you do. So you tell her that you'll send her an email with that stipulation. She increases her order, and accounting books the full amount.

With another customer, you try a second strategy. Instead of offering the discount, you offer the product at full price, but agree to pay a 20-percent credit in the next quarter. That way you can book the full price now. You pitch this offer as follows: "Our marketing department analyzed past sales using our fancy new computer system, and we know that increasing advertising will cause additional sales. So, if you order more product now, next quarter we'll give you 20 percent of the order back to pay for advertising."

In truth, you doubt the customer will spend the money on advertising. Instead, they'll just take the credit and sit on a bigger inventory. That will kill your sales to them next quarter, but you'll solve that problem then.

Even with these additional orders, you're still under quota. In desperation, you decide to sell product to a fictitious company that is "owned" by your brother-in-law. You set up a new account, and when accounting calls your brother-in-law for a credit check he cooperates with your scheme. You then sell $40,000 of product to the fictitious company and ship the product to your brother-in-law's garage. Accounting books the revenue in the quarter, and you have finally made quota. A week into the next quarter, your brother-in-law returns the merchandise.

Meanwhile, unknown to you, your company's ERP system is scheduling production. The program that creates the production schedule reads the sales from your activities (and those of the other salespeople) and finds a sharp increase in product demand. Accordingly, it generates a schedule that calls for substantial production increases and schedules workers for the production runs. The production system, in turn, schedules the material requirements with the inventory application, which increases raw materials purchases to meet the increased production schedule. ∎

Discussion Questions

1. Is it ethical for you to write the email agreeing to take the product back? If that email comes to light later, what do you think your boss will say?

2. Is it ethical for you to offer the "advertising" discount? What effect does that discount have on your company's balance sheet?

3. Is it ethical for you to ship to the fictitious company? Is it legal?

4. Describe the impact of your activities on next quarter's inventories.

5. Setting aside the ethical issues, would you say the enterprise system is more a help or a hindrance in this example?

ERP training falls into two broad categories. The first category is training about how to implement the ERP solution. This training includes topics such as obtaining top-level management support, preparing the organization for change, and dealing with the inevitable resistance that develops when people are asked to perform work in new ways. The second category is training on how to use the ERP application software; this training includes specific steps for using the ERP applications to accomplish the activities in processes like those in Figure 7-21.

ERP vendors also provide on-site consulting for implementing and using the ERP system. Additionally, an industry of third-party ERP consultants has developed to support new ERP customers and implementations. These consultants provide knowledge gained through numerous ERP implementations. Such knowledge is valued because most organizations only go through an ERP conversion once. Ironically, having done so, they now know how to do it. Consequently, some employees, seasoned by an ERP conversion with their employer, leave that company to become ERP consultants

Industry-Specific Solutions

As you can tell, considerable work needs to be done to customize an ERP application to a particular customer. To reduce that work, ERP vendors provide starter kits for specific industries called **industry-specific solutions**. These solutions contain program and database configuration files as well as process blueprints that apply to ERP implementations in specific industries. Over time, SAP, which first provided such solutions, and other ERP vendors created dozens of such starter kits for manufacturing, sales and distribution, health care, and other major industries.

What Companies Are the Major ERP Vendors?

Although more than 100 different companies advertise ERP products, not all of those products meet the minimal ERP criteria. Even of those that do, the bulk of the market is held by the five vendors shown in Figure 7-22. This figure shows market rank rather than market share because it is difficult to obtain comparable revenue numbers. Infor is owned by private equity investors and does not publish financial data.

Figure 7-22
Characteristics of
Top ERP Vendors

Company	ERP Market Rank	Remarks	Future
Epicor	5	Strong-industry specific solutions, especially retail.	Epicor 9 designed for flexibility (SOA). Highly configurable ERP. Lower cost.
Microsoft Dynamics	4	Four products acquired: AX, Nav, GP, and Solomon. AX and Nav more comprehensive. Solomon on the way out? Large VAR channel.	Products not well integrated with Office. Not integrated at all with Microsoft development languages. Product direction uncertain. Watch for Microsoft ERP announcement on the cloud (Azure).
Infor	3	Privately held corporation that has acquired an FRP product named Baan, along with more than 20 others.	Span larger small companies to smaller large companies. Offers many solutions.
Oracle	2	Combination of in-house and acquired (PeopleSoft, Siebel) products.	Intensely competitive company with strong technology base. Large customer base. Flexible SOA architecture. Expensive. Oracle CEO Ellison owns 70% of NetSuite.
SAP	1	Led ERP success. Largest vendor, most comprehensive solution. Largest customers.	Technology older. Expensive and seriously challenged by less expensive alternatives. Huge customer base. Future growth uncertain.

Microsoft's ERP revenue is combined with its CRM revenue, and its true ERP revenue is unknown. Similarly, Oracle and SAP combine ERP revenue with revenue from other products.

Q6 What Are the Challenges of Implementing New Enterprise Information Systems?

Implementing new enterprise systems, whether CRM, ERP, or EAI, is challenging, difficult, expensive, and risky. It is not unusual for enterprise system projects to be well over budget and a year or more late. The expense and risks arise from four primary factors (see Figure 7-23).

Collaborative Management

Unlike departmental systems in which a single department manager is in charge, enterprise systems have no clear boss. Examine the discharge process in Figure 7-10; there is no manager of discharge. The discharge process is a collaborative effort among many departments (and customers).

With no single manager, who resolves the disputes that inevitably arise? All of these departments ultimately report to the CEO, so there is a single boss over all of them, but employees can't go to the CEO with a problem about, say, coordinating discharge activities between nursing and housekeeping. The CEO would throw them out of his or her office. Instead, the organization needs to develop some sort of collaborative management for resolving process issues.

Usually this means that the enterprise develops committees and steering groups for providing enterprise process management. Although this can be an effective solution, and in fact may be the *only* solution, the work of such groups is both slow and expensive.

Requirements Gaps

As stated in Q3, few organizations today create their own enterprise systems from scratch. Instead, they license an enterprise product that provides specific functions and features and that includes inherent procedures. But, such licensed products are never a perfect fit. Almost always there are gaps between the organization's requirements and the application's capabilities.

The first challenge is identifying the gaps. To specify a gap, an organization must know both what it needs and what the new product does. However, it can be very difficult for an organization to determine what it needs; that difficulty is one reason organizations choose to license rather than to build. Further, the features and functions of complex products like CRM or ERP are not easy to identify. Thus, gap identification is a major task when implementing enterprise systems.

The second challenge is deciding what to do with gaps, once they are identified. Either the organization needs to change the way it does things to adapt to the new

- Collaborative management
- Requirements gaps
- Transition problems
- Employee resistance

Figure 7-23
Four Primary Factors

application, or the application must be altered to match what the organization does. Either choice is problematic. Employees will resist change, but paying for alterations is expensive and, as noted in Chapter 4, the organization is committing to maintaining those alterations as the application is changed over time. Here, organizations fill gaps by choosing their lesser regret.

Transition Problems

Transitioning to a new enterprise system is also difficult. The organization must somehow change from using isolated departmental systems to using the new enterprise system, while continuing to run the business. It's like having heart surgery while running a 100-yard dash.

Such transitions require careful planning and substantial training. Inevitably, problems will develop. Knowing this will occur, senior management needs to communicate the need for the change to the employees and then stand behind the new system as the kinks are worked out. It is an incredibly stressful time for all involved. We will discuss development techniques and implementation strategies further in Chapter 10.

Employee Resistance

People resist change. Change requires effort and it engenders fear. Considerable research and literature exists about the reasons for change resistance and how organizations can deal with it. Here we will summarize the major principles.

Some companies may change too often. See the Guide on pages 246–247 for a discussion on how management fads can grow tiresome for employees.

First, senior-level management needs to communicate the need for the change to the organization, and reiterate this, as necessary, throughout the transition process. Second, employees fear change because it threatens **self-efficacy**, which is a person's belief that he or she can be successful at his or her job. To enhance confidence, employees need to be trained and coached on the successful use of the new system. Word-of-mouth is a very powerful factor, and in some cases key users are trained ahead of time to create positive buzz about the new system. Video demonstrations of employees successfully using the new system are also effective.

Third, employees may need to be given extra inducement to change to the new system. As one experienced change consultant said, "Nothing succeeds like praise or cash, especially cash." Straight-out pay for change is bribery; but contests with cash prizes among employees or groups can be very effective at inducing change.

Implementing new enterprise systems can solve many problems and bring great efficiency and cost savings to an organization, but it is not for the faint of heart.

Q7 How Will Service-Oriented Architecture (SOA) Impact Enterprise Information Systems?

Service-oriented architecture (SOA) is a software design philosophy in which activities are organized into modules of functionality called *Web services* that are requested and delivered over the Internet[3] using **SOA standards**. In this question, we will first describe SOA principles and then explain how SOA will impact enterprise information systems like ERP.

What Is SOA?

It is difficult to explain SOA directly without delving into details of computer program design and implementation. Instead, consider the analogy of a pizza stand. The stand publishes a menu of pizzas that it is capable of producing. As everyone knows, the

---

[3] Actually, any internet that uses TCP/IP could be used. Here, to simplify, we'll assume the Internet.

customer studies the menu, orders a pizza, the pizza is created, and the customer pays. The menu specifies the content, size, and price of the pizza. As a customer, you have no idea how or where the pizza is being made. The pizza stand could be buying frozen pizzas from a grocery down the street and baking them, or it could make the sauces in-house but buy the dough elsewhere, or it could make everything in-house. You have no idea how it is done, and as long as the pizza is delivered in accordance with the terms in the menu, you don't need to. The pizza stand can make major changes in the ways that it makes pizzas, and you need never know about those changes. You still get the pizza you've ordered at the price on the menu.

Using SOA terminology, we would say that the pizza stand provides a service that is consumed by the customer. The production of the service (pizza) is **encapsulated**, which means that the methodology and location of the service is private. Users of the service do not know how or where the service is performed, and they need not know. All they need to know is the menu.

A **Web service** is an encapsulated software service provided over the Internet using standard protocols. A service provider creates a **service description**, which documents how to use the service, and publishes that description using a standardized language called **Web Service Description Language (WSDL)**.

All service providers publish WSDL descriptions of their services. For example, Amazon.com offers a Web service for programs to use to search its Web site. If you want to write a program to access that service, you first need to access the Web service's WSDL service description. You can find it at http://soap.amazon.com/schemas2/ AmazonWebServices.wsdl. That code has meaning to computer programmers; they know how to use it to write programs to search Amazon.com. Check it out just for fun.

Because the service is encapsulated, no one knows how or where that service is provided. Amazon.com could employ millions of people who madly search printed catalogs in a dusty back room in Chicago, or, that service could be distributed over thousands of computers using Amazon.com's own Elastic Cloud 2 (EC2; see Case Study 1, page 28). Or it could be something else. But, because of encapsulation, the search method and location can change tomorrow without impacting any program that accesses that service.

Programmers who want to develop programs to request the service use the service description to design their programs. Later, the services are delivered and consumed using standards such as XML, SOAP, REST, and others.

Why Is SOA Important for Enterprise Systems?

The major enterprise applications like SAP and Oracle ERP were developed long before the Internet and long before the SOA standards were developed. They consist of hundreds of thousands of lines of computer code, all written to use pre-Internet technology.

Today, however, ERP customers do not want to be restricted to thick-client applications on their desktop computer at work. They want to be able to access ERP and other enterprise applications using a Web browser, an iPad, a smartphone, and HTML 5 devices yet to come. The changing technical landscape poses an enormous challenge and burden on enterprise solution vendors. Rewriting all of the SAP code, for example, to enable use of these other devices is too costly and would take too long. Even if SAP could afford the redevelopment investment, by the time it has rewritten its software a new standard or device will have come along.

Web services provide a solution to this problem. Rather than rewriting all of the ERP code, SAP can build an SOA interface around particular features and functions in their existing code and expose the functionality of that older code via a Web service.

For example, all ERP applications maintain a vendor list and a list of items and prices of products each vendor provides. The existing thick-client, desktop application is accessed via forms and reports built into the code. Now suppose SAP or another ERP vendor has customers that want to access this list and these prices using an iPad or an Android phone, something that the current SAP or other ERP or CRM packages do not do.

Figure 7-24
Using Enterprise Application
SOA Services

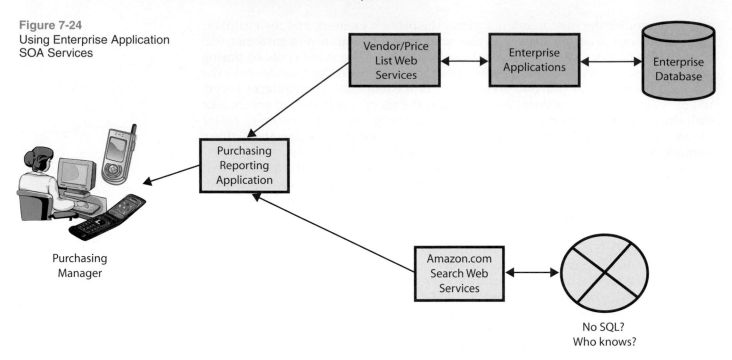

In this case, SAP or another solution provider can expose the vendor and price lists as a Web service. They can provide Web services for querying for a vendor, querying for all parts provided by a vendor, updating prices, removing a vendor or item from a list, and so forth. As shown in Figure 7-24, once they have done that, customers or third-party vendors can write code that will expose these services on a wide variety of devices.

Furthermore, the customer can use this ERP data in ways that no one ever envisioned. Suppose, for example, that the customer wants to compare prices of the items it purchases to prices for the same items on Amazon.com. No one at SAP or any other ERP vendor ever planned on that requirement, but a customer could use data from both the ERP and Amazon.com Web services to develop a report application.

We think of HTML and Web browsers as having provided most of the utility of the Web. However, in terms of nontrivial Internet applications with deep functionality, SOA Web services are at least of equal importance.

Q8 2022?

Because of the exceedingly low processing costs, we can expect that more and more enterprise IS solutions will move to the cloud. Because of the flexibility and adaptability of Web services, we can further expect that those cloud-based enterprise solutions will be exposed as Web services. All of this is happening right now, in 2012.

But, let's take the next step. What happens when cloud-based SOA enterprise applications have moved to the iPad and the Android phone and are hosted in Office 365 and SharePoint Online? You'll learn about tribes and their relationship to Google+ in the next chapter, but what happens when users have taken their data from their smartphone and posted it in a work circle on Google+ with a link for more data back to SharePoint Online?

This evolving, but real, scenario creates enormous security challenges that we'll discuss in Chapter 12. But what else?

It's inevitable: **islands of automation**, **version 2.0**. A new type of island of automation will result from the storing of data in the iCloud, in Google+, in SharePoint Online, and so on, while other versions of the data are stored in the corporate data center in SAP or whatever—maybe no longer the current version, but some version.

Using this perspective, examine Figure 7-10 again. It's likely that doctors, nurses, and families will want to access and process patient data on whatever devices are convenient for them. In that case, where is the integrated data for any given patient? The enterprise database shown in that figure has some version of it. But where is the rest? And where is the current version? The data are spread over devices used by people all over the hospital, at doctors' clinics, and in their homes. In truth, there is no data integration in this scenario.

We have re-created information silos, but these version 2.0 silos are more isolated and less secure than the previous ones. The cost savings of the cloud and the convenience of personal devices ensure the success of this new scenario. But, then what? You and your classmates will find out as you manage your way through this problem in the next 10 years.

Guide
The Flavor-of-the-Month Club

"Oh, come on. I've been here 30 years and I've heard it all. All these management programs. . . . Years ago, we had Zero Defects. Then it was Total Quality Management, and after that, Six Sigma. We've had all the pet theories from every consultant in the Western Hemisphere. No, wait, we had consultants from Asia, too.

"Do you know what flavor we're having now? We're redesigning ourselves to be 'customer-centric.' We are going to integrate our functional systems into a CRM system to transform the entire company to be 'customer-centric.'

"You know how these programs go? First, we have a pronouncement at a 'kick-off meeting' where the CEO tells us what the new flavor is going to be and why it's so important. Then a swarm of consultants and 'change management' experts tell us how they're going to 'empower' us. Then HR adds some new item to our annual review, such as, 'Measures taken to achieve customer-centric company.'

"So, we all figure out some lame thing to do so that we have something to put in that category of our annual review. Then we forget about it because we know the next new flavor of the month will be along soon. Or worse, if they actually force us to use the new system, we comply, but viciously. You know, go out of our way to show that the new system can't work, that it really screws things up.

"You think I sound bitter, but I've seen this so many times before. The consultants and rising stars in our company get together and dream up one of these programs. Then they present it to the senior managers. That's when they make their first mistake: They think that if they can sell it to management, then it must be a good idea. They treat senior management like the customer. They should have to sell the idea to those of us who actually sell, support, or make things. Senior management is just the banker; the managers should let us decide if it's a good idea.

"If someone really wanted to empower me, she would listen rather than talk. Those of us who do the work have hundreds of ideas of how to do it better. Now it's customer-centric? As if we haven't been trying to do that for years!

"Anyway, after the CEO issues the pronouncements about the new system, he gets busy with other things and forgets about it for a while. Six months might go by, and then we're either told we're not doing enough to become customer-centric (or whatever the flavor is) or the company announces another new flavor.

"In manufacturing they talk about push versus pull. You know, with push style, you make things and push them onto the sales force and the customers. With pull style, you let the customers' demand pull the product out of manufacturing. You build when you have holes in inventory. Well, they should adapt those ideas to what they call 'change management.' I mean, does anybody need to manage real change? Did somebody have a 'Use the Google+ program'? Did some CEO announce, 'This year, we're all going to use Google+? Did the HR department put a line into our annual evaluation form that asked how many times we'd used Google+? No, no, no, and no. Customers pulled Google+

through. We wanted it, so we started using it. Same with Kindles, iPads, Twitter, and Facebook.

"That's pull. You get a group of workers to form a network, and you get things going among the people who do the work. Then you build on that to obtain true organizational change. Why don't they figure it out?

"Anyway, I've got to run. We've got the kick-off meeting of our new initiative—something called business process management. Now they're going to empower me to manage my own activities, I suppose. Like, after 30 years, I don't know how to do that. Oh, well, I plan to retire soon.

"Oh, wait. Here, take my T-shirt from the knowledge management program 2 years ago. I never wore it. It says, 'Empowering You Through Knowledge Management.' That one didn't last long." ■

Discussion Questions

1. Clearly, this person is cynical about new programs and new ideas. What do you think might be the cause of her antagonism? What seems to be her principal concern?

2. What does she mean by "vicious" compliance? Give an example of an experience you've had that exemplifies such compliance.

3. Consider her point that the proponents of new programs treat senior managers as the customer. What does she mean? To a consultant, is senior management the customer? What do you think she's trying to say?

4. What does she mean when she says, "If someone wants to empower me, she would listen rather than talk"? How does listening to someone empower that person?

5. Her examples of "pull change" all involve the use of new products. To what extent do you think pull works for new management programs?

6. How do you think management could introduce new programs in a way that would cause them to be pulled through the organization? Consider the suggestion she makes, as well as your own ideas.

7. If you managed an employee who had an attitude like this, what could you do to make her more positive about organizational change and new programs and initiatives?

Guide

ERP and the Standard, Standard Blueprint

Designing business processes is difficult, time consuming, and very expensive. Highly trained experts conduct seemingly countless interviews with users and domain experts to determine business requirements. Then, even more experts join those people, and together this team invests thousands of labor hours to design, develop, and implement effective business processes that meet those requirements. All of this is a very high-risk activity, prone to failure. And it all must be done before IS development can even begin.

ERP vendors such as SAP have invested millions of labor hours into the business blueprints that underlie their ERP solutions. Those blueprints consist of hundreds or thousands of different business processes. Examples are processes for hiring employees, processes for acquiring fixed assets, processes for acquiring consumable goods, and processes for custom "one-off" (a unique product with a unique design) manufacturing, to name just a few.

Additionally, ERP vendors have implemented their business processes in hundreds of organizations. In so doing, they have been forced to customize their standard blueprint for use in particular industries. For example, SAP has a distribution-business blueprint that is customized for the auto parts industry, for the electronics industry, and for the aircraft industry. Hundreds of other customized solutions exist as well.

Even better, the ERP vendors have developed software solutions that fit their business-process blueprints. In theory, no software development is required at all if the organization can adapt to the standard blueprint of the ERP vendor.

As described in this chapter, when an organization implements an ERP solution, it identifies any differences that exist between its business processes and the standard blueprint. Then, the organization must remove that difference, which can be done in one of two ways: It changes business processes to fit the standard blueprint. Or, the ERP vendor or a consultant modifies the standard blueprint (and software solution that matches that blueprint) to fit the unique requirements.

In practice, such variations from the standard blueprint are rare. They are difficult and expensive to implement, and they require the using organization to maintain the variations from the standard as new versions of the ERP software are developed. Consequently, most organizations choose to *modify their processes* to meet the blueprint, rather than the other way around. Although such process changes are also difficult to implement, once the organization has converted to the standard blueprint, they need no longer support a "variation."

So, from a standpoint of cost, effort, risk, and avoidance of future problems, there is a huge incentive for organizations to adapt to the standard ERP blueprint.

Initially, SAP was the only true ERP vendor, but other companies have developed and acquired ERP solutions as well. Because of competitive pressure across the software industry, all of these products are beginning to have the same sets of features and functions. ERP solutions are becoming a commodity.

All of this is fine, as far as it goes, but it introduces a nagging question: If, over time, every organization tends to implement the standard ERP blueprint, and if, over time, every software company develops essentially the same ERP features and functions, then won't every business, worldwide, come to look just like every other business, worldwide? How will organizations gain a competitive advantage if they all use the same business processes?

If every auto parts distributor uses the same business processes, based on the same software, are they not all clones of one another? How will one distinguish itself? How will innovation occur? Even if one parts distributor does successfully innovate a business process that gives it a competitive advantage, will the ERP vendors be conduits to transfer that innovation to competitors? Does the use of "commoditized" standard blueprints mean that no company can sustain a competitive advantage? ■

Source: iStockphoto.com.

Discussion Questions

1. Explain in your own words why an organization might choose to change its processes to fit the standard blueprint. What advantages accrue by doing so?

2. Explain how competitive pressure among software vendors will cause the ERP solutions to become commodities. What does this mean to the ERP software industry?

3. If two businesses use exactly the same processes and exactly the same software, can they be different in any way at all? Explain why or why not.

4. Explain the following statement: An ERP software vendor can be a conduit to transfer innovation. What are the consequences to the innovating company? To the software company? To the industry? To the economy?

5. In theory, such standardization might be possible, but worldwide, there are so many different business models, cultures, people, values, and competitive pressures, can any two businesses ever be exactly alike?

Active Review

Use this Active Review to verify that you understand the ideas and concepts that answer the chapter's study questions.

Q1 What are the basic types of structured processes?

Define *structured* and *dynamic processes* and compare and contrast them. Define *departmental processes, enterprise processes,* and *interenterprise processes* and explain their differences. Define those same levels of information systems.

Q2 How can information systems improve process quality?

Name, define, and give an example of two dimensions of process quality. Name and describe three ways that organizations can improve process quality. Name and describe three ways that information systems can be used to improve process quality.

Q3 How do enterprise systems eliminate the problem of information silos?

Define *information silo,* and explain how such silos come into existence. When do such silos become a problem? Explain how the information silo at Fox Lake led to the conflict between wedding events and facilities at Fox Lake. Describe how the system in Figure 7-9 solves this problem. Describe a situation in which an enterprise system creates a burden for one department without any benefit to that department. Explain a key difference between the enterprise system at Fox Lake and the one at the hospital in Figure 7-10. Describe a key benefit to kitchen operations of the enterprise system to the hospital.

Q4 How do CRM, ERP, and EAI support structured enterprise processes?

Define *business process reengineering,* and explain why it is difficult and expensive. Explain two major reasons why developing enterprise information systems in-house is expensive. Explain the advantages of inherent processes. Define and differentiate among *CRM, ERP,* and *EAI.* Explain how the nature of CRM and ERP is more similar than that of EAI.

Q5 What are the elements of an ERP system?

Describe the minimum capability of a true ERP product. Explain the nature of each of the following ERP solution components: programs, data, procedures, and training and consulting. For each, summarize the work that customers must perform. List the top five ERP vendors in decreasing order of market share.

Q6 What are the challenges of implementing new enterprise information systems?

Name and describe four sources of challenges when implementing enterprise systems. Describe why enterprise systems management must be collaborative. Explain two major tasks required to identify requirements gaps. Summarize the challenges of transitioning to an enterprise system. Explain why employees resist change, and describe three ways of responding to that resistance.

Q7 How will service-oriented architecture (SOA) impact enterprise information systems?

Using the analogy of a pizza stand, explain the nature of SOA. Define and explain the importance of *encapsulation.* Define *Web service* and *service description.* Explain the importance of WSDL. Explain why SOA offers advantages to both enterprise solution providers as well as solution customers. Describe what is unique about the application shown in Figure 7-21.

Q8 2022?

Explain why it is reasonable to expect more use of the cloud and of Web services in the next 10 years. Describe the situation that is likely to occur and explain the term *islands of automation, version 2.0.* Explain the two major problems of such silos.

Using Your Knowledge at Fox Lake

Using the terminology of this chapter, explain the problem illustrated by the discussion between Anne and Mike at the start of this chapter. Explain why the departmental systems in Figure 7-5 will cause information silos. Describe how the solution shown in Figure 7-9 will help to solve this problem. Summarize management problems that Fox Lake can anticipate when implementing the solutions shown in Figure 7-9.

Key Terms and Concepts

Using Your Knowledge

1. Using the example of your university, give examples of information systems for each of the three levels of scope shown in Figure 7-4. Describe three departmental information systems that are likely to duplicate data. Explain how the characteristics of information systems in Figure 7-4 relate to your examples.

2. In your answer to question 1, explain how the three departmental information systems create information silos. Describe the kinds of problems that these silos are likely to cause. Use Figure 7-8 as a guide.

3. Using your answer to question 2, describe an enterprise information system that will eliminate the silos. Explain whether your information system is more like the one in Figure 7-9 or more like the one in Figure 7-10. Would the implementation of your system require business process reengineering? Explain why or why not.

4. Using the patient discharge process in Figure 7-10, explain how the hospital benefits from an ERP solution. Describe why integration of patient records has advantages over separated databases. Explain the value of an industry-specific ERP solution to the hospital.

5. Consider the problem at Fox Lake at the start of this chapter. Explain why this problem was caused by a lack of integration. In what ways would ERP help Fox Lake? If Fox Lake decided to implement ERP, which vendors are likely to have suitable products? Do you think you would recommend an ERP system to Fox Lake? Why or why not?

6. Google or Bing each of the five vendors in Figure 7-19. In what ways have their product offerings changed since this text was written? Do these vendors have new products? Have they made important acquisitions? Have they been acquired? Have any new companies made important inroads into their market share? Update Figure 7-19 with any important late-breaking news.

7. Reread the explanation of SOA in Q7. In your own words, explain how an SOA-designed ERP system enables ERP customers to better integrate existing and new company applications into the vendor's ERP package. Explain how SOA creates an opportunity for smaller companies to develop and sell ERP-related applications.

Collaboration Exercise 7

With a team of your fellow students, develop an answer to the following questions. Use Google Docs, Google+, Windows Live SkyDrive, SharePoint, Office 365, or some other collaboration tool to conduct your meetings.

The county planning office issues building permits, septic system permits, and county road access permits for all building projects in a county in an eastern state. The planning office issues permits to homeowners and builders for the construction of new homes and buildings and for any remodeling projects that involve electrical, gas, plumbing, and other utilities, as well as the conversion of unoccupied spaces, such as garages, into living or working space. The office also issues permits for new or upgraded septic systems and permits to provide driveway entrances to county roads.

Figure 7-25 shows the permit process that the county used for many years. Contractors and homeowners found this process to be slow and very frustrating. For one, they did not like its sequential nature. Only

Figure 7-25
Building Permit Process, Old
Version

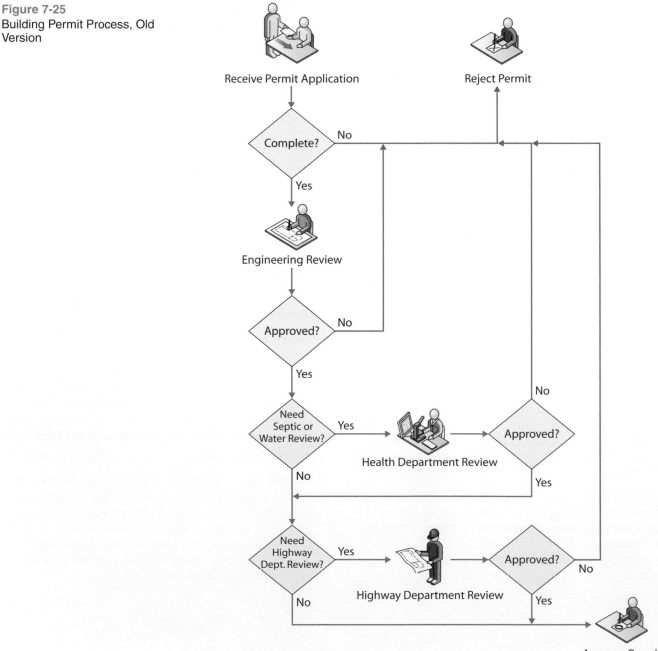

after a permit had been approved or rejected by the engineering review process would they find out that a health or highway review was also needed. Because each of these reviews could take 3 or 4 weeks, applicants requesting permits wanted the review processes to be concurrent rather than serial. Also, both the permit applicants and county personnel were frustrated because they never knew where a particular application was in the permit process. A contractor would call to ask how much longer, and it might take an hour or longer just to find which desk the permits were on.

Accordingly, the county changed the permit process to that shown in Figure 7-26. In this second process, the permit office made three copies of the permit and distributed one to each department. The departments reviewed the permits in parallel; a clerk would analyze the results and, if there were no rejections, approve the permit.

Unfortunately, this process had a number of problems, too. For one, some of the permit applications were

lengthy; some included as many as 40 to 50 pages of large architectural drawings. The labor and copy expense to the county was considerable.

Second, in some cases departments reviewed documents unnecessarily. If, for example, the highway department rejected an application, then neither the engineering nor health departments needed to continue their reviews. At first, the county responded to this problem by having the clerk who analyzed results cancel the reviews of other departments when he or she received a rejection. However, that policy was exceedingly unpopular with the permit applicants, because once an application was rejected and the problem corrected the permit had to go back through the other departments. The permit would go to the end of the line and work its way back into the departments from which it had been pulled. Sometimes this resulted in a delay of 5 or 6 weeks.

Canceling reviews was unpopular with the departments as well, because permit-review work had to

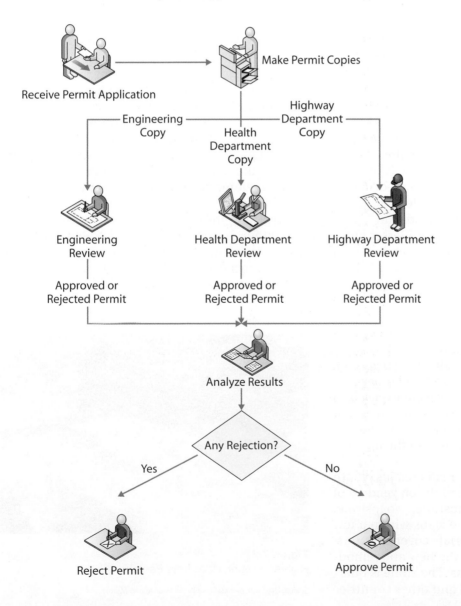

Figure 7-26
Building Permit Process, Revised Version

be repeated. An application might have been nearly completed when it was cancelled due to a rejection in another department. When the application came through again, the partial work results from the earlier review were lost.

1. Explain why the processes in Figures 7-25 and 7-26 are classified as enterprise processes rather than as departmental processes. Why are these processes not interorganizational processes?

2. Using Figure 7-8 as an example, redraw Figure 7-25 using an enterprise information system that processes a shared database. Explain the advantages of this system over the paper-based system in Figure 7-25.

3. Using Figure 7-10 as an example, redraw Figure 7-26 using an enterprise information system that processes a shared database. Explain the advantages of this system over the paper-based system in Figure 7-26.

4. Assuming that the county has just changed from the system in Figure 7-25 to the one in Figure 7-26, which of your answers in questions 2 and 3 do you think is better? Justify your answer.

5. Assume your team is in charge of the implementation of the system you recommend in your answer to question 4. Describe how each of the four challenges discussed in Q5 pertain to this implementation. Explain how your team will deal with those challenges.

6. Read the Guide on the Flavor of the Month on page 246, if you have not already done so. Assume that person is a key player in the implementation of the new system. How will your team deal with her?

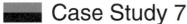

Case Study 7

Process Cast in Stone

Bill Gates and Microsoft were exceedingly generous in the allocation of stock options to Microsoft employees, especially during Microsoft's first 20 years. Because of that generosity, Microsoft created 4 billionaires and an estimated 12,000 millionaires as Microsoft succeeded and the value of employee stock options soared. Not all of those millionaires stayed in the Seattle/Redmond/Bellevue, Washington, area, but thousands did. These thousands of millionaires were joined by a lesser number who made their millions at Amazon.com and, to a lesser extent, at RealNetworks, Visio (acquired by Microsoft), and Aldus (acquired by Adobe). Today, some Google employees who work at Google's Seattle office are joining these ranks.

The influx of this wealth had a strong impact on Seattle and the surrounding communities. One result has been the creation of a thriving industry in high-end, very expensive homes. These Microsoft and other millionaires are college educated; many were exposed to fine arts at the university. They have created homes that are not just large and situated on exceedingly valuable property, but that also are appointed with the highest-quality components.

Today, if you drive through a small area just south of central Seattle, you will find a half dozen vendors of premium granite, marble, limestone, soapstone, quartzite, and other types of stone slabs within a few blocks of each other. These materials cover counters, bathrooms, and other surfaces in the new and remodeled homes of this millionaire class. The stone is quarried in Brazil, India, Italy, Turkey, and other countries and either cut at its origin or sent to Italy for cutting. Huge cut slabs, 6 feet by 10 feet, arrive at the stone vendors in south Seattle, who stock them in their warehouses. The stone slabs vary not only in material, but also in color, veining pattern, and overall beauty. Choosing these slabs is like selecting fine art (see Figure 7-27). (Visit www.pentalonline.com or http://metamarbleandgranite.com to understand the premium quality of these vendors and products.)

Typically, the client (homeowner) hires an architect who either draws plans for the kitchen, bath, or other stone area as part of the overall house design or who hires a specialized kitchen architect who draws those plans. Most of these clients also hire interior decorators

Figure 7-27
High-end countertops from Pental

Source: Used with permission of Pental Granite and Marble.

who help them select colors, fabrics, furniture, art, and other home furnishings. Because selecting a stone slab is like selecting a work of art, clients usually visit the stone vendors' warehouses personally. They walk through the warehouses, often accompanied by their interior designer, and maybe also their kitchen architect, carrying little boxes into which stone vendor employees place chips of slabs in which the client expresses interest.

Usually, the team selects several stone slabs for consideration, and those are set aside for that client. The name of the client or the decorator is written in indelible ink on the side of the stone to reserve it. When the client or design team makes a final selection, the name is crossed out on the stone slabs they do not purchase. The purchased slabs are set aside for shipping.

During the construction process, the contractor will have selected a stone fabricator, who will cut the stone slab to fit the client's counters. The fabricator will also treat the stone's edges, possibly repolish the stone, and cut holes for sinks and faucets. Fabricators move the slabs from the stone vendor to their workshops, prepare the slab, and eventually install it in the client's home.

Questions

1. Identify the key actors in this scenario. Name their employer (if appropriate), and describe the role that they play. Include as a key player the operations personnel who move stones in the warehouse as well as who load stones on the fabricators' trucks.

2. Using Figure 7-20 as an example, diagram the stone-selection process. Classify this process as a personal, a departmental, an enterprise, or an interenterprise process.

3. The current system is not a paper-based system; it is a stone-based system. Explain why this is so.

4. Create an enterprise system that uses a shared database. Change the diagram you created in your answer to question 2 to include this database. (Assume every slab of stone and every location in the warehouse have a unique identifier.) Does the shared database system solve the problems of the stone-based system? Why or why not?

5. Do you think the customers, designers, and fabricators would prefer the stone-based system or the database system? Explain.

6. Suppose you manage the stone vendor company. If you implement the system in your answer to question 4, what problems can you expect? If you do not implement that system, what problems can you expect? What course of action would you take and why?

7. Explain how a knowledge of enterprise systems can help you become a stone slab client rather than a stone chipper.

Fox Lake Country Club, Part 3 and Chapter 7

GOALS

Use Fox Lake Country Club to:

- Illustrate the need for enterprise processes and information systems in the context of a country club that students should be able to understand.

- Demonstrate problems that occur when management fails to think through process and systems consequences of new business activities, acquisitions, mergers, etc.

- Set up Fox Lake for use in Chapters 7–12.

BACKGROUND

1. Many students find it difficult to appreciate the differences between departmental and enterprise processes and systems. They can learn the definitions, but often they don't think about the difference in human aspects of departmental and cross-departmental processes. The point of the argument between Anne and Mike is to bring home some of those differences.

2. I chose a country club for use in Chapters 7–12 because I thought it would be interesting to the students and it had process problems that would be easy to understand and yet complex enough to be realistic. Fox Lake, *per se*, does not exist, but this case is loosely based upon several existing country clubs.

3. Every student understands weddings, and almost all have played golf or tennis or swum at a community center if not a country club. These multiple departments provide ample evidence for the needs and problems of cross-functional applications.

4. Country clubs are losing members and revenue. See, for example, *www.boston.com/yourtown/news/framingham/2010/02/as_golf_course_closes_others_s.html*. The problem is the recession, as well as the fact that young people are not relating to country club life. (Bonus: How does holding wedding events at the club counter that trend?)

5. The long-run solution is for Fox Lake to develop business processes for reserving facilities and for scheduling maintenance on facilities. Those processes need to be augmented by information systems. We'll pick this up in Chapter 10.

6. Anne Foster is a good role model for a highly motivated professional who uses and benefits from information systems. Chapter 7 reveals a need for a facilities planning or reservation system. Chapter 8 will show her responding to critical user-generated content, and Chapter 9 will illustrate one potential use for business intelligence for marketing.

7. Advise the students to read the information about Fox Lake in the Part 3 opening. The students will be tempted to skip that material, and it contains background data that they will need to understand the examples in Chapters 7–12.

HOW TO GET STUDENTS INVOLVED

1. Discuss the differences between departmental and cross-functional processes:

   ■ **How is Anne incentivized? How is Mike incentivized? In what ways will these differences affect their approach to the use of facilities?**

   ■ **Why is it likely that it will be easier for Anne to work with wedding events personnel and for Mike to work with facilities personnel than it will be for them to work together?**

   ■ **Is this situation unusual? Have any of you seen such differences in your workplace?**

2. Why haven't these problems occurred before?

   ■ **How do wedding events differ from other Fox Lake activities?**

   ■ **Should Jeff and Fox Lake's management have anticipated these differences?**

   ■ **What should Jeff have done when he and Fox Lake first thought about the new wedding event business?**

3. What are potential solutions?

   ■ **What data is missing?**

   ■ **Would a roster of room use by date be sufficient?**

   Probably not. Fox Lake would need multiple copies of the roster kept at different locations around the club. How would they be kept consistent?

   ■ **How about a shared database of facility use?**

A database would work, but business processes would have to be adjusted to use that system (more in Chapter 10).

- **What can Jeff do to solve the problem now?**

4. Relate this situation to chapter questions:

- **Give a Fox Lake example of departmental and enterprise IS.**

- **In what sense does this situation indicate the presence of an information silo?**

- **How would an IS eliminate that silo?**

- **Is there a role for CRM, ERP, or EAI here?**

No, that would be overkill. Fox Lake needs a simple reservation system *with attendant business processes to use it.*

- **What challenges will Fox Lake face when implementing a facility reservation system?**

VIDEO

Unlike GearUp, Fox Lake has multiple, independent departments. These departments give rise to the need for cross-functional, enterprise systems.

This first Fox Lake video introduces the characters and illustrates a cross-functional process problem in what we hope is an entertaining, yet educational,
manner. The students need to focus on the underlying problem, the processes that are involved, and possible IS solutions to those problems.

The primary goal of these videos, is to engage the students, to make them care about the characters in the story. The videos set the stage for the need for IS but make no attempt to teach it. Use the videos to set the stage for the importance of what you are going to teach.

BOTTOM LINE

- **Business professionals have different perspectives because they have different goals and objectives and are incentivized differently.**

- **Even relatively small organizations have a need for cross-functional, enterprise systems.**

- **Information silos cause serious organizational problems and can be expensive to solve.**

- **Numerous IS alternatives exist for facilities scheduling, but business processes that use them will have to be created.**

- **Jeff and the other Fox Lake managers should have considered the need for new or altered cross-functional systems when they started the wedding events business.**

YOU BE THE GUIDE

Using the Ethics Guide: Dialing for Dollars (page 238–239)

GOALS

- Understand how business pressures motivate people to act unethically and sometimes illegally.

- Discuss ethical principles among three different aggressive sales techniques.

- Illustrate how deception in the use of an interdepartmental information system may cause unintended consequences.

BACKGROUND AND PRESENTATION STRATEGIES

The stock market is brutal to companies that miss their quarterly sales projections. The pressure on a company to make its numbers can be over the top—especially on small-cap companies that are new, have a limited track record, and have limited cash reserves. Stock prices on such companies can fall by two-thirds of their value in a day.

The software industry has used all three of the techniques in this guide, especially during the 1990s and early 2000s. These techniques, when applied to distributor-customers, are often referred to as *stuffing the channel*. It's a risky strategy; the company is just putting this quarter's problem into the next quarter, where, unless there is a substantial increase in sales demand, the problem will be worse. Managers do it or look the other way when it's being done, because putting off the stock price slaughter for one quarter is at least putting it off for one quarter.

The three techniques used here are:

1. The side letter
2. The delayed discount
3. The fictitious account

I believe that *all three of the stuffing techniques are unethical*. Furthermore, the first and third violate SEC rules and regulations, and the *last one is criminally fraudulent*

In class, I've used the following sequence of questions to introduce this guide:

- **Why is the company doing this?**
- **What are the techniques used here?**

- **Which of these techniques is criminally fraudulent?**
- **Which are violations of SEC rules and regulations?**
- **Which are unethical?**

The surprise in this guide is the impact these actions have on manufacturing scheduling. Given enterprise systems, the fictitious increased sales activity *generates increased production activity*, thus compounding the company's problems in the next quarter. The company will have a huge finished goods inventory—from returns and also from the increased production activity. The stock market will note the increased inventory, and even more pressure will come to the beleaguered company (though they brought it on themselves).

Such ethical issues are, by the way, not new: "Oh, the tangled web we weave, when first we practice to deceive!" (Sir Walter Scott, *Marmion*). Here, we've automated the tangled web.

This company is in serious trouble. At this point, *all choices are bad*. It's a "pick your least regret" situation. I believe that this company is a company to leave, and soon. These practices are unethical, and the company will ultimately fail. The bloodbath, when it happens, will be huge.

SUGGESTED RESPONSES FOR DISCUSSION QUESTIONS

1. To me, *the email involves deception*. The reason for writing it is to avoid a control placed by the accounting department. In almost every case, actions taken for the purpose of deception are unethical. The second part of this question is a good one to ask the class:

- **If the email comes to light later, what will your boss say?**

Your boss will likely deny direct involvement. Your boss won't deny that such letters are written, but he or she will never admit (nor will there be evidence to prove) that it was encouraged. You'll be left holding the bag, so to speak.

Additional questions to add reality to this vignette:

- **What would you do if you found yourself employed by a company that encouraged such practices?**

Suppose you like where you live, your kids are happy in school, and your spouse has a great job.

- **Would you change jobs just because of this problem?**

2. I think the delayed discount via the advertising letter is deceptive, and hence unethical. But sometimes I play devil's advocate as follows:

- **Is this clearly less unethical than the email? The customer might use the discount for advertising. If they don't, it's not my fault.**

Yes, that might be, but the entire action is based on deception. And there's an additional lie:

- **How likely is it that the salesperson's "fancy new computer system" produced data about the utility of advertising?**

- **Can any course of action that involves a lie ever be ethical? Why or why not?**

To answer the rest of the question in the text, the impact on the balance sheet is to overstate revenue in this quarter.

3. Shipping to the fictitious company is both illegal and unethical. This is "Go to jail" activity. DO NOT engage in such activity! Enough said.

4. The email and the fictitious company actions will cause excessive inventory next quarter. All this is "behind the scenes," so no information system will have been programmed to expect the large returns that are going to occur. And, as pointed out in the next question, the sales this quarter may cause the ERP to increase production.

Another question to ask:

- **What would you do if you worked as an inventory manager in this company? How would you plan your inventory?**

This organization is in a very interesting bind. Inventories are going to go up unless someone tells production to ignore the depletion of inventory. But this means that someone has to explain why. If they explain why, however, then what was a "dirty little secret" in sales becomes a "dirty little secret" across the company. Is this the culture that any company wants to create? And yet, if they miss their numbers badly, the organization will be in trouble.

- **Which is better: Work in a company with a culture of keeping "dirty little secrets" or work in a troubled company?**

The sales manager will probably begin to reduce sales activity by some factor in his planning. He'll have to guess because no one is likely to tell him which sales are phony. Long-term production planning becomes impossible.

To me, this is a fascinating consequence of these unethical practices. If top management is not aware of the channel stuffing that sales is doing (unlikely, but possible), the production manager might be called on the carpet—at least for increasing production because of the perceived phony sales.

In my experience, production people and salespeople have very different personalities with very different values. Production people crave organization, accuracy, and quality. Salespeople crave human interaction, flexibility, optimism, and "we can do it" attitudes. The two types are like oil and water. I see a possibly explosive meeting between these two groups.

If the class is willing, it might be worthwhile to conduct a mock hallway interchange—have one student (majoring in, for example, marketing) represent the salesperson and another (majoring in, for example, production management) represent the production manager. You can be the CEO!

Cue the students: The production manager is irate and righteous; the salesperson is guilty, but thrilled to have made the numbers. The salesperson feels like he or she has pulled the company out of a disaster.

5. I think the ERP system, while most inconvenient to this company in the short run, will ultimately be beneficial because it will make it harder and harder to hide these unethical practices.

WRAP UP

- **The easiest response to this scenario is to say "I'll never work for a company like that." But, what if you like the company and situations like this only come around every 18 months or so—and then it's only the occasional side letter?**

- **Would you stay here?**

- **Last point: With process-based, enterprise systems, the actions of one department influence those of another. In this case, deception breeds deception (and disaster!).**

Using the Guide: The Flavor-of-the-Month Club (pages 246–247)

GOALS

- Understand sources of resistance to change-management activities.

- Encourage students to think about the reality of change management and how to deal with forces that oppose it.

- Understand how change management relates to BPM.

BACKGROUND AND PRESENTATION STRATEGIES

Changing business processes looks so simple in class. Just move some symbols around on a diagram, and presto! Change has occurred. Except, people resist change. The goal of this guide is to explore some of the problems and issues that process change involves.

The person on whom this vignette is based believed that *management never listened* to her. She thought she was *smarter than management* (and she was at the particular work she did), and she thought most attempts at change management were silly—almost as if management went to a training program, learned certain words to recite, and then recited those words, without any real care for the employees.

People who deal closely with the customer often identify more with the customers' needs and problems than they do with their own management. Because they spend more time with the customer than they do with their managers, they begin to identify more with the customer than with the company. They blame management for the customers' problems. This is especially true if they have no ready fix for the customers' problems.

Outside consultants can be highly demotivating to employees. Employees quite naturally feel resentful when some highly paid person from outside comes along and "tells management what I've been telling them all along." They feel, "Management won't listen to me, but they will listen to them."

A single "kick-off" meeting is insufficient to launch a new program. The program must have *regular, recurring follow-up* at all levels of management (especially first-line management).

Companies sometimes encounter *vicious compliance:* "You control my paycheck, but you don't control my heart and mind. I'll do what you say, but angrily, and I won't do a very good job at it." This is an incredibly immature response, but sometimes employees feel that is their only possible response. Communication is nil.

Scenario for class discussion: To illustrate how difficult change management can be, consider the following scenario: Suppose an organization changes its competitive strategy from a *differentiating strategy* to a *cost-leader strategy*. (See also the Yikes! Bikes guide in Chapter 3.)

- **How will this change alter the way the organization treats its existing customers?**

- **How will the customers respond to those changes?**

- **How will the employees respond to the customers' responses?**

- **What kind of change-management program needs to be created when shifting to a cost-leader strategy?**

- **What changes, besides customer service, will be affected? For example, how might that strategy change employee travel accommodations or computer equipment?**

- **How will the employees respond to those changes?**

Ask the students to specify five or six features of a change-management program to implement a change to a cost-leader strategy.

- **Even with such a program, how popular will such a change be?**

- **Is it conceivable that there could be a pull style of change management? If so, how?**

- **Is it even possible for an organization to make the shift from a differentiation strategy to a cost-leadership strategy?**

- **How popular will management be during such a change? Does unpopularity justify not making the change?**

SUGGESTED RESPONSES FOR DISCUSSION QUESTIONS

1. Begin by asking the students:

   ■ **What causes someone to have such an attitude?**

   ■ **What has management done in the past to cause her to feel this way?**

   ■ **What would you do if you had an employee like this?**

   Some of the causes I perceive: Management doesn't listen to her good ideas, but they will listen to an outside consultant. Management is insincere in its efforts to help employees deal with changes.

2. Vicious compliance means employees do something because they have to. They don't believe in it, but they'll do it because they want their paychecks. It is horrible to feel like this and horrible to manage people who act like this.

   ■ **Have you ever worked in an organization in which vicious compliance was practiced?**

   ■ **What causes vicious compliance?**

   ■ **What would you do if you managed a department with employees who were complying viciously?**

   ■ **Can information systems play a role in causing vicious compliance?**

3. She wants to focus on the needs of the company's customers, not the needs of the company's managers. Sometimes, senior management is treated as the person to convince, yet revenue depends on the customers' response.

   For example, you can convince management that a new IS will be terrific, but if its features cause employees to hate it, then it was not terrific. By the way, employees have a different relationship to senior managers than consultants do. If management buys the consultants' story, the consultants have convinced their customer, but the employees will be left with the duty of convincing the company's customers.

   ■ **What does she mean by the statement, "Senior management is just the banker"?**

   ■ **What happens when employees are more focused on pleasing their management than on pleasing the customer?**

   ■ **What is the proper balance between pleasing management and pleasing the customer?**

4. The employee is saying that she has great ideas that she believes no one listens to. She doesn't need

someone to give her more power; she needs someone to let her use the power she already has.

   ■ **How does listening to someone empower them?**

   ■ **What is the difference between *telling* someone what they should do and *listening* to them say what they want to do?**

   ■ **How does that difference empower someone?**

5. The contrarian has a point: When people truly see the benefit of something, there really is no need to manage change. But, is all change like that?

   ■ **Is there a way, for example, to pull the changes to implement a new ERP system through the organization? How?**

   ■ **If not, how could management push the changes for the new ERP system?**

   Pull can work if employees have been the source of a change or have had a vital role in implementing that change. Maybe quality circles succeed because employees will pull the change to them.

6. Management could listen to the employees, incorporate employees' ideas for implementation, communicate early and often, and take active steps to show value for employees. Management also must deal with self-efficacy issues.

7. She needs to be listened to, and more than once. She will be quick to sense any insincerity, and if she's promised anything she'll be furious (as well as smug because she *knew* it was only a ruse) that management has let her down once again. Involve her in a leadership role for new programs and initiatives. This employee will be high-maintenance for a long time. The extra effort might be worth the manager's time, if she has lots to add to the group.

WRAP UP

■ **What did you learn about change management from this exercise?**

■ **What does change management have to do with BPM?**

■ **How does change management pertain to IS in particular?**

■ **Side note: Interesting career opportunities are available in helping organizations adapt to changes brought by information systems, but such jobs can be hard to find. Not all go by the title of change-management consultant. Sometimes the titles are user support, user training, systems analyst, and related titles. If you're interested in this topic, you should take our systems development class.**

YOU BE THE GUIDE

Using the Guide: ERP and the Standard, Standard Blueprint

(pages 248–249)

GOALS

- Reinforce the importance of inherent processes in ERP and other licensed software and the expense and challenges of variances from those processes.

- Introduce possible longer-range consequences of adapting to vendors' inherent processes.

- Demonstrate an example of long-range thinking.

BACKGROUND AND PRESENTATION STRATEGIES

Warning: Before using this guide, ensure the students understand what an ERP system is and how much it integrates the organization's activities. It may be a good idea to start with a review of ERP systems.

Are organizations that enforce the standard ERP blueprint for their industry condemning themselves to industry-wide uniformity?

I don't know how serious this problem is. But, in theory, as ERP packages become commodities (and we do know that competitive software products always become a commodity), then every business will be run just like every other business. If that is the case, then how will one business gain a competitive advantage? Possibly, the company that executes the ERP processes most efficiently becomes the leader, but that is a difference in scale more than a difference in kind.

Even more worrisome, once ERP systems are solidly integrated into the organization, will they stifle creativity? Employees already complain that they are forced to do silly things because the "software requires them to." Will the software mean that it is a waste of time to develop improved ways of doing business, because the improved way is incompatible with the "always-enforced" ERP way?

I posed this question to a PeopleSoft (now Oracle) salesperson who said the answer lay with business intelligence applications of the data generated by the ERP system. "Organizations can gain a competitive advantage," he said, "by reporting and mining the data that we generate in their databases."

Is that answer credible? If the information created by the business intelligence system can be applied in the context of the existing ERP or other system, then his answer may have merit. But what if the information

created indicates the need for a change to a system that cannot be changed because of the structure of an existing ERP system?

Side effect: When an organization requests a feature change in the ERP system, that action may mean that every other customer of that vendor, and ultimately the entire industry, will have that change. Thus, the competitive advantage will be unsustainable.

What to do? No organization today that can benefit from ERP would choose not to implement it. But, having done so, has the organization entered a conformity trap?

SUGGESTED RESPONSES FOR DISCUSSION QUESTIONS

1. The vendors would say that customers should adapt because the standard blueprint, the inherent processes, are the "best-of-class solutions." They also know that variances are expensive and difficult to maintain. Life for the vendor and for the IT department is a lot easier if the company converts to the standard process.

   ■ **What does the organization lose by converting to the standard blueprint?**

   ■ **What are the costs of that conversion? (Also consider nonmonetary costs.)**

2. Ask the marketing students what causes products to become commodities. Software is no different. (This point, by the way, opens the door to talk about careers in software sales, marketing, and support. These are great, high-paying jobs, and this class is the first step toward one.)

   The process: No vendor can allow another vendor to have a competitive advantage, so they all copy the features and functions from one another. Ultimately, like cans of tomatoes on the grocery shelf, they all look the same.

3. This is the key question, and I don't know a definite answer. The answer may come down to the issue of whether they can be better in the execution of the inherent processes in the software.

   ■ **If a company executes the standard blueprint better than its competitors, will that give it a competitive advantage?**

   ■ **Is it possible for a company to engage in a differentiation strategy if all companies use the same inherent processes?**

- **Consider Lowe's and Home Depot. They have the same business processes. What will make one better than the other? If they're both using the same ERP package, the differentiation won't be in IS innovation.**

There is no obvious nor easy answer.

4. Such transfer of innovation happens when a company has an exception to the ERP system for which it asks the ERP vendor to program supporting software. If the exception represents an improved process, the ERP vendor can put it into its new software versions.

   Voila! The ERP vendor has been a conduit of innovation from one company to an industry.

   Ultimately, this phenomenon is beneficial to the industry and the economy. That may be small consolation to the company that cannot maintain its competitive advantage. Then again, innovation should be a continuous process. As Rudyard Kipling wrote,

   > "They copied all they could follow, but they couldn't copy my mind,
   >
   > And I left 'em sweating and stealing a year and a half behind."
   >
   > (*The Mary Gloster*, 1894)

5. It is probably not possible for two companies ever to be completely alike, but they may be close enough to make sustainable competitive advantages difficult, if not impossible. Example: Lowe's versus Home Depot.

One way to teach this is to play devil's advocate (or, depending on your views, an honest critic). Say something like:

- **This essay is much ado about nothing. It has no real issue; the points it makes are hair-splitting, unrealistic, theoretical, and vapid. We're wasting our time.**

See how the students respond. If they take an opposing position, continue in this vein. If they don't, ask them if they think they've wasted their time by considering this essay. To me, thinking about something that might be important and concluding that it is not important is hardly a waste of time.

WRAP UP

- **From time to time, it's worth thinking about the long-range consequences of technology trends. In this case, we find that adapting to industry-wide inherent processes may create competitive advantages but—at least for interdepartmental processes—those advantages may not be sustainable.**

- **By the way, most medium- to large-scale companies have a person called the CTO, or chief technology officer. You'll learn more about that person in Chapter 11. One of the key roles of that person is to think about the longer-range consequences of technology use. The job of CTO is fascinating, and it is one that some of you might want to consider.**

Social Media Information Systems

I would totally recommend Fox Lake Country Club for your wedding reception if you want to be told to disinvite your close friends and family. I dreamed my whole life about having my wedding reception there, and I was so excited . . . little did I know that they were TOTAL liars who planned ballroom renovations DURING my wedding reception—told me to cut 35 people from my guest list!! What is the point of having your dream wedding if the people you love aren't there to enjoy it with you!!?? They are just greedy businesspeople who want to get your money no matter what!!! Whatever you do, don't ever work with Fox Lake Country Club!!!!!

—Posting on Fox Lake's Facebook Page

"She said WHAT?" asked Jeff Lloyd, general manager of Fox Lake Country Club.

"She said that we're a bunch of greedy businesspeople who want to get your money, no matter what,'" Anne responded.

"On our Facebook page????" Jeff is incredulous.

"Yup."

"Well, delete it then. That shouldn't be too hard." Jeff turns to look out the window at the golfers headed to the first tee.

"Jeff, we can do that, but I think we should be careful here," Anne offers this opinion cautiously as she pushes back.

"No, of course, let's leave it out there. Let's tell the whole world that you and I are greedy businesspeople out to take advantage of our customers. What did she say, 'Don't ever work with Fox Lake?' Yeah, let's leave that there, too . . . maybe put a link to it on our Web site.

That'll help at the next board meeting." Sarcasm drips from his voice.

"Well, Jeff, here's the deal. You don't want to enrage the connected . . . they have power. Remember what happened to Nestlé?"

"No, what? Are they greedy businesspeople, too?"

"They got some bad PR on their site and just deleted it. Bingo, it came back, but a thousandfold. Worse, someone at Nestlé got high handed and posted a criticism of the commenters; it was pouring gas on a raging fire."

"Anne, you're tedious. Tell me what we CAN do!"

"Be open. The key is open, honest communication. We fix the problem—get the maintenance done ahead of schedule or delay, I don't care. Then, we tell our upset and nervous bride that we fixed it . . . maybe ask her, gently, to write that on our page. Possibly we follow up with our side of the story, briefly and not defensively."

"Too passive for me. Let's sue her for defamation." Jeff's sarcasm turns to anger.

"No, Jeff. No. That's not the way. You have any idea of the comments we'd get?"

"A lot."

"Besides, we have another problem." Anne represses a smile as she thinks.

"What's that, Anne?"

"Her father. He's a partner in the club's law firm. You gonna hire him to sue his own daughter? Over her wedding plans?" Anne tries hard not to chuckle.

Jeff stares at the golfers out the window, "Weddings. Why did I think weddings were a good idea? What's the matter with golf? It's a good business . . . you water the grass, put out the flags, move the tees around. . . ." ■

Study Questions

Q1 What is a social media information system (SMIS)?

Q2 How do SMIS advance organizational strategy?

Q3 How do SMIS increase social capital?

Q4 What roles do SMIS play in the hyper-social organization?

Q5 How do organizations use Web 2.0?

Q6 How can organizations manage the risks of social media and Web 2.0?

Q7 2022?

Changes are happening so rapidly to social media that we all struggle to keep up with the latest developments. We revise this textbook every year, and even still, writing in August, I know that by the time you read this in January or later, a good portion of it will be obsolete. Unfortunately, I don't know which parts they will be.

In my experience, the best response to rapid technological change is to learn and understand underlying principles. Rather than show you Facebook or Google+ features that we know will change before the ink on this page is dry, let's instead focus on principles, conceptual frameworks, and models that will be useful when you address the opportunities and risks of social media systems in the early years of your professional career.

That knowledge will also help you avoid mistakes. Every day, you can hear businesspeople saying, "We're using Twitter." "We've connected our Facebook page to our Web site." Or, creating ads and news releases that say, "Follow us on Twitter." The important question is, for what? To be modern? To be hip? And, do they have a social media plan?

We'll begin in Q1 by defining and describing the components of a social media information system, which will help you understand the commitment that organizations make when they use social media. As you've learned, the purpose of information systems is to help organizations achieve their strategy, and, in Q2, we'll consider how social media IS do. Next, Q3 addresses how social media information systems increase social capital; Q4 will examine the role of social media information systems in creating the hyper-social organization. Q5 will address Web 2.0, a precursor to today's social networking systems, but one that is still relevant to businesses today. We then describe in Q6 how organizations can manage the risks of social media. We'll wrap up in Q7 with an odd analogy about the change in the relationship between individuals and organizations heading into 2022.

Be aware that this text takes the position that social media, especially as manifested in the hyper-social organization, is a new business phenomenon. Consequently, it breaks social media out of the definition of Web 2.0. You will find sources that define social media as part of Web 2.0, so do not be confused by this difference.

Q1 What Is a Social Media Information System (SMIS)?

Social media (SM) is the use of information technology to support the sharing of content among networks of users. Social media enables people to form **communities**, **tribes**, or **hives**, all of which are synonyms that refer to a group of people related by a common interest. (The latter two terms are in vogue among business and technology writers.) A **social media information system (SMIS)** is an information system that supports the sharing of content among networks of users.

As illustrated in Figure 8-1, social media is the merger of many disciplines. In this book, we will focus on the MIS portion of this diagram by discussing SMIS and how they contribute to organizational strategy. If you decide to work in the SM field as a professional, you will need some knowledge of all these disciplines, except possibly computer science.

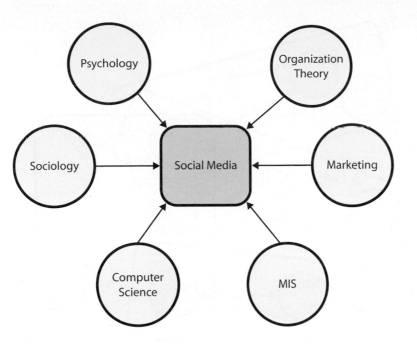

Figure 8-1
Social Media Is a Convergence
of Disciplines

Three SMIS Roles

To discuss the components of an SMIS, you need to understand the roles played by the three organizational units shown in Figure 8-2:

- User communities
- Social media sponsors
- Social media application providers

User Communities

Forming communities is a natural human trait; anthropologists claim that the ability to form them is responsible for the progress of the human race. In the past, however, communities were based on family relationships or geographic location. Everyone in the village formed a community. The key difference of SM communities is that they are formed based on mutual interests and transcend familial, geographic, and organizational boundaries.

Because of this transcendence, most people belong to several, or even many, different user communities. Google+ recognized this fact when it created user circles that enable users to allocate their connections (*people*, using Google+ terminology) to one or more community groups. Facebook and other SM application providers are adapting in similar ways.

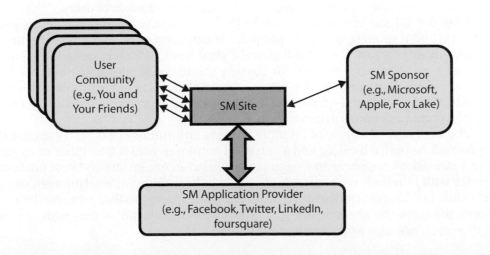

Figure 8-2
SMIS Organizational Roles

Figure 8-3
SM Communities

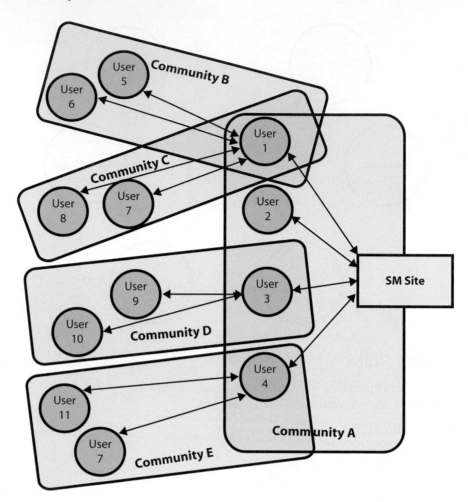

Figure 8-3 expands on the community–SM site relationship in Figure 8-2. From the point of view of the SM site, Community A is a first-tier community that consists of users that have a direct relationship to that site. User 1, in turn, belongs to three communities: A, B, and C (these could be, say, classmates, professional contacts, and friends). From the point of view of the SM site, Communities B–E are second-tier communities because the relationships in those communities are intermediated by first-tier users. The number of second- and first-tier community members grows exponentially. If each community had, for example, 100 members, then the SM site will have 100×100, or 10,000, second-tier members and $100 \times 100 \times 100$ third-tier members (not shown in Figure 8-3). However, that statement is not quite true, because communities overlap; in Figure 8-3, for example, user 7 belongs to communities C and E. Thus, these calculations are the maximum number of users.

How the SM site chooses to relate to these communities depends on its goals. If the SM site is interested in pure publicity, it will want to relate to as many tiers of communities as it can. If so, it will create a **viral hook**, which is some inducement, such as a prize or other reward, for passing the message along through the tiers. If, however, the purpose of the SM site is to solve an embarrassing problem, say to fix a product defect, then the sponsors of the SM site endeavor to constrain, as much as it can, the communications to community A.

The exponential nature of relationships via community tiers offers sponsoring organizations both a blessing and a curse. An employee who is a member of community A can share her sincere and legitimate pride in her organization's latest product or service with hundreds or thousands of people in her communities. However, she can also blast her disappointment at some recent development to that same audience, or, worse, inadvertently share private and proprietary organizational data with someone in that audience who works for the competition.

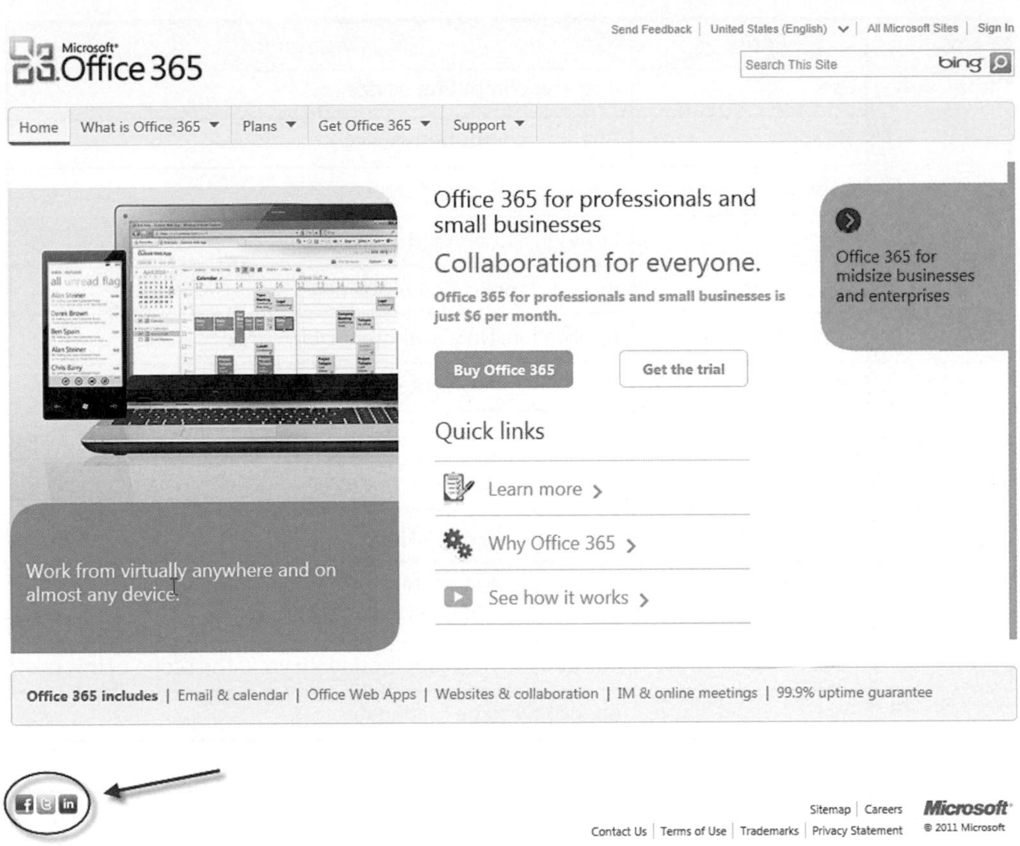

Figure 8-4
Not a Casual Commitment

Social media is a powerful tool, and organizations should know their goals and plan accordingly, as you'll learn.

Social Media Sponsors

Social media sponsors are companies and other organizations that choose to support a presence on one or more SM sites. Figure 8-4 shows Microsoft's Office365.com page with links to Facebook, Twitter, and LinkedIn in the bottom-left corner of that page. When Microsoft places those icons on its promotional pages, it is making a commitment to invest considerable employee time and other costs to support social media. It needs to develop procedures and staff and train people to support that site, as you'll learn in the next section.

Social Media Application Providers

Social media application providers are the companies that operate the SM sites. Facebook, Twitter, LinkedIn, and Google are all SM application providers. These providers create the features and functions of the site, and they compete with one another for the attention of user communities and SM sponsors.

Social media have evolved in such a way that users expect to use SM applications without paying a license fee or other charge. Sponsors may or may not pay a fee, depending on the application and on what they do with it. On Facebook, for example, creating a company page is free, but Facebook charges a fee to advertise to communities that Like that page. Most SM applications earn revenue through some type of advertising model.

SMIS Components

Because they are information systems, SMIS have the same five components as all IS: hardware, software, data, procedures, and people. Consider each component for each of the three organizational roles summarized in Figure 8-5.

Figure 8-5
The Five Components of SMIS

Component	Entity	Description
Hardware	User	Any user computing device
	SM sponsor	Any user computing device
	Application provider	Elastic, cloud- based servers
Software	User	Browser, iOS, and other applications
	SM sponsor	Browser, application tools
	Application provider	Application, NoSQL or other DBMS
Data	User	User- generated content, connection data
	SM sponsor	Sponsor content
	Application provider	Content and connection data storage and rapid retrieval
Procedures	User	Informal, copy each other
	SM sponsor	Create, manage, remove content; extract value from content and connections; manage risk
	Application provider	Run and maintain application (beyond the scope of this text)
People	User	Adaptive, can be irrational
	SM sponsor	Key users
	Application provider	Staff to run and maintain application (beyond the scope of this text)

Hardware

Both community users and employees of SM sponsors process SM sites using desktops, laptops, smartphones, iPads, HTML 5 devices, and, indeed, any intelligent, communications device. In most cases, SM application providers host the SM presence using elastic servers in the cloud.

Software

Users employ browsers and client applications, such as iOS applications, to read and submit data and to add and remove connections to communities and other users. SM sponsors contribute to the site via browsers or using specialized sponsor applications provided by the SM application provider. In some cases, like, say, Facebook applications, SM sponsors create their own applications and interface those applications with the SM site.

SM application providers develop and operate their own custom, proprietary, social networking application software. As you learned in Chapter 4, supporting custom software is expensive over the long term; SM application vendors must do so because the features and functions of their applications are fundamental to their competitive strategy. They can do so because they spread the development costs over the revenue generated by millions of users.

As you learned in Case Study 5, many social networking vendors use a NoSQL database management system to process their data, although traditional relational DBMS products are used as well. Recall, too, that Facebook began development of Cassandra in-house (Case Study 5, page 174), but donated it to the open-source community when it realized the expense and commitment of maintaining it.

Data

SM data falls into two categories: content and connections. **Content data** is data and responses to data that are contributed by users and SM sponsors. You provide the source content data for your Facebook site, and your friends provide response content when they write on your wall, make comments, tag you, or otherwise publish on your site.

Connection data is data about relationships. On Facebook, for example, the relationships to your friends are connection data. The fact that you've liked particular organizations is also connection data. Connection data differentiates SMIS from Web site applications. Both Web sites and social networking sites present user and responder content, but only social networking applications store and process connection data.

SM application providers store and retrieve SM data on behalf of sponsors and user communities. As explained in Case Study 5, they must do so in the presence of network and server failures, and they must do so rapidly. The problem is made somewhat easier, however, because SM content and connection data have a relatively simple structure.

How honest are people with social media? Reflect on ethical issues for social media in the Ethics Guide on pages 280–281.

Procedures

For social networking users, procedures are informal, evolving, and socially oriented. You do what your friends do. When the members of your tribe learn how to do something new and interesting, you copy them. Software is designed to be easy to learn and use.

Such informality makes using SMIS easy; it also means that unintended consequences are common. The most troubling examples concern user privacy. Many people have learned not to post pictures of themselves in front of their house numbers on the same publicly accessible site on which they're describing their new high-definition television. Many others, alas, have not.

For SM sponsors, social networking procedures cannot be so informal. Before initiating a social networking presence, organizations must develop procedures for creating content, managing user responses, removing obsolete or objectionable content, and extracting value from content. For an example of the latter, setting up an SMIS to gather data on product problems is a wasted expense unless procedures exist to extract knowledge from that social networking data. Organizations also need to develop procedures to manage SM risk, as described in Q6.

Procedures for operating and maintaining the SM application are beyond the scope of this text.

Be careful what you publish! Social networking at work can be problematic. The Guide on pages 288–289 explores social networking opinion of employees at Pearson Education (the publisher of this text).

People

Users of social media do what they want to do depending on their goals and their personalities. They behave in certain ways and observe the consequences. They may or may not change their behavior. By the way, note that SM users aren't necessarily rational, at least not in purely monetary ways. See, for example, the study by Vernon Smith in which people walked away from free money because they thought someone else was getting more![1]

SM sponsors, however, cannot be casual. Anyone who contributes to an organization's SM site or who uses his or her position in a company to speak for an organization needs to be trained on both SMIS user procedures as well as on the organization's social networking policy. We will discuss such procedures and policies in Q6.

Social media are creating new job titles, new responsibilities, and the need for new types of training. For example, what makes for a good tweeter? What makes for an effective wall writer? What type of person should be hired for such jobs? What education should they have? How does one evaluate candidates for such positions? All of these questions are being asked and answered today. Clearly it's a hot field, and because social media reinforces inherent human behavior, SM jobs are not likely to disappear anytime soon.

The staff to operate and maintain the SM application is beyond the scope of this text.

---

[1] Vernon Smith, *Rationality in Economics: Constructivist and Ecological Forms* (Cambridge, UK: Cambridge University Press, 2007), pp. 247–250.

Not Free

Before we go on, you will sometimes read that SMIS are free. It is true that Facebook, Twitter, LinkedIn, and other sites do not charge for hardware, software, or data storage. However, unless the using organization takes the foolish and irresponsible posture of letting its social networking presence do whatever it will, someone will need to develop, implement, and manage the social networking procedures just described. Furthermore, employees who contribute to and manage social networking sites will generate direct labor costs.

Q2 How Do SMIS Advance Organizational Strategy?

In Chapter 3, Figure 3-1 (page 76), you learned the relationship of information systems to organizational strategy. In brief, strategy determines value chains, which determine business processes, which determine information systems. Insofar as value chains determine *structured* business processes, like those discussed in Chapter 7, this chain is straightforward. However, social media is by its very nature *dynamic*; its flow cannot be designed or diagrammed, and, if it were, no sooner would the diagram be finished than the SM process would have changed.

Therefore, we need to back up a step and consider how value chains determine dynamic processes and thus set SMIS requirements. As you will see, social media fundamentally changes the balance of power between users, their communities, and organizations.

Before we consider each of the primary value chain activities, you need to know two important terms. Gossieaux and Moran, creators of the hyper-social organization theory, identify two kinds of communities that are important to commerce:[2]

- Defenders of belief
- Seekers of the truth

Defenders of belief share a common belief and form their hive around that belief. They seek conformity and want to convince others of the wisdom of their belief. A group that believes that Google+ is far superior to Facebook will engage in behaviors to convince others that this is true. When confronted with contrary evidence, they do not change their opinion, but become more firmly convinced in their belief.[3] Defenders-of-belief communities facilitate activities like sales and marketing. They are not effective for activities that involve innovation or problem solving. Such groups can form strong bonds and allegiance to an organization.

Seekers of the truth share a common desire to learn something, solve a problem, or make something happen. A group of CFOs who want to learn how to manage the risk of placing financial data in the cloud seek "the truth." They share a common problem, but not a common solution to that problem. Not surprisingly, such tribes are incredible problem solvers and excel at innovation. They can be useful in customer service activity, as long as they don't conclude that the best way to solve a product problem is to use another company's product, something they might do because such groups seldom form a strong bond to an organization. The only organizational bond seekers of the truth are likely to form occurs when the organization demonstrates behavior that demonstrates that it, too, is committed to solving the community's shared problem.

Figure 8-6 summarizes how social media contributes to the five primary value chain activities and to the human resources support activity. Consider each row of this table.

---

[2] Francois Gossieaux and Edward K. Moran, *The Hyper-Social Organization* (New York: McGraw-Hill), pp. 22, 23–25.
[3] Daniel Kahneman, Paul Slovic, and Amos Tversky, *Judgment Under Uncertainty: Heuristics and Biases* (Cambridge, UK: Cambridge University Press, 1982), p. 144.

Activity	Community type	Focus	Dynamic process	Risks
Sales and marketing	Defender of belief	Outward to prospects	Social CRM Peer-to-peer sales	Loss of credibility Bad PR
Customer service	Seeker of the truth	Outward to customers	Peer-to-peer support	Loss of control
Inbound logistics	Seeker of the truth	Upstream supply chain providers	Problem solving	Privacy
Outbound logistics	Seeker of the truth	Downstream supply chain shippers	Problem solving	Privacy
Manufacturing and operations	Seeker of the truth	Outward for user design Inward to operations and manufacturing	User-guided design Enterprise 2.0 Knowledge management	Efficiency/effectiveness
Human resources	Defender of belief	Employment candidates Employee communications	Employee prospecting, recruiting, and evaluation SharePoint & Enterprise 2.0 for employee-to-employee communication	Error Loss of credibility

Figure 8-6
Social Media in Value Chain Activities

Social Media and the Sales and Marketing Activity

In the past, organizations controlled their relationships with customers using structured processes and related information systems. In fact, the primary purpose of traditional CRM was to manage customer touches. Traditional CRM ensured that the organization spoke to customers with one voice and that it controlled the messages, offers, and even the support that customers received based on the value of a particular customer. In 1990, if you wanted to know something about an IBM product you'd contact its local sales office, that office would classify you as a prospect and use that classification to control the literature, documentation, and your access to IBM personnel.

Social CRM is a dynamic, SM-based CRM process. The relationships between organizations and customers emerge in a dynamic process as both parties create and process content. In addition to the traditional forms of promotion, employees in the organization create wikis, blogs, discussion lists, frequently asked questions, sites for user reviews and commentary, and other dynamic content. Customers search this content, contribute reviews and commentary, ask more questions, create user groups, and so forth. With social CRM, each customer crafts his or her own relationship with the company.

Social CRM flies in the face of the principles of traditional CRM. Because relationships emerge from joint activity, customers have as much control as companies. This characteristic is an anathema to traditional sales managers who want control over what the customer is reading, seeing, and hearing about the company and its products. The general manager at Fox Lake is incensed because a negative review was published on his organization's Facebook page. He wants to delete it but cannot for fear of the backlash.

Further, traditional CRM is centered on lifetime value; customers that are likely to generate the most business get the most attention and have the most impact on the organization. However, with social CRM the customer who spends 10 cents but who is an effective reviewer, commentator, or blogger can have more influence than the quiet customer who purchases $10 million a year. Such imbalance is incomprehensible to traditional sales managers.

However, traditional sales managers *are* happy to have defenders-of-belief groups sell their products using peer-to-peer recommendations. A quick look at products and their reviews on Amazon.com will show how frequently customers are willing to write long, thoughtful reviews of products they like or do not like. Amazon.com and other online retailers also allow readers to rate the helpfulness of reviews. In that way, substandard reviews are revealed for the unwary.

However, using social media for sales and marketing does present some risks. In March 2011, Microsoft tweeted the following after the Japanese earthquakes: "How you can #SupportJapan- http://bingedit/fEh7iT. For every retweet, @bing will give $1 to Japan quake victims, up to $100k." The URL was for a page that detailed how to use Bing Maps and other services to help with the disaster. Users expressed their disgust at what they saw as Microsoft using a tragedy to promote its search engine. Seven hours later, Bing apologized with the following tweet: "We apologize the tweet was negatively perceived. Intent was to provide a way for people to help Japan. We have donated $100k."[4] The risks of social media for sales and marketing are loss of credibility and bad public relations.

Social Media and Customer Service

Product users are amazingly willing to help each other solve problems. Even more, they will do so without pay; in fact, payment can warp and ruin the support experience as customers fight with one another. SAP learned that it was better to reward its SAP Developer Network with donations on their behalf to charitable organizations than it was to give them personal rewards.[5]

Not surprisingly, organizations whose business strategy involves selling to or through developer networks have been the earliest and most successful at SM-based customer support. In addition to SAP, Microsoft has long sold through its network of partners. Its MVP (Most Valuable Professional) program is a classic example of giving praise and glory in exchange for customer-provided customer assistance (http://mvp.support.microsoft.com). Of course, the developers in their networks have a business incentive to participate because that activity helps them sell services to the communities in which they participate.

However, users with no financial incentive are also willing to help others. Amazon.com offers badges to users who provide high levels of service, such as the Top Reviewer badge, which is simply an icon that appears next to a reviewer's name. You'll need your psychology course to explain what drives people to strive for such recognition. MIS just provides the platform!

The primary risk of peer-to-peer support is loss of control. As stated, seekers of the truth will seek the truth, even if that means recommending another vendor's product over yours. We address that risk in Q6.

Social Media and Inbound and Outbound Logistics

For more on supply chain IS, see the International Dimension, pages 452–467.

Companies whose profitability depends on the efficiency of their supply chain have long used information systems to improve both the effectiveness and efficiency of structured supply chain processes. Because supply chains are tightly integrated into structured manufacturing processes, there is less tolerance for the unpredictability of dynamic, adaptive processes. Problems are an exception. The Japanese earthquake in the spring of 2011 created havoc in the automotive supply chain when major Japanese manufacturers lacked power and, in some cases, facilities to operate. Social media was used to dispense news, allay fears of radioactive products, and solve problems.

Seekers-of-the-truth communities provide better and faster problem solutions to complex supply chain problems. Social media is designed to foster content creation and feedback among networks of users, and that characteristic facilitates the iteration and feedback needed for problem solving, as described in Chapter 2.

Loss of privacy is, however, a significant risk. Problem solving requires the open discussion of problem definitions, causes, and solution constraints. Suppliers and

---

[4] Greg Lamm, "Microsoft Apologizes for Bing Japan Earthquake Tweet," March 13, 2011, www.techflash.com/seattle/2011/03/microsoft-sorry-for-bing-quake-tweet.html, access date September 7, 2011.
[5] Francois Gossieaux and Edward K. Moran, *The Hyper-Social Organization* (New York: McGraw-Hill), pp. 8, 9.

shippers work with many companies; supply chain problem solving via social media is problem solving in front of your competitors.

Social Media and Manufacturing and Operations

Operations and manufacturing activities are dominated by structured processes. The flexibility and adaptive nature of social media would result in chaos if applied to the manufacturing line or to the warehouse. However, social media does play a role in product design as well as in employee knowledge sharing and management.

Crowdsourcing is the dynamic social media process of employing users to participate in product design or product redesign. eBay often solicits customers to provide feedback on their eBay experience. As that site says, "there's no better group of advisors than our customers." User-guided design has been used for the design of video games, shoes, and many other products.

Enterprise 2.0 is the application of social media to facilitate the cooperative work of people inside organizations. Enterprise 2.0 can be used in operations and manufacturing to enable users to share knowledge and problem-solving techniques.

Andrew McAfee, the originator of the term *Enterprise 2.0*, defined six characteristics that he refers to with the acronym **SLATES** (see Figure 8-7).[6] Workers want to be able to *search* for content inside the organization just like they do on the Web. Most workers find that searching is more effective than navigating content structures such as lists and tables of content. Workers want to access organizational content by *link*, just as they do on the Web. They also want to *author* organizational content using blogs, wikis, discussion groups, published presentations, and so on.

Enterprise 2.0 content is *tagged*, just like content on the Web, and tags are organized into structures, as is done on the Web at sites like Delicious (www.delicious.com). These structures organize tags as a taxonomy does, but, unlike taxonomies, they are not preplanned; they emerge. A **folksonomy** is content structure that has emerged from the processing of many user tags. Additionally, Enterprise 2.0 workers want applications to enable them to rate tagged content and to use the tags to predict content that will be of interest to them (as with Pandora), a process McAfee refers to as *extensions*. Finally, Enterprise 2.0 workers want relevant content pushed to them; they want to be *signaled* when something of interest to them happens in organizational content.

Enterprise 2.0 Component	Remarks
Search	People have more success searching than they do in finding from structured content
Links	Links to enterprise resources (like on the Web)
Authoring	Create enterprise content via blogs, wikis, discussion groups, presentations ...
Tags	Flexible tagging (like delicious) results in folksonomies of enterprise content
Extensions	Using usage patterns to offer enterprise content via tag processing (like the style of Pandora)
Signals	Pushing enterprise content to users based on subscriptions and alerts

Figure 8-7
McAffee's SLATES Enterprise 2.0 Model

---

[6] Andrew McAfee, "Enterprise 2.0: The Dawn of Emergent Collaboration," *MIT Sloan Management Review*, Spring 2006, http://sloanreview.mit.edu/the-magazine/files/saleablepdfs/47306.pdf (accessed August 2011).

Social media is increasingly used to recruit and evaluate potential employees. See Guide on pages 290–291.

The potential problem with Enterprise 2.0 is the quality of its dynamic process. Because the benefits of Enterprise 2.0 result from emergence, there is no way to control for either effectiveness or efficiency. It's a messy process about which little can be predicted.

Social Media and Human Resources

The last row in Figure 8-6 concerns the use of social media and human resources. Social media is used for finding employee prospects; for recruiting candidates; and, in some organizations, for candidate evaluation.

Social media are also used for employee communications, using internal, personnel sites such as MySite and MyProfile in SharePoint, or other, similar Enterprise 2.0 facilities. SharePoint provides a place for employees to post their expertise in the form of "Ask me about" questions. When employees are looking for an internal expert, they can search SharePoint for people who have posted the desired expertise.

The risks of social media in human resources concern the possibility of error when using sites such as Facebook to form conclusions about employees. A second risk is that the SM site becomes too defensive as a defender of belief or is obviously promulgating an unpopular management message.

Study Figure 8-6 to understand the general framework by which organizations can accomplish their strategy via dynamic process supported by SMIS. We will now turn to an economic perspective on the value and use of SMIS.

Q3 How Do SMIS Increase Social Capital?

Business literature defines three types of capital. Karl Marx defined **capital** as the investment of resources for future profit. This traditional definition refers to investments into resources such as factories, machines, manufacturing equipment, and the like. **Human capital** is the investment in human knowledge and skills for future profit. By taking this class, you are investing in your own human capital. You are investing your money and time to obtain knowledge that you hope will differentiate you from other workers and ultimately give you a wage premium in the workforce.

According to Nan Lin, **social capital** is the investment in social relations with the expectation of returns in the marketplace.[7] When you attend a business function for the purpose of meeting people and reinforcing relationships, you are investing in your social capital. Similarly, when you join LinkedIn or contribute to Facebook, you are (or can be) investing in your social capital.

What Is the Value of Social Capital?

According to Lin, social capital adds value in four ways:

- Information
- Influence
- Social credentials
- Personal reinforcement

Relationships in social networks can provide *information* about opportunities, alternatives, problems, and other factors important to business professionals. They also provide an opportunity to *influence* decision makers in one's employer or in other organizations who are critical to your success. Such influence cuts across formal organizational structures, such as reporting relationships. Third, being linked to a network of highly regarded contacts is a form of *social credential*. You can bask in the glory of those with whom you are related. Others will be more inclined to work with you if they

---

[7] Nan Lin, *Social Capital: The Theory of Social Structure and Action* (Cambridge, UK: Cambridge University Press, 2002), Location 310 of the Kindle Edition.

Using MIS InClass 8 *A Group Exercise*

Computing Your Social Capital

Source: Superstock.

Social capital is not an abstract concept that applies only to organizations; it applies to you as well. You and your classmates are accumulating social capital now. What is the value of that capital? To see, form a group and complete the following items:

1. Define *capital, human capital,* and *social capital.* Explain how these terms differ.

2. How does the expression "It's not what you know, but who you know that matters" pertain to the terms you defined in item 1?

3. Do you, personally, agree with the statement in item 2? Form your own opinion before discussing it with your group.

4. As a group, discuss the relative value of human and social capital. In what ways is social capital more valuable than human capital? Form a group consensus view on the validity of the statement in item 2.

5. Visit the Facebook, LinkedIn, Twitter, or other social networking presence site of each group member.
   a. Using the definition of social capital value in this chapter, assess the value of each group member's social networking presence.
   b. Recommend at least one way to add value to each group member's social capital at each site.

6. Suppose you each decide to feature your Facebook or other social networking page on your professional résumé.
   a. How would you change your presence that you evaluated in item 5 in order to make it more appropriate for that purpose?
   b. Describe three or four types of professionals that you could add to your social network that would facilitate your job search.

7. Imagine that you are the CEO of a company that has just one product to sell: You:
   a. Review the Enterprise 2.0 SLATES principles in Figure 8-7 and assess how each could pertain to the selling of your "product" (i.e., obtaining a quality job that you want). You can find the McAfee article at http://sloanreview.mit.edu/the-magazine/2006-spring/47306/enterprise-the-dawnof-emergent-collaboration/
   b. Explain how you could use your social networking presence to facilitate social CRM selling of your product.
   c. Devise a creative and interesting way to use this exercise as part of your social CRM offering.

8. Present your answers to items 4 and 7 to the rest of the class.

believe critical personnel are standing with you and may provide resources to support you. Finally, being linked into social networks reinforces a professional's image and position in an organization or industry. It reinforces the way you define yourself to the world (and to yourself).

Social networks differ in value. The social network you maintain with your high school friends probably has less value than the network you have with your business associates, but not necessarily so. According to Henk Flap, the **value of social capital** is determined by the number of relationships in a social network, by the strength of those relationships, and by the resources controlled by those related.[8] If your high

---

[8] Henk D. Flap, "Social Capital in the Reproduction of Inequality," *Comparative Sociology of Family, Health, and Education,* Vol. 20 (1991), pp. 6179–6202. Cited in Nan Lin, *Social Capital: The Theory of Social Structure and Action* (Cambridge, UK: Cambridge University Press, 2002), Kindle location 345.

school friends happened to have been Bill Gates and Larry Page, and if you maintain strong relations with them via your high school network, then the value of that social network far exceeds any you'll have at work. For most of us, however, the network of our current professional contacts provides the most social capital.

So, when you use social networking professionally, consider those three factors. You gain social capital by adding more friends and by strengthening the relationships you have with existing friends. Further, you gain more social capital by adding friends and strengthening relationships with people who control resources that are important to you. Such calculations may seem cold, impersonal, and possibly even phony. When applied to the recreational use of social networking, they may be. But when you use social networking for professional purposes, keep them in mind.

How Do Social Networks Add Value to Businesses?

Organizations have social capital just as humans do. Historically, organizations created social capital via salespeople, via customer support, and via public relations. Endorsements by high-profile people are a traditional way of increasing social capital, but there are tigers in those woods.

Today, progressive organizations maintain a presence on Facebook, LinkedIn, Twitter, and possibly other sites. They include links to their social networking presence on their Web sites and make it easy for customers and interested parties to leave comments. In most cases, such connections are positive, but they can backfire, as you saw at Fox Lake in the opening vignette.

To understand how social networks add value to businesses, consider each of the elements of social capital: number of relationships, strength of relationships, and resources controlled by "friends."

Using Social Networking to Increase the Number of Relationships

In a traditional business relationship, a client (you) has some experience with a business, such as the restaurant at Fox Lake. Traditionally, you may express your opinions about that experience by word of mouth to your social network. However, such communication is unreliable and brief: You are more likely to say something to your friends if the experience was particularly good or bad; but, even then, you are likely only to say something to those friends whom you encounter while the experience is still recent. And once you have said something, that's it; your words don't live on for days or weeks.

Figure 8-8 shows the same relationships as shown in Figure 8-3 but cast into the framework of Fox Lake. Users 1–4 in this example have a direct relationship with Fox Lake's SM site (Facebook, or whatever is popular). Here, communities B–D in Figure 8-3 have been replaced by weddings. (We'll assume that user 1 has two children who were married at Fox Lake and not that user 1 is divorced and chose to have both of her weddings at Fox Lake.)

This diagram indicates that weddings can potentially contribute more than just revenue to Fox Lake. If Fox Lake can find a way to induce members of the wedding party, or wedding attendees, to form a relationship with Fox Lake, weddings will contribute substantially to the number of relationships in Fox Lake's social network and, depending on the strength and value of those connections, possibly contribute substantially to Fox Lake's social capital.

Fox Lake has a waiting list for new memberships, so it is unlikely to use social networking to induce people to become members. However, brides need not be club members to have their weddings at Fox Lake, so Fox Lake would be interested in inducing one Fox Lake bride to convince a friend to have her wedding at Fox Lake as well.

Such relationship sales have been going on by word of mouth for centuries; the difference here is that SMIS allow such sales to scale to levels not possible in the past; SMIS also make those relationships visible and available for other purposes.

Figure 8-8
SM Communities

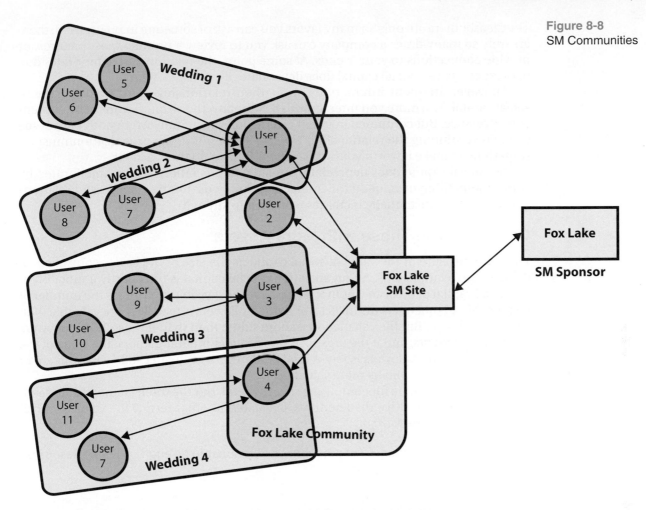

Using Social Networks to Increase the Strength of Relationships

To an organization, the **strength of a relationship** is the likelihood that the entity (person or other organization) in the relationship will do something that benefits the organization. An organization has a strong relationship with you if you buy its products, write positive reviews about it, post pictures of you using the organization's products or services, and so on.

As stated earlier, social networks provide four forms of value: influence, information, social credentials, and reinforcement. If an organization can induce those in its relationships to provide more of any of those factors, it has strengthened that relationship.

In his autobiography, Benjamin Franklin provided a key insight.[9] He said that if you want to strengthen your relationship with someone in power, ask them to do you a favor. Before he invented the public library, he would ask powerful strangers to lend him their expensive books. In that same sense, organizations have learned that they can strengthen their relationships with you by asking you to do them a favor. In Q4, we will discuss information systems that encourage the creation of user-generated content as a way of getting you to do them a favor. When you provide that favor, it strengthens your relationship with the organization.

Traditional capital depreciates. Machines wear out, factories get old, technology and computers become obsolete, and so forth. Does social capital also depreciate? Do relationships wear out from use? So far, the answer seems to be both yes and no.

---

[9] Founding father of the United States. Author of *Poor Richard's Almanac*. Successful businessman; owner of a chain of print shops. Discoverer of groundbreaking principles in the theory of electricity. Inventor of bifocals, the potbelly stove, the lightning rod, and much more. Founder of the public library and the postal service. Darling of the French court and salons, and now, contributor to social network theory!

Clearly, there are only so many favors you can ask of someone in power. And, there are only so many times a company can ask you to review a product, post pictures, or provide connections to your friends. At some point, the relationship deteriorates due to overuse. So, yes, social capital does depreciate.

However, frequent interactions strengthen relationships and hence increase social capital. The more you interact with a company, the stronger your commitment and allegiance. But continued frequent interactions occur only when both parties see value in continuing the relationship. Thus, at some point, the organization must do something to make it worth your while to continue to do them a favor.

So, social capital does depreciate, but such depreciation can be ameliorated by adding something of value to the interaction. And, continuing a successful relationship over time substantially increases relationship strength.

Connecting to Those with More Assets

The third measure of the value of social capital is the size of the assets controlled by those in the relationships. An organization's social capital is thus partly a function of the social capital of those to whom it relates. The most visible measure is the number of relationships. Someone with 1,000 loyal Twitter followers is usually more valuable than someone with 10. But the calculation is more subtle than that; if those 1,000 followers are college students, and if the organization's product is adult diapers, the value of the relationship to the followers is low. A relationship with 10 Twitter followers who are in retirement homes would be more valuable.

There is no formula for computing social capital, but the three factors would seem to be more multiplicative than additive. Or, stated in other terms, the value of social capital is more in the form of

$$\text{Social Capital} = \text{Number of Relationships} \times \text{Relationship Strength} \times \text{Entity Resources}$$

Than it is:

$$\text{Social Capital} = \text{Number of Relationships} + \text{Relationship Strength} + \text{Entity Resources}$$

Again, do not take these equations literally; take them in the sense of the multiplicative interaction of the three factors.

This multiplicative nature of social capital means that a huge network of relationships to people who have few resources may be lower than that of a smaller network with people with substantial resources. Furthermore, those resources must be relevant to the organization. Students with pocket change are relevant to Pizza Hut; they are irrelevant to a BMW dealership.

This discussion brings us to the brink of social networking practice. Most organizations today (2011) ignore the value of entity assets and simply try to connect to more people with stronger relationships. This area is ripe for innovation. Data aggregators like ChoicePoint and Acxiom maintain detailed data about people, worldwide. It would seem that such data could be used by information systems to calculate the potential value of a relationship to a particular individual. This possibility would enable organizations to better understand the value of their social networks as well as guide their behavior with regard to particular individuals.

Stay tuned; many possibilities exist, and some ideas, maybe yours, will be very successful.

Q4 What Roles Do SMIS Play in the Hyper-Social Organization?

Social capital is an economic perspective on social media. Another perspective is the sociological one developed by Gossieaux and Moran in a model they call the *hyper-social organization*. According to this model, using social media in an old-style,

Figure 8-9
Four Pillars of the Hyper-Social
Organization

Consumers → Humans

Market Segments → Tribes

Channels → Networks

Structure & Control→ Messiness

organization-centric manner is ineffective. The true value of social media can only be achieved when organizations use social media to interact with customers, employees, and partners in a more humane, relationship-oriented way. Rather than sending *messages* that attempt to manage, influence, and control, hyper-social organizations create *relationships* in which both parties perceive and gain value.

Thus, a **hyper-social organization** is an organization that uses social media to transform its interactions with customers, employees, and partners into mutually satisfying relationships with them and their communities. In particular, a hyper-social organization is one that has made the four transitions, called *pillars*, shown in Figure 8-9. The concepts and language of this model are marketing-oriented, but in this model marketing is broadly conceived to pertain to employees and partners as well as customers. Consider each of the transitions in Figure 8-9.

Consumers Become Humans

According to recent studies, consumers are skeptical of organizational messages and no longer listen. A 2009 McKinsey study found that two-thirds of purchase-decision touch points involve SM-based reviews and recommendations outside the realm of organizational messaging.[10] Such skepticism may not be new, it could be that consumers have always held it, but until social media, advertising and PR were the consumers' only data source. New or not, that skepticism gives a competitive advantage to hyper-social organizations.

Today, customers want informed, useful interactions that help them solve particular problems and satisfy unique needs. Customers increasingly ignore prepackaged organizational messages that tout product benefits. An example of this new style is the sales force in Apple stores that has been trained to act as customer problem-solving consultants and not as sellers of products. (See Case Study 4, page 137.) Organizations' SM sites need to mirror this behavior, otherwise social media is nothing more than another channel for classic advertising.

For example, at Fox Lake, an email advertising campaign directed to the communities of users 1, 3, and 4 (Figure 8-8) would use social media in the pre-hyper-social way. Prospects are treated as entities to be influenced, and while such an advertising campaign might be cheaper than printed media, it isn't more effective. However, if Fox Lake creates an SM environment in which families that have already held their wedding at Fox Lake offer advice to families that are planning weddings, then Fox Lake will be relating to potential wedding customers as humans with important hopes and fears. By doing so, Fox Lake will increase its social capital, regardless of whether the prospective family holds its wedding at Fox Lake or elsewhere.

Market Segments Becomes Tribes

The second pillar of the hyper-social organization is the transformation of thinking from market segments to tribes. Market segments have key traits and characteristics; tribes, as we have seen, have relationships for defending beliefs or seeking the truth.

Using traditional market-segment thinking, GearUp, the company discussed in the first part of this book, would promote an upcoming soccer event to a market

---

[10] David Court, Dave Elzinga, Susan Mulder, and Ole Jørgen Vetvik, "The Consumer Decision Journey," *McKinsey Quarterly*, June 2009, www.mckinseyquarterly.com/The_consumer_decision_journey_2373 (accessed August 2011).

segment, of, say, 20- to 25-year-old women who work in retail and live in certain zip codes. Using tribal thinking, GearUp would market to communities that defend the belief that soccer is a great game or to communities that grieved over the last game of the 2011 Women's World Soccer Cup. Such tribal marketing would enable GearUp to follow relationships beyond 25-year-old women to customers and markets that are ripe for sales, but of which GearUp is ignorant. It might be, for example, that the community that is grieving that last World Cup game includes 65-year-old grandfathers who are predisposed to buy soccer balls for their granddaughters. Relating to the community will bring those customers into GearUp's network.

A similar transformation is important within organizations. A company with an employee morale problem would, using market-segment thinking, find the categories of employees who are most discontented using the "market segment" of, say, job titles. They might find a major source of discontent among customer support representatives who are working with customers frustrated by failures in a defective product. The traditional management response would be something like, "That's always a problem in customer support; give 'em a bonus." If, instead, the organization were to focus on the seeker-of-the-truth community inside the organization that wants the defective product fixed, it would engage engineers, parts purchasing agents, manufacturing quality assurance employees, as well as customer support. By relating to and supporting a solution by that internal tribe, the company will not only improve morale but also solve the problem and increase internal social capital.

Channels Become Networks

Prior to 1980, organizational communication was highly restricted to a few channels. The United States had three major, national TV networks and no more than a half a dozen major national newspapers. Consumers got their news twice a day; in the morning in the paper and in the evening at the 6:00 nightly news.

In that highly constrained environment, organizations could control messaging via paid advertising and public relations efforts to manipulate editors and writers. It was easy to get the consumers' attention because there were no alternatives. The Internet, Web sites, broadcast email, cable TV, and smartphones have blown those existing channels apart. Only old people watch the evening news, and they are notoriously poor consumers. With the myriad of communications channels available today, there is so much traffic that organizations find it nearly impossible to obtain attention in these channels.

As stated earlier, social media enables people to form communities based on common interests, and to obtain any of the consumers' attention organizations must today engage with networks in those communities, based on those interests. And, the communities are bored with, even disdainful of, traditional product data.

According to Gossieaux and Moran, another key difference is that channels transmit *data*, whereas networks transmit *knowledge*. Actually, many consumers would disagree that ads, at least, carry data. They carry the subliminal message that if you, too, buy that car, or paint, or soap, you too will be handsome, admired, or clean and happy. In any case, that kind of "data" has no power in today's networks. At Fox Lake, people want to know how to save money on catering, what musicians to avoid, or what to do with leftover wedding flowers. They want assistance reducing stress and expense and increasingly the likelihood of hosting a memorable and successful event. To the extent that Fox Lake can join or create networks to that end, it will increase both sales and social capital.

Structure and Control Becomes Messy

The final pillar of the hyper-social organization is, using our terms, a transition from a structured process to a dynamic one. Organizations and executives no longer plan and control organizational messaging. Such messaging emerges via a dynamic,

Activity	Description
Sense	Important communities. What they do, where they hang out, what they care about, how your organization can relate to them.
Engage	In relationships. Talk *with*, not to, community members (customers, employees, partners).
Activate	Connect communities to your internal value chains and processes (Figure 8-6).
Measure	Success in terms of social capital.
Story tell	Publicize community successes. Take a backseat role to the community.

Figure 8-10
SEAMS Dynamic Process
Activities

SM-based process. That concept is an anathema to traditional organizations and managers, and in the early years of your career you are likely to be part of helping your organization overcome resistance to it.

To facilitate that transition, the hyper-social organization model defines a dynamic process, called **SEAMS,** with the five major activities shown in Figure 8-10. The theme that runs through all five of these activities is to engage with communities with authentic relationships that are important to the community. Having done so, in the activate activity, connect your efforts to whatever value chain and process will achieve your organization's strategies. Make it easy to order your product, if sales are your goal, but not the obvious nor the immediate purpose of your relationship. Publish the successes of community members in ways that favor your organization, but that take a back seat to the community.

How Can SMIS Foster Hyper-Social Organizations?

SMIS play a key role for implementing the SEAMS process. Figure 8-11 summarizes important systems for each of the activities in Figure 8-10. Before discussing that figure, however, realize that all of these activities require the involvement of personnel in the hyper-social organization. Organizations need to staff and manage this activity, just as they formerly did for their media buying activity.

Sense Activities

Sensing involves two functions: (1) determining what the communities you care about are saying about you and (2) identifying the structure, goals, and dynamic of communities with which you want to relate. For the first, many organizations hire reputation management services like those provided by Reputation.com and others. These services can be expensive because they must be staffed by human beings who read, comprehend, filter, and synthesize SM conversations about

Activity	SMIS
Sense	Reputation management services (e.g., www.reputation.com) Twitter, Facebook, LinkedIn, blogs, other
Engage	Social media, Twitter, Facebook, LinkedIn, blogs, other
Activate	Integrate SM presence with CRM, ERP, other operational systems SOA useful
Measure	Social monitoring services (e.g., WebiMax) in-house metrics
Story tell	Blogs, videos, YouTube, white papers for benefit of SM communities

Figure 8-11
SMIS and SEAMS Activities

your organization. Of course, an organization can also do its own reputation management as well.

The second function is to identify communities with which you wish to engage and determine their type (defender of belief or seeker of truth), their structure, their key contributors, their goals and objectives, and their willingness to engage with organizations like yours. Given that data, you can then craft the best way of engaging those communities.

Engage

Once you have identified your important communities and have a plan, the next activity is to engage with those communities by creating relationships. Today, organizations use Facebook, Twitter, LinkedIn, and others for this purpose. They also support employee and partner blogs and other social media.

Personnel who perform these functions need to be trained in organizational policy and know the strategy and tactics to be used for the engagement. Many organizations have a few **key users** who are personnel trained to perform SM engagement tasks. Nonkey users submit ideas and responses to key users for publication in communities. In this way, the key users serve as a buffer and a filter for possible inappropriate content.

Activate

Although it is important that organizations engage in authentic relationships with the community and not attempt to use the community as a pure advertising and sales channel, it is also important that the organization make it easy for community members to obtain sales-oriented materials and to purchase when they want to. Thus, hooks into the organization's CRM, ERP, and other operational systems need to be provided in a discrete and appropriate manner. By the way, designing applications according to SOA principles greatly facilitates this task.

Measure

As with the sensing activity, many organizations use outside social monitoring services such as WebiMax to assess the effectiveness of the organization's SM efforts. In addition, organizations also staff in-house measuring activities.

Measurements include not only the number of mentions in the target communities, but also the response to the organization's own SM presence. These measurements answer questions like: How many commenters? How many reviewers? What is the traffic rate on the organization's SM sites, and how is it changing?

Gossieaux and Moran caution that such measurements are likely to overlook the **active lurker**, someone who reads, consumes, and observes activity in one social medium and then broadcasts it in some other medium. An example is someone who sees an interesting feature in Fox Lake's wedding SM presence and sends a link to that feature to their friends. Fox Lake will be able to measure the traffic generated from the shared link, but they are unable to determine which traffic is due to the active lurker.

Story Tell

Given relationships to important communities, the organization should then develop stories about their interaction with the community or interaction in the community that involves them and publish those stories back to the community. Fox Lake might, for example, commission a video crew to "tell the story" of someone's wedding planning and then post that on a wedding planning SM site. YouTube is, of course, a common site for such videos. For more technical products, white papers on the appropriate use or solution to problems are also popular.

Storytelling must observe one limit, however. Stories must be authentic accounts of interactions that are important to the SM community. Thinly disguised advertisements will be ignored at best and ridiculed at worst. You can find a story example that Microsoft did of an early user of Office 365 at www.youtube.com/watch?v=2O4Uc5mUSLA.

Q5 How Do Organizations Use Web 2.0?

Social media and SMIS are the leading edge in Internet commerce today. However, Web 2.0, the name for another set of Internet capabilities, emerged in the early 2000s and is still important. We will address Web 2.0 here because it includes features and functions that you need to know.

Prior to Web 2.0, e-commerce sites duplicated the experience of shopping in a grocery store or other retail shop. The customer moved around the store, placed items in a shopping cart, and then checked out. Such e-commerce sites were, and still are, effective at selling goods online, but they do not take full advantage of the Web's potential.

Amazon.com was one of the first to recognize other possibilities when it added the "Customers Who Bought This Book Also Bought" feature to its Web site. With that feature, e-commerce broke new ground. No grocery store could or would have a sign that announced, "Customers who bought this tomato soup, also bought. . . ." That idea was the first step toward what has come to be known as Web 2.0.

What Is Web 2.0?

Although the specific meaning of **Web 2.0** is hard to pin down, it generally refers to a loose grouping of capabilities, technologies, business models, and philosophies. Figure 8-12 compares Web 2.0 to traditional processing. (For some reason, the term *Web 1.0* is not used.)

Warning: As stated in the chapter preview, some people define *Web 2.0* to include social media. We separate Web 2.0 and social media here because social media, and especially hyper-social organizations, represent a difference in the nature of the relationship between organizations and humans. Pre-hyper-social

Web 2.0 Processing	Traditional Processing
Major winners: Google, Amazon.com, eBay	Major winners: Microsoft, Oracle, SAP
Software as a (Free) Service	Software as product
Frequent releases of thin-client applications	Infrequent, controlled releases
Business model relies on advertising or other revenue-from-use	Business model relies on sale of software licenses
Viral marketing	Extensive advertising
Product value increases with use and users	Product value fixed
Organic interfaces, mashups encouraged	Controlled, fixed interface
Participation	Publishing
Some rights reserved	All rights reserved

Figure 8-12
Comparison of Web 2.0 with Traditional Processing

organizations can use the tools and techniques described here for Web 2.0 without any fundamental change in their relationship to consumers.

Software as a (Free) Service

Google, Amazon.com, and eBay exemplify Web 2.0. These companies do not sell software licenses, because software is not their product. Instead, they provide software as a service (SaaS) in the cloud. You can search Google, run Google Docs, use Google Earth, process Gmail, and access Google Maps—all from a thin-client browser, with the bulk of the processing occurring in the cloud, somewhere on the Internet. Like all Web 2.0 programs, Google releases new versions of its programs frequently. Instead of software license fees, the Web 2.0 business model relies on advertising or other revenue that results as users employ the software as a service.

Figure 8-13 shows features that Google was at one time considering adding to Google Maps. Notice the warning that they "may change, break, or disappear at any time." By providing frequent updates this way, Google maintains it reputation as an innovative company while obtaining testing and usability feedback on new features.

Software as a service clashes with the revenue model used by traditional software vendors, such as Microsoft, Oracle, and SAP. Software is the traditional vendors' product. They release new versions and new products infrequently. For example, 3 years separated the release of Microsoft Office 2007 from 2010. Releases are made in a very controlled fashion, and extensive testing and true beta programs precede every release.

Traditional software vendors depend on software license fees. If a large number of Office users switched to free word processing and spreadsheet applications, the hit on Microsoft's revenue would be catastrophic. (See Case 6, page 210 for an example.) Because of the importance of software licensing revenue, substantial marketing efforts are made to convert users to new releases.

In the Web 2.0 world, no such marketing is done; new features are released and vendors wait for users to spread the news to one another, one friend sending a

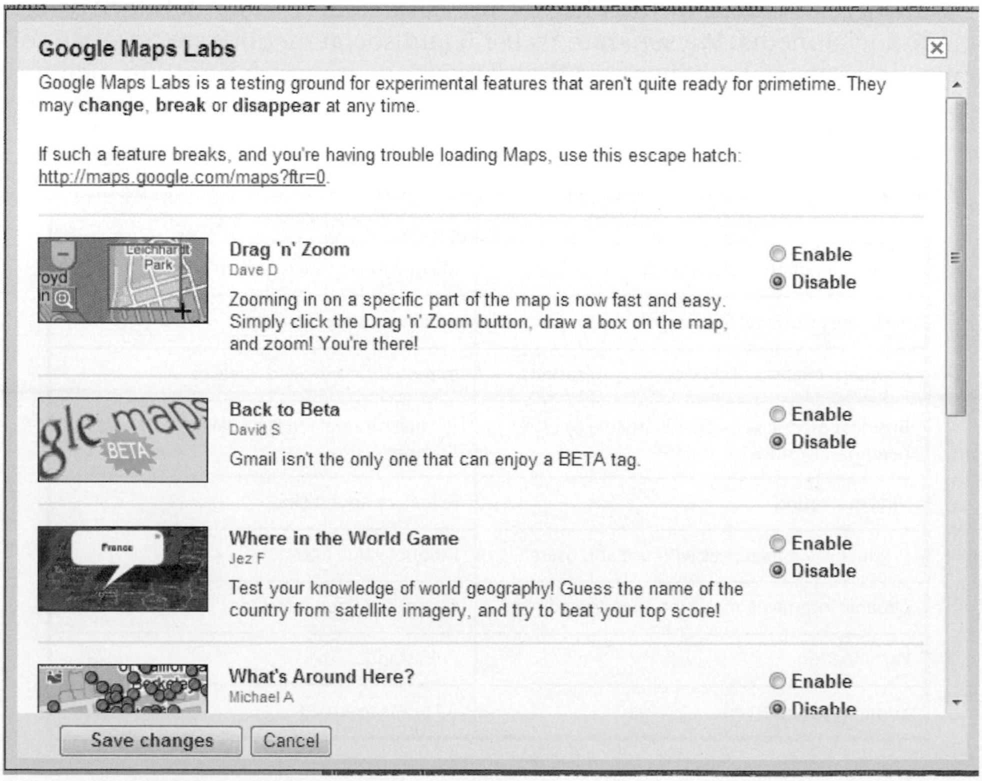

Figure 8-13
Testing of New Features, Web 2.0 Style

Source: Google Maps.

Google Maps Labs

Google Maps Labs is a testing ground for experimental features that aren't quite ready for primetime. They may **change**, **break** or **disappear** at any time.

If such a feature breaks, and you're having trouble loading Maps, use this escape hatch:
http://maps.google.com/maps?ftr=0

Drag 'n' Zoom
Dave D
Zooming in on a specific part of the map is now fast and easy. Simply click the Drag 'n' Zoom button, draw a box on the map, and zoom! You're there!
○ Enable
◉ Disable

Back to Beta
David S
Gmail isn't the only one that can enjoy a BETA tag.
○ Enable
◉ Disable

Where in the World Game
Jez F
Test your knowledge of world geography! Guess the name of the country from satellite imagery, and try to beat your top score!
○ Enable
◉ Disable

What's Around Here?
Michael A
○ Enable
◉ Disable

Save changes   Cancel

message to many friends; most of whom send that message, in turn, to their friends; and so forth, in a process called **viral marketing**. Google has never announced any software in a formal marketing campaign. Users carry the message to one another. In fact, if a product requires advertising to be successful, then it is not a Web 2.0 product.

By the way, traditional software companies do use the term *software as a service*. However, they use it only to mean that they will provide their software products via the cloud rather than having customers install that software on their computers. Software licenses for their products still carry license fees. You can, for example, obtain a license to use Office as part of the Office 365 SaaS offering.

Use Increases Value

Another characteristic of Web 2.0 is that the value of the site increases with users and use. Amazon.com gains more value as more users write more reviews. Amazon.com becomes *the* place to go for information about books or other products. Similarly, the more people who buy or sell on eBay, the more eBay gains value as a site.

Organic User Interfaces and Mashups

The traditional software model carefully controls the users' experience. All Office programs share a common user interface; the ribbon (toolbar) in Word is similar to the ribbon in PowerPoint and in Excel. In contrast, Web 2.0 interfaces are organic. Users find their way around eBay and PayPal, and if the user interface changes from day to day, well, that is just the nature of Web 2.0. Further, Web 2.0 encourages **mashups**, which occur when the output from two or more Web sites is combined into a single user experience.

Google's **My Maps** is an excellent mashup example. Google publishes Google Maps and provides tools for users to make custom modifications to those maps. Thus, users mash the Google Map product with their own knowledge. One user demonstrated the growth of gang activity to the local police by mapping new graffiti sites on Google Maps. Other users share their experiences or photos of hiking trips or other travel. See Figure 8-14 for another example.

Figure 8-14
Mashup Example

Source: © 2011 Google.

Ethics Guide

Hiding the Truth?

No one is going to publish their ugliest picture on their Facebook page, but how far should you go to create a positive impression? If your hips and legs are not your best features, is it unethical to stand behind your sexy car in your photo? If you've been to one event with someone very popular in your crowd, is it unethical to publish photos that imply you meet as an everyday occurrence? Surely there is no obligation to publish pictures of yourself at boring events with unpopular people just to balance the scale for those photos in which you appear unrealistically attractive and overly popular.

As long as all of this occurs on a Facebook or MySpace account that you use for personal relationships, well, what goes around comes around. But consider social networking in the business arena:

a. Suppose that a river rafting company starts a group on a social networking site for promoting rafting trips. Graham, a 15-year-old high school student who wants to be more grown-up than he is, posts a picture of a handsome 22-year-old male as a picture of himself. He also writes witty and clever comments on the site photos and claims to play the guitar and be an accomplished masseuse. Are his actions unethical? Suppose someone decided to go on the rafting trip, in part because of Graham's postings, and was disappointed with the truth about Graham. Would the rafting company have any responsibility to refund that person's fees?

b. Suppose you own and manage the rafting company. Is it unethical for you to encourage your employees to write positive reviews about your company? Does your assessment change if you ask your employees to use an email address other than the one they have at work?

c. Again, suppose you own and manage the rafting company and that you pay your employees a bonus for every client they bring to a rafting trip. Without specifying any particular technique, you encourage your employees to be creative in how they obtain clients. One employee invites his Facebook friends to a party at which he shows photos of prior rafting trips. On the way to the party, one of the friends has an automobile accident and dies. His spouse sues your company. Should your company be held accountable? Does it matter if you knew about the presentation? Would it matter if you had not encouraged your employees to be creative?

d. Suppose your rafting company has a Web site for customer reviews. In spite of your best efforts at camp cleanliness, on one trip (out of dozens) your staff accidentally served contaminated food and everyone became ill with food-poisoning. One of those clients from that trip writes a poor review because of that experience. Is it ethical for you to delete that review from your site?

e. Assume you have a professor who has written a popular textbook. You are upset with the grade you received in his class, so you write a scandalously poor review of that professor's book on Amazon.com. Are your actions ethical?

f. Instead of owner, suppose you were at one time employed by this rafting company and you were, undeservedly you think, terminated. To get even, you use Facebook to spread rumors to your friends (many of whom are river guides) about the safety of the company's trips. Are your actions unethical? Are they illegal? Do you see any ethical distinctions between this situation and that in item d?

g. Again, suppose that you were at one time employed by the rafting company and were undeservedly terminated. You notice that the company's owner does not have a Facebook account, so you create one for her. You've known her for many years and have dozens of photos of her, some of which were taken at parties and are unflattering and revealing. You post those photos along with critical comments that she made about clients or employees. Most of the comments were made when she was tired or frustrated, and they are hurtful, but because of her wit, also humorous. You send friend invitations to people whom she knows, many of whom are the target of her biting and critical remarks. Are your actions unethical? ∎

Discussion Questions

1. Read the situations in items a through g and answer the questions contained in each.

2. Based on your answers in question 1, formulate ethical principles for creating or using social networks for business purposes.

3. Based on your answers in question 1, formulate ethical principles for creating or using user-generated content for business purposes.

4. Summarize the risks that a business assumes when it chooses to sponsor user-generated content.

5. Summarize the risks that a business assumes when it uses social media for business purposes.

Source: Rubberball/Superstock.

281

In Web 2.0 fashion, Google provides users a means for sharing their mashed-up map over the Internet and then indexes that map for Google search. If you publish a mashup of a Google map with your knowledge of a hiking trip on Mt. Pugh, anyone who performs a Google search for Mt. Pugh will find your map. Again, the more users who create My Maps, the greater the value of the My Maps site.

Participation and Ownership Differences

Mashups lead to another key difference. Traditional sites are about publishing; Web 2.0 is about participation. Users provide reviews, map content, discussion responses, blog entries, and so forth. A final difference, listed in Figure 8-12, concerns *ownership*. Traditional vendors and Web sites lock down all the legal rights they can. For example, Oracle publishes content and demands that others obtain written permission before reusing it. Web 2.0 locks down only some rights. Google publishes maps and says, "Do what you want with them. We'll help you share them."

How Can Businesses Benefit from Web 2.0?

Amazon.com, Google, eBay, and other Web 2.0 companies have pioneered Web 2.0 technology and techniques to their benefit. A good question today, however, is how these techniques might be used by non-Internet companies. How might 3M, Alaska Airlines, Procter & Gamble, or the bicycle shop down the street use Web 2.0?

Advertising

Consider an ad for Oracle CRM that appears in the print version of the *Wall Street Journal*. Oracle has no control over who reads that ad, nor does it know much about the people who do (just that they fit the general demographic of *Wall Street Journal* readers). On any particular day, 10,000 qualified buyers for Oracle products might happen to read the ad, or then again, perhaps only 1,000 qualified buyers read it. Neither Oracle nor the *Wall Street Journal* knows the number, but Oracle pays the same amount for the ad, regardless of the number of readers or who they are.

In the Web 2.0 world, advertising is specific to user interests. Someone who searches online for "customer relationship management" is likely an IT person (or a student) who has a strong interest in Oracle and its competing products. Oracle would like to advertise to that person.

Google pioneered Web 2.0 advertising. With its **AdWords** software, vendors pay a certain amount for particular search words. For example, GearUp might agree to pay $2 for the term *soccer ball*. When someone Googles that term, Google will display a link to GearUp's Web site. If the user clicks that link (and *only* if the user clicks that link), Google charges GearUp's account $2. GearUp pays nothing if the user does not click.

The amount that a company pays per word can be changed from day to day, and even hour to hour. If GearUp is about to offer a new spinning bicycle, it will be willing to pay for the word *spinning* just before the event starts. The value of a click on *spinning* is zero after the event has closed.

AdSense is another advertising alternative. Google searches an organization's Web site and inserts ads that match content on that site. When users click those ads, Google pays the organization a fee. Other Web 2.0 vendors offer services similar to AdWords and AdSense.

With Web 2.0, the cost of reaching a particular, qualified person is much smaller than in the traditional advertising model. As a consequence, many companies are switching to the new lower-cost medium, and newspapers and magazines are struggling with a sharp reduction in advertising revenue.

Mashups

How can two non-Internet companies mash the content of their products? Suppose you're watching a hit movie and you would like to buy the jewelry, dress, or watch worn by the leading actress. Suppose that Nordstrom sells all those items. With Web 2.0 technology, the movie's producer and Nordstrom can mash their content together so that you, watching the movie on computer at home, can click the item you like and be directed to Nordstrom's e-commerce site that will sell it to you. Or, perhaps Nordstrom is disintermediated out of the transaction, and you are taken to the e-commerce site of the watch's manufacturer.

Q6 How Can Organizations Manage the Risks of Social Media and Web 2.0?

Social media and Web 2.0 represent a revolution in the way that organizations communicate. Twenty years ago, most organizations managed all public and internal messaging with the highest degree of control. Every press conference, press release, public interview, presentation, and even academic paper needed to be preapproved by both the legal and marketing departments. Such approval could take weeks or months.

Today, progressive hyper-social organizations have turned that model on its head. Employees are encouraged to engage with communities and, in most organizations, to identify themselves with their employer while doing so. All of this participation, all of this engagement, however, comes with risks. In this question, we will consider risks from employee communication and risks from nonemployee, user-generated content.

Managing the Risk of Employee Communication

The first step that any hyper-social organization should take is to develop and publicize a **social media policy**, which is a statement that delineates employees' rights and responsibilities. You can find an index to 100 different policies at the Social Media Today Web site.[11] In general, the more technical the organization, the more open and lenient are the social policies. The U.S. military has, perhaps surprisingly, endorsed social media with enthusiasm, tempered by the need to protect classified data.

Intel Corporation created an open and employee-trusting SM policy that is a model for hyper-social organizations to emulate. Intel's six guiding principles to its employees are:

1. Stick to your area of expertise.
2. Post meaningful, respectful comments.
3. Pause and think before posting.
4. Respect proprietary information and content, and confidentiality.
5. When disagreeing with others, keep it appropriate and polite.
6. Know and follow company code of conduct and privacy policy.[12]

This policy is supplemented with a statement of Rules of Engagement for social media, which is excerpted and summarized in Figure 8-15. Read this list carefully; it contains great advice and considerable wisdom. Also, visit the full description at www.intel.com/content/www/us/en/legal/intel-social-media-guidelines.html.

---

[11] "Social Media Employee Policy Examples from Over 100 Organizations," Social Media Today, http://socialmediatoday.com/ralphpaglia/141903/social-media-employee-policy-examples-over-100-companies-and-organizations (accessed August 2011).
[12] "Intel Social Media Guidelines," Intel, www.intel.com/content/www/us/en/legal/intel-social-media-guidelines.html (accessed November 2011).

Rule	Remarks
Be transparent.	Your honesty—or dishonesty—will be quickly noticed in the social media environment. If you are blogging about your work at Intel, use your real name, identify that you work for Intel, and be clear about your role....
Be judicious.	Make sure your efforts to be transparent don't violate Intel's privacy, confidentiality, and legal guidelines for external commercial speech...
Write what you know.	Make sure you write and post about your areas of expertise, especially as related to Intel and our technology. If you are writing about a topic that Intel is involved with but you are not the Intel expert on the topic, you should make this clear to your readers. And write in the first person...
Perception is reality.	In online social networks, the lines between public and private, personal and professional are blurred. Just by identifying yourself as an Intel employee, you are creating perceptions about your expertise and about Intel by our shareholders, customers, and the general public-and perceptions about you by your colleagues and managers. Do us all proud...
It's a conversationn.	Talk to your readers like you would talk to real people in professional situations. ...Don't be afraid to bring in your own personality and say what's on your mind. Consider content that's open-ended and invites response. Encourage comments.
Are you adding value?	There are millions of words out there. The best way to get yours read is to write things that people will value. Social communication from Intel should help our customers, partners, and co-workers...
Your responsibility.	What you write is ultimately your responsibility. Participation in social computing on behalf of Intel is not a right but an opportunity, so please treat it seriously and with respect...
Create some excitement.	As a business and as a corporate citizen, Intel is making important contributions to the world, to the future of technology, and to public dialogue on a broad range of issues. Our business activities are increasingly focused on high-value innovation. Let's share with the world the exciting things we're learning and doing—and open up the channels to learn from others.
Be a leader.	There can be a fine line between healthy debate and incendiary reaction. Do not denigrate our competitors or Intel. Nor do you need to respond to every criticism or barb...Did you screw up? If you make a mistake, admit it. Be upfront and be quick with your correction. If you're posting to a blog, you may choose to modify an earlier post—just make it clear that you have done so.
If it gives you pause, pause.	If you're about to publish something that makes you even the slightest bit uncomfortable, don't shrug it off and hit 'send.' Take a minute to review these guidelines and try to figure out what's bothering you, then fix it...

Two elements in this list are particularly noteworthy. The first is the call for transparency and truth. As an experienced and wise business professional once told me, "Nothing is more serviceable than the truth." It may not be convenient, but it is serviceable, long term. Second, SM contributors and their employers should be open and above board. If you make a mistake, don't obfuscate; instead correct it, apologize, and make amends. The SM world is too open, too broad, and too powerful to fool.

When singer Amy Winehouse died in July 2011, both Microsoft and Apple tweeted messages about where to buy her music that the Twittersphere found distasteful and objectionable.[13] After a loud outcry, both organizations were prompt with apologies, made amends to her family and friends, and the errors were forgotten by day's end. Had they done otherwise, we would still be hearing about them. See also Using Your Knowledge Question 8 on page 291.

Managing the Risk of User-Generated Content

User-generated content (UGC), which simply means content on your SM site that is contributed by nonemployee users, is the essence of SM relationships. As with any relationship, however, UGC comments can be inappropriate or excessively negative in tone or otherwise problematic. Organizations need to determine how they will deal with such content before engaging in social media.

[13] Sarah Kessler, "Microsoft Apologizes for 'Crass' Amy Winehouse Tweet," CNN.com, July 26, 2011, www.cnn.com/2011/TECH/social.media/07/25/apology.winehouse.tweet.mashable/index.html?iref=allsearch (accessed August 2011).

Problem Sources

The major sources of UGC problems are:

- Junk and crackpot contributions
- Inappropriate content
- Unfavorable reviews
- Mutinous movements

When a business participates in a social network or opens its site to UGC, it opens itself to misguided people who post junk unrelated to the site's purpose. Crackpots may also use the network or UGC site as a way of expressing passionately held views about unrelated topics, such as UFOs, government cover-ups, fantastic conspiracy theories, and so forth. Because of the possibility of such content, SM sponsors should regularly monitor the site and remove objectionable material immediately. Monitoring can be done by employees, or companies like Bazaarvoice offer services not only to collect and manage ratings and reviews, but also to monitor the site for irrelevant content.

Unfavorable reviews are another risk. Research indicates that customers are sophisticated enough to know that few, if any, products are perfect. Most customers want to know the disadvantages of a product before purchasing it so they can determine if those disadvantages are important for their application. However, if every review is bad, if the product is rated 1 star out of 5, then the company is using social media to publish its problems. In this case, some action must be taken as described next.

Mutinous movements are an extension of bad reviews. When President Obama used Twitter to explain and justify one element of the federal budget debate in August 2011, it backfired. He lost 33,000 followers as a result.

Responding to Social Networking Problems

The first task in managing social networking risk is to know the sources of potential problems and to monitor sites for problematic content. Once such content is found, however, organizations must have a plan for creating the organization's response. Three possibilities are:

- Leave it
- Respond to it
- Delete it

If the problematic content represents reasonable criticism of the organization's products or services, the best response may be to leave it where it is. Such criticism indicates that the site is not just a shill for the organization, but contains legitimate user content. Such criticism also serves as a free source of product reviews, which can be useful for product development. To be useful, the development team needs to know about the criticism, so, as stated, processes to ensure that the criticism is found and communicated to the development team are necessary.

A second alternative is to respond to the problematic content. However, this alternative is dangerous. If the response could be construed, in any way, as patronizing or insulting to the content contributor, the response can enrage the community and generate a strong backlash. Also, if the response appears defensive, it can become a public relations negative.

In most cases, responses are best reserved for when the problematic content has caused the organization to do something positive as a result. For example, suppose a user publishes that he or she was required to hold for customer support for 45 minutes. If the organization has done something to reduce wait times, then an effective response to the criticism is to recognize it as valid and state, nondefensively, what had been done to reduce wait times.

If a reasoned, nondefensive response generates continued and unreasonable UGC from that same source, it is best for the organization to do nothing. "Never wrestle with a pig; you'll get dirty and the pig will enjoy it." Instead, allow the community to constrain the user. It will.

Deleting content should be reserved for contributions that are inappropriate because they are contributed by crackpots, because they have nothing to do with the site, or because they contain obscene or otherwise inappropriate content. However, deleting legitimate negative comments can result in a strong user backlash. As Anne mentions in the Fox Lake case that opens this chapter, Nestlé created a PR nightmare on its Facebook account with its response to criticism it received about its use of palm oil. Someone altered the Nestlé logo, and in response Nestlé decided to delete all Facebook contributions that used that altered logo, and did so in an arrogant, heavy-handed way. The result was a negative firestorm on Twitter.[14]

A sound principle in business is to never ask a question to which you do not want the answer. We can extend that principle to social networking; never set up a site that will generate content for which you have no effective response!

Q7 2022?

So much change is in the air: social media, hyper-social organizations, Web 2.0, Enterprise 2.0. Is there a hyper-hyper-social organization or an Enterprise 3.0 around the corner? We don't know. However, new versions of the iOS devices and their copycats, along with dynamic and agile information systems based on cloud computing and virtualization, guarantee that monumental changes will continue to occur in between now and 2022.

In Brazil, Unilever placed GPS devices in 50 packages of its Omo detergent.[15] The GPS devices were activated when customers removed the package from the shelf. The devices then reported the customer's home location to Unilever. Unilever employees then contacted the customers at home and gave them pocket video cameras. The point? Promotion. But what's next?

Advance the clock 10 years. You're now the product marketing manager for an important new product series for your company . . . the latest in a line of, say, intelligent home appliances. How are you going to promote your products? GPS, with a team following them home? No, you'll have to do something even more creative by 2022, something that will involve social media that does not exist today.

Think about your role as a manager in 2022. Your team has 10 people, 3 of whom report to you; 2 report to other managers; and 5 work for different companies. Your company uses Office Gizmo 2022, augmented by Google Whammo ++ Star, both of which have many features that enable employees to publish their ideas in blogs, wikis, videos, and whatever other means have become available. Your employees have computers assigned to them at work; computers that they almost never use. Instead, they use their $19 slate computers that are always connected via wireless WAN to an ISP that they pay for themselves. Of course, your employees have their own Facebook, Twitter, LinkedIn, foursquare, and other social networking sites to which they regularly contribute.

How do you manage this team? If "management" means to plan, organize, and control, how can you accomplish any of these functions in this emergent network of employees? But, if you and your organization follow the lead of tech-savvy companies

---

[14] Bernhard Warner, "Nestlé's 'No Logo' Policy Triggers Facebook Revolt," Social Media Influence, March 19, 2010, http://socialmediainfluence.com/2010/03/19/nestles-no-logo-policy-triggers-facebook-revolt/ (accessed August 2010).

[15] Laurel Wentz, "Is Your Detergent Stalking You?" *Advertising Age,* July 29, 2010, http://adage.com/globalnews/article?article_id=145183 (accessed August, 2010).

like Intel, you'll know you cannot close the door on your employee's SM lives, nor will you want to. Instead, you'll harness the power of the social behavior of your employees and partners to advance your strategy.

In the context of CRM, hyper-social means that the vendor loses control of the customer relationship. Customers use all the vendor's touch points they can find to craft their own relationships. Emergence in the context of management means loss of control of employees. Employees craft their own relationships with their employers, whatever that might mean by 2022. Certainly it means a loss of control, one that is readily made public, to the world.

In the 1960s, when someone wanted to send an email to Don Draper at Sterling Cooper, his or her secretary addressed the envelope to Sterling Cooper and down at the bottom added, "Attention: Don Draper." The letter was to Sterling Cooper, oh, by the way, also to Don Draper.

Email changed that. Today, someone would send an email to DonDraper@Sterling Cooper.com, or even just to Don@SterlingCooper.com. That address is to a person and then to the company.

Social media changes addresses further. When Don Draper creates his own blog, people respond to Don's Blog, and, only incidentally do they notice in the About Don section of the blog that Don works for Sterling Cooper. In short, the focus has moved in 50 years from organizations covering employee names to employees covering organization names.

Does this mean that organizations go away by 2022? Hardly. They are needed to raise and conserve capital and to organize vast groups of people and projects. No group of loosely affiliated people can envision, design, develop, manufacture, market, sell, and support an iPad. Organizations are required.

So what, then? Maybe we can take a lesson from biology. Crabs have an external exoskeleton. Deer, much later in the evolutionary chain, have an internal endoskeleton. When crabs grow, they must endure the laborious and biologically expensive process of shedding a small shell and growing a larger one. They are also vulnerable during the transition. When deer grow, the skeleton is inside and it grows with the deer. No need for vulnerable molting. And, considering agility, would you take a crab over a deer?

In the 1960s, organizations were the exoskeleton around employees. By 2022, they will be endoskeleton, supporting the work of people on the exterior.

Does that analogy offer guidance to the future? Maybe.

Guide

Blending the Personal and the Professional

Many businesses are beginning to use social networking sites such as Facebook and Twitter for professional purposes. It began with coworkers sharing their accounts with each other socially, just as they did in college. The first interactions concerned activities such as photos of the company softball team or photos at a cocktail party at a recent sales meeting. However, as stated in the networking guide in Chapter 6, every business social function is a *business* function, so even sharing photos and pages with the work softball team began to blur the personal–professional boundary.

The employees of Pearson, the publisher of this textbook, are no exception. When I began work on this chapter, I started a Facebook group called "Using MIS." I then queried Facebook for Pearson employees I guessed might have Facebook accounts and invited them to be "friends." Most accepted, and I asked them to join the Using MIS group.

The first day I checked my account, I found an entry from Anne, one of my new friends, who stated that she had been out too late the prior night. That day she happened to be working on the sales plan for this book, and I realized that I didn't want to know her current condition. So, in the group, I asked whether the blending of the personal and the professional is a good thing, and the following conversation resulted:

Anne: I think that for a lot of reasons it is a good thing . . . within reason. I think that people seeing a personal side of you can humanize you. For example, my "I was out too late last night" post didn't mean that I was not into work early and ready to go (which I was, just with a larger coffee than usual), just that I like to have a good time outside of my work life. Also, with all the time we spend at work, our social lives are intertwined with our work lives.

Also, 9–5 work hours are becoming more and more obsolete. I may be updating my Facebook page at noon on a Friday, but you will surely find me working at least part of my day on Saturday and Sunday.

Bob: I definitely see Anne's point of view. There is the temptation to believe that we are all family. I am too old to believe that, but corporate advancement is always going to be predicated to some degree on your willingness to surrender the personal for the professional and/or allow blur. Technology may give you the illusion that you can safely have it both ways.

I am skeptical of business applications for Facebook. My guess is most folks find them lame in the way that business blogs and Xmas cards from your insurance agent are.

Lisa: I actually think there is a place for Facebook in business . . . For example, think about how it's connected a team like ours—where everyone is located all over the country—to have a place where we actually get to know each other a little better. It's corny, perhaps, but reading people's status updates on my iPhone gives me a better sense of who they are in "real life," not just on the job. I'd get that if we all sat in the same office every day; given that we don't, it's a pretty decent substitute.

I totally agree with Anne's notion that, in many ways, the personal and the professional already do blur . . . but I think that's more to do with who we are and what we do, than any specific notion of "corporations." Our work is portable and always on—and judged by results, not hours logged (I think!). In a work universe like that, the lines sort of slowly and inevitably blur . . . PS: Anne, I was out too late too. :)

Clearly, I am the curmudgeon here. But, just as I was reflecting on these comments, I received a private email from another person who chose not to be identified:

Other person: A few weeks ago, Pearson started getting really into Facebook. I went from not really using it to getting tons of "friend requests" from coworkers. Then, I got a request from somebody in an executive position at Pearson. I was worried at first—I had heard so many stories of people who had lost their jobs due to social networking, blogging, or other information they posted on the Internet. When I received this request, I must have gone over my profile 10 times to ensure there was nothing that could any way be misconstrued as offensive or illegal. I think many people at the company already know a lot about me, but I . . . I think you would have to be more careful if you're in the introductory months of a new job. ∎

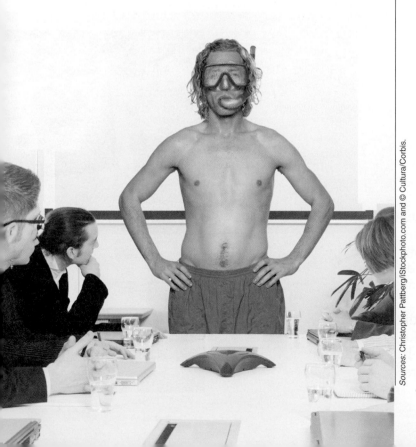

Sources: Christopher Pattberg/iStockphoto.com and © Cultura/Corbis.

Discussion Questions

1. Do you think Anne's post that she was "Out too late last night" was inappropriate, given that she knew that her professional colleagues were reading her page? Explain your answer.

2. Anne and Lisa contend that Facebook allows employees to get to know each other better in "real life" and not just on the job. Both of these women are very successful business professionals, and they believe such knowledge is important. Do you? Why or why not?

3. Bob is skeptical that Facebook has potential business applications. He thinks social networking sites will become as lame and as uninteresting as business blogs and corporate holiday cards. Do you agree? Why or why not?

4. In the olden days before social networking, instant messaging, email, and "free" long-distance phone calls, social networking was restricted to the people in your department, or maybe those who worked on your floor. You knew the people to whom you revealed personal data, and they were close to you in the organizational hierarchy. You would have had almost no contact with your manager's manager's manager, and what contact you did have would have been in the context of a formal meeting. How do you think management is affected when personal data is readily shared far up and down the organizational hierarchy?

5. Do you think it was appropriate for the senior manager to invite distant subordinates in the organization to be friends? Why did this action put the junior employees in a tight spot? What advantages accrue to the senior manager of having very junior friends? What advantages accrue to the junior professional of having a senior friend?

6. All of the people in this dialog update Facebook using intelligent phones and iOS devices that they purchased with their own money. Because they are not using a corporate asset, managers at Pearson would be unable to stop these employees from using Facebook, if they wanted to. How does this fact change the power structure within an organization? Consider, for example, what would happen if senior management announced an unpopular change in employee benefits or some other program.

7. As the lawyers say, "You cannot un-ring the bell." Once you've revealed something about yourself, you cannot take it back. Knowing that, what criteria will you use to decide what you will post on a social networking site that is read by your professional colleagues? How do those criteria differ from the criteria you use at school?

Guide
Social Recruiting

Social recruiting makes

sense. Recruiting has always been a social process—prospecting for candidates, matching candidates' qualifications against job needs, interviewing employees to determine how they fit the organizational culture, background checks—all of these have a social component that can be enhanced with social media.

Today, some hyper-social organizations use their communities to locate prospects. In the recent downturn, some have created communities of "alumni" employees, meaning those who have been laid off, to keep track of them in case an opportunity to rehire good performers occurs. Professional recruiters also build and use existing communities to locate prospects for openings they have.

In addition to prospecting, employers also use candidates' SM sites, particularly LinkedIn, Facebook, and Twitter, to get a sense of the candidate as a person and to find any potential behavior or attitude problems. However, using social data exposes **protected data**, which is data about candidates' sex, race, religion, sexual orientation, and disabilities that is illegal to use for hiring decisions. In most cases, it is clear that none of this data should influence such decisions, but the issues can sometimes be cloudy. Can an organization reject a person shown sitting in a wheelchair for a job that requires walking? The legal precedents are not clear.

What is clear, however, is that by consuming that data the organization loses a common defense against bias lawsuits: "We didn't know." Because the organization does know, it must be careful not to use such data inappropriately and also to appear not to have done so.

The general guideline is to treat every candidate the same. If social media are used for screening for one candidate, use it for all. If social media are used only after the first interview, conduct that same process for all. Furthermore, keep screenshots of every Web page that informs the hiring decision. Finally, when organizations do find worrisome indicators on SM sites, they may want to allow the candidate an opportunity to address any concerns during an interview. Data that appears problematic may be harmless or an error.

Now, put the shoe on the other foot. What should you, as a job candidate, do? First, as of 2012 at least, join LinkedIn and use it only for professional purposes. Fill your profile with appropriate professional data. Strive to ensure that your data indicates an ambitious interest in whatever field you choose. Build your connections and check out LinkedIn tools like the JobsInsider for using your contacts to obtain references inside organizations.

Second, until Facebook adds an equivalent capability, use Google+ circles. Keep your personal

social data out of any circle that can be publicly accessed. If you use sites that do not have a similar capability, remove inappropriate content from sites that can be publicly accessed. You should assume that any prospective employer will use all of your public SM data.

By the way, what is funny or innocent to you and your friends may not appear so to a potential employer. If you're in doubt, ask professional people who are 10 or 20 years older than you to assess your social data.

Finally, keep in mind that social media is a double-edged sword. Check out the blogs, commentary, and any other postings of people who already work at prospective employers. You're not necessarily looking for organizational dirt; you're looking for a good fit between you and the organization's culture. If, for example, an employee's blog or social data indicates employees travel frequently, that can be good or bad for you, depending on whether you want to travel. But at least you'll know from a reliable source. Human resources may say, "We have flexible working hours," and employees may agree, "Yes, we do. Work any 65 hours a week you want." If you do find employee social data that concerns you, at an appropriate time and in a polite way, review those concerns during your job interview process. ■

Sources: Derren Nugent/Newscom.

1. Define *protected data*. In your opinion, what kind of protected data should never be used for hiring decisions? Name and describe three situations in which it is at least debatable whether such data should be used.

2. Think of two organizations for which you would like to work. Assume both organizations review job candidates' SM data as part of their initial screening process.
   a. Name and describe three positive criteria that both companies could use to evaluate applicants. If you think the companies might use different criteria, explain the difference.
   b. Name and describe three indications of problematic issues that both companies could use to evaluate candidates. If you think the companies might use different criteria, explain the difference.
   c. If you were rejected because of a lack of social data supporting your criteria for item a or because of the presence of social data in the criteria for item b, would you know it?

3. Evaluate your own social data in light of your answer to question 2.
   a. Describe elements in your social data that support positive criteria.
   b. Describe elements in your social data that could indicate problematic issues.

4. Ask someone else to evaluate your social data in light of both sets of criteria in question 2. You can ask a friend, but you will likely obtain better information if you pick someone whom you do not know well. Most human resource screening personnel are in their 30s. Try to pick someone in that age group to evaluate your criteria, if you can.

5. Choose the most negative social data according to your answers to questions 3 and 4. Suppose you are in a job interview and you are asked about that problematic data. Explain your response.

6. Consider the job you would most like to obtain after you graduate. Assume you are the hiring decision maker for that job. Name and describe five indications that would positively influence you toward a job candidate.

7. Join LinkedIn if you have not already done so. Build your personal profile in accordance with your answer to question 6.

8. Regardless of whether the steps in this guide were assigned to you, if you have read them and not taken the steps recommended here, explain why.

Active Review

Use this Active Review to verify that you understand the ideas and concepts that answer this chapter's study questions.

Q1 What is a social media information system (SMIS)?

Define *social media, communities, tribes, hives,* and *social media information systems.* Name and describe three SMIS organizational roles. Explain the elements of Figure 8-3. Explain why placing a LinkedIn icon on a company Web site is not a casual decision. In your own words, explain the nature of the five components of SMIS for each of the three SMIS organizational roles.

Q2 How do SMIS advance organizational strategy?

Explain the terms *defenders of belief* and *seekers of the truth.* How do the goals of each type of community differ? Summarize how social media contributes to sales and marketing, customer support, inbound logistics, outbound logistics, manufacturing and operations, and human resources. Name SM risks for each activity. Define *social CRM, crowdsourcing,* and *Enterprise 2.0.* Explain each element in the SLATES model.

Q3 How do SMIS increase social capital?

Define *social capital* and explain four ways that social capital adds value. Name three factors that determine social capital and explain how "they are more multiplicative than additive."

Q4 What roles do SMIS play in the hyper-social organization?

Define *hyper-social organization.* Name the four pillars of hyper-social organization, explain each, and give an example of differences of each state in each transition. Explain how the term *messy* pertains to process types. Explain the nature of each SEAMS activity and give an example of the user of SMIS for each.

Q5 How do organizations use Web 2.0?

Explain how Amazon.com ushered in Web 2.0. Explain the term *software as a (free) service* and how it differs from traditional software licensing. Describe the difference in business models between Web 2.0 and traditional software companies. Explain the statement, "If a product requires advertising, then it is not Web 2.0." Explain how use increases value in Web 2.0. Define *mashup.* In what way are Web 2.0 interfaces organic? How does rights management differ between Web 2.0 and traditional software? Summarize the ways that businesses can benefit from Web 2.0.

Q6 How can organizations manage the risks of social media and Web 2.0?

Name and describe two types of SM risk. Describe the purpose of an SM policy and summarize Intel's six guiding principles. Describe an SM mistake, other than one in this text, and explain the wise response to it. Name four sources of problems of UGC; name three possible responses, and give the advantages and disadvantages of each.

Q7 2022?

Summarize possible management challenges when controlling employees in 2022. Describe the text's suggested response. How does the change in forms of address since the 1960s indicate a change in the relationship of employees and organizations to the business world. Explain the relationship of the differences between crab and deer to this change.

Using Your Knowledge at Fox Lake

Summarize the problem that Fox Lake has with regard to the bride and her family. Recommend a course of action for Fox Lake to deal with this problem. Describe ways that Fox Lake can turn this potential reputation disaster into increased social capital.

Key Terms and Concepts

Active lurker   276
AdSense   282
AdWords   282
Capital   268
Communities   258
Connection data   263
Content data   262
Crowdsourcing   267
Defenders of belief   264
Enterprise 2.0   267
Folksonomy   267
Hives   258
Human capital   268

Hyper-social organization   273
Key users   276
Mashup   279
My Maps   279
Protected data   290
SEAMS   275
Seekers of the truth   264
SLATES   267
Social capital   268
Social CRM   265
Social media (SM)   258
Social media application
    providers   261

Social media information system
    (SMIS)   258
Social media policy   283
Social media sponsors   261
Strength of a relationship   271
Tribes   258
User generated content
    (UGC)   284
Value of social capital   269
Viral hook   260
Viral marketing   279
Web 2.0   277

Using Your Knowledge

1. Using the Facebook page of a company that you have Liked (or would choose to), fill out the grid in Figure 8-5. Strive to replace the phrases in that grid with specific statements that pertain to Facebook, the company you like, and you and users whom you know. For example, if you and your friends access Facebook using an Android phone, enter that specific device.

2. Name a company for which you would like to work. Using Figure 8-6 as a guide, describe, as specifically as you can, how that company could use social media. Include community type, specific focus, processes involved, risks, and any other observations.

   a. Sales and marketing
   b. Customer service
   c. Inbound logistics
   d. Outbound logistics
   e. Manufacturing and operations
   f. Human resources

3. Visit www.lie-nielsen.com or www.sephora.com. On the site you chose, find links to social networking sites. In what ways are those sites sharing their social capital with you? In what ways are they attempting to cause you to share your social capital with them? Describe the business value of social networking to the business you chose.

4. According to Paul Greenberg, Amazon.com is the master of the 2-minute relationship and Boeing is the master of the 10-year relationship.[16] Visit www.boeing.com and www.amazon.com. From Greenberg's statement and from the appearance of these Web sites, it appears that Boeing is committed to traditional CRM and Amazon.com to social CRM.

Give evidence from each site that this might be true. Explain why the products and business environment of both companies cause this difference. Is there any justification for traditional CRM at Amazon.com? Why or why not? Is there any justification for social CRM at Boeing? Why or why not? Based on these companies, is it possible that a company might endorse Enterprise 2.0 but not endorse social CRM? Explain.

5. Google or Bing "Chloe" and search for sites that deal with Chloe fashion products. Identify companies that have purchased the Chloe AdWord. Follow three or four such links. Identify as many Web 2.0 features in the sites that you encounter as you can. Explain what you think the business rationale is for each site.

6. Visit www.intel.com/content/www/us/en/legal/intel-social-media-guidelines.html. Using the four pillars that define a hyper-social organization, explain why Intel appears to be hyper-social.

7. Visit http://socialmediatoday.com/ralphpaglia/141903/social-media-employee-policy-examples-over-100-companies-and-organizations. Find an organization with a very restricted employee SM policy. Name the organization and explain why you find that policy restrictive. Does that policy cause you to feel positive, negative, or neutral about that company? Explain.

8. Reread the paragraph about Microsoft and Apple's Twitter problems on page 263. In your opinion, what is it about this situation that is distasteful? We could have increased the visual appeal of this textbook by including a picture of Amy Winehouse in this chapter. Would including a photo have been distasteful? Why or why not?

---

[16] Paul Greenberg, *CRM at the Speed of Light*, 4th ed. (New York: McGraw-Hill, 2010), p. 105.

▬ Collaboration Exercise 8

With a team of your fellow students, develop an answer to the following questions. Use Google Docs, Google1, Windows Live SkyDrive, SharePoint, Office 365, or some other collaboration tool to conduct your meetings.

Suppose your team has been hired by Anne Foster to make Fox Lake's wedding events department a hyper-social organization. Work with your group to answer the following questions:

1. Is your assignment valid? Is it possible to make a department within Fox Lake hyper-social without making all of Fox Lake hyper-social? Why or why not? If you conclude it is not, then broaden this assignment to include all of Fox Lake.

2. Identify five actions that the wedding events department can take to transform its orientation from consumers to humans.

3. Describe how the wedding events department would define its customers using market segments.

Explain how it would define its customers using tribes. Explain how a tribe orientation would change the content and structure of the wedding events department's SM presence.

4. Explain why the wedding events department sending an email solicitation to its communities would be an example of a channel-based orientation. Describe two actions that it could take to demonstrate a network-based orientation.

5. Using Figures 8-10 and 8-11 as a guide, give specific examples of tasks for the wedding events department for each of the activities in the SEAMS dynamic process. For each, describe how information systems could be used to facilitate the task.

6. Prepare a 2-minute summary of what you have learned from this exercise that your group's members could use in a job interview. Give your presentation to the rest of the class.

▬ Case Study 8

Tourism Holdings Limited (THL)

Note: Because this case involves concepts from both this chapter and from Chapter 9, it is continued at the end of that chapter.

Tourism Holdings Limited (THL) is a publicly listed New Zealand corporation that owns multiple brands and businesses in the tourism industry. THL's principal holdings include:

- New Zealand tourist attractions, including Waitomo Black Water Rafting and Waitomo Glowworm Caves
- Kiwi Experience and Feejee Experience, hop-on, hop-off tourist bus services
- Four brands of holiday rental vehicles
- Ci Munro, a van-customization manufacturing facility

In 2009, THL earned $5 million in profit before interest and taxes on $170 million in revenue. It operates in New Zealand, Australia, and Fiji and has sales offices in Germany and the United Kingdom as well.

THL originated as The Helicopter Line, which provided scenic helicopter flights over New Zealand. Over the years, THL sold the helicopter business and has since owned and operated numerous tourism organizations and brands. THL continues to frequently buy and sell tourism businesses. For the current list of businesses, visit www.thlonline.com/THLBusinesses.

According to Grant Webster, THL's CEO, "THL is a house of brands and not a branded house." Thus, in the holiday rental business, THL owns and operates four different van rental brands: Maui, Britz, Backpacker, and

ExploreMore. These brands are differentiated on price; Maui is the most expensive line, whereas ExploreMore appeals to the most budget-conscious traveler. Britz is the next step down in price from Maui, and Backpacker falls between Britz and ExploreMore.

Tourism Market

In 2008, an estimated 866 million international visitors toured the world. That number is expected to grow to more than 1.6 billion by 2020, according to *Tourism Business Magazine*. In 2008, travel and tourism was the world's largest business sector, accounting for 230 million jobs and over 10 percent of the world's GDP.

In spite of these long-term growth prospects, international tourism has contracted recently, following the financial crisis of fall 2008. As of June 2009, an annual total of 1.15 million international travelers visited New Zealand, a decrease of 5 percent from the year before, and 5.5 million international travelers visited Australia, a decline of 2 percent.

According to Webster, "While we believe the long-term prospects of tourism in our traditional markets of New Zealand, Australia, and Fiji will remain strong, THL's substantial growth opportunities will be achieved by expanding to other countries, possibly the United States, or Europe."

Investment in Information Systems

THL considers information systems and technology as a core component of its business value and has invested in a variety of innovative information systems and Web 2.0 technologies. Webster speaks knowledgeably about information technologies, including SharePoint, Microsoft

Office SharePoint Services (MOSS), Microsoft Report Server, OLAP, and data mining (discussed in Chapter 9).

Because of its acquisition of multiple brands and companies, THL accumulated a disparate set of information systems, based on a variety of different technologies. These disparate technologies created excessive software maintenance activity and costs. To reduce costs and simplify IS management, THL converted its customer-facing Web sites to use Microsoft SharePoint and MOSS. "Having a single development platform reduced our maintenance expenses and enabled us to focus management attention, development, and personnel training on a single set of technologies," according to Steve Pickering, manager of Interactive Information Systems.

THL uses SharePoint not for collaboration, as discussed in Chapter 2, but rather as a development and hosting platform for sophisticated, highly interactive Web sites. You can find an example of such sophisticated capability at www.kiwiexperience.com. Click "Design Your Own Trip . . ." and the Web site will display a map of New Zealand as well as a menu of instructions. You can then select different locations, experiences, and sites from a menu, and the Web site will recommend particular tours, as shown in the right-hand pane in Figure 8-16. Visit the site to get a sense of the interactivity and sophistication of processing.

Web 2.0 technologies enable the tourism industry to disintermediate sales channels. According to the New Zealand Ministry of Tourism, in 2006 the Internet was used by 49 percent of international travelers to research travel options. That percentage has increased dramatically, and it is likely well over 50 percent today.

As with all disintermediation, when THL sells directly to the consumer it saves substantial distribution costs. To facilitate direct sales, THL actively uses Google AdWords and Google Analytics, a Google-supplied information system that enables AdWords customers to better understand how their sites are processed. THL is also experimenting with online chat, both voice and video. "A camper rental can cost $5,000 to $10,000 or more, and we believe our customers want a trusted relationship with a salesperson in order to commit," according to Webster. "We think that video online chat might give us that relationship with our customers."

Sources: Tourism Business Magazine, November 2009, p. 20; www.tourismbusinessmag.co.nz (accessed July 2010); New Zealand Ministry of Tourism, www.tourismresearch.govt.nz (accessed July 2010); Tourism of Australia, www.tourism.australia.com (accessed July 2010).

Questions

1. This case implies that the frequent acquisition and disposition of tourism brands poses problems for information systems. Summarize what you think those problems might be. Consider all five components of an information system. To what extent does standardizing on a single development platform solve those problems? Which of the five components does such standardization help the most?

2. Using Figure 3-12 (page 88) as a guide, summarize the ways in which IS gives THL a competitive advantage. Discuss each of the elements in Figure 3-12.

3. Visit www.kiwiexperience.com and click "Design Your Own Trip." Select a variety of locations in the Adrenalin, Nature, and Kiwi Culture menus. Select several locations in each category and then select a pass that fits your destinations.

   a. Evaluate this user interface. Describe its strengths and weaknesses.

   b. Evaluate the Map Instructions. Do you find these instructions to be adequate? Explain why or why not.

   c. Summarize the ways in which this site uses social networking.

   d. Explain why this site is an example of a mashup.

4. Consider the Kiwi Experience site in the context of social CRM.

   a. Identify the customer touch points.

   b. Which elements of the SLATES model does this site contain?

   c. Consider the SLATES model elements that this site does not contain. Which ones do you think might be appropriate?

   d. Explain one way to implement each of the elements you identified in part c.

   e. Describe how your recommended social CRM capabilities would help to generate a trusted relationship.

5. Does your experience working with the Kiwi Experience site cause you to believe that either it or THL is a hyper-social organization? Explain why or why not.

Figure 8-16
Interactive Map of New Zealand at www.KiwiExperience.com

Source: Used with permission of Tourism Holdings Limited.

TEACHING SUGGESTIONS

Fox Lake Country Club, Chapter 8

GOALS

- Give students a business perspective on some of the risks of social media.
- Consider options for dealing with negative user-generated content.
- Discuss change in power in control of the customer/business relationship.

BACKGROUND

1. User-generated content (UGC) is a double-edged sword. It's great to have favorable customer comments on the company's Facebook and other social media pages, but companies must also be prepared for dealing with critical feedback.

2. Jeff is over his head in dealing with negative UGC. Anne is right; just deleting critical feedback can be problematic if that deletion motivates viral anger, as happened at Nestlé. Anne is right to counsel discretion.

3. The critical comments came about because of the process problem discussed in Chapter 7. If changes to the wedding plans had not been requested, the bride wouldn't have posted this feedback. So, the cost of that process problem keeps getting bigger. However, even without this incident, Fox Lake should be prepared to deal with critical feedback.

4. Weddings are a great candidate for use of social networking groups and applications, as described in this chapter.

HOW TO GET STUDENTS INVOLVED

1. What do the students think of the bride's critical post?

   - **Was the bride's post outlandish? Was it unfair to Fox Lake?**

   - **If you were the bride, what would you post?**

   - **If you were the bride, besides Fox Lake's Facebook page, where else would you post critical feedback?**

2. How does management learn about critical UGC?

   - **The case doesn't say, but how do you suppose that Anne learned about the posting on the Facebook page?**

   - **How would Anne or Jeff learn about posts on other user review and social networking sites?**

   - **In general, how can organizations keep tabs on the feedback that they're getting?**

3. What should Fox Lake do?

   - **Do you agree that Fox Lake ought not to simply delete the critical feedback? Why or why not?**

   - **If you were the bride and you learned that your feedback had been deleted, what would you do?**

   - **In your opinion, what should Fox Lake do about this feedback?**

   - **How can companies like Fox Lake learn about negative PR on social networking/user review sites?**

   - **State a general policy that Fox Lake could use for dealing with critical UGC.**

4. Is social networking "free"?

   - **Often, you will hear people say that the beauty of sites like Facebook and Twitter is that they are free. In what respect is this true?**

   - **What indirect costs accrue to companies that have a social networking presence?**

   - **What steps should a company take before creating a social networking presence?**

   (Set up procedures and personnel to review SN sites; have a policy for responding to critical feedback; designate responsibility for monitoring and responding to and mitigating the damages of negative UGC.)

5. Social networking and UGC increase customer power.

   - **In what ways do social networking and UGC change the balance of power between vendors and customers?**

   - **Do you think that this change in power is beneficial or harmful to commerce? List reasons why it is not. List reasons why it is.**

   - **How can organizations respond to this change in power relationships?**

VIDEO

Jeff learns that maintaining a presence on social networking sites isn't free. He needs to understand that critical feedback is common and to be expected. He needs to know what his options are and be prepared. He also needs to realize that the customer base in the wedding business is, by its nature, very social. Setting up SN groups and a wedding planning SN application may be good marketing, but they have a downside.

BOTTOM LINE

■ Fox Lake needs to expect negative UGC from time to time and be prepared to productively respond to it.

■ Responses to critical feedback need to be more nuanced than "just delete it."

■ Maintaining an SN presence is not "free."

■ Social networking, and UGC in particular, give more power to the customer.

YOU BE THE GUIDE

Using the Ethics Guide: Hiding the Truth? (pages 280–281)

GOALS

- Distinguish between using social networking for fun and for business.
- Explore ethical questions about deception on business social networking sites.
- Formulate ethical principles when creating or using social networks for business

BACKGROUND AND PRESENTATION STRATEGIES

Many students are surprised and delighted to learn that the knowledge and skills they have with social networking sites can transfer over to business sites. However, there is a danger. Habits formed when using social sites may be inappropriate, harmful, or unethical when applied to a business site. The purpose of this guide is to explore the ethical dimension of that danger.

You can use this guide in conjunction with the "Human Networks Matter More" guide in Chapter 6.

In my experience, students are naïve about the dangers of social networking in business. They project their ideas about privacy and self-disclosure onto others and, at least early in their career, this attitude is unwise. Many of the people with whom they will work will be older and more conservative. Also, business is competitive in ways that social life is not. Someone who is your friend today may turn out to be your competitor tomorrow. Do students really want to give that much potential harmful ammunition away?

■ **How is social networking different in business than in private life?**

■ **Do the ethics vary between private and business use of social networking?**

SUGGESTED RESPONSES FOR DISCUSSION QUESTIONS

1. a. His actions are immature but, in my opinion, not unethical. I don't think his behavior would surprise too many people. Maybe disappoint them. I doubt that the company would have to refund money, but the event wouldn't help the company accomplish its competitive strategy.

b. I think it would be unethical for you to ask your employees to lie. It's a gray area, in my opinion, if you tie employee compensation to what they write. But, is this just another form of marketing? If you ask them to use a different email address, you're asking them to perpetuate a deception, and that seems unethical to me.

c. I'm not a lawyer, but it does not seem that the rafting company has any legal responsibility here (unless, perhaps, your employee served too much alcohol to someone). The event is horrible, but it doesn't seem to me that you or the company has any ethical or legal problem.

d. An important question. It would seem to me that because the rafting company is paying for the site, then it has the right to control the site's content, just as it would control any marketing message. I think readers of reviews on company sites should expect such censorship. I suppose, too, that it matters how you position the reviews. If you say "here are some reviews," you're probably OK. BTW, it is my understanding that not all of the "Customers who bought this also bought that" features of Web sites are honest. I understand that some companies just couple a product they'd like to sell with a popular product, regardless of the underlying purchasing patterns.

e. Yes, this happened to me. I thought it was unethical.

f. I think your actions are not only unethical, they are libelous. The difference is that the student was ostensibly offering an honest opinion; in this case, you are perpetuating a lie.

g. An interesting situation. You are not her and you are perpetuating a deception by publishing a false Facebook account. If all statements are true, and if no photos are altered, then you aren't spreading libelous material. I doubt your actions are illegal, but they are very much unethical.

2. Answer depends on the student. I'd say that any action that perpetuates a deception is unethical.

3. Answer depends on the student. I'd say that the UGC needs to be honestly presented. If UGC is being filtered, then the site should say, "This is some of our user feedback" or words to that effect. Interestingly, though, Bazaarvoice claims that user confidence in a site increases if the site contains some negative commentary. (See the Resources section at *www.bazaarvoice.com*.)

4. The major risk is loss of control. And, in order to gain control, the company may need to dedicate one or more employees or consultants to patrolling the site, leading to greater cost. Also, some damage to brand or reputation may occur before any offensive content is removed from the site.

5. Loss of control. Mitigating damages may be more difficult than for UGC, however. Once people have been connected, the sponsoring business cannot necessarily disconnect them. For example, if a group gets together on the company's site and decides that a competitor offers a better product, the company can remove those users, but they likely still know about each other and will move to the competitor. Also, it may not be possible to remove the group without serious consequences.

WRAP UP

■ It's great that your knowledge and skills of social networking transfer to the business world. However, think twice before you transfer your private site social networking ethics and behavior to a business social networking site. Your actions can impact your career, not just your social life.

Using the Guide: Blending the Personal and the Professional

(pages 288–289)

GOALS

- Explore the appropriateness of self-disclosure on a social networking site that includes business professionals.

- Understand that there are generational differences in attitudes about social networking in business.

- Consider implications of social networking on organizational hierarchies.

BACKGROUND AND PRESENTATION STRATEGIES

The students will undoubtedly have strong opinions on this topic. You shouldn't have any trouble getting a discussion going. Encourage the students to read all of the comments in this guide before expressing their own ideas.

One possibility is to encourage them to conduct the conversation using a social networking group on Facebook or Google+.

The conversation will be more interesting if it involves students and people from a different generation (parents, other faculty, local businesspeople). When I discuss this among my friends, I find very different age-related attitudes. I imagine this is true more widely.

SUGGESTED RESPONSES FOR DISCUSSION QUESTIONS

1. First, Anne has graciously allowed me to use her name in this guide. For the record, Anne is *not* a lush and is a very successful and accomplished business professional. I am grateful that she allowed me to publish this example.

   Having said that, I think it was inappropriate because, among other factors, it misrepresents Anne. And, although it might be appropriate for friends, it seems inappropriate for business colleagues to know. However, my answer was disputed by other professionals at Pearson.

2. I don't see much business value in knowing details about the social life of most of the people with whom I work. I appreciate knowing their hobbies and interests and family situation, but I don't need nor value knowing personal details. It seems unnecessary and invasive of their lives. But, I'm the curmudgeon here. You and your students may hold different opinions.

3. Given the success of Facebook and Twitter, Bob is probably wrong. It seems to me that Fox Lake has real and important needs for social networking. I think it can strongly contribute to the success of the wedding events business.

4. Again, I don't want to share my personal life with my manager's manager's manager. I wouldn't want to burden myself with wondering if every comment that I share with my friends is appropriate for senior management to read. To me, I think it makes life simpler to have friends that I trust with personal data and business associates whom I treat more carefully.

5. I think it was inappropriate for the senior manager to issue the friend request to someone so junior. The senior manager put the employee in an awkward and difficult circumstance. The employee didn't truly want to be friends with the manager, but didn't want to rebuff the manager, either. I don't know if the manager did this to demonstrate a contemporary attitude about technology or if the manger wanted another source of employee feedback. The manager learns more about what's motivating and driving junior employees, and, given the existence of an employee-based social network, this may be important (see the next question). The junior person has a chance to connect with the senior person on a more personal basis.

6. By connecting employees using their own devices, social media gives employees more power through their group. Management cannot deal with issues on a one-by-one basis. Management needs to be careful not to offend the group. In the final analysis, it means less power for management vis-à-vis employees.

7. I think people need to be much more careful about what they put on their sites if they know that professional colleagues have access to that site.

One strategy is to have one account and name for friends and another for work. However, given easy searching and the presence of photos, it may be difficult to keep the two accounts separate.

WRAP UP

■ **Think carefully about what you post on a social networking site that is accessed by professional colleagues.**

■ **The consequences of too much self-revelation on a social site is social stigma and embarrassment. The consequences if that site is read by business colleagues is loss of opportunity, loss of professional respect, lower pay raises, and even a lost job.**

■ **Use sites like Google+ and the new features of Facebook that allow you to segregate your content by friend group.**

■ **Think about it!**

YOU BE THE GUIDE

Using the Guide: Social Recruiting
(pages 290–291)

GOALS

- Encourage students to think seriously about the work they need to do to obtain the job they want.

- Help students to understand the consequences of their social media sites on potential job opportunities.

- Encourage students to use capabilities like Google+ circles to isolate and protect their private data and the data they reveal to their friends.

- Consider some of the ethical consequences of using social media data in hiring decisions.

BACKGROUND AND PRESENTATION STRATEGIES

1. Students will likely have strong thoughts and feelings about this subject. It shouldn't be hard to get the students discussing. To encourage thought, you might want to assume a strong position from an employer's standpoint. Tell the students that you'll use anything you can get to avoid hiring the wrong person. Sure, you might make a mistake or two, eliminating candidates with quick and inappropriate judgments, but hey, right now it's an employers' market. You have many quality candidates from which to choose.

2. Students most likely have already thought about this matter and probably have made up their minds on what they're going to do. The question is, are they doing it? Do they really think all of their public social media content is appropriate?

3. The discussion around question 1 could be awkward. Easy examples are that blind people ought not to work at archery ranges, and those in wheelchairs can't carry heavy boxes. But, should someone who has evidence of a drinking problem be hired as a bartender? Should someone who is grossly overweight work behind the counter at a doughnut shop? Should someone who is white

work as a bouncer at a popular black nightclub? Sticky issues.

 SUGGESTED RESPONSES FOR DISCUSSION QUESTIONS

1. See item 3.

2. Specific answers depend on the organizations the students choose. General guidelines:

   a. In general, positive criteria would be evidence that the student has been engaging in activities that are related to the job and that demonstrate that someone has trusted the student with significant responsibilities. General mature demeanor on the site.

   b. Evidence of immaturity, irresponsibility, or negativity.

   c. Most likely not.

3. Answer depends on the student.

4. The most important activity here. The student doesn't know what he or she is communicating; they're too close to it. It is important to choose someone not in their age group.

5. Answer depends on the student. Again, an important task, however.

6. Answer depends on the student.

7. Important activity.

8. Another important activity. Students need to take themselves, their need for a job, and these exercises seriously.

WRAP UP

■ Most likely, you already know what you should be doing with regard to social media content.

■ Reflect on your answers to these questions, especially question 4, and then do something about it.

■ This is important!

Business Intelligence Systems

"I'm not sure." Jeff rocks back in his chair, looks out the window, and watches two sweaty tennis players come in from their match.

"Come on, Jeff, the data's there. Just let me have it." Anne is pleading about her need for information.

"Let me be sure I get this. You want to go into our membership database and extract the names of all the members who have daughters between 20 and 30 years of age?"

"Right."

"Why not older than 30?" Jeff asks out of curiosity.

"Because they'll be less influenced by their families. But, OK, let's say 35. And I want their email addresses, too." Anne's not letting up the pressure.

"You gonna send out a blanket email? 'Hey, you've got a daughter, how about a wedding right here at Fox Lake?'"

"No, I'm going to write something quite a bit more sophisticated than that."

"What if their daughter is already married?"

"Well, that's a problem. I've got two ways to go. I can either write the promotion in a general way . . . you know, 'Fox Lake is a wonderful wedding site, blah, blah, and if your daughter or any of her friends are recently engaged, consider Fox . . .' Something like that."

"That's not too bad. I'm warming up to this idea."

"Or, I could be a lot more direct. We buy the marital data. My brother-in-law was telling me it's amazing the data you can buy about people's personal lives."

"Oh, no. We're not spying on our membership."

"He says this isn't spying. All the data is from public records. They just put all this public data together and sell it."

"Two problems: One, members are going to feel like they're being spied on. And two, that data's got to be pricey."

"Ah, now we're just talking price!"

"No, I said two problems: price and I don't like the appearance of spying."

"Look, Jeff, how will they know? I'm not gonna say, 'Hey, our records indicate you've got a pregnant, unmarried daughter, better hurry in to set up the wedding.'"

"Like, you've got 60,000 miles on your car, time for an oil change?"

"Yeah, no, I mean, no, I'm not going to say that."

"What are you going to say?"

"I don't say anything about them. It's about us! It looks like the promo went out to everyone, but, in truth, it just goes to families that we learn have unmarried, 20-something daughters. If we do it that way, I can spend a lot more on each promo piece. Maybe send out a package by courier. That'd be classy . . . with a flower for the Mom. Or . . ."

"Hey, kid, stop dreaming and get back to this meeting. If I agree, can we do this? Does anyone know how to get qualified names from the database?"

"I talked to Mike. He's got this groundskeeper guy who's a techno-whiz. Anyway, that guy knows how to query our database. In fact, he already looked at the data; we've got nearly 450 families with daughters of the right age."

"And sons? What about sons?"

"Yeah, I know. Just because the daughter's family traditionally pays . . . Maybe. But, for now, let's start with daughters."

"I have a bad feeling about this."

"Jeff, you told me to increase the wedding revenue. We're sitting on all this data. I want to make it pay. Let's do it!"

"OK. Find out what data we can buy and how much it costs. Make sure it's all public data. And, all the expenses, including any data purchases, come out of your budget. Got it?"

"I have it. I'll get going. Thanks, Jeff!" ■

Study Questions

Q1 How do organizations use business intelligence (BI) systems?

Q2 What are the three primary activities in the BI process?

Q3 How do organizations use data warehouses and data marts to acquire data?

Q4 How do organizations use typical reporting applications?

Q5 How do organizations use typical data mining applications?

Q6 What is the role of knowledge management systems?

Q7 What are the alternatives for publishing BI?

Q8 2022?

The information systems described in Chapters 7 and 8 generate enormous amounts of data. Most of these data are used for operational purposes, such as tracking orders, inventories, payables, and so forth. These operational data have a potential windfall: They contain patterns, relationships, and clusters and can be used to make predictions. This chapter considers business intelligence (BI) systems; information systems that can produce such results from organizational data, as well as from external data that can be purchased. In addition to such data, another rich source of knowledge is employees themselves. Employees come to the organization with expertise, and as they gain experience in the organization they add to that expertise. Vast amounts of collective knowledge exist in every organization's employees. How can that knowledge be shared?

This chapter begins by summarizing the ways organizations use business intelligence. It then describes the three basic activities in the BI process and illustrates those activities using the GearUp problem that was presented at the beginning of Chapter 5. We then discuss the role of data warehouses and data marts and then survey reporting, data mining, and knowledge management BI applications. After that, you'll learn alternatives for publishing the results of BI applications. We will wrap up the chapter with a 2022 observation that many people find frightening.

Q1 How Do Organizations Use Business Intelligence (BI) Systems?

Business intelligence (BI) systems are information systems that process operational and other data to identify patterns, relationships, and trends for use by business professionals and other knowledge workers. These patterns, relationships, trends, and predictions are referred to as **business intelligence**. As information systems, BI systems have the five standard components: hardware, software, data, procedures, and people. The software component of a BI system is called a **BI application**.

In the context of their day-to-day operations, organizations generate enormous amounts of data. According to McKinsey & Company, as of 2009, companies with more than 1,000 employees in "nearly all sectors in the U.S. economy had at least an average of 200 terabytes of stored data."[1] Business intelligence is buried in that data, and the function of a BI system is to extract it and make it available to those who need it.

The boundaries of BI systems are blurry. In this text, we will take the broad view shown in Figure 9-1. Source data for a BI system can be the organization's own operational data, it can be data that the organization purchases from data vendors, or it can be human knowledge. The BI application processes the data to produce business intelligence for use by knowledge workers. As you will learn, this broad definition encompasses reporting applications, data mining applications, and knowledge management applications.

As shown in Figure 9-2, business intelligence is used for all four of the collaborative tasks described in Chapter 2. Starting with the last row of this figure, business intelligence is used just for informing. At Fox Lake, management may want to know how frequently meeting rooms and other facilities are used. At the time of the analysis, the manager may not have any particular purpose in mind, but is just browsing the BI results for some future, unspecified purpose. Kelly at GearUp may just want to know

---

[1] "Big Data: The Next Frontier for Innovation, Competition, and Productivity," McKinsey & Company, May 2011. Available at www.mckinsey.com/mgi/publications/big_data/index.asp (accessed July 2011).

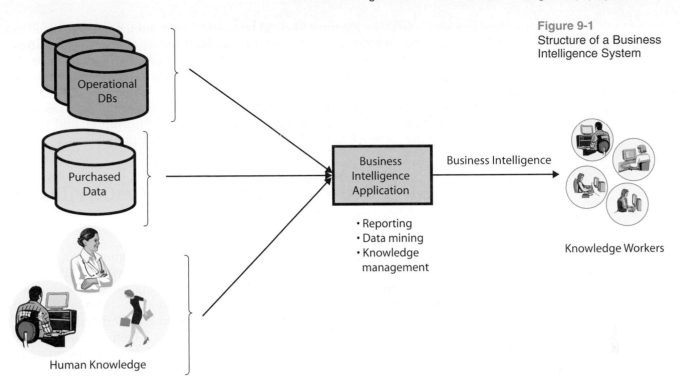

Figure 9-1
Structure of a Business
Intelligence System

how GearUp's current sales compare to the forecast; she may have no particular purpose in mind, she just wants to know "how we're doing."

Moving up a row in Figure 9-2, some managers use BI systems for decision making. At the start of this chapter, Anne wants to decide which Fox Lake members are the best targets for wedding event solicitations. Addison at GearUp may have an opportunity to purchase 10,000 soccer balls; she needs to use business intelligence to determine how many she thinks GearUp can sell prior to her negotiation with the vendor.

(By the way, some authors define BI systems as supporting decision making only, in which case they use the older term **decision support systems** as a synonym for decision-making BI systems. We take the broader view here to include all four of the tasks in Figure 9-2 and will avoid the term *decision support systems.*)

Problem solving is a third category of business intelligence use. Again, a problem is a perceived difference between what is and what ought to be. Business intelligence can be used for both sides of that definition: determining *what is* as well as *what should be.* At Fox Lake, if Jeff wants to increase membership referrals for new memberships, he'll need to know both the current referral rate and what he can realistically ask for it to become. Business intelligence can be used to determine both.

Finally, business intelligence can be used during project management. If Fox Lake decides to winterize its tennis facilities, it might use business intelligence to

Task	Fox Lake Example	GearUp Example
Project management	Winterize tennis facilities	Create GearUp Europe
Problem solving	How can we increase membership referrals?	How can we reduce operational expenses?
Deciding	Which of our members should receive a wedding solicitation?	How many soccer balls can we sell?
Informing	How much use do our facilities have in the spring and autumn seasons?	How do our actual sales compare to our sales forecast?

Figure 9-2
Example Uses of Business
Intelligence

determine which facilities are most likely to be used in the winter, how many facilities can be used in the winter, and what particular features or characteristics these facilities need to have. When GearUp decides to open its European office, it can use business intelligence to determine which gear it should sell first and which vendors to contact to obtain that gear.

As you study this figure, recall the hierarchical nature of these tasks. Deciding requires informing; problem solving requires deciding (and informing); and project management requires problem solving (and deciding [and informing]).

Q2 What Are the Three Primary Activities in the BI Process?

Figure 9-3 shows the three primary activities in the BI process: acquire data, perform analysis, and publish results. These activities directly correspond to the BI elements in Figure 9-1. **Data acquisition** is the process of obtaining, cleaning, organizing, relating, and cataloging source data. We will illustrate a simple data acquisition example for GearUp later in this question and discuss data acquisition in greater detail in Q3.

BI analysis is the process of creating business intelligence. The three fundamental categories of BI analysis are reporting, data mining, and knowledge management. We will illustrate a simple example of a reporting system for GearUp later in this question, and describe each of the three categories of BI analysis in greater detail in Q4, Q5, and Q6, respectively.

Publish results is the process of delivering business intelligence to the knowledge workers who need it. **Push publishing** delivers business intelligence to users without any request from the users; the BI results are delivered according to a schedule or as a result of an event or particular data condition. **Pull publishing** requires the user to request BI results. Publishing media include print as well as online content delivered via Web servers, specialized Web servers known as *report servers*, and BI results that are sent via automation to other programs. We will discuss these publishing options further in Q7. For now, consider a simple example of the use of business intelligence at GearUp.

Using Business Intelligence for Problem-Solving at GearUp

At the start of Chapter 5, personnel at GearUp were attempting to reduce operational expenses. Buyers and operations personnel believed that some vendors were causing GearUp lost sales and extra expense when they agreed to deliver more items than they had, resulting in GearUp having to cancel or reduce customer orders. Also, some vendors seem to have more goods damaged in shipment than others. However, other than a general notion that some vendors were especially problematic or especially not-problematic, they didn't know how serious this problem was, nor did they know

Figure 9-3
Three Primary Activities in the BI Process

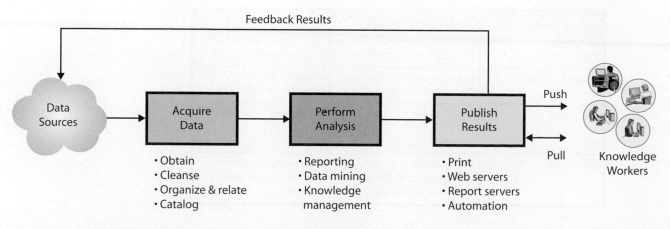

the particular pattern for each vendor. The following summarizes the process and potential problems:

1. GearUp obtains a commitment from a vendor for a maximum number of an item at a given price, say up to 10,000 soccer balls at $15 each.
2. GearUp runs a sales event for the item for which it has a commitment.
3. GearUp sells as many of the items as it can during the 3 days of each event, up to the promised amount (here 10,000).
4. At the end of the event, GearUp orders from the vendor the amount it actually sold (10,000 or fewer).
5. Normally, GearUp receives the number of items that it has ordered. However, some vendors fail to ship the full amount to which they committed or some items are damaged in shipment.
6. If GearUp receives fewer items than it orders, it must reduce the items that it ships to its customers.
7. Some customers, upon notification that the quantity they will receive will be less than the quantity they order, cancel their entire order.

Addison, a buyer, and Drew, the operations manager, met with Lucas, the IT director, who agreed to provide data that Addison and Drew could analyze. In terms of Figure 9-3, Lucas agreed to acquire data by extracting it from GearUp's customer order and shipping databases as well as its accounts payable systems and to deliver that extracted data to Addison in a Microsoft Access database.

Acquire Data

The top section of Figure 9-4 shows three of the tables in GearUp's operational database that Lucas used to produce the data extract. The *Order_Item* table contains records of items on customer orders. The columns are self-explanatory except for EventItemNumber, which is a number that identifies an item from a particular vendor that is to be sold during a particular event. Thus, for example, EventItemNumber 10 identifies the purchase of soccer balls from San Diego Sports for sales for the July 14, 2011, event.

Source tables from operational database:

Order_Item (InvoiceNumber, LineItemNumber, EventItemNumber, QuantityOrdered)

Shipment_Item (ShipmentID, EventItemNumber, InvoiceNumber, QuantityShipped)

Item_Received (PurchaseOrderNumber, DateReceived, VendorID, EventItemNumber,

QuantityReceived, QuantityAccepted)

Lucas creates the following tables in an Access BI database:

Item_Shipped (InvoiceNumber, EventItemNumber, QuantityOrdered, QuantityShipped)

Item_Not_Shipped (InvoiceNumber, EventItemNumber, QuantityOrdered)

Quantity_Received (VendorID, EventItemNumber, TotalQuantityReceived,

TotalQuantityAccepted)

Also places the Order_Item in the BI database

Addison creates a new table in the Access BI database:

Item_Summary_Data (VendorID, EventItemNumber, TotalOrdered, TotalReceived,

TotalDamaged, TotalCancelled, NetSold)

Note: Underline indicates primary key.

Figure 9-4
Tables Used for BI Analysis at GearUp

Figure 9-5
Extract of the
Item_Summary_Data

EventItemNumber	VendorID	TotalOrdered	TotalReceived	TotalDamaged	TotalCancelled	NetSold
100	1000	7500	7500	800	1500	5200
200	2000	11000	11000	0	0	11000
300	4000	10000	9000	100	1400	8500
400	1000	10500	10500	6500	200	3800
500	4000	7500	7500	400	300	6800
600	3000	27000	15000	0	17250	9750
700	2000	700	700	0	0	700
800	4000	12000	12000	0	0	12000
900	1000	6300	6300	0	0	6300
1000	2000	19800	19800	600	-600	19800
1100	3000	8000	6500	200	2000	5800
1200	4000	8000	7800	0	200	7800
1300	5000	14500	14500	0	0	14500
1400	1000	900	900	400	25	475
1500	4000	7500	7200	0	700	6800

Shipment_Item is similar to *Order_Item*, but it contains records of the items that were actually shipped to customers. If all promised items were delivered to GearUp with no damage, then the QuantityOrdered in *Order_Item* and the QuantityShipped in *Shipment_Item* will be equal.

The data in *Item_Received* is generated when vendor shipments are received at the GearUp loading dock. It shows the number of items received and the number that were accepted; the difference between the number received and the number accepted is the number that were damaged.

Lucas uses the data in these source tables to create the *Item_Shipped, Item_Not_Shipped,* and *Quantity_Received* tables shown in the middle part of Figure 9-4. He placed those tables into the data extract database along with the *Order_Item* table.

When Addison received that database, she summed quantities from the tables that Lucas had given her to create the *Item_Summary_Data* table shown in the last part of Figure 9-4. We will not explain the SQL statements she used, but you should verify that the source data given is sufficient to be able to construct it. See Using Your Knowledge Questions 1 and 2, page 333.

Analyze Data

Figure 9-5 shows sample data for the *Item_Summary_Data* table. The actual table contains more than 700 rows, but this sample will do for our purposes. TotalOrdered is the number that GearUp sold to its customers and, in turn, ordered from the vendor. TotalReceived is the number sent by the vendor, including damaged items. TotalDamaged is the number that were received in damaged condition. TotalCancelled is the number of units that customers cancelled if they were told that they would receive only a portion of their order. Finally, NetSold is the number of items that were actually shipped to the customers, after accounting for shortage, damage, and cancellation.

To determine the extent of sales lost due to short shipments or damage, Addison created an Access report (Figure 9-6) to sum data from the *Item_Summary_Data* table. SumOfTotalOrdered is the number of items ordered from each vendor. SumOfNetSold is the total number of items actually shipped to customers for each vendor.

Figure 9-6
Lost Sales Summary
Report

Lost Sales Summary

VendorID	SumOfTotalOrdered	SumOfNetSold	SumOfLostSales
5000	14500	14500	0
2000	31500	31500	0
4000	45000	41900	3100
1000	25200	15775	9425
3000	35000	15550	19450

Lost Sales Detail

VendorID	EventItemNumber	TotalOrdered	NetSold	LostSales
1000				
	100	7500	5200	2300
	400	10500	3800	6700
	900	6300	6300	0
	1400	900	475	425
2000				
	200	11000	11000	0
	700	700	700	0
	1000	19800	19800	0
3000				
	600	27000	9750	17250
	1100	8000	5800	2200
4000				
	300	10000	8500	1500
	500	7500	6800	700
	800	12000	12000	0
	1200	8000	7800	200
	1500	7500	6800	700
5000				
	1300	14500	14500	0

Figure 9-7
Lost Sales Detail
Report

SumOfLostSales is the difference between these two. From this report, she can see that vendors 5000 and 2000 have never had a shortage or quality problem. Vendor 4000 has a modest problem, but vendors 1000 and 3000 have caused numerous lost sales, either due to shortages or damaged goods. In fact, more than half of the sales of vendor 3000's items have been lost (19,450/35,000).

Drew wonders if these lost sales are due to one or two events or if they represent a recurring problem. To investigate, Addison creates the report shown in Figure 9-7. From this report, they can see that vendor 3000's problems, although substantial, are primarily due to one problem on EventItemNumber 600. However, vendor 4000 has a regular pattern of shortages or damage, or both. To learn which, Addison creates more reports, as you will see below.

But first, notice that these reports are difficult to interpret because they show vendor IDs and not vendor names. Also, Figure 9-7 shows items by EventItemNumber and not by item name and event date. Drew, as operations manager, keeps a Microsoft Excel spreadsheet that has event data, including vendor and item names. A sample of that spreadsheet is shown in Figure 9-8.

Figure 9-8
Event Data Spreadsheet

GearUpEventData

	A	B	C	D	E	F	G
1							
2		Event:	7/11/2011	Addison			
3							
4			Items:				
5							
6			Soccer Balls	General Sports	$ 12.75	$ 27.00	100
7			Orange Cones	San Diego Sports	$ 17.00	$ 35.00	200
8			Coaching Manuals	Green Lake	$ 3.50	$ 7.00	300
9							
10		Event:	7/12/2011	Julie			
11							
12			Items:				
13							
14			Mountain Tent	General Sports	$ 112.00	$ 185.00	400
15			Camp Stove	Americana Sports	$ 37.50	$ 85.00	500

Figure 9-9
Short and Damaged Shipments
Summary

Short and Damaged Summary

VendorID	SumOfItemsShort	SumOfItemsDamaged
5000	0	0
2000	0	600
1000	0	7700
4000	1500	500
3000	13500	200

Figure 9-9
Short and Damaged Shipments
Summary

If Drew's spreadsheet were in tabular format, it would be easy to import this data from Excel to Access. However, it is not, and someone must go through this spreadsheet and either put it into tabular format or extract the data from the spreadsheet and manually enter it into the Access database. This situation is typical of the kinds of data conversion and integration activities that business intelligence requires. We will leave that problem for now, however, and turn to other issues.

Drew wants to determine how many of the lost sales are due to short vendor shipments and how many are due to damage. To make that determination, Addison produces the report shown in Figure 9-9. As you can see, all of Vendor 1000's problems are caused by damage; that vendor always shipped the appropriate number. This damage could have occurred as the result of catastrophe to a single shipment, or it might be a persistent damage problem. To check out that possibility, Addison prepares the report shown in Figure 9-10. From this report, they determine that vendor 1000 has persistent damage problems. Addison and other buyers can use this knowledge when negotiating with that vendor in the future.

However, if you're reading closely, you see a problem. According to the report in Figure 9-6, vendor 2000 has never had a shortage of any type. However, the report in Figure 9-9 shows that that same vendor, 2000, had 600 units rejected as damaged. Figure 9-10 shows that those damaged items occurred with EventItem-Number 1000.

Look back to the data extraction in Figure 9-5 and you will see the problem. In the row for EventItemNumer 1000 (sixth row from the bottom), the value of TotalCancelled

Figure 9-10
Short and Damaged Shipments
Details Report

Short and Damaged Details

VendorID	EventItemNumber	ItemsShort	ItemsDamaged
1000			
	100	0	800
	400	0	6500
	900	0	0
	1400	0	400
2000			
	200	0	0
	700	0	0
	1000	0	600
3000			
	600	12000	0
	1100	1500	200
4000			
	300	1000	100
	500	0	400
	800	0	0
	1200	200	0
	1500	300	0
5000			
	1300	0	0

is shown to be –600. This result, an error, occurred because the operational data showed that 19,800 units were ordered and 19,800 units were sold. However, the operational data also showed that 600 units were damaged. Clearly, something is wrong, somewhere. It could be due to a keying mistake by someone on the receiving dock, it could be that the vendor subsequently shipped replacement items that were not charged and therefore did not appear in the accounts payable database that Lucas queried, or it could be due to some other reason.

Such a discrepancy is not unusual for BI analyses. When data are integrated from several or many different sources, the resulting collection is frequently inconsistent. The only safeguard against inaccurate analyses from such inconsistent data is for the analysts and knowledge workers to know that such inconsistencies are possible, to be on the lookout for them, and to apply a critical eye to BI results.

Publish Results

Addison, Drew, and Lucas would use a process similar to that just discussed to finish their analysis. They would likely add costs to the data they've already gathered and analyze it so as to produce an average cost per item for each vendor and other similar results. The particulars are not important here; just realize they would continue in a similar vein until they were finished.

At that point, according to the process summary in Figure 9-3, they would publish their results. Several possibilities exist:

- Print and distribute the results via email or a collaboration tool.
- Publish via a Web server or SharePoint.
- Publish on a BI server.
- Automate the results via a Web service.

We will discuss these alternatives in more detail in Q7. For now, just realize that GearUp would choose among these alternatives according to its needs. If the business intelligence is only created to provide guidance for buyers, Addison and Drew might be content just to print their results and email them to buyers or share them using a collaboration tool. As an alternative, they could also produce the report in HTML and place it on a Web server. As an extension to that option, they could use SharePoint to publish the results. Although we didn't discuss them in Chapter 2, SharePoint has extensive features and functions for BI reporting. Addison and Drew could integrate their analyses with these features and functions so that users could go to a SharePoint site for the latest data. Fourth, they could publish via a BI server, which is a Web server application that is specialized for publishing BI results. Finally, Lucas might assign a programmer in his department to create a Web service that would make it possible for other programs to obtain the BI results programmatically. Most likely, for their situation, they will print the results and email them or share them via a collaboration tool.

With this example in mind, we will now discuss each of the elements of Figure 9-3 in greater detail.

Q3 How Do Organizations Use Data Warehouses and Data Marts to Acquire Data?

Although it is possible to create basic reports and perform simple analyses from operational data, this course is not usually recommended. For reasons of security and control, IS professionals do not want business analysts like Addison processing operational data. If Addison makes an error, that error could cause a serious disruption in GearUp's operations. Also, operational data is structured for fast and reliable transaction processing. It is seldom structured in a way that readily supports BI

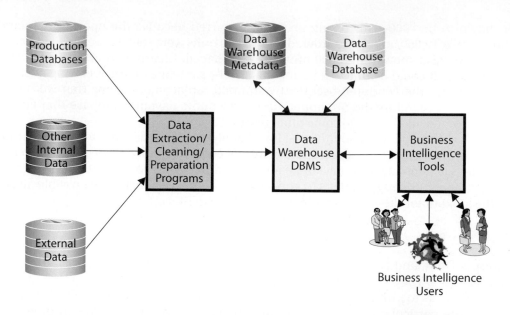

analysis. Finally, BI analyses can require considerable processing; placing BI applications on operational servers can dramatically reduce system performance.

For these reasons, most organizations extract operational data for BI processing. For a small organization like GearUp, the extraction may be as simple as an Access database. Larger organizations, however, typically create and staff a group of people who manage and run a **data warehouse**, which is a facility for managing an organization's BI data. The functions of a data warehouse are to:

- Obtain data
- Cleanse data
- Organize and relate data
- Catalog data

Figure 9-11 shows the components of a data warehouse. Programs read production and other data and extract, clean, and prepare that data for BI processing. The prepared data are stored in a data warehouse database using a data warehouse DBMS, which can be different from the organization's operational DBMS. For example, an organization might use Oracle for its operational processing, but use SQL Server for its data warehouse. Other organizations use SQL Server for operational processing, but use DBMSs from statistical package vendors such as SAS or SPSS in the data warehouse.

Data warehouses include data that are purchased from outside sources. The purchase of data about other companies is not unusual or particularly concerning from a privacy standpoint. However, some companies, like Fox Lake, might choose to buy personal, consumer data (like marital status) from data vendors like Acxiom Corporation. Figure 9-12 lists some of the consumer data

- Name, address, phone
- Age
- Gender
- Ethnicity
- Religion
- Income
- Education
- Voter registration
- Home ownership
- Vehicles

- Magazine subscriptions
- Hobbies
- Catalog orders
- Marital status, life stage
- Height, weight, hair and eye color
- Spouse name, birth date
- Children's names and birth dates

that can be readily purchased. An amazing (and from a privacy standpoint, frightening) amount of data is available.

Metadata concerning the data—its source, its format, its assumptions and constraints, and other facts about the data—is kept in a data warehouse metadata database. The data warehouse DBMS extracts and provides data to BI applications.

Problems with Operational Data

Most operational and purchased data have problems that inhibit their usefulness for business intelligence. Figure 9-13 lists the major problem categories. First, although data that are critical for successful operations must be complete and accurate, data that are only marginally necessary need not be. For example, some systems gather demographic data in the ordering process. But, because such data are not needed to fill, ship, and bill orders, their quality suffers.

Problematic data are termed dirty data. Examples are a value of B for customer gender and of 213 for customer age. Other examples are a value of 999–999–9999 for a U.S. phone number, a part color of gren, and an email address of WhyMe@Guess WhoIAM.org. All of these values can be problematic for BI purposes.

Purchased data often contain missing elements. Most data vendors state the percentage of missing values for each attribute in the data they sell. An organization buys such data because for some uses some data are better than no data at all. This is especially true for data items whose values are difficult to obtain, such as Number of Adults in Household, Household Income, Dwelling Type, and Education of Primary Income Earner. However, care is required here because for some BI applications a few missing or erroneous data points can seriously bias the analysis.

Inconsistent data, the third problem in Figure 9-13, is particularly common for data that have been gathered over time. When an area code changes, for example, the phone number for a given customer before the change will not match the customer's number after the change. Likewise, part codes can change, as can sales territories. Before such data can be used, they must be recoded for consistency over the period of the study.

Some data inconsistencies occur from the nature of the business activity. Consider a Web-based order-entry system used by customers worldwide. When the Web server records the time of order, which time zone does it use? The server's system clock time is irrelevant to an analysis of customer behavior. Coordinated Universal Time (formerly called Greenwich Mean Time) is also meaningless. Somehow, Web server time must be adjusted to the time zone of the customer.

Another problem is nonintegrated data. A particular BI analysis might require data from an ERP system, an e-commerce system, and a social networking application. Analysts may wish to integrate that organizational data with purchased consumer data. Such a data collection will likely have relationships that are not represented in primary key/foreign key relationships. It is the function of personnel in the data warehouse to integrate such data, somehow.

Data can also have the wrong **granularity**, a term that refers to the level of detail represented by the data. Granularity can be too fine or too coarse. For the former, suppose we want to analyze the placement of graphics and controls on an order-entry Web page. It is possible to capture the customers' clicking behavior in what is termed

- Dirty data
- Missing values
- Inconsistent data
- Data not integrated
- Wrong granularity
  - Too fine
  - Not fine enough
- Too much data
  - Too many attributes
  - Too many data points

Figure 9-13
Possible Problems with Source Data

clickstream data. Those data, however, include everything the customer does at the Web site. In the middle of the order stream are data for clicks on the news, email, instant chat, and a weather check. Although all of that data may be useful for a study of consumer browsing behavior, it will be overwhelming if all we want to know is how customers respond to an ad located differently on the screen. To proceed, the data analysts must throw away millions and millions of clicks.

Data can also be too coarse. For example, a file of regional sales totals cannot be used to investigate the sales in a particular store in a region, and total sales for a store cannot be used to determine the sales of particular items within a store. Instead, we need to obtain data that is fine enough for the lowest-level report we want to produce.

In general, it is better to have too fine a granularity than too coarse. If the granularity is too fine, the data can be made coarser by summing and combining. Only analysts' labor and computer processing are required. If the granularity is too coarse, however, there is no way to separate the data into constituent parts.

The final problem listed in Figure 9-13 is to have too much data. As shown in the figure, we can have either too many attributes or too many data points. Think back to the discussion of tables in Chapter 5. We can have too many columns or too many rows.

Consider the first problem: too many attributes. Suppose we want to know the factors that influence how customers respond to a promotion. If we combine internal customer data with purchased customer data, we will have more than a hundred different attributes to consider. How do we select among them? Because of a phenomenon called the *curse of dimensionality*, the more attributes there are, the easier it is to build a model that fits the sample data but that is worthless as a predictor. There are other good reasons for reducing the number of attributes, and one of the major activities in data mining concerns efficient and effective ways of selecting attributes.

The second way to have too much data is to have too many data points—too many rows of data. Suppose we want to analyze clickstream data on CNN.com. How many clicks does that site receive per month? Millions upon millions! In order to meaningfully analyze such data we need to reduce the amount of data. One good solution to this problem is statistical sampling. Organizations should not be reluctant to sample data in such situations.

Data Warehouses Versus Data Marts

To understand the difference between data warehouses and data marts, think of a data warehouse as a distributor in a supply chain. The data warehouse takes data from the data manufacturers (operational systems and purchased data), cleans and processes the data, and locates the data on the shelves, so to speak, of the data warehouse. The people who work with a data warehouse are experts at data management, data cleaning, data transformation, data relationships and the like. However, they are not usually experts in a given business function.

A data mart is a data collection, smaller than the data warehouse, that addresses the needs of a particular department or functional area of the business. If the data warehouse is the distributor in a supply chain, then a data mart is like a retail store in a supply chain. Users in the data mart obtain data that pertain to a particular business function from the data warehouse. Such users do not have the data management expertise that data warehouse employees have, but they are knowledgeable analysts for a given business function.

Figure 9-14 illustrates these relationships. The data warehouse takes data from the data producers and distributes the data to three data marts. One data mart is used to analyze clickstream data for the purpose of designing Web pages. A second analyzes store sales data and determines which products tend to be purchased together. This information is used to train salespeople on the best way to up-sell to customers. The third data mart is used to analyze customer order data for the

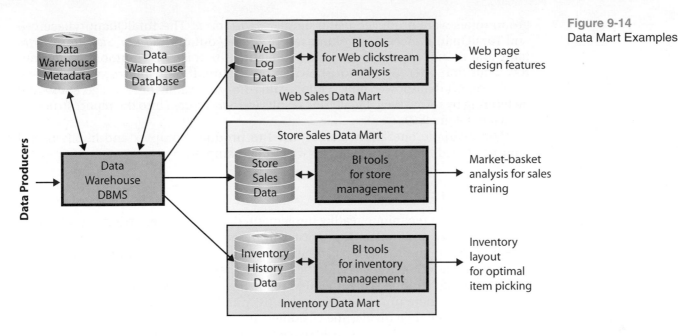

Figure 9-14
Data Mart Examples

purpose of reducing labor for item picking from the warehouse. A company like Amazon.com, for example, goes to great lengths to organize its warehouses to reduce picking expenses.

As you can imagine, it is expensive to create, staff, and operate data warehouses and data marts. Only large organizations with deep pockets can afford to operate a system like that shown in Figure 9-11. Smaller organizations like GearUp operate subsets of this system, but they must find ways to solve the basic problems that data warehouses solve, even if those ways are informal.

Q4 How Do Organizations Use Typical Reporting Applications?

A **reporting application** is a BI application that inputs data from one or more sources and applies reporting operations to that data to produce business intelligence. We will first summarize reporting operations and then illustrate two important reporting applications: RFM analysis and OLAP.

Basic Reporting Operations

Reporting applications produce business intelligence using five basic operations:

- Sorting
- Filtering
- Grouping
- Calculating
- Formatting

None of these operations is particularly sophisticated; they can all be accomplished using SQL and basic HTML or a simple report writing tool.

Addison at GearUp used Access to apply all five of these operations in the preparation of the reports discussed in Q2. Examine, for example, Figure 9-7 (page 301). The results are *sorted* and *grouped* by VendorID and, within a vendor, *sorted* in decreasing order by value of SalesShortage. The value of SalesShortage as well as the group totals were produced using simple *calculations*. The TotalQuantityReceived and TotalQuantityAccepted columns were *filtered* out of the *Item_Summary_Data* table and do not appear in the report in Figure 9-6. It is also common to filter out rows, but that operation is not shown in this figure. If Addison were to prepare a similar report that showed only vendors with a nonzero value for Shortage, she would be filtering by row as well. Finally, the results were *formatted* into the report structure shown in Figure 9-7.

These simple operations can be used to produce complex and highly useful reports. Consider RFM and OLAP as two prime examples.

RFM Analysis

RFM analysis, a technique readily implemented with basic reporting operations, is used to analyze and rank customers according to their purchasing patterns.[2] RFM considers how *recently* (R) a customer has ordered, how *frequently* (F) a customer ordered, and how much *money* (M) the customer has spent.

To produce an RFM score, the RFM reporting tool first sorts customer purchase records by the date of their most recent (R) purchase. In a common form of this analysis, the tool then divides the customers into five groups and gives customers in each group a score of 1 to 5. The 20 percent of the customers having the most recent orders are given an R score of 1, the 20 percent of the customers having the next most recent orders are given an R score of 2, and so forth, down to the last 20 percent, who are given an R score of 5.

The tool then re-sorts the customers on the basis of how frequently they order. The 20 percent of the customers who order most frequently are given an F score of 1, the next 20 percent of most frequently ordering customers are given a score of 2, and so forth, down to the least frequently ordering customers, who are given an F score of 5.

Finally, the tool sorts the customers again according to the amount spent on their orders. The 20 percent who have ordered the most expensive items are given an M score of 1, the next 20 percent are given an M score of 2, and so forth, down to the 20 percent who spend the least, who are given an M score of 5.

Figure 9-15 shows sample RFM results. The first customer, Big 7 Sports, has ordered recently and orders frequently. Big 7 Sports's M score of 3 indicates, however, that it does not order the most expensive goods. From these scores, the sales team can conclude that Big 7 Sports is a good, regular customer, and that they should attempt to up-sell more-expensive goods to Big 7 Sports.

The second customer in Figure 9-15 could represent a problem. St. Louis Soccer Club has not ordered in some time, but when it did order in the past it ordered

Figure 9-15
Example RFM Scores

Customer	RFM Score		
Big 7 Sports	1	1	3
St. Louis Soccer Club	5	1	1
Miami Municipal	5	4	5
Central Colorado State	3	3	3

---

[2] Arthur Middleton Hughes, "Boosting Response with RFM," *Marketing Tools*, May 1996. See also http://dbmarketing.com.

frequently, and its orders were of the highest monetary value. This data suggests that St. Louis Soccer Club might have taken its business to another vendor. Someone from the sales team should contact this customer immediately.

No one on the sales team should even think about the third customer, Miami Municipal. This company has not ordered for some time; it did not order frequently; and, when it did order, it bought the least-expensive items, and not many of them. Let Miami Municipal go to the competition; the loss will be minimal.

The last customer, Central Colorado State, is right in the middle. Central Colorado State is an OK customer, but probably no one in sales should spend much time with it. Perhaps sales can set up an automated contact system or use the Central Colorado State account as a training exercise for an eager departmental assistant or intern.

Online Analytical Processing

Online analytical processing (OLAP), a second type of reporting application, is more generic than RFM. OLAP provides the ability to sum, count, average, and perform other simple arithmetic operations on groups of data. The remarkable characteristic of OLAP reports is that they are dynamic. The viewer of the report can change the report's format, hence the term *online*.

An OLAP report has measures and dimensions. A **measure** is the data item of interest. It is the item that is to be summed or averaged or otherwise processed in the OLAP report. Total sales, average sales, and average cost are examples of measures. A **dimension** is a characteristic of a measure. Purchase date, customer type, customer location, and sales region are all examples of dimensions.

Figure 9-16 shows a typical OLAP report. Here, the measure is *Net Store Sales*, and the dimensions are *Product Family* and *Store Type*. This report shows how net store sales vary by product family and store type. Stores of type *Supermarket* sold a net of $36,189 worth of nonconsumable goods, for example.

A presentation like that in Figure 9-16 is often called an **OLAP cube**, or sometimes simply a *cube*. The reason for this term is that some software products show these displays using three axes, like a cube in geometry. The origin of the term is unimportant here, however. Just know that an *OLAP cube* and an *OLAP report* are the same thing.

The OLAP report in Figure 9-16 was generated by Microsoft SQL Server Analysis Services and is displayed in an Excel pivot table. The data were taken from a sample instructional database, called Food Mart, that is provided with SQL Server.

It is possible to display OLAP cubes in many ways besides with Excel. Some third-party vendors provide more extensive graphical displays. For more information about such products, check for OLAP vendors and products at the Data Warehousing Review at http://dwreview.com/OLAP/index.html.

Figure 9-16
Example Grocery Sales OLAP Report

	A	B	C	D	E	F	G
1							
2							
3	Store Sales Net	Store Type ▼					
4	Product Family ▼	Deluxe Supermarket	Gourmet Supermarket	Mid-Size Grocery	Small Grocery	Supermarket	Grand Total
5	Drink	$8,119.05	$2,392.83	$1,409.50	$685.89	$16,751.71	$29,358.98
6	Food	$70,276.11	$20,026.18	$10,392.19	$6,109.72	$138,960.67	$245,764.87
7	Non-Consumable	$18,884.24	$5,064.79	$2,813.73	$1,534.90	$36,189.40	$64,487.05
8	Grand Total	$97,279.40	$27,483.80	$14,615.42	$8,330.51	$191,901.77	$339,610.90

	A	B	C	D	E	F	G	H	I
1									
2									
3	Store Sales Net			Store Type ▼					
4	Product Family ▼	Store ▼	Store State	Deluxe Superma	Gourmet Supermar	Mid-Size Groce	Small Grocery	Supermarket	Grand Total
5	Drink	USA	CA		$2,392.83		$227.38	$5,920.76	$8,540.97
6			OR	$4,438.49				$2,862.45	$7,300.94
7			WA	$3,680.56		$1,409.50	$458.51	$7,968.50	$13,517.07
8		USA Total		$8,119.05	$2,392.83	$1,409.50	$685.89	$16,751.71	$29,358.98
9	Drink Total			$8,119.05	$2,392.83	$1,409.50	$685.89	$16,751.71	$29,358.98
10	Food	USA	CA		$20,026.18		$1,960.53	$47,226.11	$69,212.82
11			OR	$37,778.35				$23,818.87	$61,597.22
12			WA	$32,497.76		$10,392.19	$4,149.19	$67,915.69	$114,954.83
13		USA Total		$70,276.11	$20,026.18	$10,392.19	$6,109.72	$138,960.67	$245,764.87
14	Food Total			$70,276.11	$20,026.18	$10,392.19	$6,109.72	$138,960.67	$245,764.87
15	Non-Consumable	USA	CA		$5,064.79		$474.35	$12,344.49	$17,883.63
16			OR	$10,177.89				$6,428.53	$16,606.41
17			WA	$8,706.36		$2,813.73	$1,060.54	$17,416.38	$29,997.01
18		USA Total		$18,884.24	$5,064.79	$2,813.73	$1,534.90	$36,189.40	$64,487.05
19	Non-Consumable Total			$18,884.24	$5,064.79	$2,813.73	$1,534.90	$36,189.40	$64,487.05
20	Grand Total			$97,279.40	$27,483.80	$14,615.42	$8,330.51	$191,901.77	$339,610.90

Figure 9-17
Example of Expanded Grocery
Sales OLAP Report

As stated earlier, the distinguishing characteristic of an OLAP report is that the user can alter the format of the report. Figure 9-17 shows such an alteration. Here, the user added another dimension, *Store Country* and *Store State*, to the horizontal display. Product-family sales are now broken out by store location. Observe that the sample data only includes stores in the United States, and only in the western states of California, Oregon, and Washington.

With an OLAP report, it is possible to **drill down** into the data. This term means to further divide the data into more detail. In Figure 9-18, for example, the user has drilled down into the stores located in California; the OLAP report now shows sales data for the four cities in California that have stores.

Notice another difference between Figures 9-17 and 9-18. The user has not only drilled down, she has also changed the order of the dimensions. Figure 9-17 shows *Product Family* and then store location within *Product Family*. Figure 9-18 shows store location and then *Product Family* within store location.

Both displays are valid and useful, depending on the user's perspective. A product manager might like to see product families first and then store location data. A sales manager might like to see store locations first and then product data. OLAP reports provide both perspectives, and the user can switch between them while viewing the report.

Unfortunately, all of this flexibility comes at a cost. If the database is large, doing the necessary calculating, grouping, and sorting for such dynamic displays will require substantial computing power. Although standard commercial DBMS products do have the features and functions required to create OLAP reports, they are not designed for such work. They are designed, instead, to provide rapid response to transaction-processing applications, such as order entry or manufacturing planning. Consequently, some organizations tune DBMS products on dedicated servers for this purpose. Today, many OLAP servers are being moved to the cloud.

Store Sales Net				Store Type ▼					
Store Country ▼	Store Sta	Store City	Product Family ▼	Deluxe Super	Gourmet Supermar	Mid-Size Groce	Small Grocery	Supermarket	Grand Total
USA	CA	Beverly Hills	Drink		$2,392.83				$2,392.83
			Food		$20,026.18				$20,026.18
			Non-Consumable		$5,064.79				$5,064.79
		Beverly Hills Total			$27,483.80				$27,483.80
		Los Angeles	Drink					$2,870.33	$2,870.33
			Food					$23,598.28	$23,598.28
			Non-Consumable					$6,305.14	$6,305.14
		Los Angeles Total						$32,773.74	$32,773.74
		San Diego	Drink					$3,050.43	$3,050.43
			Food					$23,627.83	$23,627.83
			Non-Consumable					$6,039.34	$6,039.34
		San Diego Total						$32,717.61	$32,717.61
		San Francisco	Drink				$227.38		$227.38
			Food				$1,960.53		$1,960.53
			Non-Consumable				$474.35		$474.35
		San Francisco Total					$2,662.26		$2,662.26
	CA Total				$27,483.80		$2,662.26	$65,491.35	$95,637.41
	OR		Drink	$4,438.49				$2,862.45	$7,300.94
			Food	$37,778.35				$23,818.87	$61,597.22
			Non-Consumable	$10,177.89				$6,428.53	$16,606.41
	OR Total			$52,394.72				$33,109.85	$85,504.57
	WA		Drink	$3,680.56		$1,409.50	$458.51	$7,968.50	$13,517.07
			Food	$32,497.76		$10,392.19	$4,149.19	$67,915.69	$114,954.83
			Non-Consumable	$8,706.36		$2,813.73	$1,060.54	$17,416.38	$29,997.01
	WA Total			$44,884.68		$14,615.42	$5,668.24	$93,300.57	$158,468.91
USA Total				$97,279.40	$27,483.80	$14,615.42	$8,330.51	$191,901.77	$339,610.90
Grand Total				$97,279.40	$27,483.80	$14,615.42	$8,330.51	$191,901.77	$339,610.90

Figure 9-18
Example of Drilling Down into Expanded Grocery Sales OLAP Report

313

Using MIS InClass 9 *A Group Exercise*

Do You Have a Club Card?

Sources: Shutterstock.com and Superstock.

A **data aggregator** is a company that obtains data from public and private sources and stores, combines, and publishes it in sophisticated ways. When you use your grocery store club card, the data from your grocery shopping trip are sold to a data aggregator. Credit card data, credit data, public tax records, insurance records, product warranty card data, voter registration data, and hundreds of other types of data are sold to aggregators.

Not all of the data are identified in the same way (or, in terms of Chapter 5, not all of it has the same primary key). But, using a combination of phone number, address, email address, name, and other partially identifying data, such companies can integrate that disparate data into an integrated, coherent whole. They then query, report, and mine the integrated data to form detailed descriptions about companies, communities, zip codes, households, and individuals.

As you will learn in Chapter 12, laws limit the types of data that federal and other governmental agencies can acquire and store. There are also some legal safeguards on data maintained by credit bureaus and medical facilities. However, no such laws limit data storage by most companies (nor are there laws that prohibit governmental agencies from buying results from data aggregators).

Acxiom Corporation, a data aggregator with $1.2 billion in sales in 2009, has been described as the "biggest company you never heard of." Visit www.acxiom.com and complete the following tasks:

1. Navigate the Acxiom Web site and make a list of 10 different products that Acxiom provides.

2. Describe Acxiom's top customers.

3. Examine your answers to items 1 and 2 and describe, in general terms, the kinds of data that Acxiom must collect to be able to provide these products to its customers.

4. In what ways might companies like Acxiom need to limit their marketing so as to avoid a privacy outcry from the public?

5. According to the Web site, what is Acxiom's privacy policy? Are you reassured by its policy? Why or why not?

6. Should there be laws governing companies like Acxiom? Why or why not?

7. Prepare a 3-minute presentation of your answers to items 3, 4, 5, and 6. Give your presentation to the rest of the class.

Q5 How Do Organizations Use Typical Data Mining Applications?

Data mining and other business intelligence systems are useful, but they are not without problems, as discussed in the Guide on pages 330–331.

Data mining is the application of statistical techniques to find patterns and relationships among data for classification and prediction. As shown in Figure 9-19, data mining resulted from a convergence of disciplines. Data mining techniques emerged from statistics and mathematics and from artificial intelligence and machine-learning fields in computer science. As a result, data mining terminology is an odd blend of terms from these different disciplines. Sometimes people use the term *knowledge discovery in databases (KDD)* as a synonym for data mining.

Data mining techniques take advantage of developments in data management for processing the enormous databases that have emerged in the last 10 years. Of course, these data would not have been generated were it not for fast and cheap computers, and without such computers the new techniques would be impossible to compute.

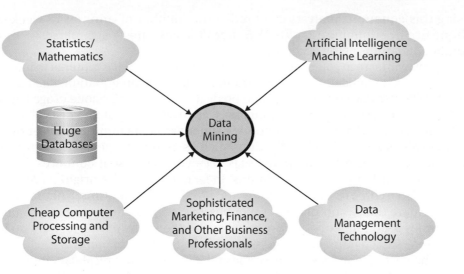

Figure 9-19
Data Mining Origins

Most data mining techniques are sophisticated, and many are difficult to use well. Such techniques are valuable to organizations, however, and some business professionals, especially those in finance and marketing, have become expert in their use. In fact, today there are many interesting and rewarding careers for business professionals who are knowledgeable about data mining techniques.

Data mining techniques fall into two broad categories: unsupervised and supervised. We explain both types in the following sections.

Unsupervised Data Mining

With **unsupervised data mining**, analysts do not create a model or hypothesis before running the analysis. Instead, they apply a data mining application to the data and observe the results. With this method, analysts create hypotheses *after the analysis*, in order to explain the patterns found.

One common unsupervised technique is **cluster analysis**. With it, statistical techniques identify groups of entities that have similar characteristics. A common use for cluster analysis is to find groups of similar customers from customer order and demographic data.

For example, suppose a cluster analysis finds two very different customer groups: One group has an average age of 33, owns three Android phones, two iPads, has an expensive home entertainment system, drives a Lexus SUV, and tends to buy expensive children's play equipment. The second group has an average age of 64, owns Arizona vacation property, plays golf, and buys expensive wines. Suppose the analysis also finds that both groups buy designer children's clothing.

These findings are obtained solely by data analysis. There is no prior model about the patterns and relationships that exist. It is up to the analyst to form hypotheses, after the fact, to explain why two such different groups are both buying designer children's clothes.

Many problems arise with classification schemes, especially those that classify people. The Ethics Guide on pages 318–319 examines some of these problems.

Supervised Data Mining

With **supervised data mining**, data miners develop a model *prior to the analysis* and apply statistical techniques to data to estimate parameters of the model. For example, suppose marketing experts in a communications company believe that cell phone usage on weekends is determined by the age of the customer and the number of months the customer has had the cell phone account. A data mining analyst would then run an analysis that estimates the impact of customer and account age.

One such analysis, which measures the impact of a set of variables on another variable, is called a **regression analysis**. A sample result for the cell phone example is:

$$CellphoneWeekendMinutes = 12 + (17.5 \times CustomerAge) + (23.7 \times NumberMonths\ OfAccount)$$

Using this equation, analysts can predict the number of minutes of weekend cell phone use by summing 12, plus 17.5 times the customer's age, plus 23.7 times the number of months of the account.

As you will learn in your statistics classes, considerable skill is required to interpret the quality of such a model. The regression tool will create an equation, such as the one shown. Whether that equation is a good predictor of future cell phone usage depends on statistical factors, such as *t* values, confidence intervals, and related statistical techniques.

Neural networks are another popular supervised data mining application used to predict values and make classifications such as "good prospect" or "poor prospect" customers. The term *neural networks* is deceiving because it connotes a biological process similar to that in animal brains. In fact, although the original *idea* of neural nets may have come from the anatomy and physiology of neurons, a neural network is nothing more than a complicated set of possibly nonlinear equations. Explaining the techniques used for neural networks is beyond the scope of this text. If you want to learn more, search http://kdnuggets.com for the term *neural network*.

In the next sections, we will describe and illustrate two typical data mining tools—market-basket analysis and decision trees—and show applications of those techniques. From this discussion, you can gain a sense of the nature of data mining. These examples should give you, a future manager, a sense of the possibilities of data mining techniques. You will need additional coursework in statistics, data management, marketing, and finance, however, before you will be able to perform such analyses yourself.

Market-Basket Analysis

Suppose you run a dive shop, and one day you realize that one of your salespeople is much better at up-selling to your customers. Any of your sales associates can fill a customer's order, but this one salesperson is especially good at selling customers items *in addition* to those for which they ask. One day, you ask him how he does it.

"It's simple," he says. "I just ask myself what is the next product they would want to buy. If someone buys a dive computer, I don't try to sell her fins. If she's buying a dive computer, she's already a diver and she already has fins. But, these dive computer displays are hard to read. A better mask makes it easier to read the display and get the full benefit from the dive computer."

A **market-basket analysis** is an unsupervised data mining technique for determining sales patterns. A market-basket analysis shows the products that customers tend to buy together. In marketing transactions, the fact that customers who buy product X also buy product Y creates a **cross-selling** opportunity; that is, "If they're buying X, sell them Y" or "If they're buying Y, sell them X."

Figure 9-20 shows hypothetical sales data from 400 sales transactions at a dive shop. The first row of numbers under each column is the total number of times an item was sold. For example, the 270 in the first row of Mask means that 270 of the 400 transactions included masks. The 90 under Dive Computer means that 90 of the 400 transactions included dive computers.

We can use the numbers in the first row to estimate the probability that a customer will purchase an item. Because 270 of the 400 transactions were masks, we can estimate the probability that a customer will buy a mask to be 270/400, or .675.

In market-basket terminology, **support** is the probability that two items will be purchased together. To estimate that probability, we examine sales transactions and count the number of times that two items occurred in the same transaction. For the data in Figure 9-20, fins and masks appeared together 250 times, and thus the support for fins and a mask is 250/400, or .625. Similarly, the support for fins and weights is 20/400, or .05.

These data are interesting by themselves, but we can refine the analysis by taking another step and considering additional probabilities. For example, what proportion of the customers who bought a mask also bought fins? Masks were purchased 270 times, and of those individuals who bought masks, 250 also bought fins. Thus, given that a customer bought a mask, we can estimate the probability that he or she will buy fins to be 250/270, or .926. In market-basket terminology such a conditional probability estimate is called the **confidence**.

	Mask	Tank	Fins	Weights	Dive Computer
Mask	270	10	250	10	90
Tank	10	200	40	130	30
Fins	250	40	280	20	20
Weights	10	130	20	130	10
Dive Computer	90	30	20	10	120
	Support				
Num Trans	400				
Mask	0.675	0.025	0.625	0.025	0.225
Tank	0.025	0.5	0.1	0.325	0.075
Fins	0.625	0.1	0.7	0.05	0.05
Weights	0.025	0.325	0.05	0.325	0.025
Dive Computer	0.225	0.075	0.05	0.025	0.3
	Confidence				
Mask	1	0.05	0.892857143	0.076923077	0.75
Tank	0.037037037	1	0.142857143	1	0.25
Fins	0.925925926	0.2	1	0.153846154	0.166666667
Weights	0.037037037	0.65	0.071428571	1	0.083333333
Dive Computer	0.333333333	0.15	0.071428571	0.076923077	1
	Lift (Improvement)				
Mask		0.074074074	1.322751323	0.113960114	1.111111111
Tank	0.074074074		0.285714286	2	0.5
Fins	1.322751323	0.285714286		0.21978022	0.238095238
Weights	0.113960114	2	0.21978022		0.256410256
Dive Computer	1.111111111	0.5	0.238095238	0.256410256	

Figure 9-20
Market-Basket Analysis at a Dive Shop

Reflect on the meaning of this confidence value. The likelihood of someone walking in the door and buying fins is 250/400, or .625. But the likelihood of someone buying fins, given that he or she bought a mask, is .926. Thus, if someone buys a mask, the likelihood that he or she will also buy fins increases substantially, from .625 to .926. Thus, all sales personnel should be trained to try to sell fins to anyone buying a mask.

Now consider dive computers and fins. Of the 400 transactions, fins were sold 250 times, so the probability that someone walks into the store and buys fins is .625. But of the 90 purchases of dive computers, only 20 appeared with fins. So the likelihood of someone buying fins, given he or she bought a dive computer, is 20/90, or .1566. Thus, when someone buys a dive computer, the likelihood that she will also buy fins falls from .625 to .1566.

The ratio of confidence to the base probability of buying an item is called **lift**. Lift shows how much the base probability increases or decreases when other products are purchased. The lift of fins and a mask is the confidence of fins given a mask, divided by the base probability of fins. In Figure 9-20, the lift of fins and a mask is .926/.625, or 1.32. Thus, the likelihood that people buy fins when they buy a mask increases by 32 percent. Surprisingly, it turns out that the lift of fins and a mask is the same as the lift of a mask and fins. Both are 1.32.

We need to be careful here, though, because this analysis only shows shopping carts with two items. We cannot say from this data what the likelihood is that customers, given that they bought a mask, will buy both weights and fins. To assess that probability, we need to analyze shopping carts with three items. This statement illustrates, once again, that we need to know what problem we're solving before we start to build the information system to mine the data. The problem definition will help us decide if we need to analyze three-item, four-item, or some other sized shopping cart.

Many organizations are benefiting from market-basket analysis today. You can expect that this technique will become a standard CRM analysis during your career.

Ethics Guide

The Ethics of Classification

Classification is a useful human skill. Imagine walking into your favorite clothing store and seeing all of the clothes piled together on a center table. T-shirts and pants and socks intermingle, with the sizes mixed up. Retail stores organized like this would not survive, nor would distributors or manufacturers who managed their inventories this way. Sorting and classifying are necessary, important, and essential activities. But those activities can also be dangerous.

Serious ethical issues arise when we classify people. What makes someone a good or bad "prospect"? If we're talking about classifying customers in order to prioritize our sales calls, then the ethical issue may not be too serious. What about classifying applicants for college? As long as there are more applicants than positions, some sort of classification and selection process must be done. But what kind?

Suppose a university collects data on the demographics and the performance of all of its students. The admissions committee then processes these data using a decision tree data mining program. Assume the analysis is conducted properly and the tool uses statistically valid measures to obtain statistically valid results. Thus, the following resulting tree accurately represents and explains variances found in the data; no human judgment (or prejudice) was involved. ■

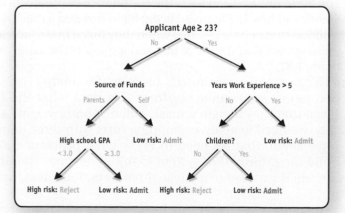

Discussion Questions

1. Explain what conditions in the data could have caused this particular structure to emerge. For example, what conditions may have existed for self-funding students under the age of 23 to be classified as low risk? Explain how you think the three other branches in this tree may have come about.

2. Consider this tree from the standpoint of:
  a. A 23-year-old woman whose job experience is 3 years as a successful Wall Street financial analyst.
  b. A 28-year-old gay male with 4 years' job experience who has no children and pays his own college education.
  c. The university fund-raising committee that wants to raise money from parent donations.
  d. A student who was seriously ill while attending a top-notch high school but managed to graduate with a GPA of 2.9 by working independently on her classes from her hospital room.

3. Suppose you work in admissions and your university's public relations department asks you to meet with the local press for an article they are preparing regarding your admittance policy. How do you prepare for the press meeting?

4. Would your answer to question 3 change if you work at a private rather than public institution? Would it change if you work at a small liberal arts college rather than a large engineering-oriented university?

5. What conclusions do you make regarding the use of decision trees for categorizing student applicants?

6. What conclusions do you make regarding the use of decision trees for categorizing prospects in general?

Decision Trees

A **decision tree** is a hierarchical arrangement of criteria that predict a classification or a value. Here we will consider decision trees that predict classifications. Decision tree analyses are an unsupervised data mining technique: The analyst sets up the computer program and provides the data to analyze, and the decision tree program produces the tree.

A Decision Tree for Student Performance

The basic idea of a decision tree is to select attributes that are most useful for classifying entities on some criterion. Suppose, for example, that we want to classify students according to the grades they earn in the MIS class. To create a decision tree, we first gather data about grades and attributes of students in past classes.

We then input that data into the decision tree program. The program analyzes all of the attributes and selects an attribute that creates the most disparate groups. The logic is that the more different the groups, the better the classification will be. For example, if every student who lived off campus earned a grade higher than 3.0, and every student who lived on campus earned a grade lower than 3.0, then the program would use the variable *live-off-campus* or *live-on-campus* to classify students. In this unrealistic example, the program would be a perfect classifier, because each group is pure, with no misclassifications.

More realistically, consider Figure 9-21, which shows a hypothetical decision tree analysis of MIS class grades. Again, assume we are classifying students depending on whether their grade was greater than 3.0 or less than or equal to 3.0.

The decision tree tool that created this tree examined student characteristics such as students' class (junior or senior), their major, their employment, their age, their club affiliations, and other student characteristics. It then used values of those characteristics to create groups that were as different as possible on the classification grade above or below 3.0.

For the results shown here, the decision tree program determined that the best first criterion is whether the students are juniors or seniors. In this case, the classification was imperfect, as shown by the fact that neither of the senior nor the junior groups consisted only of students with GPAs above or below 3.0. Still, it did create groups that were less mixed than in the *All Students* group.

Figure 9-21
Decision Tree Example for MIS
Classes (hypothetical data)

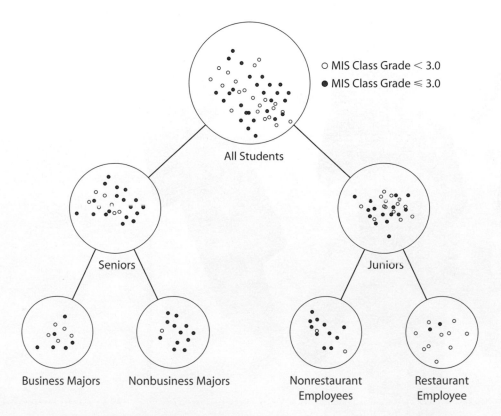

Next, the program examined other criteria to further subdivide *Seniors* and *Juniors* so as to create even more pure groups. The program divided the senior group into subgroups: those who are business majors and those who are not. The program's analysis of the junior data, however, determined that the difference between majors is not significant. Instead, the best classifier (the one that generated the most different groups) is whether the junior worked in a restaurant.

Examining this data, we see that junior restaurant employees do well in the class, but junior nonrestaurant employees and senior nonbusiness majors do poorly. Performance in the other senior group is mixed. (Remember, these data are hypothetical.)

A decision tree like the one in Figure 9-21 can be transformed into a set of decision rules having the format, **If . . . then . . . .** Decision rules for this example are:

- If student is a junior and works in a restaurant, then predict grade >3.0.
- If student is a senior and is a nonbusiness major, then predict grade ≤ 3.0.
- If student is a junior and does not work in a restaurant, then predict grade ≤ 3.0.
- If student is a senior and is a business major, then make no prediction.

As stated, decision tree algorithms create groups that are as pure as possible, or, stated otherwise, as different from each other as possible. The algorithms use several metrics for measuring difference among groups. Further explanation of those techniques is beyond the scope of this text. For now, just understand that maximum difference among groups is used as the criterion for constructing the decision tree.

Let's now apply the decision tree technique to a business situation.

A Decision Tree for Loan Evaluation

A common business application of decision trees is to classify loans by likelihood of default. Organizations analyze data from past loans to produce a decision tree that can be converted to loan-decision rules. A financial institution could use such a tree to assess the default risk on a new loan. Sometimes, too, financial institutions sell a group of loans (called a *loan portfolio*) to one another. An institution considering the purchase of a loan portfolio can use the results of a decision tree program to evaluate the risk of a given portfolio.

Figure 9-22 shows an example provided by Insightful Corporation, a vendor of BI tools. This example was generated using its Insightful Miner product. This tool examined data from 3,485 loans. Of those loans, 72 percent had no default and 28 percent did default. To perform the analysis, the decision tree tool examined six different loan characteristics.

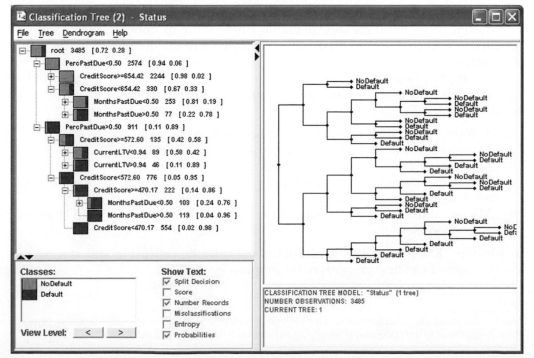

Figure 9-22
Credit Score Decision Tree

Source: Used with permission of Insightful Corporation. Copyright © 1999–2005 Insightful Corporation. All Rights Reserved.

In this example, the decision tree program determined that the percentage of the loan that is past due (*PercPastDue*) is the best first criterion. Reading Figure 9-22, you can see that of the 2,574 loans with a *PercPastDue* value of 0.5 or less (amount past due is less than half the loan amount), 94 percent were not in default. Reading down several lines in this tree, 911 loans had a value of *PercPastDue* greater than 0.5; of those loans, 89 percent were in default.

These two major categories are then further subdivided into three classifications: *CreditScore* is a creditworthiness score obtained from a credit agency; *MonthsPastDue* is the number of months since a payment; and *CurrentLTV* is the current ratio of out-standing balance of the loan to the value of the loan's collateral.

With a decision tree like this, the financial institution can develop decision rules for accepting or rejecting the offer to purchase loans from another financial institution. For example:

- If percent past due is less than 50 percent, then accept the loan.
- If percent past due is greater than 50 percent *and*
    - If *CreditScore* is greater than 572.6 *and*
    - If *CurrentLTV* is less than .94, then accept the loan.
- Otherwise, reject the loan.

Of course, the financial institution will need to combine these risk data with an economic analysis of the value of each loan to determine which loans to take.

Decision trees are easy to understand and, even better, easy to implement using decision rules. They also can work with many types of variables, and they deal well with partial data. Organizations can use decision trees by themselves or combine them with other techniques. In some cases, organizations use decision trees to select variables that are then used by other types of data mining tools. For example, decision trees can be used to identify good predictor variables for neural networks.

Q6 What Is the Role of Knowledge Management Systems?

Knowledge management (KM) is the process of creating value from intellectual capital and sharing that knowledge with employees, managers, suppliers, customers, and others who need it. Whereas reporting and data mining are used to create new information from data, knowledge management systems concern the sharing of knowledge that is known to exist, either in libraries of documents or in the heads of employees.

KM applications enable employees and others to leverage organizational knowledge to work smarter. Santosus and Surmacz cite the following as the primary benefits of KM:

1. KM fosters innovation by encouraging the free flow of ideas.
2. KM improves customer service by streamlining response time.
3. KM boosts revenues by getting products and services to market faster.
4. KM enhances employee retention rates by recognizing the value of employees' knowledge and rewarding them for it.
5. KM streamlines operations and reduces costs by eliminating redundant or unnecessary processes.[3]

In addition, KM preserves organizational memory by capturing and storing the lessons learned and best practices of key employees.

---

[3] Megan Santosus and John Surmacz, "The ABCs of Knowledge Management," *CIO Magazine*, May 23, 2001. Available at http://cio.com/research/knowledge/edit/kmabcs.html (accessed July 2005).

The three major categories of knowledge assets are data, documents, and employees. We addressed information derived from data in the reporting and data mining sections of this chapter. In this section, we will consider KM as it pertains to sharing of document content and employee knowledge.

Sharing Document Content

In Chapter 2, we discussed content management in the context of collaboration systems. The focus on content for KM applications is slightly different. Whereas collaboration systems are concerned with document creation and change management, KM applications are concerned with maximizing content use. In this section, we focus on two key technologies for sharing content: indexing and RSS.

Indexing

Indexing is the single most important content function in KM applications. KM users need an easily accessible and robust means of determining whether the content they need exists, and, if so, a link to obtain that content. Users need a keyword search that provides quick response and high document relevancy. The higher the relevancy, the more productive users will be.

The largest collection of documents ever assembled exists on the Internet, and the world's best-known indexing engine is operated by Google. When you Google a term, you are tapping into the world's largest content-indexing system. Google's limitation is that it can index only publicly accessible documents.

When organizations protect their content by placing it behind firewalls, Google's indexing software cannot find it. If you want to access documents published in, say, *Forbes*, you will have to use an indexing service that has an indexing agreement with *Forbes*. Similarly, organizations must develop their own indexing systems, or license indexing systems from others, in order to make their own protected content available to their employees and other authorized users.

Real Simple Syndication (RSS)

Real Simple Syndication (RSS) is a standard for subscribing to content sources. You can think of RSS as an email system for content. With a program called an **RSS reader**, you can subscribe to magazines, blogs, Web sites, and other content sources. The RSS reader will periodically check the sources to which you subscribe to determine whether any content has changed. If so, the RSS reader will place a summary of the change and link to the new content in what is essentially an RSS inbox. You can process your RSS inbox just like your email inbox. You read content changes, delete them in your RSS inbox, and, depending on your reader's features, forward notices of changes to others via email.

Figure 9-23 shows the interface of a typical RSS reader. The left-hand pane shows the RSS sources to which this user is subscribed. Entries are grouped into categories such as Mashable!, Quotes of the Day, and so forth. In order to subscribe, the data source must provide what is termed an **RSS feed**. This simply means that the site posts changes according to one of the RSS standards.

Today, the employees in many organizations share their knowledge via personal blogs. Figure 9-24 shows the blog posts of one of the key employees on the Microsoft Office 365 team. Blogs like this include RSS feeds so that you can subscribe to them using an RSS reader. You can also configure SharePoint and other content-management systems to provide an RSS feed on lists or document libraries. Users who subscribe to those feeds will be notified whenever content changes.

Content-sharing systems are flexible and organic. They are closer to Web 2.0 applications than are applications such as reporting and data mining. In fact, some people would say that content-sharing systems *are* Web 2.0 applications. In fact, the domain of content sharing may be merged into Enterprise 2.0 applications like those discussed in Chapter 8.

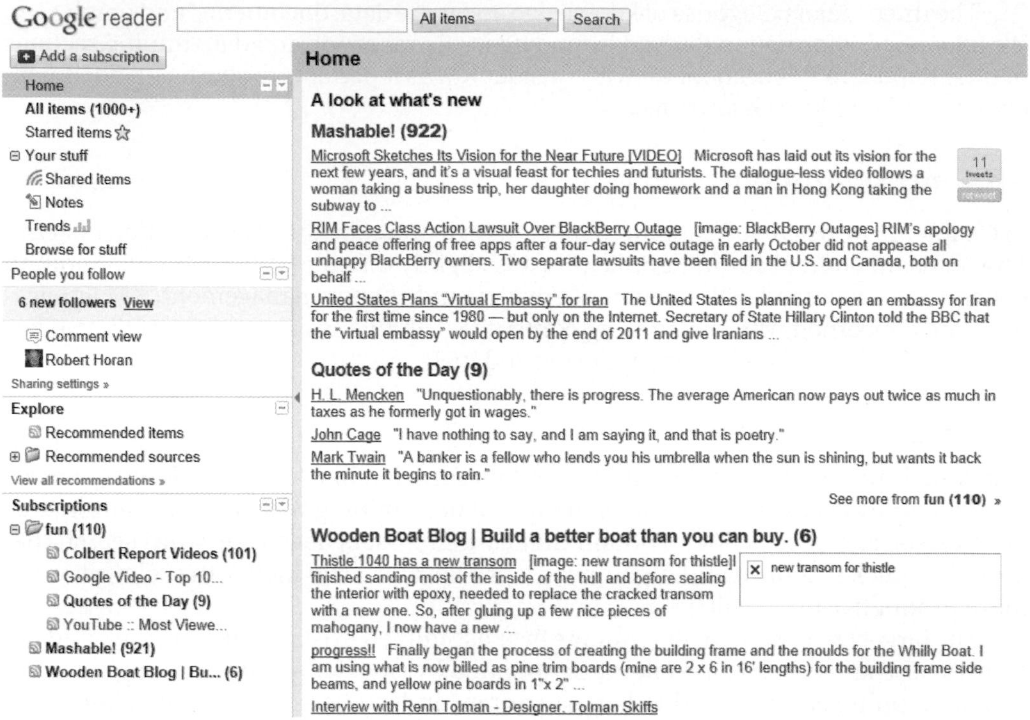

Figure 9-23
Example RSS Reader

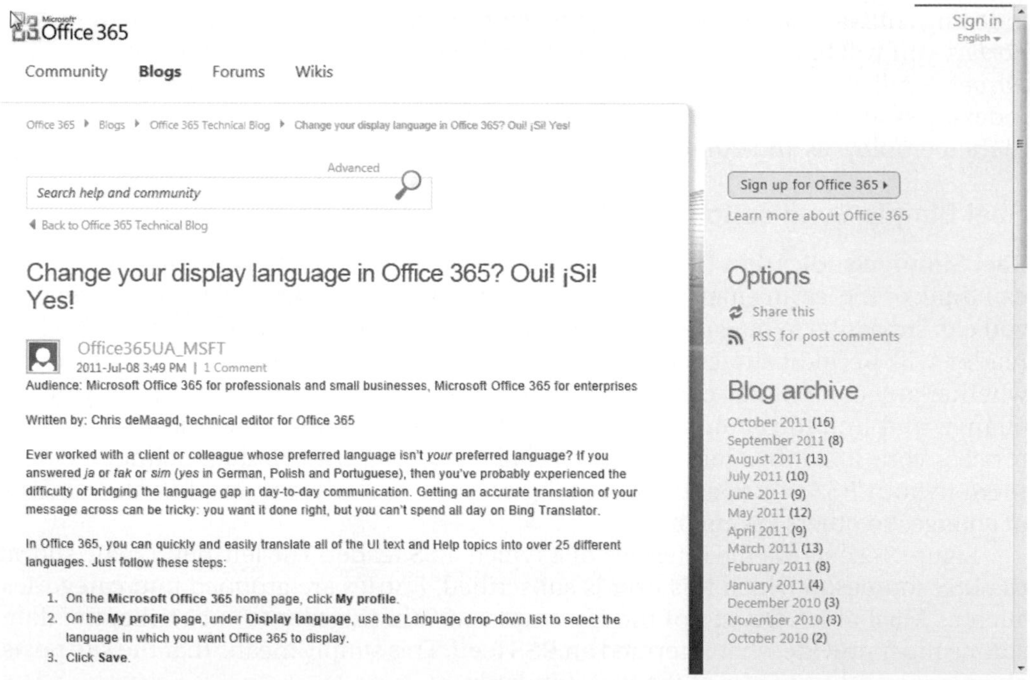

Figure 9-24
Blog Posts by Office 365 Team Member

Expert Systems

Expert systems attempt to capture human expertise and put it into a format that can be used by nonexperts. Expert systems are rule-based systems that use If . . . then rules similar to those created by decision tree analysis. However, decision trees' If . . . then rules are created by mining data. The If . . . then rules in expert systems are created by interviewing experts in a given business domain and codifying the rules stated by those experts. Also, decision trees typically have fewer than a dozen rules, whereas expert systems can have hundreds or thousands of rules.

Problems of Expert Systems

Many expert systems were created in the late 1980s and early 1990s, and a few of them have been successful. However, most suffer from three major disadvantages:

- Expensive to develop
- Unpredictable to maintain
- Overhyped

Expert systems are difficult and expensive to develop. They require many labor hours from both experts in the domain under study and designers of expert systems. This expense is compounded by the high opportunity cost of tying up domain experts. Such experts are normally some of the most sought-after employees in the organization.

Second, expert systems are difficult to maintain. Because of the nature of rule-based systems, the introduction of a new rule in the middle of hundreds of others can have unexpected consequences. Unfortunately, such side effects cannot be predicted or eliminated.

Finally, expert systems have been unable to live up to the high expectations set by their name. Initially, proponents of expert systems hoped to be able to duplicate the performance of highly trained experts, such as cardiologists. It turned out, however, that no expert system has the same diagnostic ability as a knowledgeable, skilled, and experienced cardiologist.

Today, however, there are successful, less-ambitious expert systems. Typically, these systems address more restricted problems than duplicating a doctor's diagnostic ability. We consider one next.

Expert Systems for Pharmacies

The Medical Informatics group at Washington University School of Medicine in St. Louis, Missouri, develops innovative and effective information systems to support decision making in medicine. The group has developed several expert systems that are used as a safety net to screen the decisions of doctors and other medical professionals. These systems help to achieve the hospital's goal of state-of-the-art, error-free care.

Medical researchers developed early expert systems to support, and in some cases to replace, medical decision making. MYCIN was an expert system developed in the early 1970s for the purpose of diagnosing certain infectious diseases. Physicians never routinely used MYCIN, but researchers used its expert system framework as the basis for many other medical systems. For one reason or another, however, none of those systems has seen extensive use.

In contrast, the systems developed at Washington University are routinely used, in real time, every day. One of the systems, DoseChecker, verifies appropriate dosages on prescriptions issued in the hospital. Another application, PharmADE, ensures that patients are not prescribed drugs that have harmful interactions. The pharmacy order-entry system invokes these applications as a prescription is entered. If either system detects a problem with the prescription, it generates an alert like the one shown in Figure 9-25.

A pharmacist screens an alert before sending it to the doctor. If the pharmacist disagrees with the alert, it is discarded. If the pharmacist agrees there is a problem with either the dosage or a harmful drug interaction, she sends the alert to the doctor. The doctor can then alter the prescription or override the alert. If the doctor does not respond, the system will escalate the alert to higher levels until the potential problem is resolved.

Neither DoseChecker nor PharmADE attempts to replace the decision making of medical professionals. Rather, they operate behind the scenes, as a reliable assistant helping to provide error-free care.[4]

---

[4] The Division of Medical Informatics at Washington University School of Medicine for the Department of Pharmacy at Barnes Jewish Hospital. http://informatics.wustl.edu (accessed January 2005). Used with permission of Medical Informatics at Washington University School of Medicine and BJC Healthcare.

Figure 9-25
Alert from Pharmacy
Expert System

Source: The Division of Medicine
at Washington University School
of Medicine for the Department
of Pharmacy at Barnes Jewish Hospital
Informatics. www.wustl.edu. Used with
permission of Medical Informatics
at Washington University School
of Medicine and BJC Healthcare.

**Pharmacy Clinical Decision Support
Version 2.0**

Developed by The Division of Medical Informatics at Washington University School of Medicine
for the Department of Pharmacy at Barnes Jewish Hospital.

Data as of: Mar 10 2000 4:40 AM   **Alert #: 13104**   **Satellite: CHNE**

Patient Name	Registration	Age	Sex	Weight(kg)	Height(in)	IBW(kg)	Location
SAMPLE,PATIENT	9999999	22	F	114	0	0	528

Creatinine Clearance Lab Results (last 3):

Collection Date	Serum Creatinine	Creatinine Clearance
Mar 9 2000 9:55 PM	7.1	14

DoseChecker Recommendations and Thoughts:

Order	Start Date	Drug Name	Route	Dose	Frequency
295	Mar 10 2000 12:00 AM	MEPERIDINE INJ 25MG	IV	25 MG	Q4H
Recommended Dose/Frequency:				0.0 MG	PER DAY
Comments:	0 <= CrCl < 20. Mependine should not be used for more than 48 hours or at doses > 600 mg per day in patients with renal or CNS disease. Serious consideration should be given to using an alternative analgesic in this patient population.				

Q7 What Are the Alternatives for Publishing BI?

The previous discussions have illustrated the power and utility of reporting, data mining, and knowledge management BI applications. But, for BI to be actionable, it must be published to the right user at the right time. In this question, we will discuss the primary publishing alternatives and discuss the functionality of BI servers, a special type of Web server.

Characteristics of BI Publishing Alternatives

Figure 9-26 lists four server alternatives for BI publishing. **Static reports** are BI documents that are fixed at the time of creation and do not change. A printed sales analysis is an example of a static report. In the BI context, most static reports are published as PDF documents.

Dynamic reports are BI documents that are updated at the time they are requested. A sales report that is current as of the time the user accessed it on a Web server is a dynamic report. In almost all cases, publishing a dynamic report requires the BI application to access a database or other data source at the time the report is delivered to the user.

Pull options for each of the servers in Figure 9-26 are the same. The user goes to the site, clicks a link (or opens an email), and obtains the report. Because they're the same for all four server types, they are not shown in Figure 9-26.

Push options vary by server type. For email or collaboration tools, push is manual; someone, say a manager, an expert, or an administrator, creates an email with the report as an attachment (or URL to the collaboration tool) and sends it to the users

Figure 9-26
BI Publishing Alternatives

Server	Report Type	Push Options	Skill Level Needed
Email or collaboration tool	Static	Manual	Low
Web server	Static/Dynamic	Alert/RSS	Low for static High for dynamic
SharePoint	Static/Dynamic	Alert/RSS Workflow	Low for static High for dynamic
BI server	Dynamic	Alert/RSS Subscription	High

known to be interested in that report. For Web servers and SharePoint, users can create alerts and RSS feeds to have the server push content to them when the content is created or changed, with the expiration of a given amount of time, or at particular intervals. SharePoint workflows can also push content.

A BI server extends alert/RSS functionality to support user **subscriptions**, which are user requests for particular BI results on a particular schedule or in response to particular events. For example, a user can subscribe to a daily sales report, requesting that it be delivered each morning. Or, the user might request that RFM analyses be delivered whenever a new result is posted on the server, or a sales manager might subscribe to receive a sales report whenever sales in his region exceed $1 million during the week. We explain the two major functions of a BI server in the next section.

The skills needed to create a publishing application are either low or high. For static content, little skill is needed. The BI author creates the content, and the publisher (usually the same person) attaches it to an email or puts it on the Web or a SharePoint site, and that's it. Publishing dynamic BI is more difficult; it requires the publisher to set up database access when documents are consumed. In the case of a Web server, the publisher will need to develop or have a programmer write code for this purpose. In the case of SharePoint and BI servers, program code is not necessarily needed, but dynamic data connections need to be created, and this task is not for the technically faint-of-heart. You'll need knowledge beyond the scope of this class to develop dynamic BI solutions. You should be able to do this, however, if you take a few more IS courses or major in IS.

What Are the Two Functions of a BI Server?

A **BI server** is a Web server application that is purpose-built for the publishing of business intelligence. The Microsoft SQL Server Report manager (part of Microsoft SQL Server Reporting Services) is the most popular such product today, but there are other products as well.

BI servers provide two major functions: management and delivery. The management function maintains metadata about the authorized allocation of BI results to users. The BI server tracks what results are available, what users are authorized to view those results, and the schedule upon which the results are provided to the authorized users. It adjusts allocations as available results change and users come and go.

As shown in Figure 9-27, all management data needed by any of the BI servers is stored in metadata. The amount and complexity of such data depends, of course, on the functionality of the BI server.

BI servers use metadata to determine what results to send to which users and, possibly, on which schedule. Today, the expectation is that BI results can be delivered to "any" device. In practice, *any* is interpreted to mean computers; smartphones; iPads and other tablets; applications such as Microsoft Office; and SOA web services.

Figure 9-27
Components of a Generic
BI System

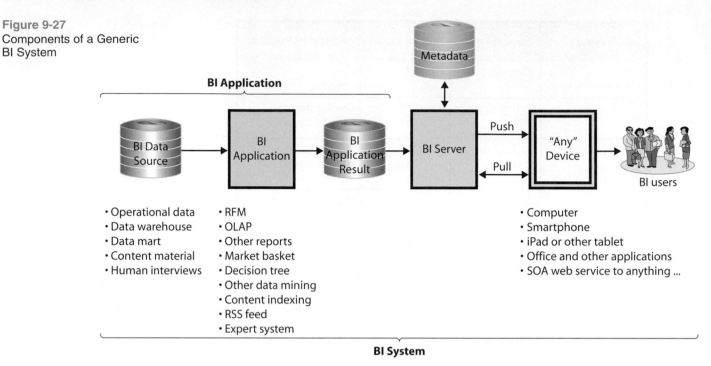

Q8 2022?

BI systems truly add value. As described in the Guide on page 330, not every system is a success, but simple ones like RFM and OLAP often are, and even complicated and expensive data mining applications can generate tremendous return if they are applied to appropriate problems and are well-designed and implemented.

For example, suppose you never buy expensive jewelry on your credit card. If you travel to South America and attempt to buy a $5,000 diamond bracelet using that credit card, watch what happens! Especially if you make the attempt on a credit card other than the one for which you paid for the travel. A data mining application integrated into the credit card agency's purchase-approval process will detect the unusual pattern, on the spot, and require you to personally verify the purchase on the telephone or in some other way before it will accept the charge. Such applications are exceedingly accurate because they are well designed and implemented by some of the world's best data miners.

How will this change by 2022? We know that data storage is free, that CPU processors are becoming nearly so, that the world is generating and storing exponentially more information about customers, and that data mining techniques are only going to get better. I think it likely that by 2022 some companies will know more about your purchasing psyche than you, your mother, or your analyst.

In fact, it may be important to ask the question: How unsupervised do we want unsupervised data mining to be? Today, a data miner extracts a dataset and inputs it into an unsupervised data mining application for analysis. The application finds patterns, trends, and other business intelligence and reports the results to the human analyst. The BI analyst examines the results and possibly iterates by finding more data and running more analyses.

But what happens when BI applications become sophisticated enough to replace the BI analyst? What happens when the unsupervised data mining application has features and functions to find its own datasets and to evaluate those datasets based on the results of a prior BI analysis? And then decides which BI analysis to perform next?

Biology (New York: Penguin, 2006). Machines work faster than humans and they work 24/7. At some point, will machines know so much about us that we are incapable of understanding the results? What happens when, because of complexity, such BI machines can only communicate with other BI machines?

Ray Kurzweil, futurist, successful inventor, and entrepreneur has developed a theory around a social *singularity* that is reached when machines are skilled at building their own information systems.[5] Apply that thinking to unsupervised data mining. What happens when machines can direct their own data mining activities? There will be an accelerating positive feedback loop among the BI machines. Then, what will they know about us? Is it important that at that date we will lack the capacity to know what the machines will know?

This line of thinking exposes a future flaw that runs through this text. We've defined information as something possessed only by humans. If it's on a piece of paper or on a screen, it's data. If it's in the mind of a human, it is (or can be) information. When we're talking about simple reporting operations such as grouping and filtering, etc., that's legitimate. But, in the day when unsupervised data mining truly is unsupervised, machines will possess and create information for themselves.

Do you know what your data mining application is doing tonight?

---

[5] Ray Kurzweil. *The Singularity Is Near: When Humans Transcend.*

Guide
Semantic Security

Security is a very difficult problem— and risks grow larger every year. Not only do we have cheaper, faster computers (remember Moore's Law). We also have more data, more systems for reporting and querying that data, and easier, faster, and broader communication. We have organizational data in the cloud that is not physically under our control. All of these combine to increase the chances that private or proprietary information is inappropriately divulged.

Access security is hard enough: How do we know that the person (or program) who signs on as Megan Cho really is Megan Cho? We use passwords, but files of passwords can be stolen. Setting that issue aside, we need to know that Megan Cho's permissions are set appropriately. Suppose Megan works in the HR department, so she has access to personal and private data of other employees. We need to design the reporting system so that Megan can access all of the data she needs to do her job, and no more.

Also, the delivery system must be secure. A BI server is an obvious and juicy target for any would-be intruder. Someone can break in and change access permissions. Or, a hacker could pose as someone else to obtain reports. Application servers help the authorized user, resulting in faster access to more information. But, without proper security reporting, servers also ease the intrusion task for unauthorized users.

All of these issues relate to access security. Another dimension to security is equally serious and far more problematic: **semantic security**. Semantic security concerns the unintended release of protected information through the release of a combination of reports or documents that are independently not protected.

Take an example from class. Suppose I assign a group project, and I post a list of groups and the names of students assigned to each group. Later, after the assignments have been completed and graded, I post a list of grades on the Web site. Because of university privacy policy, I cannot post the grades by student name or identifier; so instead, I post the grades for each group. If you want to get the grades for each student, all you have to do is combine the list from Lecture 5 with the list from Lecture 10. You might say that the release of grades in this example does no real harm—after all, it is a list of grades from one assignment.

But go back to Megan Cho in HR. Suppose Megan evaluates the employee compensation program. The COO believes salary offers have been inconsistent over time and that they vary too widely by department. Accordingly, the COO authorizes Megan to receive a report that lists *SalaryOfferAmount* and *OfferDate* and a second report that lists *Department* and *AverageSalary*.

Those reports are relevant to her task and seem innocuous enough. But Megan realizes that she could use the information they contain to determine individual salaries—information she does not have and is not authorized to receive. She proceeds as follows.

Like all employees, Megan has access to the employee directory on the Web portal. Using the directory, she can obtain a list of employees in each department, and using the facilities of her ever-so-helpful report-authoring system she combines that list with the department and average-salary report. Now she has a list of the names of employees in a group and the average salary for that group.

Megan's employer likes to welcome new employees to the company. Accordingly, each week the company publishes an article about new employees who have been hired. The article makes pleasant comments about each person and encourages employees to meet and greet them.

Megan, however, has other ideas. Because the report is published on SharePoint, she can obtain an electronic copy of it. It's an Acrobat report, and using Acrobat's handy Search feature, she soon has a list of employees and the week they were hired.

She now examines the report she received for her study, the one that has *SalaryOfferAmount* and the offer date, and she does some interpretation. During the week of July 21, three offers were extended: one for $35,000, one for $53,000, and one for $110,000. She also notices from the "New Employees" report that a director of marketing programs, a product test engineer, and a receptionist were hired that same week. It's unlikely that they paid the receptionist $110,000; that sounds more like the director of marketing programs. So, she now "knows" (infers) that person's salary.

Next, going back to the department report and using the employee directory, she sees that the marketing director is in the marketing programs department. There are just three people in that department, and their average salary is $105,000. Doing the arithmetic, she now knows that the average salary for the other two people is $102,500. If she can find the hire week for one of those other two people, she can find out both the second and third person's salaries.

You get the idea. Megan was given just two reports to do her job. Yet she combined the information in those reports with publicly available information and is able to deduce salaries, for at least some employees. These salaries are much more than she is supposed to know. This is a semantic security problem. ■

Discussion Questions

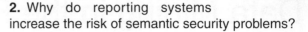

1. In your own words, explain the difference between access security and semantic security.

2. Why do reporting systems increase the risk of semantic security problems?

3. What can an organization do to protect itself against accidental losses due to semantic security problems?

4. What legal responsibility does an organization have to protect against semantic security problems?

5. Suppose semantic security problems are inevitable. Do you see an opportunity for new products from insurance companies? If so, describe such an insurance product. If not, explain why not.

Source: iStockphoto.com.

SALARY INFORMATION

Guide
Data Mining in the Real World

"I'm not really a contrarian about data mining. I believe in it. After all, it's my career. But data mining in the real world is a lot different from the way it's described in textbooks.

"There are many reasons it's different. One is that the data are always dirty, with missing values, values way out of the range of possibility, and time values that make no sense. Here's an example: Somebody sets the server system clock incorrectly and runs the server for a while with the wrong time. When they notice the mistake, they set the clock to the correct time. But all of the transactions that were running during that interval have an ending time before the starting time. When we run the data analysis, and compute elapsed time, the results are negative for those transactions.

"Missing values are a similar problem. Consider the records of just 10 purchases. Suppose that two of the records are missing the customer number and one is missing the year part of transaction date. So you throw out three records, which is 30 percent of the data. You then notice that two more records have dirty data, and so you throw them out, too. Now you've lost half your data.

"Another problem is that you know the least when you start the study. So you work for a few months and learn that if you had another variable; say the customer's Zip code, or age, or something else, you could do a much better analysis. But those other data just aren't available. Or, maybe they are available, but to get the data you have to reprocess millions of transactions, and you don't have the time or budget to do that.

"Overfitting is another problem, a huge one. I can build a model to fit any set of data you have. Give me 100 data points and in a few minutes, I can give you 100 different equations that will predict those 100 data points. With neural networks, you can create a model of any level of complexity you want, except that none of those equations will predict new cases with any accuracy at all. When using neural nets, you have to be very careful not to overfit the data.

"Then, too, data mining is about probabilities, not certainty. Bad luck happens. Say I build a model that predicts the probability that a customer will make a purchase. Using the model on new-customer data, I find three customers who have a .7 probability of buying something. That's a good number, well over a 50–50 chance, but it's still possible that none of them will buy. In fact, the probability that none of them will buy is $.3 \times .3 \times .3$, or .027, which is 2.7 percent.

"Now suppose I give the names of the three customers to a salesperson who calls on them, and sure enough, we have a stream of bad luck and none of them buys. This bad result doesn't mean the model is wrong. But what does the salesperson think? He thinks the model is worthless and can do better on his own. He tells his manager who tells her associate, who tells the Northeast Region, and sure enough, the model has a bad reputation all across the company.

"Another problem is seasonality. Say all your training data are from the summer. Will your model be valid for the winter? Maybe, but maybe not. You might even know that it won't be valid for predicting winter sales, but if you don't have winter data, what do you do?

"When you start a data mining project, you never know how it will turn out. I worked on one project for 6 months, and when we finished, I didn't think our model was any good. We had too many problems with data: wrong, dirty, and missing. There was no way we could know ahead of time that it would happen, but it did.

"When the time came to present the results to senior management, what could we do? How could we say we took 6 months of our time and substantial computer resources to create a bad model? We had a model, but I just didn't think it would make accurate predictions. I was a junior member of the team, and it wasn't for me to decide. I kept my mouth shut, but I never felt good about it. Fortunately, the project was cancelled later for other reasons.

"However, I'm only talking about my bad experiences. Some of my projects have been excellent. On many, we found interesting and important patterns and information, and a few times I've created very accurate predictive models. It's not easy, though, and you have to be very careful. Also, lucky!" ■

Discussion Questions

1. Summarize the concerns expressed by this contrarian.

2. Do you think the concerns raised here are sufficient to avoid data mining projects altogether?

3. If you were a junior member of a data mining team and you thought that the model that had been developed was ineffective, maybe even wrong, what would you do? If your boss disagrees with your beliefs, would you go higher in the organization? What are the risks of doing so? What else might you do?

Active Review

Use this Active Review to verify that you understand the ideas and concepts that answer the chapter's study questions.

Q1 How do organizations use business intelligence (BI) systems?

Define *business intelligence* and *BI system*. Explain the elements in Figure 9-1. Give an example, other than in this text, of one way that an organization could use business intelligence for each of the four collaborative tasks in Figure 9-2.

Q2 What are the three primary activities in the BI process?

Name and describe the three primary activities in the BI process. Summarize how Addison and Drew used these activities to produce BI results for GearUp.

Q3 How do organizations use data warehouses and data marts to acquire data?

Describe the need and functions of data warehouses and data marts. Name and describe the role of data warehouse components. List and explain the problems that can exist in data used for data mining and sophisticated reporting. Use the example of a supply chain to describe the differences between a data warehouse and data mart.

Q4 How do organizations use typical reporting applications?

Name and describe five basic reporting operations and summarize how Addison used them at GearUp. Define *RFM analysis* and explain the actions that should be taken with customers who have the following scores: [1, 1, 1,], [5, 1, 1,], [1, 1, 3], and [1, 4, 1]. Explain OLAP and describe its unique characteristics. Explain the roles for measure and dimension in an OLAP cube. Illustrate an OLAP cube with a single measure and five dimensions, two dimensions on one axis and three on another. Show how drill down applies to your example.

Q5 How do organizations use typical data mining applications?

Define *data mining,* and explain how its use typically differs from reporting applications. Explain why data mining tools are difficult to use well. Describe the differences between unsupervised and supervised data mining. Use an example to illustrate cluster analysis and regression analysis. Define *neural networks,* and explain why the term is a misnomer. Define *support, confidence*, and *lift,* and describe these terms using the data in Figure 9-21. Describe a good application for market-basket analysis results. Describe the purpose of decision trees and explain how the data in Figure 9-23 is used to evaluate loans for possible purchase.

Q6 What is the role of knowledge management systems?

Define *knowledge management,* and describe its primary benefits. Explain how KM document sharing differs from content management. Explain the importance of indexing, and describe when Google indexing is useful and when it is not. Explain the statement, "RSS is like email for content." Define *RSS reader* and *RSS feed,* and explain how they interact. Define *expert system,* and explain why expert systems have a checkered reputation. Describe the purpose of the expert systems in use at the Washington University School of Medicine.

Q7 What are the alternatives for publishing BI?

Name four alternative types of server used for publishing business intelligence. Explain the difference between static and dynamic reports; explain the term *subscription*. Describe why dynamic reports are difficult to create.

Q8 2022?

Summarize the function of the credit card approval application. Explain how you think that application uses data. Summarize the way that unsupervised data mining could spiral out of the control of humans. In your opinion, is this a problem? Why or why not? Describe the singularity that could occur for data mining applications. Explain the information flaw that runs throughout this text.

Using Your Knowledge at Fox Lake

Summarize what Anne wants to do. Assume that Anne has been able to obtain the members' data regarding their children's ages and marital status. Which of the following BI techniques described in this chapter would be most appropriate for her to use. Reporting? OLAP? RFM? Data mining? Explain your answer.

Key Terms and Concepts

Using Your Knowledge

1. Using words, not SQL, explain the logic of the steps that Lucas must have used to use the tables in the top part of Figure 9-4 to create the tables in the center part of the figure. Verify that all necessary data are present. Make and justify assumptions, if required.

2. Using words, not SQL, explain the logic of the steps that Addison must have used to use the tables in the middle part of Figure 9-4 to create the *Item_ Summary_Data* table. Verify that all necessary data are present. Make and justify assumptions, if required.

3. Reflect on the differences between reporting systems and data mining systems. What are their similarities and differences? How do their costs differ? What benefits does each offer? How would an organization choose between these two BI tools?

4. Suppose you are a member of the Audubon Society, and the board of the local chapter asks you to help them analyze its member data. The group wants to analyze the demographics of its membership against members' activity, including events attended, classes attended, volunteer activities, and donations. Describe two different reporting applications and one data mining application that they might develop. Be sure to include a specific description of the goals of each system.

5. Suppose you are the director of student activities at your university. Recently, some students have charged that your department misallocates its resources. They claim the allocation is based on outdated student preferences. Funds are given to activities that few students find attractive, and insufficient funds are allocated to new activities in which students do want to participate. Describe how you could use reporting and/or data mining systems to assess this claim.

6. Suppose you work at Costco or another major, national, big-box store, and you do a market-basket analysis and identify the 25 pairs of items in the store that have the highest lift and the 25 pairs of items that have the lowest lift. What would you do with this knowledge? Costco (or your big-box store) doesn't have salespeople, so up-selling is not an option. What else might you do with information about these items' lift? Consider advertising, pricing, item location in stores, and any other factor that you might adjust. Do you think the lift calculations are valid for all stores in the United States (or other country)? Why or why not? Are the 50 pairs of products with the highest and lowest lift the best place to focus your attention? What other 50 pairs of products might you want to consider? Explain.

7. Describe a use for RFM analysis at Fox Lake. Consider golf, tennis, the restaurant, or the pro shop as candidates. Which do you think is best suited to RFM? Explain your rationale. For your application, explain what you would do for customers who have the following scores: [1, 1, 1], [3, 1, 1], [1, 4, 1], [3, 3, 1], [1, 1, 3].

8. Describe an application for market-basket analysis for the Fox Lake restaurant. Explain how you would use the knowledge that two menu items have a lift of 7. Explain how you would use the knowledge that two items have a lift of .003. If they have a lift of 1.03? If they have a lift of 2.1?

▬ Collaboration Exercise 9

With a team of your fellow students, develop an answer to the following four questions. Use Google Docs, Google+, Windows Live SkyDrive, SharePoint, Office 365, or some other collaboration tool to conduct your meetings.

Mary Keeling owns and operates Carbon Creek Gardens, a retailer of trees, garden plants, perennial and annual flowers, and bulbs. "The Gardens," as her customers call it, also sells bags of soil, fertilizer, small garden tools, and garden sculptures. Mary started the business 16 years ago when she bought a section of land that, because of water drainage, was unsuited for residential development. With hard work and perseverance, Mary has created a warm and inviting environment with a unique and carefully selected inventory of plants. The Gardens has become a favorite nursery for serious gardeners in her community.

"The problem," she says, "is that I've grown so large, I've lost track of my customers. The other day, I ran into Tootsie Swan at the grocery store, and I realized I hadn't seen her in ages. I said something like, 'Hi, Tootsie, I haven't seen you for a while,' and that statement unleashed an angry torrent from her. It turns out that she'd been in over a year ago and had wanted to return a plant. One of my part-time employees waited on her and had apparently insulted her, or at least didn't give her the service she wanted. So, she decided not to come back to The Gardens.

"Tootsie was one of my best customers. I'd lost her, and I didn't even know it! That really frustrates me. Is it inevitable that as I get bigger, I lose track of my customers? I don't think so. Somehow, I have to find out when regular customers aren't coming around. Had I known Tootsie had stopped shopping with us, I'd have called her to see what was going on. I need customers like her.

"I've got all sorts of data in my sales database. It seems like the information I need is in there, but how do I get it out?"

In this exercise, you will apply the knowledge of this chapter to Mary Keeling's problem.

1. Mary wants to know when she's lost a customer. One way to help her would be to produce a report, say in PDF format, showing the top 50 customers from the prior year. Mary could print that report or we could place it on a private section of her Web site so that she can download it from wherever she happens to be.

   Periodically—say, once a week—Mary could request a report that shows the top buyers for that week. That report could also be in PDF format, or it could just be produced onscreen. Mary could compare the two reports to determine who is missing. If she wonders whether a customer such as Tootsie has been ordering, she could request a query report on Tootsie's activities.

   Describe the advantages and disadvantages of this solution.

2. Describe the best possible application of an OLAP tool at Carbon Creek. Can it be used to solve the lost-customer problem? Why or why not? What is the best way, if any, for Mary to use OLAP at The Gardens? If none, explain why.

3. Describe the best possible application of decision tree analysis at Carbon Creek. Can it be used to solve the lost-customer problem? Why or why not? What is the best way, if any, for Mary to use decision tree analysis at The Gardens? If none, explain why.

4. Describe the best possible application of RFM analysis at Carbon Creek. Can it be used to solve the lost-customer problem? Why or why not? What is the best way, if any, for Mary to use RFM at The Gardens? If none, explain why.

5. Describe the best possible application of market-basket analysis at Carbon Creek. Can it be used to solve the lost-customer problem? Why or why not? What is the best way, if any, for Mary to use market-basket analysis at The Gardens? If none, explain why.

6. Which of the applications of BI tools in this exercise will provide Mary the best value? If you owned Carbon Creek Gardens and you were going to implement just one of these applications, which would you choose? Why?

▬ Case Study 9

THL (cont.)

Before proceeding, reread Case 8, page 294, which introduces THL, Tourism Holdings Limited, a New Zealand–based company that owns and operates multiple businesses. In this case, we will examine how THL uses information systems to support vehicle leasing in its four camper-leasing business lines.

Leasing camper vehicles to customers has three fundamental phases:

1. Matching customer requirements with vehicle availability
2. Reserving vehicles and operations support
3. Billing and customer service

Online Reservations Systems

Customers access a Web site for whichever brand of vehicle they wish to rent. On that site, they specify the dates and locations from which they want to rent and return a vehicle. THL information systems access the vehicle inventory to determine which vehicles might be available.

That determination is complex. THL may not have the wanted vehicle in the desired location, but it might have a higher-priced vehicle available and choose to offer the customer a free upgrade. Or, it might have the desired vehicle in a different city and choose to move the vehicle to that location. However, moving the vehicle might impact prior reservations for that vehicle, making such movement infeasible. Finally, this complexity is compounded because certain vehicles are not to be rented from particular locations. (Two-wheel drive standard vehicles cannot be rented for the Australian outback, for example). And, of course, vehicles undergo both scheduled and unscheduled maintenance.

Pricing is another complicated decision in the reservation process. Like hotels and airlines, THL engages in flex pricing, whereby prices are determined not only by the vehicle and rental period, but also by customer demand.

To accommodate this complexity, THL developed a rule-based availability information system known as Aurora. Business analysts create business rules like those shown in Figure 9-28. Figure 9-28 shows an example of rules that block vehicles from rental; Figure 9-29 shows a screen that is used to set up or modify a rule. All rules are stored in a SQL Server database, a database that also contains all of the vehicle reservation data. Application programs in the Aurora system access and process the business rules when determining vehicle availability. Because rules are set up and managed with easy-to-use interfaces like that in Figure 9-28, nonprogrammer business analysts are able to change reservation policy without the assistance of technical personnel.

THL also operates information systems for vehicle check-in and customer billing.

The Aurora reservation system off-loads data to a second SQL Server database that operates a Report Server (see Figure 9-30). By off-loading the data, THL produces numerous sophisticated reports without impacting the performance of the online reservation system.

Reports from the server guide both operational and managerial activities. One report, for example, shows the vehicles that are to be checked out and returned to each rental location. Other reports show which vehicles need to be transferred to other locations, which vehicles are to be sent for maintenance, which vehicles are to be retired from the fleet, and so forth.

BI Systems

"We know our operational data contains a wealth of information about our customers, their rental needs, trends in rental activity and vehicle needs, and other key business drivers," Grant Webster, CEO, stated. "We've already developed numerous OLAP cubes and we're working on other types of business intelligence applications."

As shown in Figure 9-30 data from the report server is downloaded to a third server that provides OLAP services. Operational data is processed, and OLAP cubes

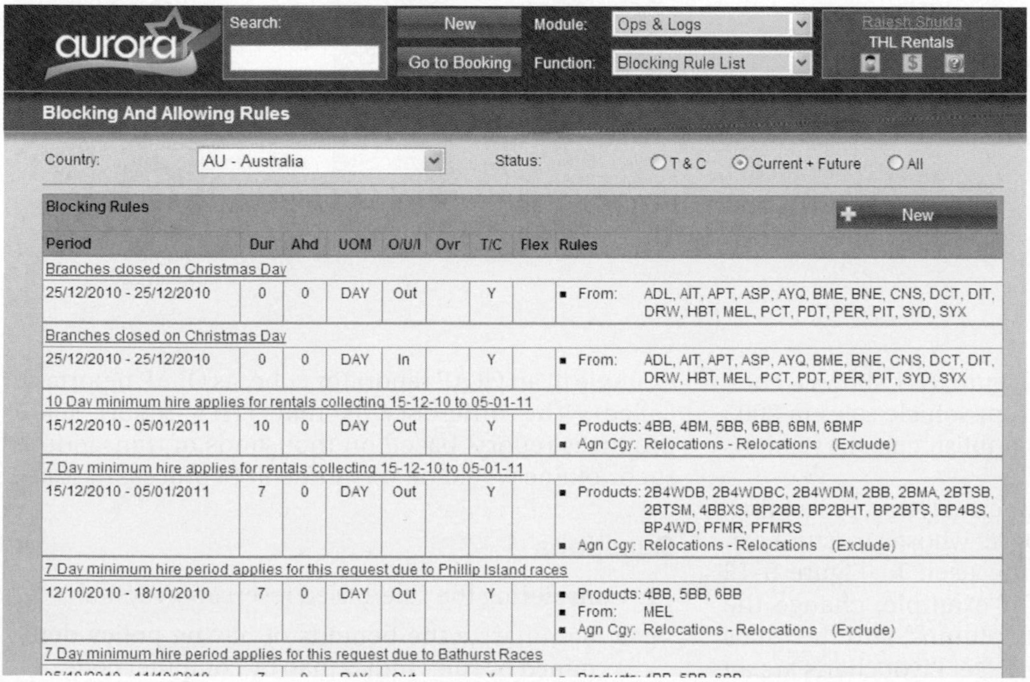

Figure 9-28
Example Rental Rules

Source: © Tourism Holdings Limited. Used with permission.

Figure 9-29
Setting up a Blocking Rule

Source: © Tourism Holdings Limited. Used with permission.

Edit Blocking Rule

Country:	AU - Australia	Rule Type:	Blocking
Reason / Message:	Branches closed on Christmas Day		
Duration of Booking:	0 ∨ *	Book Ahead Period :	0 ∨ *
By Date:	⊙ Out ○ Use ○ In	Unit of Measure:	Calendar Day ∨
Flags:	☐ Overrideable ☐ Only Flex Bookings ☐ Bypass Availability Check		☑ T&C rule
Period From:	25/12/2010 📅 *	To:	25/12/2010 📅 *

Rule Components: — Remove

Type	Items	Excl	Add
▪ Products:		☐	(Select) ∨
▪ Brands:		☐	(Select) ∨
▪ Packages:		☐	[____] 📋 ➕
▪ Locations From:	☐ ADL ☐ AIT ☐ APT ☐ ASP ☐ AYQ ☐ BME ☐ BNE ☐ CNS ☐ DCT ☐ DIT ☐ DRW ☐ HBT ☐ MEL ☐ PCT ☐ PDT ☐ PER ☐ PIT ☐ SYD ☐ SYX	☐	(Select) ∨
▪ Locations To:		☐	(Select) ∨
▪ Agent Countries:		☐	(Select) ∨
▪ Agent Categories:		☐	(Select) ∨
▪ Agents:		☐	[____] 📋 ➕

— Delete   💾 Save   ◄ Back

Figure 9-30
THL Information Systems

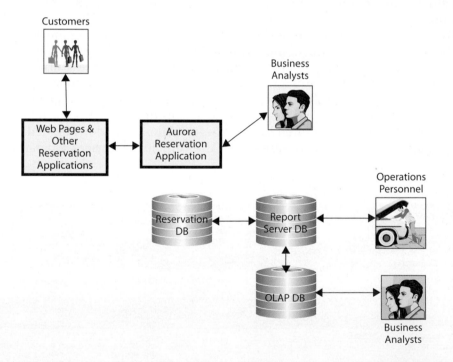

are created on a weekly basis. Figure 9-31 shows a cube that displays revenue earned from vehicle sales in 2005 (THL is, naturally, reluctant to publish current versions of such private data).

OLAP, which stands for online analytical processing, refers to the production of reports whose structure can be changed dynamically by the user. In Figure 9-18 (page 311), the user could, for example, change the brand and geographic market columns, and the totals would be adjusted accordingly. Excel Pivot charts are an

example of an OLAP report (or cube, as OLAP reports are called). The difference is that THL's report server produces reports based on thousands of transactions; such volume would be very difficult to process in Excel.

Questions

1. Considering the rule-based reservation system:

   a. Summarize the benefits of having policy determined by rules rather than by computer code.

Figure 9-31
The OLAP Report

Source: © Tourism Holdings Limited.
Used with permission.

PowerPlay - [Monthly S & M Report.ppx of CombinedVehicleSales (Reporter)]
File Edit View Insert Explore Calculate Format Tools Window Help

Vehicle | Out City | Package | Relocation | To City | Brand | Inclusive | Oneway | Country | Cancelled | Cancelled | BookDate | OutDate | Hire Length | Flex

			April 05	May 05	June 05	2006	July 2006	August 2006	September 2006
			Book Week (36) 2005	Book Week (36) 2005	Book Week (36) 2005	Book Week (36) 2006	36	36	36
Van	Asia	Backpacker	AU	$0	$0	$0	$0	$0	$0	$0
			NZ	$0	$0	$0	$0	$0	$0	$0
			Total	$0	$0	$0	$0	$0	$0	$0
		Explore More	AU	$0	$0	$0	$0	$0	$0	$0
			NZ	$0	$0	$0	$0	$0	$0	$0
			Total	$0	$0	$0	$0	$0	$0	$0
Car	Agent Market	TOTAL	AU	$3,697	$973	$1,926	$21,592	$0	$0	$0
			NZ	$23,016	$5,751	$5,920	$40,694	$0	$0	$0
			Total	$26,713	$6,725	$7,846	$62,286	$0	$0	$0
		Maui	AU	$1,577	$183	$0	$3,502	$0	$0	$0
			NZ	$7,047	$2,145	$2,038	$27,598	$0	$0	$0
			Total	$8,624	$2,327	$2,038	$31,099	$0	$0	$0
		Britz	AU	$2,121	$791	$1,926	$18,090	$0	$0	$0
			NZ	$15,855	$3,607	$3,882	$13,096	$0	$0	$0
			Total	$17,976	$4,398	$5,808	$31,186	$0	$0	$0
		Backpacker	AU	$0	$0	$0	$0	$0	$0	$0
			NZ	$113	$0	$0	$0	$0	$0	$0
			Total	$113	$0	$0	$0	$0	$0	$0
		Explore More	AU	$0	$0	$0	$0	$0	$0	$0
			NZ	$0	$0	$0	$0	$0	$0	$0

For Help, press F1.

b. What are the consequences of someone entering an incorrect rule? Offer both mundane and drastic examples.

c. Considering your answer to part b, if you managed the reservation system at THL what process would you use for the modification of rules?

2. Examine the OLAP cube in Figure 9-31. The values in this report (or cube, as OLAP reports are called) are sums of rental revenue from vehicles.

a. Using your intuition and business knowledge, what do you think the value $3,697 means? What do $1,587 and $2,121 mean?

b. State three conclusions that you can make from this data.

c. The principal advantage of OLAP is that columns and rows can be switched and the report values will be recalculated automatically. Explain what would happen if the user of this report were to switch the first column (geographic area) with the third column (brand). You do not have sufficient data to compute values, but explain in words what will happen.

3. Considering customer reservation data, give an example of the use of each of the following:

a. Reporting application (other than OLAP)
b. Market-basket analysis
c. Unsupervised data mining
d. Supervised data mining
e. Rank your answers to parts a–d on the basis of their desirability. Justify your ranking.

4. Suppose that THL decides to start a van rental business in the United States. Suppose that it is considering opening operations in Alaska, California, Arizona, New Mexico, or Florida.

a. Given the nature of THL's current camper-vehicle rental activities, which of those states do you think would be best? Justify your decision. Consider potential competition, market size, applicability of THL's experience, and other factors you deem relevant.

b. Summarize THL's competitive strengths for this new operation.

c. Summarize THL's competitive vulnerabilities for this new operation.

d. Describe how its reservation system adds value to this new operation.

e. Summarize the problems that you think THL might have in running a business 7,500 miles (or more) from its headquarters.

5. Name and describe information systems and technologies that THL could use to mitigate the problems in your answer to part e in question 4.

Fox Lake Country Club, Chapter 9

GOALS

Use Fox Lake Country Club to:

- Illustrate a practical application for business intelligence (BI) systems.

- Show how a BI system can improve decision making and save costs.

- Illuminate some of the social and ethical problems that occur when using customer data for promotions.

- Evaluate uses for RFM.

- Evaluate uses for OLAP.

- Set up security problem for Chapter 12.

BACKGROUND

1. This vignette is entirely plausible. Any member who has a family membership will have given Fox Lake data about his or her children. It's possible that members on individual memberships may have given that data as well.

2. Obtaining the marital status of members' daughters is more difficult. There are agencies, however, that might have that data. Both ChoicePoint and Acxiom are two possibilities. You might ask the students to look at the Web sites for those companies to see if such data are available. If not, look for other vendors that might have data like that.

3. Having the groundskeeper access the database is probably not a good idea. You might ask the class what they think about that. Ask what steps Fox Lake should take before it turns over its data to someone with unknown credentials.

4. To bring this home to the students, ask how they would respond if their parents received such a solicitation. Of course, as Anne points out, the parents won't necessarily know that they received the promotion only because of their daughter's age.

5. If you want to show how easy this is, create the tables shown in item 4 in the next section. In Access, add a bit of data, and then run the Access queries in class.

Or, if the students have been learning Access, have them do so.

6. Although not part of the story, Fox Lake presents a good example for evaluating the use of both RFM and OLAP.

7. Heads up: The groundskeeper is going to steal data and more, as we'll learn in Chapter 12.

HOW TO GET STUDENTS INVOLVED

1. Is Anne's request of Jeff reasonable?

   - **Jeff has told Anne to increase revenue. Is she making a reasonable request?**

   - **Will having this data save Fox Lake costs? If so, how? Does it have any benefit other than cost? Why or why not?**

   - **Is buying data about members' daughters' marital status legal? Is it ethical? Is it a good business decision? Why or why not?**

   - **Does Fox Lake have any other data that Anne can use to advantage? If so, what is that data? How would she obtain it?**

2. Other than buying the data, how else might Fox Lake obtain data about the marital status of its members?

   - **Can you think of ways of obtaining marital status data without buying it?**

   - **Describe a marketing campaign that is likely to yield this data.**

   One possibility: Get the wedding anniversary date for each member. Members who do not have an anniversary will say they are unmarried. How can Fox Lake get its members to reveal anniversary data?

3. Suppose Fox Lake buys data about members' daughters' marital status and the word gets out. Several club members call Jeff to register shock and anger.

   - **What can Jeff do?**

   - **Is there anything Fox Lake might have done in anticipation of this problem?**

   - **Does the risk of unfavorable member response override the value of the purchased data? How would Jeff or Anne approach this question?**

Obtaining the data about families with daughters who could be wedding events prospects is not difficult. In this exercise, we explore the nature of the queries involved.

■ **We don't have sufficient information to know specifically the data that exist and how they are to be processed, but let's make some guesses. Suppose Fox Lake has the following tables of data:**

Membership (Number, PrincipalMemberName, PrincipalMemberEmail, Birthdate, Address and other data . . .)

Club_Member (MemberNumber, Name, Email, Birthdate, DateOfBirth, Gender, Membership_Number)

where

Number is key of Membership, and MemberNumber is key of Club_Member.

Member_Number is a foreign key to Membership.

(Thus, the person who buys a membership has his or her personal data included in the Membership table. Additional family members, including spouse and children, have data stored in a row of Club_Member.)

■ **In words, how would you go about obtaining a list of all the club members who are female and between 19 and 36 years of age?**

■ **In words, how would you go about obtaining the principal name, address, and other data for any of those members you identified?**

■ **Using Access, how would you obtain the names of the principle members of memberships having an eligible wedding prospect?**

(By the way, an eligible prospect could be a principle member, i.e., have her own membership. So, two different queries are required.)

4. There might be good applications for RFM at Fox Lake. Consider three possibilities:

■ **How might Fox Lake use RFM for golf course reservations? What would a score of {2, 3, 1} mean? What would scores of {4, 1, 2} and {1, 2, 4} mean? How could Fox Lake use this data?**

■ **How might Fox Lake use RFM for the restaurant? What would a score of {2, 3, 1} mean? What would scores of {4, 1, 2} and {1, 2, 4} mean? How could Fox Lake use this data?**

■ **How might Fox Lake use RFM for the pro shop? What would a score of {2, 3, 1} mean? What would**

scores of {4, 1, 2} and {1, 2, 4} mean? How could Fox Lake use this data?

■ **Which of these applications seems best, and why?**

5. Fox Lake might have uses for OLAP. Consider the possibilities:

■ **Describe ways that Fox Lake could use OLAP for its restaurant. Name two different measures and four different dimensions.**

■ **Describe ways that Fox Lake could use OLAP for the pro shop. Name two different measures and four different dimensions.**

■ **Which, if either of these, would be worth doing? Why?**

6. Consider membership activity reporting:

■ **Identify three different reports about membership activity that would be helpful to Jeff for understanding how Fox Lake is performing.**

VIDEO

Anne's intuition is telling her that Fox Lake has the data she needs, and even though she doesn't know quite how to get it she knows it will save her costs and/or help her do a better marketing plan. So, she has the courage to press Jeff on this issue. Once again we see the need for a business professional to have some knowledge and courage when dealing with technology.

Notice that she's already been to Mike with this idea. She can be sure that he can and will support her if Jeff approves the program. The video also touches on privacy issues that you might amplify in class.

Again, however, Mike's groundskeeper is going to cause problems before this is over . . . in Chapter 12 in fact.

BOTTOM LINE

■ **Operational data has considerable information to save costs and guide decision making.**

■ **Fox Lake can learn potential prospects from a relatively simple report, even if it doesn't buy the marital data.**

■ **Buying data about members has financial and possibly public relations costs. Fox Lake should tread lightly here.**

■ **Fox Lake has meaningful applications for:**
- **RFM**
- **OLAP**
- **Membership reporting**

It is unlikely that Fox Lake is doing either RFM or OLAP, however. I doubt they even know about them. Thus, an opportunity for an informed student . . .

YOU BE THE GUIDE

Using the Ethics Guide: The Ethics of Classification (pages 318–319)

GOAL

- Explore ethical issues about using decision trees for classifying people.

BACKGROUND AND PRESENTATION STRATEGIES

Classification, especially the classification of people, poses many ethical problems. But, organizations must classify; they must decide which students to admit, which people to promote, or which people to deny loans. *It has to be done.*

Decision trees are a classification scheme that analyzes data to create the most dissimilar groups. As such, it is *free of human bias.* The analysis is performed, and the data speak for themselves.

Thus, even though the results of such an analysis may be *unpopular,* such as the example in the guide, these results come directly from the data. The data are speaking for themselves. No subjective human judgment entered into this analysis, and the results *should be less biased* than when using human categorizers.

However, *not all decision trees are equally valid.* Like all statistics techniques, decision tree analyses vary in the degree of fit. Some data analyses have clear separation of groups—the criteria really do split the data. For others, the split is less clear, even murky. However, the analysis software will show the criteria, even if they are weak. Unless the analysts know to interpret standard errors, confidence intervals, and related measures, they will not be able to discriminate a strong classification scheme from a weak one. From the data presented, we have no idea of how strong this decision tree analysis was.

However, the results of a decision tree analysis may tend to reinforce negative social stereotypes and may be organizationally, legally, and socially infeasible.

SUGGESTED RESPONSES FOR DISCUSSION QUESTIONS

1. Of course, this question has no correct answer. Often, the students' answers are fascinating. Sometimes the students become angry, even though they know this is an example, and I need to remind them that this is only an example.

2. None of these people will like this scheme. The people in a, b, and d would be furious. You might let students role-play and speak for each of them. By the way, what relevance is the sexual preference of the person in b? It will have been more difficult for him to have children by 28 than it would have been for a straight man. He might prevail in a discrimination suit against the university.

   The university fund-raising committee in c won't like this scheme because it is biased toward students who are paying their own way. There may be many students younger than age 23 with a high school GPA under 3.0 who have parents who would be pleased to donate, but not if their children aren't admitted.

3. First, would anyone want that job? What will happen if the press finds out about the person in 2(d)? It will be a public relations nightmare.

   To respond to this question, one teaching possibility: *Conduct a mock press interview in class.* Divide the students into two groups—one group of university admissions personnel who must defend this scheme and a second group of press reporters. Conduct the interview. If the class is large, bring three to five members of each group to the front of the class and conduct the interview in front of the class.

Cues for the University Personnel:

- **Our analysis is based on reliable data about the success of past students.**

- **We provided no human input to obtain these results. We are only responding to what the data tell us.**

- **We used the best, most up-to-date statistical techniques.**

- **We will review this policy each year and rerun our analysis when appropriate.**

Questions from the Press:

- **We hear you are operating a harsh and inhumane computer-based system for school admissions. Is this true?**

- **Are you actually turning away people because they were sick in high school?**

- **Please describe the scheme you use.**

- **We've heard of a discrimination suit from one of the rejected students. Does the system, in fact, discriminate against gay people?**

Good luck!

4. Private institutions may have some leeway that public institutions don't. I doubt there would be much difference depending on the type of school. The students may have other opinions.

5. You might also ask:

- **Does the answer depend on the statistical strength of the results?**

I think that any university using decision trees would at least have to (a) ensure that its tree was defensible to the public, (b) provide human review to overrule the classification for exceptional situations, and (c) ensure the results are *statistically* valid.

6. Ensure that the results are statistically strong. Be sure that the results are publicly defensible. Consult corporate legal about the risk of antidiscriminatory practices and other legal risks.

WRAP UP

To wrap up, I say that many different opinions are possible with regard to the use of decision trees, but that each business professional should take the time to consider what his or her own opinions are. Here are some questions that help the students form their own opinions. The answers depend on each student's perspective and values.

- **Do individuals who are classified by an automated process have a right to know that this is being done? For example, when applying for a loan, does the applicant have a right to know that the approval or rejection notification is made by an automated process and not by a human?**

- **Are decision tree classification schemes more appropriate for single events, such as a loan approval, than they are for life-changing events, such as college admissions?**

- **Can decision trees be used to advantage to eliminate situations that have substantial human bias?**

- **Should decision trees be used when they reinforce negative social stereotypes? Does it matter if the data strongly support the negative social stereotype?**

- **Can techniques like decision trees offer an organization an easy way to hide its social bias? What if the organization chooses to use analyses that have results that reinforce their biases, but ignore those that do not reinforce them? Isn't this just a smokescreen to hide behind?**

YOU BE THE GUIDE

Using the Guide: Semantic Security (pages 330–331)

GOALS

- Discuss the trade-off between data availability and security.

- Introduce, explain, and discuss ways to respond to *semantic security*.

BACKGROUND AND PRESENTATION STRATEGIES

This guide briefly discusses access security and mentions some of its problems, especially authorization. We will address authorization safeguards in Chapter 12, thus here I recommended focusing on the second theme: *semantic security*.

Semantic security is the "unintended release of protected information through the release of a combination of reports or documents that individually do not contain protected information."

In this guide, Megan was able to combine data in reports that she receives for her job with data in a combination of public documents to infer at least one employee's salary, and possibly several others. She is not supposed to have this data. The fact that both the new-employee report and the employee newsletter were *delivered electronically* greatly simplified her task. This fact enabled her to readily search those documents.

In truth, this problem has existed for as long as records have been kept. It is becoming a larger factor today because more reports are being produced, and those reports are being produced *in readily searchable form*. Thus, more data can be searched faster.

The critical question is: *What can be done about it?* Who has the time to consider every possible inference from combinations of every available document? Who has the ability to make every possible inference? No one.

We consider those issues in the following questions.

SUGGESTED RESPONSES FOR DISCUSSION QUESTIONS

1. *Access security* ensures that only authorized users can take authorized actions at appropriate times. *Semantic security* concerns information that is inadvertently released via a combination of information that is obtained via authorized methods. Questions to ask:

   - **Did Megan break into any security system?** (No.)

   - **Did Megan violate any corporate policy?** (No.)

   - **Was she able to obtain, through her efforts, data that she was not authorized to have?** (Yes.)

2. Reporting systems increase the risk because they deliver data in formats that are readily searched electronically.

   - **Should (or even can) anything be done to make electronic documents not searchable?** (No.)

   - **So, do we stop producing electronic reports?** (Obviously not, but this leads to question 3.)

3. This is a tough question to answer. Organizations need to understand that combinations of documents can give away sensitive data. With that awareness, managers need to manage with the expectation that some confidential data will ultimately be released. We just don't know what or when.

   - **Is there a way for organizations to eliminate this possibility?**

     It is difficult to imagine that there is a way. Even investigating the possibilities would be incredibly expensive.

   - **How would you know if you found all the possibilities?**

   - **If you know your organization is subject to a threat, what can you do?**

     One answer: While hoping that confidential data stays that way, manage as if it won't. See the Wrap Up discussion. Also, the next two questions provide some guidance.

4. Organizations have a responsibility to comply with privacy law. Federal organizations must comply with the Privacy Act of 1974. Medical offices must comply with HIPAA. The Gramm-Leach-Bliley (GLB) Act requires financial institutions to protect their clients' data. (See the Ethics Guide in Chapter 12, pages 426–427, for more.)

   Most of these laws require basic accounting controls for security. They do not address semantic security. However, I believe lawyers will require corporations to take reasonable and prudent steps to avoid obvious semantic security problems.

5. Most business insurance policies contain clauses that cover some liability for semantic security lapses. There might be an opportunity for a new type of policy that addresses such risks. It seems doubtful, but for enough money you can get someone to insure anything. These are good questions for students to ask their insurance-course professor.

WRAP UP

It is not possible to protect against all semantic security problems. Too much information is published, and the world is full of clever, curious people.

■ **Given this fact, what can we do?**

Where possible, *design business programs for transparency.* Insofar as possible, design business programs *assuming sensitive data will become known.*

In the encryption discipline, it has long been recognized that any security technique that relies on a secret algorithm will *eventually be breached.* The technique must assume that the algorithm is in the public domain; secrecy is provided by the keys that are used with the technique.

Salary data is a particularly sensitive topic for most people:

■ **Suppose you manage a department in which salaries are to be kept confidential. Are they?**

■ **Knowing that salaries may not always be confidential, what do you do if there's a serious salary imbalance in your department?**

You can hope it never becomes public; you can try to correct it by raising someone's salary; you can prepare yourself for the lower-paid employee to come angrily in your door some day. There's no way around it, you're exposed to a risk.

For a second example, if it is important that the number of employees and the revenue of a given division remain confidential, then do all you can to keep that data confidential. But, expect that reporters, business analysts, stock pickers, and many others will be able to infer that data. *Do not construct a business plan that relies on such secrecy.* Someone will find a way to discover the data.

YOU BE THE GUIDE

Using the Guide: Data Mining in the Real World (pages 332–333)

GOAL

- Teach real-world issues and limitations for data mining.

BACKGROUND AND PRESENTATION STRATEGIES

The contrarian whom I interviewed for this guide had 15 years' experience as a data miner, most of that in the automotive industry. He'd come back to the university because he was having a career crisis. He wasn't sure that data mining was worth it. He'd begun to question the validity of many data mining techniques. His concerns and misgivings are summarized in this guide.

Judging by his experience, especially his last comment about luck, we can conclude that data mining shares risk characteristics with other forms of mining. Sometimes you find the gold or the oil, and sometimes you do not.

A *difficult ethical dilemma* is buried in this guide—one that I softened in writing the text. At the end of 6 months, this person had determined that the model that he had developed was, in fact, useless. They had overfit the data, and *he believed the predictive power of the model was nil*. He did not believe that the model should be implemented. But he was a junior member of the team, and his boss did not want to admit the model they had developed would be a bad predictor. His response was to leave that company within a few months. He still feels guilty about it—guilty that he didn't get a better result and guilty that he wasn't more honest and forthcoming. See question 3, that follows.

SUGGESTED RESPONSES FOR DISCUSSION QUESTIONS

1. The problems he identifies are:
   - Dirty data
   - Missing values
   - Lack of knowledge at start of project
   - Overfitting
   - Probabilistic—good model may have unlucky first uses
   - Seasonality
   - High risk—cannot know outcome

The students may not understand *overfitting*. It's not discussed in the main part of the text. Overfitting occurs when you create a model that is too complicated. Basically, your model captures not only the essence of the underlying phenomena, but also the random error that happened to be present in the data you analyzed. When you try to use that model to predict, it predicts both the phenomena and the error; but the error, because it's random, will be different than it was for the sample study data. Thus, the model is terrific for explaining the sample data, but horrible as a predictor.

Overfitting is a huge problem in data mining, especially when using neural nets. They can produce such a complicated set of equations that they can predict any sample, including all of the sample's error.

2. No. That would be throwing the baby out with the bath water. However, I would say:

   - **Have a clear business objective in mind. Don't just "see what the data show."**

   - **Understand how the results of data mining can lead to action—not just insight.**

   - **If possible, run a pilot study with a limited amount of data and determine the utility of the analysis.**

   (A pilot study may not be possible. If the only difference between the pilot and the full analysis is the amount of data processed, then the complete study infrastructure may need to be finished just to do the pilot.)

   - **Be aware of the problem of overfitting—one can create a model that will fit the sample data perfectly, but that will have no utility for prediction.**

   - **Keep in mind the risky nature of data mining.**

3. Some possible responses: First, discuss your misgivings with your boss. Maybe you are wrong about the quality of the model. Maybe there are other factors in the background that make your fears ungrounded. Maybe your boss agrees and wants to strategize with you about what to do.

   - **If your boss disagrees, would you go higher in the organization?**

   Maybe. But only after very careful questioning of my situation and motives. I'd ask myself whether the problems and risks of going higher are worth the gain.

Risks:

- This will end my relationship with my boss.
- My boss will become my enemy within the company.
- I may expose both of us to substantial career risk.
- My boss's boss may think I'm a whiner and a problem maker.
- My boss's boss may not want to know.

Gain:

- Saving the organization time and money.
- If the data mining project involves people, saving the harm that will be done by miscategorizing people.
- Preserving the reputation of data mining within the organization.

Other courses of action are to quit the company, to transfer to another group, or to not do anything at all.

Or, you could do as the real contrarian did, go back to graduate school.

All in all, this is a very difficult situation with no clear and obvious solution.

WRAP UP

■ **This case has two major themes: realistic problems in data mining and an ethical dilemma—when you know something that will be possibly self-defeating to reveal. Both are important.**

■ **You may not be a data miner in your career, but you will most likely encounter, sometime during your career, a situation when you may have to take self-defeating actions in order to act ethically. You need to keep thinking about such situations and what YOU will do.**

Information Systems Management

Part 4 addresses the management of information systems development, IS resources, and IS security in Chapters 10, 11, and 12, respectively. Even if you are not an IS major, you need to know about these functions so that you can be a successful and effective consumer of IS professionals' services.

GearUp and Fox Lake are both small companies with well under $100 million a year in sales. Like most small companies, neither has a formal organization for managing information systems development, resources, and security. However, small organizations are not exempt from these responsibilities, and, in fact, in a small business without professional IS personnel, those responsibilities fall more heavily on business managers. So, pay close attention to the

user and management responsibilities in these three chapters.

If you work for a medium-size or larger organization that does have the support of a professional staff, these chapters will help you understand the responsibilities and activities of IS professionals, which will enable you to work more effectively with them.

In Chapter 10, we will examine how Fox Lake could define new business processes and an information system to support those processes. In Chapter 11, we will investigate what Fox Lake is and is not doing with regard to the management of IS resources. Finally, in Chapter 12 we will see why Fox Lake's information systems are particularly vulnerable to computer misuse and crime. It's not going to be pretty!

Business Process and Information Systems Development

"**Jeff, we clean** the clubhouse restrooms twice a day . . . in the morning before 7 and again just before lunch. We've been doing that for years. Never been a problem." Mike Stone, facilities manager, is defending his department in a meeting with Jeff Lloyd, Fox Lake's general manager, and Anne Foster, manager of the newly formed wedding events department.

"That's just great Mike. Just great." Anne raises her voice, "And what if, like on the PAST THREE SATUR-DAYS, we have two weddings in the afternoon? Do you think maybe guests at the second wedding would like clean bathrooms?" Anne is incredulous that she has to ask for clean bathrooms, of all things. "It's your friends and family at a wedding . . . at Fox Lake! You would hope the bathrooms will be clean!"

Jeff sits impatiently, he doesn't like the direction of this discussion, but he doesn't know where to take it . . .

Mike continues. "Look, Anne, I can hire staff to clean the bathrooms on whatever schedule you want. I DO have a budget to pay attention to, however, so I'm not going to hire people to clean bathrooms that are already clean because we DIDN'T have two weddings that day."

"Well, Mike, should we talk about our problem with the toilet in the ladies room?"

"What do you mean?"

"I mean for a whole month, we've had a toilet that overflows . . . "

"Mike, is that right?" Jeff jumps in.

"Look. I don't have a plumber on staff. Steve's the weekend manager. He knows we watch our expenses, and he's not going to call a plumber on Saturday, week-end rates and all. So, he does the right thing. He goes over there and tries to fix it himself."

"Seems like a good response, doesn't it?" Jeff asks, wondering where this one is going.

"I thought so, too. Saves us money and solves the problem. Turns out that plumbing equipment was never designed to have 250 people at an event. It's designed for one or two people from the restaurant, maybe a party of four golfers. Anyway, he fixes the toilet with spare parts and whatnot and, with that heavy use, it breaks again, and Anne comes unglued! Besides, if I had notice, I could bring in some Porta Potties . . ."

"Mike!!! This is a wedding! You're not going take your Vera Wang gown into a Porta Potty. I CAN'T BELIEVE I'M HAVING THIS DISCUSSION!!!" Anne is stupefied at his comment.

Jeff steps in. "OK, you two. Clearly, we've got some work to do. We're almost at the end of the big wedding season. Take a break and then sit down together and schedule it out. Figure out what it will take to get us through this year. Mike, let me know if you need more money and I'll see what I can come up with. But, I don't mean a lot. Meanwhile, I'll start thinking about a longer-term solution."

Next week, Jeff meets in his office with Laura Shen, who'd been recommended to him as someone who could help solve the wedding events and facilities problems.

"Laura, I don't really know what you do. Margaret Silvester, one of our board members, said you'd helped with some computer problems at her company, and she insisted I meet with you. This doesn't seem like a problem for a computer programmer, though."

"Jeff, I'm not a programmer. I'm what's called a 'business analyst.' I know technology, and while I have written computer programs, that's not what I do. I specialize in understanding business needs, strategies, and goals and helping businesses implement systems to accomplish those needs. Often that involves computer-based systems, but not always."

"Well, what do you know about us?"

"Margaret gave me a quick rundown. You've recently acquired a wedding events business and you've had problems integrating it with the rest of Fox Lake."

"That's about right. But, we didn't acquire a business . . . we hired someone who owned a small business and she hoped to make it bigger working for Fox Lake. I was looking for a source of more revenue."

"So, what's the problem?"

"Facilities, mostly. We had some issues about using membership data for marketing, but not serious ones. The big problems are sharing facilities, timely maintenance, and tracking repairs. And, these wedding events stress us in ways we're not used to. The crew at the restaurant can serve up a few burgers and fries to the club members, but when we start putting high-end caterers into their kitchen space, well, like I said, it's stressful . . ."

"I might be able to help. Did you see this coming when you started wedding events?"

"No, not really. We just thought we could use our buildings for weddings . . . I didn't understand how it would impact everything else."

"Well, let me talk with your key people for a bit, and I'll get back to you with some ideas and a proposal." ■

Study Questions

Q1 Why do organizations need to manage business processes?

Q2 What are the stages of business process management (BPM)?

Q3 How can BPMN process diagrams help identify and solve process problems?

Q4 Which comes first, business processes or information systems?

Q5 What are systems development activities?

Q6 Why are business processes and systems development difficult and risky?

Q7 What are the keys for successful process and systems development projects?

Q8 2022?

Suppose Fox Lake had hired you instead of Laura. How would you proceed? According to Jeff, "The big problems are sharing facilities, timely maintenance, and tracking repairs." How would you address these problems? What would you advise Fox Lake to do? Would you start by creating a spreadsheet or a database to schedule maintenance? If so, how would Fox Lake use either to solve these problems? Or, would you start by creating some sort of information system that has procedures for scheduling the use of facilities? Or, would you begin with a business process, say the process of planning weddings, and work from there to the need for information systems, and from there to the need for a spreadsheet or a database?

To answer these questions, we will address two major themes in this chapter: business process management and information systems development. The two themes are closely related and overlap in important ways. We begin in Q1 through Q3 by describing the need for process management, the stages in the business process management cycle, and BPMN, a notation used for documenting business processes.

Next, in Q4, we investigate the relationship of processes and systems by asking the question: Which should organizations create first? The response to that question sets up the discussion of systems development activities in Q5 and the challenges and keys to success in development projects in Q6 and Q7. We'll wrap up this chapter with a discussion of how information systems careers are likely to change between now and 2022.

Q1 Why Do Organizations Need to Manage Business Processes?

In order to discuss process design, we will extend the definition of business processes that we used in Chapter 3. Here we will define a **business process** as a network of activities, repositories, roles, resources, and data flows that interact to accomplish a business function. As stated in Chapter 3, *activities* are collections of related tasks that receive inputs and produce outputs. A *repository* is a collection of something; an inventory is a physical repository and a database is a data repository. The new terms in this definition are **roles**, which are collections of activities, and **resources,** which are people or computer applications that are assigned to roles. Finally, a **data flow** is the movement of data from one activity or another or from an activity to a repository, or the reverse.

To make this more clear, you can think of roles as job titles. Example roles are *salesperson, credit manager, inventory supervisor*, and the like. Thus, an organization might assign three people (resources) to the salesperson role, or it might create an information system (resource) to perform the credit manager role.

To better understand this definition, consider a simple, but common, example.

A Sample Ordering Business Process

Suppose that you work in sales for a company that sells equipment and supplies to the hotel industry. Your products include hotel furniture, cleaning equipment, and supplies, such as towels and linens and staff uniforms. Processing an order involves the five steps shown in Figure 10-1. You are one of many people (resources) that perform the salesperson role.

As a salesperson, you do not perform all of the activities shown; rather, you orchestrate their performance. You are the customer's representative within the firm. You ensure that the operations department verifies that the product is available and can be delivered to the customer on the requested schedule. You check with accounting to

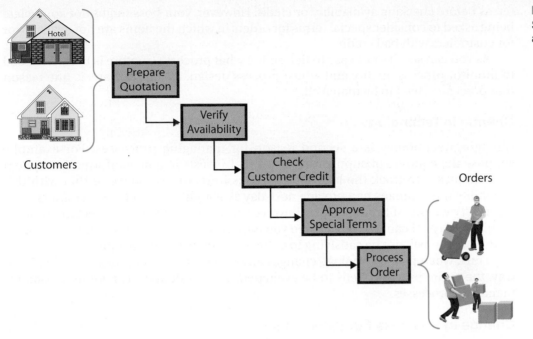

Figure 10-1
Steps in Processing
an Order

verify the credit required to process the order, and you check with your boss, a sales manager, to approve any special terms the customer might request (discounts, free shipping, extended return policy, etc.). We will document this process further in Q2.

Why Does This Process Need Management?

When you joined the firm, they taught you to follow this process, and you've been using for it 2 years. It seems to work, so why does it need to be managed? The fundamental answer to this question is that processes are dynamic and often need to be changed. This need can arise because of a process quality problem, because of a change in technology, or because of a change in some business fundamental.

Improve Process Quality

As you learned in Chapter 7, process quality has two dimensions: efficiency (use of resources) and effectiveness (accomplish strategy). The most obvious reason for changing a process is that it has efficiency or effectiveness problems. Consider a sales process. If the organization's goal is to provide high-quality service, then if the process takes too long or if it rejects credit inappropriately it is ineffective and needs to be changed.

With regard to efficiency, the process may use its resources poorly. For example, according to Figure 10-1, salespeople verify product availability before checking customer credit. If checking availability means nothing more than querying an information system for inventory levels, that sequence makes sense. But suppose that checking availability means that someone in operations needs not only to verify inventory levels, but also to verify that the goods can be shipped to arrive on time. If the order delivery is complex, say the order is for a large number of beds that have to be shipped from three different warehouses, an hour or two of labor may be required to verify shipping schedules.

After verifying shipping, the next step is to verify credit. If it turns out the customer has insufficient credit and the order is refused, the shipping-verification labor will have been wasted. So, it might make sense to check credit before checking availability.

Similarly, if the customer's request for special terms is disapproved, the cost of checking availability and credit is wasted. If the customer has requested special terms that are not normally approved, it might make sense to obtain approval of special terms before checking availability or credit. However, your boss might not appreciate being asked to consider special terms for orders in which the items are not available or for customers with bad credit.

As you can see, it's not easy to determine what process structure is best. The need to monitor process quality and adjust process design, as appropriate, is one reason that processes need to be managed.

Change in Technology

Changing technology is a second reason for managing processes. For example, suppose the equipment supplier in Figure 10-1 invests in a new information system that enables it to track the location of trucks in real time. Suppose that with this capability the company can provide next-day availability of goods to customers. That capability will be of limited value, however, if the existing credit-checking process requires 2 days. "I can get the goods to you tomorrow, but I can't verify your credit until next Monday" will not be satisfying to either customers or salespeople.

Thus, when new technology changes any of a process's activities in a significant way, the entire process needs to be evaluated. That evaluation is another reason for managing processes.

Change in Business Fundamentals

A third reason for managing business processes is a change in business fundamentals. A substantial change in any of the following factors might result in the need to modify business processes:

- Market (e.g., new customer category, change in customer characteristics)
- Product lines
- Supply chain
- Company policy
- Company organization (e.g., merger, acquisition)
- Internationalization
- Business environment

To understand the implications of such changes, consider just the sequence of verifying availability and checking credit in Figure 10-1. A new category of customers could mean that the credit-check process needs to be modified; perhaps a certain category of customers is too risky to be extended credit. All sales to such customers must be cash. A change in product lines might require different ways of checking availability. A change in the supply chain might mean that the company no longer stocks some items in inventory but ships directly from the manufacturer instead.

Or, the company might make broad changes to its credit policy. It might, for example, decide to accept more risk and sell to companies with lower credit scores. In this case, approval of special terms becomes more critical than checking credit, and the sequence of those two activities might need to be changed.

Of course, a merger or acquisition will mean substantial change in the organization and its products and markets, as does moving portions of the business offshore or engaging in international commerce. Finally, a substantial change in the business environment, say, the onset of a recession, might mean that credit checking becomes vitally important and needs to be moved to first in this process.

Q2 What Are the Stages of Business Process Management (BPM)?

The factors just discussed will necessitate changes in business processes, whether the organization recognizes that need or not. Organizations can either plan to develop and modify business processes, or they can wait and let the need for change just

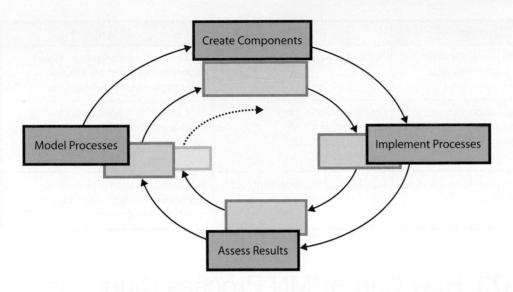

Figure 10-2
Stages in the BPM Cycle

happen to them. In the latter case, the business will continually be in crisis, dealing with one process emergency after another.

Figure 10-2 shows the basic activities in **business process management (BPM),** a cyclical process for systematically creating, assessing, and altering business processes. This cycle begins by creating models of business processes. The business users who have expertise and are involved in the particular process (this could be you!) adjust and evaluate those models. Usually teams build an **as-is model** that documents the current situation and then changes that model to make adjustments necessary to solve process problems.

Given the model, the next step is to create system components. Those components have the five elements of every information system, although some are entirely automated (no people and procedures) and some are entirely manual (no hardware or software). Next, needed business processes or changes to existing business processes are implemented.

Well-managed organizations don't stop there. Instead, they create policy, procedures, and committees to continually assess business process effectiveness. The Information Systems Audit and Control Association has created a set of standard practices called **COBIT (Control Objectives for Information and related Technology)** that are often used in the assessment stage of the BPM cycle. Explaining these standards is beyond the scope of this discussion, but you should know that they exist. See www.isaca.org/cobit for more information.

When the assessment process indicates that a significant need for change has arisen, the BPM cycle is repeated. Adjusted and new process models are developed, and components are created, implemented, and assessed.

Effective BPM enables organizations to attain continuous process improvement. Like quality improvement, process improvement is never finished. Process effectiveness is constantly monitored, and processes are adjusted as and when required.

Business process management has the same scope as discussed for information systems in Chapter 7: departmental, enterprise, and interenterprise. As shown in Figure 10-3, BPM becomes more difficult as the scope of the underlying processes increases.

Finally, do not assume that business process management applies only to commercial, profit-making organizations. Nonprofit and government organizations have all three types of processes shown in Figure 10-3, but most of these processes are service-oriented, rather than revenue-oriented. Your state's Department of Labor, for example, has a need to manage its processes, as does the Girl Scouts of America. BPM applies to all types of organizations.

Scope	Description	Example	BPM Role
Departmental	Business process resides within a single business function.	Accounts payable	BPM authority belongs to a single departmental manager who has authority to resolve BPM issues.
Enterprise	Business process crosses into multiple departments within a single organization.	Customer relationship management (CRM); enterprise resource management (ERP)	BPM authority shared across several or many departments. Problem resolution via committee and policy.
Interenterprise	Business process crosses into multiple organizations.	Supply chain management (SCM)	BPM authority shared by multiple companies. Problem resolution via negotiation and contract.

Figure 10-3
Scope of Business Process
Management

Q3 How Can BPMN Process Diagrams Help Identify and Solve Process Problems?

One of the four stages of BPM, and arguably the most important stage, is to model business processes. It is so important because such models are the blueprint for the new process and system components. If models are incomplete and incorrect, components cannot be created correctly. In this question, you will learn standard notation for creating process documentation.

Need for Standard for Business Processing Notation

As stated, we define a *business process* as a network of activities, repositories, roles, resources, and data flows that interact to accomplish a business function. This definition is commonly accepted, but unfortunately dozens of other definitions are used by other authors, industry analysts, and software products. For example, IBM, a key leader in business process management, has a product called WebSphere Business Modeler that uses a different set of terms. It has activities and resources, but it uses the term *repository* more broadly that we do, and it uses the term *business item* for *data flow*. Other business-modeling software products use still other definitions and terms. These differences and inconsistencies can be problematic, especially when two different organizations with two different sets of definitions must work together.

Accordingly, a software-industry standards organization called the **Object Management Group (OMG)** created a standard set of terms and graphical notations for documenting business processes. That standard, called **Business Process Modeling Notation (BPMN),** is documented at www.bpmn.org. A complete description of BPMN is beyond the scope of this text. However, the basic symbols are easy to understand, and they work naturally with our definition of business process. Hence, we will use the BPMN symbols in the illustrations in the chapter. All of the diagrams in this chapter were drawn using Microsoft Visio, which includes several BPMN symbol templates. Figure 10-4 summarizes the basic BPMN symbols.

Documenting the As-Is Business Order Process

Figure 10-5 shows the as-is, or existing, order process introduced in Figure 10-1. First, note that this process is a model, an abstraction that shows the essential elements of the process but omits many details. If it were not an abstraction, the model would be as large as the business itself. This diagram is shown in **swim-lane layout.** In this format, each role in the business process is given its own swim lane. In Figure 10-5, there are five roles and hence five swim lanes. All activities for a given role are shown

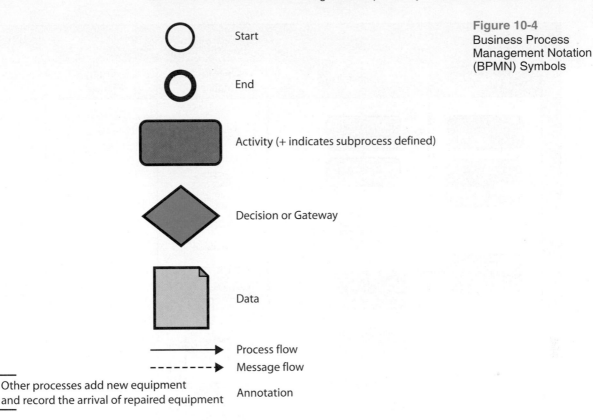

Figure 10-4
Business Process
Management Notation
(BPMN) Symbols

in that role's swim lane. Swim-lane layout simplifies process diagrams and draws attention to interactions among components of the diagram.

Two kinds of arrows are shown. Dotted arrows depict the flow of messages and data flows. Solid arrows depict the flow or sequence of the activities in the process. Some sequence flows have data associated with them as well. According to Figure 10-5, the customer sends an RFQ (request for quotation) to a salesperson (dotted arrow). That salesperson prepares a quotation in the first activity and then (solid arrow) submits the quotation back to the customer. You can follow the rest of the process in this diagram. Allocate inventory means that if the items are available they are allocated to the customer so that they will not be sold to someone else.

Diamonds represent decisions and usually contain a question that can be answered with yes or no. Process arrows labeled Yes and No exit two of the points of the diamond. Three of the activities in the as-is diagram contain a square with a plus (+) sign. This notation means that the activity is considered to be independent of this process and that it is defined in greater detail in another diagram.

For example, the Check Customer Credit subprocess is shown in Figure 10-6. Note the role named *CRM* in this subprocess. In fact, this role is performed entirely by an information system, although we cannot determine that fact from this diagram. Again, each role is fulfilled by some set of resources, either people or information systems, or both.

Using Process Diagrams to Identify Process Problems

The processes shown in Figures 10-5 and 10-6 have problems. Before you continue, examine these figures and see if you can determine what they are.

....

The problems in these processes involve allocations. The Operations Manager role allocates inventory to the orders as they are processed and the Credit Manager role allocates credit to the customer of orders in process. These allocations are correct as long as the order is accepted. However, if the order is rejected, these allocations are

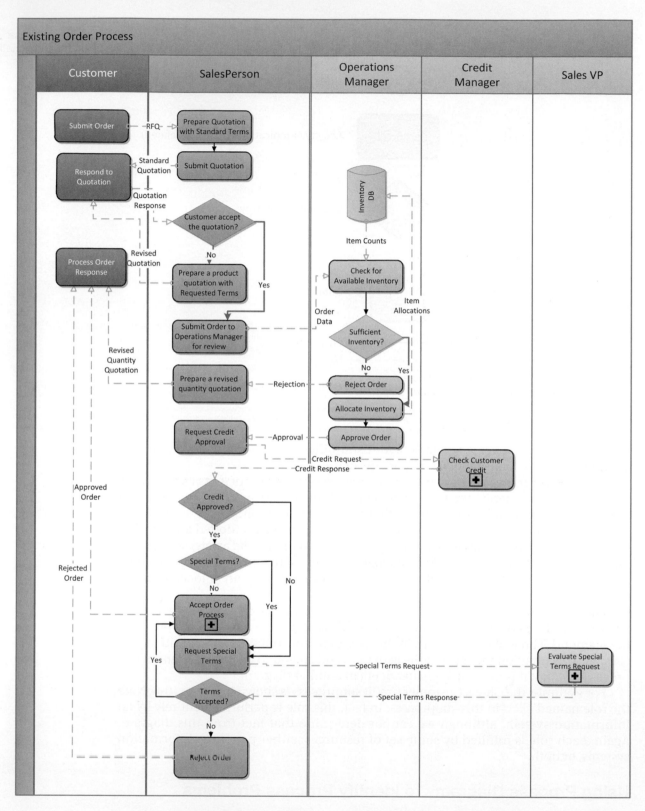

Figure 10-5
Existing Ordering Process

not freed. Thus, inventory is allocated that will not be ordered, and credit is extended for orders that will not be processed.

One fix (several are possible) is to define an independent process for Reject Order (in Figure 10-5 that would mean placing a box with a + in the Reject Order activity) and then designing the Reject Order subprocess to free allocations. Creating such a diagram is left as exercise 3 in Using Your Knowledge (page 381).

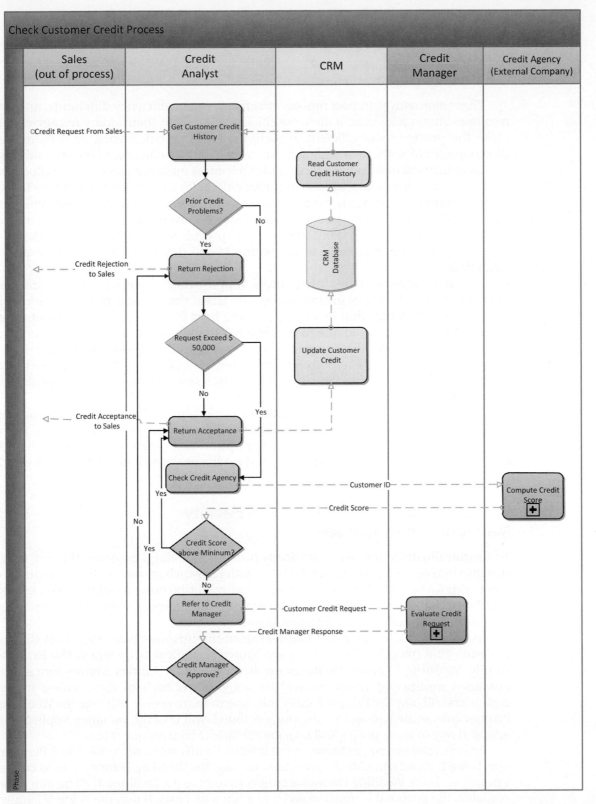

Figure 10-6
Check Customer Credit
Process

How Can Business Process Quality Be Improved?

Two ways of improving process quality are to:

- Add more resources
- Change process structure

These alternatives impact process effectiveness and efficiency differently. Adding resources always adds cost. If there are efficiencies of scale, then adding resources will make the process more efficient. If there are no scale efficiencies, or if there are diseconomies of scale, then adding resources will reduce efficiency. However, adding resources may still make sense if those added resources make the process more effective.

Changing process structure can improve either efficiency or effectiveness or both. In some situations, changing the process structure reduces work, and hence reduces cost. In other situations, cost increases, but effectiveness increases sufficiently to justify the added costs. Ideally, the change to process structure improves both.

Of course, it is also possible to add resources and change process structure at the same time.

To better understand these alternatives, suppose the company having the process in Figure 10-5 finds that its inventory costs are larger than it expects. Investigation of the causes determines that inventory is being held for excessive amounts of time because orders are delayed due to the time required to check the customer's credit. To solve this problem, the company could speed up the process by adding more people resources to the Credit Analyst role shown in Figure 10-6. Or, the company might add resources by investing in an information system to augment or replace the humans who perform the credit-checking role.

Instead of adding resources, the company could address this problem by changing the structure of the process to check credit before checking inventory availability. Such a change is shown in Figure 10-7. Another option is for the company to both add resources to the credit-checking process and to change the sequence of inventory and credit checking.

Fox Lake Wedding Planning and Facility Maintenance Processes

To further illustrate the use of business process modeling, consider the Fox Lake scenario that opened this chapter. It ended with Laura, a business analyst, planning to meet with Anne and Mike to determine what might be done to address Fox Lake's problems. Because Fox Lake has no existing maintenance scheduling system, this team of people needed to model a new business process.

Assume that after they met Laura created the business process model shown in Figure 10-8 (page 352). Four roles are shown in vertical swim lanes: The Bride & Family, Wedding Planner, Facilities Application, and Facilities Maintenance. An unknown number of resources will be assigned to each of these roles; many customers will play the Bride & Family role, one or more people will take the Wedding Planner role, some person or computing resource will take the Facilities Application role, and one or more people will take the Facilities Maintenance role.

Examine the exchanges between the Bride & Family role and the Wedding Planner role. Bride & Family provide the requirements that the Wedding Planner uses to create a proposal. Then, Wedding Planner attempts to reserve the facilities. If all facilities are available, the proposal is transformed into a bid with costs. If not, the Bride & Family are asked to revise their requirements (smaller number of guests, different date, reception outside, etc.). If the Bride & Family accept the bid and sign the bid, then the facility reservations are confirmed and a deposit is collected. That collection activity is documented as a separate process.

This process model, like all models, is an abstraction. It does not include every detail, but it captures the essence of the process and the need to reserve Fox Lake facilities. It might seem odd to you to formalize the process of planning a wedding

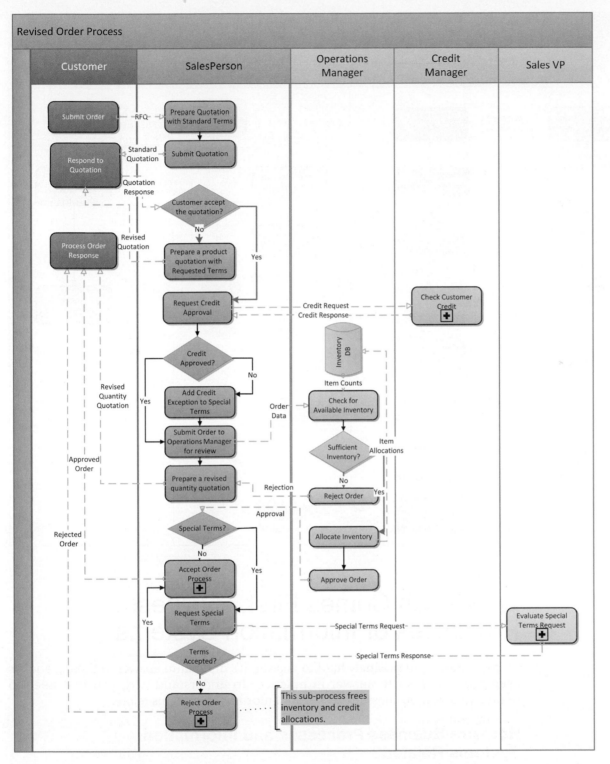

Figure 10-7
Revised Order Process

in this way, but such formalization is needed to create and implement business processes and related information systems.

By the way, this model is incomplete. Many activities at Fox Lake besides wedding planning need to reserve facilities. Most likely, Laura would document those processes as well, or she might generalize this process into one that would work for all facility users, not just wedding planning. We needn't be concerned with those extensions here, however.

The next step in the BPM process is to create components. That step leads us into the topic of systems development, and we begin by discussing the relationship of business processes and information systems.

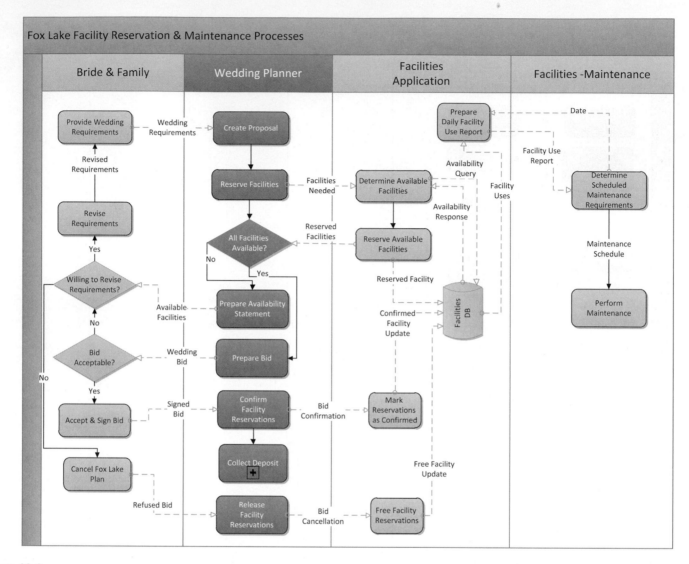

Figure 10-8
Fox Lake Wedding Planning
and Facilities Maintenance
Processes

Q4 Which Comes First, Business Processes or Information Systems?

This question is surprisingly hard to answer. It's difficult to answer in theory, and it's even more difficult to answer in practice. To understand why, you first need to understand how business processes and information systems relate.

How Are Business Processes and Information Systems Related?

To learn the relationship between business processes and information systems, examine Figure 10-9, which is a color-coded version of Figure 10-8. Information system elements are shown in bold colors. The Facilities database is shown in red, Facilities Reservation application programs are shown in orange, and procedures for using the Facilities Reservation system are shown in blue. This process involves a second, separate billing information system that is processed in the Collect Deposit subprocess shown in green. The other activities in this process are not part of any information system.

We can deduce three important principles from this figure. First, information systems and business processes are not the same thing. Information system elements

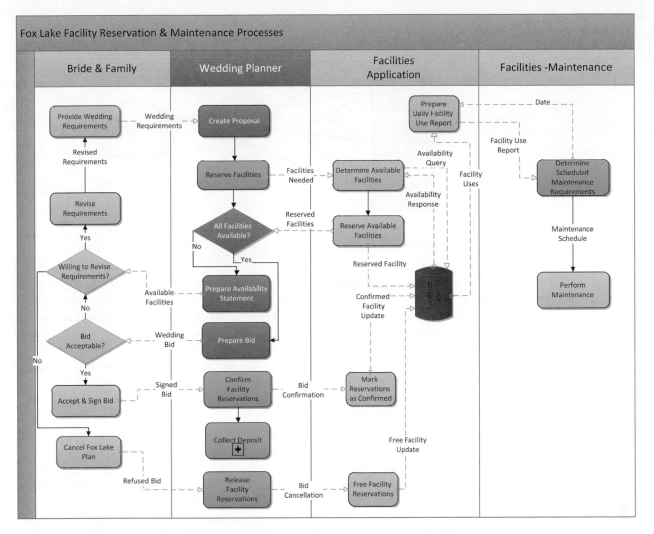

Figure 10-9
Fox Lake Processes Showing
IS Components

are embedded within business processes, but there are activities in business processes that are not part of the information system. Second, this business process uses two separate information systems; and, in general, a business process can utilize zero, one, or more information systems.

The third principle is not visible in Figure 10-9, but we can infer it. The Facilities Reservation information system is likely to be used by other business processes. In fact, the Fox Lake billing process uses this system to bill customers for facility use. In addition, the budgetary process uses the Facility Reservation system to determine a budget for future facility revenue, and so forth. Thus, a particular information system may be used by one or more business processes.

Recalling the cardinality principles from Chapter 5, we can say that the relationship of business processes and information systems is many-to-many, as illustrated in Figure 10-10. For example, the Wedding Planning process uses two information systems (many), and, at the same time, the Facilities Scheduling system is used in four different business processes (also many).

Which Comes First?

Why do we care about this? What difference it make? The many-to-many relationship between business processes and information systems poses a dilemma when it comes time to build them. Which should we do first? Should we specify one or more business processes and then build the information systems that they require? Or, do we attempt to determine, in the abstract, all of the ways that someone might use an information system, build it, and then construct the business processes around it?

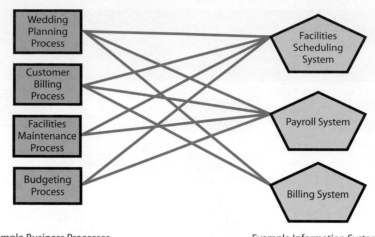

Example Business Processes   Example Information Systems

If you reflect on this situation, you can see why ERP systems, which promise to do everything, are both wonderful and terrible. They're wonderful because they include all the business processes and all the system components that an organization will need, at least as determined by the ERP vendor. They're terrible because, to implement ERP, an organization must attempt to do everything at once.

But, for non-ERP business processes and information systems, and for small organizations like Fox Lake, which should come first? Consider the alternatives.

Business Processes First

Suppose we decide to design business processes first and then build information system components as a consequence of that process design. If we take this approach, we'll have a development process that looks like that in Figure 10-11. The organization will engage in business process management and construct system components in the create components stage of the BPM cycle.

This approach works well for the business processes that are being constructed, but what about others in the future? Suppose the Facilities Reservation system is constructed to reserve facilities like rooms in buildings and the restaurant and that it works well for that purpose. But what if Fox Lake's golf operations department wants to be able to reserve one or both golf courses for special events? The golf course reservation process was not part of the requirements when the Facilities

Figure 10-11
BPM and Systems
Development

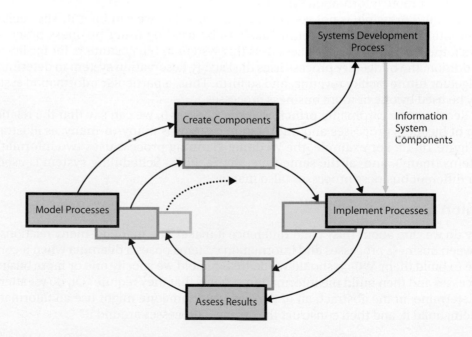

Reservation system was constructed for Wedding Events, and the system won't work for that process.

So, starting from processes and working toward information systems is likely to work well for the business processes under consideration, but will cause problems later, for other processes that use the same information systems. So, what if we start with the information system, first?

Information System First

To start with systems first, a development team would talk with representative future users of the system and attempt to determine all of the ways that someone at Fox Lake might want to reserve facilities. From those requirements, they would then design components and construct the system.

Systems development is the process of creating and maintaining an information system. The most common technique for developing information systems is the **systems development life cycle (SDLC)**, and it has the five steps shown in Figure 10-12. A high-level business planning process determines that a system is needed for some function; at Fox Lake that function would be to reserve facilities. Given that system need, the development team would then refine the system definition, determine requirements, design system components, and then implement the system.

This development process makes business processes a poor step-child of the information systems development process. The focus is on hardware, software, data, procedures (for using the system only), and user training. Some aspects of business processes will be constructed as part of the system implementation, but, as you saw in Figure 10-9, business processes can include many activities that are not part of the information system. Those activities are unlikely to be considered when the system is constructed.

Another Factor: Off-the-Shelf Software

A missing factor in this discussion is off-the-shelf software. Few organizations today can afford to create computer programs and design databases in-house. It is unlikely that Fox Lake, for example, will do so. Instead, most organizations attempt to license software off-the-shelf and adapt it to their needs, or adapt their needs to it.

So, if an organization knows that it will most likely license off-the-shelf software, is it better to design processes first or to develop information systems first? Unfortunately, again, there is no demonstrably correct answer. If an organization starts with business processes first, it is likely to choose a package that will work well for the processes being

Figure 10-12
Classic Five-Step Systems Development Life Cycle

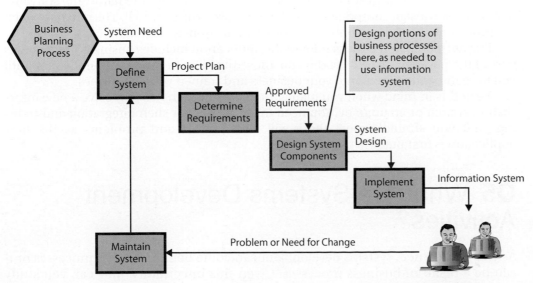

developed, but that may not work well for other processes that may come along later (like golf operations wanting to reserve golf courses). However, if it starts with information systems and collects all the requirements, it is likely to find a package that will work better for all users, but, again, business processes will receive short shrift.

And the Answer Is . . .

In theory, it is better to start with business processes. As discussed in Chapter 3, business processes are closer to the organization's competitive strategy and other goals and objectives. Starting with processes and working toward systems is more likely to result in processes and systems that are aligned with the organization's strategy and direction.

In practice, however, the answer is not clear. Organizations today take both approaches. Sometimes the same organization takes one approach with one set of processes and systems and a second approach with a different set.

The factor that overtakes all is off-the-shelf software. The vendor of the software knows the features that are most commonly needed by its customers. Therefore, if an organization starts with business processes and selects an application that works for those processes, it is likely that the application will also include features and functions that will be needed by other business processes to be designed in the future. At Fox Lake, an application that can be used to reserve buildings and rooms is likely to be adaptable enough to also reserve golf courses and golf facilities.

Most likely, an application software vendor includes procedures for using that software as part of its offering. So, the procedure components in Figure 10-9 (shown in blue) are most likely part of the package. However, the entire business process in Figure 10-9 is unlikely to be part of the vendor's package.

Therefore, in most cases, if an organization is likely to license an application from a vendor, it is better to begin with processes. This rule is not ironclad, however. You should expect to find both approaches used in organizations during your career.

Not Possible to Buy Processes or Systems Off-the-Shelf

Before we continue with systems development, do not be misled by the last few paragraphs. It is possible to buy an off-the-shelf computer application that will fulfill the Facilities Application role. Laura, and possibly others, will most likely search for just such an application rather than creating it in-house.

However, it is *not* possible to buy an information system off-the-shelf. The procedures for reserving facilities, confirming reservations, and so on all need to be integrated into Fox Lake's business processes. Employees who fulfill process roles need to be trained on those procedures. The most we can say is that the hardware, software, and database design components can be purchased off-the-shelf. The database data, the procedures, and the people are all provided in-house.

Furthermore, even if the vendor of the application includes business processes as part of the package, as ERP vendors do, those business processes are not yours until you have integrated them into your business and trained your employees.

Keep this in mind when you manage a department that is to receive a new information system or an upgrade. You need to allow time for such integration and training, and you should expect there will be mistakes and problems as the new application is first put into use.

Q5 What Are Systems Development Activities?

As you just learned, systems development can come before business processes or it can be a result of business processes. Given this uncertainty, how can you study systems development activities?

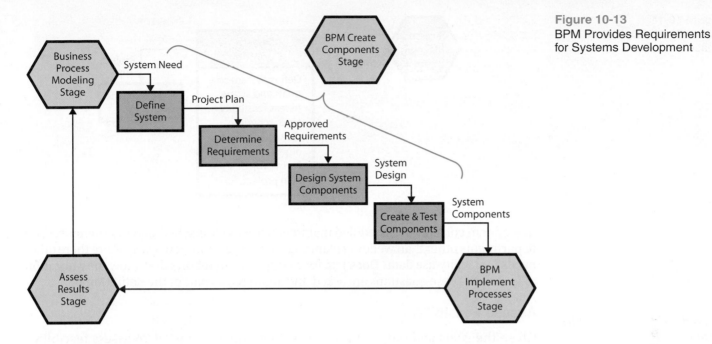

Figure 10-13
BPM Provides Requirements
for Systems Development

Examine Figure 10-12 again. It shows the basic phases of the systems development life cycle, the most commonly used process for creating information systems. If we put those phases into the context of Figure 10-11, we will obtain the diagram in Figure 10-13. Whether you use the process in Figure 10-12 (systems first) or the process in Figure 10-13 (processes first), the same basic activities are involved in creating IS components:

- Define the system
- Determine requirements
- Design system components
- Implementation:
  - If using Figure 10-12, implement the system
  - If using Figure 10-13, create and test components
- Maintenance:
  - If using Figure 10-12, maintain the system
  - If using Figure 10-13, assess results

So, if you learn the nature of the work for each of these activities, you will be well prepared to participate as a user, manager, and business professional in development activities regardless of which approach your organization takes. As indicated, there are some important differences in the implementation and maintenance activities, but we can deal with those differences as we go.

So, consider the nature of the work for each of these activities.

Define the System

In response to the need for the new system, the organization will assign a few employees, possibly on a part-time basis, to define the new system, assess its feasibility, and plan the project. In a large organization, someone from the IS department leads the initial team, but the members of that initial team are both users and IS professionals. For an organization like Fox Lake, the team would most likely be led by an outside consultant like Laura.

Define System Goals and Scope

As shown in Figure 10-14, the first step is to define the goals and scope of the new information system. Is the goal of the new system only to implement the elements required for the processes in Figure 10-11? Or, is the new system broader in scope? Should the

Figure 10-14
SDLC: System Definition
Phase

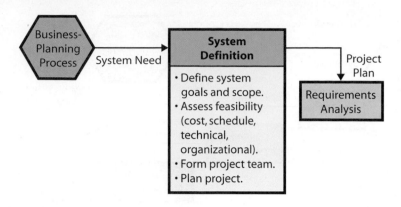

new system consider unscheduled maintenance as well as scheduled maintenance? Are departments other than wedding planning going to use this new system? Are there other needs for facility use data? Does Jeff, for example, want reports that show the utilization of facilities? These questions are asked and answered as part of the definition phase.

Assess Feasibility

For a discussion of the ethical issues relating to cost estimates, see the Ethics Guide on pages 362–363.

Given the goals and scope of the new system, the next task is to assess feasibility. "Does this project make sense?" The aim here is to eliminate obviously nonsensical projects before forming a project development team and investing significant labor.

Feasibility has four dimensions: **cost**, **schedule**, **technical**, and **organizational feasibility**. Because IS development projects are difficult to budget and schedule, cost and schedule feasibility can be only an approximate, back-of-the-envelope analysis. The purpose is to eliminate any obviously infeasible ideas as soon as possible.

Technical feasibility refers to whether existing information technology is likely to be able to meet the needs of the new system. The new system at Fox Lake is well within the capabilities of existing technology. For more advanced systems, this is not always the case. Between 1995 and 2005, the IRS engaged in a 10-year information systems project disaster when it attempted to use new technology to revamp tax return processing without assessing the technical feasibility. Finally, *organizational feasibility* concerns whether the new system fits within the organization's customs, culture, charter, or legal requirements. At Fox Lake, for example, is a daily maintenance schedule appropriate? Are there union regulations that stipulate that workers need to have advanced notice of hours to be worked? Does the system need to prepare a weekly or monthly schedule to comply with these rules?

Form a Project Team

If the defined project is determined to be feasible, the next step is to form the project team. Normally, the team consists of both IT personnel and user representatives. The project manager and IT personnel can be in-house personnel or outside contractors. We will describe various means of obtaining IT personnel using outside sources and the benefits and risks of outsourcing when we discuss IS management in the next chapter.

Typical personnel on a development team are a manager (or mangers for larger projects), business analysts, system analysts, programmers, software testers, and users. A **business analyst** is someone who is well versed in Porter's models, organizational strategy, and systems alignment theory, like COBIT, and who also understand the proper role for technology. As shown in Figure 10-15, business analysts work primarily with business processes as well as with systems development at a high level.

Systems analysts are IS professionals who understand both business and technology. They are active throughout the systems development process and play a key role in moving the project through the systems development process. Systems analysts integrate the work of the programmers, testers, and users. Depending on the nature of the project, the team may also include hardware and communications specialists, database designers and administrators, and other IT specialists. As shown

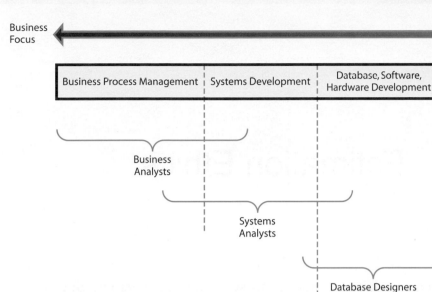

in Figure 10-15, systems analysts work with process design as well, but their primary focus is information systems development.

The team composition changes over time. During requirements definition, the team will be heavy with business and systems analysts. During design and implementation, it will be heavy with programmers, testers, and database designers. During integrated testing and conversion, the team will be augmented with testers and business users.

User involvement is critical throughout the system development process. Depending on the size and nature of the project, users are assigned to the project either full or part time. Sometimes users are assigned to review and oversight committees that meet periodically, especially at the completion of project phases and other milestones. Users are involved in many different ways. *The important point is for users to be actively involved in and take ownership of the project throughout the entire development process.*

The first major task for the assembled project team is to plan the project. Members of the project team specify tasks to be accomplished, assign personnel, determine task dependencies, and set schedules. We will discuss this further in Q6.

Determine Requirements

Determining the system's requirements is the most important phase in the systems development process. If the requirements are wrong, the system will be wrong. If the requirements are determined completely and correctly, then design and implementation will be easier and more likely to result in success.

Examples of requirements in Figure 10-9 are the contents of the Facility Use Report or the fields to be provided in the Facilities Needed data flow. Requirements include not only what is to be produced, but also how frequently and how fast it is to be produced. Some requirements specify the volume of data to be stored and processed.

If you take a course in systems analysis and design, you will spend weeks on techniques for determining requirements. Here, we will just summarize that process. Typically, systems analysts interview users and record the results in some consistent manner. Good interviewing skills are crucial; users are notorious for being unable to describe what they want and need. Users also tend to focus on the tasks they are performing at the time of the interview. Tasks performed at the end of the quarter or end of the year are forgotten if the interview takes place mid-quarter. Seasoned and experienced systems analysts know how to conduct interviews to bring such requirements to light.

Ethics Guide   Estimation Ethics

A *buy-in* occurs when a company agrees to produce a system or product for less than it knows the project will require. Laura could buy in at Fox Lake if she agreed to build the system for, say, $50,000, when good estimating techniques indicate it will take $75,000. If the contract for the system or product is written for "time and materials," Fox Lake will ultimately pay Laura the $75,000 for the finished system. Or, Fox Lake will cancel the project once the true cost is known. If the contract for the system or product is written for a fixed cost, then Laura will eat the extra costs. She'd use the latter strategy if the contract opens up other business opportunities that are worth the $25,000 loss.

Buy-ins always involve deceit. Most would agree that buying in on a time-and-materials project, planning to stick the customer with the full cost later, is unethical and wrong. Opinions on buying in on a fixed-priced contract vary. You know you'll take a loss, but why? For a favor down the road? Or some other unethical reason? Some would say that because buying in is always deceitful, it should always be avoided. Others say that it is just one of many different business strategies.

What about in-house projects? Do the ethics change if an in-house development team is building a system for use in-house? If team members know there is only $50,000 in the budget, should they start the project if they believe that its true cost is $75,000? If they do start, at some point senior management will either have to admit a mistake and cancel the project or find the additional $25,000. Project sponsors can make all sorts of excuses for such a buy-in. For example, "I know the company

needs this system. If management doesn't realize it and fund it appropriately, then we'll just force their hand."

These issues become even stickier if team members disagree about how much the project will cost. Suppose one faction of the team believes the project will cost $35,000, another faction estimates $50,000, and a third thinks $65,000. Can the project sponsors justify taking the average? Or, should they describe the range of estimates?

Other buy-ins are more subtle. Suppose you are a project manager of an exciting new project that is possibly a career-maker for you. You are incredibly busy, working 6 days a week and long hours each day. Your team has developed an estimate for $50,000 for the project. A little voice in the back of your mind says that maybe not all costs for every aspect of the project are included in that estimate. You mean to follow up on that thought, but more pressing matters in your schedule take precedence. Soon you find yourself in front of management, presenting the $50,000 estimate. You probably should have found the time to investigate the estimate, but you didn't. Is your behavior unethical?

Or, suppose you approach a more senior manager with your dilemma. "I think there may be other costs, but I know that $50,000 is all we've got. What should I do?" Suppose the senior manager says something like, "Well, let's go forward. You don't know of anything else, and we can always find more budget elsewhere if we have to." How do you respond?

You can buy in on schedule as well as cost. If the marketing department says, "We have to have the new product for the trade show," do you agree, even if you know it's highly unlikely? What if marketing says, "If we don't have it by then, we should just cancel the project." Suppose it's not impossible to make that schedule, it's just highly unlikely. How do you respond? ■

Discussion Questions

1. Do you agree that buying in on a cost-and-materials project is always unethical? Explain your reasoning. Are there circumstances in which it could be illegal?

2. Suppose you learn through the grapevine that your opponents in a competitive bid are buying in on a time-and-materials contract. Does this change your answer to question 1?

3. Suppose you are a project manager who is preparing a request for proposal on a cost-and-materials systems development project. What can you do to prevent buy-ins?

4. Under what circumstances do you think buying in on a fixed-price contract is ethical? What are the dangers of this strategy?

5. Explain why in-house development projects are always time-and-materials projects.

6. Given your answer to question 5, is buying in on an in-house project always unethical? Under what circumstances do you think it is ethical? Under what circumstances do you think it is justifiable, even if it is unethical?

7. Suppose you ask a senior manager for advice as described in the guide. Does the manager's response absolve you of guilt? Suppose you ask the manager and then do not follow her guidance. What problems result?

8. Explain how you can buy in on schedule as well as costs.

9. For an in-house project, how do you respond to the marketing manager who says that the project should be cancelled if it will not be ready for the trade show? In your answer, suppose that you disagree with this opinion—suppose you know the system has value regardless of whether it is done by the trade show.

Figure 10-16
SDLC: Requirements Analysis
Phase

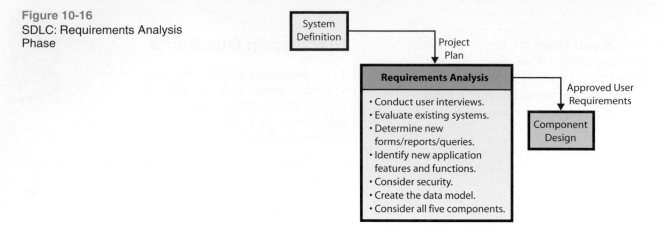

As listed in Figure 10-16, sources of requirements include existing systems as well as the forms, reports, queries, and application features and functions desired in the new system. Security is another important category of requirements.

If the new system involves a new database or substantial changes to an existing database, then the development team will create a data model. As you learned in Chapter 5, that model must reflect the users' perspective on their business and business activities. Thus, the data model is constructed on the basis of user interviews and must be validated by those users.

Sometimes the requirements determination is so focused on the software and data components that other components are forgotten. Experienced project managers ensure consideration of requirements for all five IS components, not just for software and data. Regarding hardware, the team might ask: Are there special needs or restrictions on hardware? Is there an organizational standard governing what kinds of hardware can, or cannot, be used? Must the new system use existing hardware? What requirements are there for communications and network hardware? Can we use the cloud?

Similarly, the team should consider requirements for procedures and personnel: Do accounting controls require procedures that separate duties and authorities? Are there restrictions that some actions can be taken only by certain departments or specific personnel? Are there policy requirements or union rules that restrict activities to certain categories of employees? Will the system need to interface with information systems from other companies and organizations? In short, requirements need to be considered for all of the components of the new information system.

These questions are examples of the kinds of questions that must be asked and answered during requirements analysis.

Design System Components

Each of the five components is designed in this stage. Typically, the team designs each component by developing alternatives, evaluating each of those alternatives against the requirements, and then selecting from among those alternatives. Accurate requirements are critical here; if they are incomplete or wrong, then they will be poor guides for evaluation.

Figure 10-17 shows that design tasks pertain to each of the five IS components. For hardware, the team determines specifications for the hardware the system will need. (The team is not designing hardware in the sense of building a CPU or a disk drive.) Program design depends on the source of the programs. For off-the-shelf software, the team must determine candidate products and evaluate them against the requirements. For off-the-shelf with alteration programs, the team identifies products to be acquired off-the-shelf and then determines the alterations required. For custom-developed programs, the team produces design documentation for writing program code.

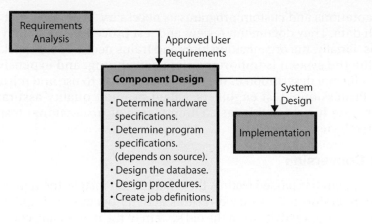

Figure 10-17
SDLC: Component Design
Phase

If the project includes constructing a database, then during this phase database designers convert the data model to a database design using techniques like those described in Chapter 5. If the project involves off-the-shelf programs, then little database design needs to be done; the programs will have been coded to work with a pre-existing database design.

Procedure design differs depending on whether the project is part of a BPM process (processes first) or is part of a systems development process (systems first). If the former, then business processes will already be designed, and all that is needed is to create procedures for using the application (like those shown in blue in Figure 10-9). If the latter, then procedures for using the system need to be developed, and it is possible that business processes that surround the system need to be developed as well.

With regard to people, design involves developing job descriptions for the various roles. These descriptions will detail responsibilities, skills needed, training required, and so forth.

Implementation Activities

The term *implementation* has two meanings for us. It could mean to implement the information systems components, only, or it could mean to implement the information system and the business processes that use the information system. As you read the following task descriptions, keep in mind that the tasks can apply to both interpretations of implementation.

Tasks in the implementation phase are to build and test system components and to convert users to the new system and possibly new business processes (see Figure 10-18). Developers construct each of the components independently. They obtain, install, and test hardware. They license and install off-the-shelf programs; they

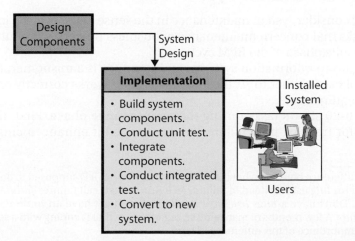

Figure 10-18
SDLC: Implementation Phase

write adaptations and custom programs as necessary. They construct a database and fill it with data. They document, review, and test procedures, and they create training programs. Finally, the organization hires and trains needed personnel.

Testing the system is important, time consuming, and expensive. A **test plan**, which is a formal description of the system's response to use and misuse scenarios, is written. Professional test engineers, called product quality assurance (PQA) test engineers, are hired for this task. Often teams of professional test engineers are augmented by users as well.

System Conversion

Once the system has passed testing, the organization installs the new system. The term **system conversion** is often used for this activity because it implies the process of *converting* business activity from the old system to the new. Again, conversion can be to the new system, only, or it can be to the new system, including new business processes.

Four types of conversion are possible: pilot, phased, parallel, and plunge. Any of the first three can be effective. In most cases, companies should avoid "taking the plunge"!

With **pilot installation**, the organization implements the entire system/business processes on a limited portion of the business. An example would be for Fox Lake to use the new system for a few wedding events. The advantage of pilot implementation is that if the system fails, the failure is contained within a limited boundary.

As the name implies, with **phased installation** the new system/business processes are installed in phases across the organization(s). Once a given piece works, then the organization installs and tests another piece of the system, until the entire system has been installed. Some systems are so tightly integrated that they cannot be installed in phased pieces. Such systems must be installed using one of the other techniques.

With **parallel installation**, the new system/business processes run in parallel with the old one until the new system is tested and fully operational. Parallel installation is expensive, because the organization incurs the costs of running both the existing and new system/business processes. Users must work double-time, if you will, to run both systems. Then, considerable work is needed to reconcile the results of the new with the old.

The final style of conversion is **plunge installation** (sometimes called *direct installation*). With it, the organization shuts off the old system/business processes and starts the new one. If the new system/business processes fail, the organization is in trouble: Nothing can be done until either the new system/business processes are fixed or the old system/business processes are reinstalled. Because of the risk, organizations should avoid this conversion style if possible. The one exception is if the new system is providing a new capability that will not disrupt the operation of the organization if it fails.

Figure 10-19 summarizes the tasks for each of the five components during the design and implementation phases. Use this figure to test your knowledge of the tasks in each phase.

What Are the Tasks for System Maintenance?

Here, we will consider system maintenance in the sense of the process in Figure 10-12, only. The tasks that concern maintenance of business processes are subsumed under the assess results phase of the BPM cycle.

With regard to information systems, **maintenance** is a misnomer; the work done during this phase is either to *fix* the system so that it works correctly or to *adapt* it to changes in requirements.

Figure 10-20 shows tasks during the maintenance phase. First, there needs to be a means for tracking both failures[1] and requests for enhancements to meet new

---

[1] A *failure* is a difference between what the system does and what it is supposed to do. Sometimes you will hear the term *bug* used instead of failure. As a future user, call failures *failures*, because that's what they are. Don't have a *bugs list*, have a *failures list*. Don't have an *unresolved bug*, have an *unresolved failure*. A few months of managing an organization that is coping with a serious failure will show you the importance of this difference in terms.

	Hardware	**Software**	**Data**	**Procedures**	**People**
Design	Determine hardware specifications.	Select off-the-shelf programs. Design alterations and custom programs as necessary.	Design database and related structures.	Design user and operations procedures.	Develop user and operations job descriptions.
Implementation	Obtain, install, and test hardware.	License and install off-the-shelf programs. Write alterations and custom programs. Test programs.	Create database. Fill with data. Test data.	Document procedures. Create training programs. Review and test procedures.	Hire and train personnel.
	Integrated Test and Conversion				

Unit test each component

Note: Cells shaded purple represent software development.

Figure 10-19
Design and Implementation for the Five Components

requirements. For small systems, organizations can track failures and enhancements using word-processing documents. As systems become larger, however, and as the number of failure and enhancement requests increases, many organizations find it necessary to develop a tracking database. Such a database contains a description of the failure or enhancement. It also records who reported the problem, who will make the fix or enhancement, what the status of that work is, and whether the fix or enhancement has been tested and verified by the originator.

Typically, IS personnel prioritize system problems according to their severity. They fix high-priority items as soon as possible, and they fix low-priority items as time and resources become available.

Because an enhancement is an adaptation to new requirements, developers usually prioritize enhancement requests separate from failures. The decision to make an enhancement includes a business decision that the enhancement will generate an acceptable rate of return.

Figure 10-20
SDLC: System Maintenance Phase

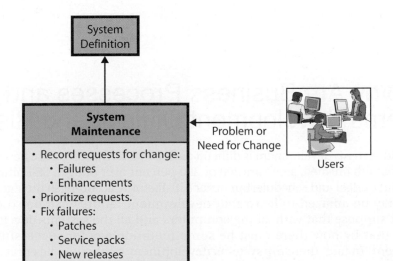

Using MIS InClass 10 *A Group Exercise*

Fox Lake Facilities' Future

Source: Laura Gangi Pond/Shutterstock.com.

Suppose that Fox Lake wants to create a facilities reservation system. How should it proceed? As described in Q4, it could model business processes first (Figure 10-12), and then select an information system. The problem, as described in Q4, is that in the future, if the golf operations, tennis operations, the pro shop, the restaurant, or any other department wants to make a reservation, that system may not have the features and functions needed. They could attempt to model business processes for all of these potential users, and then build the system, but that's a big job.

So, instead, they could follow Figure 10-13. They would begin by asking users in every department about their interest in a reservation system and interviewing users of departments that have such an interest. The disadvantage of this approach is that they would then need to develop business processes to fit the software, after the fact.

These three scenarios can be summarized as follows:

a. Model business processes for wedding planning and facilities maintenance, similar to that shown in Figure 10-9. Develop a facility reservation information system that will meet the needs of these departments. Future departments may or may not be able to use the reservation system as built; if not, the system can be altered.

b. Model business processes for every major facility user at Fox Lake. Model processes for wedding events, golf, tennis, the swimming pool, and any other potential facility reservation system user. Develop a facility reservation information system that will meet all of these needs.

c. Identify departments that have a need for a facilities reservation system. Without attempting to specify business processes for these departments, collect requirements for a facilities reservation system. (This alternative amounts to identifying the requirements for the blue, orange, and red elements of Figure 10-9 for each potential user.)

Fox Lake has to decide. If you were Jeff, what would you do? Form a team, answer the following questions, and make a recommendation to Jeff.

1. List the criteria that you think Fox Lake should use in deciding its development strategy.

2. Score alternatives a–c based on your criteria.

3. Recommend a course of action for Fox Lake to take. Justify your recommendation.

4. Present your recommendation to the rest of the class.

Q6 Why Are Business Processes and Systems Development Difficult and Risky?

Process and systems development is difficult and risky. Many projects are never finished. Of those that are finished, some are 200 or 300 percent over budget. Still other projects finish within budget and schedule, but never satisfactorily accomplish their goals.

You may be amazed to learn that development failures can be so dramatic. You might suppose that with all the computers and all the systems developed over the years that by now there must be some methodology for successful systems development. In fact, there *are* systems development methodologies that can result in success; the SDLC, just discussed, is the most popular such method. But, even when competent people follow this or some other accepted methodology, the risk of failure is still high.

User involvement is critical to the systems success, as described in the Guide on pages 378–379.

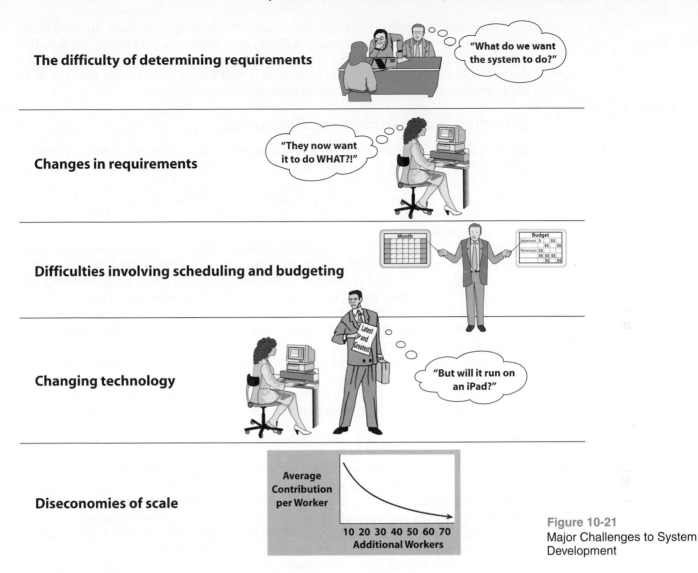

Figure 10-21
Major Challenges to System Development

In the following sections, we will discuss the five major challenges to systems development displayed in Figure 10-21.

The Difficulty of Requirements Determination

First, requirements are difficult to determine. The processes and system diagrammed in Figure 10-8 are a good first start. But, what steps need to be taken to fulfill an activity? What specific data items appear in data flows? What is the specific format of the Facility Use Report?

The proposed Fox Lake system/processes are simple. Consider, instead, the development of a new interorganizational system to be used by the suppliers of the Boeing 787 airplane. What features and functions should it have? What is to be done if different companies have different ideas about the IS features required? Companies may disagree about the data they are willing to share. How are those differences to be resolved? Hundreds of hours of labor will be required to determine the requirements.

The questions could go on and on. One of the major purposes of the systems development process is to create an environment in which such questions are both asked and answered.

Changes in Requirements

Even more difficult, systems development aims at a moving target. Requirements change as the system is developed, and the bigger the system and the longer the project, the more the requirements change.

When requirements do change, what should the development team do? Stop work and rebuild the system in accordance with the new requirements? If they do that, the system will develop in fits and starts and may never be completed. Or, should the team finish the system, knowing that it will be unsatisfactory the day it is implemented and will, therefore, need immediate maintenance?

Scheduling and Budgeting Difficulties

Other challenges involve scheduling and budgeting. How long will it take to build a system? That question is not easy to answer. Suppose you are developing a new facilities maintenance database at Fox Lake. How long will it take to create the data model? Even if you know how long it takes to create the data model, others may disagree with you and with each other. How many times will you need to rebuild the data model until everyone agrees?

Again, the Fox Lake system is a simple problem. What if you are building the new database for the Boeing supply chain system? How many hours will it take to create the data model, review, and approve it? Consider database applications. How long will it take to build the forms, reports, queries, and application programs? How long will it take to test all of them? What about procedures and people? What procedures need to be developed, and how much time should be set aside to create and document them, develop training programs, and train the personnel?

Further, how much will all of this cost? Labor costs are a direct function of labor hours; if you cannot estimate labor hours, you cannot estimate labor costs. Moreover, if you cannot estimate how much a system costs, then how do you perform a financial analysis to determine if the system generates an appropriate rate of return?

Changing Technology

Yet another challenge is that while the project is underway, technology continues to change. For example, say that while you are developing your facilities maintenance application, Apple, Microsoft, and Google and their business partners all release new versions of their devices and software. You know that with these new devices you can create a better facilities scheduling capability for wedding planners and maintenance workers, but using them means a major change in requirements.

Do you want to stop your development to switch to the new technology? Would it be better to finish developing according to the existing plan? Such decisions are tough. Why build an out-of-date system? But, can you afford to keep changing the project?

Diseconomies of Scale

Unfortunately, as development teams become larger, the average contribution per worker decreases. This is true because as staff size increases, more meetings and other coordinating activities are required to keep everyone in sync. There are economies of scale up to a point, but beyond a workgroup of, say, 20 employees, diseconomies of scale begin to take over.

A famous adage known as **Brooks' Law** points out a related problem. *Adding more people to a late project makes the project later.*[2] Brooks' Law is true not only because a larger staff requires increased coordination, but also because new people need to be trained. The only people who can train the new employees are the existing team members, who are, thus, taken off productive tasks. The costs of training new people can overwhelm the benefit of their contribution.

In short, managers of software development projects face a dilemma: They can increase work per employee by keeping the team small, but in doing so they extend

---

[2] Fred Brooks was a successful executive at IBM in the 1960s. After retiring from IBM, he wrote a classic book on IT project management called *The Mythical Man-Month*. Published by Addison-Wesley in 1975, the book is pertinent today and should be read by every IT or IS project manager. It's an enjoyable book, as well as informative.

the project's timeline. Or, they can reduce the project's timeline by adding staff, but because of diseconomies of scale they will have to add 150 or 200 hours of labor to gain 100 hours of work. And, due to Brooks' Law, once the project is late, both choices are bad.

Furthermore, schedules can be compressed only so far. According to one other popular adage, "Nine women cannot make a baby in one month."

Q7 What Are the Keys for Successful Process and Systems Development Projects?

Process and systems development projects, whether they begin with processes and work toward systems or begin with systems and work toward processes, are challenging to manage. In this question we will consider five keys to success:

- Create a work-breakdown structure.
- Estimate time and costs.
- Create a project plan.
- Adjust the plan via trade-offs.
- Manage development challenges.

Create a Work-Breakdown Structure

The key strategy for process and systems development—and, indeed, the key strategy for any project—is to divide and conquer. The project is too large, too complicated, and the duration is too long to attempt to manage it as one piece. Instead, successful project managers break the project into smaller and smaller tasks until each task is small enough to estimate and to manage. Every task should culminate in one or more results called **deliverables.** Examples of deliverables are documents, designs, prototypes, data models, database designs, working data entry screens, and the like. Without a defined deliverable, it is impossible to know if the task was accomplished.

Tasks are interrelated, and to prevent them from becoming a confusing morass project teams create a **work-breakdown structure (WBS),** which is a hierarchy of the tasks required to complete a project. The WBS for a large project is huge; it might entail hundreds or even thousands of tasks. Figure 10-22 shows the WBS for the system definition phase for a typical IS project.

In this diagram, the overall task, *System definition,* is divided into *Define goals and scope, Assess feasibility, Plan project,* and *Form project team.* Each of those tasks is broken into smaller tasks until the work has been divided into small tasks that can be managed and estimated.

Estimate Time and Costs

As stated, it is exceedingly difficult to determine duration and labor requirements for many development tasks. Fred Brooks defined software as "logical poetry." Like poetry, software is not made of wood or metal or plastic; it is pure thought-stuff. Some years ago, when I pressed a seasoned software developer for a schedule, he responded by asking me, "What would Shakespeare have said if someone asked him how long it would take him to write *Hamlet?*" Another common rejoinder is, "What would a fisherman say if you ask him how long will it take to catch three fish? He doesn't know, and neither do I."

Organizations take three approaches to this challenge. The first is to avoid the major schedule risks and never develop systems and software in-house. Instead, they license packages, such as ERP systems, that include both business processes and information systems components. As stated earlier, even if the vendor provides workable processes, those processes will need to be integrated into the business.

Figure 10-22
Example Work-Breakdown
Structure (WBS)

	System definition		
1.1		Define goals and scope	
	1.1.1		Define goals
	1.1.2		Define system boundaries
	1.1.3		Review results
	1.1.4		Document results
1.2		Assess feasibility	
	1.2.1		Cost
	1.2.2		Schedule
	1.2.3		Technical
	1.2.4		Organizational
	1.2.5		Document feasibility
	1.2.6		Management review and go/no go decision
1.3		Plan project	
	1.3.1		Establish milestones
	1.3.2		Create WBS
		1.3.2.1	Levels 1 and 2
		1.3.2.2	Levels 3+
	1.3.3		Document WBS
		1.3.3.1	Create WBS baseline
		1.3.3.2	Input to Project
	1.3.4		Determine resource requirements
		1.3.4.1	Personnel
		1.3.4.2	Computing
		1.3.4.3	Office space
		1.3.4.4	Travel and Meeting Expense
	1.3.5		Management review
		1.3.5.1	Prepare presentation
		1.3.5.2	Prepare background documents
		1.3.5.3	Give presentation
		1.3.5.4	Incorporate feedback into plan
		1.3.5.5	Approve project
1.4		Form project team	
	1.4.1		Meet with HR
	1.4.2		Meet with IT Director
	1.4.3		Develop job descriptions
	1.4.4		Meet with available personnel
	1.4.5		Hire personnel

However, the schedule risk of integration activities is far less than those for developing processes, programs, databases, and other components.

But what if no suitable package exists? In that case, companies take one of two remaining approaches. They can admit the impossibility of systems development scheduling and plan accordingly. They abandon any confidence in their estimates and invest a certain level of resources into a project, manage it as best they can, and take the schedule that results. Only loose commitments are made regarding the completion date and final system functionality. Project sponsors dislike this approach because they are signing a blank check. But sometimes it is just a matter of admitting the reality that exists: "We don't know, and it's worse to pretend that we do."

The third approach is to attempt to schedule the development project in spite of all the difficulties. Several different estimation techniques can be used. If the project is similar to a past project, the schedule data from that past project can be used for planning. When such similar past projects exist, this technique can produce quality schedule estimates. If there is no such past project, managers can make the best estimates they can. For computer coding, some managers estimate the number of lines of code that will need to be written and apply industry or company averages to estimate the time required. Other coding estimation techniques exist, visit http://sunset.usc.edu/csse/research/COCOMOII/cocomo_main.html. Of course, lines of code and other advanced techniques estimate schedules only for software components. The schedules for processes, procedures, databases, and the other components must be estimated using other methods.

Create a Project Plan

A project plan is a list of WBS tasks, arranged to account for task dependencies, with durations and resources applied. Some tasks cannot be started or finished until other tasks are completed. You can't, for example, put electrical wires in a house until you've built the walls. You can define task dependencies in planning software such as Microsoft Project, and it will arrange the plan accordingly.

	Task Name	Duration
1	□ 1 System definition	57 days
2	□ 1.1 Define goals and scope	18 days
3	1.1.1 Define goals	1 wk
4	1.1.2 Define system boundaries	2 wks
5	1.1.3 Review results	3 days
6	1.1.4 Document results	2 days
7	□ 1.2 Assess feasibility	7 days
8	1.2.1 Cost	1 wk
9	1.2.2 Schedule	3 days
10	1.2.3 Technical	3 days
11	1.2.4 Organizational	3 days
12	1.2.5 Document feasibility	2 days
13	1.2.6 Management review and go/no go decision	0 days
14	□ 1.3 Plan project	36 days
15	1.3.1 Establish milestones	2 days
16	□ 1.3.2 Create WBS	10 days
17	1.3.2.1 Levels 1 and 2	2 wks
18	1.3.2.2 Levels 3 +	2 wks
19	□ 1.3.3 Document WBS	5 days
20	1.3.3.1 Create WBS baseline	1 wk
21	1.3.3.2 Input to MS Project	3 days
22	□ 1.3.4 Determine resource requirements	10 days
23	1.3.4.1 Personnel	2 wks
24	1.3.4.2 Computing	2 days
25	1.3.4.3 Office sapce	3 days
26	1.3.4.4 Travel and meeting expense	1 day
27	□ 1.3.5 Management review	9 days
28	1.3.5.1 Prepare presentation	3 days
29	1.3.5.2 Prepare background docs	1 wk
30	1.3.5.3 Give presentation	1 day
31	1.3.5.4 Incorporate feedback into plan	3 days
32	1.3.5.5 Approve project	0 days
33	□ 1.4 Form project team	10 days
34	1.4.1 Meet with HR	1 day
35	1.4.2 Meet with IT Director	1 day
36	1.4.3 Develop job descriptions	4 days
37	1.4.4 Meet with available personnel	3 days
38	1.4.5 Hire personnel	2 days

Figure 10-23

Gantt Chart of the WBS for the Definition Phase of a Project

Given dependencies, estimates for task duration and resource requirements are then applied to the WBS to form a project plan. Figure 10-23 shows the WBS as input to Microsoft Project, with task dependencies and durations defined. The display on the right, called a **Gantt chart**, shows tasks, dates, and dependencies.

The user has entered all of the tasks from the WBS and has assigned each task a duration. She has also specified task dependencies, although the means she used are beyond our discussion. The two red arrows emerging from task 4, *Define system boundaries,* indicate that neither the *Review results* task nor the *Assess feasibility* task can begin until *Define system boundaries* is completed. Other task dependencies are also shown; you can learn about them in a project management class.

The **critical path** is the sequence of activities that determine the earliest date by which the project can be completed. Reflect for a moment on that statement: The *earliest date* is the date determined by considering the *longest path* through the network of activities. Paying attention to task dependencies, the planner will compress the tasks as much as possible. Those tasks that cannot be further compressed lie on the critical path. Microsoft Project and other project-planning applications can readily identify critical path tasks.

Figure 10-23 shows the tasks on the critical path in red. Consider the first part of the WBS. The project planner specified that task 4 cannot begin until 2 days before task 3 starts. (That's the meaning of the red arrow emerging from task 3.) Neither task 5 nor task 8 can begin until task 4 is completed. Task 8 will take longer than tasks 5 and 6, and so task 8—not tasks 5 or 6—is on the critical path. Thus, the critical path to this point is tasks 3, 4, and 8. You can trace the critical path through the rest of the WBS by following the tasks shown in red, though the entire WBS and critical path are not shown.

Using Microsoft Project or a similar product, it is possible to assign personnel to tasks and to stipulate the percentage of time that each person devotes to a task. Figure 10-24 shows a Gantt chart for which this has been done. The notation means that Eleanore works only 25 percent of the time on task 3; Lynda and Richard work full time. Additionally, one can assign costs to personnel and compute a labor budget for each task and for the overall WBS. One can assign resources to tasks and use Microsoft Project to detect and prevent two tasks from using the same resources. Resource costs can be assigned and summed as well.

Managers can use the critical path to perform critical path analysis. First, note that if a task is on the critical path, and if that task runs late, the project will be late.

The Guide on pages 381–381 states the challenges and difficulties with project estimation in the real world.

Figure 10-24
Gantt Chart with Resources
Assigned

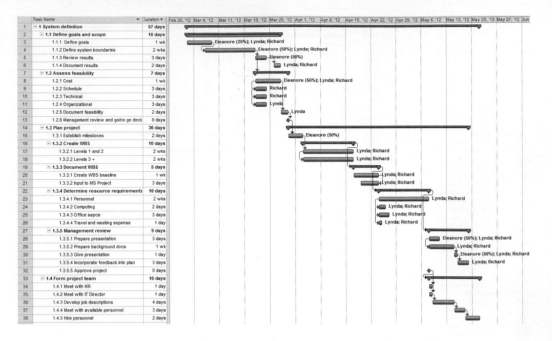

Hence, tasks on the critical path cannot be allowed to run late if the project is to be delivered on time. Second, tasks not on the critical path can run late to the point at which they would become part of the critical path. Hence, up to a point, resources can be taken from noncritical path tasks to shorten tasks on the critical path. **Critical path analysis** is the process by which project managers compress the schedule by moving resources, typically people, from noncritical path tasks onto critical path tasks.

Adjust Plan via Trade-offs

The project plan for the entire project results in a finish date and a total cost. During my career, I've been involved in about a dozen major development projects, and in every one the first response to a completed project plan has been, "Good heavens! No way! We can't wait that long or pay that much!" And my experience is not unusual.

Thus, the first response to a project plan is to attempt to reduce time and costs. Reductions can be made, but not out of thin air. An old adage in planning development projects is, "Believe your first number." Believe what you have estimated before your desires and wishes cloud your judgment.

So, how can schedules and costs be responsibly reduced? By considering trade-offs. A **trade-off** is a balancing of three critical factors: requirements, cost, and time. To understand this balancing challenge, consider the construction of something relatively simple—say, a piece of jewelry like a necklace or the deck on the side of a house. The more elaborate the necklace or the deck, the more time it will take. The less elaborate, the less time it will take. Further, if we embellish the necklace with diamonds and precious gems, it will cost more. Similarly, if we construct the deck from old crates it will be cheaper than if we construct it of clear-grained, prime Port Orford cedar.

We can summarize this situation as shown in Figure 10-25. We can *trade off* requirements against time and against cost. If we make the necklace simpler, it will take less time. If we eliminate the diamonds and gems, it will be cheaper. The same trade-offs exist in the construction of anything: houses, airplane interiors, buildings, ships, furniture, *and* information systems.

The relationship between time and cost is more complicated. Normally, we can reduce time by increasing cost *only to a point*. For example, we can reduce the time it takes to produce a deck by hiring more laborers. At some point, however, there will be so many laborers working on the deck that they will get in one another's way, and the time to finish the deck will actually increase. As discussed earlier, at some point, adding more people creates **diseconomies of scale,** the situation that occurs when

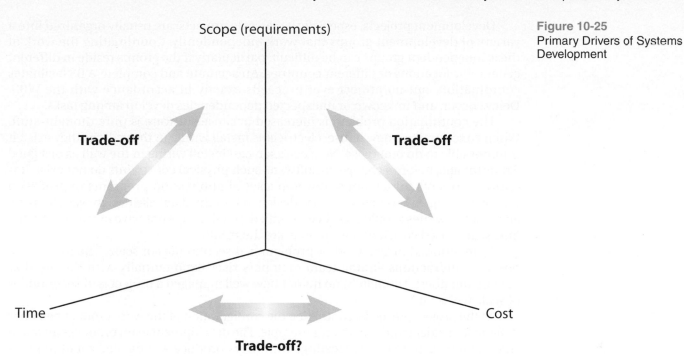

Figure 10-25
Primary Drivers of Systems
Development

adding more resources creates inefficiencies, such as those that occur when adding more people to a late project (recall Brooks' Law).

In some projects, we can reduce costs by increasing time. If, for example, we are required to pay laborers time-and-a-half for overtime, we can reduce costs by eliminating overtime. If finishing the deck—by, say, Friday—requires overtime, then it may be cheaper to avoid overtime by completing the deck sometime next week. This trade-off is not always true, however. Extending the project interval means that we need to pay labor and overhead for a longer period; thus, adding more time can also increase costs.

Consider how these trade-offs pertain to information systems. We specify a set of requirements for the new information system, and we schedule labor over a period of time. Suppose the initial schedule indicates the system will be finished in 3 years. If business requirements necessitate the project be finished in 2 years, we must shorten the schedule. We can proceed in two ways: reduce the requirements or add labor. For the former, we eliminate functions and features. For the latter, we hire more staff or contract with other vendors for development services. Deciding which course to take will be difficult and risky.

Using trade-offs, the WBS plan can be modified to shorten schedules or reduce costs. But they cannot be reduced by management fiat.

Manage Development Challenges

Given the project plan and management's endorsement and approval, the next stage is to do it. The final WBS plan is denoted as the **baseline WBS**. This baseline shows the planned tasks, dependencies, durations, and resource assignments. As the project proceeds, project managers can input actual dates, labor hours, and resource costs. At any point in time, planning applications can be used to determine whether the project is ahead or behind schedule and how the actual project costs compare to baseline costs.

However, nothing ever goes according to plan, and the larger the project and the longer the development interval, the more things will violate the plan. Four critical factors need to be considered:

1. Coordination
2. Diseconomies of scale
3. Configuration control
4. Unexpected events

Development projects, especially large-scale projects, are usually organized into a variety of development groups that work independently. Coordinating the work of these independent groups can be difficult, particularly if the groups reside in different geographic locations or different countries. An accurate and complete WBS facilitates coordination, but no project ever proceeds exactly in accordance with the WBS. Delays occur, and unknown or unexpected dependencies develop among tasks.

The coordination problem is increased because software is pure thought-stuff. When constructing a new house, electricians install wiring in the walls as they exist; it is impossible to do otherwise. No electrician can install wiring in the wall as designed 6 months ago, before a change. In software, such physical constraints do not exist. It is entirely possible for a team to develop a set of application programs to process a database using an obsolete database design. When the database design was changed, all involved parties should have been notified, but this may not have occurred. Wasted hours, increased cost, and poor morale are the result.

As mentioned in Q6, another problem is diseconomies of scale. The number of possible interactions among team members rises exponentially with the number of team members. Ultimately, no matter how well managed a project is, diseconomies of scale will set in.

As the project proceeds, controlling the configuration of the work product becomes difficult. Consider requirements, for example. The development team produces an initial statement of requirements. Meetings with users produce an adjusted set of requirements. Suppose an event then occurs that necessitates another version of requirements. After deliberation, assume the development team decides to ignore a large portion of the requirements changes resulting from the event. At this point, there are four different versions of the requirements. If the changes to requirements are not carefully managed, changes from the four versions will be mixed up, and confusion and disorder will result. No one will know which requirements are the correct, current requirements.

Similar problems occur with designs, program code, database data, and other system components. The term **configuration control** refers to a set of management policies, practices, and tools that developers use to maintain control over the project's resources. Such resources include documents, schedules, designs, program code, test suites, and any other shared resource needed to complete the project. Configuration control is vital; a loss of control over a project's configuration is so expensive and disruptive that it can result in termination for senior project managers.

The last major challenge to large-scale project management is unexpected events. The larger and longer the project, the greater the chance of disruption due to an unanticipated event. Critical people can change companies; even whole teams have been known to pack up and join a competitor. A hurricane may destroy an office; the company may have a bad quarter and freeze hiring just as the project is staffing up; technology will change; competitors may do something that makes the project more (or less) important; or the company may be sold and new management may change requirements and priorities.

Because software is thought-stuff, team morale is crucial. I once managed two strong-headed software developers who engaged in a heated argument over the design of a program feature. The argument ended when one threw a chair at the other. The rest of the team divided its loyalties between the two developers, and work came to a standstill as subgroups sneered and argued with one another when they met in hallways or at the coffee pot. How do you schedule that event into your WBS? As a project manager, you never know what strange event is heading your way. Such unanticipated events make project management challenging, but also incredibly fascinating!

Q8 2022?

Process and systems development will evolve in the next 10 years in four important ways. First, we will see a continuing focus on aligning business processes and information systems with business strategy, goals, and objectives. You and your classmates will be an important factor in that alignment. Unlike earlier generations of business professionals, you are truly computer literate. Although it might seem trivial, your skills with Facebook, Twitter, and foursquare have given you confidence in your ability to master computer-based systems. You also know that such systems can be easy or difficult to use.

Given this background, as future managers in accounting, finance, marketing, operations, and so forth you will be less willing, perhaps unwilling, to compromise. You know that information systems can be constructed to do what you want, and you'll be likely to insist on it.

Second, computer systems will be more easily changed and adapted in the future. Software vendors know that the key to their future growth is not having the single best solution, but rather on having a solution that is readily tailored to their customers' idiosyncrasies. When ERP was new, customers were willing to adapt their business processes to those of the vendors because there was no other choice. But, as indicated by the popularity of ERP industry-specific solution templates, customers want more. They want to be able to do whatever it is they do to gain a competitive advantage over their customers, and adapting their business processes to the same processes used by everyone else isn't going to get them there. So, software vendors will find ways to make their solutions more agile using SOA and other techniques, and, as a result, systems and processes will be more agile and better able to adapt to changing needs.

The third major change involves the cloud. Until very recently, when systems development teams wanted to build and test a new project, they would need to start a formal project and request funds to buy or lease development computers and communications infrastructure. Today, with elastic cloud computing, prototypes and even finished systems can be constructed in the cloud within very small hardware budgets. The result will be substantially more innovation, hard as that is to imagine!

Finally, the next 10 years will see the emergence of new software vendor business models. The Firm (www.thefirmmpls.com) a workout studio in Minneapolis pays almost nothing in license fees for the full-service operations application that it obtains from the SaaS vendor MindBody, Inc. Instead, all of the credit card charges that Firm customers make are processed by MindBody. Inc. This processing enables MindBody to earn a small amount on every customer transaction. MindBody supports more than 6,000 studios and trainers in the United States. Its software is a veritable money machine.

A key element of this new business model is the alignment between the goals of workout studios and MindBody. Both make more money when customers purchase. Therefore, MindBody's software includes features and functions that enable studio managers to determine which products, classes, trainers, and even ads and marketing campaigns are the most successful. Furthermore, MindBody has a window on the best practices in the industry. To motivate studios to adapt to new practices that will create more revenue, MindBody provides comparative statistics on any given studio's performance against similar companies in its region.

MindBody's business model is an example of a potentially monumental change in the way that business software is provided. Stay tuned!

Guide
Dealing with Uncertainty

In the mid-1970s, I worked as a database disaster repairman. As an independent consultant, I was called by organizations that licensed the then-new database management systems but had little idea of what to do with them.

One of my memorable clients had converted the company's billing system from an older-technology system to the new world of database processing. Unfortunately, after they cut off the old system, serious flaws were found in the new one, and from mid-November to mid-January the company was unable to send a bill. Of course, customers who do not receive bills do not pay, and my client had a substantial cash-flow problem. Even worse, some of its customers used a calendar-year tax basis and wanted to pay their bills prior to the end of the year. When those customers called to find the amount they owed, accounts receivable clerks had to say, "Well, we don't know. The data's in our computer, but we can't get it out." That was when the company called me for database disaster repair.

The immediate cause of the problem was that the client used the plunge conversion technique. But looking deeper, how did that organization find itself with a new billing system so full of failures?

In this organization, management had little idea about how to communicate with IT, and the IT personnel had no experience in dealing with senior management. They talked past one another.

Fortunately, this client was, in most other respects, a well-managed company. Senior management only needed to learn to manage their IS projects with the same discipline as they managed other departments. So, once we had patched the billing system together to solve the cash-flow problem, the management team began work to implement policies and procedures to instill the following principles:

- Business users, not IS, would take responsibility for the success of new systems.
- Users would actively work with IS personnel throughout systems development, especially during the requirements phase.
- Users would take an active role in project planning, project management, and project reviews.
- No development phase would be considered complete until the work was reviewed and approved by user representatives and management.
- Users would actively test the new system.
- All future systems would be developed in small increments.

I cannot claim that all future development projects at this company proceeded smoothly after the users began to practice these principles. In fact, many users were slow to take on their new responsibilities; in some cases, the users resented the time they were asked to invest in the new practices. Also, some were uncomfortable in these new roles. They wanted to work in their business specialty and not be asked to participate in IS projects about which they knew little. Still others did not take their responsibilities seriously; they would come to meetings ill prepared, not fully engage in the process, or approve work they did not understand.

However, after that billing disaster, senior management understood what needed to be done. They made these practices a priority, and over time user resistance was mostly overcome. When it was not overcome, it was clear to senior management where the true problem lay. ■

Discussion Questions

1. In general terms, describe how the billing system might have been implemented using pilot conversion. Describe how it might have been implemented using parallel conversion.

2. If you were the billing system project manager, what factors would you consider when deciding the style of conversion to use?

3. If the billing system had been converted using either pilot or parallel, what would have happened?

4. Explain in your own words the benefits that would accrue using the new principles.

5. Summarize the reasons that users resisted these new principles. What could be done to overcome that resistance?

6. Suppose you work in a company where users have little to no active involvement in systems development. Describe likely consequences of this situation. Describe six actions you could take to correct this situation.

Guide
The Real Estimation Process

"I'm a software developer.

I write programs in an object-oriented language called C# (pronounced 'C-sharp'). I'm a skilled object-oriented designer, too. I should be—I've been at it 12 years and worked on major projects for several software companies. For the last 4 years, I've been a team leader. I lived through the heyday of the dot-com era and now work in the development group at a Windows Series 7 Mango application vendor.

"All of this estimating theory is just that—theory. It's not really the way things work. Sure, I've been on projects in which we tried different estimation techniques. But here's what really happens: You develop an estimate using whatever technique you want. Your estimate goes in with the estimates of all the other team leaders. The project manager sums all those estimates together and produces an overall estimate for the project.

"By the way, in my projects, time has been a much bigger factor than money. At one software company I worked for, you could be 300 percent over your dollar budget and get no more than a slap on the wrist. Be 2 weeks late, however, and you were finished.

"Anyway, the project managers take the project schedule to senior management for approval, and what happens? Senior management thinks they are negotiating. 'Oh, no,' they say, 'that's way too long. You can surely take a month off that schedule. We'll approve the project, but we want it done by February 1 instead of March 1.'

"Now, what's their justification? They think that tight schedules make for efficient work. You know that everyone will work extra hard to meet the tighter timeframe. They know Parkinson's Law—'the time required to perform a task expands to the time available to do it.' So, fearing the possibility of wasting time because of too-lenient schedules, they lop a month off our estimate.

"Estimates are what they are; you can't knock off a month or two without some problem, somewhere. What does happen is that projects

get behind, and then management expects us to work longer and longer hours.

"Not that our estimation techniques are all that great, either. Most software developers are optimists. They schedule things as if everything will go as planned, and things seldom do. Also, schedulers usually don't allow for vacations, sick days, trips to the dentist, training on new technology, peer reviews, and all the other things we do in addition to writing software.

"So we start with optimistic schedules on our end, then management negotiates a month or two off, and voilà, we have a late project. After a while, management has been burned by late projects so much that they mentally add the month or even more back onto the official schedule. Then both sides work in a fantasy world, where no one believes the schedule, but everyone pretends they do.

"I like my job. I like software development. Management here is no better or worse than in other places. As long as I have interesting work to do, I'll stay here. But I'm not working myself silly to meet these fantasy deadlines." ■

Discussion Questions

1. What do you think of this developer's attitude? Do you think he's unduly pessimistic or do you think there's merit to what he says?

2. What do you think of his idea that management thinks they're negotiating? Should management negotiate schedules? Why or why not?

3. Suppose a project actually requires 12 months to complete. Which do you think is likely to cost more: (a) having an official schedule of 11 months with at least a 1-month overrun or (b) having an official schedule of 13 months and, following Parkinson's Law, having the project take 13 months?

4. Suppose you are a business manager and an information system is being developed for your use. You review the scheduling documents and see that little time has been allowed for vacations, sick leave, miscellaneous other work, and so forth. What do you do?

5. Describe the intangible costs of having an organizational belief that schedules are always unreasonable.

6. If this developer worked for you, how would you deal with his attitude about scheduling?

7. Do you think there is something different when scheduling information systems development projects than when scheduling other types of projects? What characteristics might make such projects unique? In what ways are they the same as other projects?

8. What do you think managers should do in light of your answer to question 7?

Active Review

Use this Active Review to verify that you understand the ideas and concepts that answer the chapter's study questions.

Q1 Why do organizations need to manage business processes?

Define *business process* using the new definition in this chapter. Define *roles, resources,* and *data flows.* Summarize three reasons that processes need to be changed and give an example of each.

Q2 What are the stages of business process management (BPM)?

Describe the need for BPM and explain why it is a cycle. Name the four stages of the BPM process and summarize the activities in each. Explain the role of COBIT.

Q3 How can BPMN process diagrams help identify and solve process problems?

Explain the need for a process documentation standard. Explain each of the symbols in Figures 10-5 and 10-6. Summarize the process problems in these two diagrams and explain how the process in Figure 10-7 solves those problems. Describe two ways of improving business process quality. Explain each of the elements of Figure 10-8.

Q4 Which comes first, business processes or information systems?

Explain how information systems and business processes differ. Give an example, other than one in this text, of a business process that uses two or more information systems. Give an example, other than one in this text, of an information system that is part of two or more business processes. Explain the problems that occur if we develop business processes first, with IS as a component. Explain the problems that occur if we develop information systems first, with business processes as a component. Explain the differences between Figures 10-11 and 10-12. Summarize the issues to address when answering which comes first. Explain why it is not possible to buy processes or systems off-the-shelf.

Q5 What are systems development activities?

Name five basic systems development activities. Explain how they pertain whether developing processes first or information systems first. Describe tasks required for the definition, requirements, and design steps. Explain the role of business analysts and systems analysts. Explain the tasks required to implement and maintain the system and assess the process. Describe four types of process/system conversion. Describe how activities in these last two steps differ depending on whether the processes or systems are developed first.

Q6 Why are business processes and systems development difficult and risky?

Name five major challenges that occur when developing processes and systems. For each, explain how that challenge could arise in the development of the processes and systems to solve the Fox Lake facility reservation problem.

Q7 What are the keys for successful process and systems development projects?

Name five keys for successful development projects. Explain the purpose of a work-breakdown structure. Summarize the difficulties of development estimation and describe three ways of addressing it. Explain the elements in the Gantt chart in Figure 10-24. Define *critical path,* and explain critical path analysis. Summarize requirements, cost, and schedule trade-offs. List and explain four critical factors for development project management.

Q8 2022?

Name four ways that process and systems development will evolve in the next 10 years. Explain how the computer literacy of you and your classmates contribute to process and systems alignment. Summarize the key to growth for software vendors and explain how that contributes process and system agility. Describe how the elastic cloud will foster innovation. Using the example of MindBody, explain how new business models will enable software to be delivered to customers in innovative ways.

Using Your Knowledge at Fox Lake

Examine alternatives a, b, and c in Using MIS InClass 10 on page 366. Explain how each alternative could solve Fox Lake's problem. Which is likely to be the most expensive? Which is likely to be the most robust?

Key Terms and Concepts

Using Your Knowledge

1. Assume that you are in intern working with Laura and you are present in the initial conversations she has with Fox Lake. Assume that Laura asks you to help her investigate this new system.

   a. Using Figure 10-13 as a guide, develop a plan for implementing the process in Figure 10-9. Ignore the Collect Deposit activity. Assume that it has been developed and works.

   b. Specify in detail the tasks to accomplish during the system definition phase.

   c. Write a memo to Laura explaining how you think Fox Lake should proceed.

2. The process documented in Figure 10-9 does not include unscheduled maintenance. Assume that requests for such maintenance arise during wedding events (they arise from other sources as well, but ignore those sources here) and that they are handled by facilities personnel who are on-call 24 hours a day. Create a process diagram, similar to that in Figure 10-9, that documents a business process and need for a facilities tracking system.

Assume there will be a Wedding Operations role, and Unscheduled Maintenance Application role, and a Facilities Maintenance Person role. If possible, use Visio to create your diagram, otherwise use PowerPoint.

3. Using your own experience and knowledge, create a process diagram for a Reject Order activity that would fix the allocation problem in Figure 10-5. Use Figure 10-6 as an example. Use Visio 2010 and the standard BPMN shapes, if possible. Explain how your process fixes the allocation problem.

4. Search Google or Bing for the phrase "what is a business analyst." Investigate several of the links that you find and answer the following questions:

   a. What are the primary job responsibilities of a business analyst?

   b. What knowledge do business analysts need?

   c. What skills/personal traits do business analysts need?

   d. Would a career as a business analyst be interesting to you? Explain why or why not.

Collaboration Exercise 10

With a team of your fellow students, develop an answer to the following questions. Use Google Docs, Google+, Windows Live SkyDrive, SharePoint, Office 365, or some other collaboration tool to conduct your meetings.

Wilma Baker, Jerry Barker, and Chris Bickel met in June 2010 at a convention of resort owners and tourism operators. They sat next to each other by chance while waiting for a presentation; after introducing themselves and laughing at the odd sound of their three names, they were surprised to learn that they managed similar businesses.

Wilma Baker lives in Santa Fe, New Mexico, and specializes in renting homes and apartments to visitors to Santa Fe. Jerry Barker lives in Whistler Village, British Columbia, and specializes in renting condos to skiers and other visitors to the Whistler/Blackcomb Resort. Chris Bickel lives in Chatham, Massachusetts, and specializes in renting homes and condos to vacationers to Cape Cod.

The three agreed to have lunch after the presentation. During lunch, they shared frustrations about the difficulty of obtaining new customers, especially in the current economic downturn. Barker was especially concerned about finding customers in to fill the facilities that had been constructed to host the Olympics in the prior year.

As the conversation developed, they began to wonder if there was some way to combine forces (i.e., they were seeking a competitive advantage from an alliance). So, they decided to skip one of the next day's presentations and meet to discuss ways to form an alliance. Ideas they wanted to discuss further were sharing customer data, developing a joint reservation service, and exchanging property listings.

As they talked, it became clear they had no interest in merging their businesses; each wanted to stay independent. They also discovered that each was very concerned, even paranoid, about protecting their existing customer base from poaching. Still, the conflict was not as bad as it first seemed. Barker's business was primarily the ski trade, and winter was his busiest season; Bickel's business was mostly Cape Cod vacations, and she was busiest during the summer. Baker's high season was the summer and fall. So, it seemed there was enough difference in their high seasons that they would not necessarily cannibalize their businesses by selling the others' offerings to their own customers.

The question then became how to proceed. Given their desire to protect their own customers, they did not want to develop a common customer database. The best idea seemed to be to share data about properties. That way they could keep control of their customers but still have an opportunity to sell time at the others' properties.

They discussed several alternatives. Each could develop her or his own property database, and the three could then share those databases over the Internet. Or, they could develop a centralized property database that they would all use. Or, they could find some other way to share property listings.

Because we do not know Baker, Barker, and Bickel's detailed requirements, you cannot develop a plan for a specific system. In general, however, they first need to decide how elaborate an information system they want to construct. Consider the following two alternatives:

a. They could build a simple system centered on email. With it, each company sends property descriptions to the others via email. Each independent company then forwards these descriptions to its own customers, also using email. When a customer makes a reservation for a property, that request is then forwarded back to the property manager via email.

b. They could construct a more complex system using a Web-based, shared database that contains data on all their properties and reservations. Because reservations tracking is a common business task, it is likely that they can license an existing application with this capability.

1. Create a process diagram for alternative a, using Figure 10-8 as a guide. Each company will need to have a role for determining its available properties and sending emails to the other companies that describe them. They will also need to have a role for receiving emails and a role for renting properties to customers. Assume the companies have from three to five agents who can fulfill these roles. Create a role for the email system if you think it is appropriate. Specify roles, activities, repositories, and data flows.

2. Create a process diagram for alternative b, using Figure 10-8 as a guide. Each company will need to have a role for determining its available properties and adding them to the reservation database. They will also need a role for renting properties that accesses the shared database. Assume the companies have from three to five agents who can fulfill these roles. Create a role for the property database application. Specify roles, activities, repositories, and data flows.

In your answers to 1 and 2, use Microsoft Visio and BPMN templates to construct your diagram. If you don't have those templates, use the cross-functional and basic flowchart templates. If you do not have access to Visio, use PowerPoint instead.

3. Compare and contrast your answers in questions 1 and 2. Which is likely to be more effective in generating rental income? Which is likely to be more expensive to develop? Which is likely to be more expensive to operate?

4. If you were a consultant to Baker, Barker, and Bickel, which alternative would you recommend? Justify your recommendation.

Case Study 10

Slow Learners, or What?

In 1974, when I was teaching at Colorado State University, we conducted a study of the causes of information systems failures. We interviewed personnel on several dozen projects and collected survey data on another 50 projects. Our analysis of the data revealed that the single most important factor in IS failure was a lack of user involvement. The second major factor was unclear, incomplete, and inconsistent requirements.

At the time, I was a devoted computer programmer and IT techie, and, frankly, I was surprised. I thought that the significant problems would have been technical issues.

I recall one interview in particular. A large sugar producer had attempted to implement a new system for paying sugar-beet farmers. The new system was to be implemented at some 20 different sugar-beet collection sites, which were located in small farming communities, adjacent to rail yards. One of the benefits of the new system was significant cost savings, and a major share of those savings occurred because the new system eliminated the need for local comptrollers. The new system was expected to eliminate the jobs of 20 or so senior people.

The comptrollers, however, had been paying local farmers for decades; they were popular leaders not just within the company, but in their communities as well. They were well liked, highly respected, important people. A system that caused the elimination of their jobs was, using a term from this chapter, *organizationally infeasible*, to say the least.

Nonetheless, the system was constructed, but an IS professional who was involved told me, "Somehow, that new system just never seemed to work. The data were not entered on a timely basis, or they were in error, or incomplete; sometimes the data were not entered at all. Our operations were falling apart during the key harvesting season, and we finally backed off and returned to the old system." Active involvement of system users would have identified this organizational infeasibility long before the system was implemented.

That's ancient history, you say. Maybe, but in 1994 the Standish Group published a now famous study on IS failures. Entitled "The CHAOS Report," the study indicated the leading causes of IS failure are, in descending order: (1) lack of user input, (2) incomplete requirements and specifications, and (3) changing requirements and specifications. That study was completed some 20 years after our study.

In 2004, Professor Joseph Kasser and his students at the University of Maryland analyzed 19 system failures to determine their cause. They then correlated their analysis of the cause with the opinions of the professionals involved in the failures. The correlated results indicated that the first-priority cause of system failure was "Poor requirements"; the second-priority cause was "Failure to communicate with the customer." (Google or Bing "Joseph Kasser" to learn more about this work.)

In 2003, the IRS Oversight Board concluded that the first cause of a massive, expensive failure in the development of a new information system for the IRS was "inadequate business unit ownership and sponsorship of projects. This resulted in unrealistic business cases and continuous project scope 'creep.'"

For over 30 years, studies have consistently shown that leading causes of system failures are a lack of user involvement and incomplete and changing requirements. Yet failures from these very failures continue to mount.

Sources: Standish Group, www.standishgroup.com; IRS Oversight Board, "Independent Analysis of IRS Business Systems Modernization, Special Report," December 2003, http://www.treas.gov/irsob/reports/special_report1203.pdf.

Questions

1. Using the knowledge you have gained from this chapter, summarize the roles that you think users should take during an information systems development project. What responsibilities do users have? How closely should they work with the IS team? Who is responsible for stating requirements and constraints? Who is responsible for managing requirements?

2. If you ask users why they did not participate in requirements specification, some of the common responses are the following:
   a. "I wasn't asked."
   b. "I didn't have time."
   c. "They were talking about a system that would be here in 18 months, and I'm just worried about getting the order out the door today."
   d. "I didn't know what they wanted."
   e. "I didn't know what they were talking about."
   f. "I didn't work here when they started the project."
   g. "The whole situation has changed since they were here; that was 18 months ago!"
   Comment on each of these statements. What strategies do they suggest to you as a future user and as a future manager of users?

3. If you ask IS professionals why they did not obtain a complete and accurate list of requirements, common responses are:
   a. "It was nearly impossible to get on the users' calendars. They were always too busy."
   b. "The users wouldn't regularly attend our meetings. As a result, one meeting would be dominated by the needs of one group, and another meeting would be dominated by the needs of another group."
   c. "Users didn't take the requirement process seriously. They wouldn't thoroughly review the requirements statements before review meetings."
   d. "Users kept changing. We'd meet with one person one time and another person a second time, and they'd want different things."
   e. "We didn't have enough time."
   f. "The requirements kept changing."
   Comment on each of these statements. What strategies do they suggest to you as a future user and a future manager of users?

4. If it is widely understood that one of the principal causes of IS failures is a lack of user involvement, and if this factor continues to be a problem after 30+ years of experience, does this mean that the problem cannot be solved? For example, everyone knows that you can maximize your gains by buying stocks at their annual low price and selling them at their annual high price, but doing so is very difficult. Is it equally true that although everyone knows that users should be involved in requirements specification, and that requirements should be complete, it just cannot be done? Why or why not?

TEACHING SUGGESTIONS

Fox Lake Country Club, Chapter 10

GOALS

Use Fox Lake Country Club to:

- Illustrate the need for a new information system.

- Introduce the job description of business analyst.

- Reiterate that organizations must think about the need for cross-functional processes when acquiring or starting new business units.

BACKGROUND

1. Clearly, the wedding events and facilities maintenance departments need to have processes and an IS by which wedding events can record its facilities requirements and maintenance can respond to those requirements appropriately.

2. You can use this case to make it clear to students that Fox Lake needs *both* new business processes and new information systems. Neither, by itself, will do the job. Figure 10-9 illustrates this. The processes have many activities, but only the colored activities involve an information system. Both are needed.

3. Buried in the details is that fact that the bathrooms weren't designed for that many people at a time. This is an indication of a larger problem; neither Jeff nor Anne thought through the consequences on existing Fox Lake operations when they started the wedding events business.

4. Laura is an experienced and capable business analyst. That job is different than the classic systems analyst. A business analyst is primarily a business professional who is involved in business processes that may or may not use information systems. A business analyst works at the very earliest stage of the systems development process, when the need for a new system or a change to an existing system is first recognized. See Figure 10-15. Students should consider the job of business analyst. They can be a dual major of something, perhaps accounting or management, with IS.

5. BTW, this chapter only addresses the facilities reservation problem. A system for recording and responding to the need for unscheduled maintenance (like the broken toilets) is left as an exercise. You might discuss/develop processes and system needs for that system in class.

HOW TO GET STUDENTS INVOLVED

1. Is this opening scenario realistic?

   - **Is this a credible situation? Could such problems really happen?**

   - **Is either Mike or Anne incompetent?**

     (I don't think so . . . they're just doing their jobs, from their perspectives. Mike is attempting to help when he offers the Porta Potties.)

   - **In what ways does this opening scene illustrate how differences in goals and incentives make enterprise systems and processes difficult?**

   - **How did Jeff choose to proceed?**

   - **Do you think he should have done something different?**

   - **Is there a way that Jeff might have anticipated these problems?**

2. Consider the text's solution to these problems in Figure 10-9. Use this diagram to discuss the differences between processes and systems procedures. Figure 10-9 shows two business processes: wedding planning and facilities maintenance. Some of the activities involve an IS and some do not. For the activities that do involve an IS, say Reserve Facilities, procedures for using the IS to access the Determine Available Facilities application will need to be written.

   - **What is the difference between business processes and IS procedures?**

   - **How many business processes are in Figure 10-9?**

   - **Where are the IS procedures in Figure 10-9?**

   - **Who develops the processes?**

   - **Who develops the procedures?**

3. With regards to the job of business analyst:

   - **What does a business analyst do?**

   - **Where would a diagram like Figure 10-9 come from? Could Jeff, Mike, or Anne have produced it?**

   - **Would a computer programmer or database designer have produced Figure 10-9?**

   - **Suppose you were Anne, are you able to review Figure 10-9? Are you able to produce it?**

   - **What skills do you think a business analyst like Laura needs?**

■ **Figure 10-15 shows the difference in scope for systems analysts and business analysts.**

(Might be worth saying that a systems analyst really needs to be a full IS major. A business analyst could have another major, say Strategy, coupled with a number of IS courses.)

4. Which comes first, processes or systems?

■ **Use Figure 10-12 to discuss how Fox Lake would proceed if it decided to gather systems requirements first and then work the system into business processes.**

■ **Use Figure 10-13 to discuss how Fox Lake would proceed if it decided to begin with business processes and then develop system components as part of the BPM process.**

I would ask the students at this point to discuss how these two strategies differ in character. One will feature users and their activities, with and without the system. The other will feature the system and back into users and activities.

■ **So, at Fox Lake, which should come first?**

■ **In general, which should come first?**

(I don't think you can make a general statement. It depends on what exists and whether the N:M relationship between processes and systems is heavier on the N or on the M. Better system or process requirements result, IMO, if we start with the one that is on the lighter side of N or M.)

5. This situation illustrates the naiveté of thinking that licensing off-the-shelf software will solve the problem. Where do either the processes or the procedures come from?

■ **If Fox Lake finds a facilities reservation software package, has it wasted is time creating Figure 10-9?**

■ **Where will the business processes come from?**

■ **Where will the systems procedures come from?**

VIDEO

The video demonstrates how the need for a new process and a new system arises in a small organization, one that definitely does not practice business process management. Problems have occurred, and are still occurring, that could have been prevented. Jeff buys time by asking them to figure out some way of managing until the end of the wedding season. Then they can find a longer-term solution.

Laura is a seasoned, experienced, and competent business analyst. She plays a key role in this video and those for Chapters 11 and 12 as well. The major purpose for her is to illustrate the business analyst job role and to pique the students' interest in it.

BOTTOM LINE

■ **Fox Lake has a need for new business processes for the scheduling of facilities use and maintenance.**

■ **Fox Lake most likely needs a computer-based information system to augment those business processes documented in Figure 10-9.**

■ **Licensing software won't solve the problem by itself.**

■ **Fox Lake needs a business analyst like Laura to help it solve this problem. Business analysis is an interesting career that you should consider.**

■ **BTW, we have not solved the unscheduled maintenance problem; this still needs to be done.**

YOU BE THE GUIDE

Using the Ethics Guide:
Estimation Ethics (pages 362–363)

GOALS

- Introduce the concept of *buy-in* as it pertains to information systems.

- Assess the ethics of buy-ins in different settings.

BACKGROUND AND PRESENTATION STRATEGIES

I was first introduced to *buy-in* when I worked in procurement in the defense industry in the late 1960s. At that time, it was common for large government contractors to buy in on initial system production and to make up the difference by selling expensive spare parts over the 20-year or more life of that system. Senator Proxmire attained national prominence when he discovered the U.S. Navy was paying $250 for submarine toilet seats. Another cost-recovery technique was to claim that all but the most obvious corrections to plans were "out of scope" changes that required supplemental payment.

I was a very junior person, and I do not know what the thinking was at senior levels. But, I suspect it involved a degree of "wink-wink" collusion between high-level defense and aerospace executives. Congress had only so much money in the budget for a given system. The contractor would bid within that limit and make up the differences via supplemental appropriations in later years. I suspect that none of this was a surprise to Congress. It was a way of obtaining a system in the face of competing demands for the government budget. Some called it a "game that we must play." It was not illegal, and it involved some risk on the contractor's part; there was always the chance that a project would be cancelled before the buy-in costs could be recovered.

Buy-ins are prevalent in everyday life, too. We all know the ads for cars that loudly announce a price of $15,000, but the small print indicates that there will be supplemental charges for "additional items."

All types of custom building also can involve buy-ins. Building a custom home, a custom boat, a custom airplane interior—all are susceptible to buy-ins.

The best defense against buy-ins is experience in the industry. Or, as Donald Trump put it during his Senate testimony on the United Nations remodeling project, if you don't have experience working with New York construction contractors, "You'll go to school while they eat your lunch."

So, one of the major goals of this guide is to see how buy-ins apply to information systems projects. Future managers need to know this so that they can guard against, or at least consider the possibility of a buy-in.

Future managers also need to consider their own values and principles. At what point is a buy-in within accepted boundaries of conduct, and when does it exceed those boundaries? When will you be willing to put your job on the line when resisting a buy-in on ethical principles?

Finally, note that the guide points out that buy-ins can occur for both cost and schedule. They also can occur for technical feasibility when a team asserts that some new technology is further developed than it is. Ultimately, however, technical buy-ins become both cost and schedule buy-ins.

SUGGESTED RESPONSES FOR DISCUSSION QUESTIONS

1. Again using the definition of *ethical* as "consistent with agreed principles of correct moral conduct," I don't think it's possible to say that every buy-in is unethical. All buy-ins involve deceit, but that deceit may be an accepted practice in the industry (see previous comments). It's a very slippery slope, however. What level of deceit is allowable? Senator Proxmire's discovery of a $250 submarine toilet seat seems to indicate that someone went over the line.

   Yes, a buy-in could be illegal, especially for public projects. The contractor might have agreed to comply with a law that pertains to honesty in bidding. Also, some states may have enacted laws that require a certain level of truth in advertising. Such laws lie behind the auto ads in which someone quickly reads the serial number of autos that are being advertised.

2. First, your company may have a policy about buy-ins that requires you to submit a complete and honest bid. If so, you should follow that policy. If not, you need to wonder how reliable the grapevine is and assess how widespread and accepted buy-ins are in your industry. You also need to check with your management. Consider the impact of a buy-in on your reputation for future jobs (see question 3). As a general rule, I'd say avoid the buy-in, bid honestly, and keep looking for other jobs on which to bid, but

this general rule, in some industries, might be hopelessly naive.

3. Create as comprehensive a list of features and functions as you can. Ensure that the proposal requires an estimate for every feature and function. Check bids to ensure that every item was included. Employ experts to determine the reasonableness of the bid items. For this activity, there is no substitute for experience. Check the reputation of the vendor. Are they known for buy-ins or for honest bids? What percent overrun is typical for the vendor's projects?

4. Some vendors buy in to gain experience and/or reputation on a particular technology. Someone might buy in, for example, on building a database for a Web site so as to learn how to build such databases. If the vendor considers the difference between the buy-in bid and the actual cost as an investment and has no intent of recovering that loss, then the behavior is ethical, at least to my mind. Otherwise, is the buy-in consistent with agreed-on principles in that industry?

   The obvious danger is that you never have a chance to get your money back. The customer never approves any "out of scope" changes and cancels the project before you have a chance to recoup losses on spare or replacement parts.

5. There is no fixed bid.

6. What difficult questions! Is it ever appropriate to deceive your own management? If so, when? I think, over the long haul, nothing is more serviceable than the truth. I don't think I'd ever recommend deceiving one's own management. There may be exceptions to that, but I'd say they'd be very rare. I'd say it's unethical, unwise, and seldom justifiable. In some organizations, that attitude might be called naïve. (If so, I'd rather work somewhere else.)

7. If I were the junior person, I'd go with the manager's recommendation. The statement, "We can always find the money someplace else," suggests to me that the manager has flexibility in the budget that I don't know about. I think the statement "absolve you of guilt" puts it a little strongly, but, yes, I think I could go forward on solid ethical ground. Not following the advice is a form of betrayal. If you aren't going to follow that advice, at least tell your manager ahead of time and explain why you cannot. Or, determine the other costs and show them to your manager.

8. You can buy in on schedule by agreeing to produce something on a schedule that you believe you cannot meet. When schedule delays occur, the customer is so committed to the project that they cannot cancel it.

9. Again, nothing is more serviceable than the truth. I'd call the marketing manager's bluff: "OK, let's cancel the project." If the project is important enough, that person will back down. Then, I'd say, "We'll do the best we can, but we operate under the risk that it won't be done by then. Plan accordingly." I'd then try to negotiate having some limited version of the project ready by the trade show.

   This happened to me once when a senior sales manager said a version of a software product had to be ready by that year's fall Comdex show. I did exactly as described previously. It turned out he was speaking rashly and backed down. We delivered a solid working version for use in the computers in the trade-show booth. The full version was shipped to customers 2 months later.

WRAP UP

■ **Be aware that buy-ins occur and that some vendors make a practice of them. Scrutinize unbelievably low bids. They probably are unbelievable.**

■ **There is no substitute for experience. Hire expertise to evaluate bids.**

■ **Consider your own position on buy-ins. When can you justify one? Ever? If so, when?**

YOU BE THE GUIDE

Using the Guide: Dealing with Uncertainty (pages 378–379)

GOALS

- Reinforce the dangers of the plunge style of implementation.
- Introduce basic policies and procedures for user management of IS projects.

BACKGROUND AND PRESENTATION STRATEGIES

System conversion of critical business functions like billing is important and often difficult. Regardless of the style of implementation, problems usually occur. Pilot and piecemeal conversion reduce the risk, but they still demand careful attention—from both users and developers. Parallel implementation is expensive and requires users to perform double duty. If parallel implementation is used, the plan should include hiring additional, temporary personnel to ease the users' workload.

The story recounted in this guide occurred around 1980. I hope that the plunge conversion of a critical system like billing would be rare today. I suppose, though, that in smaller companies, it still must occur.

At the time of the billing system disaster, this company had about $70 million in sales. Its credit was excellent, and borrowing money for the cash flow crisis was thankfully not a problem. Interest rates were high then, however, and borrowing was expensive.

The person in charge of the company's IT department had been promoted from within. He was in over his head. I worked with him for a year or so after this billing system disaster; the company wanted him to succeed. Ultimately, however, the job required him to grow faster than he could. He left the company and took a job managing computer operations at another company. That job was a better fit for his skills. The company then hired a more senior and experienced person as its IS director.

The billing disaster caught the attention of the CEO. Up until then, he'd not paid too much attention to his information systems. Until the billing system, the company's information systems were primarily calculating systems and had been managed with a light touch by the CFO. The billing system changed the CEO's posture.

At the time of the disaster, the attitude of the entire company mirrored that of the CEO. No one knew exactly what the IS department did, and as long as they got their paychecks on time, they didn't much care. Once the CEO decided that users need to be more closely involved, once he understood and believed the criticality of user involvement in information systems, he embarked on a program to get the users involved.

As stated in the guide, employee attitudes did not change overnight, however. To facilitate a change in attitude, he asked me to conduct a series of meetings with key users in headquarters and other major offices, explaining the importance of user involvement in information systems development and use. (By the way, it was in one of those meetings that I first thought of the five component model of an information system.)

You might forewarn your students about how difficult it can be to choose to actively participate in systems requirements:

- It's easy to deprioritize requirement meetings because the new system is usually months away, and you'll have jobs that need to be done today.

- The new system may involve discussions about technology that you find tedious and boring.

- The systems development personnel may not be terribly skilled at communicating with you.

- Meetings may require lots of preparation.

- Possibly none of your managers will see the importance of your involvement and will not reinforce your activities.

- You may know that you'll be long gone into a new position or new job by the time the system comes along.

- Users may differ with each other and with you.

- Meetings can become tedious.

All these factors can make it difficult for you to participate. It's still very important for you to do so, however.

Over time, user resistance was overcome, at least for most user managers. The next system the company developed was an order entry and production scheduling system. It had active user involvement, and though that process, too, had problems, that system's development was a vast improvement over the billing system.

See Case Study 10. Even today, active user management of requirements is a serious problem. We have 30 years' experience with this phenomenon, and yet it still continues. Why? I hope someone will someday do research that will lead us out of this continuing, unsolved problem. It's a puzzle.

SUGGESTED RESPONSES FOR DISCUSSION QUESTIONS

1. Pilot conversion: Implement for one product line, for a set of a few customers, or for one production plant. Parallel conversion: Run both the old billing system and the new one at the same time. Reconcile the two systems.

2. Risk, cost, and disruption of business activities would be good factors to consider. It's a balancing of trade-offs.

3. It would have become obvious that the system was not finished and was not ready for use. For piecemeal conversion, the damage would have been limited to a section of the business, and the company would have needed to borrow less money, or possibly none at all. Damage to the company's reputation by not being able to send bills would have been limited to a few customers. In the case of parallel conversion, no customers would have been impacted at all, and there would have been no need to borrow money.

4. The ultimate result is better information systems: information systems that meet user requirements; information systems that are easy to use; information systems with appropriate security. I think, too, that ultimately, it results in lower cost. Although the cost of development may be higher because of the cost of users' labor in creating such systems, over the long haul an information system that meets user needs and is easy to use will result in less operations labor and, if the system is in use long enough, will recoup the greater initial investment.

5. Users resisted because the system required more work from them. They had to devote time and attention to the new system. Also, they could no longer sit on the sidelines and criticize whatever result occurred because they became partly responsible for the new system. If the system did not meet user needs, they would be held accountable for the failure by their peers. In this particular company, however, the major form of resistance was from the extra work.

   Some of the factors in this company were senior management's posture that user involvement and user training were going to be required. Consistency was also important; when users balked at attending meetings, senior management made it clear that attendance at such meetings was required. When users came to meetings ill-prepared, senior management objected. (Relate this situation to the change-management discussions in Chapter 7.)

6. Systems for which users have little active involvement will not meet users' needs; they will be difficult to use; they will constantly be "in development." Users will be frustrated and unproductive. They will hold the IS department responsible for the systems failures.

   What the student could do depends on his or her job description and management level in the organization. Apply the six principles stated in the middle of the guide in a way that is appropriate for that job and level.

WRAP UP

■ **Unless the system has an inconsequential impact on operations, do not take the plunge. (And why develop a system that has an inconsequential impact?)**

■ **Active user involvement is key! As a future manager and business professional, take the principles in the middle of this guide seriously.**

■ **The bottom, bottom line:** *Users are ultimately responsible for the quality of the information systems they have!*

YOU BE THE GUIDE

Using the Guide: The Real Estimation Process (pages 380–381)

GOALS

- Sensitize students to the challenges of software scheduling.

- Alert students to possible consequences when negotiating a schedule.

BACKGROUND AND PRESENTATION STRATEGIES

There are many formal methods for scheduling, and I've worked at companies that have attempted to implement some of those methods. But invariably, requirements change, personnel depart, management loses patience with the discipline required to manage to schedules, or some other factor invalidates the good intentions of the project's managers. Companies that have an effective process for scheduling software projects are extremely rare.

If anyone had figured software scheduling out, you'd think it would be Microsoft. But look how late both Vista and Office 2007 were. Clearly, Microsoft doesn't know how to do it, either.

The Software Institute at Carnegie Mellon developed the software maturity model that rates organizations on their use of effective development processes. Perhaps some of that model's level-4 or level-5 companies know how to schedule software development and how to manage to that schedule.

For complex software, with real users and with real requirements-management problems, I'm skeptical that anyone has figured it out. I think schedule risk is one of the major reasons that organizations choose to license software. The schedule (and attendant cost) risks of in-house software development are just too great.

Perhaps there's something about the nature of software that means you can't know how long it will take until you've done it. If so, the only organizations that can afford that kind of risk are vendors who can amortize the cost (whatever it turns out to be) over hundreds or thousands of users.

The protagonist of this guide has been burned many times. He's been asked to work weekends, holidays, and nights and to put in 80- and 90-hour workweeks during "crunch time," and he's not doing it anymore. He'll give what he thinks is a fair contribution—and he'll

probably do quite a bit more than that—but he no longer believes in heroics. "The more rabbits you pull out of the hat, the more rabbits they expect you to pull out of a hat, until all you're doing is pulling rabbits out of the hat. Nope, not anymore!"

Two important takeaways for the students:

■ **Software developers are optimists. Ensure that they have not planned schedules assuming that people work full time. People can't work all the time—they get sick, go to the dentist, serve jury duty, write employee evaluations, sit on design reviews, apply for patents, and so on. Plans should apply a factor like 0.6 to compute the number of effective labor hours for each employee.**

■ **Be aware of the consequences of negotiating a schedule. If the developers have used a sensible process for creating the schedule, it is seldom worth reducing it. They're optimists, anyway, and chances are the project will take longer than they think. If you trust that developer management is making effective use of the developers' time, leave the schedules alone.**

One important point not brought out by this guide: *Large projects are much harder to schedule than small ones.* Also, if the project lasts longer than a year, watch out! Longer projects mean more chance for technology change, requirements change, and employee turnover. All these factors increase the likelihood of schedule delays.

SUGGESTED RESPONSES FOR DISCUSSION QUESTIONS

1. I think the developer has been burned many times. We can learn a lot by understanding his points.

2. There's a risk when management attempts to negotiate schedules. As stated in the takeaway, noted previously, if management trusts that development management has used a sensible process to obtain the schedules, and if they trust development management to effectively utilize developers' time, leave the schedule alone.

   Alternatively, if the product must be produced more quickly, remove requirements. But do so realistically, and not as part of a negotiating ploy.

   As a manager, consider, too, the implications of negotiating a schedule. You're essentially telling the developers that you do not trust them, that you think they're attempting to deceive you with a relaxed schedule.

Rather than a harsh negotiation with the implications just stated, you might ask the developers to show you their schedule, to discuss their scheduling methodology with you, and then, as a team, work together to determine if there are any tasks for which the schedule could be compressed, or ways of rearranging tasks for greater schedule efficiency.

3. Without any further data about the costs of the 1-month difference, I'd prefer the 13-month shipment. Software that is produced when in "late mode" is typically lower in quality than software that is produced on a planned schedule. I'd bet (absent more knowledge) that such quality matters will translate into costs high enough to swamp the costs of the 2 extra months of development.

4. Return the plan to development management and tell them to plan more realistically. This planning mistake would raise serious flags in my mind about the competency of the development team. I'd do something to get that team more training, bring in consulting expertise, or start looking for new development managers.

5. If schedules are always unreasonable, then nobody believes anything. Schedules lose relevance, importance, and meaning. "Everybody knows this is a phony schedule. Don't knock yourself out."

6. I'd listen. I'd ask him to help me develop a plan and a process that would not have the result he fears. I'd work with him to develop that plan and to implement it.

7. This is a good question for the students to discuss. Some factors that may make software scheduling harder are:

   • Changing technology.
   • Changing requirements.

   • Software is mental—it's logical poetry. It's as varied as the human mind.
   • Large differences exist in the amount of quality code that different developers generate. These differences complicate planning.
   • Different tasks require different amounts of time. Writing an application where the tools and techniques are known is far simpler than inventing or applying a new technology. This complicates the planning process.

   In other ways, software is similar to managing any other complex project. It requires clearly defined tasks and schedules, unambiguous assignments of personnel to tasks, careful follow-up on assignments, management of critical paths and schedules, effective communication, and other skills students will learn in their project management classes.

8. Learn project management skills. Be aware of the difficulty of scheduling software projects. Understand the need to manage requirements creep. Be willing to remove features and functions if the schedule must be kept. Always plan on delays in software projects. Don't assume that because a project is late that software management is incompetent. It may be, but it may also be that unavoidable factors intervened.

WRAP UP

■ **What did you learn from this guide?**

■ **As a future manager, how will you plan your activities around software schedules?**

■ **How useful are the insights of this contrarian?**

■ **What characteristics make some contrarians' comments more useful than others?**

Information Systems Management

"Jeff, want to talk about information systems?" Laura Shen, a business analyst that Fox Lake hired to help solve process and systems problems, is proceeding cautiously with Jeff, Fox Lake's general manager.

"Sure, Laura, I've been wondering what you're up to."

"Well, I found some process problems that Mike, Anne, and I are working out. I think we're well on our way there." Laura's starting with the good news.

"Great."

"And, some of those processes use information systems, so I've been looking at them as well."

"Good."

"Jeff, you've hired me to help resolve some problems and help Fox Lake with IS and IT, and I really want to do that," Laura continues, still warming up to her point.

"That's what we want, Laura."

"Well, OK, then, Jeff, I think you need to manage the IS function more directly."

"WHAT?"

"I see some problems, some lack of organization, some IS issues that need to be addressed, and you're the person to do it." Laura waits for that news to settle.

"Laura, I'm not an IT guy. I can barely do my email, or schedule a tee time on our Web site. I don't know anything about IT."

"I understand. That's not your background, and it's nothing you thought you'd be doing as a GM."

"You can bet on it."

"Well, in a larger company, you'd have a senior manager in charge. You'd have a chief information officer or at least an IS/IT manager to do it. You'd manage him . . . or her. But, you don't."

"You're right, Laura, we don't have anyone by that title. That's why I look to Mike to do it."

"Jeff, there are a couple of problems with that. For one, it's not Mike's background, and, as you know, Mike's a new manager. If he were more senior he might be able to handle it, but he's not. He's a hard-working maintenance supervisor who's struggling to manage all of Fox Lake's facilities."

"And he's done a good job at it."

"OK, Jeff, but set that aside. The second problem of having Mike do it is that you've got the fox in charge of the hen house."

"What do you mean?"

"He's incentivized to stay in budget. Including all of the IT/IS that he's managing, he's also manager of facilities and needs some of the IT/IS budget for support to facilities. He has no incentive, other than professional courtesy, to provide any new IS capability to wedding events, or any other function."

"You think he's got a conflict of interest?" Jeff sits back in his chair reflecting.

"Like you said, 'You can bet on it.' Plus, Fox Lake is vulnerable." Laura finally brings up the issue that concerns her.

"Vulnerable? How?"

"Well, you're running servers and your network from the facilities building. They're in the backroom, but access to the servers is wide open. I'm not worried about someone running into them with a golf cart, though that could happen. I'm more worried that anyone with access to that building has access to all of the servers, the applications, and all of your data."

"I thought we moved some of those systems to the cloud, whatever that is. At least, I approved the budget to do that."

"That was for the new facilities scheduling system. The Fox Lake membership applications, all the accounting systems, and all the older systems still run on those servers." Laura thinks she's making some headway.

"Hmpf. I don't know. Maybe I should hire someone to manage it."

"You could. It would be expensive, and you may not need to. Why not get involved yourself, clean it up, and then hire someone if necessary?"

"OK, you've got my attention. Let's talk some more. I've got to run now, but put down your thoughts and let me take a look. Then, we'll see."

"Will do. Thanks, Jeff." Laura leaves, much relieved.

She had deeper suspicions than she stated but not enough data to bring them up. "At least, we'll get him on track," she thinks as she walks to her car. ■

Study Questions

Q1 What are the functions and organization of the IS department?

Q2 How do organizations plan the use of IS?

Q3 What are the advantages and disadvantages of outsourcing?

Q4 What are your user rights and responsibilities?

Q5 2022?

Information systems are critical to organizational success, and like all critical assets, need to be managed responsibly, in organizations both large and small. In this chapter, we will survey the management of IS and IT resources. We begin by discussing the major functions and the organization of the IS department. Then we will consider planning the use of IT/IS. Outsourcing is the process of hiring outside vendors to provide business services and related products. For our purposes, outsourcing refers to hiring outside vendors to provide information systems, products, and applications. We will examine the pros and cons of outsourcing and describe some of its risks. Finally, we will conclude this chapter by discussing the relationship of users to the IS department. In this last section, you will learn both your own and the IS department's rights and responsibilities.

The purpose of this chapter is not to teach you how to manage information systems. Such management, in truth, requires many years of experience. Instead, the goal of this chapter is to give you an appreciation for the responsibilities of IS management and to help you become an effective consumer of IS services.

And, if you work for a small company like Fox Lake, you will at least know the elements of IS management and be able to help people like Jeff understand what needs to be done. By the way, GearUp doesn't have issues like Fox Lake, primarily because it employs an in-house IT person.

Q1 What Are the Functions and Organization of the IS Department?

The major functions of the information systems department[1] are as follows:

- Plan the use of IS to accomplish organizational goals and strategy.
- Manage outsourcing relationships.
- Protect information assets.
- Develop, operate, and maintain the organization's computing infrastructure.
- Develop, operate, and maintain applications.

We will consider the first two functions in questions Q2 and Q3 of this chapter. The protection function is the topic of Chapter 12. The last two functions are important for IS majors, but less so for other business professionals, and we will not consider them in this text. To set the stage, consider the organization of the IS department.

How Is the IS Department Organized?

Figure 11-1 shows typical top-level reporting relationships. As you will learn in your management classes, organizational structure varies depending on the organization's size, culture, competitive environment, industry, and other factors. Larger organizations

---

[1] Often, the department we are calling the *IS department* is known in organizations as the *IT department*. That name is a misnomer however, because the IT department manages systems as well as technology. If you hear the term *IT department* in industry, don't assume that the scope of that department is limited to technology.

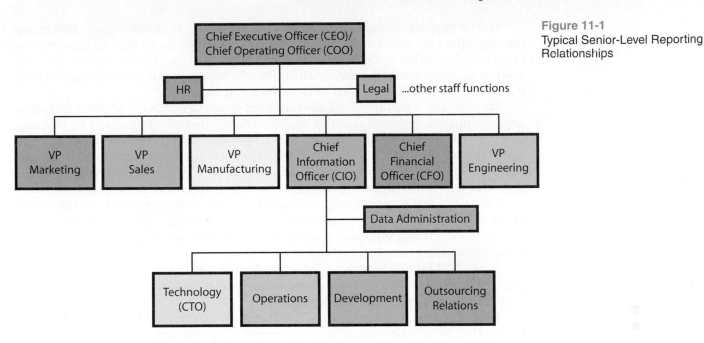

Figure 11-1
Typical Senior-Level Reporting
Relationships

with independent divisions will have a group of senior executives like those shown here for each division. Smaller companies may combine some of these departments. Consider the structure in Figure 11-1 as typical.

The title of the principal manager of the IS department varies from organization to organization. A common title is **chief information officer,** or **CIO**. Other common titles are *vice president of information services, director of information services*, and, less commonly, *director of computer services*.

In Figure 11-1, the CIO, like other senior executives, reports to the *chief executive officer* (CEO), though sometimes these executives report to the *chief operating officer* (COO), who, in turn, reports to the CEO. In some companies, the CIO reports to the *chief financial officer* (CFO). That reporting arrangement might make sense if the primary information systems support only accounting and finance activities. In organizations such as manufacturers that operate significant nonaccounting information systems, the arrangement shown in Figure 11-1 is more common and effective.

The structure of the IS department also varies among organizations. Figure 11-1 shows a typical IS department with four groups and a data administration staff function.

Most IS departments include a *technology* office that investigates new information systems technologies and determines how the organization can benefit from them. For example, today many organizations are investigating social media and elastic cloud opportunities and planning how they can use those capabilities to better accomplish their goals and objectives. An individual called the **chief technology officer,** or **CTO**, often heads the technology group. The CTO evaluates new technologies, new ideas, and new capabilities and identifies those that are most relevant to the organization. The CTO's job requires deep knowledge of information technology and the ability to envision and innovate applications in the organization.

The next group in Figure 11-1, *Operations,* manages the computing infrastructure, including individual computers, in-house server farms, networks, and communications media. This group includes system and network administrators. As you will learn, an important function for this group is to monitor the user experience and respond to user problems.

The third group in the IS department in Figure 11-1 is *Development*. This group manages the process of creating new information systems as well as maintaining existing information systems. (Recall from Chapter 10 that in the context of information systems *maintenance* means either fixing problems or adapting existing information systems to support new features and functions.)

The size and structure of the development group depends on whether programs are developed in-house. If not, this department will be staffed primarily by business and systems analysts who work with users, operations, and vendors to acquire and install licensed software and to set up the system components around that software. If the organization develops programs in-house, then this department will include programmers, test engineers, technical writers, and other development personnel.

The last IS department group in Figure 11-1 is *Outsourcing Relations*. This group exists in organizations that have negotiated outsourcing agreements with other companies to provide equipment, applications, or other services. You will learn more about outsourcing later in this chapter.

Figure 11-1 also includes a *Data Administration* staff function. The purpose of this group is to protect data and information assets by establishing data standards and data management practices and policies.

There are many variations on the structure of the IS department shown in Figure 11-1. In larger organizations, the operations group may itself consist of several different departments. Sometimes, there is a separate group for data warehousing and data marts.

As you examine Figure 11-1, keep the distinction between IS and IT in mind. *Information systems (IS)* exist to help the organization achieve its goals and objectives. Information systems have the five components we have discussed throughout this text. *Information technology (IT)* is simply technology. It concerns the products, techniques, procedures, and designs of computer-based technology. IT must be placed into the structure of an IS before an organization can use it.

What IS-Related Job Positions Exist?

IS departments provide a wide range of interesting and well-paying jobs. Many students enter the MIS class thinking that the IS departments consist only of programmers and computer technicians. If you reflect on the five components of an information system, you can understand why this cannot be true. The data, procedures, and people components of an information system require professionals with highly developed interpersonal communications skills.

Figure 11-2 summarizes the major job positions in the IS industry. With the exception of computer technician and possibly of PQA test engineer, all of these positions require a 4-year degree. Furthermore, with the exception of programmer and PQA test engineer, all of these positions require business knowledge. In most cases, successful professionals have a degree in business. Note, too, that most positions require good verbal and written communications skills. Business, including information systems, is a social activity.

Many of the positions in Figure 11-2 have a wide salary range. Lower salaries are for professionals with limited experience or for those who work in smaller companies or work on small projects. The larger salaries are for those with deep knowledge and experience who work for large companies on large projects. Do not expect to begin your career at the high end of these ranges. As noted, all salaries are for positions in the United States and are shown in U.S. dollars.

(By the way, for all but the most technical positions, knowledge of a business specialty can add to your marketability. If you have the time, a dual major can be an excellent choice. Popular and successful dual majors are accounting and information systems, marketing and information systems, and management and information systems.)

Figure 11-2

Job Positions in
the Information
Systems Industry

Title	Responsibilities	Knowledge, Skill, and Characteristics Requirements	United States 2011 Salary Range (USD)
Business analyst	Work with business leaders and planners to develop processes and systems that implement business strategy and goals.	Knowledge of business planning, strategy, process management, and technology. Can deal with complexity. See big picture but work with details. Strong interpersonal and communication skills needed.	$75,000–$125,000
System analyst	Work with users to determine system requirements, design and develop job descriptions and procedures, help determine system test plans.	Strong interpersonal and communications skills. Knowledge of both business and technology. Adaptable.	$65,000–$125,000
Programmer	Design and write computer programs.	Logical thinking and design skills, knowledge of one or more programming languages.	$50,000–$150,000
PQA test engineer	Develop test plans, design and write automated test scripts, perform testing.	Logical thinking, basic programming, superb organizational skills, eye for detail.	$40,000–$95,000
Technical writer	Write program documentation, help-text, procedures, job descriptions, training materials.	Quick learner, clear writing skills, high verbal communications skills.	$40,000–$95,000
User support representative	Help users solve problems, provide training.	Communications and people skills. Product knowledge. Patience.	$40,000–$65,000
Computer technician	Install software, repair computer equipment and networks.	Associate degree, diagnostic skills.	$30,000–$65,000
Network administrator	Monitor, maintain, fix, and tune computer networks.	Diagnostic skills, in-depth knowledge of communications technologies and products.	$75,000–$200,000+
Consultant	Wide range of activities: programming, testing, database design, communications and networks, project management, security and risk management, social media, strategic planning.	Quick learner, entrepreneurial attitude, communications and people skills. Respond well to pressure. Particular knowledge depends on work.	From $35 per hour for a contract tester to more than $500 per hour for strategic consulting to executive group.
Salesperson	Sell software, network, communications, and consulting services.	Quick learner, knowledge of product, superb professional sales skills.	$65,000–$200,000+
Small-scale project manager	Initiate, plan, manage, monitor, and close down projects.	Management and people skills, technology knowledge. Highly organized.	$75,000–$150,000
Large-scale project manager	Initiate, plan, monitor, and close down complex projects.	Executive and management skills. Deep project management knowledge.	$150,000–$250,000+
Database administrator	Manage and protect database (see Chapter 5).	Diplomatic skills, database technology knowledge.	$75,000–$250,000
Chief technology officer (CTO)	Advise CIO, executive group, and project managers on emerging technologies.	Quick learner, good communication skills, business background, deep knowledge of IT.	$125,000–$300,000+
Chief information officer (CIO)	Manage IT department, communicate with executive staff on IT- and IS-related matters. Member of the executive group.	Superb management skills, deep knowledge of business and technology, and good business judgment. Good communicator. Balanced and unflappable.	$150,000–$500,000, plus executive benefits and privileges.

Q2 How Do Organizations Plan the Use of IS?

We begin our discussion of IS functions with planning. Figure 11-3 lists the major IS planning functions.

Align Information Systems with Organizational Strategy

The purpose of an information system is to help the organization accomplish its goals and objectives. In order to do so, all information systems must be aligned with the organization's competitive strategy.

Recall the four competitive strategies from Chapter 3: An organization can be a cost leader either across an industry or within an industry segment. Alternatively, an organization can differentiate its products or services either across the industry or within a segment. Whatever the organizational strategy, the CIO and the IS department must constantly be vigilant to align IS with it.

Maintaining alignment between IS direction and organizational strategy is a continuing process. As strategies change, as the organization merges with other organizations, as divisions are sold, IS must evolve along with the organization.

Unfortunately, however, IS infrastructure is not malleable. Changing a network requires time and resources. Integrating disparate information systems applications is even slower and more expensive. This fact often is not appreciated in the executive suite. Without a persuasive CIO, IS can be perceived as a drag on the organization's opportunities.

Communicate IS Issues to the Executive Group

This last observation leads to the second IS planning function in Figure 11-3. The CIO is the representative for IS and IT issues within the executive staff. The CIO provides the IS perspective during discussions of problem solutions, proposals, and new initiatives.

For example, when considering a merger, it is important that the company consider integration of information systems in the merged entities. This consideration needs to be addressed during the evaluation of the merger opportunity. Too often, such issues are not considered until after the deal has been signed. Such delayed consideration is a mistake; the costs of the integration need to be factored into the economics of the purchase. Involving the CIO in high-level discussions is the best way to avoid such problems.

Develop Priorities and Enforce Them Within the IS Department

The next two IS planning functions in Figure 11-3 are related. The CIO must ensure that priorities consistent with the overall organizational strategy are developed and communicated to the IS department. At the same time, the CIO must also ensure that the department evaluates proposals and projects for using new technology in light of those communicated priorities.

Technology is seductive, particularly to IS professionals. The CTO may enthusiastically claim, "With SOA services we can do this and this and this." Although true, the question that the CIO must continually ask is whether those new possibilities are consistent with the organization's strategy and direction.

Figure 11-3
Planning the Use of IS/IT

- Align information systems with organizational strategy; maintain alignment as organization changes.
- Communicate IS/IT issues to executive group.
- Develop/enforce IS priorities within the IS department.
- Sponsor steering committee.

Thus, the CIO must not only establish and communicate such priorities, but enforce them as well. The department must evaluate every proposal, at the earliest stage possible, as to whether it is consistent with the organization's goals and aligned with its strategy.

Furthermore, no organization can afford to implement every good idea. Even projects that are aligned with the organization's strategy must be prioritized. The objective of everyone in the IS department must be to develop the most appropriate systems possible, given constraints on time and money. Well thought out and clearly communicated priorities are essential.

Sponsor the Steering Committee

The final planning function in Figure 11-3 is to sponsor the steering committee. A **steering committee** is a group of senior managers from the major business functions that works with the CIO to set the IS priorities and decide among major IS projects and alternatives.

The steering committee serves an important communication function between IS and the users. In the steering committee, information systems personnel can discuss potential IS initiatives and directions with the user community. At the same time, the steering committee provides a forum for users to express their needs, frustrations, and other issues they have with the IS department.

Typically, the IS department sets up the steering committee's schedule and agenda and conducts the meetings. The CEO and other members of the executive staff determine the membership of the steering committee.

One other task related to planning the use of IT is to establish the organization's computer-use policy. For more on computer-use issues, read the Ethics Guide on pages 394–395.

Q3 What Are the Advantages and Disadvantages of Outsourcing?

Outsourcing is the process of hiring another organization to perform a service. Outsourcing is done to save costs, to gain expertise, and to free management time.

The father of modern management, Peter Drucker, is reputed to have said, "Your back room is someone else's front room." For instance, in most companies, running the cafeteria is not an essential function for business success; thus, the employee cafeteria is a "back room." Google wants to be the worldwide leader in search and mobile computing hardware and applications, all supported by ever-increasing ad revenue. It does not want to be known for how well it runs cafeterias. Using Drucker's sentiment, Google is better off hiring another company, one that specializes in food services, to run its cafeterias.

Because food service is some company's "front room," that company will be better able to provide a quality product at a fair price. Outsourcing to a food vendor will also free Google's management from attention on the cafeteria. Food quality, chef scheduling, plastic fork acquisition, waste disposal, and so on, will all be another company's concern. Google can focus on search, mobile computing, and advertising-revenue growth.

Outsourcing Information Systems

Many companies today have chosen to outsource portions of their information systems activities. Figure 11-4 lists popular reasons for doing so. Consider each major group of reasons.

Management Advantages

First, outsourcing can be an easy way to gain expertise. Suppose, for example, that an organization wants to upgrade its thousands of user computers on a cost-effective basis. To do so, the organization would need to develop expertise in automated software installation, unattended installations, remote support, and

Ethics Guide

Using the Corporate Computer

Suppose you work at a company that has the following computer use policy:

Computers, email, social networking, and the Internet are to be used primarily for official company business. Small amounts of personal email can be exchanged with friends and family, and occasional usage of the Internet is permitted, but such usage should be limited and never interfere with your work.

Suppose you are a manager and you learn that one of your employees has been engaged in the following activities:

1. Playing computer games during work hours
2. Playing computer games on the company computer before and after work hours
3. Responding to emails from an ill parent
4. Watching DVDs during lunch and other breaks
5. Sending emails to plan a party that involves mostly people from work
6. Sending emails to plan a party that involves no one from work
7. Searching the Web for a new car
8. Reading the news on CNN.com
9. Checking the stock market over the Internet
10. Bidding on items for personal use on eBay
11. Selling personal items on eBay
12. Paying personal bills online
13. Paying personal bills online when traveling on company business
14. Buying an airplane ticket for an ill parent over the Internet

Source: Superstock.

15. Changing the content of a personal Facebook page
16. Changing the content of a personal business Web site
17. Buying an airplane ticket for a personal vacation over the Internet
18. Responding to personal Twitter messages ■

Discussion Questions

1. Explain how you would respond to each situation.

2. Suppose someone from the IS department notifies you that one of your employees is spending 3 hours a day writing Twitter messages. How do you respond?

3. For question 2, suppose you ask how the IS department knows about your employee and you are told, "We secretly monitor computer usage." Do you object to such monitoring? Why or why not?

4. Suppose someone from the IS department notifies you that one of your employees is sending many personal emails. When you ask how they know the emails are personal, you are told that IS measures account activity and when suspicious email usage is suspected the IS department reads employees' email. Do you think such reading is legal? Is it ethical? How do you respond?

5. As an employee, if you know that your company occasionally reads employees' email, does that change your behavior? If so, does that justify the company reading your email? Does this situation differ from having someone read your personal postal mail that happens to be delivered to you at work? Why or why not?

6. Write what you think is the best corporate policy for personal computer usage at work. Specifically address Facebook, MySpace, Twitter, and other personal social networking activity.

Figure 11-4
Popular Reasons for
Outsourcing IS Services

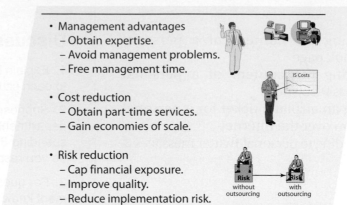

other measures that can be used to improve the efficiency of software management. Developing such expertise is expensive, and it is not in the company's strategic direction. Efficient installation of software to thousands of computers is not in the "front room." Consequently, the organization might choose to hire a specialist company to perform this service.

Another reason for outsourcing is to avoid management problems. Suppose Carbon Creek Gardens (Chapter 9 Collaboration Exercise, page 334) decides to share its inventory with its suppliers using SOA services. How will Mary Keeling hire the appropriate staff? She doesn't know if she needs a C++ programmer or an HTML programmer. Even if she could find and hire the right staff, how would she manage them? How would she create a good work environment for a C++ programmer, when she does not know what such a person does? To avoid such management problems, Carbon Creek would hire an outside firm to develop and maintain the Web service.

Similarly, some companies choose to outsource to save management time and attention. Lucas at GearUp has the skills to manage a new software development project, but he may choose to not invest the time.

Note, too, that it's not just Lucas' time. It is also time from more senior managers who approve the purchase and hiring requisitions for that activity. And, those senior managers, like Kelly, will need to devote the time necessary to learn enough about Web farms to approve or reject the requisitions. Outsourcing saves both direct and indirect management time.

Cost Reduction

Other common reasons for choosing to outsource concern cost reductions. With outsourcing, organizations can obtain part-time services. Another benefit of outsourcing is to gain economies of scale. If 25 organizations develop their own payroll applications in-house, then when the tax law changes 25 different groups will have to learn the new law, change their software to meet the law, test the changes, and write the documentation explaining the changes. However, if those same 25 organizations outsource to the same payroll vendor, then that vendor can make all of the adjustments once, and the cost of the change can be amortized over all of them (thus lowering the cost that the vendor must charge).

Risk Reduction

Another reason for outsourcing is to reduce risk. First, outsourcing can cap financial risk. In a typical outsourcing contract, the outsource vendor will agree to provide, say, computer workstations with certain software connected via a particular network. Typically, each new workstation will have a fixed cost, say, $2,500 per station. The company's management team might believe that there is a good chance that they can provide workstations at a lower unit cost, but there is also the chance that they will get in over their heads and have a disaster. If so, the cost per computer could be much higher than $2,500. Outsourcing caps that financial risk and leads to greater budgetary stability.

Second, outsourcing can reduce risk by ensuring a certain level of quality, or avoiding the risk of having substandard quality. A company that specializes in food service knows what to do to provide a certain level of quality. It has the expertise to ensure, for example, that only healthy food is served. So, too, a company that specializes in, say, cloud-server hosting, knows what to do to provide a certain level of service for a given workload.

Note that there is no guarantee that outsourcing will provide a certain level of quality or quality better than could be achieved in-house. If it doesn't outsource the cafeteria, Google might get lucky and hire only great chefs. Carbon Creek Gardens might get lucky and hire the world's best software developer. But, in general, a professional outsourcing firm knows how to avoid giving everyone food poisoning or developing new applications. And, if that minimum level of quality is not provided, it is easier to hire another vendor than it is to fire and rehire internal staff.

Finally, organizations choose to outsource IS in order to reduce implementation risk. Hiring an outside vendor reduces the risk of picking the wrong hardware or the wrong software, using the wrong network protocol, or implementing tax law changes incorrectly. Outsourcing gathers all of these risks into the risk of choosing the right vendor. Once the company has chosen the vendor, further risk management is up to that vendor.

International Outsourcing

Many firms headquartered in the United States have chosen to outsource overseas. Microsoft and Dell, for example, have outsourced major portions of their customer support activities to companies outside the United States. India is a popular source because it has a large, well-educated, English-speaking population that will work for 20 to 30 percent of the labor cost in the United States. China and other countries are used as well. In fact, with modern telephone technology and Internet-enabled service databases, a single service call can be initiated in the United States, partially processed in India, then Singapore, and finalized by an employee in England. The customer knows only that he has been put on hold for brief periods of time.

International outsourcing is particularly advantageous for customer support and other functions that must be operational 24/7. Amazon.com, for example, operates customer service centers in the United States, India, and Ireland. During the evening hours in the United States, customer service reps in India, where it is daytime, handle the calls. When night falls in India, customer service reps in Ireland handle the early morning calls from the east coast of the United States. In this way, companies can provide 24/7 service without requiring employees to work night shifts.

By the way, as you learned in Chapter 1, the key protection for your job is to become someone who excels at nonroutine symbolic analysis. Someone with the ability to find innovative applications of new technology also is unlikely to lose his or her job to overseas workers.

What Are the Outsourcing Alternatives?

Organizations have found hundreds of different ways to outsource information systems and portions of information systems. Figure 11-5 organizes the major categories of alternatives according to information systems components.

Some organizations outsource the acquisition and operation of computer hardware. Electronic Data Systems (EDS) has been successful for more than 30 years as an outsource vendor of hardware infrastructure. Figure 11-5 shows another alternative, outsourcing the computers in the cloud.

Acquiring licensed software, as discussed in Chapters 4 and 10, is a form of outsourcing. Rather than develop the software in-house, an organization licenses it from another vendor. Such licensing allows the software vendor to amortize the cost of software maintenance over all of the users, thus reducing that cost for all users. Software as a service (SaaS) is another outsourcing alternative that provides hosted applications and data storage. Salesforce.com is a typical example of a company that offers SaaS.

Figure 11-5
IS/IT Outsourcing Alternatives

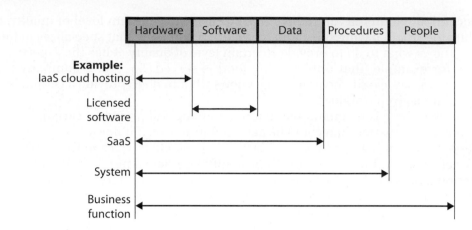

Another outsourcing alternative is to outsource an entire system. PeopleSoft (now owned by Oracle) attained prominence by providing the entire payroll function as an outsourced service. In such a solution, as the arrow in Figure 11-5 implies, the vendor provides hardware, software, data, and some procedures. The company need provide only employee and work information; the payroll outsource vendor does the rest.

A Web storefront is another form of application outsourcing. Amazon.com, for example, provides a Web storefront for product vendors and distributors who choose not to develop their own Web presence. In this case, rather than pay a fixed fee for the storefront service, the product vendors and distributors pay Amazon.com a portion of the revenue generated. Such Web-service hosting has become a major profit center for Amazon.com.

Finally, some organizations choose to outsource an entire business function. For years, many companies have outsourced to travel agencies the function of arranging for employee travel. Some of these outsource vendors even operate offices within the company facilities. Such agreements are much broader than outsourcing IS, but information systems are key components of the applications that are outsourced.

Not everyone agrees on the desirability of outsourcing. For potential pitfalls, read the example in the Guide on pages 404–405.

What Are the Risks of Outsourcing?

With so many advantages and with so many different outsourcing alternatives, you might wonder why any company has any in-house IS/IT functions. In fact, outsourcing presents significant risks, as listed in Figure 11-6.

Figure 11-6
Outsourcing Risks

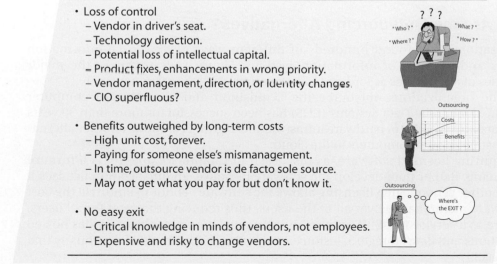

Loss of Control

The first risk of outsourcing is a loss of control. Outsourcing puts the vendor in the driver's seat. Each outsource vendor has methods and procedures for its service. The organization and its employees will have to conform to those procedures. For example, a hardware infrastructure vendor will have standard forms and procedures for requesting a computer, for recording and processing a computer problem, or for providing routine maintenance on computers. Once the vendor is in charge, employees must conform.

When outsourcing the cafeteria, employees have only those food choices that the vendor provides. Similarly, when obtaining computer hardware and services, the employees will need to take what the vendor supports. Employees who want equipment that is not on the vendor's list will be out of luck.

The outsource vendor chooses the technology that it wants to implement. If the vendor, for some reason, is slow to pick up on a significant new technology, then the hiring organization will be slow to attain benefits from that technology. An organization can find itself at a competitive disadvantage because it cannot offer the same IS services as its competitors.

Another concern is a potential loss of intellectual capital. The company may need to reveal proprietary trade secrets, methods, or procedures to the outsource vendor's employees. As part of its normal operations, that vendor may move employees to competing organizations, and the company may lose intellectual capital as that happens. The loss need not be intellectual theft; it could simply be that the vendor's employees learned to work in a new and better way at your company, and then they take that learning to your competitor.

Similarly, all software has failures and problems. Quality vendors track those failures and problems and fix them according to a set of priorities. When a company outsources a system, it no longer has control over prioritizing those fixes. Such control belongs to the vendor. A fix that might be critical to your organization might be of low priority to the outsource vendor.

Other problems are that the outsource vendor may change management, adopt a different strategic direction, or be acquired. When any of those changes occur, priorities may change, and an outsource vendor that was a good choice at one time might be a bad fit after it changes direction. It can be difficult and expensive to change an outsource vendor when this occurs.

The final loss-of-control risk is that the company's CIO can become superfluous. When users need a critical service that is outsourced, the CIO must turn to the vendor for a response. In time, users learn that it is quicker to deal directly with the outsource vendor, and soon the CIO is out of the communication loop. At that point, the vendor has essentially replaced the CIO, who has become a figurehead. However, employees of the outsource vendor work for a different company, with a bias toward their employer. Critical managers will thus not share the same goals and objectives as the rest of the management team. Biased, bad decisions can result.

Benefits Outweighed by Long-Term Costs

The initial benefits of outsourcing can appear huge. A cap on financial exposure, a reduction of management time and attention, and the release of many management and staffing problems are all possible. (Most likely, outsource vendors promise these very benefits.) Outsourcing can appear too good to be true.

In fact, it *can be* too good to be true. For one, although a fixed cost does indeed cap exposure, it also removes the benefits of economies of scale. If the Web storefront takes off, and suddenly the organization needs 200 servers instead of 20, the using organization will pay 200 times the fixed cost of supporting one server. It is likely, however, that because of economies of scale, the costs of supporting 200 servers are far less than 10 times the costs of supporting 20 servers.

Also, the outsource vendor may change its pricing strategy over time. Initially, an organization obtains a competitive bid from several outsource vendors. However, as the winning vendor learns more about the business and as relationships develop

Using MIS InClass 11   *A Group Exercise*

What's That Humming Sound?

Source: Shutterstock.com.

Green computing is environmentally conscious computing consisting of three major components: power management, virtualization, and e-waste management. In this exercise, we focus on power.

You know, of course, that computers (and related equipment, such as printers) consume electricity. That burden is light for any single computer or printer. But consider all of the computers and printers in the United States that will be running tonight, with no one in the office. Proponents of green computing encourage companies and employees to reduce power and water consumption by turning off devices when not in use.

Is this issue important? Is it just a concession to environmentalists to make computing professionals appear virtuous? Form a team and develop your own, informed opinion by considering computer use at your campus.

1. Search the Internet to determine the power requirements for typical computing and office equipment. Consider laptop computers, desktop computers, CRT monitors, LCD monitors, and printers. For this exercise, ignore server computers. As you search, be aware that a *watt* is a measure of electrical power. It is *watts* that the green computing movement wants to reduce.

2. Estimate the number of each type of device in use on your campus. Use your university's Web site to determine the number of colleges, departments, faculty, staff, and students. Make assumptions about the number of computers, copiers, and other types of equipment used by each.

3. Using the data from items 1 and 2, estimate the total power used by computing and related devices on your campus.

4. A computer that is in screensaver mode uses the same amount of power as one in regular mode. Computers that are in sleep mode, however, use much less power, say 6 watts per hour. Reflect on computer use on your campus and estimate the amount of time that computing devices are in sleep versus screensaver or use mode. Compute the savings in power that result from sleep mode.

5. Computers that are automatically updated by the IS department with software upgrades and patches cannot be allowed to go into sleep mode because if they are sleeping they will not be able to receive the upgrade. Hence, some universities prohibit sleep mode on university computers (sleep mode is never used on servers, by the way). Determine the cost, in watts, of such a policy.

6. Calculate the monthly cost, in watts, if:
   a. All user computers run full time night and day.
   b. All user computers run full time during work hours and in sleep mode during off-hours.
   c. All user computers are shut off during nonwork hours.

7. Given your answers to items 1–6, is computer power management during off-hours a significant concern? In comparison to the other costs of running a university, does this issue really matter? Discuss this question among your group and explain your answer.

between the organization's employees and those of the vendor, it becomes difficult for other firms to compete for subsequent contracts. The vendor becomes the *de facto* sole source and, with little competitive pressure, might increase its prices.

Another problem is that an organization can find itself paying for another organization's mismanagement, with little knowledge that that is the case. If GearUp outsources its auction site, it is difficult for it to know if the vendor is well managed.

GearUp may be paying for poor management; even worse, it may suffer the consequences of poor management, such as lost data. It will be very difficult for GearUp to learn about such mismanagement.

No Easy Exit

The final category of outsourcing risk concerns ending the agreement. There is no easy exit. For one, the outsource vendor's employees have gained significant knowledge of the company. They know the server requirements in customer support, they know the patterns of usage, and they know the best procedures for downloading operational data into the data warehouse. Consequently, lack of knowledge will make it difficult to bring the outsourced service back in-house.

Also, because the vendor has become so tightly integrated into the business, parting company can be exceedingly risky. Closing down the employee cafeteria for a few weeks while finding another food vendor would be unpopular, but employees would survive. Shutting down the enterprise network for a few weeks would be impossible; the business would not survive. Because of such risk, the company must invest considerable work, duplication of effort, management time, and expense to change to another vendor. In truth, choosing an outsource vendor can be a one-way street.

Choosing to outsource is a difficult decision. In fact, the correct decision might not be clear, but time and events could force the company to decide.

It may not always be clear whether a company should outsource. The Guide on pages 406–407 considers different scenarios.

Q4 What Are Your User Rights and Responsibilities?

As a future user of information systems, you have both rights and responsibilities in your relationship with the IS department. The items in Figure 11-7 list what you are entitled to receive and indicate what you are expected to contribute.

Your User Rights

You have a right to have the computing resources you need to perform your work as proficiently as you want. You have a right to the computer hardware and programs that you need. If you process huge files for data-mining applications, you have a right to the huge disks and the fast processor that you need. However, if you merely receive email and consult the corporate Web portal, then your right is for more modest requirements (leaving the more powerful resources for those in the organization who need them).

Figure 11-7
User Information Systems
Rights and Responsibilities

You have a right to:
- Computer hardware and programs that allow you to perform your job proficiently
- Reliable network and Internet connections
- A secure computing environment
- Protection from viruses, worms, and other threats
- Contribute to requirements for new system features and functions
- Reliable systems development and maintenance
- Prompt attention to problems, concerns, and complaints
- Properly prioritized problem fixes and resolutions
- Effective training

You have a responsibility to:
- Learn basic computer skills
- Learn standard techniques and procedures for the applications you use
- Follow security and backup procedures
- Protect your password(s)
- Use computer resources according to your employer's computer use policy
- Make no unauthorized hardware modifications
- Install only authorized programs
- Apply software patches and fixes when directed to do so
- When asked, devote the time required to respond carefully and completely to requests for requirements for new system features and functions
- Avoid reporting trivial problems

You have a right to reliable network and Internet services. *Reliable* means that you can process without problems almost all of the time. It means that you never go to work wondering, "Will the network be available today?" Network problems should be a rare occurrence.

You also have a right to a secure computing environment. The organization should protect your computer and its files, and you should not normally even need to think about security. From time to time, the organization might ask you to take particular actions to protect your computer and files, and you should take those actions. But such requests should be rare and related to specific outside threats.

You have a right to participate in requirements meetings for new applications that you will use and for major changes to applications that you currently use. You may choose to delegate this right to others, or your department may delegate that right for you, but if so, you have a right to contribute your thoughts through that delegate.

You have a right to reliable systems development and maintenance. Although schedule slippages of a month or two are common in many development projects, you should not have to endure schedule slippages of six months or more. Such slippages are evidence of incompetent systems development.

Additionally, you have a right to receive prompt attention to your problems, concerns, and complaints about information services. You have a right to have a means to report problems, and you have a right to know that your problem has been received and at least registered with the IS department. You have a right to have your problem resolved, consistent with established priorities. This means that an annoying problem that allows you to conduct your work will be prioritized below another's problem that interferes with his ability to do his job.

Finally, you have a right to effective training. It should be training that you can understand and that enables you to use systems to perform your particular job. The organization should provide training in a format and on a schedule that is convenient to you.

Your User Responsibilities

You also have responsibilities toward the IS department and your organization. Specifically, you have a responsibility to learn basic computer skills and to learn the techniques and procedures for the applications you use. You should not expect hand-holding for basic operations. Nor should you expect to receive repetitive training and support for the same issue.

You have a responsibility to follow security and backup procedures. This is especially important because actions that you fail to take might cause problems for your fellow employees and your organization as well as for you. In particular, you are responsible for protecting your password(s). In the next chapter, you will learn that this is important not only to protect your computer, but, because of intersystem authentication, it is important to protect your organization's networks and databases as well.

You have a responsibility for using your computer resources in a manner that is consistent with your employer's policy. Many employers allow limited email for critical family matters while at work, but discourage frequent and long casual email. You have a responsibility to know your employer's policy and to follow it.

You also have a responsibility to make no unauthorized hardware modifications to your computer and to install only authorized programs. One reason for this policy is that your IS department constructs automated maintenance programs for upgrading your computer. Unauthorized hardware and programs might interfere with these programs. Additionally, the installation of unauthorized hardware or programs can cause you problems that the IS department will have to fix.

You have a responsibility to install computer patches and fixes when asked to do so. This is particularly important for patches that concern security and backup and recovery. When asked for input to requirements for new and adapted systems, you have a responsibility to take the time necessary to provide thoughtful and complete responses. If you do not have that time, you should delegate your input to someone else.

Finally, you have a responsibility to treat information systems professionals professionally. Everyone works for the same company, everyone wants to succeed, and professionalism and courtesy will go a long way on all sides. One form of professional behavior is to learn basic computer skills so that you avoid reporting trivial problems.

Q5 2022?

Many changes and developments will have a major impact on the organizational management of IS and IT resources in the next 10 years. Most organizations will move their internal hardware infrastructure into the cloud. Sure, some companies will be concerned enough about security that they'll keep some data on their own, privately controlled servers, but vast amounts of hardware infrastructure will migrate to the cloud. Running a computer center for anyone other than a cloud vendor is not a promising career.

Licensed, off-the-shelf software will become more configurable, more adaptable, and more flexible. Fewer and fewer applications will be developed in-house, and software customization will become easier. Fewer and less-skilled employees will be needed to adapt software to increasingly unique organizational needs.

The iOS devices and other, small computing devices will become cheaper and even more popular. Powerful computing devices will be as available as cheap cell phones are today. More so, actually.

All of these changes will dramatically impact IS and IT management, but none of them are even close in importance to another challenge that will emerge in the next 10 years: Loss of control.

How will organizations maintain control of their employees' use of IT? When employees come to work with their own computing devices that are more powerful than any computer they have at work, and when those devices access networks that are paid for by the employees, how does the IS department maintain control?

For a few years, organizations may be able to maintain some semblance of control by limiting access to organizational networks. "You can only sign on to the corporate network using a device that the company provides and approves." That policy will work for a while, but ultimately it's doomed. For one, at some point that policy will put employees at a competitive disadvantage. Employees will want to access the network using whatever hardware they have, wherever they happen to be. If they can't, their competitors will.

But there's a second reason limiting access to the corporate network won't work. Employees will move off the network! "Ah, we can't access SharePoint from our iPads, so let's use my SkyDrive instead of the corporate SharePoint site. I'll share my folder with the whole team and then we can get to it using our own latest-version iOS devices. Here, I'll copy the data from the computer at work onto my SkyDrive, and we can take it from there." Or, "Let's create a Google+ circle." Or . . .

Now, all the corporate data are out on someone's SkyDrive or Google+ account or somewhere else and has been shared with, well, who knows? Employee Jones made a mistake; instead of sharing her Google+ circle with her teammates at work, she shared it on a public circle. Now, anyone, or any crawler, that stumbles over that data has access to it.

Over the past 40 years, IS departments have waged a losing battle for control over corporate data. Is there an answer? In high-security military sites, personal computing devices are not allowed and local area networks are not connected, in any way, with the Internet. Security policy dictates that if an employee takes a personal computing device, including an iPhone, an iPad, or a thumb drive—in fact, any device with memory—into a secure area, that device will be confiscated and never returned. It will never leave the secure area again.

Can corporations take that posture? Hardly. There doesn't seem to be an answer, except perhaps buying insurance. Which sets the stage for Chapter 12 . . . on security.

Guide

Is Outsourcing Fool's Gold?

"People are kidding themselves. It sounds so good—just pay a fixed, known amount to some vendor, and all your problems go away. Everyone has the computers they need, the network never goes down, and you never have to endure another horrible meeting about network protocols, HTTPs, and the latest worm. You're off into information systems nirvana. . . .

"Except it doesn't work that way. You trade one set of problems for another. Consider the outsourcing of computer infrastructure. What's the first thing the outsource vendor does? It hires all of the employees who were doing the work for you. Remember that lazy, incompetent network administrator that the company had—the one who never seemed to get anything done? Well, he's baaaaack, as an employee of your outsource company. Only this time he has an excuse, 'Company policy won't allow me to do it that way.'

"So the outsourcers get their first-level employees by hiring the ones you had. Of course, the outsourcer says it will provide management oversight, and if the employees don't work out, they'll be gone. What you're really outsourcing is middle-level management of the same IT personnel you had. But there's no way of knowing whether the managers they supply are any better than the ones you had.

"Also, you think you had bureaucratic problems before? Every vendor has a set of forms, procedures, committees, reports, and other management 'tools.' They will tell you that you have to do things according to the standard blueprint. They have to say that because if they allowed every company to be different, they'd never be able to gain any leverage themselves, and they'd never be profitable.

"So now you're paying a premium for the services of your former employees, who are now managed by strangers who are paid by the outsource vendor, who evaluates those managers on how well they follow the outsource vendor's profit-generating procedures. How quickly can they turn your operation into a clone of all their other clients? Do you really want to do that?

"Suppose you figure all this out and decide to get out of it. Now what? How do you undo an outsource agreement? All the critical knowledge is in the minds of the outsource vendor's employees, who have no incentive to work for you. In fact, their employment contract probably prohibits it. So now you have to take an existing operation within your own company, hire employees to staff that function, and relearn everything you ought to have learned in the first place.

"Gimme a break. Outsourcing is fool's gold, an expensive leap away from responsibility. It's like saying, 'We can't figure out how to manage an important function in our company, so you do it!' You can't get away from IS problems by hiring someone else to manage them for you. At least you care about *your* bottom line." ■

Source: Matthew Benoit/Shutterstock.com.

Discussion Questions

1. Hiring an organization's existing IS staff is common practice when starting a new outsourcing arrangement. What are the advantages of this practice to the outsource vendor? What are the advantages to the organization?

2. Suppose you work for an outsource vendor. How do you respond to the charge that your managers care only about how they appear to their employer (the outsource vendor), not how they actually perform for the organization?

3. Consider the statement, "We can't figure out how to manage an important function in our company, so you do it!" Do you agree with the sentiment of this statement? If this is true, is it necessarily bad? Why or why not?

4. Explain how it is possible for an outsource vendor to achieve economies of scale that are not possible for the hiring organization. Does this phenomenon justify outsourcing? Why or why not?

5. In what ways is outsourcing IS infrastructure like outsourcing the company cafeteria? In what ways is it different? What general conclusions can you make about infrastructure outsourcing?

Source: Tom McNemar/iStockphoto.com.

Guide

What If You Just Don't Know?

What if you have to make a decision and you just don't know which way to go? For complex issues like outsourcing, it can be difficult to know what the right decision is. In many cases, more analysis won't necessarily reduce the uncertainty.

Consider outsourcing as a typical, complex, real-life decision problem. The question is, will outsourcing save your organization money? Will the cap on financial exposure be worth the loss of control? Or, is your organization avoiding managing the IS function because you would just like to have the whole IS mess out of your hair?

Suppose the CIO is adamantly opposed to the outsourcing of computer infrastructure to the cloud. Why is that? He is obviously biased, because such outsourcing will mean a huge cut in his department and a big loss of control for him. It might even mean he loses his job. But is that all there is to it? Or does he have a point? Are the projected savings real? Or are they the result of a paper analysis that misses many of the intangibles? For that matter, does that analysis miss some of the tangibles?

You could do another study; you could commission an independent consultant to examine this situation and make a recommendation. However, is that avoiding the issue, yet again? Further, what if there is no time? Your servers are down for two days for the third time this quarter, and you've got to act. You've got to do something. But what? Take it to the board of directors? No, they don't know. That's just another way of avoiding a tough decision. You've got to decide.

In some ways, higher education does you a disservice. In school, you're taught that a bit more study, another report, or a little more analysis will help you find a better answer. But many decisions don't work that way. There might not be the time or money for another study or another study might just cloud the cloud-issue more. Or maybe it's just not possible to know. What will be the price of Google stock on January 1, 2015? You just don't know. ■

Discussion Questions

1. Suppose you are the CIO and you are opposed, on what you perceive as legitimate grounds, to a cloud outsourcing proposal. Suppose you know that everyone on the steering committee thinks you're biased because your department will shrink. What can you do to increase your credibility?

2. Suppose you're on the steering committee and you know that the CIO is biased about the cloud proposal. What questions can you ask to assess the degree to which his bias is influencing his position?

3. Describe a situation where you were in a biased situation and you needed to convince others to believe you, despite your bias. What did you do? Did it work?

4. Suppose you have to make a decision and you feel you don't know what you need to know to make that decision with confidence. Does it help to consider the cost of a mistake? How? Does it help to consider the cost of undoing your mistake? How?

5. Some executives say there's always more time than you think. You can always find a temporizing measure to buy yourself more time. Others say that it is critical to be decisive; make decisions when you have to, with the best knowledge you have; and get on with the next issue. Which view do you take with regard to the situation described here? Why?

6. One theory holds that some people are just better decision makers—that when given very little data, some people just have the knack for making good decisions. Others contend that there is no such difference; some people are just luckier. Or, some people have the knack for managing their affairs so that they never have to make a decision with little data. What do you think?

7. In the scenario presented, the CEO is frustrated and wants to get the IS mess out of her hair. How do her emotions cause her to second-guess her decision process? What role do you think emotions should play in a decision?

Active Review

Use this Active Review to verify that you understand the ideas and concepts that answer the chapter's study questions.

Q1 What are the functions and organization of the IS department?

List the five primary functions of the IS department. Define *CIO* and explain the CIO's typical reporting relationships. Name the four groups found in a typical IS department and explain the major responsibilities of each. Define *CTO* and explain typical CTO responsibilities. Explain the purpose of the data administration function.

Q2 How do organizations plan the use of IS?

Explain the importance of strategic alignment as it pertains to IS planning. Explain why maintaining alignment can be difficult. Describe the CIO's relationship to the rest of the executive staff. Describe the CIO's responsibilities with regard to priorities. Explain challenges to this task. Define *steering committee* and explain the CIO's role with regard to it.

Q3 What are the advantages and disadvantages of outsourcing?

Define *outsourcing*. Explain how Drucker's statement, "Your back room is someone else's front room" pertains to outsourcing. Summarize the management advantages,

cost advantages, and risks of outsourcing. Explain why international outsourcing can be particularly advantageous. Describe skills you can develop that will protect you from having your job outsourced. Summarize the outsourcing risks concerning control, long-term costs, and exit strategy.

Q4 What are your user rights and responsibilities?

Explain in your own words the meaning of each of your user rights as listed in Figure 11-7. Explain in your own words the meaning of each of your user responsibilities in Figure 11-7.

Q5 2022?

List the changes and developments that will have an impact on an organization's management of IS and IT. Explain why loss of control is inevitable and discuss why controlling access to the corporate network is ultimately not a viable control. Describe how employees may move off that network and discuss the security threat that occurs. Explain how the military secures some computing facilities. State the only available protection today.

Using Your Knowledge at Fox Lake

List the five functions of the IS department. Explain who is performing those functions at Fox Lake now. Summarize important IS management tasks that Jeff should either do or delegate and manage.

▬▬ Key Terms and Concepts

Chief information officer (CIO)   389
Chief technology officer (CTO)   389
Green computing   400
Outsourcing   393
Steering committee   393

Using Your Knowledge

1. According to this chapter, information systems, products, and technology are not malleable; they are difficult to change, alter, or bend. How do you think senior executives other than the CIO view this lack of malleability? For example, how do you think IS appears during a corporate merger?

2. Suppose you represent an investor group that is acquiring hospitals across the nation and integrating them into a unified system. List five potential problems and risks concerning information systems. How do you think IS-related risks compare to other risks in such an acquisition program?

3. What happens to IS when corporate direction changes rapidly? How will IS appear to other departments? What happens to IS when the corporate strategy changes frequently? Do you think such frequent changes are a greater problem to IS than to other business functions? Why or why not?

4. Consider the following statement: "In many ways, choosing an outsource vendor is a one-way street." Explain what this statement means. Do you agree with it? Why or why not? Does your answer change depending on what systems components are being outsourced? Why or why not?

Collaboration Exercise 11

With a team of your fellow students, develop an answer to the following questions. Use Google Docs, Google+, Windows Live SkyDrive, SharePoint, Office 365, or some other collaboration tool to conduct your meetings.

Suppose that you and a team of fellow students are interns working for Laura. She has asked you to gather information on Fox Lake's computing infrastructure and to write a one-page memo to Jeff outlining what he should be doing to manage IS at Fox Lake.

1. Reread the chapter introductions regarding Fox Lake in Chapters 7 through 11. List and briefly describe the information systems that are being used at Fox Lake. Although we have not considered accounting systems, add them to your list.

2. Describe the Fox Lake computing infrastructure. Assume that Fox Lake servers are located in the facilities building and that Fox Lake operates a local area network among its buildings and facilities. Portions of the network are wired and others are wireless. Assume that the network is supported by a third party. Use your knowledge of business to list other computing equipment that Fox Lake must have.

3. With the exception of the new facilities scheduling system that will be operated in the cloud, assume that Fox Lake's data are stored on servers in the facilities building. List major categories of data that must exist to support the golf, tennis, restaurant, pro shop, and wedding activities.

4. Using Figure 11-5 as a guide, identify one potential use for each of the five types of outsourcing at Fox Lake. Choose realistic uses from which Fox Lake could benefit and explain how each use can be beneficial.

5. Describe why Mike has a conflict of interest in the management of IS at Fox Lake (see the chapter introduction). Assuming that Jeff wants to continue to have Mike manage the IS facilities and resources, how can he reduce the impact of this conflict?

6. Given your answers to questions 1-5, write a one-page memo to Jeff explaining how he should be involved in management of the IS department.

7. Generalize the memo in your answer to question 6 to describe the responsibilities for IS management for owners of small businesses of any type. Write this memo in such a way that you might use it in a job interview with the owner of a small business.

▬ Case Study 11

iApp$$$$ 4 U

Let's suppose that you have a great idea for an iOS application. It doesn't matter what it is; it could be something to make life easier for college students or your parents or something to track health care expenses and payments for your grandparents. Whatever it is, let's assume that the idea is a great one.

First, what is the value of that idea? According to Raven Zachary, writing on the O'Reilly blog, it is zero. *Nada.* According to Zachary, no professional iPhone developer (he wrote this in 2008 about iPhone apps) will take equity or the promise of future revenue sharing in exchange for cash. There is too much cash-paying work. And, ideas are only as good as their implementation, a fact that is true for every business project, not just iOS applications.

So, how can you go about getting your iOS application developed? According to *OS X Daily*, in 2010 iOS developers in the United States and countries in the European Union were charging $50 to $250 per hour, and a typical, smaller application required 4 to 6 weeks to create. TechCrunch polled 124 developers and found that the average cost of creating an iPhone app was $6,453, but that number included projects that were programmed using cheaper, offshore developers.

These costs are incomplete. They include programming time, but not time to specify requirements nor to design the user interface, both of which are time-consuming tasks. Also, it is not clear that these costs include testing time nor the time needed to marshal the app through the Apple review process before it can appear in the App Store.

So, what are your options? First, do as much work as you can. Reread the stages in the systems development life cycle in Chapter 10 (pages 358–367). Determine how many of those stages you can do yourself. Unless you are already a skilled object-oriented programmer and comfortable writing in Objective-C, you cannot do the coding yourself. You might, however, be able to reduce development costs if you design the user interface and specify the ways that your users will employ it. You can also develop at least the skeleton of a test plan. You might also perform some of the testing tasks yourself.

If you have, let's round up, say $10,000 that you're willing to invest, then you could outsource the development to a U.S. or EU programmer. If not, you have two other possible choices: outsource offshore or hire a computer science student. Elance is a clearinghouse for iOS development experts; it lists developers, their locations, typical costs, and ratings provided by previous customers. As you can see, you can hire developers in India, Russian, the Ukraine, Romania, and other countries. Costs tend to be in the $2,000 range for a simple app, but again, that estimate probably does not include all the costs you will incur getting your application into the App Store.

What about hiring a local computer science student? The price might be right, certainly far less than a professional developer, but this alternative is fraught with problems. First, good students are in high demand, and, second, good students are, well, students. They need to study and don't have as much time to devote to your app. And, hard as it is to believe, some students are flakes. However, if you have a friend whom you trust, you might make this option work.

One other option is to divide and conquer. Break your really great idea up into smaller apps. Pick one that is sure to be a hit, and sell it cheaply, say for $.99. Use the money that you earn from that application to fund the next application, one that you might sell for more.

Questions

1. What characteristics make an iOS app great? Describe at least five characteristics that compel you to buy applications. What characteristics would make an application easy and cheap to develop? Difficult and expensive?

2. Visit http://techcrunch.com/2010/05/16/iphone-app-sales-exposed. Summarize the returns earned by both the top and more typical applications.

3. Reread pages 356–366 of Chapter 10 about the SDLC process. List tasks to perform and assess whether you could perform each task. If you cannot perform that task, describe how you could outsource that task and estimate how much you think it would cost for a simple application.

4. Visit www.elance.com and identify five potential outsource vendors that you could use to develop your app. Describe criteria you would use for selecting one of these vendors

5. Explain how you think Google's purchase of Motorola Mobility changes the opportunity for iOS apps. In theory, does this purchase cause you to believe it would be wiser for you to develop on the Android or on the Windows 7 phone?

6. Search the Web for "Android developers" and related terms. Does it appear that the process of creating an Android app is easier, cheaper, or more desirable than creating an iOS app?

7. Search the Web for "Windows Phone 7 developers" and related terms. Does it appear that the process of creating an Windows Phone 7 app is easier, cheaper, or more desirable than creating an iOS app?

8. Prepare a 1-minute summary of your experience with this exercise that you could use in a job interview to demonstrate innovative thinking. Give your summary to the rest of your class.

Sources: Raven Zachary, "Turning Ideas into iPhone Applications," November 21, 2008, http://blogs.oreilly.com/iphone/2008/11/turning-ideas-into-application.html (accessed August 2011); "iPhone Development Costs," OS X Daily, September 7, 2010, http://osxdaily.com/2010/09/07/iphone-development-costs/ (accessed August 2011); Alex Ahlund, "iPhone App Sales, Exposed," TechCrunch, May 16, 2010, http://techcrunch.com/2010/05/16/iphone-app-sales-exposed/ (accessed August 2011); "iPhone Development Experts," Elance, www.elance.com/groups/iPhone_Development_Experts (accessed August 2011).

Fox Lake Country Club, Chapter 11

GOALS

Use Fox Lake Country Club to:

- Illustrate the need for IS management, even at small companies.

- Illustrate that non-IS business professionals need more knowledge of IS at small companies than they do at large ones.

- Demonstrate that anyone thinking of starting, managing, or taking a key role in a small business should take as many IS classes as possible.

- Set the stage for problems that will occur in Chapter 12.

BACKGROUND

1. Fox Lake's IS management is an out-of-control mess. Mike has no background in IS, and he's a new manager. He inherited some IS that were developed by contractors in the past. He has no idea how to manage IS.

2. As Laura indicates, Mike has a disincentive to provide service to Anne or any department other than facilities. Right now, it all comes out of his budget, and he's incentivized not to exceed his budget. That arrangement is guaranteed to cause problems.

3. Senior managers who want to avoid IS management and IS involvement like the plague used to be very common. Thankfully, they are less common today. Fox Lake is too small to have a full-time CIO or manager of IS. Jeff can do the job, it's just management like he already does. IS does have some technical issues that he needs help with . . . he might hire Laura to advise him in the beginning.

4. Laura is trying to point out, in the gentlest way possible, that Jeff isn't doing his job. He needs to get involved with IS management, just as much as he's involved with the management of any other department at Fox Lake.

5. I've used a small company for Chapters 10–12 for two reasons: (1) so that students would see the need for knowledge and involvement in IS by all business professionals, not just IS managers, and (2) so that the problems would be small enough to be comprehended in a short period of time. Of course, companies like Boeing, 3M, Microsoft, and Procter & Gamble have

huge needs for IS management, and huge IS departments to support it. However, such departments are beyond the scope of this text.

HOW TO GET STUDENTS INVOLVED

1. What issue is Laura trying to raise?

  - **What's going on here? Why is Laura proceeding so cautiously?**
  - **What does Jeff need to do?**
  - **What is Mike's conflict of interest?**
  - **What is Laura's chief concern?**

2. Consider the four IS responsibilities:

  - **Plan information systems and infrastructure.**
  - **Develop and adapt IS and infrastructure.**
  - **Maintain IS and operate and manage infrastructure.**
  - **Protect infrastructure and data.**
    - **Given what you know about Fox Lake, assess it on each of the items above.**
    - **What should Fox Lake be doing?**
    - **What is Fox Lake doing?**

3. Fox Lake cannot afford an IS department, yet it has certain responsibilities with regards to IS.

  - **What's realistic for a small company?**
  - **What should Jeff be doing?**
  - **What should Mike be doing?**
  - **What should Anne be doing?**

VIDEO

Laura is an experienced and capable consultant. She needs to provide critical feedback to Jeff and, for the most part, she does a good job of it. Jeff hears that he needs to get more involved in IS management, but (1) doesn't want to and (2) doesn't feel qualified. Even still, if he doesn't do it, who will?

Mike was promoted from within, and like many people in that circumstance he has his hands full managing what he views as his primary responsibility, facilities. He figures that as long as no one is stealing equipment or running golf carts into servers, everything must be OK.

Both Jeff and Mike have a lot to learn . . . and soon will.

BOTTOM LINE

■ Some IS management functions can be ignored for a while, but lack of planning and security will be a problem in the long run.

■ Even small companies need to think about IS planning, development, management, and protection. Appropriate tasks and procedures need to be developed and employees trained and assigned to those tasks.

■ In many ways, IS management is harder in small companies than in large ones because small companies can seldom afford qualified IS staff.

■ If you're thinking about starting, managing, or working in a small company, take as many IS classes as you can.

■ At a small company, if you, as a manager, don't manage IS, who will?

YOU BE THE GUIDE

Using the Ethics Guide: Using the Corporate Computer (pages 394–395)

GOALS

- Evaluate the ethics of employee activities in terms of a particular computer-use policy.
- Forewarn students that employers have the right to monitor computer usage, and many do.
- Develop techniques for managing employees' computer use.

BACKGROUND AND PRESENTATION STRATEGIES

This subject is a follow-on to the Ethics Guide in Chapter 6. This discussion differs from that one because it considers a specific computer-use policy. It also focuses on the student's role as a manager rather than as a computer user.

Many students use their computers in the classroom for email, Web surfing, and instant messaging. If that is the case in your classroom, you might consider the *following hoax*:

- **Did you know that the university monitors your use of its network? In fact, I receive a report after each class period on the emails you've sent, the Web sites you've visited, and the number of minutes you've spent in IM chat.**

- **Frankly, I'm a little shocked. The content of some of your emails is, well, embarrassing. . . . What is this world coming to, anyway?**

  Pause. Let those statements settle in . . .

- **OK, those statements *are not true*, but they *could be at your job*. What do you think about that?**

  - If you choose to spend your time in class surfing the Web or chatting with friends, that's your choice. You're wasting your time and money, but that's your choice.

  - However, if I were paying you to be here, if you were my employees, I'd want to know that you are actually engaged in accomplishing your job and not gossiping about your fellow employees with your sister-in-law across the state.

- **How intrusive do you think an employer should be in making assessments about computer use?**

- **Suppose you manage a department and you suspect your employees are wasting time on their computers at work. What would you do?**

- **What do you think causes employees to waste time on their computers at work? Would they be wasting time staring out the window, if they did not have a computer?**

  By the way, I disagree with that last justification. The Web, IM, email, and computer games are attractive, even addictive, in ways that staring out the window is not.

- **In theory at least, if employees have been given appropriate assignments, and if there is regular follow-up on employee progress on those assignments, then employees ought not to have time to waste on their computers. They should be so busy doing their work that there isn't time to surf or chat.**

- **This may be naïve, but excessive personal computer use is a symptom of poorly directed or poorly motivated employees. Put everyone in the right job, get them excited about what they're doing, follow up on their progress on a regular basis, and excessive personal computer use will not be a problem.**

- **Some senior managers will agree with that statement, too. So, if your department is known to have many employees excessively using their computers for personal work, that fact will reflect negatively on your management ability.**

  In the early days of blogging, Michelle Malkin received a series of abusive, racist, and sexist emails in response to one of her blog entries. One of those exceedingly offensive emails was generated by a legal secretary from his desk at a law office in Los Angeles.

  The email system automatically generated a trailer that included the name of the law firm. Ms. Malkin posted the abusive email in its entirety, including the trailer with the firm's name, on her Web site. The law firm was inundated with criticism for its employee's behavior. The employee was promptly fired, but the public relations scandal continued to plague the firm for weeks.

- **If you managed that law firm, how would you have responded to this situation?**

SUGGESTED RESPONSES FOR DISCUSSION QUESTIONS

1. This is a long list of situations. One approach is to ask the students to group the situations into categories according to the severity of the violation. Three possible categories are: *OK, Questionable,* and *Definitely Wrong.* I'd put the following in the *Definitely Wrong* category: situations 1, 6, 10, 11, 12, 15, 16, and 18. In the *OK* category, I'd put situations 3, 5, 13, and 14. I'd place all of the others in the *Questionable* category. It will be interesting to see how your students respond to this!

2. If I was told that an employee was spending 3 hours a day using Twitter, I'd evaluate that employee's recent performance. I'd find out what jobs the employee was supposed to have been doing and find out how well those jobs were done. Clearly, something's wrong. I'd talk with the employee. Perhaps this person is ready for new responsibilities; perhaps the employee has lost interest in work. I'd try to get to the root of the problem and make a change.

3. I personally find secret monitoring of employees computer use a bit creepy, but the employer *is* paying for the employees' time and for the equipment. I grant an employer's right to perform such monitoring. I think that the monitoring ought to be done in such a way, however, so as to minimize the intrusion on the employees' privacy. If someone is using the Web for personal business, neither I nor the company needs to know what sites were visited. Similarly, the company may monitor email, but the intrusion should be limited to the minimum possible needed to accomplish the company's goals.

4. It is certainly legal for companies to read employees' emails, and, because the employer is paying for the employees' time and the computer and network equipment, I think it's ethical. When employees use their employer's equipment for personal use, I believe they give up any right to privacy. But, see the limitations stated for question 3.

5. I personally dislike a style of management that relies on the hammer of discovery to limit employees' misuse of computers. I'd prefer to manage by giving people work they want to do, by creating tight but not impossible schedules, by following up with them on progress, and by focusing on what they *should be* doing rather than on what they *ought not* to be doing.

   But, my management experience is limited to managing highly skilled, motivated, ambitious employees in the software business. When employees must spend hours performing dreary, repetitive work, the motivational situation is entirely different. I can see how the hammer might need to be used in those circumstances.

   I think the postal mail situation is different. For one, postal mail uses few company resources. Also, an employee reading a single letter is different from an employee sending out hundreds of emails.

6. I like the policy at the start of the guide. One could say it should be more specific, but the problem with that is that employees will be able to say about some behavior, "Well, that's not on the list." I think the key phrase is *never interfere with your work.* One could strengthen that statement by specifically excluding the use of the computer for personal business. Some of the wording depends on other HR policies as well.

WRAP UP

■ **As a future employee, be forewarned that employers have the right, both legally and ethically, to monitor your computer use. Many do.**

■ **As a future manager, consider how you will deal with employees who are misusing their computer resources. Know the organization's official policy.**

■ **Understand, too, that excessive personal computer use by your employees reflects negatively on your management ability.**

■ **If possible, manage positively. Give the employees sufficient work that they will not have time to misuse computer resources. Follow up with schedules and deadlines. Make sure that missed schedules are not caused by computer misuse.**

YOU BE THE GUIDE

Using the Guide: Is Outsourcing Fool's Gold? (pages 404–405)

GOAL

- Investigate advantages and disadvantages of computer infrastructure outsourcing.

BACKGROUND AND PRESENTATION STRATEGIES

Here is a real-world case that you might use as an opening narrative:

When I worked for Wall Data in the mid-1990s, senior management gave up managing the firm's computing infrastructure and hired EDS to take over the IS function. From my perspective (a business-unit manager for an offsite development group), I didn't think the service was much better—but it wasn't worse—and senior management of the company no longer needed to devote so much of its time and attention to infrastructure management.

Prior to the change to EDS, our group, which was remote from headquarters, was supported by an individual who never seemed to be able to get anything done. Whenever I had a problem, it seemed to me that he had an excuse, but no fix. I'll never forget my shock and dismay when, after the switch to EDS, I rounded the corner in the hallway one morning, only to run into that same person, wearing an EDS shirt!

In fairness to the employee, and in fairness to EDS, his performance did improve. He wasn't much better at fixing problems on the spot, but the EDS reporting systems required him to keep better track of open problems, and eventually someone from his new management team would insist that he find a solution. Problem reports did not disappear into a black hole as they had prior to EDS involvement.

As an aside, I can't imagine a worse client for an outsourcing vendor than a company of professional software developers! Developers aren't prone to keeping their machines in the "standard configuration." They add all sorts of bells and whistles to their machines, and they're good at hiding it, too. Making additions to their computers tends to make the developers happy, and a happy developer is a more productive developer, so I'd look the other way unless the changes were particularly egregious.

I wasn't involved in the contract negotiation or the justification of the switch to EDS. I suspect it was quite expensive—certainly more expensive than the prior internal IS had been. But if you compute the opportunity cost of lost labor from the regular network failures that we'd had, and if you consider the savings in management time that resulted, it may have been more than worth it.

This contrarian employee makes an excellent point about conflicting management goals. During crunch time, we stressed our computing infrastructure just when we needed the highest reliability. The development team commonly put in 80-hour workweeks. It was a management challenge when we watched the outsourcing vendor's employees leave in the middle of a problem because they were not authorized to work overtime. We were exhausted from our long hours, the network was inhibiting our progress, and we needed a solution. Such events were rare, but they are memorable. They also made it difficult to convince developers of the need to keep their machines in the "standard configuration."

From this anecdotal experience from a single data point, I'd say that outsourcing computer infrastructure removes the highs and the lows from internal support. Although we didn't have heroic support during crunch time, we stopped having infrastructure disasters, too. The support provided by EDS middle management gave us reliability, if not immediate solutions.

By the way, an outsourcing vendor has an advantage that an in-house staff never has. *The outsource vendor can say no.* It is difficult for in-house staff to say no, especially to senior management. So the in-house staff finds itself supporting all sorts of "special situations" that an outsource vendor avoids. "It's not in the contract. Would you like to negotiate an out-of-scope change?" puts a severe damper on special requests.

SUGGESTED RESPONSES FOR DISCUSSION QUESTIONS

1. Advantages to the vendor: reduced recruitment costs; quicker staffing; and reduced training time, because existing employees know much of the computing infrastructure. Advantages to the customer: no downtime while vendor hires personnel, working relationships already established, less customer time for training new personnel.

2. Good question for the students:

   ■ **If you worked for EDS, how would you respond to a customer's complaint, "You care only about the EDS bottom line"?**

I think the response has to be that the vendor's bottom line and the customer's bottom line are inextricably related. In the long run, the vendor succeeds only if the customer succeeds. Also, part of the evaluation of vendor employees' performance is customer satisfaction.

3. This statement need not be true. It could be that the company knows how to manage the infrastructure but finds the management opportunity cost to be too high. But, it probably is true for many outsourcing situations. It doesn't seem necessarily bad—if you say it about the company cafeteria, it seems innocuous enough, and, at bottom, how is outsourcing the cafeteria fundamentally different from outsourcing the computer infrastructure? See question 5.

4. Economies of scale are the key for outsourcing vendors' success. When an outsourcing vendor develops a system for problem recording, tracking, and resolution, it can amortize the cost of that system over all its clients. A single company must pay for the development of such a system by itself.

Consider, too, the use of new technology. An outsourcing vendor can dedicate personnel to learning new technology and developing the means of utilizing the technology for its customers. It then amortizes the cost of that technology assessment and development over all its clients.

An outsourcing vendor can also afford to train specialists in particular problems and to make those specialists available on an as-needed basis to all its clients. An outsourcing vendor can afford to pay someone to know, for example, all the dials and knobs and options on a Cisco router of a particular type and to understand how that router works with certain types of ACLs in particular firewalls. Such specialized knowledge is not available to a single company. Again, the cost of that specialized expertise is amortized over all clients.

5. I think the cafeteria is more separable than the computing infrastructure. It would be relatively easy to change the cafeteria vendor—just move one group out and another one in. Also, in most cases, the cafeteria could be closed for a period of time, if necessary. Employees can eat elsewhere.

The computing infrastructure is akin to the nervous system of the organization. Outsourcing personnel are integrated into the organization, removing them will be more problematic than removing cafeteria personnel. Also, the computing infrastructure is required—the organization cannot close it down for a period of time while it's being repaired.

Because of the difficulty and expense of recovering from a mistaken vendor choice, I believe there is considerably more risk when choosing a computer infrastructure outsource firm than when considering someone to run the cafeteria.

WRAP UP

■ **Outsourcing computer infrastructure has both advantages and disadvantages.**

■ **What are two advantages?**

(Figure 11-4 has a list of possibilities.)

■ **What are two disadvantages?**

(Figure 11-6 has a list of possibilities.)

■ **Suppose you're working as a department manager and you learn that your company has decided to outsource its computing infrastructure. In a weekly meeting, one of your employees asks you what you think about that. How do you respond?**

The answer depends on what I know: If I've been informed about the reasons for the change, then I explain those reasons. If this is a surprise to me, I would say I don't know anything about it, but will learn more and pass along information as I obtain it. I'd also say something positive about the company.

YOU BE THE GUIDE

Using the Guide: What If You Just Don't Know? (pages 406–407)

GOALS

- Sensitize students to problems that cannot be solved by quantitative analysis.
- Discuss the impact of bias and emotions in such decisions.

BACKGROUND AND PRESENTATION STRATEGIES

One of the joys of working in business is the tremendous variety of problems that one encounters and the many different solution strategies that those problems require. Consider some examples:

■ If you want to know the financial impact of a 2 percent raise in loan interest rate on the 5-year cost of purchasing an item of equipment, do a financial analysis. The quantitative techniques you are learning in your accounting and finance classes will serve you well.

■ But *what about less quantitative decisions*? Or what about decisions for which there is no agreed-on procedure? Marketing is replete with examples of such decisions. For example:

■ How do you select a product name? Suppose you have created a new super-smart television/entertainment device. Suppose you hire a name-development consultant who creates a list of the following alternative names: Baton, Watch!, and Kenya. How do you *decide which is the best name*?

■ Or, consider strategic marketing. To whom do you sell your new entertainment product? How do you decide who will be most likely to buy?

■ Although you can commission analytical studies, convene focus groups, conduct surveys, and so on, these measures may not appreciably improve the quality of your decision. And often you don't have time.

■ So you must make a subjective decision. But suppose the person who knows the most about the situation has a bias, as in the scenario in this guide. The person who knows the most about moving to the cloud is the person whose budget and responsibilities will be dramatically reduced—maybe even eliminated.

■ How do you use the input from such a source when making a subjective decision?

Some business decisions, like the interest rate computation, are quantitative in nature. Others are very subjective—like choosing the best advertising campaign. (I know you can try them on focus groups, but still, ultimately, it's a subjective decision.) *Outsourcing* is a decision between these two extremes: Parts of the decision are quantitative, but other parts are subjective. The management decision team's decision-making capability is greatly hampered by the clear bias of the person who knows the most about the organization's IS infrastructure.

SUGGESTED RESPONSES FOR DISCUSSION QUESTIONS

1. First, raise the objection! Tell everyone you know you're biased; tell everyone that you are, of course, concerned about the reduction in your budget and responsibilities. Then, having made your bias clear, make as fact-based a quantitative analysis as you can. Do not be emotional. State the facts in a calm professional manner.

   If you cannot make a solid analysis against the outsourcing proposal, don't try. Be a professional, take your hit, and move on. Take the time to adjust your career goals and aspirations in light of the likely future dominance of cloud-based infrastructure. Become, for example, an expert in security in the cloud. Be a professional about it. Guard your reputation as a businessperson with high integrity; you need it for the long run.

2. In the case of the CIO's bias, look at the quality of the analysis. Is it solidly based on facts, or is it full of difficult-to-prove subjective judgments? Does the CIO appear to be defensive or balanced? This is tough—on everyone. It may be that you just have to discount the CIO's input.

3. The students should have good examples to share. You could start the discussion by asking for examples from academia. Though I have to be careful bringing it up, lest I have a line of students outside my door after the next exam, one example is the student who's arguing for 10 extra points on an exam score.

4. The circumstances are such that you may make a bad decision. You can use the best process available to you and still not have a solid basis for the decision. In this case, do consider the cost of the wrong decision. If the cost is likely to be catastrophic, seek more input; find out what you need to know; strive to find another way to analyze the situation. Use your professional network; talk to others. If the cost of a mistake is modest, it may make sense just to make the decision and move on, preparing as best you can for dealing with a mistake. If the cost of undoing the decision is not great, just make the decision. Or, try to alter the situation so that the cost of undoing it will not be great.

   ■ **By the way, it is important to distinguish between a bad decision and a bad result. You can use a superb decision-making process and be unlucky. If so, you'll have a good decision but a bad result. That happens, but it's important to know, for future decisions, that your decision making was not defective.**

5. My answer to these opinions is that both may be right—it just depends. Usually, there is more time than you think. Usually, you don't have to decide right now, and usually you can take the time for further consideration, more points of view, or additional analysis. But not always!

   At the same time, in some situations any decision, even a bad one, will be better than further temporizing. This occurs when the organization is "holding its breath," waiting for a signal about which way to go. In my experience, such situations in business are, thankfully, rare.

   With regard to outsourcing, I think the steering committee should listen to the CIO, review the proposals from the cloud vendors, do its homework investigating the performance of the cloud vendors at other companies that are similar, and make a decision. The only reason I'd wait would be if there is a suspicion, based on the analysis of the vendors' reputations, that cloud-based solutions do not work for companies like yours.

6. To my mind, there is no question that some people are better decision makers with limited data than others. Some people just seem to make a long string of good decisions. Bill Gates is one of them. There were many, perhaps dozens, of young men like Gates who had successful early products and companies. Philippe Kahn (Borland) and Mitch Kapor (Lotus) are two examples. Neither of these two, nor the others, seemed to be able to thread the complexities of the early PC world as well as Gates. Recall that Gates outfinagled IBM when IBM was *the* powerhouse of the industry. Famous stock pickers like Peter Lynch are another example. Lynch would say that he just did his homework, but so did everyone else in that business, and no one had the success he had at Magellan.

   I think part of it is that some people have an excellent sense of timing for their decisions. They delay a risky decision until the situation has clarified itself, and then they make the decision. For example, in the late 1980s Microsoft supported both DOS/Windows and IBM's OS/2. Gates went out on the road, touting OS/2 along with IBM. He pushed both operating systems until the point when it was clear that DOS/Windows would be the winner. Then, when Windows was clearly the winner, he broke from IBM with Windows 95. (Of course, Microsoft heavily influenced that result. Microsoft Office ran only on Windows. OS/2 had few desktop applications, so no one wanted to use it. There was no way that Microsoft was going to put Office on OS/2 unless OS/2 started gaining market share. Had that occurred, Microsoft would have inundated the market with Office for OS/2, which it never had to do.)

7. She'll be concerned that her desire to be rid of the problem will overcome sound business judgment. Regarding the proper role of emotions, I'd say be guided, be informed, by one's emotions. They're pointing you in some direction. But, make the decision on as rational a basis as you can.

WRAP UP

■ **Not every decision can be analyzed quantitatively. Some require subjective judgment.**

■ **We've identified a few ways of dealing with difficult decisions. Keep thinking about them. For an exercise, consider this subjective decision:**

■ **Try this personal example: Cast out every thought you've ever had about what job you want. From that blank slate, what job do you want?**

Information Security Management

"It's weird, Jeff. I don't get it. Someone's stealing wedding presents . . . five times in the last month! I thought it was bad luck, but five times???" Anne Foster, manager of wedding events, is talking with Jeff, Fox Lake's general manager.

"We'd better assign someone for security, Anne."

"Yeah, I guess, but I hate to have a guard standing around. It doesn't happen all the time . . . we had 23 weddings this month."

"Do you remember which five?" Jeff asks.

"Maybe, let's see, the Kibby, the Horan, the Grant, the Yagan, the Svendson . . . hey, that's odd, those families are all members here. And, those could be the only member weddings we've had this month. How weird!" Anne looks puzzled.

"Any idea what was taken?" Jeff asks, feeling more and more uncomfortable about this conversation.

"That's odd, too. All expensive things. Sonos speakers, Bose radios, that kind of stuff."

"Anne, let me look into this. I'll get back to you. Meanwhile, move the presents out of the lobby, somewhere less public . . . back of the reception room or something."

"OK."

After Anne leaves, Jeff picks up his phone to call Laura.

"Laura, I think we've got a problem."

"What's up?"

"Someone's stealing wedding presents . . . but only from weddings of members."

"That is odd." Laura sounds hesitant on the phone.

"Could someone be getting to our data? Find out when members are having weddings?"

"Maybe, but why just steal gifts from members' weddings?" Laura asks.

"Because members are well-to-do. Their presents are expensive." Jeff's not happy at all.

"Ah. Well, like I said last week, those servers are open to anyone with a key to the facilities building. If someone knew how to get into the system, how to access the database, maybe a little SQL . . . sure, it could be done."

"Laura, can you come over here for a meeting this afternoon? Say 1:30?"

That afternoon, Jeff and Laura walk into Mike's office. Laura looks over Mike's shoulder and sees little yellow sticky notes on the screen . . . the writing looks like passwords . . .

"That takes care of access," she says to herself.

"Mike, do you remember several months ago, when Anne needed a report about members with daughters?"

"Yeah, I do . . . " Mike looks concerned. Why are Jeff and Laura popping in on him?

"Who created that report?" Jeff asks.

"Jason and Chris—they did a good job, too." Mike sounds defensive.

"Who are they?" Laura asks, although she's already figured it out.

"Groundskeepers. Chris took computer courses somewhere. He knows a lot! Anne was really pleased with their results. She upset now?" Mike looks worried.

"No, not at all." Jeff tries to reassure Mike.

"They have a key to the building?" Laura asks.

"Well, they did when they were working on that job. But I got the keys back."

"They could make a copy . . . Mike, I think you better call the police." Jeff looks down at his feet while Mike calls. ■

Study Questions

Q1 What is the goal of information systems security?

Q2 How should you respond to security threats?

Q3 How should organizations respond to security threats?

Q4 What technical safeguards are available?

Q5 What data safeguards are available?

Q6 What human safeguards are available?

Q7 2022?

This chapter provides an overview of the major components of information systems security. We begin in Q1 by defining the goals of IS security. Next, in Q2, we address how you, both as a student today and as a business professional in the future, should respond to security threats. Then, in Q3, we ask what organizations need to do to respond to security threats. After that, questions Q4 through Q6 address security safeguards. Q4 discusses technical safeguards that involve hardware and software components; Q5 addresses data safeguards; and Q6 discusses human safeguards that involve procedure and people components. We wrap up the chapter with a preview of IS security in 2022.

Unfortunately, threats to data and information systems are increasing and becoming more complex. In fact, the U.S. Bureau of Labor Statistics estimates that demand for security specialists will increase by more than 50 percent between 2008 and 2018.[1] If you find this topic interesting, majoring in information systems with a security specialty would open the door to many interesting jobs.

Q1 What Is the Goal of Information Systems Security?

Information systems security involves a trade-off between cost and risk of loss. To understand the nature of this trade-off, we begin with a description of the security threat/loss scenario and then discuss the sources of security threats. Following that, we will summarize the size of the security problem and then state the goals of information systems security.

The IS Security Threat/Loss Scenario

Figure 12-1 illustrates the major elements of the security problem that individuals and organizations confront today. A **threat** is a person or organization that seeks to obtain data or other assets illegally, without the owner's permission and often without the owner's knowledge. A **vulnerability** is an opportunity for threats to gain access to individual or organizational assets. For example, when you buy something online, you provide your credit card data; when that data is transmitted over the Internet, it is vulnerable to threats. A **safeguard** is some measure that individuals or organizations take to block the threat from obtaining the asset. Notice in Figure 12-1 that safeguards

Figure 12-1
Threat/Loss Scenario

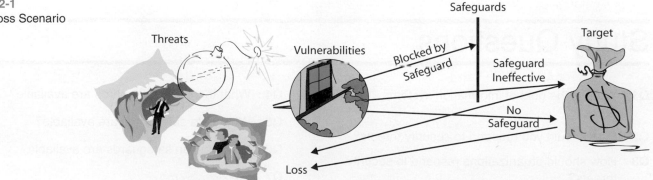

[1] U.S. Bureau of Labor Statistics, *Occupational Outlook Handbook, 2010–2011 Edition.* www.bls.gov/oco/ocos305.htm#outlook (accessed August 2011). The information security specialty is included in the network systems and data communications category.

Threat/Target	Vulnerability	Safeguard	Result	Explanation
Xbox Live gamer wants your credit card data.	You use your credit card to buy online.	HTTPS	No loss.	Effective safeguard
	You send credit card data to friend via email.	None	Loss of credit card data.	No safeguard
Part-time Fox Lake employees want wedding data.	Event guest names and addresses stored in Fox Lake database.	Passwords Locked rooms	Loss of data. Passwords readily accessible. Room keys not controlled.	Ineffective safeguard

Figure 12-2
Examples of Threat/Loss

are not always effective; some threats achieve their goal despite safeguards. Finally, the **target** is the asset that is desired by the threat.

Figure 12-2 shows examples of threats/targets, vulnerabilities, safeguards, and results. In the first two rows, an Xbox gamer (the threat) wants your credit card data (the target) to buy more games on your account. As stated previously, when you provide your credit card data for an online transaction, that data is vulnerable to the threat as it travels over the Internet. However, if, as shown in the first row of Figure 12-2, you conduct your transaction using HTTPS rather than HTTP (discussed in Q4), you will be using an effective safeguard, and you will successfully counter the threat.

If, however, as described in the second row of Figure 12-2, you send your credit card data to a friend via email, you will, in most cases, have no safeguard at all. That data is open to any threat that happens to sniff your traffic on the Internet. In this case, you may soon be paying for hours and hours of Xbox games for a person who you do not even know.

The bottom row of Figure 12-2 shows the situation at Fox Lake. Two part-time employees want access to the Fox Lake wedding data so they can know when members' weddings are scheduled. That data is protected by passwords and physical locks on computer access. However, both of these safeguards are weak; the passwords are written on yellow sticky notes on Mike's computer, and the room keys are not effectively controlled. In this case, there were safeguards, but they were ineffective.

What Are the Sources of Threats?

Figure 12-3 summarizes the sources of security threats. The type of threat is shown in the columns and the type of loss is shown in the rows.

Human Error

Human errors and mistakes include accidental problems caused by both employees and nonemployees. An example is an employee who misunderstands operating procedures and accidentally deletes customer records. Another example is an employee who, in the course of backing up a database, inadvertently installs an old database on top of the current one. This category also includes poorly written application programs and poorly designed procedures. Finally, human errors and mistakes include physical accidents, such as driving a forklift through the wall of a computer room.

Computer Crime

The second threat type is *computer crime*. This threat type includes employees and former employees who intentionally destroy data or other system components. It also includes hackers who break into a system and virus and worm writers who infect computer systems. Computer crime also includes those who break into a system to steal for financial gain and also includes some form of terrorism.

Figure 12-3
Security Problems and Sources

		Threat		
		Human Error	**Computer Crime**	**Natural Disasters**
Loss	**Unauthorized data disclosure**	Procedural mistakes	Pretexting Phishing Spoofing Sniffing Hacking	Disclosure during recovery
	Incorrect data modification	Procedural mistakes Incorrect procedures Ineffective accounting controls System errors	Hacking	Incorrect data recovery
	Faulty service	Procedural mistakes Development and installation errors	Usurpation	Service improperly restored
	Denial of service (DOS)	Accidents	DOS attacks	Service interruption
	Loss of infrastructure	Accidents	Theft Terrorist activity	Property loss

Natural Events and Disasters

Natural events and disasters are the third type of security threat. This category includes fires, floods, hurricanes, earthquakes, tsunamis, avalanches, and other acts of nature. Problems in this category include not only the initial loss of capability and service, but also losses stemming from actions to recover from the initial problem.

What Types of Security Loss Exist?

Five types of security loss exist: unauthorized data disclosure, incorrect data modification, faulty service, denial of service, and loss of infrastructure. Consider each.

Unauthorized Data Disclosure

Unauthorized data disclosure occurs when a threat obtains data that is supposed to be protected. It can occur by human error when someone inadvertently releases data in violation of policy. An example at a university is a department administrator who posts student names, identification numbers, and grades in a public place, when the releasing of names and grades violates state law. Another example is employees who unknowingly or carelessly release proprietary data to competitors or to the media. Wikileaks is another famous example.

The popularity and efficacy of search engines has created another source of inadvertent disclosure. Employees who place restricted data on Web sites that can be reached by search engines might mistakenly publish proprietary or restricted data over the Web.

Of course, proprietary and personal data can also be released and obtained maliciously. **Pretexting** occurs when someone deceives by pretending to be someone else. A common scam involves a telephone caller who pretends to be from a credit card company and claims to be checking the validity of credit card numbers: "I'm checking your MasterCard number; it begins with 5491. Can you verify the rest of the number?" Thousands of MasterCard numbers start with 5491; the caller is attempting to steal a valid number.

Phishing is a similar technique for obtaining unauthorized data that uses pretexting via email. The **phisher** pretends to be a legitimate company and sends an email requesting confidential data, such as account numbers, Social Security numbers, account passwords, and so forth. Phishing compromises legitimate brands and trademarks.

Spoofing is another term for someone pretending to be someone else. If you pretend to be your professor, you are spoofing your professor. **IP spoofing** occurs when an intruder uses another site's IP address to masquerade as that other site. **Email spoofing** is a synonym for phishing.

Sniffing is a technique for intercepting computer communications. With wired networks, sniffing requires a physical connection to the network. With wireless networks, no such connection is required: **Drive-by sniffers** simply take computers with wireless connections through an area and search for unprotected wireless networks. They can monitor and intercept wireless traffic at will. Even protected wireless networks are vulnerable, as you will learn. Spyware and adware are two other sniffing techniques discussed later in this chapter.

Other forms of computer crime include **hacking**, which is breaking into networks to steal data such as customer lists, product inventory data, employee data, and other proprietary and confidential data.

Finally, people might inadvertently disclose data during recovery from a natural disaster. During a recovery, everyone is so focused on restoring system capability that they might ignore normal security safeguards. A request like "I need a copy of the customer database backup" will receive far less scrutiny during disaster recovery than at other times.

Incorrect Data Modification

The second type of security loss in Figure 12-3 is *incorrect data modification*. Examples include incorrectly increasing a customer's discount or incorrectly modifying an employee's salary, earned days of vacation, or annual bonus. Other examples include placing incorrect information, such as incorrect price changes, on a company's Web site or company portal.

Incorrect data modification can occur through human error when employees follow procedures incorrectly or when procedures have been designed incorrectly. For proper internal control on systems that process financial data or control inventories of assets, such as products and equipment, companies should ensure separation of duties and authorities and have multiple checks and balances in place.

A final type of incorrect data modification caused by human error includes *system errors*. An example is the lost-update problem discussed in Chapter 5 (page 155).

Computer criminals can make unauthorized data modifications by hacking into a computer system. For example, hackers could hack into a system and transfer people's account balances or place orders to ship goods to unauthorized locations and customers.

Finally, faulty recovery actions after a disaster can result in incorrect data changes. The faulty actions can be unintentional or malicious.

Faulty Service

The third type of security loss, *faulty service*, includes problems that result because of incorrect system operation. Faulty service could include incorrect data modification, as just described. It also could include systems that work incorrectly by sending the wrong goods to a customer or the ordered goods to the wrong customer, incorrectly billing customers, or sending the wrong information to employees. Humans can inadvertently cause faulty service by making procedural mistakes. System developers can write programs incorrectly or make errors during the installation of hardware, software programs, and data.

Usurpation occurs when computer criminals invade a computer system and replace legitimate programs with their own unauthorized ones that shut down legitimate applications and substitute their own processing to spy, steal and manipulate data, or other purposes. Faulty service can also result when service is improperly restored during recovery from natural disasters.

Denial of Service

Human error in following procedures or a lack of procedures can result in **denial of service (DOS)**, the fourth type of loss. For example, humans can inadvertently shut down a Web server or corporate gateway router by starting a computationally intensive application. An OLAP application that uses the operational DBMS can consume so many DBMS resources that order-entry transactions cannot get through.

Computer criminals can launch denial-of-service attacks in which a malicious hacker floods a Web server, for example, with millions of bogus service requests that so occupy the server that it cannot service legitimate requests. Also, computer worms can infiltrate a network with so much artificial traffic that legitimate traffic cannot get through. Finally, natural disasters may cause systems to fail, resulting in denial of service.

Loss of Infrastructure

Many times, human accidents cause loss of infrastructure, the last loss type. Examples are a bulldozer cutting a conduit of fiber-optic cables and the floor buffer crashing into a rack of Web servers.

Theft and terrorist events also cause loss of infrastructure. For instance, a disgruntled, terminated employee might walk off with corporate data servers, routers, or other crucial equipment. Terrorist events also can cause the loss of physical plants and equipment.

Natural disasters present the largest risk for infrastructure loss. A fire, flood, earthquake, or similar event can destroy data centers and all they contain.

You may be wondering why Figure 12-3 does not include viruses, worms, and Trojan horses. The answer is that viruses, worms, and Trojan horses are techniques for causing some of the problems in the figure. They can cause a denial-of-service attack, or they can be used to cause malicious, unauthorized data access or data loss.

How Big Is the Computer Security Problem?

We do not know the full extent of losses due to computer security threats. Certainly, the losses due to human error are enormous, but few organizations compute those losses and even fewer publish them. Losses due to natural disasters are also enormous and impossible to compute. The earthquake in Japan shut down Japanese manufacturing, and losses rippled through the supply chain from the Far East to Europe and the United States. One can only imagine the enormous expense for Japanese companies as they restored their information systems.

With regard to computer crime losses, the U.S. Justice Department publishes a list of computer crime news on its site at www.justice.gov/criminal/cybercrime/cc.html. Some of the major arrests, charges, and convictions for a 3-month period in 2011 are shown in Figure 12-4. By no means is this a comprehensive list of computer crime during those months in the United States. Take it as anecdotal evidence of the kinds of crimes that are being committed. For every one crime that results in an arrest, there are likely 10, or even hundreds or thousands, that go unreported or unsolved.

In September 2011, Norton, a maker of antivirus software licensed by Symantec, claimed that total computer crime losses in 24 countries during the prior 12 months exceeded $388 billion. They estimated that $114 billion of that were direct cash losses and that the remainder, $274 billion, were costs associated with time that victims invested in recovering from crime incidents. According to this report, in those same countries, over one million people per day were victims of a computer crime. Not surprisingly, heavy users of the Internet (more than 49 hours per week) were the most common victims.[2]

---

[2] http://us.norton.com/content/en/us/home_homeoffice/html/cybercrimereport (accessed September 2011).

Date	Event	Loss
8/10/11	Credit card theft using credit card data purchased from Russian individuals.	$770,000
7/19/11	Denial-of-service attack on PayPal by disgruntled customers.	Unknown
7/13/11	Former employee stole former coworkers' email credentials and hacked their email accounts to obtain customer and sales data.	Unknown
6/29/11	Fraudulent sales of nonexistent items on eBay, Craigslist, and AutoTrader.com.	Unknown
6/22/11	Spoofing of IRS tax preparation services.	$209,000
6/29/11	Two individuals from Latvia phished antivirus software to obtain credit card data and payments for nonexistent software from more than 1 million users.	$74 million
5/19/11	Former Bank of America computer programmer altered cash machine code to dispense money without a transaction record.	$419,000

Figure 12-4
Sample Arrests and Convictions Reported by the U.S. Department of Justice

Source: www.justice.gov/criminal/cybercrime/cc.html.

One of the oldest and most respected surveys of computer crimes is conducted by the Computer Security Institute (CSI; previously known as the FBI/CSI survey). This survey has been conducted since 1995, and the organizations involved in the survey are balanced among for-profit and nonprofit organizations and government agencies. They are also balanced for size of organization, from small to very large. You can obtain a copy of the most recent survey at http://gocsi.com (registration is required).

In the 2009 report, CSI stated that it had no estimate of the total loss to computer crime experienced by its survey respondents. Only 144 of the 522 responding organizations provided cost data on losses to computer crime. Furthermore, some losses are difficult to quantify. For example, what is the cost of a denial-of-service attack on an organization's Web site? If a company's Web site is unavailable for 24 hours, what potential sales, prospects, or employees have been lost? What reputation problem was created for the organization? Certainly, some financial loss has occurred, but it is impossible to quantify.

Of those organizations that did report data on financial losses, financial fraud had the highest average incident cost—$463,100—and losses due to bots (see Q4) averaged $345,600.[3] Given the paucity of data and the bias in the survey because responding organizations are security-conscious members of the CSI community, we should follow CSI's lead and simply say that we have no idea of the true cost of computer crime.

However, the CSI survey does provide useful data about the percentage of different types of attacks. Figure 12-5 shows the trend in computer crime incidents over the past 10 years. As shown, as a general trend, the percent of organizations reporting incidents of all types has been gradually decreasing. Considering types of crime, the number of virus attacks during this period has steadily decreased, indicating the success of antivirus programs. Financial fraud has remained relatively stable, however, affecting approximately 12 percent of the respondents over this period. Laptop theft has declined from around 70 percent in 1999 to 44 percent in 2008. Still, laptop theft does occur, and it is the cause of a considerable portion of the loss of proprietary, customer, and employee data. Every 6 months or

---

[3] 2008 CSI Computer Crime and Security Survey, p. 16.

Figure 12-5
Percent of Security Incidents

Source: 2008 CSI Computer Crime
and Security Survey, p. 15.

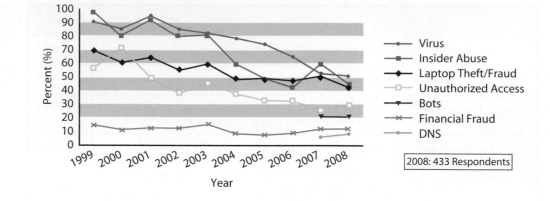

so, the press reports another incident in which an organization was exposed to risk when an employee lost his or her laptop.

Be careful with your interpretation of Figure 12-5. Note that it shows the percent of companies reporting incidents, not the cost of the loss. For the cost of loss data that CSI did receive, financial fraud had the highest average cost, yet it has the lowest frequency in Figure 12-5.

Unfortunately, it is impossible to obtain accurate data about the losses incurred by individuals and organizations due to computer security problems. Many incidents, possibly most, go unreported. Organizations are, understandably, reluctant to release news of monetary and data losses due to computer crime. However, based on the plethora of products that can be purchased for less than $1,000, including credit card details, fake credit cards, bank credentials, online pay service credentials, and so on, we know that the losses must be substantial.

One of the most sobering facts, however, was observed by Professor Randy Boyle of the University of Utah, author of *Applied Information Security* and *Corporate Computer and Network Security.* Dr. Boyle writes of intrusion detection systems. An **intrusion detection system (IDS)** is a computer program that senses when another computer is attempting to scan the disk or otherwise access a computer. According to Boyle, "When I run an IDS on a computer on the public Internet, some nights I get more than 1,000 attempts, mostly from foreign countries. There is nothing you can do about it except use reasonable safeguards."[4]

Goal of Information Systems Security

Computer security losses are serious. As Professor Boyle notes, there is no way to control or eliminate threats from computer criminals, nor can we stop earthquakes or tornadoes. Human error is constant. So, what is the goal of IS security?

As shown in Figure 12-1, threats can be stopped—or, if not stopped, the costs of threat loss can be reduced by creating appropriate safeguards. Safeguards are, however, expensive to create and maintain. They also reduce work efficiency by making common tasks more difficult, adding additional labor expense. The goal for you, as an individual, and for the organization is to find an appropriate trade-off between the risk of loss and the cost of implementing safeguards. We will explore methods for doing that in the next two questions, and then we'll discuss particular safeguards in the three questions after that.

---

[4] Private correspondence with the author, August 20, 2011.

Using MIS InClass 12   *A Group Exercise*

Phishing for . . . Credit Cards, Identifying Numbers, and Bank Accounts

Source: iStockphoto.com.

A phisher is an individual or organization that spoofs legitimate companies in an attempt to illegally capture personal data, such as credit card numbers, email accounts, and driver's license numbers. Some phishers install malicious program code on users' computers as well.

Phishing is usually initiated via email. Phishers steal legitimate logos and trademarks and use official sounding words in an attempt to fool users into revealing personal data or clicking a link. Phishers do not bother with laws about trademark use. They place names and logos like Visa, MasterCard, Discover, and American Express on their Web pages and use them as bait. In some cases, phishers copy the entire look and feel of a legitimate company's Web site.

In this exercise, you and a group of your fellow students will be asked to investigate phishing attacks. If you search the Web for phishing, be aware that your search may bring the attention of an active phisher. Therefore, do not give any data to any site that you visit as part of this exercise!

1. To learn phishing fundamentals, visit www.microsoft.com/protect/fraud/phishing/symptoms.aspx. To see recent examples of phishing attacks, visit www.fraudwatchinternational.com/phishing/.
   a. Using examples in these links, describe how phishing works.
   b. Explain why a link that appears to be legitimate, such as www.microsoft.mysite.com, may, in fact, be a link to a phisher's site.
   c. List five indicators of a phishing attack.
   d. Write an email that you could send to a nontechnical friend or relative that explains what phishing is and how he or she can avoid it.

2. Suppose you received the email in Figure 1 and mistakenly clicked "See more details here." When you did so, you were taken to the Web page shown in Figure 2. List each phishing symptom that you find in these figures and explain why it is a symptom.

3. Suppose you work for an organization that is being phished.
   a. How would you learn that your organization has been attacked?
   b. What steps should your organization take in response to the attack?
   c. What liability, if any, do you think your organization has for damages to customers that result from a phishing attack that carries your brand and trademarks?

4. Summarize why phishing is a serious problem to commerce today.

5. Describe actions that industry organizations, companies, governments, or individuals can take to help reduce phishing.

Your Order ID: "17152492"
Order Date: "09/07/12"
Product Purchased: "Two First Class Tickets to Cozumel"
Your card type: "CREDIT"
Total Price: "$349.00"

Hello, when you purchased your tickets you provided an incorrect mailing address.
See more details here
Please follow the link and modify your mailing address or cancel your order. If you have questions, feel free to contact us account@usefulbill.com

Figure 1
Fake Phishing Email

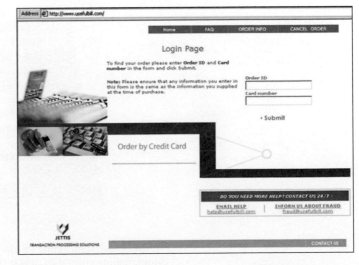

Figure 2
Fake Phishing Screen

Q2 How Should You Respond to Security Threats?

As stated at the end of Q1, your personal IS security goal should be to find an effective trade-off between the cost of safeguards and the risk of loss. Few individuals, however, take security as seriously as they should, and most fail to implement even low-cost safeguards. Figure 12-6 lists recommended personal security safeguards, and with the possible exception of cookie clearing (discussed below), all of them are low cost and easy to implement.

The first safeguard is to take security seriously. You cannot see the attempts that are being made, right now, to compromise your computer. Even though you are unaware of these threats, they are present, as you just learned. When your security is compromised, the first indication you will receive will be bogus charges on your credit card or messages from friends complaining about the disgusting email they just received from your email account.

If you decide to take computer security seriously, the single most important safeguard you can implement is to create and use strong passwords. We discussed ways of doing this in Chapter 1 (page 22). To summarize, do not use any word, in any language, as part of your password. Use passwords with a mixture of upper- and lowercase letters and numbers.

Such nonword passwords are still vulnerable to a **brute force attack** in which the password cracker tries every possible combination of characters. John Pozadzides estimates that a brute force attack can crack a six-character password of either upper- or lowercase letters in about 5 minutes. However, brute force requires 8.5 days to crack a password having a mixture of upper- and lowercase letters, numbers, and special characters. A 10-digit password of only upper- and lowercase letters takes 4.5 years to crack, but one using a mix of letters, numbers, and special characters requires nearly 2 million years. A 12-digit, letter-only password requires 3 million years, and a 12-digit mixed password will take many, many millions of years.[5] All of these estimates assume, of course, that the password contains no word in any language. The bottom line is this: Use long passwords with no words, at least 10 characters, and a mix of letters, numbers, and special characters.

In addition to using long, complex passwords, you should also use different passwords for different sites. That way, if one of your passwords is compromised, you do not lose control of all of your accounts.

Figure 12-6
Personal Security Safeguards

- Take security seriously.
- Create strong passwords.
- Use multiple passwords.
- Send no valuable data via email or IM.
- Use HTTPS at trusted, reputable vendors.
- Remove high-value assets from computers.
- Clear browsing history, temporary files, and cookies (CCleaner or equivalent).
- Update antivirus software.
- Demonstrate security concern to your fellow workers.
- Follow organizational security directives and guidelines.
- Consider security for all business initiatives.

---

[5] John Pozadzides, "How I'd Hack Your Weak Passwords." One Man's Blog, March 26, 2007. http://onemansblog.com/2007/03/26/how-id-hack-your-weak-passwords/ (accessed August 2011). When Pozadzides wrote this in 2007, it was for a personal computer. Using 2012 technology, these times would be half or less. Using a cloud-based network of servers for password cracking would cut these times by 90 percent or more.

Most email and IM is not protected by encryption (see Q4), and you should assume that anything you write in email or IM could find its way to the front page of the *New York Times* tomorrow. Never send passwords, credit card data, or any other data in email or IM.

Buy only from reputable vendors, and when buying online, use only HTTPS. If the vendor does not support HTTPS in its transactions (look for https:// in the address line of your browser), do not buy from that vendor.

You can reduce your vulnerability to loss by removing high-value assets from your computers. Now, and especially later as a business professional, make it your practice not to travel out of your office with a laptop or other device that contains any data that you do not need. In general, store proprietary data on servers or removable devices that do not travel with you. (Office 365, by the way, uses HTTPS to transfer data to and from SharePoint. You can use it or a similar application for storing documents that you need to access on the road.)

Your browser automatically stores a history of your browsing activities and temporary files that contain sensitive data about where you've visited, what you've purchased, what your account names and passwords are, and so forth. It also creates **cookies**, which are small files that your browser stores on your computer when you visit Web sites. Cookies enable you to access Web sites without having to sign in every time, and they speed up processing of some sites. Unfortunately, they also contain sensitive security data. The best safeguard is to remove history, temporary files, and cookies from your computer and to set your browser to disable history and cookies. Doing so will mean that you must always sign in to the sites you visit. CCleaner is a free, open source product that will do a thorough job of removing all such data (http://download.cnet.com/ccleaner/). You should make a backup of your computer before using CCleaner, however.

Removing and disabling cookies presents an excellent example of the trade-off between improved security and cost. Your security will be substantially improved, but it will be more difficult for you to use your computer. You decide, but make a conscious decision; do not let ignorance of the vulnerability of such data make the decision for you.

We will address the use of antivirus software in Q4. The last three items in Figure 12-6 apply once you become a business professional. With your coworkers, and especially with those whom you manage, you should demonstrate a concern and respect for security. You should also follow all organizational security directives and guidelines. Finally, unlike Jeff or Laura at Fox Lake, consider security in all of your business initiatives.

Q3 How Should Organizations Respond to Security Threats?

Management has a crucial role in organizational IS security. Management establishes security policy and has the responsibility of making the trade-off between the risk of loss and the cost of safeguards. The National Institute of Standards and Technology (NIST) published an excellent security handbook that addresses management's responsibility, available online at http://csrc.nist.gov/publications/nistpubs/800-12/800-12-html/. We will follow its discussion in this section.

The *NIST Handbook* of Security Elements

Figure 12-7 lists elements of computer security described in the *NIST Handbook*. First, computer security must support the organization's mission. There is no "one size fits all" solution to security problems. Security systems for a diamond mine and security systems for a wheat farm will differ.

According to the second point in Figure 12-7, when you manage a department, you have a responsibility for information security in that department, even if no one tells you that you do. Do appropriate safeguards exist? Are your employees properly trained? Will

Figure 12-7
Management Guidelines for
IS Security

1. Computer security should support the mission of the organization.
2. Computer security is an integral element of sound management.
3. Computer security should be cost-effective.
4. Computer security responsibilities and accountability should be made explicit.
5. System owners have computer security responsibilities outside their own organizations.
6. Computer security requires a comprehensive and integrated safeguards.
7. Computer security should be periodically reassessed.
8. Computer security is constrained by societal factors.

your department know how to respond when the computer system fails? If these issues are not addressed in your department, raise the issue to higher levels of management.

Security can be expensive. Therefore, as shown in the third principle of Figure 12-7, computer security should have an appropriate cost-benefit ratio. Costs can be direct, such as labor costs, and they can be intangible, such as employee or customer frustration. Organizations such as Fox Lake and GearUp cannot afford to provide the same level of security as Pearson Education or the IRS. All the same, they should pay attention to security and manage security risk, as described in the next section.

According to the fourth principle in Figure 12-7, security responsibilities and accountabilities must be explicit. General statements like "everyone in the department must adequately safeguard company assets" are worthless. Instead, managers should assign specific tasks to specific people or specific job functions.

Because information systems integrate the processing of many departments, security problems originating in your department can have far-reaching consequences. If one of your employees neglects procedures and enters product prices incorrectly on your Web storefront, the consequences will extend to other departments, other companies, and your customers. Understanding that computer system owners have security responsibilities outside their own departments and organizations is the fifth principle of computer security.

As the sixth principle in Figure 12-7 implies, there is no magic bullet for security. No single safeguard, such as a firewall, a virus-protection program, or increased employee training, will provide effective security. The problems described in Figure 12-3 require the specification of integrated safeguards that provide comprehensive protection.

Once the integrated safeguards have been specified, the company cannot simply forget about them. As the seventh principle in Figure 12-7 indicates, security is a continuing need, and every company must periodically evaluate its security threats and safeguards.

Finally, social factors put some limits on security. Employees resent physical searches when arriving at and departing from work. Customers do not want to have their retinas scanned before they can place an order. Computer security conflicts with personal privacy, and a balance may be hard to achieve.

What Are the Elements of a Security Policy?

As stated, senior management has two overarching security tasks: defining a security policy and managing computer-security risk. Although management may delegate specific tasks, it maintains responsibility for the organization's security and must approve and endorse all such work.

A good **security policy** has three elements. The first is a general statement of the organization's security goals and of the assets to be protected. This statement also designates a department for managing the organization's security. In general terms, this statement specifies *how* the organization will ensure enforcement of security safeguards and policies.

The second security policy element is the *issue-specific policy*. For example, management might formulate a policy on personal use of computers at work and email privacy. The organization has the legal right to limit personal use of its computer systems and to inspect personal email for compliance. Employees have a right to know such policies.

The third security policy element is the *system-specific policy*, which concerns specific information systems. For example, what customer data from the order-entry system will be sold or shared with other organizations? Or, what policies govern the design and operation of systems that process employee data? Companies should address such policies as part of the standard systems development process.

Management sets security policies to ensure compliance with security law, as discussed in the Ethics Guide on pages 426–427.

How Is Risk Managed?

Management's second overarching security task is risk management. **Risk** is the likelihood of an adverse occurrence. Management cannot manage threats directly, but it *can* manage the likelihood that threats will be successful. Thus, management cannot keep hurricanes from happening, but it can limit the security consequences of a hurricane by creating a backup processing facility at a remote location.

As stated, companies can reduce risks with safeguards, but always at a cost. It is management's responsibility to decide which safeguards to implement, or, stated differently, how much risk to assume.

Unfortunately, risk management takes place in a sea of uncertainty. Uncertainty is different from risk. Risk refers to threats and consequences that we know about. **Uncertainty** refers to the things we do not know that we do not know. For example, an earthquake could devastate a corporate data center on a fault that no one knew about. An employee might have found a way to steal inventory using a hole in the corporate Web site that no expert knew existed. Because of uncertainty, risk management is always approximate.

Risk Assessment

The first step in risk management is to assess threats, vulnerabilities, and assets that are subject to those threats and vulnerabilities. Management must also assess the potential consequences of loss of assets.

Consequences can be tangible or intangible. *Tangible* consequences are those whose financial impact can be measured. The costs of *intangible* consequences, such as loss of customer goodwill due to an outage, cannot be measured. Normally, when analyzing consequences, companies estimate the costs of tangible consequences and simply list intangible consequences.

The final two factors in risk assessment are likelihood and probable loss. *Likelihood* is the probability that a given asset will be compromised by a given threat, despite the safeguards. **Probable loss** is the "bottom line" of risk assessment. To obtain a measure of probable loss, companies multiply likelihood by the cost of the consequences. Probable loss also includes a statement of intangible consequences.

Risk-Management Decisions

Given the probable loss from the risk assessment just described, senior management must decide what to do. In some cases, the decision is easy. Companies can protect some assets by use of inexpensive and easily implemented safeguards. Installing virus-protection software is an example. However, some vulnerability is expensive to eliminate, and management must determine if the costs of the safeguard are worth the benefit of probable loss reduction. Such risk-management decisions are difficult because the true effectiveness of the safeguard is seldom known, and the probable loss is subject to uncertainty.

Uncertainty, however, does not absolve management from security responsibility. Management has a fiduciary responsibility to the organization's owners, and senior managers must make reasonable and prudent decisions in light of available information.

Ethics
Guide   Security Privacy

Some organizations have legal requirements to protect the customer data they collect and store, but the laws may be more limited than you think. The **Gramm-Leach-Bliley (GLB) Act**, passed by Congress in 1999, protects consumer financial data stored by financial institutions, which are defined as banks, securities firms, insurance companies, and organizations that provide financial advice, prepare tax returns, and provide similar financial services.

The **Privacy Act of 1974** provides protections to individuals regarding records maintained by the U.S. government, and the privacy provisions of the **Health Insurance Portability and Accountability Act (HIPAA)** of 1996 give individuals the right to access health data created by doctors and other health-care providers. HIPAA also sets rules and limits on who can read and receive your health information.

The law is stronger in other countries. In Australia, for example, the Privacy Principles of the Australian Privacy Act of 1988 govern not only government and health-care data, but also records maintained by businesses with revenues in excess of AU$3 million.

To understand the importance of these limitations, consider online retailers that routinely store customer credit card data. Do Dell, Amazon.com, airlines, and other e-commerce businesses have a legal requirement to protect their customers' credit card data? Apparently not—at least not in the United States. The activities of such organizations are not governed by the GLB, the Privacy Act of 1974, or HIPAA.

Most consumers would say, however, that online retailers have an ethical requirement to protect a customer's credit card and other data, and most online retailers would agree. Or at least the retailers would agree that they have a strong business reason to protect that data. A substantial loss of credit card data by any large online retailer would have detrimental effects on both sales and brand reputation.

Data aggregators like Acxiom Corporation further complicate the risk to individuals because they develop a complete profile of households and individuals. And, no federal law prohibits the U.S. government from buying information products from the data accumulators.

But let's bring the discussion closer to home. What requirements does your university have on the data it maintains about you? State law or university policy may govern those records, but no federal law does. Most universities consider it their responsibility to provide public access to graduation records. Anyone can determine when you graduated, your degree, and your major. (Keep this service in mind when you write your resume.)

Most professors endeavor to publish grades by student number and not by name, and there may be state law that requires that separation. But what about your work? What about the papers you write, the answers you give on exams? What about the emails you send to your professor? The data are not protected by federal law, and they are probably not protected by state law. If your professor chooses to cite your work in research, she will be subject to copyright law, but not privacy law. What you write is no longer your personal data; it belongs to the academic community. You can ask your professor what she intends to do with your coursework, emails, and office conversations, but none of that data is protected by law.

The bottom line is this: Be careful with your personal data. Large, reputable organizations are likely to endorse ethical privacy policy and to have strong and effective safeguards to effectuate that policy. But individuals and small organizations might not. If in doubt, ask. ■

Discussion Questions

1. As stated in the case, when you order from an online retailer, the data you provide is not protected by U.S. privacy law. Does this fact cause you to reconsider setting up an account with a stored credit card number? What is the advantage of storing the credit card number? Do you think the advantage is worth the risk? Are you more willing to take the risk with some companies than with others? Why or why not?

2. Suppose you are the treasurer of a student club, and you store records of club members' payments in a database. In the past, members have disputed payment amounts; therefore, when you receive a payment, you scan an image of the check or credit card invoice and store the scanned image in a database.

One day, you are using your computer in a local coffee shop when a malicious student breaks into your computer over the shop's wireless network and steals the club database. You know nothing about this until the next day, when a club member complains that a popular student Web site has published the names, bank names, and bank account numbers for everyone who has given you a check.

What liability do you have in this matter? Could you be classified as a financial institution because you are taking students' money? (You can find the GLB at www.ftc.gov/privacy/privacyinitiatives/glbact.html) If so, what liability do you have? If not, do you have any other liability? Does the coffee shop have liability?

3. Suppose you are asked to fill out a study questionnaire that requires you to enter identifying data, as well as answers to personal questions. You hesitate to provide the data, but the top part of the questionnaire states, "All responses will be strictly confidential." So, you fill out the questionnaire.

Unfortunately, the person who is conducting the study visits the same wireless coffee shop that you visited (in question 2), and the same malicious student breaks in and steals the study results. Your name and all of your responses appear on that same student Web site. Did the person conducting the study violate a law? Does the confidentiality assurance on the form increase that person's requirement to protect your data? Does your answer change if the person conducting the study is (a) a student, (b) a professor of music, or (c) a professor of computer security?

4. In truth, only a talented and motivated hacker could steal databases from computers using a public wireless network. Such losses, although possible, are unlikely. However, any email you send or files you download can readily be sniffed at a public wireless facility. Knowing this, describe good practice for computer use at public wireless facilities.

5. Considering your answers to the above questions, state three to five general principles to guide your actions as you disseminate and store data.

Q4 What Technical Safeguards Are Available?

Technical safeguards involve the hardware and software components of an information system. Figure 12-8 lists primary technical safeguards.

Identification and Authentication

Every information system today should require users to sign on with a user name and password. The user name *identifies* the user (the process of **identification**), and the password *authenticates* that user (the process of **authentication**).

Passwords

All forms of computer security involve passwords. Review the material on strong passwords and password etiquette in Chapter 1, as well as the password discussion in Q2.

Smart Cards

A **smart card** is a plastic card similar to a credit card. Unlike credit, debit, and ATM cards, which have a magnetic strip, smart cards have a microchip. The microchip, which holds far more data than a magnetic strip, is loaded with identifying data. Users of smart cards are required to enter a **personal identification number (PIN)** to be authenticated.

Biometric Authentication

Biometric authentication uses personal physical characteristics such as fingerprints, facial features, and retinal scans to authenticate users. Biometric authentication provides strong authentication, but the required equipment is expensive. Often, too, users resist biometric identification because they feel it is invasive.

Biometric authentication is in the early stages of adoption. Because of its strength, it likely will see increased usage in the future. It is also likely that legislators will pass laws governing the use, storage, and protection requirements for biometric data.

You can remember authentication methods by understanding they fall into three categories: what you know (password or PIN), what you have (smart card), and what you are (biometric).

Single Sign-on for Multiple Systems

Information systems often require multiple sources of authentication. For example, when you sign on to your personal computer, you need to be authenticated. When you access the LAN in your department, you need to be authenticated again. When you traverse your organization's WAN, you will need to be authenticated to even more networks. Also, if your request requires database data, the DBMS server that manages that database will authenticate you yet again.

It would be annoying to enter a name and password for every one of these resources. You might have to use and remember five or six different passwords just to

Figure 12-8
Technical Safeguards

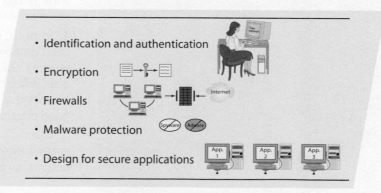

- Identification and authentication
- Encryption
- Firewalls
- Malware protection
- Design for secure applications

access the data you need to perform your job. It would be equally undesirable to send your password across all of these networks. The further your password travels, the greater the risk it can be compromised.

Instead, today's operating systems have the capability to authenticate you to networks and other servers. You sign on to your local computer and provide authentication data; from that point on, your operating system authenticates you to another network or server, which can authenticate you to yet another network and server, and so forth.

A system called **Kerberos** authenticates users without sending their passwords across the computer network. Developed by the Massachusetts Institute of Technology (MIT), Kerberos uses a complicated system of "tickets" to enable users to obtain services from networks and other servers. Windows, Linux, Unix, and other operating systems employ Kerberos and thus can authenticate user requests across networks of computers using a mixture of these operating systems.

This discussion indicates another reason why you must protect your user name and password. Once you have authenticated yourself on your local system, your operating system will authenticate you to networks and other servers. Someone who obtains your name and password will gain access not only to your computer, but via intersystem authentication, to many other computers and servers as well. Once more, with feeling: Protect your passwords!

Despite all that we know about the need for protecting passwords, compliance with password-protection guidelines is still lacking, as the Guide on pages 444–445 demonstrates.

Wireless Access

For a wired network, a potential intruder must obtain physical access to the network. For a wireless network, however, no direct connection is needed. Drive-by sniffers can walk or drive around business or residential neighborhoods with a wireless computer and locate dozens, or even hundreds, of wireless networks. The wireless network will broadcast whether it is protected. If it is not, the sniffer can use it to obtain free access to the Internet or to connect to LANs that are connected to the access point.

It is possible to protect wireless networks. Businesses with sophisticated communications equipment use elaborate techniques—techniques that require the support of highly trained communications specialists. Common protections are the use of VPNs and special security servers.

For the less sophisticated SOHO (small office, home office) market, wireless networks are less secure. The IEEE 802.11 Committee, the group that develops and maintains wireless standards, first developed a wireless security standard called **Wired Equivalent Privacy (WEP)**. Unfortunately, WEP was insufficiently tested before it was deployed, and it has serious flaws. In response, the IEEE 802.11 Committee developed improved wireless security standards called **Wi-Fi Protected Access (WPA)** and **WPA2**. Fortunately, most wireless devices today can use WPA techniques.

Encryption

Encryption is the process of transforming clear text into coded, unintelligible text for secure storage or communication. Considerable research has gone into developing **encryption algorithms** (procedures for encrypting data) that are difficult to break. Commonly used methods are DES, 3DES, and AES; search the Web for these terms if you want to know more about them. Encryption concepts are summarized in Figure 12-9 (on the next page).

A **key** is a number used to encrypt the data. It is called a key because it unlocks a message, but it is a number used with an encryption algorithm and not a physical thing like the key to your apartment.

To encode a message, a computer program uses the encryption method with the key to convert a noncoded message into a coded one. The resulting coded message looks like gibberish. Decoding (decrypting) a message is similar; a key is applied to the coded message to recover the original text. In **symmetric encryption**, the same key (again, a number) is used to encode and to decode the message. With **asymmetric encryption**, two keys are used; one key encodes the message, and the other key decodes the message. Symmetric encryption is simpler and much faster than asymmetric encryption.

Figure 12-9
Basic Encryption Techniques

Technique	How It Works	Characteristics
Symmetric	Sender and receiver transmit message using the same key.	Fast, but difficult to get the same key to both parties.
Asymmetric	Sender and receiver transmit message using two keys, one public and one private. Message encrypted with one of the keys can be decrypted with the other.	Public key can be openly transmitted; slower than symmetric encryption.
SSL/TLS	Works between Levels 4 and 5 of the TCP-OSI architecture. Sender uses public/private key to transmit symmetric key, which both parties use for symmetric encryption—for a limited, brief period.	Used by most Internet applications. A useful and workable hybrid of symmetric and asymmetric encryption. Look for https:// in your browser's address field.

A special version of asymmetric encryption, **public key/private key**, is used on the Internet. With this method, each site has a public key for encoding messages and a private key for decoding them. Before we explain how that works, consider an analogy.

Suppose you send a friend an open combination lock (like you have on your gym locker). Suppose you are the only one who knows the combination to that lock. Now, suppose your friend puts something in a box and locks the lock. Now, neither your friend nor anyone else can open that box. Your friend sends the locked box to you, and you apply the combination to open the box.

A public key is like the combination lock, and the private key is like the combination. Your friend uses the public key to code the message (lock the box), and you use the private key to decode the message (use the combination to open the lock).

Now, suppose we have two generic computers, A and B. Suppose A wants to send an encrypted message to B. To do so, A sends B its public key (in our analogy, A sends B an open combination lock). Now B applies A's public key to the message and sends the resulting coded message back to A. At that point, neither B nor anyone other than A can decode that message. It is like the box with a locked combination lock. When A receives the coded message, A applies its private key (the combination in our analogy) to unlock or decrypt the message.

Again, public keys are like open combination locks. A will send a lock to anyone who asks for one. But A never sends its private key (the combination) to anyone. Private keys stay private.

Most secure communication over the Internet uses a protocol called **HTTPS**. With HTTPS, data are encrypted using a protocol called the **Secure Socket Layer (SSL)**, also known as **Transport Layer Security (TLS)**. SSL/TLS uses a combination of public key/private key and symmetric encryption.

The basic idea is this: Symmetric encryption is fast and is preferred. But, the two parties (say you and a Web site) don't share a symmetric key. So, the two of you use public/private encryption to share the same symmetric key. Once you both have that key, you use symmetric encryption.

Figure 12-10 summarizes how SSL/TLS works when you communicate securely with a Web site:

1. Your computer obtains the public key of the Web site to which it will connect.
2. Your computer generates a key for symmetric encryption.
3. Your computer encodes that key using the Web site's public key. It sends the encrypted symmetric key to the Web site.
4. The Web site then decodes the symmetric key using its private key.
5. From that point forward, your computer and the Web site communicate using symmetric encryption.

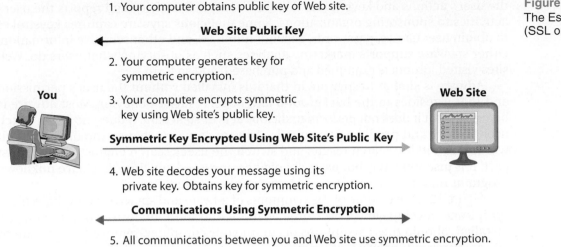

Figure 12-10
The Essence of HTTPS
(SSL or TLS)

1. Your computer obtains public key of Web site.

Web Site Public Key

2. Your computer generates key for symmetric encryption.

You

3. Your computer encrypts symmetric key using Web site's public key.

Web Site

Symmetric Key Encrypted Using Web Site's Public Key

4. Web site decodes your message using its private key. Obtains key for symmetric encryption.

Communications Using Symmetric Encryption

5. All communications between you and Web site use symmetric encryption.

At the end of the session, your computer and the secure site discard the keys. Using this strategy, the bulk of the secure communication occurs using the faster symmetric encryption. Also, because keys are used for short intervals, there is less likelihood they can be discovered.

Firewalls

Firewalls are the third technical safeguard listed in Figure 12-8. A firewall is a computing device that prevents unauthorized network access. A firewall can be a special purpose computer or it can be a program on a general-purpose computer or on a router.

Malware Protection

The next technical safeguard in our list in Figure 12-8 is malware. The term *malware* has several definitions. Here we will use the broadest one: **Malware** is viruses, worms, Trojan horses, spyware, and adware.

Viruses, Trojan Horses, and Worms

A **virus** is a computer program that replicates itself. Unchecked replication is like computer cancer; ultimately, the virus consumes the computer's resources. Furthermore, many viruses also take unwanted and harmful actions.

The program code that causes unwanted activity is called the **payload**. The payload can delete programs or data—or even worse, modify data in undetected ways. Imagine the impact of a virus that changed the credit rating of all customers. Some viruses publish data in harmful ways—for example, sending out files of credit card data to unauthorized sites.

There are many different virus types. **Trojan horses** are viruses that masquerade as useful programs or files. The name refers to the gigantic mock-up of a horse that was filled with soldiers and moved into Troy during the Trojan War. A typical Trojan horse appears to be a computer game, an MP3 music file, or some other useful innocuous program.

A **worm** is a virus that propagates using the Internet or other computer network. Worms spread faster than other virus types because they are specifically programmed to spread. Unlike nonworm viruses, which must wait for the user to share a file with a second computer, worms actively use the network to spread. Sometimes, worms so choke a network, making it unusable.

Spyware, Adware, and Beacons

Spyware programs are installed on the user's computer without the user's knowledge or permission. Spyware resides in the background and, unknown to the user, observes the user's actions and keystrokes, monitors computer activity, and reports the user's activities to sponsoring organizations. Some malicious spyware captures keystrokes to obtain user names, passwords, account numbers, and other sensitive information. Other spyware supports marketing analyses such as observing what users do, Web sites visited, products examined and purchased, and so forth.

Adware is similar to spyware in that it is installed without the user's permission and that it resides in the background and observes user behavior. Most adware is benign in that it does not perform malicious acts or steal data. It does, however, watch user activity and produce pop-up ads. Adware can also change the user's default window or modify search results and switch the user's search engine. For the most part, it is just annoying, but users should be concerned any time they have unknown programs on their computers that perform unknown functions.

Figure 12-11 lists some of the symptoms of adware and spyware. Sometimes these symptoms develop slowly over time as more and more malware components are installed. Should these symptoms occur on your computer, remove the spyware or adware using antimalware programs.

As you learned in Q2, your browser stores data about sites you visit in small files called cookies. In some cases, cookies contain data about what you have recently purchased or searched on. Since cookies were introduced, some companies have become even more sophisticated in mining data about your behavior.

Beacons, tiny files that gather demographic information, use a single code to identify users by age, gender, location, likely income, and online activity. A beacon code can contain your favorite movies, whether you read the online news, your shopping habits, your online dating habits, and what type of research you conduct on their computer. A beacon is placed on Web sites and is downloaded into your computer, automatically, without your being aware. The information is refreshed in real time and sold to other companies. For example, if you like classic movies, then your personal details could be sold to a company selling DVDs of recently restored old films, and this company, in turn, would target you with ads. Your information can be sold over and over again, several times a day. The chief marketing officer of Lotame Solutions, a company that specializes in beacons, says, "We can segment it all the way down to one person." As of 2011, no laws have been introduced or passed to prevent the use of beacons. Most users are unaware that they are being tracked this way.[6]

Malware Safeguards

Fortunately, it is possible to avoid most malware using the following malware safeguards:

1. **Install antivirus and antispyware programs on your computer.** Your IS department will have a list of recommended (perhaps required) programs for this purpose. If you choose a program for yourself, choose one from a reputable vendor. Check reviews of antimalware software on the Web before purchasing.
2. **Set up your antimalware programs to scan your computer frequently.** You should scan your computer at least once a week and possibly more. When you detect

Figure 12-11
Spyware and Adware
Symptoms

- Slow system start up
- Sluggish system performance
- Many pop-up advertisements
- Suspicious browser homepage changes
- Suspicious changes to the taskbar and other system interfaces
- Unusual hard-disk activity

---

[6] Julia Angwin, "The Web's New Gold Mine: Your Secrets," *Wall Street Journal*, July 30, 2010.

malware code, use the antimalware software to remove them. If the code cannot be removed, contact your IS department or antimalware vendor.

3. **Update malware definitions. Malware definitions**—patterns that exist in malware code—should be downloaded frequently. Antimalware vendors update these definitions continuously, and you should install these updates as they become available.

4. **Open email attachments only from known sources.** Also, even when opening attachments from known sources, do so with great care. According to professor and security expert Ray Panko, about 90 percent of all viruses are spread by email attachments.[7] This statistic is not surprising, because most organizations are protected by firewalls. With a properly configured firewall, email is the only outside-initiated traffic that can reach user computers.

   Most antimalware programs check email attachments for malware code. However, all users should form the habit of *never* opening an email attachment from an unknown source. Also, if you receive an unexpected email from a known source or an email from a known source that has a suspicious subject, odd spelling, or poor grammar, do not open the attachment without first verifying with the known source that the attachment is legitimate.

5. **Promptly install software updates from legitimate sources.** Unfortunately, all programs are chock full of security holes; vendors are fixing them as rapidly as they are discovered, but the practice is inexact. Install patches to the operating system and application programs promptly.

6. **Browse only in reputable Internet neighborhoods.** It is possible for some malware to install itself when you do nothing more than open a Web page. Don't go there!

Bots, Botnets, and Bot Herders

Recently, new terms have been introduced into the computer security vocabulary. A **bot** is a computer program that is surreptitiously installed and that takes actions unknown and uncontrolled by the computer's owner or administrator. The term *bot* is a new catch-all term that refers to any type of virus, worm, Trojan Horse, spyware, adware, or other program not installed and controlled by the computer's owner or manager. Some bots are very dangerous and malicious; some steal credit card data, banking data, and e-mail addresses. Others cause denial-of-service attacks and still others just produce pop-ups and other annoyances.

A **botnet** is a network of bots that is created and managed by the individual or organization that infected the network with the bot program. The individual or organization that controls the botnet is called a **bot herder**. Botnets and bot herders are potentially serious problems not only to commerce, but also to national security. It is believed that a unit of the North Korean Army served as a bot herder for a botnet that caused denial-of-service attacks on Web servers in South Korea and in the United States in July 2009.

The safeguards discussed for malware are the best protection against bots. Stay tuned, however; the end of the bot story has not yet been written.

Design Secure Applications

The final technical safeguard in Figure 12-8 concerns the design of applications. As a future IS user, you will not design programs yourself. However, you should ensure that any information system developed for you and your department includes security as one of the application requirements.

---

[7] Ray Panko, *Corporate Computer and Network Security* (Upper Saddle River, NJ: Prentice Hall, 2004), p. 165.

Q5 What Data Safeguards Are Available?

Data safeguards are measures used to protect databases and other organizational data. Figure 12-12 summarizes some important data safeguards. First, the organization needs to inventory its sensitive data and specify the degree of protection that such data requires. Next, the organization should assign data rights and responsibilities and enforce those rights with users' accounts having appropriate permission levels and password authentication, at least.

The organization should protect especially sensitive data by storing it in encrypted form. Such encryption uses one or more keys in ways similar to that described for data communication encryption. One potential problem with stored data, however, is that the key might be lost or that disgruntled or terminated employees might destroy it. Because of this possibility, when data are encrypted, a trusted party should have a copy of the encryption key. This safety procedure is sometimes called **key escrow**.

Another data safeguard is to periodically create backup copies of database contents. The organization should store at least some of these backups off premises, possibly in a remote location. Additionally, IT personnel should periodically practice recovery, to ensure that the backups are valid and that effective recovery procedures exist. Do not assume that just because a backup is made the database is protected.

Physical security is another data safeguard. The computers that run the DBMS and all devices that store database data should reside in locked, controlled-access facilities. If not, they are subject not only to theft, but also to damage. For better security, the organization should keep a log showing who entered the facility, when, and for what purpose.

Physical security was one of the problems that Fox Lake had when its data was stolen. The member data were stored on a database in the facilities building. Although the building was locked, short-term contractors were given keys that they could easily make copies of.

It is unrealistic for a small company like Fox Lake to lock up users' computers in a controlled-access facility. It is likely feasible, however, for Fox Lake to lock a data server in a secure place and allow access to it over their LAN. Then, as long as passwords protect computer access, sensitive data would not be readily accessible.

In the case of cloud data storage, the organization needs to ensure that the security requirements of the data match the security measures provided by the cloud vendor. Most cloud vendors have their public auditors prepare an SAS 70 report, which is an audited report on the vendor's capabilities. In addition, some vendors have obtained an ISO certification as well.[8]

Figure 12-12
Data Safeguards

- Inventory sensitive data and specify protection required.
- Assign data rights and responsibilities.
- Enforce rights with user accounts authenticated by passwords.
- Encrypt data, as needed.
- Implement backup and recovery procedures.
- Create physical security, as needed.
- Ensure that cloud vendors provide appropriate security for the data they store.

---

[8] For example, visit www.microsoft.com/download/en/details.aspx?id=26552 to learn the security measures for Office 365.

Q6 What Human Safeguards Are Available?

Human safeguards involve the people and procedure components of information systems. In general, human safeguards result when authorized users follow appropriate procedures for system use and recovery. Restricting access to authorized users requires effective authentication methods and careful user account management. In addition, appropriate security procedures must be designed as part of every information system, and users should be trained on the importance and use of those procedures. In this section, we will consider the development of human safeguards first for employees and then for nonemployee personnel.

Human Safeguards for Employees

Figure 12-13 lists security considerations for employees. The first is the creation of appropriate position definitions.

Position Definitions

It is impossible to have effective human safeguards unless job tasks and responsibilities are clearly defined for each employee position. In general, job descriptions should provide a separation of duties and authorities. For example, no single individual should be allowed to approve expenses, write checks, and account for the disbursement. Instead, one person should approve expenses, another person pay them, and a third account for the transaction. Similarly, in inventory, no single person should be allowed

- Position definition
  - Separate duties and authorities.
  - Determine least privilege.
  - Document position sensitivity.

"OK to pay this"

- Hiring and screening

"Where did you last work?"

- Dissemination and enforcement (responsibility, accountability, compliance)

"Let's talk security..."

- Termination
  - Friendly

"Congratulations on your new job"

  - Unfriendly

"We've closed your accounts. Goodbye"

Figure 12-13
Human Safeguards for Employees

to authorize an inventory withdrawal, remove the items from inventory, and account for the removal.

Given appropriate job descriptions, users' computer accounts should give users the least possible privilege necessary to perform their jobs. For example, users whose job description does not include modifying data should be given accounts with read-only privilege. Similarly, user accounts should prohibit users from accessing data they do not need. Because of the problem of semantic security (Chapter 9, page 328), access to seemingly innocuous data should be limited if the employee does not need that data for his or her job.

Finally, the security sensitivity should be documented for each position. Some jobs involve highly sensitive data (e.g., employee compensation, salesperson quotas, and proprietary marketing or technical data). Other positions involve no sensitive data. Documenting *position sensitivity* enables security personnel to prioritize their activities in accordance with the possible risk and loss.

Hiring and Screening

Security considerations should be part of the hiring process. Of course, if the position involves no sensitive data and no access to information systems, then screening for information systems security purposes will be minimal. When hiring for high-sensitivity positions, however, extensive interviews, references, and background investigations are appropriate. Note, too, that security screening applies not only to new employees, but also to employees who are promoted into sensitive positions.

Dissemination and Enforcement

Obviously, employees cannot be expected to follow security procedures if they do not know about them. Therefore, employees need to be trained on security policies, procedures, and the responsibilities they will have.

Employee security training begins during new-employee training, with the explanation of general security policies and procedures. That general training must be amplified in accordance with the position's sensitivity and responsibilities. Promoted employees should receive security training that is appropriate to their new positions. The company should not provide user accounts and passwords until employees have completed required security training.

Enforcement consists of three interdependent factors: responsibility, accountability, and compliance. First, the company should clearly define the security *responsibilities* of each position. The design of the security responsibility should be such that employees can be held *accountable* for security violations. Procedures should exist so that when critical data are lost, it is possible to determine how the loss occurred and who is accountable. Finally, the security program should encourage security *compliance*. Employee activities should regularly be monitored for compliance, and management should specify disciplinary action to be taken in light of noncompliance.

Management attitude is crucial: Employee compliance is greater when management demonstrates, both in word and deed, a serious concern for security. If managers write passwords on staff bulletin boards, shout passwords down hallways, or ignore physical security procedures, then employee security attitudes and employee security compliance will suffer. Note, too, that effective security is a continuing management responsibility. Regular reminders about security are essential.

Termination

Companies also must establish security policies and procedures for the termination of employees. Most employee terminations are friendly and occur as the result of promotion, retirement, or when the employee resigns to take another position. Standard human resources policies should ensure that system administrators receive notification in advance of the employee's last day, so that they can remove accounts and passwords. Procedures for recovering keys for encrypted data and any other security assets must be part of the employee's out-processing.

Unfriendly termination is more difficult because employees may be tempted to take malicious or harmful actions. In such a case, system administrators might need to remove user accounts and passwords prior to notifying the employee of her termination. Other actions may be needed to protect the company's information assets. A terminated sales employee, for example, might attempt to take the company's confidential customer and sales-prospect data for future use at another company. The terminating employer should take steps to protect those data prior to the termination.

The human resources department should be aware of the importance of giving IS administrators early notification of employee termination. No blanket policy exists; the information systems department must assess each case on an individual basis.

Human Safeguards for Nonemployee Personnel

Business requirements may necessitate opening information systems to non-employee personnel—temporary personnel, vendors, partner personnel (employees of business partners), and the public. Although temporary personnel can be screened, to reduce costs the screening will be abbreviated from that for employees. In most cases, companies cannot screen either vendor or partner personnel. Of course, public users cannot be screened at all. Similar limitations pertain to security training and compliance testing.

In the case of temporary, vendor, and partner personnel, the contracts that govern the activity should call for security measures appropriate to the sensitivity of the data and the IS resources involved. Companies should require vendors and partners to perform appropriate screening and security training. The contract also should mention specific security responsibilities that are particular to the work to be performed. Companies should provide accounts and passwords with the least privilege and remove those accounts as soon as possible.

The situation differs with public users of Web sites and other openly accessible information systems. It is exceedingly difficult and expensive to hold public users accountable for security violations. In general, the best safeguard from threats from public users is to *harden* the Web site or other facility against attack as much as possible. **Hardening** a site means to take extraordinary measures to reduce a system's vulnerability. Hardened sites use special versions of the operating system, and they lock down or eliminate operating systems features and functions that are not required by the application. Hardening is actually a technical safeguard, but we mention it here as the most important safeguard against public users.

Finally, note that the business relationship with the public, and with some partners, differs from that with temporary personnel and vendors. The public and some partners use the information system to receive a benefit. Consequently, safeguards need to protect such users from internal company security problems. A disgruntled employee who maliciously changes prices on a Web site potentially damages both public users and business partners. As one IT manager put it, "Rather than protecting ourselves from them, we need to protect them from us." This is an extension of the fifth guideline in Figure 12-7.

Account Administration

The third human safeguard is account administration. The administration of user accounts, passwords, and help-desk policies and procedures are important components of the security system.

Account Management

Account management concerns the creation of new user accounts, the modification of existing account permissions, and the removal of unneeded accounts. Information system administrators perform all of these tasks, but account users have the responsibility to notify the administrators of the need for these actions. The IS department should create standard procedures for this purpose. As a future user, you can improve your relationship with IS personnel by providing early and timely notification of the need for account changes.

The existence of accounts that are no longer necessary is a serious security threat. IS administrators cannot know when an account should be removed; it is up to users and managers to give such notification.

Password Management

Passwords are the primary means of authentication. They are important not just for access to the user's computer, but also for authentication to other networks and servers to which the user may have access. Because of the importance of passwords, NIST recommends that employees be required to sign statements similar to that shown in Figure 12-14.

When an account is created, users should immediately change the password they are given to a password of their own. In fact, well-constructed systems require the user to change the password on first use.

Additionally, users should change passwords frequently thereafter. Some systems will require a password change every three months or perhaps more frequently. Users grumble at the nuisance of making such changes, but frequent password changes reduce not only the risk of password loss, but also the extent of damage if an existing password is compromised.

Some users create two passwords and switch back and forth between those two. This strategy results in poor security, and some password systems do not allow the user to reuse recently used passwords. Again, users may view this policy as a nuisance, but it is important.

Help-Desk Policies

In the past, help desks have been a serious security risk. A user who had forgotten his password would call the help desk and plead for the help-desk representative to tell him his password or to reset the password to something else. "I can't get this report out without it!" was (and is) a common lament.

The problem for help-desk representatives is, of course, that they have no way of determining that they are talking with the true user and not someone spoofing a true user. But, they are in a bind: If they do not help in some way, the help desk is perceived to be the "unhelpful desk."

To resolve such problems, many systems give the help-desk representative a means of authenticating the user. Typically, the help-desk information system has answers to questions that only the true user would know, such as the user's birthplace, mother's maiden name, or last digits of an important account number. Often, too, the method by which the new password can be obtained is sent to the user in an email. Email, as you learned, is sent as plaintext, however, so the new password itself ought not to be emailed. If you ever receive notification that your password was reset when you did not request such a reset, immediately contact IS security. Someone has compromised your account.

Figure 12-14
Sample Account
Acknowledgment Form

Source: National Institute of Standards and Technology, *Introduction to Computer Security: The NIST Handbook,* Publication 800-12, p. 114.

> I hereby acknowledge personal receipt of the system password(s) associated with the user IDs listed below. I understand that I am responsible for protecting the password(s), will comply with all applicable system security standards, and will not divulge my password(s) to any person. I further understand that I must report to the Information Systems Security Officer any problem I encounter in the use of the password(s) or when I have reason to believe that the private nature of my password(s) has been compromised.

Figure 12-15
Systems Procedures

	System Users	Operations Personnel
Normal Operation	Use the system to perform job tasks, with security appropriate to sensitivity.	Operate data center equipment, manage networks, run Web servers, and related operational tasks.
Backup	Prepare for loss of system functionality.	Back up Web site resources, databases, administrative data, account and password data, and other data.
Recovery	Accomplish job tasks during failure. Know tasks to do during system recovery.	Recover systems from backed up data. Role of help desk during recovery.
Incident Response	Know what to do when security breach occurs, such as whom to contact and what data to gather.	Know how to investigate security breaches, know whom to contact, and follow guidelines from legal department. Set up and practice disaster recovery.

All such help-desk measures reduce the strength of the security system, and, if the employee's position is sufficiently sensitive, they might create too large a vulnerability. In such a case, the user may just be out of luck. The account will be deleted, and the user must repeat the account-application process.

Systems Procedures

Figure 12-15 shows a grid of procedure types—normal operation, backup, recovery, and incident response. Procedures of each type should exist for each information system. For example, the order-entry system will have procedures of each of these types, as will the Web storefront, the inventory system, and so forth. The definition and use of standardized procedures reduces the likelihood of computer crime and other malicious activity by insiders. It also ensures that the system's security policy is enforced.

Normal Use Procedures

Procedures should be created for both users and operations personnel. For each type of user, the company should develop procedures for accomplishing work. Within a business process, for example, procedures need to describe how to use the information system to accomplish particular activity tasks. Normal-use procedures should provide safeguards appropriate to the sensitivity of the information system.

Backup and Recovery Procedures

Backup procedures concern the creation of backup data to be used in the event of failure. Whereas operations personnel have the responsibility for backing up system databases and other systems data, departmental personnel have the need to back up data on their own computers. Good questions to ponder are, "What would happen if I lost my computer or iPhone tomorrow?" "What would happen if someone dropped my computer during an airport security inspection?" "What would happen if my computer were stolen?" Employees should ensure that they back up critical business data on their computers. The IS department can help in this effort by designing backup procedures and making backup facilities available.

Finally, systems developers should develop procedures for system recovery. First, how will the department manage its affairs when a critical system is unavailable? Customers will want to order, and manufacturing will want to remove items from inventory even though a critical information system is unavailable. How will the department respond? Once the system is returned to service, how will records of business activities during the outage be entered into the system? How will service be resumed? The system developers should ask and answer these questions and others like them and develop procedures accordingly.

Responding to Security Incidents

The final category of procedures concerns the response to security incidents. As stated in Q1, security problems can arise from human error, computer crime, or natural disaster. Both users and operations personnel need procedures for each category.

Concerning human error, when users realize that they or others have made serious errors, they need to know what to do and whom to contact. They need to know what data they need to gather to document the problem and guide the best response. Operations personnel need procedures on how best to affect the problem resolution and how to help users avoid such problems in the future.

With regard to computer crime, no organization should wait until some asset has been lost or compromised before deciding what to do. Both users and operations personnel should have procedures in place that indicate how to respond to security problems, whom they should contact, the data they should gather, and steps they can take to reduce further loss.

Consider, for example, a virus. Incident response procedures should stipulate what an employee should do when he notices the virus. It should specify whom to contact and what to do. It may stipulate that the employee should turn off his computer and physically disconnect from the network. The plan should also indicate what users with wireless connections should do.

Procedures should provide centralized reporting of all security incidents. Such reporting will enable an organization to determine if it is under systematic attack or whether an incident is isolated. Centralized reporting also allows the organization to learn about security threats, take consistent actions in response, and apply specialized expertise to all security problems.

When computer crime occurs, speed is frequently important. Viruses and worms can spread very quickly across an organization's networks, and a fast response will help to mitigate the consequences. Because of the need for speed, preparation pays. The incident-response plan should identify critical personnel and their off-hours contact information. These personnel should be trained on where to go and what to do when they get there. Without adequate preparation, there is substantial risk that the actions of well-meaning people will make the problem worse.

Emergency procedures also need to be created for the response to natural disasters. As always, the best way to solve a problem is not to have it, and the best safeguard against a natural disaster is appropriate location. If possible, place computing centers, Web farms, and other computer facilities in locations not prone to floods, earthquakes, hurricanes, tornados, or avalanches. Even in those locations, place infrastructure in unobtrusive buildings, basements, backrooms, and similar locations well within the physical perimeter of the organization. Also, locate computing infrastructure in fire-resistant buildings designed to house expensive and critical equipment.

However, sometimes business requirements necessitate locating the computing infrastructure in undesirable locations. Also, even at a safer location, disasters do occur. Therefore, many businesses prepare backup processing centers in locations geographically removed from the primary processing site.

Figure 12-16 lists major disaster-preparedness tasks. After choosing a safe location for the computing infrastructure, the organization should identify all mission-critical applications. These are applications without which the organization cannot carry on and which, if lost for any period of time, could cause the organization's failure. The next

Figure 12-16
Disaster-Preparedness Tasks

- Locate infrastructure in safe location.
- Identify mission-critical systems.
- Identify resources needed to run those systems.
- Prepare remote backup facilities.
- Train and rehearse.

step is to identify all resources necessary to run those systems. Such resources include computers, operating systems, application programs, databases, administrative data, procedure documentation, and trained personnel.

Next, the organization creates backups for the critical resources at the remote processing center. A **hot site** is a utility company that can take over another company's processing with no forewarning. Hot sites are expensive; organizations pay $250,000 or more per month for such services. **Cold sites**, in contrast, provide computers and office space. They are cheaper to lease, but customers install and manage systems themselves. The total cost of a cold side, including all customer labor and other expenses, might not necessarily be less than the cost of a hot site.

Once the organization has backups in place, it must train and rehearse cutover of operations from the primary center to the backup. In the case of a hot site, employees must know how to ensure the hand off occurs without incident, how to run systems while the hot site is active, and how to recover processing when the primary site is again operational. For cold sites, employees must know how to apply backups, how to start systems, and how to run systems from the cold site location. As with all emergency procedures, periodic refresher rehearsals are mandatory.

The need to prepare for natural disasters is a major advantage of storing data in the cloud. Reputable vendors such as Microsoft, Oracle, Amazon.com, Apple, Rackspace, and others have already created backup sites to take over from their primary sites. Users of these cloud vendors can benefit by sharing the cost of these preparations with all of the cloud vendor's customers.

Security Monitoring

Security monitoring is the last of the human safeguards we will consider. Important monitoring functions are activity log analyses, security testing, and investigating and learning from security incidents.

Many information system programs produce *activity logs*. Firewalls produce logs of their activities, including lists of all dropped packets, infiltration attempts, and unauthorized access attempts from within the firewall. DBMS products produce logs of successful and failed log-ins. Web servers produce voluminous logs of Web activities. The operating systems in personal computers can produce logs of log-ins and firewall activities.

None of these logs add any value to an organization unless someone looks at them. Accordingly, an important security function is to analyze these logs for threat patterns, successful and unsuccessful attacks, and evidence of security vulnerabilities.

Today, most large organizations actively investigate their security vulnerabilities. They may employ utilities such as Nessus or AppScan to assess their vulnerabilities. Many companies create **honeypots**, which are false targets for computer criminals to attack. To an intruder, a honeypot looks like a particularly valuable resource, such as an unprotected Web site, but in actuality the only site content is a program that determines the attacker's IP address. Organizations then use IP traceback programs, such as Sam Spade, to determine who has attacked them.[9] If you are technically minded, detail oriented, and

---

[9] For this reason, do *not* attempt to scan servers for fun. It won't take the organization very long to find you, and they will not be amused!

curious, a career as a security specialist in this field is almost as exciting as it appears on *CSI*. To learn more, check out Sam Spade, HotBot, or AppScan. See also *Applied Information Security*.[10]

Security, like BPM, is a process that requires process management. There is no final state that represents a secure system or company. Instead, companies must monitor security on a continuing basis.

Q7 2022?

What will be the status of information security by 2022? Will we have found a magic bullet to eliminate security problems? No. Human error is a constant; well-managed organizations will plan better for it and know how to respond better when it does occur, but as long as we have humans, we'll have error. Natural disasters are similar. The horrific events surrounding Hurricane Katrina in 2005 and the Japanese tsunami in 2011, as well as the serious but not horrific Hurricane Irene in 2011, have alerted the world that we need to be better prepared, and more companies will set up hot or cold sites and put more data in well-prepared clouds. So, we'll be better prepared, but natural disasters are natural, after all.

What about computer crime? It is a field of cat and mouse. Computer criminals find a vulnerability to exploit, and they exploit it. Computer security experts discover that vulnerability and create safeguards to thwart it. Computer criminals find a new vulnerability to exploit, computer security forces thwart it, and so it goes. The next major challenges will likely be those affecting iOS and other intelligent, portable devices. But, security on these devices will be improved as threats emerge that exploit their vulnerabilities. This cat-and-mouse game is likely to continue for at least the next 10 years. No super-safeguard will be devised to prevent computer crime, nor will any particular computer crime be impossible to thwart. However, the skill level of this cat-and-mouse activity is likely to increase, and substantially so. Because of increased security in operating systems and other software, and because of improved security procedures and employee training, it will become harder and harder for the lone hacker to find some vulnerability to exploit. Not impossible, but vastly more difficult.

So, what will happen? Cloud vendors and major organizations will continue to invest in safeguards; they'll hire more people (maybe you), train them well, and become ever more difficult to infiltrate. Although some criminals will continue to attack these fortresses, most will turn their attention to less protected, more vulnerable, mid-sized and smaller organizations, and to individuals. You can steal $50 million from one company or $50 from a million people with the same cash result. And, in the next 10 years, because of improved security at major Web sites, the difficultly and cost of stealing that $50 million will be much higher than stealing $50 a million times. Take another look at Figure 12-6—and not for the purpose of the exam!

Part of the problem is porous national borders. As Professor Boyle states:

> People can freely enter the U.S. electronically without a passport. They can commit numerous crimes with few repercussions. There are no real electronic IDs. There are very few lawmen that know anything about electronic crimes beyond what they read in the news. Gangs, well organized and motivated by money, commit most of the crime. Electronic lawlessness is the order of the day.[11]

If someone in Romania steals from Google or Apple or Microsoft or Boeing or AirBus and then disappears into a cloud of networks in Uzbekistan, those large

---

[10] Randall Boyle, *Applied Information Security* (Upper Saddle River, NJ: Pearson Education, 2010).
[11] Private correspondence with the author, August 24, 2011.

organizations have the expertise to know how to proceed and whether it will be worth it. They also have the needed financial resources. But if that same criminal steals from you in Nashville, what do the local law enforcement authorities know to do? Or even the Tennessee state authorities? And, if your portion of the crime is for $50, how many calls to Uzbekistan do they want to make?

Again, according to Professor Boyle:

> At the federal level, finances and politics take precedence over electronic security. The situation will likely be solved as it was in the past. Strong local "electronic" sheriffs will take control of the electronic border and enforce existing laws. It will take a couple decades (at least). Technology is moving faster than either the public or elected officials can educate themselves.[12]

That's it! You've reached the end of this text. Take a moment to consider how you will use what you learned, as described in the Guide on pages 446–447.

Take yet another look at Figure 12-6. Send a copy to your loved ones.

---

[12] Private correspondence with the author, August 24, 2011.

Guide
Security Assurance, Hah!

"If I have to go to one more employee meeting about security policy, I'm going to scream. The managers talk about threats, and safeguards, and risk, and uncertainty, and all the things they want us to do to improve security. Has any manager ever watched people work in this department?

"Walk through the cubicles here and watch what is happening. I'll bet half the employees are using the password they were assigned the day they started work. I'll bet they've never changed their password, ever! And for the people who have changed their passwords, I'll bet they've changed them to some simpleton word like 'Sesame' or 'MyDogSpot' or something equally absurd.

"Or, open the top drawer of any of my coworkers' desks and guess what you'll find? A little yellow sticky with entries like OrderEntry: 748QPt#7ml, Compensation: RXL87MB, System: ti5587Y. What do you suppose those entries are? Do you think anyone who worked here on a weekend wouldn't know what to do with them? And the only reason they're in the desk drawers is that Martha (our manager) threw a fit when she saw a yellow sticky like that on Terri's monitor.

"I've mentioned all this to Martha several times, but nothing happens. What we need is a good scare. We need somebody to break into the system using one of those passwords and do some damage. Wait—if you enter a system with a readily available password, is that even breaking in? Or is it more like opening a door with a key you were given? Anyway, we need someone to steal something, delete some files, or erase customer balances. Then maybe the idiotic management here would stop talking about security risk assurance and start talking about real security, here on the ground floor!" ■

Discussion Questions

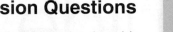

1. Summarize the point that this contrarian is making.

2. What do you think Martha should do about the points the contrarian makes? Surmise why nothing has been done to this point.

3. Explain three ways that our contrarian could make his point more effectively.

4. We've now heard from numerous contrarians. What do you think about them? What are the advantages of having a contrarian in a group or meeting? What are the disadvantages?

5. Contrarians can be amusing, and they often make excellent points, but they become tiresome. Using your answers to question 4, explain why that is. What would drive you to the point of becoming a contrarian? What other strategy could you employ?

Guide
The Final, Final Word

Congratulations! You've made it through the entire book. With this knowledge, you are well prepared to be an effective user of information systems. And with work and imagination, you can be much more than that. Many interesting opportunities are available to those who can apply information in innovative ways. Your professor has done what she can do, and the rest, as they say, is up to you.

So what's next? Back in Chapter 1, we claimed that Introduction to MIS is the most important course in the business curriculum today. That claim was based on the organization's innovative use of nearly free data communications and data storage. By now, you've learned many of the ways that businesses and organizations use these resources and information systems based upon those resources. You've also seen how businesses like GearUp and Fox Lake use information systems to solve problems and further their competitive strategies. In some cases, particularly with Fox Lake, they *struggled* to use information systems for those purposes.

How can you use that knowledge? Chapter 1 claimed that future business professionals must be able "to assess, evaluate, and apply emerging information technology to business." Have you learned how to do that? At least, are you better able to do that than you were prior to this class? You probably know the meaning of many more terms than you did when you started this class, and such knowledge is important. But, even more important is the ability to use that knowledge to apply MIS to your business interests.

Chapter 1 also reviewed the work of the RAND Corporation and that of Robert Reich on what professional workers in the twenty-first century need to know. Those sources state that such workers need to know how to innovate the use of technology and how to "collaborate, reason abstractly, think in terms of systems, and experiment." Have you learned those behaviors? Or, at least, are you better at them than when you started this course?

As of August 2011, the official national unemployment rate was about 9.2 percent, with the real unemployment rate, which includes those who have stopped looking for work, much higher. Under these circumstances, good jobs will be difficult to obtain. You need to apply every asset you have. One of those assets is the knowledge you've gained in this class. Take the time to do the exercises at the end of this Guide, and then use the answers in your job interviews!

Look for the job you truly want to do, get that job, and work hard. In the movie *Phillip Glass in 12 Acts,* the composer Phillip Glass claimed he knew the secret to success. It was, he said, "Get up early and work hard all day." That quotation seems obvious and hardly worth stating. Except that it has the ring of truth. And, if you can find a job you truly love, it isn't even hard. Actually, it's fun, most of the time. So, use what you've learned in this class to obtain the job you truly want! ∎

Discussion Questions

1. Reflect on what you have learned from this course. Write two paragraphs on how the knowledge you have gained will help you to "assess, evaluate, and apply emerging information technology to business." Shape your writing around the kind of job that you want to obtain upon graduation.

2. Write two paragraphs on how the knowledge and experiences you've had in this class will help you "collaborate, reason abstractly, think in terms of systems, and experiment." Again, shape your writing around the kind of job you wish to obtain.

3. Using your answer to question 1, extract three or four sentences about yourself that you could use in a job interview.

4. Using your answer to question 2, extract three or four sentences about yourself that you could use in a job interview.

5. Practice using your answers to questions 3 and 4 in a job interview with a classmate, roommate, or friend.

Active Review

Use this Active Review to verify that you understand the ideas and concepts that answer the chapter's study questions.

Q1 What is the goal of information systems security?

Define *threat, vulnerability, safeguard,* and *target.* Give an example of each. List three types of threats and five types of security losses. Summarize each of the elements in the cells of Figure 12-3. Summarize indications that computer security losses are a problem. Define *IDS.* Explain the goal of IS security.

Q2 How should you respond to security threats?

Explain each of the elements in Figure 12-6. Define *brute force attack.* Define *cookie* and explain why using a program like CCleaner is a good example of the security trade-off.

Q3 How should organizations respond to security threats?

Broadly describe senior management's security role. Explain the meaning of each element in Figure 12-7. State three elements of a security policy and explain each. Define *risk* and *uncertainty* and explain the difference between them. Define *safeguard* and *vulnerability* and explain their relationship. Describe two types of consequences of data loss. Define *likelihood* and *probable loss* and explain their relationship. Explain computer security risk-management decisions that senior management must make. Explain why uncertainty does not absolve management from security responsibility.

Q4 What technical safeguards are available?

Define *technical safeguard* and explain which of the five components are involved in such safeguards. Explain the use of identification and authentication and describe three types of authentication. Describe the purpose of Kerberos. Explain the security problem posed by wireless networks and describe safeguards that exist for the SOHO market. Describe symmetric and asymmetric encryption and explain how they are used for SSL/TLS. Name the five types of malware as defined in this text and briefly describe each. Describe the six antimalware techniques presented.

Q5 What data safeguards are available?

Define *data safeguards* and give four examples. Explain each.

Q6 What human safeguards are available?

Name the components involved in human safeguards. Name and describe four human safeguards that pertain to employees. Explain how human safeguards pertain to nonemployee personnel. Summarize account administration safeguards. Describe eight types of procedures for system users and system operations personnel. Summarize security monitoring functions. Define *honeypot.*

Q7 2022?

Explain how the phrase *cat and mouse* pertains to computer security. Describe the types of security problems are likely to occur in the next 10 years. Explain how the focus of computer criminals will likely change in the next 10 years? Explain how this is likely to impact smaller organizations, and you.

Using Your Knowledge at Fox Lake

Using the knowledge you have gained from this chapter, summarize the security mistakes that Fox Lake made. Explain how Jeff, Mike, and Anne should have acted differently.

▬▬ Key Terms and Concepts

Adware 432	Authentication 428	Biometric authentication 428
Asymmetric encryption 429	Beacons 432	Bot 433

Using Your Knowledge

1. Search online to find a way to obtain your own credit report. Several sources to check are www.equifax.com, www.experian.com, and www.transunion.com. Look for a source that provides the report for free.

   a. Review your credit report for obvious errors. However, other checks are appropriate. Search the Web for guidance on how best to review your credit records. Summarize what you learn.

   b. What actions should you take if you find errors in your credit report?

   c. Define identity theft. Search the Web and determine the best course of action if someone thinks he has been the victim of identity theft.

2. Suppose you work in a small business and your boss has asked you to explain proper individual security practices to your fellow workers. Using Figure 12-6 as a guide, develop a PowerPoint presentation that you could use to present your ideas. Incorporate ideas from Q7 as well.

3. Suppose that a particular financial institution has never had a serious security problem. Can they use this fact in their marketing? If so, explain how. If not, explain why not.

4. Consider the categories of threat in Figure 12-3. Describe the three most serious threats to each of the following businesses:

   a. GearUp
   b. A neighborhood accounting firm
   c. A dentist's office
   d. A Honda dealership

5. Describe a potential technical safeguard for each of the threats you identified in your answer to question 4.

6. Describe a potential data safeguard for each of the threats you identified in your answer to question 4. If no data safeguard is appropriate to a business, explain why.

7. Describe a potential human safeguard for each of the threats you identified in your answer to question 4.

8. Describe how each of the businesses in question 4 should prepare for security incidents.

9. How likely are the threats you identified in question 4? If you owned these businesses, which of the items you described in questions 5 through 8 would you implement?

Collaboration Exercise 12

With a team of your fellow students, develop an answer to the following questions. Use Google Docs, Google+, Windows Live SkyDrive, SharePoint, Office 365, or some other collaboration tool to conduct your meetings.

Suppose Chris and Jason, the groundskeepers at Fox Lake, are the same Chris and Jason that appeared in the Guide on pages 150–151. After Chris was fired from his job, he wandered around, couldn't find professional work, and settled for cutting the grass at Fox Lake. He happened to tell Mike about his computer knowledge the day before Anne made her request for a report on membership data (see Chapter 9, pages 294–295). Mike thought giving Chris that task would possibly help Chris's professional job prospects, as well as solve a problem for Fox Lake. Jason was working at Fox Lake part time, and it was he who hatched the scheme to steal expensive wedding presents. Chris provided the data, and Jason did the stealing. Assume that the wedding events data and the membership data are stored in separate databases on the server in the facilities building. Access to both is protected via user account and password, but Mike leaves his passwords on his desktop computer monitor. The machines themselves are located in a backroom of the facilities building.

Meeting with your group, answer the following questions:

1. In what ways did weaknesses in technical safeguards allow this situation to occur?

2. In what ways did weaknesses in data safeguards allow this situation to occur?

3. In what ways did weaknesses in human safeguards allow this situation to occur?

4. How should Fox Lake respond to this incident?

5. What security mistakes, if any, did each of the following individuals make:
   a. Anne
   b. Mike
   c. Jeff
   d. Laura

6. If you were Jeff, how would you remedy the weaknesses you identified in your answers to questions 1–3?

7. Suppose you were on a job interview with the owner of a small business with IS systems and IT infrastructure similar to that of Fox Lake. If that owner were to ask you what the top three issues for IS security in a small business are, how would you respond?

Case Study 12

Moore's Law, One More Time . . .

According to Stewart Baker, former counsel for the National Security Agency, "What we've been seeing, over the last decade or so, is that Moore's Law is working more for the bad guys than the good guys." Should we agree?

If you are in the business of cracking passwords using brute force techniques, then doubling the speed of a CPU will halve the time needed to crack a password. That seems like a real benefit to the criminal, but for a reasonably strong password—one that takes, say, 200 years to crack—halving that time is still 100 years, which is too long for computer crime. But, if the infiltrator uses 1000 computers, then 100 years becomes 36 days, which may or may not be timely for the criminal's purposes. Certainly, then, faster CPUs benefit password cracking, at least.

Also, the availability of cheap, large, fast disks, and hence cheap storage, enables criminals to inexpensively store millions of common passwords, all the words in all the world's languages, and other useful password-cracking data. Furthermore, cheap storage

enables criminals to store the gigabytes of data they reap from snooping; data that can be mined at leisure for user identities, passwords, birth dates, Social Security numbers, credit card accounts, and so forth. Certainly, nearly free data storage benefits computer crime as well.

But maybe we're missing the greatest benefit. Thirty minutes of searching the terms *data breach* and *data loss* with Google in August 2011 netted the following seven events, all of which occurred in 2011:

1. In June, 1.3 million Sega game players lost birth date, email, and encrypted password data due to a security breach.

2. In April, 70 million Sony game players had their credit card data stolen.

3. A flaw in iOS 3.0 enabled criminals to invade the email accounts of 144,000 people, including former White House Chief of Staff Rahm Emanuel. In fairness to Apple, the problem seemed to lie more with AT&T than Apple.

4. A flaw in iOS, up to version 4.3, enabled hackers to obtain administration account privileges from users who downloaded Acrobat PDF files. The problem was Apple's, not Adobe's. It has since been fixed.

5. Friendly neighbor Ian Wood stole $57,000 from his neighbors by using personal data he obtained on Facebook to access their online accounts. He followed the "forget your password" instructions and responded to questions using the Facebook data. When he gained access to the accounts, he requested new credit cards, which he then stole from his neighbors' mailboxes.

6. Phishers spoofing Twitter obtained Twitter account data by claiming that Twitter was about to start charging for its services. To object, all the user had to do was to register his or her Twitter ID and password at a fake Twitter account. The phisher took the objectors' data.

7. In the too-ironic-to-believe category, a Chinese television program promoting the Chinese military showed a screenshot of an attempt to hack into the IP address 138.26.72.17. At the time, that address belonged to a university in the United States. Apparently the editor of the program didn't know what an IP address was.

This 30-minute search actually yielded many more examples than listed here; try it yourself.

What can we learn from these seven scenarios? What technology do they share? Data communications. Recall from Chapter 1 that Moore's Law makes data communications essentially free. These seven events are some of the consequences of that fact.

Now consider that iOS, Android phones, and literally millions of other mobile devices will further increase data communications, and you can see that the opportunities for computer criminals will only increase—exponentially, in fact.

Questions

1. Explain why Moore's Law makes it increasingly more important to create strong passwords.

2. Use one or more of the crime scenarios listed in this case study to explain why it is important to use different passwords for different accounts.

3. Explain how data communications played an important role in each of the crime scenarios listed in this case study.

4. Do you agree that Moore's Law is helping the "bad guys" more than the "good guys"? Why or why not? Use evidence in this case, knowledge from this chapter, and your own experience in your answer.

5. Suppose you had a disk full of a day's Internet traffic into your university's primary router. Explain how you could mine this data. Name at least seven different types of data you are likely to find and, in words, explain how you would go about finding it.

6. Describe, in your own words, why increased use of portable devices is likely to create even greater opportunities for computer criminals.

7. Review Figure 12-6 and explain how the measures recommended in the figure would have helped anyone who had the misfortune to be a victim in any of the seven scenarios presented in the case study.

Sources: David Talbot, "Moore's Outlaws," *MIT Technology Review*, Vol. 113, No. 4, August 2010; "Sega Says 1.3 Million Users Affected by Cyber Attack," Reuters, www.reuters.com/article/2011/06/19/us-sega-hackers-idUSL3E7HJ01520110619; Garrett Martin, "Sony Data Loss Biggest Ever," *Boston Herald,* April 27, 2011, www. bostonherald.com/business/technology/general/view.bg?articleid=1333548; 8bitjay, "5 of the Most Notable iOS Security Holes We've Seen," iSmashPhone.com, November 1, 2010, http://ismashphone.com/2010/11/5-of-the-most-notable-ios-security-holes-weve-seen.html; Matthew Calamia, "IOS Security Flaw Discovered," Mobiledia.com, July 7, 2011, www.mobiledia.com/news/97150.html; Helen A. S. Popkin, "Man Steals $57K from Neighbors Using Their Facebook Info," MSNBC Technolog, August 16, 2011, http://technolog.msnbc.msn.com/_news/2011/08/16/7387638-man-steals-57k-from-neighbors-using-their-facebook-info?GT1=43001; Rosa Golijan, "No, You Won't Have to Pay to Use Twitter in October," Digital Life, http://digitallife.today.com/_news/2011/08/19/7416549-no-you-wont-have-to-pay-to-use-twitter-in-october?GT1=43001; "Chinese Government Caught on Film Hacking the West," Security Watchdog, www.v3.co.uk/v3-uk/security-watchdog-blog/2103749/chinese-government-caught-tv-film-hacking-west.

TEACHING SUGGESTIONS

Fox Lake Country Club, Chapter 12

GOALS

Use Fox Lake Country Club to:

- Underline the importance of IT's management and protection functions.

- Emphasize the importance of professional IT development.

- Show the need for background checks on employees who access organizational data.

- Show the need for employee termination safeguards.

BACKGROUND

1. This problem started back in Chapter 9 when Anne asked Mike for the BI report about members who were prospects for wedding events. Mike hired his groundskeepers, Jason and Chris, and left them alone with the servers.

2. Mike has passwords written on yellow sticky notes on his monitor. That sounds and looks ridiculous, but right now, in hundreds of businesses, this exact scenario is being repeated. If nothing else, students should learn from this not to do that, no matter how aggravating it is to remember passwords.

3. Numerous mistakes were made that led to this problem. Laura saw it coming when she first started to work with Fox Lake. Having servers in unsecured locations where many part-time employees and contractors passed through was a sure invitation to trouble.

HOW TO GET STUDENTS INVOLVED

1. What caused this problem?

   ■ Numerous mistakes were made that led to the theft of data and, subsequently, to the theft of gifts. Identify as many of these mistakes as you can.

2. What is the extent of this problem?

   ■ Does Fox Lake know the extent of the damages? What else might have been done with the member data?

■ Should Fox Lake inform the membership that member data have been compromised? Why or why not?

3. With regards to the yellow sticky notes:

   ■ Why were the yellow sticky notes a problem? Would it be much different if those yellow sticky notes were in a locked drawer?

   ■ The best way to protect passwords is not to write them down. Review the material on creating passwords in Chapter 1 (page 22). How could Mike have used the strategy described there?

   ■ Remember this story. Always protect your passwords!

4. With regards to Fox Lake security threats and safeguards:

   ■ For each threat in Figure 12-3:

   • Give an example of how that threat could compromise IS, data, or IT at Fox Lake.

   • How is Fox Lake particularly vulnerable to that threat because of its inattention to protecting IS and IT infrastructure?

   • Describe a safeguard that a company like Fox Lake could use to protect itself from data loss. Be realistic; keep in mind Fox Lake's size and financial situation.

5. Consider human safeguards, in particular:

   ■ Explain why the data loss resulted from a lack of human safeguards.

   ■ Do you think Fox Lake should have performed a background check on Chris before letting him access the company's data? Why or why not?

   ■ Even though Fox Lake is small, describe appropriate hiring and termination procedures as they relate to IS and IT.

VIDEO

We wanted to have fun with this video and so we cast it in the form of a Dashell Hammett mystery (like the *Thin Man*). It's intended to be playful and a good capstone for this series. In this final segment, Laura's suspicions are confirmed, Jeff learns that he should have been paying more attention to IS management, and Mike learns many lessons, not the least of which is not to write passwords on yellow sticky notes on his monitor.

The problems began when Anne asked Mike for the data about members who fit her qualifications for wedding event prospects. Mike did what he thought was right . . . use the skills of the employees he has. Just as he has a nonplumber repairing the restrooms, he had an amateur (who turned out to be a famous hacker) obtain the data for Anne.

Everyone learns a lesson. Fox Lake will have to deal with the PR problems of the stolen gifts. And, they can hope that the data haven't been sold or used for any other purpose. If so, they may have to confront their membership with an announcement that Fox Lake members' data have been compromised. Regardless, Jeff is going to be in even more trouble for starting the wedding events business, and may lose his job.

One possible class exercise would be to review the Fox Lake case and to list the mistakes that Fox Lake made and what it could have (realistically) done to prevent those mistakes. Students then might ponder how they can use this knowledge in their future careers!

BOTTOM LINE

■ **Information systems security management is important. Every business professional has a responsibility for security, even if the organization, like Fox Lake, pays little attention to security.**

■ **As a future manager, understand that you have important security responsibilities, even if no one tells you that you do.**

■ **Don't write passwords on yellow sticky notes on your computer screen!**

■ **As a manager in a small business, if you don't manage IS security, who will?**

YOU BE THE GUIDE

Using the Ethics Guide: Security Privacy (pages 426–427)

GOALS

- Understand the legal requirements, ethical considerations, and business consequences of data acquisition, storage, and dissemination.

- Help students formulate personal principles with regard to data acquisition, storage, and dissemination.

BACKGROUND AND PRESENTATION STRATEGIES

Throughout this text, we've discussed three categories of criteria for evaluating business actions and employee behavior:

- Legal
- Ethical
- Good business practice

We can clearly see the differences in these criteria with regard to data security. A doctor's office that does not create systems to comply with HIPAA is violating the law. An e-commerce business that collects customer data and sells it to spammers is behaving unethically (at least according to the accepted principles of behavior of most business professionals). An e-commerce business that is lackadaisical about securing its customer data is engaging in poor business practices.

Business professionals need to be worried, much more so than they are, about sending email over wireless networks. Unless the email is encrypted, and it almost never is, its contents are readily available. Recently, in 2011, I received an email from a small vendor that stated, here is your new user name and here is your new password. All open.

I don't think we can over-emphasize the importance of creating and using long, effective passwords. Professor Boyle's observation that he receives over 1,000 intrusion attempts per night on a computer that is open to the Internet is sobering! Also, see the argument in Q7 that as major sites become more difficult to infiltrate, criminals will turn to smaller, less hard sites. Stealing $50 from a million people nets $50 million.

Two guidelines that apply the principle, "The best way to solve a problem is not to have it" are:

■ **Resist providing sensitive data.**

■ **Don't collect data you don't need.**

I have become very aggressive in not divulging personal data. At least 95 percent of the time, when I challenge someone as to why they need some piece of personal data, they respond, "Oh, don't bother—we don't have to have it." I recommend a similar strategy to my students.

When someone says, "All answers are strictly confidential," consider the source. If that statement comes from the university computer security staff, I believe they understand what they are claiming to provide and will take every professional effort to comply with that statement. If it is made by a team of undergraduates with majors that predispose me to believe they know little of computer security, then I suspect they may not know what they are claiming to provide. Furthermore, in the event of a security system failure, the university has a deep enough pocket to provide compensation for damages. It would be difficult to obtain compensation from a group of undergraduates.

■ **Don't provide data to sources with questionable data security!**

 ## SUGGESTED RESPONSES FOR DISCUSSION QUESTIONS

1. The advantage of an account is you don't have to enter credit card data every time you buy. The problem is that your credit card data is stored on at least one of their disks, and hence it is vulnerable to theft. (The order entry software may also store your credit card data for a one-time purchase, but that storage should be temporary.)

   I recommend four general principles:

   ■ **Never set up an account with a vendor unless you know that vendor has substantial financial assets (Amazon.com versus Mom-and-Pop Plant Sales).**

   ■ **Set up accounts only with companies with which you do enough business that the time-savings benefits of the account justify the risk of a security problem.**

   ■ **If you do set up an account, protect it with a long, strong password!**

   ■ **Send credit card data only to organizations that are using SSL/TLS (https).**

   ■ **Never send your Social Security number, driver's license number, or any password to anyone.**

(Caveat: Maybe it would be OK to send your SSN to the IRS. The alternative is paying by mail, but is that any more secure? The IRS stores your SSN, regardless of how you pay. A good question.)

2. You probably do have some liability in this instance, but unless you have substantial personal assets, it's probably not worth anyone's time to sue you. Your club or university may have liability, however. I doubt anyone could claim that you are a financial institution, but there may be other liability. The possible liability of the coffee shop is interesting. I suspect there is some language somewhere that limits its liability. These are questions to explore with a business law professor because the relevant case law is evolving.

   As a practical matter, whenever you collect any sort of confidential computer-sensible data, don't store it on the notebook computer you carry around campus or use for wireless access. Store it in the cloud, using a high-quality company like Microsoft or Google that knows how to protect data. Protect your cloud account with a long, strong password. Do not access sensitive data over public, wireless networks unless you are using https.

3. Use the three categories of criteria: Collecting sensitive data and not protecting it is *poor business practice*, even if you provide no confidentiality statement. Collecting data and not protecting becomes *unethical* if you do provide a confidentiality statement.

   As to the *legality*, I am not an attorney, but I don't believe this event violates any commonly enacted law. However, you may have violated an implied contract between you and the responder. If your statement does constitute a contract, you are expected to do what a reasonable and prudent person would do to protect that data. If you do not take such precautions, you are in violation of the contract and could be held financially accountable.

   The three different backgrounds alter what the reasonable and prudent person would be expected to do. The student would have the least responsibility, because of his or her assumed immaturity and inexperience. The professor of music would have greater responsibilities because his or her position as a professor would imply greater experience and world knowledge. The professor of computer security would have a very high level of expectation of behavior for protecting that data.

4. I think the following is the very best guideline for email:

   - **Never send an email, from anywhere, unless you would be pleased to see it published on the front page of the *New York Times* or your local newspaper the next day. If you'd be embarrassed, likely to be sued, or likely to go to jail were that email published, don't send it.**

5. One possible list of general principles for storing and disseminating data:

   - **Don't disseminate data when you can avoid it.**

   - **Don't collect data when you can avoid it.**

   - **When you do collect sensitive data, store it in the cloud, using reputable cloud vendors, and protect your account with long, strong passwords. Avoid public, wireless networks unless you are using https. (This guideline is appropriate for an individual; obviously a business has other requirements.)**

   - **Never generate an email that you'd regret seeing on the front page of the *New York Times*.**

   - **Secure your personal/home/SOHO wireless networks.**

WRAP UP

- **As a business professional, you have the responsibility to consider the legality, the ethics, and the wisdom when you request, store, or disseminate data. The more knowledge and experience you have, the greater that responsibility is.**

- **Think about this and develop your own code of behavior. Then, follow that code. The best way to solve a problem is not to have it!**

YOU BE THE GUIDE

Using the Guide: Security Assurance, Hah! (pages 444–445)

GOALS

- Remind the students, one more time, to protect their passwords and to manage their employees to protect passwords as well.

- Discuss the differences between a *contrarian position* and a *contrarian,* and assess the proper role for each.

BACKGROUND AND PRESENTATION STRATEGIES

These contrarians are becoming tedious! They always do. Although we have learned much from the contrarians in the various guides, they can begin to seem like whiners.

■ **What's the difference between a *contrarian position* and a *contrarian*?**

A *contrarian position* is a posture on an idea, a concept, a strategy, or a tactic that runs counter to the accepted perception, belief, or line of thinking. When the child in Hans Christian Anderson's *The Emperor's New Clothes* says, "But he has nothing on at all," in reference to the emperor's nakedness, the child was taking a contrarian position.

Were someone to say, "Wireless network security is unimportant," that person would be taking a contrarian position.

Contrarian positions can be right (the emperor was naked), or wrong (wireless security is very important). Often the value of a contrarian position is not so much in whether it is right or wrong, but rather because it causes people to reevaluate their thinking on some topic. When the late Seattle newspaper columnist Emmett Watson ran his *Lesser Seattle* campaign with the slogan, "Keep the bastards out!" he forced citizens and the city to reconsider its population growth objectives.

A *contrarian* is someone who always takes the opposing position. Contrarians take a particular joy in conflict and opposition. They are predictable because they will choose whatever side no one else seems to be on. Although contrarians make great newspaper columnists, cartoonists, and bloggers, they seldom achieve notable success in business. They become a nuisance and tiresome. It's as if they enjoy butting their heads against the wall, often seeming to rejoice in what they perceive as the "stupidity" of coworkers, their managers, the company, their industry, whatever.

I think the contrarian in this chapter has crossed into nuisance territory. His protests are adding little value. He's made his security opinion known, and both his manager and his fellow employees have taken some action. He's probably right that not much else will happen until a disaster occurs, and, having made as much contribution as he can, further expostulations won't create a solution.

The inappropriate password behavior he cites is not really his problem; it's his manager's and his company's problem. Having said what he has, he should let it go.

Advice to the future business professional:

■ **Although taking a contrarian position from time to time on important issues can be an effective behavior that leads to a successful business career, becoming a contrarian can limit your career.**

■ **Contrarians are fundamentally destructive; they say only what's wrong. The bulk of their words are critical rather than constructive. When a business looks for leaders and managers, it needs to find people who can construct and build, not people who constantly complain. Contrarians are usually relegated to a corner, but seldom to the corner office.**

■ **What's this contrarian's point?**

His point is that sophisticated security management will never be possible without proper password management. That statement is obviously true.

■ **Does that mean that security management and planning ought not to be done?**

No, of course not. So, make your point and move on!

SUGGESTED RESPONSES FOR DISCUSSION QUESTIONS

1. The contrarian's point is that effective security cannot occur unless employees appropriately protect their passwords. He doesn't want to think about larger security issues when he knows that his fellow employees are reckless with their passwords.

   He's frustrated that his manager hasn't taken more action than she has.

2. Martha should listen to him, and consistent with her own priorities and those of the department (meaning she should make this a high priority, but not to the

exclusion of other important tasks that need to be done), she should instigate a program to improve password use in her department.

If she thinks that she and her employees can handle it, she should consider putting the contrarian in charge of the new password management program. She could also enlist the help of her IS department. There may be ways that they can require employees to regularly change their passwords to strong passwords and to ensure that they are not reusing prior passwords too frequently.

Why hasn't Martha done more? Possibly she's busy with other problems, possibly she doesn't understand the importance of good password use, possibly she thinks the contrarian is a crank and dismisses most of what he says. Maybe she's avoiding the problem because she just hates to meet with him!

3. Three ways for the contrarian to make his point more effectively:
   - Use empathic thinking—consider the perspectives of fellow employees and Martha.
   - Write a memo suggesting, specifically, how the department could develop better password management. Perform all of the staff work needed for Martha to implement the plan.
   - Prepare a PowerPoint or other presentation that shows employees easy ways to generate and remember strong passwords. (See the guide on security in Chapter 1.)

4. See commentary in the Guidelines. Contrarians identify problems, and usually they are important problems. Contrarians don't "wear well" in organizations, though; over time, they become a nuisance.

5. See comments in the Guidelines. It would be tempting to become a contrarian if a person believed, even knew, that he or she had excellent ideas but those ideas were continually and consistently ignored. In some ways, contrarians have turned bitterness into words.

- **If you are communicating on some issue, and your communications seems to have no effect, change tactics. Don't keep blasting the same horn. Either find another way to make your case or give up. Is it really your job to force change on this issue? Or, are you frustrated about something else?**

- **If you don't have the power to force a change, if no one seems open to that change, and if the issue is very important, you may have to change jobs. Blasting the same horn is tiresome for you and for everyone else.**

WRAP UP

- **We've considered numerous contrarians and contrarian positions in this text. We've learned a lot from them; they've helped us focus our thinking.**

- **I do not, however, want to leave you with the impression that becoming a contrarian is a good pathway to a successful career. An occasional *contrarian position* on an important matter can be effective and useful. Seldom, however, do perpetual contrarians go far.**

- **If you're prone to critical commentary, give these warnings some thought!**

YOU BE THE GUIDE

Using the Guide: The Final, Final Word (pages 446–447)

GOAL

- Inspire the students to use their learning from this class to find, create, and manage innovative applications of information systems and technology.

BACKGROUND AND PRESENTATION STRATEGIES

Thanks to Moore's Law, the costs of computing, storage, and data communication continue to fall. As discussed in Chapter 1, data storage and communication are today essentially free. As long as this trend continues, new technology will emerge and new opportunities for innovation will develop.

In the mid-1990s, some people looked at Bill Gates' wealth and despaired because "all the great opportunities were gone." But, along came the Internet, and soon Jeff Bezos illustrated that great opportunities were still available. Of course, after that followed Google, and after Google came YouTube, then Facebook, then Twitter, LinkedIn, and Groupon. What's next? As the industry solves the problem of the last mile, there will be yet another story of incredible success.

And these are just the stars, the headlines of the industry. Behind them are hundreds—thousands—of people in industry who have found ways to gain competitive advantage for themselves and their organizations by developing new technology and by finding new ways to apply emerging technology in innovative ways.

In the last lectures, I like to refer back to Chapter 1 and readdress the ideas in Robert Reich's *The Work of Nations* and his study of labor needs in the twenty-first century.

■ With globalization, work will migrate to lowest-cost sources.

■ Routine work will migrate to lower-labor-cost countries; workers who live in North America or other high-labor-cost areas cannot depend on jobs that involve routine work.

■ In-person services cannot be moved overseas, but most such jobs are low-paying, service-oriented jobs that business school graduates will not want.

■ Symbolic-analytic workers will have ample opportunity. Such workers need to learn:

- Abstract thinking (including meta-level thinking)
- How to experiment
- Systems thinking
- Collaboration

■ This class has prepared you for those four attributes.

■ As you write your memo, think about these ideas and focus on knowledge you have gained from this class that will enable you to be a more successful symbolic thinker.

SUGGESTED RESPONSES FOR DISCUSSION QUESTIONS

I think these questions are quite important, and I assign them for substantial credit. They are in many ways, the students' real final exam.

1,2. These exercises reference the reasons given in Chapter 1 that MIS is the most important course in the business curriculum. Students are asked to score themselves. For students who have engaged with the material and worked hard in the course, these should be easy to answer. For those who have not worked very hard, these questions at least ask them to address that fact; perhaps the frank appraisal of their performance will help them in the next term.

3,4,5. These questions are intended to leave the student with a practical memento of this class. I ask the students to share their ideas in class . . . and, assuming the students have taken the assignment seriously, I devote considerable class time to it. I hope that they will learn from each other in this exercise.

WRAP UP

■ The best is yet to come!

■ What that best is, what happens next, will be in large measure up to you!

■ We started this book with a firing and we're ending it, we hope, with a hiring . . . yours!

■ Prosper, do good work, and have fun!

International MIS

Q1 How Does the Global Economy Impact Organizations and Processes?

Businesses compete today in a global market. International business has been sharply increasing since the middle of the twentieth century. After World War II, the Japanese and other Asian economies exploded when those countries began to manufacture and sell goods to the West. The rise of the Japanese auto industry and the semiconductor industry in southeastern Asia greatly expanded international trade. At the same time, the economies of North America and Europe became more closely integrated.

Since then, a number of other factors have caused international business to explode. The fall of the Soviet Union opened the economies of Russia and Eastern Europe to the world market. Even more important, the telecommunications boom during the dot-com heyday caused the world to be encircled many times over by optical fiber that can be used for data and voice communications.

After the dot-com bust, optical fiber was largely underutilized and could be purchased for pennies on the dollar. Plentiful, cheap telecommunications enabled people worldwide to participate in the global economy. Prior to the advent of the Internet, for a young Indian professional to participate in the Western economy he or she had to migrate to the West—a process that was politicized and limited. Today, that same young Indian professional can sell his or her goods or services over the Internet without leaving home. During this same period, the Chinese economy became more open to the world, and it, too, benefits from plentiful, cheap telecommunications.

Columnist and author Thomas Friedman estimates that from 1991 until 2007 some 3 billion people were added to the world economy.[1] Not all of those people speak English, and not all of them are well enough educated (or equipped) to participate in the world economy. But even if just 10 percent are, then 300 million people were added to the English-speaking world economy.

But this discussion has a U.S./North American bias. The strengthening world economy is important in its own right, and not just because of the way that it impacts the United States. As of 2011, auto manufacturing in the European Union (EU) and North America is in the doldrums, but it is booming in the developing

---

[1] Thomas L. Friedman, *The World Is Flat: A Brief History of the Twenty-First Century 3.0* (New York: Farrar, Strauss and Giroux, 2007).

economies of China, India, and Brazil. Economic activity and trade among those nations prosper outside the sphere of the EU and the United States. It remains to be seen whether this activity is strong enough to overcome the consumption slowdown in the developed world, but, in 2011, many EU- and U.S.-based companies find their greatest opportunities outside their national markets.

How Does the Global Economy Change the Competitive Environment?

To understand the impact of globalization, consider each of the elements in Figure ID-1.

The enlarged and Internet-supported world economy has altered every one of the five competitive forces. Suppliers have to reach a wider range of customers, and customers have to consider a wider range of vendors. Suppliers and customers benefit not just from the greater size of the economy, but also by the ease with which businesses can learn of each other using tools such as Google and Bing.

Because of the data available on the Internet, customers can more easily learn of substitutions. The Internet has made it easier for new market entrants, although not in all cases. Amazon.com, Apple, and Google, for example, have garnered such a large market share that it would be difficult for any new entrant to challenge them. Still, in other industries, the global economy facilitates new entrants. Finally, the global economy has intensified rivalry by increasing product and vendor choices and by accelerating the flow of information about price, product, availability, and service.

How Does the Global Economy Change Competitive Strategy?

Today's global economy changes thinking about competitive strategies in two major ways. First, the sheer size and complexity of the global economy means that any organization that chooses a strategy allowing it to compete industry-wide is taking a very big bite! Competing in many different countries, with products localized to the language and culture of those countries, is an enormous and expensive task.

For example, to promote Windows worldwide, Microsoft must produce a version of Windows in dozens of different languages. Even in English, Microsoft produces a U.K. version, a U.S. version, an Australian version, and so forth. The problem for Microsoft is even greater, because different countries use different character sets. In some languages, writing flows from left to right. In other languages, it flows from right to left. When Microsoft set out to sell Windows worldwide, it embarked on an enormous project.

The second major way today's world economy changes competitive strategies is that its size, combined with the Internet, enables unprecedented product differentiation.

Figure ID-1
Organizational Strategy Determines Information Systems

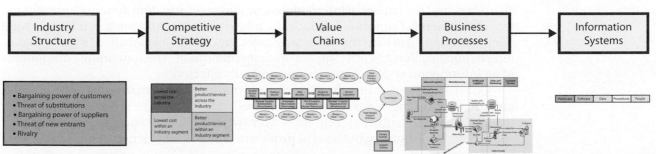

If you choose to produce the world's highest quality and most exotic oatmeal—and if your production costs require you to sell that oatmeal for $350 a pound—your target market might contain only 200 people worldwide. The Internet allows you to find them— and them to find you.

The decision involving a global competitive strategy requires the consideration of these two changing factors.

How Does the Global Economy Change Value Chains and Business Processes?

Because of information systems, any or all of the value chain activities in Figure ID-1 can be performed anywhere in the world. An international company can conduct sales and marketing efforts locally, for every market in which it sells. 3M divisions, for example, sell in the United States with a U.S. sales force, in France with a French sales force, and in Argentina with an Argentinean sales force. Depending on local laws and customs, those sales offices may be owned by 3M, or they may be locally owned entities with which 3M contracts for sales and marketing services. 3M can coordinate all of the sales efforts of these entities using the same CRM system. When 3M managers need to roll up sales totals for a sales projection, they can do so using an integrated, worldwide system.

Manufacturing of a final product is frequently distributed throughout the world. Components of the Boeing 787 are manufactured in Italy, China, England, and numerous other countries and delivered toWashington and South Carolina for final assembly. Each manufacturing facility has its own inbound logistics, manufacturing, and outbound logistics activity, but those activities are linked together via information systems.

For example, Rolls-Royce manufactures an engine and delivers that engine to Boeing via its outbound logistics activity. Boeing receives the engine using its inbound logistics activity. All of this activity is coordinated via shared, interorganizational information systems. Rolls-Royce's CRM is connected with Boeing's supply processes, using techniques such as CRM and enterprise resource planning (ERP). We discuss global supply chains further in Q4.

Because of the abundance of low-cost, well-educated, English-speaking professionals in India, many organizations have chosen to outsource their service and support functions to India. Some accounting functions are outsourced to India as well.

World time differences enable global virtual companies to operate 24/7. Boeing engineers in Los Angeles can develop a design for an engine support strut and send that design to Rolls-Royce in England at the end of their day. The design will be waiting for Rolls-Royce engineers at the start of their day. They review the design, make needed adjustments, and send it back to Boeing in Los Angeles, where the reviewed, adjusted design arrives at the start of the workday in Los Angeles. The ability to work around the clock by moving work into other time zones increases productivity.

Q2 What Are the Characteristics of International IS Components?

To understand the impact of internationalization on information systems, consider the five components. Computer hardware is sold worldwide, and most vendors provide documentation in at least the major languages, so, other than globalized supply chains, internationalization has little impact on that component. The remaining components of an information system, however, are markedly affected.

Consider the user interface for an international information system. Does it include a local-language version of Windows? What about the software application itself? Does an inventory system used worldwide by Boeing suppose that each user speaks English? If so, at what level of proficiency? If not, what languages must the user interface support?

Next, consider the data component. Suppose that the inventory database has a table for parts data and that table contains a column named Remarks. Further suppose Boeing needs to integrate parts data from three different vendors: one in China, one in India, and one in England. What language is to be used for recording remarks? Does someone need to translate all of the remarks into one language? Into three languages?

The human components—procedures and people—are obviously affected by language and culture. As with business processes, information systems procedures need to reflect local cultural values and norms. For systems users, job descriptions and reporting relationships must be appropriate for the setting in which the system is used. We will say more about this in Q5.

What's Required to Localize Software?

The process of making a computer program work in a second language is called **localizing** software. It turns out to be surprisingly hard to do. To localize a document or a Web page, all you need to do is hire a translator to convert your document or page from one language to another. The situation is much more difficult for a computer program, however.

Consider a program you use frequently—say, Microsoft Word—and ask what would need to be done to translate it to a different language. The entire user interface needs to be translated.The menu bar and the commands on the menu bar will need to be translated. It is possible that some of the icons will need to be changed, because some graphic symbols that are harmless in one culture are confusing or offensive in another.

What about an application program like CRM that includes forms, reports, and queries? The labels on each of these will need to be translated. Of course, not all labels translate into words of the same length, and so the forms and reports may need to be redesigned. The questions and prompts for queries, such as "Enter part number for back order," must also be translated.

All of the documentation will need to be translated. That should be just a matter of hiring a translator, except that all of the illustrations in the documentation will need to be redrawn in the second language.

Think, too, about error messages. When someone attempts to order more items than there are in inventory, the application produces an error message. All of those messages will need to be translated. There are other issues as well. Sorting order is one. Spanish uses accents on certain letters, and it turns out that an accented ó will sort after z when you use the computer's default sort ordering. Figure ID-2 summarizes the factors to address when localizing software.

Programming techniques can be used to simplify and reduce the cost of localization. However, those techniques must be used in design, long before any code is written. For example, suppose that when a certain condition occurs, the program is to display

- Translate the user interface, including menu bars and commands.
- Translate, and possibly redesign, labels in forms, reports, and query prompts.
- Translate all documentation and help text.
- Redraw and translate diagrams and examples in help text.
- Translate all error messages.
- Translate text in all message boxes.
- Adjust sorting order for different character set.
- Fix special problems in Asian character sets and in languages that read and write from right to left.

Figure ID-2
Issues to Address When Localizing a Computer Program

the message "Insufficient quantity in stock." If the programmer codes all such messages into the computer program, then, to localize that program, the programmer will have to find every such message in the code and then ask a translator to change that code. A preferred technique is to give every error message a unique identifier and to create a separate error file that contains a list of identifiers and their associated text. Then, when an error occurs, program code uses the identifier to obtain the text of the message to be displayed from the error file. During localization, translators simply translate the file of error messages into the second language.

The bottom line for you, as a future manager, is to understand two points: (1) Localizing computer programs is much more difficult, expensive, and time consuming than translating documents. (2) If a computer program is likely to be localized then plan for that localization from the beginning, during design. In addition, when considering the acquisition of a company in a foreign country, be sure to budget time and expense for the localization of information systems.

What Are the Problems and Issues of Global Databases?

When we discussed CRM and ERP in Chapter 7 you learned the advantage of having all data stored in a single database. In brief, a single database reduces data integrity problems and makes it possible to have an integrated view of the customer or the operations of the organization.

International companies that have a single database must, however, declare a single language for the company. Every Remark or Comment or other text field needs to be in a single language. If not, the advantages of a single database disappear. This is not a problem for companies that commit to a single company language. For example, Thomas Keidel, former CEO of the Mahr Company (www.mahr.com), states, "We standardized on English as the official company language; we use English in our meetings, in our emails, and in other correspondence. We have to do this because we have factories and offices in 20 countries, and it would be impossible to make any decision otherwise. We chose English because it is a language that most business professionals have in common."[2] For a company like this, standardizing on a language for database contents is not a problem.

A single database is not possible, however, for companies that use multiple languages. Such companies often decide to give up on the benefits of a single database to let divisions in different countries use different databases, with data in local languages. For example, an international manufacturer might allow a component manufacturing division in South Korea to have a database in Korean and a final assembly division in Brazil to have a different database in Portuguese. In this scenario, the company needs applications to export and import data among the separated databases.

Besides language, performance is a second issue that confronts global databases. Often, data transmission speeds are too slow to process data from a single geographic location. If so, companies sometimes distribute their database in locations around the world.

Distributed database processing refers to the processing of a single database that resides in multiple locations. If the distributed database contains copies of the same data items, it is called a **replicated database**. If the distributed database does not contain copies of the same data, but rather divides the database into nonoverlapping segments, it is called a **partitioned database**. In most cases, querying either type of distributed database can improve performance without too much development work. However, updating a replicated database so that changes are correctly made to all copies of the data is full of challenges that require highly skilled personnel to solve. Still, companies like Amazon.com, which operates call centers in the United States, India, and Ireland, have invested in applications that are able to successfully update distributed databases, worldwide.

---

[2] Private correspondence with the author, August 2011.

Q3 What Are the Challenges of International Cross-Functional Applications?

As you learned in Chapter 7, functional business processes and applications support particular activities within a single department or business activity. Because the systems operate independently, the organization suffers from islands of automation. Sales and marketing data, for example, are not integrated with operations or manufacturing data.

You learned that many organizations eliminate the problems of information silos by creating cross-functional systems. With international IS, however, such systems may not be worthwhile.

Advantages of Functional Systems

Lack of integration is disadvantageous in many situations, but it has *advantages*, however, for international organizations and international systems. Because an order-processing functional system located in, say, the United States is separate from and independent of the manufacturing systems located in, say, Taiwan, it is unnecessary to accommodate language, business, and cultural differences in a single system. U.S. order-processing systems can operate in English and reflect the practices and culture of the United States. Taiwanese manufacturing information systems can operate in Chinese and reflect the business practices and culture of Taiwan. As long as there is an adequate data interface between the two systems, they can operate independently, sharing data when necessary.

Cross-functional, integrated systems, such as ERP, solve the problems of data isolation by integrating data into a database that provides a comprehensive and organization-wide view. However, as discussed in Q2, that advantage requires that the company standardize on a single language, and most likely, place that database in a single location. Otherwise, separated, functional databases are needed.

Problems of Inherent Processes

Processes inherent in ERP and other applications are even more problematic. Each software product assumes that the software will be used by people filling particular roles and performing their actions in a certain way. ERP vendors justify this standardization by saying that their procedures are based on industry-wide best practices and that the organization will benefit by following these standard processes. That statement may be true, but some inherent processes may conflict with cultural norms. If they do, it will be very difficult for management to convince the employees to follow those inherent processes. Or at least it will be difficult in some cultures to do so.

Differences in language, culture, norms, and expectations compound the difficulties of international process management. Just creating an accurate as-is model is difficult and expensive; developing alternative international processes and evaluating them can be incredibly challenging. With cultural differences, it can be difficult just to determine what criteria should be used for evaluating the alternatives, let alone performing the evaluation.

Because of these challenges, in the future it is likely that international business processes will be developed more like interorganizational business processes. A high-level process will be defined to document the service responsibilities of each international unit. Then SOA standards will be used to connect those services into an integrated, cross-functional, international system. Because of encapsulation, the only obligation of an international unit will be to deliver its defined service. One service can be delivered using procedures based on autocratic management policies, and another can be delivered using procedures based on collaborative management policies. The differences will not matter to an SOA-based crossfunctional system.

Q4 How Do Interorganizational IS Facilitate Global Supply Chain Management?

A **supply chain** is a network of organizations and facilities that transforms raw materials into products delivered to customers. Figure ID-3 shows a generic supply chain. Customers order from retailers, who in turn order from distributors, who in turn order from manufacturers, who in turn order from suppliers. In addition to the organizations shown here, the supply chain also includes transportation companies, warehouses, and inventories and some means for transmitting messages and information among the organizations involved.

Because of disintermediation, not every supply chain has all of these organizations. Dell, for example, sells directly to the customer. Both the distributor and retailer organizations are omitted from its supply chain. In other supply chains, manufacturers sell directly to retailers and omit the distribution level.

The term *chain* is misleading. *Chain* implies that each organization is connected to just one company up the chain (toward the supplier) and down the chain (toward the customer). That is not the case. Instead, at each level an organization can work with many organizations both up and down the supply chain. Thus, a supply chain is a *network*.

To appreciate the international dimension of a supply chain, consider Figure ID-4. Suppose you decide to take up cross-country skiing. You go to REI (either by visiting one of its stores or its Web site) and purchase skis, bindings, boots, and poles. To fill your order, REI removes those items from its inventory of goods. Those goods have been purchased, in turn, from distributor/importers. According to Figure ID-4, REI purchases the skis, bindings, and poles from one distributor/importer and boots from a second. The distributor/importers, in turn, purchase the required items from the manufacturers, which, in turn, buy raw materials from their suppliers.

In this figure, notice the national flags on the suppliers and manufacturers. For example, the pole manufacturer is located in Brazil and imports plastic from China, aluminum from Canada, and fittings from Italy. The poles are then imported to REI in the United States by Importer/Distributor$_1$.

The only source of revenue in a supply chain is the customer. In the REI example, you spend your money on the ski equipment. From that point all the way back up the supply chain to the raw material suppliers, there is no further injection of cash into the system. The money you spend on the ski equipment is passed back up the supply chain as payments for goods or raw materials. Again, the customer is the only source of revenue.

The Importance of Information in the Supply Chain

During the global economic recession that began with the financial crisis of 2008, the focus of many businesses, worldwide, has been to reduce costs. Supply chain costs

Figure ID-3
Supply Chain Relationships

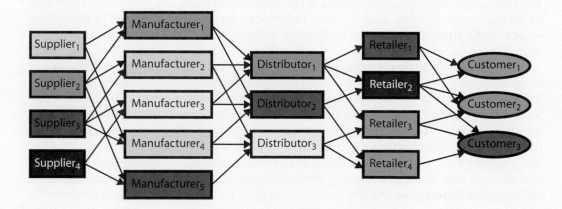

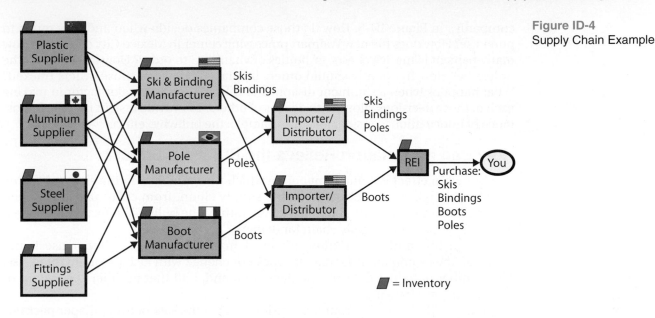

Figure ID-4
Supply Chain Example

have been a primary target for such reductions, especially among companies that have a global supply chain like that in Figure ID-5. For example, Walmart has overhauled its supply chain to eliminate intermediaries, enabling it to buy directly from manufacturers. Walmart's goal is to increase sales and revenues from its private-label goods. At the same time, it also has consolidated purchasing and warehousing into four global merchandizing centers, such as the one near Mexico City that processes goods for emerging markets.[3]

As you'll learn in your production and supply chain courses, many different factors determine the cost and performance of a supply chain. However, information is one of the most important. Consider, for example, inventory management at each of the

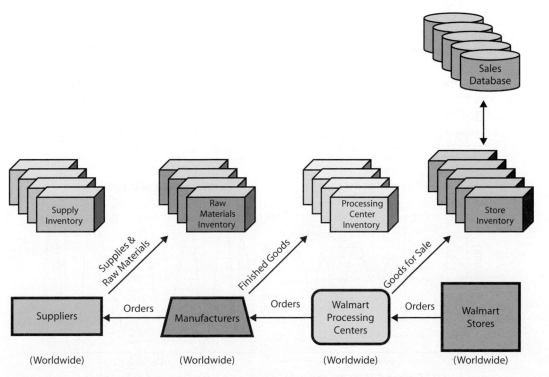

Figure ID-5
Example Walmart Supply Chain

---

[3] Jim Jubak, "China Feels Global Market Pain," *Jubak's Journal*, August 12, 2010, http://articles. moneycentral.msn.com/Investing/JubaksJournal/global-markets-pain-moves-to-china.aspx (accessed August 2010).

companies in Figure ID-5. How do those companies decide when and how much to purchase? How does the new Walmart processing center in Mexico City determine how many pairs of jeans, ice chests, or bottles of vitamin C to order? How large should the orders be? How frequently should orders be placed? How are those orders tracked? What happens when a shipment disappears? Information is a major factor in making each of those decisions, along with dozens of others. To provide insight into the importance of information, consider just one example, the bullwhip effect.

How Can Information Relieve the Bullwhip Effect?

The **bullwhip effect** is a phenomenon in which the variability in the size and timing of orders increases at each stage up the supply chain, from customer to supplier. Figure ID-6 depicts the situation. In a famous study, the bullwhip effect was observed in Procter & Gamble's supply chain for diapers.[4]

Except for random variation, diaper demand is constant. Diaper use is not seasonal; the requirement for diapers does not change with fashion or anything else. The number of babies determines diaper demand, and that number is constant or possibly slowly changing.

Retailers do not order from the distributor with the sale of every diaper package. The retailer waits until the diaper inventory falls below a certain level, called the *reorder quantity*. Then the retailer orders a supply of diapers, perhaps ordering a few more than it expects to sell to ensure that it does not have an outage.

The distributor receives the retailer's orders and follows the same process. It waits until its supply falls below the reorder quantity, and then it reorders from the manufacturer, with perhaps an increased amount to prevent outages. The manufacturer, in turn, uses a similar process with the raw-materials suppliers.

Because of the nature of this process, small changes in demand at the retailer are amplified at each stage of the supply chain. As shown in Figure ID-6, those small changes become quite large variations on the supplier end.

Figure ID-6
The Bullwhip Effect

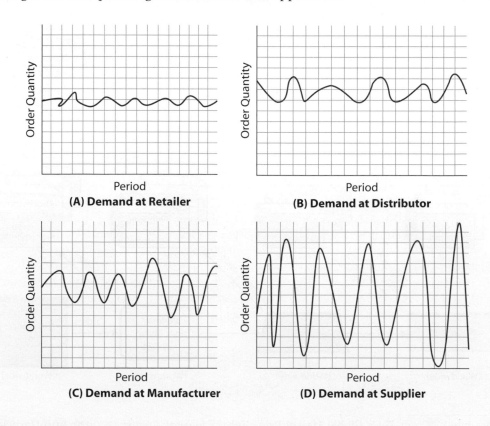

(A) Demand at Retailer

(B) Demand at Distributor

(C) Demand at Manufacturer

(D) Demand at Supplier

[4] Hau L. Lee, V. Padmanabhan, and S. Whang, "The Bullwhip Effect in Supply Chains," *Sloan Management Review*, Spring 1997, pp. 93–102.

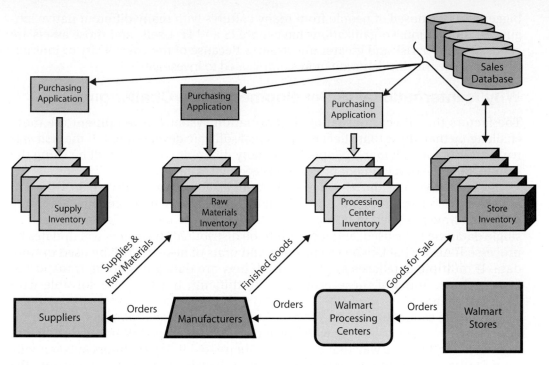

The bullwhip effect is a natural dynamic that occurs because of the multistage nature of the supply chain. It is not related to erratic consumer demand, as the study of diapers indicated. You may have seen a similar effect while driving on the freeway. One car slows down, the car just behind it slows down a bit more abruptly, which causes the third car in line to slow down even more abruptly, and so forth, until the 30th car or so is slamming on its brakes.

The large fluctuations of the bullwhip effect force distributors, manufacturers, and suppliers to carry larger inventories than should be necessary to meet the real consumer demand. Thus, the bullwhip effect reduces the overall profitability of the supply chain. Eliminating or at least reducing the bullwhip effect are particularly important for international supply chains where logistics costs are high and shipping times are long.

One way to eliminate the bullwhip effect is to give all participants in the supply chain access to consumer-demand information from the retailer. Each organization can thus plan its inventory or manufacturing based on the true demand (the demand from the only party that introduces money into the system) and not on the observed demand from the next organization up the supply chain. Of course, an *interorganizational information system* is necessary to share such data.

Consider the Walmart example in Figure ID-7. Along the bottom, each entity orders from the entity up the supply chain (the entity to its left in Figure ID-7). Thus, for example, the Walmart processing centers order finished goods from manufacturers. Without knowledge of the true demand, this supply chain is vulnerable to bullwhip effects. However, if each entity can, via an information system, obtain data about the true demand—that is, the demand from the retail customers who are the source of funds for this chain—then each can anticipate orders. The data about true demand will enable each entity to meet order requirements, while maintaining a smaller inventory.

Q5 What Are the Challenges of International IS Management?

Size and complexity make international IS management challenging. The components of international information systems are larger and more complex. Projects to develop them are larger and more complicated to manage. International IS departments are bigger and composed of people from many cultures with many different native languages. International organizations have more IS and IT assets, and those assets are exposed to more risk and greater uncertainty. Because of the complexity of international law, security incidents are more complicated to investigate.

Why Is International IS Development More Challenging?

The factors that affect international information systems development are more challenging than those that affect international software development. If the *system* is truly international, if many people from many different countries will be using the system, then the development project is exceedingly complicated.

To see why, consider the five components. Running hardware in different countries is not a problem, and localizing software is manageable, assuming programs were designed to be localized. Databases pose more difficulties. First, is a single database to be used, and if so, is it to be distributed? If so, how will updates be processed? Also, what language, currency, and units of measure will be used to store data. If multiple databases are to be used, how are data going to be transported among them. Some of these problems are difficult, but they are solvable with technical solutions.

The same cannot be said for the procedure and people components. An international system is used by people who live and work in cultures that are vastly different from one another. The way that customers are treated in Japan differs substantially from the way that customers are treated in Spain, which differs substantially from the way that customers are treated in the United States. The procedures for using a CRM will be correspondingly different.

Consider the relationship of business processes and information systems as discussed in Chapter 10. Information systems are supposed to facilitate the organization's competitive strategy and support business processes. But what if the underlying business processes differ? Customer support in Japan and customer support in Spain may involve completely different processes and activities.

Even if the purpose and scope can be defined in some unified way, how are requirements to be determined? Again, if the underlying business processes differ, then the specific requirements for the information system will differ. Managing requirements for a system in one culture is difficult, but managing requirements for international systems can be many times more difficult.

There are two responses to such challenges: (1) either define a set of standard business processes or (2) develop alternative versions of the system that support different processes in different countries. Both responses are problematic. The first response requires conversion of the organization to different work processes, and, as you learned in Chapter 7, such conversion can be exceedingly difficult. People resist change, and they will do so with vehemence if the change violates cultural norms.

The second response is easier to implement, but it creates system design challenges. It also means that, in truth, there is not one system, but many.

In spite of the problems, both responses are used. For example, SAP, Oracle, and other ERP vendors define standard business processes via the inherent procedures in their software products. Many organizations attempt to enforce those standard procedures. When it becomes organizationally infeasible to do so, organizations develop exceptions to those inherent procedures and develop programs to handle the exceptions. This choice means high maintenance expense.

What Are the Challenges of International Project Management?

Managing a global IS development project is difficult because of project size and complexity. Requirements are complex, many resources are required, and numerous people are involved. Team members speak different languages, live in different cultures, work in different time zones, and seldom meet face-to-face.

One way to understand how these factors impact global project management is to consider each of the project management knowledge areas as set out by the International Project Management Institute's document, the *PMBOK® Guide* (www.pmi.org/Marketplace/Pages/ProductDetail.aspx?GMProduct=00100035801). Figure ID-8 summarizes challenges for each knowledge area. Project integration is more difficult because international development projects require the complex integration of results from distributed work groups. Also, task dependencies can span teams working in different countries, increasing the difficulty of task management.

The scope and requirements definition for international IS is more difficult, as just discussed. Time management is more difficult because teams in different cultures and countries work at different rates. Some cultures have a 35-hour workweek, and some have a 60-hour workweek. Some cultures expect 6-week vacations, and some expect 2 weeks. Some cultures thrive on efficiency of labor, and others thrive on considerate working relationships. There is no standard rate of development for an international project.

In terms of cost, different countries and cultures pay vastly different labor rates. Using critical path analysis, managers may choose to move a task from one team to another. Doing so, however, may substantially increase costs. Thus, management may choose to accept a delay rather than move work to an available (but more expensive) team. The complex trade-offs that exist between time and cost become even more complex for international projects.

Quality and human resources are also more complicated for international projects. Quality standards vary among countries. The IT industry in some nations, like India, has invested heavily in development techniques that increase program quality. Other countries, like the United States, have been less willing to invest in quality. In any case, the integration of programs of varying quality results in an inconsistent system.

Worker expectations vary among cultures and nations. Compensation, rewards, and worker conditions vary, and these differences can lead to misunderstandings, poor morale, and project delays.

Because of these factors, effective team communication is exceedingly important for international projects, but because of language and culture differences and

Knowledge Areas	Challenge
Project integration	Complex integration of results from distributed work groups. Management of dependencies of tasks from physically and culturally different work groups.
Scope (requirements)	Need to support multiple versions of underlying business processes. Possibly substantial differences in requirements and procedures.
Time	Development rates vary among cultures and countries.
Cost	Cost of development varies widely among countries. Two members performing the same work in different countries may be paid substantially different rates. Moving work among teams may dramatically change costs.
Quality	Quality standards vary among cultures. Different expectations of quality may result in an inconsistent system.
Human resources	Worker expectations differ. Compensation, rewards, work conditions vary widely.
Communications	Geographic, language, and cultural distance among team members impedes effective communication.
Risk	Development risk is higher. Easy to lose control.
Procurement	Complications of international trade.

Figure ID-8
Challenges for International IS Project Management

geographic separation, such communication is difficult. Effective communication is also more expensive. Consider, for example, just the additional expense of maintaining a team portal in three or four languages.

If you consider all of the factors in Figure ID-8, it is easy to understand why project risk is high for international IS development projects. So many things can go wrong. Project integration is complex; requirements are difficult to determine; cost, time, and quality are difficult to manage; worker conditions vary widely; and communication is difficult. Finally, project procurement is complicated by the normal challenges of international commerce.

What Are the Challenges of International IS Management?

Chapter 11 defined the four primary responsibilities of the IS department: plan, operate, develop, and protect information systems and supporting infrastructure. Each of these responsibilities becomes more challenging for international IS organizations.

Regarding planning, the principal task is to align IT and IS resources with the organization's competitive strategy. The task does not change character for international companies; it just becomes more complex and difficult. Multinational organizations and operations are complicated, and the business processes that support their competitive strategies tend also to be complicated. Further, changes in global economic factors can mean dramatic changes in processes and necessitate changes in IS and IT support. Technology adoption can also cause remarkable change. The increasing use of cell phones in developing countries, for example, changes the requirements for local information systems. The price of oil and energy can change international business processes. So planning tasks for international IS are larger and more complex.

Three factors create challenges for international IS operations. First, conducting operations in different countries, cultures, and languages adds complexity. Go to the Web site of any multinational corporation, say www.3m.com or www.dell.com, and you'll be asked to click on the country in which you reside. When you click, you are likely to be directed to a Web server running in some other country. Those Web servers need to be managed consistently, even though they are operated by people living in different cultures and speaking different languages.

The second operational challenge of international IS is the integration of similar, but different, systems. Consider inventory. A multinational corporation might have dozens of different inventory systems in use throughout the world. To enable the movement of goods, many of these systems need to be coordinated and integrated.

Or consider customer support that operates from three different support centers in three different countries. Each support center may have its own information system, but the data among those systems will need to be exported or otherwise shared. If not, then a customer who contacts one center will be unknown to the others.

The third complication for operations is outsourcing. Many organizations have chosen to outsource customer support, training, logistics, and other backroom activities. International outsourcing is particularly advantageous for customer support and other functions that must be operational 24/7. Many companies outsource logistics to UPS, because doing so offers comprehensive, worldwide shipping and logistical support. The organization's information systems usually need to be integrated with outsource vendors' information systems, and this may need to be done for different systems, all over the world.

The fourth IS department responsibility is protecting IS and IT infrastructure. We consider that function next.

How Does the International Dimension Affect Computer Security Risk Management?

Computer security risk management is more difficult and complicated for international information systems. First, IT assets are subject to more threats. Infrastructure will be located at sites all over the world, and those sites differ in the threats to which they are exposed. Some will be subject to political threats, others to the threat of civil unrest, others to terrorists, and still others will be subject to threats of natural disasters of every conceivable type. Place your data center in Kansas, and it's subject to tornados. Place your data center internationally, and it's potentially subject to typhoons/hurricanes, earthquakes, floods, volcanic eruption, or mudslides. And don't forget epidemics that will affect the data center employees.

Second, the likelihood of a threat is more difficult to estimate for international systems. What is the likelihood that the death of Fidel Castro will cause civil unrest and threaten your data center in Havana? How does an organization assess that risk? What is the likelihood that a computer programmer in India will insert a Trojan horse into code that she writes on an outsourcing contract?

In addition to risk, international information systems are subject to far greater uncertainty. Uncertainty reflects the likelihood that something that "we don't know what we don't know" will cause an adverse outcome. Because of the multitudinous cultures, religions, nations, beliefs, political views, and crazy people in the world, uncertainty about risks to IS and IT infrastructure is high. Again, if you place your data center in Kansas, you have some idea of the magnitude of the uncertainty to which you are exposed, even if you don't know exactly what it is. Place a server in a country on every continent of the world, and you have no idea of the potential risks to which they are exposed.

Regarding safeguards, technical and data safeguards do not change for international information systems. Because of greater complexity, more safeguards or more complex ones may be needed, but the technical and data safeguards described in Chapter 12 all work for international systems. Human safeguards are another matter. For example, can an organization depend on the control of separation of duties and authorities in a culture for which graft is an accepted norm? Or, what is the utility of a personal reference in a culture in which it is considered exceedingly rude to talk about someone when they are not present? Because of these differences, human safeguards need to be chosen and evaluated on a culture-by-culture basis.

In short, risk management for both international information systems and IT infrastructure is more complicated, more difficult, and subject to greater uncertainty.

Setting Up Information Systems in Foreign Offices

To illustrate the concepts addressed by this question, suppose that GearUp decides to open an office in Europe. How might it go about developing information systems for that office?

Before answering that question, consider the experience of Thomas Keidel, chairman of the Mahr Group, a midsized, multinational firm headquartered in Germany:

> For all of our foreign offices, we obtain hardware and networking equipment from the local economy. Once we have purchased or leased a facility, local vendors supply and set up hardware, a local area network, and access to the Internet in accordance with our specifications. Then, we bring in our own IT professionals from Germany to install software. As much as possible, we use the same software, worldwide. We use the same accounting software and chart of accounts, and we use the same business processes, worldwide. Twice a year we conduct internal audits to verify compliance.
>
> One difference we do allow, however, is to conduct transactions in local currency. We assume the risk of currency fluctuations at headquarters, and if there is any currency hedging to do, we do it at headquarters. We want our foreign offices focused on sales and manufacturing and not on currency valuation opportunities and risks.[5]

Because it is a manufacturer, Mahr operates an ERP system, for which it maintains a centralized database in Germany that is accessed via its own leased communication lines, worldwide. It also requires that the same computer-assisted-design (CAD) software be used, worldwide. As Keidel notes, "That way we can exchange designs among all of our facilities without problems."

Because GearUp is a smaller, nonmanufacturing company, it does not need to consider ERP or CAD software. However, it would benefit from using Mahr's strategy: Obtain

---

[5] Private correspondence with the author, August 2011.

hardware and networks from local vendors and then install, as much as possible, software from its U.S. office.

For sales events, GearUp will need to provide advertising copy in multiple languages. Hence, it will need to alter the software it uses for setting up events and also change the basic Web design to serve event pages in different languages. To minimize software support costs, GearUp would probably develop the new multilanguage event software for Europe and then replace the U.S. event software with the European version. This would also enable GearUp to conduct North American events in English, Spanish, and Canadian French.

To provide acceptable user response time, GearUp would likely host sales events on cloud servers in Europe to avoid the slow response time of U.S. servers. Because of its size and the relative simplicity of its business model, GearUp will likely have a single, centralized database for its internal operations. If it is not already doing so, GearUp would probably use SAAS vendors for human resources and possibly for accounting.

Like Mahr, GearUp will most likely follow the same business processes in all of its offices. It is also likely to declare English as the standard language for the company; doing so will enable it to record internal systems data in English. Again, however, Web pages for sales events will need to be created in multiple languages.

If GearUp uses this model, staying with consistent software and processes as much as possible, setting up information systems should not be too difficult. Given its business model, GearUp will likely spend far more time and dollars creating vendor relationships than it will setting up its information systems.

Active Review

Use this Active Review to verify that you understand the ideas and concepts that answer the study questions.

Q1 How does the global economy impact organizations and processes?

Describe how the global economy has changed since the mid-twentieth century. Explain how the dot-com bust influenced the global economy and changed the number of workers worldwide. Summarize opportunities outside of the EU and North America. Summarize the ways in which today's global economy influences the five competitive forces. Explain how the global economy changes the way organizations assess industry structure. How does the global economy change competitive strategy? How do global information systems benefit the value chain? Using Figure 3-6 (page 79) as a guide, explain how each primary value chain activity can be performed anywhere in the world.

Q2 What are the characteristics of international IS components?

Explain how internationalization impacts the five components of an IS. What does it mean to localize software?

Summarize the work required to localize a computer program. In your own words, explain why it is better to design a program to be localized rather than attempt to adapt an existing single-language program to a second language. Explain the problems of having a single database for an international IS. Define *distributed database, replicated database,* and *partitioned database.* State a source of problems for processing replicated databases.

Q3 What are the challenges of international cross-functional applications?

Summarize the advantages of functional systems for international companies. Summarize the issues of inherent processes for multinational ERP. Explain how SOA services could be used to address the problems of international cross-functional applications.

Q4 How do interorganizational IS facilitate global supply chain management?

Define *supply chain,* and explain why the term *chain* is misleading. Under what circumstances are not all of the organizations in Figure ID-4 not part of the supply chain. Name the only source of revenue in a supply chain. Explain how Walmart is attempting to reduce supply costs. Describe the bullwhip effect, and explain why it adds costs to a supply chain. Explain how the system shown in Figure ID-7 can eliminate the bullwhip effect.

Q5 What are the challenges of international IS management?

State the two characteristics that make international IS management challenging.

Explain the difference between international systems development and international software development.

Using the five-component framework, explain why international systems development is more difficult. Give an example of one complication for each knowledge area in Figure ID-8. State the four responsibilities for IS departments. Explain how each of these responsibilities is more challenging for international IS organizations. Describe three factors that create challenges for international IS operations. Explain why international IT assets are subject to more threats. Give three examples. Explain why the likelihood of international threats is more difficult to determine. Describe uncertainty, and explain why it is higher for international IS organizations.

Summarize the strategy that Mahr uses when creating IS infrastructure in foreign offices. Explain how GearUp could use that same strategy. Describe any differences.

Key Terms and Concepts

Bullwhip effect   460
Distributed database processing   456

Localizing   455
Partitioned database   456

Replicated database   456
Supply chain   458

Using Your Knowledge

1. Suppose that you are about to have a job interview with a multinational company, such as 3M, Starbucks, or Coca-Cola. Further suppose that you wish to demonstrate an awareness of the changes for international commerce that the Internet and modern information technology have made. Using the information in Q1, create a list of three questions that you could ask the interviewer regarding the company's use of IT in its international business.

2. Suppose you work for a business that has $100 million in annual sales that is contemplating acquiring a company in Mexico. Assume you are a junior member of a team that is analyzing the desirability of this acquisition. Your boss, who is not technically savvy, has asked you to prepare a summary of the issues that she should be aware of in the merging of information systems of the two companies. She wants your summary to include a list of questions that she should ask of both your IS department and the IS department personnel in the propsective acquisition. Prepare that summary.

3. Using the data in this module as well as in Chapter 7, summarize the strengths and weaknesses of functional systems, CRM, and ERP. How do the advantages and disadvantages of each change in an international

setting? For your answer, create a table with strength and weakness columns, and with one row for each of the four systems types.

4. Suppose that you are a junior member of a newly formed, international team that will meet regularly for the next year. You have team members in Europe, North and South America, Japan, Hong Kong, Singapore, Australia, and India. All of your team meetings will be virtual; some will be synchronous, but many will be asynchronous. The team leader has asked you to help prepare the environment for these meetings. In particular, he asked you to summarize the challenges that will occur in conducting these team meetings. He also wants you to assess the strengths and weaknesses of the following collaboration tools: email, Google Docs, Google +, Windows Live SkyDrive, Microsoft SharePoint, WebEx, and Microsoft Office 365. Use Figure ID-8, the discussion in Q5, and information in Chapter 2 to prepare your assessment.

5. Assume you are Lucas at GearUp. Using your knowledge from Q5, write a one-page memo to Kelly explaining what needs to be done to set up information systems in a new European office. State and justify any assumptions you make.

Application Exercises

All exercise files can be found on the following web site: *www.pearsonhighered.com/kroenke*.

Chapter 1

1-1. The spreadsheet in Microsoft Excel file **Ch01Ex01_U5e.xlsx** contains records of employee activity on special projects. Open this workbook and examine the data that you find in the three spreadsheets it contains. Assess the accuracy, relevancy, and sufficiency of this data to the following people and problems.

   a. You manage the Denver plant, and you want to know how much time your employees are spending on special projects.
   b. You manage the Reno plant, and you want to know how much time your employees are spending on special projects.
   c. You manage the Quota Computation project in Chicago, and you want to know how much time your employees have spent on that project.
   d. You manage the Quota Computation project for all three plants, and you want to know the total time employees have spent on your project.
   e. You manage the Quota Computation project for all three plants, and you want to know the total labor cost for all employees on your project.
   f. You manage the Quota Computation project for all three plants, and you want to know how the labor-hour total for your project compares to the labor-hour totals for the other special projects.
   g. What conclusions can you make from this exercise?

1-2. The database in the Microsoft Access file **Ch01Ex02_U5e.accdb** contains the same records of employee activity on special projects as in Application Exercise 1-1. Before proceeding, open that database and view the records in the Employee Hours table.

   a. Seven queries have been created that process this data in different ways. Using the criteria of accuracy, relevancy, and sufficiency, select the single query that is most appropriate for the information requirements in Application Exercise 1-1, parts a–f. If no query meets the need, explain why.
   b. What conclusions can you make from this exercise?
   c. Comparing your experiences on these two projects, what are the advantages and disadvantages of spreadsheets and databases?

Chapter 2

2-1. Suppose that you have been asked to assist in the managerial decision about how much to increase pay in the next year. Assume you are given a list of the departments in your company, along with the average salary for employees in that department for major companies in your industry. Additionally, you are given the names and salaries of 10 people in each of three departments in your company.

   Assume you have been asked to create a spreadsheet that shows the names of the 10 employees in each department, their current salary, the difference between their current salary and the industry average salary for their department, and the percent their salary would need to be increased to meet the industry average. Your spreadsheet should also compute the average increase needed to meet the industry average for each department and the average increase, company-wide, to meet industry averages.

   a. Use the data in the file **Ch02Ex01_U5e.docx** and create the spreadsheet.
   b. How can you use this analysis to contribute to the employee salary decision? Based on this data, what conclusions can you make?
   c. Suppose other team members want to use your spreadsheet. Name three ways you can share it with them and describe the advantages and disadvantages of each.

2-2. Suppose that you have been asked to assist in the managerial decision about how much to increase pay in the next year. Specifically, you are tasked to determine if there are significant salary differences among departments in your company.

You are given an Access database with a table of employee data with the following structure:

EMPLOYEE (Name, Department, Specialty, Salary)

where *Name* is the name of an employee who works in a department, *Department* is the department name, *Specialty* is the name of the employee's primary skill, and *Salary* is the employee's current salary. Assume that no two employees have the same name. You have been asked to answer the following queries:

(1) List the names, department, and salary of all employees earning more than $100,000.
(2) List the names and specialties of all employees in the Marketing department.
(3) Compute the average, maximum, and minimum salary of employees in your company.
(4) Compute the average, minimum, and maximum salary of employees in the Marketing department.
(5) Compute the average, minimum, and maximum salary of employees in the Information Systems department.
(6) *Extra credit:* Compute the average salary for employees in every department. Use *Group By*.

a. Design and run Access queries to obtain the answers to these questions, using the data in the file **Ch02Ex02_U5e.accdb**.
b. Explain how the data in your answer contributes to the salary increase decision.
c. Suppose other team members want to use your Access application. Name three ways you can share it with them, and describe the advantages and disadvantages of each.

Chapter 3

3-1. Figure AE-1 shows an Excel spreadsheet that the resort bicycle rental business uses to value and analyze its bicycle inventory. Examine this figure to understand the meaning of the data. Now use Excel to create a similar spreadsheet. Note the following:

- The top heading is in 20-point Calibri font. It is centered in the spreadsheet. Cells A1 through H1 have been merged.

Resort Bicycle Rental							
Bicycle Inventory Valuation							
Monday, September 26, 2011							
Make of Bike	Bike Cost	Number on Hand	Cost of Current Inventory	Number of Rentals	Total Rental Revenue	Revenue per Bike	Revenue as Percent of Cost of Inventory
Wonder Bike	$325	12	$3,900	85	$6,375	$531	163.5%
Wonder Bike II	$385	4	$1,540	34	$4,570	$1,143	296.8%
Wonder Bike Supreme	$475	8	$3,800	44	$5,200	$650	136.8%
LiteLift Pro	$655	8	$5,240	25	$2,480	$310	47.3%
LiteLift Ladies	$655	4	$2,620	40	$6,710	$1,678	256.1%
LiteLift Racer	$795	3	$2,385	37	$5,900	$1,967	247.4%

Figure AE-1

Source: Microsoft product screenshot reprinted with permission from Microsoft Corporation.

- The second heading, Bicycle Inventory Valuation, is in 18-point Calibri, italics. It is centered in Cells A2 through H2, which have been merged.
- The column headings are set in 11-point Calibri, bold. They are centered in their cells, and the text wraps in the cells.

a. Make the first two rows of your spreadsheet similar to that in Figure AE-1. Choose your own colors for background and type, however.

b. Place the current date so that it is centered in cells C3, C4, and C5, which must be merged.

c. Outline the cells as shown in the figure.

d. Figure AE-1 uses the following formulas:

Cost of Current Inventory = Bike Cost × Number on Hand

Revenue per Bike = Rental Revenue × Number on Hand

Revenue as a Percent of Cost of Inventory = Total Rental Revenue × Cost of Current Inventory

Please use these formulas in your spreadsheet, as shown in Figure AE-1.

e. Format the cells in the columns, as shown.

f. Give three examples of decisions that management of the bike rental agency might make from this data.

g. What other calculation could you make from this data that would be useful to the bike rental management? Create a second version of this spreadsheet in your worksheet document that has this calculation.

3-2.   In this exercise, you will learn how to create a query based on data that a user enters and how to use that query to create a data entry form.

a. Download the Microsoft Access file **Ch03Ex02_U5e.accdb**. Open the file and familiarize yourself with the data in the Customer table.

b. Click *Create* in the Access ribbon. On the far right, select *Query Design*. Select the Customer table as the basis for the query. Drag Customer Name, Customer Email, Date Of Last Rental, Bike Last Rented, Total Number Of Rentals, and Total Rental Revenue into the columns of the query results pane (the table at the bottom of the query design window).

c. In the CustomerName column, in the row labeled Criteria, place the following text:

[Enter Name of Customer:]

Type this exactly as shown, including the square brackets. This notation tells Access to ask you for a customer name to query.

d. In the ribbon, click the red exclamation mark labeled *Run*. Access will display a dialog box with the text "Enter Name of Customer:" (the text you entered in the query Criteria row). Enter the value *Scott, Rex* and click OK.

e. Save your query with the name *Parameter Query.*

f. Click the Home tab on the ribbon and click the Design View (upper left-hand button on the Home ribbon). Replace the text in the Criteria column of the CustomerName column with the following text. Type it exactly as shown:

Like "*" & [Enter part of Customer Name to search by:] & "*"

g. Run the query by clicking Run in the ribbon. Enter *Scott* when prompted *Enter part of Customer Name to search by*. Notice that the two customers who have the name Scott are displayed. If you have any problems, ensure that you have typed the phrase above *exactly* as shown into the Criteria row of the CustomerName column of your query.

h. Save your query again under the name *Parameter Query.* Close the query window.

i. Click *Create* in the Access ribbon. Under the Forms group, select the down arrow to the right of More Forms. Choose *Form Wizard*. In the dialog that opens, in the Tables/Queries box, click the down arrow. Select *Parameter*

Query. Click the double chevron (>>) symbol and all of the columns in the query will move to the Selected Fields area.

j. Click *Next* three times. In the box under *What title do you want for your form?* enter *Customer Query Form* and click *Finish*.

k. Enter *Scott* in the dialog box that appears. Access will open a form with the values for Scott, Rex. At the bottom of the form, click the right-facing arrow and the data for Scott, Bryan will appear.

l. Close the form. Select *Object Type* and *Forms* in the Access Navigation Pane. Double-click the Customer Query Form and enter the value *James*. Access will display data for all six customers having the value James in their name.

Chapter 4

4-1. Read the Collaboration Exercise for Chapter 4, page 136. Create an Excel spreadsheet to compute the cost of new computers for the $80,000 problem. Use the spreadsheet in Figure AE-2 as an example.

Construct your spreadsheet so that you can change prices, charges, and job title employee count and Excel will update the Total Cost for Category as well as Total Cost. As stated in the note in the spreadsheet, the costs shown here are only examples, as is the choice of computer for the manager (you).

4-2. Sometimes you will have data in one Office application and want to move it to another Office application without rekeying it. Often this occurs when data was created for one purpose but then is used for a second purpose. For example, Figure AE-3 presents a portion of an Excel spreadsheet that shows the assignment of computers to employees. Lucas, at GearUp, might use such a spreadsheet to track who has which equipment.

Suppose that you (or Lucas) want to use this data to help you assess how to upgrade computers. Let's say, for example, that you want to upgrade all of the computers' operating systems to Windows 7. Furthermore, you want to first upgrade the computers that most need upgrading, but suppose you have a limited budget. To address this situation, you would like to query the data in Figure AE-3, find all computers that do not have Windows 7, and then select those with slower CPUs or smaller memory as candidates for upgrading. To do this, you need to move the data from Excel into Access.

	A	B	C	D	E	F	G
1			New Hardware & Software Cost Calculator				
2							
3							
4		Laptop	Desktop		Note for teams answering the $80,000		
5	Price of Class A Computer	$1,500	$1,000		collaboration project: Prices shown are		
6	Price of Class B Computer	$2,000	$1,500		just examples. Actual prices will likely be		
7	Price of Class C Computer	$2,500	$2,000		different. Also, the choice of Laptop B for		
8					the manager is only for example. Another		
9	Windows 7 Software Charge	$75	$75		choice may make more sense.		
10	Office 2010 Software Charge	$100	$100				
11	Network and Server Charge	$1,200	$1,200				
12							
13	Total software:	$1,375	$1,375				
14							
15	Job Title	Number of Employees	Computer System Required	Computer Type	Hardware and Software Cost	Total Cost for Category	
16	Product manager	8	B	Laptop	$3,375	$27,000	
17	Telesales	12	A	Desktop	$2,375	$28,500	
18	Department Admin	2	A	Desktop	$2,375	$4,750	
19	Marketing Communications Manager	4	B	Laptop	$3,375	$13,500	
20			C (desktop)	Both, a desktop and	$3,375	$13,500	
21	Marketing Analyst	4	B (laptop)	laptop for each analyst	$3,375	$13,500	
22	Marketing Programs Manager	6	B	Desktop	$2,875	$17,250	
23	Manager (You)	1	B	Laptop	$3,375	$3,375	
24							
25	Total Cost:					$121,375	

Figure AE-2
New-Hardware Cost Calculator

Source: Microsoft product screenshot reprinted with permission from Microsoft Corporation.

Figure AE-3
Sample Excel Data for Import

Source: Microsoft product screenshot reprinted
with permission from Microsoft Corporation.

	A	B	C	D	E	F	G	H
1	EmpLastName	EmpFirstName	Plant	Computer Brand	CPU (GHz)	Memory (GB)	Disk (GB)	OS
2	Casimiro	Amanda	Reno	Dell	1	1	120	Vista
3	McGovern	Adrian	Reno	Dell	1.2	1.512	100	XP
4	Menstell	Lori Lee	Reno	HP	1.8	2	250	XP
5	Jefferies	David	Reno	Dell	3	2	250	Vista
6	Nurul	Nicole	Reno	HP	2	2	120	Vista
7	Garrett	James	Reno	HP	2	3	120	XP
8	Austin	James	Reno	Dell	1	1	80	XP
9	Redmond	Louise	Reno	Lenova	0.5	0.512	40	Win 2000
10	Daniel	James	Reno	IBM	0.5	0.512	30	Win 2000
11								
12		Primary		James Austin				

Once you have analyzed the data and determined the computers to upgrade, you want to produce a report. In that case, you may want to move the data from Access back to Excel, or perhaps into Word. In this exercise, you will learn how to perform these tasks.

a. To begin, download the Excel file **Ch04Ex02_U5e.xlsx** into one of your directories. We will import the data in this file into Access, but before we do so familiarize yourself with the data by opening it in Excel. Notice that there are three worksheets in this workbook. Close the Excel file.

b. Create a blank Access database. Name the database *Ch04Ex02_Answer*. Place it in some directory; it may be the same directory into which you have placed the Excel file, but it need not be. Close the default table that Access creates and delete it.

c. Now, we will import the data from the three worksheets in the Excel file **Ch04Ex02_U5e.xlsx** into a single table in your Access database. In the ribbon, select *External Data* and *Import from Excel*. Start the import. For the first worksheet (Denver), you should select *Import the source data into a new table in the current database*. Be sure to click *First Row Contains Column Headings* when Access presents your data. You can use the default Field types and let Access add the primary key. Name your table *Employees* and click *Finish*. There is no need to save your import script.

For the Miami and Boston worksheets, again click *External Data, Import Excel*, but this time select *Append a copy of the records to the table Employees*. Import all data.

d. Open the *Employee* table and examine the data. Notice that Access has erroneously imported a blank line and the *Primary Contact* data into rows at the end of each data set. This data is not part of the employee records, and you should delete it (in three places—once for each worksheet). The *Employee* table should have a total of 40 records.

e. Now, create a parameterized query on this data. Place all of the columns except *ID* into the query. In the *OS* column, set the criteria to select rows for which the value is not *Windows 7*. In the *CPU* (GHz) column, enter the criterion: <=[Enter cutoff value for CPU] and in the *Memory* (GB) column, enter the criterion: <=[Enter cutoff value for Memory]. Test your query. For example, run your query and enter a value of *2* for both CPU and memory. Verify that the correct rows are produced.

f. Use your query to find values of CPU and memory that give you as close to a maximum of 15 computers to upgrade as possible.

g. When you have found values of CPU and memory that give you 15, or nearly 15, computers to upgrade, leave your query open. Now, click *External data, Word*, and create a Word document that contains the results of your query. Adjust the column widths of the created table so that it fits on the page. Write a memo around this table explaining that these are the computers that you believe should be upgraded.

4-3. Assume you have been asked to create a spreadsheet to help make a buy-versus-lease decision for the servers on your organization's Web farm. Assume that you are considering the servers for a 5-year period, but you do not know exactly how many servers you will need. Initially, you know you will need 5 servers, but you might need as many as 50, depending on the success of your organization's e-commerce activity.

a. For the buy-alternative calculations, set up your spreadsheet so that you can enter the base price of the server hardware, the price of all software, and a maintenance expense that is some percentage of the hardware price. Assume that the percent you enter covers both hardware and software maintenance. Also assume that each server has a 3-year life, after which it has no value. Assume straight-line depreciation for computers used less than 3 years, and that at the end of the 5 years you can sell the computers you have used for less than 3 years for their depreciated value. Also assume that your organization pays 2 percent interest on capital expenses. Assume the servers cost $5,000 each, and the needed software costs $750. Assume that the maintenance expense varies from 2 to 7 percent.

b. For the lease-alternative calculations, assume that the leasing vendor will lease the same computer hardware as you can purchase. The lease includes all the software you need as well as all maintenance. Set up your spreadsheet so that you can enter various lease costs, which vary according to the number of years of the lease (1, 2, or 3). Assume the cost of a 3-year lease is $285 per machine per month, a 2-year lease is $335 per machine per month, and a 1-year lease is $415 per machine per month. Also, the lessor offers a 5 percent discount if you lease from 20 to 30 computers and a 10 percent discount if you lease from 31 to 50 computers.

c. Using your spreadsheet, compare the costs of buy versus lease under the following situations. (Assume you either buy or lease. You cannot lease some and buy some.) Make assumptions as necessary and state those assumptions.

    (1) Your organization requires 20 servers for 5 years.

    (2) Your organization requires 20 servers for the first 2 years and 40 servers for the next 3 years.

    (3) Your organization requires 20 servers for the first 2 years, 40 servers for the next 2 years, and 50 servers for the last year.

    (4) Your organization requires 10 servers the first year, 20 servers the second year, 30 servers the third year, 40 servers the fourth year, and 50 servers the last year.

    (5) For the previous case, does the cheaper alternative change if the cost of the servers is $4,000? If it is $8,000?

Chapter 5

5-1. In some cases, users want to use Access and Excel together. They process relational data with Access, import some of the data into Excel, and use Excel's tools for creating professional-looking charts and graphs. You will do exactly that in this exercise.

Figure AE-4
Data Displayed in Pie-Chart
Format

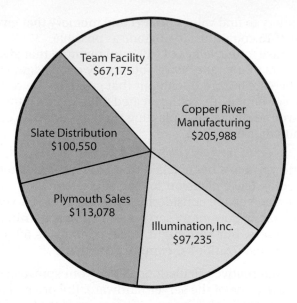

Download the Access file **Ch05Ex01_U5e.accdb**. Open the database and select *Database Tools/Relationships*. As you can see, there are three tables: *Product*, *VendorProductInventory*, and *Vendor*. Open each table individually to familiarize yourself with the data.

For this problem, we will define *InventoryCost* as the product of *IndustryStandardCost* and *QuantityOnHand*. The query *InventoryCost* computes these values for every item in inventory for every vendor. Open that query and view the data to be certain you understand this computation. Open the other queries as well so that you understand the data they produce.

a. Sum this data by vendor and display it in a pie chart like that shown in Figure AE-4 (your totals will be different than those shown). Proceed as follows:

   (1) Open Excel and create a new spreadsheet.
   (2) Click *Data* on the ribbon and select *Access* in the *Get External Data* ribbon category.
   (3) Navigate to the location in which you have stored the Access file **Ch05Ex01_U5e.accdb**.
   (4) Select the query that contains the data you need for this pie chart.
   (5) Import the data into a table.
   (6) Format the appropriate data as currency.
   (7) Select the range that contains the data, press the Function key, and proceed from there to create the pie chart. Name the data and pie chart worksheets appropriately.

b. Follow a similar procedure to create the bar chart shown in Figure AE-5. Place the data and the chart in separate worksheets and name them appropriately.

5-2. Reread the Guide on page 166. Suppose you are given the task of converting the salesperson's data into a database. Because his data is so poorly structured, it will be a challenge, as you will see.

a. Download the Excel file named **Ch05Ex02_U5e.xlsx**. This spreadsheet contains data that fits the salesperson's description in the Guide. Open the spreadsheet and view the data.

b. Download the Access file with the same name, **Ch05Ex02_U5e.accdb**. Open the database, select *Database Tools*, and click *Relationships*. Examine the four tables and their relationships.

c. Somehow, you have to transform the data in the spreadsheet into the table structure in the database. Because so little discipline was shown when creating the

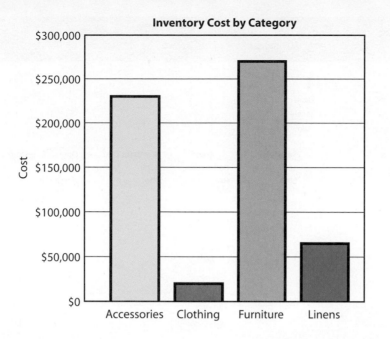

Inventory Cost by Category

spreadsheet, this will be a labor-intensive task. To begin, import the spreadsheet data into a new table in the database; call that table *Sheet1* or some other name.

d. Copy the *Name* data in *Sheet1* onto the clipboard. Then, open the *Customer* table and paste the column of name data into that table.

e. Unfortunately, the task becomes messy at this point. You can copy the *Car Interests* column into *Make or Model of Auto*, but then you will need to straighten out the values by hand. Phone numbers will need to be copied one at a time.

f. Open the *Customer* form and manually add any remaining data from the spreadsheet into each customer record. Connect the customer to his or her auto interests.

g. The data in the finished database has much more structure than that in the spreadsheet. Explain why that is both an advantage and a disadvantage. Under what circumstances is the database more appropriate? Less appropriate?

5-3.   In this exercise, you will create a two-table database, define relationships, create a form and a report, and use them to enter data and view results.

a. Download the Excel file **Ch05Ex03_U5e.xlsx**. Open the spreadsheet and review the data in the *Employee* and *Computer* worksheets.

b. Create a new Access database with the name *Ch05Ex03_Solution*. Close the table that Access automatically creates and delete it.

c. Import the data from the Excel spreadsheet into your database. Import the *Employee* worksheet into a table named *Employee*. Be sure to check *First Row Contains Column Headings*. Select *Choose my own primary key* and use the ID field as that key.

d. Import the *Computer* worksheet into a table named *Computer*. Check *First Row Contains Column Headings*, but let Access create the primary key.

e. Open the relationships window and add both *Employee* and *Computer* to the design space. Drag ID from *Employee* and drop it on *EmployeeID* in *Computer*. Check *Enforce Referential Integrity* and the two checkmarks below. Ensure you know what these actions mean.

f. Open the Form Wizard dialog box (under *Create, More Forms*) and add all of the columns for each of your tables to your form. Select *View your data by Customer*. Title your form *Employee* and your subform *Computer*.

g. Open the *Computer* subform and delete *EmployeeID* and *ComputerID*. These values are maintained by Access, and it is just a distraction to keep them. Your form should appear like the one shown in Figure AE-6.

Figure AE-6
Employee Computer
Assignment Form

Source: Microsoft product screenshot reprinted with permission from Microsoft Corporation.

Employee

ID	2
First Name	Jane
Last Name	Ashley
Department	Mkt

Computer

Serial Number ▾	Brand ▾	Purchase Cost ▾	Operating System ▾
100	Dell	$1,750	Vista
800	HP	$750	Windows XP
*			

Record: ◄ ◄ 1 of 2 ► ►I ►⊞ ⟐ No Filter Search

Record: ◄ ◄ 1 of 6 ► ►I ►⊞ ⟐ No Filter Search

h. Use your form to add two new computers to *Jane Ashley*. Both computers are Dells, and both use Vista; one costs $750, and the second costs $1,400.

i. Delete the Lenovo computer for Rex Scott.

j. Use the Report Wizard (under *Create*) to create a report having all data from both the *Employee* and *Computer* tables. Play with the report design until you find a design you like. Correct the label alignment if you need to.

Chapter 6

6-1. Numerous Web sites are available that will test your Internet data communications speed. You can find one good one at www.speakeasy.net/ speedtest/. (If that site is no longer active, Google or Bing "What is my Internet speed?" to find another speed-testing site. Use it.)

a. While connected to your university's network, go to Speakeasy and test your speed against servers in Seattle, New York City, and Atlanta. Compute your average upload and download speeds. Compare your speed to the speeds listed in Figure 6-3.

b. Go home, or to a public wireless site, and run the Speakeasy test again. Compute your average upload and download speeds. Compare your speed to those listed in Figure 6-3. If you are performing this test at home, are you getting the performance you are paying for?

c. Contact a friend or relative in another state. Ask him or her to run the Speakeasy test against those same three cities.

d. Compare the results in parts a–c. What conclusion, if any, can you make from these tests?

6-2. Suppose you work for a company that installs computer networks. Assume that you have been given the task of creating spreadsheets to generate cost estimates.

a. Create a spreadsheet to estimate hardware costs. Assume that the user of the spreadsheet will enter the number of pieces of equipment and the standard cost for each type of equipment. Assume that the networks can include the following components: NIC cards; WNIC cards; wireless access points; switches of two types, one faster, one slower, at two different prices; and routers. Also assume that the company will use both UTP and optical fiber cable and that prices for cable are stated as per foot. Use the network in Figure 6-2 (page 179) as an example.

b. Modify your spreadsheet to include labor costs. Assume there is a fixed cost for the installation of each type of equipment and a per foot cost for the installation of cable.

c. Give an example of how you might use this spreadsheet for planning network installations. Explain how you could adapt this spreadsheet for project tracking and billing purposes.

Chapter 7

7-1.   Assume that you have been hired to develop an Access database for a portion of the Fox Lake Country Club Enterprise Reservation System shown in Figure 7-9. You have been given the following design for implementation:

FACILITY   (FacilityID, FacilityName, Description, StandardRentalFee)
RESERVATION   ReservationNumber, *FacilityID,* Date, StartTime, EndTime)

Where FacilityID and ReservationNumber are AutoNumber primary keys. RESERVATION.FacilityID is a foreign key to FACILITY. Use the appropriate data types for the other columns.

a. Create these tables in Access.
b. Create the appropriate relationship in Access.
c. Import the data from the file **Ch07Ex01_U5e.txt** into the FACILITY table.
d. Create a reservation form for creating and viewing specific reservations.
e. Create a parameterized query for finding a reservation by value of Reservation-Number.
f. Create a report that shows all the reservations for all facilities.
g. Create a parameterized report that shows all of the reservations for a particular date.

7-2.   Suppose your manager asks you to create a spreadsheet to compute a production schedule. Your schedule should stipulate a production quantity for seven products that is based on sales projections made by three regional managers at your company's three sales regions.

a. Create a separate worksheet for each sales region. Use the data in the Word file **Ch07Ex02_U5e.docx**. This file contains each manager's monthly sales projections for the past year, actual sales results for those same months, and projections for sales for each month in the coming quarter.
b. Create a separate worksheet for each manager's data. Import the data from Word into Excel.
c. On each of the worksheets, use the data from the prior four quarters to compute the discrepancy between the actual sales and the sale projections. This discrepancy can be computed in several ways: You could calculate an overall average, or you could calculate an average per quarter or per month. You could also weight recent discrepancies more heavily than earlier ones. Choose a method that you think is most appropriate. Explain why you chose the method you did.
d. Modify your worksheets to use the discrepancy factors to compute an adjusted forecast for the coming quarter. Thus, each of your spreadsheets will show the raw forecast and the adjusted forecast for each month in the coming quarter.
e. Create a fourth worksheet that totals sales projections for all of the regions. Show both the unadjusted forecast and the adjusted forecast for each region and for the company overall. Show month and quarter totals.
f. Create a bar graph showing total monthly production. Display the unadjusted and adjusted forecasts using different colored bars.

Figure AE-7
Bill of Materials Example

Bill of Materials					

Ajax Toy Manufacturing
Bill of Materials

PartNumber	Level	Description
1	1	Child's Red Wagon

Parts Contained

	PartNumber	Level	Description	QuantityRequired	PartOf
⊟	2	2	Handle Bar	1	1

	PartNumber	Level	Descrption	QuantityRequir	PartOf
	3	3	Bar Grip	1	2
	4	3	Bar Tang	1	2
	14	3	Bar Stock	1	2
*	(New)			0	2

	PartNumber	Level	Description	QuantityRequired	PartOf
⊟	5	2	Wagon Body, Metal	1	1

	PartNumber	Level	Descrption	QuantityRequir	PartOf
*	(New)			0	5

	PartNumber	Level	Description	QuantityRequired	PartOf
⊟	6	2	Front Wheel Assembly	1	1

	PartNumber	Level	Descrption	QuantityRequir	PartOf
	7	3	Front Wheels	2	6
	8	3	Axel	1	6
	9	3	Wheel retainer	2	6
*	(New)			0	6

	PartNumber	Level	Description	QuantityRequired	PartOf
⊟	10	2	Rear Wheel Assembly	1	1

	PartNumber	Level	Descrption	QuantityRequir	PartOf
	11	3	Rear Wheels	2	10
	12	3	Axel	1	10

Record: ◄ ◄ 1 of 3 ► ►► ►► No Filter   Search

Record: ◄ ◄ 1 of 1 ► ►► ►► No Filter   Search

7-3. Figure AE-7 is a sample bill of materials, a form that shows the components and parts used to construct a product. In this example, the product is a child's wagon. Such bills of materials are an essential part of manufacturing functional applications as well as ERP applications.

This particular example is a form produced using Microsoft Access. Producing such a form is a bit tricky, so this exercise will guide you through the steps required. You can then apply what you learn to produce a similar report. You can also use Access to experiment on extensions of this form.

a. Create a table named *PART* with columns *Part Number, Level, Description, QuantityRequired*, and *PartOf. Description* and *Level* should be text, *PartNumber* should be AutoNumber, and *Quantity Required* and *PartOf* should be numeric, long integer. Add the *PART* data shown in Figure AE-7 to your table.

b. Create a query that has all columns of *PART*. Restrict the view to rows having a value of 1 for *Level*. Name your query *Level1*.

c. Create two more queries that are restricted to rows having values of 2 or 3 for *Level*. Name your queries *Level2* and *Level3*, respectively.

d. Create a form that contains *PartNumber, Level,* and *Description* from *Level1*. You can use a wizard for this if you want. Name the form *Bill of Materials*.

e. Using the subform tool in the Toolbox, create a subform in your form in part d. Set the data on this form to be all of the columns of *Level2*. After you have created the subform, ensure that the Link Child Fields property is set to *PartOf* and that the Link Master Fields property is set to *PartNumber*. Close the *Bill of Materials* form.

f. Open the subform created in part e and create a subform on it. Set the data on this subform to be all of the columns of *Level3*. After you have created the subform, ensure that the Link Child Fields property is set to *PartOf* and that the Link Master Fields property is set to *PartNumber*. Close the *Bill of Materials* form.

g. Open the *Bill of Materials* form. It should appear as in Figure AE-7. Open and close the form and add new data. Using this form, add sample BOM data for a product of your own choosing.

h. Following the process similar to that just described, create a *Bill of Materials Report* that lists the data for all of your products.

i. (**Optional**, **challenging extension**) Each part in the BOM in Figure AE-7 can be used in at most one assembly (there is space to show just one *PartOf* value). You can change your design to allow a part to be used in more than one assembly as follows: First, remove *PartOf* from PART. Next, create a second table that has two columns: *AssemblyPartNumber* and *ComponentPart Number*. The first contains a part number of an assembly and the second a part number of a component. Every component of a part will have a row in this table. Extend the views described above to use this second table and to produce a display similar to Figure AE-7.

Chapter 8

8-1. Microsoft created Windows Live SkyDrive and the Office Web applications as part of the Office 2010 launch. Somewhere in the middle of that launch, the Microsoft Fuse team realized that it would be a simple matter to put Facebook trappings (in tech parlance, Facebook Chrome) on top of a SkyDrive, call it Docs, and enable Windows Live SkyDrive to take advantage of Facebook's momentum. The question is, does Docs deliver value or hype?

a. Go to www.skydrive.com and create a presentation having a few slides using the Microsoft PowerPoint Web App described in Chapter 2. For the purpose of this exercise, it doesn't matter what is in your presentation; choose a presentation for another class if you want. Save that presentation and share it with several friends or team members.

b. Ask one or two of your friends to make several changes to the presentation.

c. Repeat part a, but this time go to Docs at http://docs.com and join. Add a Profile tab for Docs to your Facebook account. Share the PowerPoint presentation as in part a.

d. Ask one or two of your friends to make several changes to the presentation.

e. Reflect on your experience using Windows Live SkyDrive and Docs. Does Docs add value, or is it just hype? Explain.

8-2. Assume that you have been given the task of compiling evaluations that your company's purchasing agents make of their vendors. Each month, every purchasing agent evaluates all of the vendors that he or she has ordered from in the past month on three factors: price, quality, and responsiveness. Assume the ratings are from 1 to 5, with 5 being the best. Because your company has hundreds of vendors and dozens of purchasing agents, you decide to use Access to compile the results.

a. Create a database with three tables: VENDOR (*VendorNumber, Name, Contact*), PURCHASER (*EmpNumber, Name, Email*), and RATING (*EmpNumber, VendorNumber, Month, Year, Price Rating, QualityRating, ResponsivenessRating*). Assume that *VendorNumber* and *EmpNumber* are the keys of VENDOR and PURCHASER, respectively. Decide what you think is the appropriate key for RATING.

b. Create appropriate relationships.

c. Import the data in the Excel file **Ch08Ex02_U5e.xlsx**. Note that data for Vendor, Purchaser, and Rating are stored in three separate worksheets.

d. Create a query that shows the names of all vendors and their average scores.

e. Create a query that shows the names of all employees and their average scores. *Hint:* In this and in part f, you will need to use the *Group By* function in your query.

f. Create a parameterized query that you can use to obtain the minimum, maximum, and average ratings on each criterion for a particular vendor. Assume you will enter *VendorName* as the parameter.

g. Using the data created by your queries, what conclusions can you make about vendors or purchasers?

Chapter 9

9-1.   OLAP cubes are very similar to Microsoft Excel pivot tables. For this exercise, assume that your organization's purchasing agents rate vendors similar to the situation described in Application Exercise 8-2.

  a. Open Excel and import the data in the worksheet named *Vendors* from the Excel file **Ch09Ex01_U5e.xlsx**. The spreadsheet will have the following column names: *VendorName, EmployeeName, Date, Year*, and *Rating*.

  b. Under the *Insert* ribbon in Excel, click *Pivot Table*. A wizard will open. Select *Excel* and *Pivot table* in the first screen. Click *Next*.

  c. When asked to provide a data range, drag your mouse over the data you imported so as to select all of the data. Be sure to include the column headings. Excel will fill in the range values in the open dialog box. Place your pivot table in a separate spreadsheet.

  d. Excel will create a field list on the right-hand side of your spreadsheet. Drag and drop the field named *VendorName* onto the words "Drop Row Fields Here." Drag and drop *EmployeeName* onto the words "Drop Column Fields Here." Now drag and drop the field named *Rating* onto the words "Drop Data Items Here." Voilà! You have a pivot table.

  e. To see how the table works, drag and drop more fields onto the various sections of your pivot table. For example, drop *Year* on top of *Employee*. Then move *Year* below *Employee*. Now move *Year* below *Vendor*. All of this action is just like an OLAP cube, and, in fact, OLAP cubes are readily displayed in Excel pivot tables. The major difference is that OLAP cubes are usually based on thousands or more rows of data.

9-2.   It is surprisingly easy to create a market-basket report using table data in Access. To do so, however, you will need to enter SQL expressions into the Access query builder. Here, you can just copy SQL statements to type them in. If you take a database class, you will learn how to code SQL statements like those you will use here.

  a. Create an Access database with a table named *Order_Data* having columns *OrderNumber, ItemName*, and *Quantity*, with data types Number (*LongInteger*), Text (50), and Number (*LongInteger*), respectively. Define the key as the composite (*OrderNumber, ItemName*).

  b. Import the data from the Excel file **Ch09Ex02_U5e.xlsx** into the *Order_Data* table.

  c. Now, to perform the market-basket analysis, you will need to enter several SQL statements into Access. To do so, click the queries tab and select *Create Query* in Design view. Click *Close* when the Show Table dialog box appears. Right-click in the gray section above the grid in the *Select Query* window. Select *SQL View*. Enter the following expression exactly as it appears here:

```
SELECT    T1.ItemName as FirstItem,
          T2.ItemName as SecondItem
FROM      Order_Data T1, Order_Data T2
WHERE     T1.OrderNumber =
          T2.OrderNumber
AND       T1.ItemName <> T2.ItemName;
```

Click the red exclamation point in the toolbar to run the query. Correct any typing mistakes and, once it works, save the query using the name *TwoItem Basket*.

  d. Now enter a second SQL statement. Again, click the queries tab and select *Create Query* in Design view. Click *Close* when the Show Table dialog box appears.

Right-click in the gray section above the grid in the *Select Query* window. Select *SQL View.* Enter the following expression exactly as it appears here:

```
SELECT     TwoItemBasket.FirstItem,
           TwoItemBasket.SecondItem,
           Count(*) AS SupportCount
FROM       TwoItemBasket
GROUP BY   TwoItemBasket.FirstItem,
           TwoItemBasket.SecondItem;
```

Correct any typing mistakes and, once it works, save the query using the name *SupportCount.*

  e. Examine the results of the second query and verify that the two query statements have correctly calculated the number of times that two items have appeared together. Explain further calculations you need to make to compute support.

  f. Explain the calculations you need to make to compute lift. Although you can make those calculations using SQL, you need more SQL knowledge to do it, and we will skip that here.

  g. Explain, in your own words, what the query in part c seems to be doing. What does the query in part d seem to be doing? Again, you will need to take a database class to learn how to code such expressions, but this exercise should give you a sense of the kinds of calculations that are possible with SQL.

9-3. Suppose you are Addison at GearUp. The Access file **Ch09Ex03_U5e.accdb** contains the *ITEM_SUMMARY* table. Download that database and create the reports shown in Figures 9-6 through 9-10 as follows:

  a. Create a query that processes Item_Summary_Data to create the source data for the report shown in Figure 9-7.

  b. Using your query from part a, create the report in Figure 9-7.

  c. Modify your query in part a to create a query that processes Item_Summary_Data to create the source data for the report shown in Figure 9-6.

  d. Using your query from part c, create the report in Figure 9-6.

  e. Create a query that processes Item_Summary_Data to create the source data for the report shown in Figure 9-10.

  f. Using your query from part e, create the report in Figure 9-10.

  g. Modify your query in part e to create a query that processes Item_Summary_Data to create the source data for the report shown in Figure 9-9.

  h. Using your query from part g, create the report in Figure 9-9.

  i. Create a table from the sample data shown in Figure 9-8 (column G has values of EventItemNumber). Using that sample data, improve your report in your answer to part f. (Only five of the rows will have the additional data.)

  j. Summarize the problems of integrating data that you experienced in part i. What would you do if you had thousands of rows of data?

Chapter 10

10-1. Do Application Exercise 7-1, if you have not already done so.

  a. Add a Status column to the RESERVATION table, where Status can have values of *Not Confirmed, Confirmed,* or *Cancelled.* Explain why Fox Lake might wish to track cancelled reservations.

  b. Create a data entry form that would be appropriate for the Reserve Facilities activity in Figure 10-9. Outline procedures required for using that form. Adjust the business process in Figure 10-9 so that you can reserve one facility at a time.

  c. Create a data entry from that would be appropriate for the Confirm Facility Reservations activity in Figure 10-9. Outline procedures required for using that form.

   d. Create a data entry from that would be appropriate for the Release Facility Reservations activity in Figure 10-9. Outline procedures required for using that form.

   e. Create the Daily Facility Use Report in Figure 10-9. Assume the report has a parameterized query to produce all reservations for a given date.

   f. Input data and test your database. Use the Windows 7 Snipping Tool or some other tool to capture screenshots of your data entry screens and your report. Add them to your procedure outline and turn in the assembled document. (Or, if instructed to do so, turn in your Access database along with your procedure outlines.)

10-2. Suppose you are given the task of comparing labor costs of meetings for systems development projects to budgets. Download the Word file **Ch10Ex02_U5e.docx** and the Excel file having the same name. The Word file has records of meeting dates, times, and attendees. The document was created from informal notes taken at the meetings. The Excel file has the project budgets as well as labor costs for different categories of employees.

   Assume your company uses the traditional systems-first process illustrated in Figure 10-12. Further assume that each SDLC step requires two types of meetings: *Working meetings* involve users, business analysts, systems analysts, programmers, and PQA test engineers. *Review meetings* involve all of those people, plus level-1 and level-2 managers of both user departments and the IS department.

   a. Using either Access or Excel, whichever you think is better suited to the task, import the Word data to a work file and compute the total labor for each type of employee for each meeting.

   b. Using the file you created in part a, compute the total labor for each type of employee for each phase of the project.

   c. Combine your answer in part b with the data in the Excel file **Ch10Ex02_U5e.xlsx** to compute the total cost of meetings of each phase of the project.

   d. Use a graphic chart of the type you think best to show the differences from meeting cost and budget.

   e. Comment on your choice of Excel or Access for your work file. If you were to do this exercise over, would you use that same tool again? Why or why not?

10-3. Use Access to develop a failure-tracking database application. Use the data in the Excel file **Ch10Ex03_U5e.xlsx** for this exercise. The data includes columns for the following:

    FailureNumber
    DateReported
    FailureDescription
    ReportedBy (the name of the PQA engineer reporting the failure)
    ReportedBy_email (the email address of the PQA engineer reporting the failure)
    FixedBy (the name of the programmer who is assigned to fix the failure)
    FixedBy_email (the email address of the programmer assigned to fix the failure)
    DateFailureFixed
    FixDescription
    DateFixVerified
    VerifiedBy (the name of the PQA engineer verifying the fix)
    VeifiedBy_email (the email address of the PQA engineer verifying the fix)

   a. The data in the spreadsheet are not normalized. Normalize the data by creating a *Failure* table, a *PQA Engineer* table, and a *Programmer* table. Add other appropriate columns to each table. Create appropriate relationships.

   b. Create one or more forms that can be used to report a failure, to report a failure fix, and to report a failure verification. Create the form(s) so that the user can just pull down the name of a PQA engineer or programmer from the appropriate table to fill in the *ReportedBy*, *FixedBy*, and *VerifiedBy* fields.

   c. Construct a report that shows all failures sorted by reporting PQA engineer and then by *Date Reported*.

   d. Construct a report that shows only fixed and verified failures.

   e. Construct a report that shows only fixed but unverified failures.

Chapter 11

11-1. Suppose you have just been appointed manager of a help desk with an IS department. You have been there for just a week, and you are amazed to find only limited data to help you manage your employees. In fact, the only data kept concerns the processing of particular issues, called *Tickets*. The following data are kept: *Ticket#, Date_Submitted, Date_Opened, Date_Closed, Type (new or repeat), Reporting_ Employee_Name, Reporting_Employee_Division, Technician_Name_Problem_System,* and *Problem_Description*. You can find sample Ticket data in the Excel file **Ch11Ex01_U5e.xlsx**.

As a manager, you need more data. Among your needs are data that will help you learn who are your best- and worst-performing technicians, how different systems compare in terms of number of problems reported and the time required to fix those problems, how different divisions compare in terms of problems reported and the time required to fix them, which technicians are the best and worst at solving problems with particular systems, and which technicians are best and worst at solving problems from particular divisions.

   a. Use either Access or Excel, or a combination of the two, to produce the information listed in the Excel file **Ch11Ex01_U5e.xlsx**. In your answer, you may use queries, formulas, reports, forms, graphs, pivot tables, pivot charts, or any other type of Access or Excel display. Choose the best display for the type of information you are producing.

   b. Explain how you would use these different types of information to manage your department.

   c. Specify any additional information that you would like to have produced from this data to help you manage your department.

   d. Use either Access or Excel, or a combination, to produce the information in part c.

Chapter 12

12-1. Develop a spreadsheet model of the cost of a virus attack at an organization that has three types of computers: employee workstations, data servers, and Web servers. Assume that the number of computers affected by the virus depends on the severity of the virus. For the purposes of your model, assume that there are three levels of virus severity: *Low-severity* incidents affect fewer than 30 percent of the user workstations and none of the data or Web servers. *Medium-severity* incidents affect up to 70 percent of the user workstations, up to half of the Web servers, and none of the data servers. *High-severity* incidents can affect all organizational computers.

   a. Assume 50 percent of the incidents are low severity, 30 percent are medium severity, and 20 percent are high severity.

   b. Assume employees can remove viruses from workstations themselves, but that specially trained technicians are required to repair the servers. The time to eliminate a virus from an infected computer depends on the computer type. Let the time to remove the virus from each type be an input into your model. Assume that when users eliminate the virus themselves, they are unproductive for twice the time required for the removal. Let the average employee hourly labor cost be an input to your model. Let the average cost of a technician also be an input into your model. Finally, let the total number of user computers, data servers, and Web servers be inputs into your model.

c. Run your simulation 10 times. Use the same inputs for each run, but draw a random number (assume a uniform distribution for all random numbers) to determine the severity type. Then, draw random numbers to determine the percentage of computers of each type affected, using the constraints detailed earlier. For example, if the attack is of medium severity, draw a random number between 0 and 70 to indicate the percentage of infected user workstations and a random number between 0 and 50 to indicate the percentage of infected Web servers.

d. For each run, calculate the total of lost employee hours, the total dollar cost of lost employee labor hours, the total hours of technicians to fix the servers, and the total cost of technician labor. Finally, compute the total overall cost. Show the results of each run. Show the average costs and hours for the 10 runs.

12-2. In the Fox Lake case at the start of Chapter 12, Chris was able to use Mike's computer in the middle of the night, when no one was around, because he had access to the keys. And, Fox Lake is about to discover that Chris kept more than $2,500 worth of equipment that had been checked out to him. All of this could have been prevented if someone had known to ask Chris for keys and equipment when the reporting project was over. Accordingly, Fox Lake has decided to create an Access database to track assets that have been allocated to individuals who work at Fox Lake.

Suppose that Fox Lake has asked you to develop an Access database that tracks keys, equipment, and user accounts that have been issued to employees and contractors. Assume your database has four tables: *Person, Equipment, Key,* and *Account. Person* has data about employees and contractors, *Equipment* has data about equipment that have been allocated to individuals in the *Person* table, *Key* has data about keys that have been allocated to individuals in *Person,* and *Account* has data about accounts that have been created for individuals in *Person.* (This last table is needed because Fox Lake is about to start a policy that every user of every computer has his or her own account for using that computer. Thus, an account name is an asset, just like a building key or a paddle.)

a. Using your knowledge, experience, and intuition design the *Person, Equipment, Key,* and *Account* tables. Name and describe the columns of each table and indicate which columns are the primary key.

b. Specify the maximum cardinality of the relationships between:

(1) *Person* and *Equipment*
(2) *Person* and *Key*
(3) *Person* and *Account*

c. Modify your design in part a to include foreign keys necessary to support the relationships you specified in part b.

d. Create your database in Access and fill it with sample data.

e. Create a form for adding a new person and equipment assigned to that person.

f. Create a form for allocating a key to an existing person.

g. Create a report suitable for use when an employee quits Fox Lake. Your report should include all resources that need to be recovered as well as computer accounts that need to be removed.

h. Create a parameterized query that accepts a person's name and generates the report in part g for that person.

Glossary

10/100/1000 Ethernet A type of Ethernet that conforms to the IEEE 802.3 protocol and allows for transmission at a rate of 10, 100, or 1,000 Mbps (megabits per second). 181

32-bit processor Type of addressing used by PCs, as of 2011. Allows for addressing of up to 4 Gigabytes of main memory. 110

64-bit processor Type of addressing used by power PCs and new servers. Allows for addressing for practically unlimited main memory. 110

Abstract reasoning The ability to make and manipulate models. 6

Access A popular personal and small workgroup DBMS product from Microsoft. 147

Access point (AP) A device in a wireless network that facilitates communication among wireless devices and serves as a point of interconnection between wireless and wired networks. The access point must be able to process messages according to both the 802.3 and 802.11 standards, because it sends and receives wireless traffic using the 802.11 protocol and communicates with wired networks using the 802.3 protocol. 180

Active lurker Someone who reads, consumes, and observes activity in one social medium and then broadcasts it in another medium. 276

Activity A business function that receives inputs and produces outputs. An activity can be performed by a human, by a computer system, or by both. 84

AdSense A Web 2.0 product from Google. Google searches an organization's Web site and inserts ads that match content on that site; when users click those ads, Google pays the organization a fee. 282

Adware Programs installed on the user's computer without the user's knowledge or permission that reside in the background and, unknown to the user, observe the user's actions and keystrokes, modify computer activity, and report the user's activities to sponsoring organizations. Most adware is benign in that it does not perform malicious acts or steal data. It does, however, watch user activity and produce pop-up ads. 432

AdWords A Web 2.0 advertising product from Google. Vendors agree to pay a certain amount to Google for use of particular search words, which link to the vendor's site. 282

Alert (1) A form of report, often requested by recipients, that tells them some piece of information, usually time-related, such as notification of the time for a meeting. (2) An email text message that SharePoint sends to you when something of interest happens to a list or library. 60

Analog signal A wavy signal. A modem converts the computer's digital data into analog signals that can be transmitted over dial-up Internet connections. 182

Application software Programs that perform a business function. Some application programs are general purpose, such as Excel or Word. Other application programs are specific to a business function, such as accounts payable. 118

As-is model A model that represents the current situation and processes. 347

Asymmetric encryption An encryption method whereby different keys are used to encode and to decode the message; one key encodes the message, and the other key decodes the message. Symmetric encryption is simpler and much faster than asymmetric encryption. 429

Asynchronous communication Information exchange that occurs when all members of a work team do not meet at the same time, such as those who work different shifts or in different locations. 44

Attribute (1) A variable that provides properties for an HTML tag. Each attribute has a standard name. For example, the attribute for a hyperlink is *href*, and its value indicates which Web page is to be displayed when the user clicks the link. (2) Characteristics of an entity. Example attributes of *Order* would be *OrderNumber, OrderDate, SubTotal, Tax, Total,* and so forth. Example attributes of *Salesperson* would be *SalespersonName, Email, Phone,* and so forth. 194

Authentication The process whereby an information system verifies (validates) a user. 428

Baseline WBS The final work-breakdown structure that shows the planned tasks, dependencies, durations, and resource assignments. 375

Beacons Tiny files that gather demographic information; they use a single code to identify users by age, gender, location, likely income, and online activity. Beacons are often image files that install malware code when users open images in junk mail. Most are not malicious and simply verify users' email addresses, activities, and preferences. 432

Binary digit The means by which computers represent data; also called *bits*. A binary digit is either a zero or a one. 107

Biometric authentication The use of personal physical characteristics, such as fingerprints, facial features, and retinal scans, to authenticate users. 428

Bits The means by which computers represent data; also called *binary digit*. A bit is either a zero or a one. 107

BlackBerry OS One of the most successful early mobile operating systems and was used primarily by business users on BlackBerry devices. 115

Bluetooth A common wireless protocol designed for transmitting data over short distances, replacing cables. 182

Bot A computer program that is surreptitiously installed and that takes actions unknown and uncontrolled by the computer's owner or administrator. 433

Bot herder The individual or organization that controls a botnet. 433

Botnet A network of bots that is created and managed by the individual or organization that infected the network with the bot program. 433

Broadband Internet communication lines that have speeds in excess of 256 kbps. DSL and cable modems provide broadband access. 183

Brooks' Law The famous adage that states: *Adding more people to a late project makes the project later*. Brooks' Law is true not only because a larger staff requires increased coordination, but also because new people need to be trained. The only people who can train the new employees are the existing team members, who are thus taken off productive tasks. The costs of training new people can overwhelm the benefit of their contribution. 370

Brute force attack A password-cracking program that tries every possible combination of characters. 422

Bullwhip effect Phenomenon in which the variability in the size and timing of orders increases at each stage up the supply chain, from customer to supplier. 460

Bus Means by which the CPU reads instructions and data from main memory and writes data to main memory. 109

Business analyst (1) A person who understands business strategies, goals, and objectives and who helps businesses develop and manage business processes and information systems. (2) Someone who is well versed in Porter's models, organizational strategy, and systems alignment theory, like COBIT, and who also understands the proper role for technology. 360

Business intelligence (BI) Information containing patterns, relationships, and trends. 298

Business intelligence (BI) analysis The process of creating business intelligence. The three fundamental categories of BI analysis are reporting, data mining, and knowledge management. 298

Business intelligence (BI) application The software component of a BI system. 298

Business intelligence (BI) server A computer program that delivers BI application results in a variety of formats to various devices for consumption by BI users. 329

Business intelligence (BI) system An information system that processes operational and other source data to identify patterns, relationships, and trends and to make predictions. 298

Business process (1) A network of activities, resources, facilities, and information that interact to achieve some business function; sometimes called a *business system*. (2) A network of activities that generate value by transforming inputs into outputs. 84

Business process management (BPM) A systematic process of modeling, creating, implementing, and assessing business processes. 347

Business Process Modeling Notation (BPMN) Standard set of terms and graphical notations for documenting business processes. 348

Business process reengineering The activity of altering and designing business processes to fix defective processes, to take advantage of new technology, and to adapt to changes in the business environment or business fundamentals. 227

Byte(s) (1) A character of data. (2) An 8-bit chunk of data. 143

Cable modem A type of modem that provides high-speed data transmission using cable television lines. The cable company installs a fast, high-capacity optical fiber cable to a distribution center in each neighborhood that it serves. At the distribution center, the optical fiber cable connects to regular cable-television cables that run to subscribers' homes or businesses. Cable modems modulate in such a way that their signals do not interfere with TV signals. Like DSL lines, they are always on. 183

Cache A file on a domain name resolver that stores domain names and IP addresses that have been resolved. Then, when someone else needs to resolve that same domain name, there is no need to go through the entire resolution process. Instead, the resolver can supply the IP address from the local file. 109

Capital The investment of resources with the expectation of future returns in the marketplace. 268

Central processing unit (CPU) The CPU selects instructions, processes them, performs arithmetic and logical comparisons, and stores results of operations in memory. 107

Chief information officer (CIO) The title of the principal manager of the IT department. Other common titles are *vice president of information services, director of information services*, and, less commonly, *director of computer services*. 389

Chief technology officer (CTO) The head of the technology group. The CTO filters new ideas and products to identify those that are most relevant to the organization. The CTO's job requires deep knowledge of information technology and the ability to envision how new IT could affect an organization over time. 389

Client A computer that provides word processing, spreadsheets, database access, and usually a network connection. See also *thin* and *thick clients*. 118

Client-server applications Software applications that require code on both the client computer and the server computer. Microsoft Office Outlook email is a common example. 110

Closed source Source code that is highly protected and only available to trusted employees and carefully vetted contractors. 123

Cloud computing The elastic leasing of pooled computer resources over the Internet. The term *cloud* is used because most early diagrams of three-tier and other Internet-based systems used a cloud symbol to represent the Internet. 198

Cluster analysis An unsupervised data mining technique whereby statistical techniques are used to identify groups of entities that have similar characteristics. A common use for cluster analysis is to find groups of similar customers in data about customer orders and customer demographics. 315

COBIT (Control Objectives for Information and related Technology) A set of standard practices, created by the Information Systems Audit and Control Association, that are used in the assessment stage of the BPM cycle to determine how well an information system complies with an organization's strategy. 347

Cold sites Remote processing centers that provide office space, and possibly computer equipment, for use by a company to use to continue operations after a disaster. 441

Collaboration A group of people working together to achieve a common goal via a process of feedback and iteration. 7

Collaboration information system An information system that supports collaboration. 43

Collaboration tool The program component of a collaboration system. For the tool to be useful, it must exist as part of an information system having the other four components of an information system. 43

Columns Also called *fields*, or groups of bytes. A database table has multiple columns that are used to represent the attributes of an entity. Examples are *PartNumber*, *EmployeeName*, and *SalesDate*. 143

Commerce server An application program that runs on a server tier computer. A commerce server receives requests from users via the Web server, takes some action, and returns a response to the users via the Web server. 192

Community A group of people related by a common interest. 258

Competitive strategy The strategy an organization chooses as the way it will succeed in its industry. According to Porter, there are four fundamental competitive strategies: cost leadership across an industry or within a particular industry segment and product differentiation across an industry or within a particular industry segment. 78

Computer hardware Electronic components and related gadgetry that input, process, output, store, and communicate data according to be instructions encoded in computer programs or software. One of the five fundamental components of an information system. 8

Computer-based information system An information system that includes a computer. 9

Computers-in-a-product Computer capabilities embedded within common consumer products. 19

Confidence In market-basket terminology, the probability estimate that two items will be purchased together. 316

Configuration control A set of management policies, practices, and tools that developers use to maintain control over the project's resources. 376

Connection data In social media systems, data about relationships. 263

Content data In social media systems, data and responses to data that are contributed by users and SM sponsors. 262

Cookies Data that are stored on the user's computer by a browser. Cookies can be used for authentication, for storing shopping cart contents and user preferences, and for other legitimate purposes. Cookies can also be used to implement spyware. 423

Cooperation A group of people working together, all performing the same type of work, to accomplish a job. 32

Cost [of a business process] The cost of the inputs to a business process plus the cost of the activities involved in the process. 84

Cost feasibility Whether an information system can be developed within budget. 360

Critical path The sequence of activities that determine the earliest date by which the project can be completed. 373

Critical path analysis A project management planning process by which tasks and resources are reassigned to tasks so as to reduce the total length of the project's critical path. 374

Cross-selling The sale of related products; salespeople try to get customers who buy product X to also buy product Y. 316

Crow's foot A line on an entity-relationship diagram that indicates a 1:N relationship between two entities. 158

Crow's-foot diagram A type of entity-relationship diagram that uses a crow's foot symbol to designate a 1:N relationship. 159

Crowdsourcing The process by which organizations use Web 2.0 technologies such as user-generated content to involve their users in the design and marketing of their products. 267

Custom-developed software Software that is tailor-made for a particular organization's requirements. 120

Customer life cycle Taken as a whole, the processes of marketing, customer acquisition, relationship management, and loss/churn that must be managed by CRM systems. 229

Customer relationship management (CRM) A suite of applications, a database, and a set of inherent processes for managing all the interactions with the customer, from lead generation to customer service. 228

Data Recorded facts or figures. One of the five fundamental components of an information system. 8

Data acquisition In business intelligence systems, the process of obtaining, cleaning, organizing, relating, and cataloging source data. 300

Data aggregators Companies that obtain data from public and private sources and store, integrate, and process it in sophisticated ways. 314

Data channel Means by which the CPU reads instructions and data from main memory and writes data to main memory. 109

Data flow Movement of a data item from one activity to another activity or to or from a repository. 344

Data integrity problem In a database, the situation that exists when data items disagree with one another. An example is two different names for the same customer. 160

Data mining The application of statistical techniques to find patterns and relationships among data for classification and prediction. 314

Data model A logical representation of the data in a database that describes the data and relationships that will be stored in the database. Akin to a blueprint. 156

Data safeguards Measures used to protect databases and other data assets from threats. Includes data rights and responsibilities, encryptions, backup and recovery, and physical security. 434

Data warehouses Facilities that prepare, store, and manage data specifically for reporting and data mining. 306

Database A self-describing collection of integrated records. 143

Database administration The management, development, operation, and maintenance of the database so as to achieve the organization's objectives. This staff function requires balancing conflicting goals: protecting the database while maximizing its availability for authorized use. In smaller organizations, this function usually is served by a single person. Larger organizations assign several people to an office of database administration. 152

Database application Forms, reports, queries, and application programs for processing a database. A database can be processed by many different database applications. 152

Database application system An information system, having the standard five components, that make database data more accessible and useful. Users employ a database application that consists of forms, formatted reports, queries, and application programs. Each of these, in turn, calls on the database management system (DBMS) to process the database tables. 147

Database management systems (DBMS) A program for creating, processing, and administering a database. A DBMS is a large and complex program that is licensed like an operating system. Microsoft Access and Oracle Database are example DBMS products. 147

Database tier In the three-tier architecture, the tier that runs the DBMS and receives and processes SQL requests to retrieve and store data. 191

DB2 A popular, enterprise-class DBMS product from IBM. 147

Decision support systems Some authors define business intelligence (BI) systems as supporting decision making only, in which case they use this older term as a synonym for decision-making BI systems. 299

Decision tree A hierarchical arrangement of criteria for classifying customers, items, and other business objects. 320

Defenders of belief In social media, a community that shares a common strongly held belief; such groups seek conformity and want to convince others of the wisdom of their belief. 264

Deliverable A task that is one of many measurable or observable steps in a development project. 371

Denial of service (DOS) Security problem in which users are not able to access an information system; can be caused by human errors, natural disaster, or malicious activity. 418

Departmental information system Workgroup information systems that support a particular department. 218

Desktop virtualization Also called *client virtualization* and *PC virtualization*. The process of storing a user's desktop on a remote server. It enables users to run their desktop from many different client computers. 118

Digital divide A divide created between those who have Internet access and those who do not. 94

Digital subscriber line (DSL) A communications line that operates on the same lines as voice telephones, but do so in such a manner that their signals to not interfere with voice telephone service. 183

Dimension A characteristic of an OLAP measure. Purchase date, customer type, customer location, and sales region are examples of dimensions. 311

Discussion forum A form of asynchronous communication in which one group member posts an entry and other group members respond. A better form of group communication than email, because it is more difficult for one person to monopolize the discussion or for the discussion to go off track. 46

Diseconomy of scale A principle that states as development teams become larger, the average contribution per worker decreases. 374

Distributed database processing A technique for storing database contents on two or more computers. Partitioned databases split the database into pieces that are stored on multiple computers but that do not duplicate any data. Replicated databases duplicate data on two or more computers. Updating replicated databases is challenging. 456

Domain name A worldwide unique name that is registered in the domain name system (DNS) and is affiliated with a public IP address. The process of changing a domain name into its IP address is called *resolving the domain name*. 189

Drill down With an OLAP report, to further divide the data into more detail. 312

Drive-by sniffers People who take computers with wireless connections through an area and search for unprotected wireless networks in an attempt to gain free Internet access or to gather unauthorized data. 417

Dual processor A computer with two CPUs. 183

Dynamic processes Flexible, informal, and adaptive processes that normally involve strategic and less specific managerial decisions and activities. 107

Dynamic reports Business intelligence documents that are updated at the time they are requested. 217

Elastic In cloud computing, the situation that exists when the amount of resource leased can be dynamically increased or decreased, programmatically, in a short span of time, and organizations pay for just the resource that they use. This term was first used in this way by Amazon.com. 198

Email A form of asynchronous communication in which participants send comments and attachments electronically. As a form of group communication, it can be disorganized, disconnected, and easy to hide from. 46

Email spoofing A synonym for *phishing*. A technique for obtaining unauthorized data that uses pretexting via email. The *phisher* pretends to be a legitimate company and sends email requests for confidential data, such as account numbers, Social Security numbers, account passwords, and so forth. Phishers direct traffic to their sites under the guise of a legitimate business. 417

Encapsulation (encapsulated) An approach that isolates service logic within that service. No service user knows nor needs to know how the service is performed. 243

Encryption The process of transforming clear text into coded, unintelligible text for secure storage or communication. 429

Encryption algorithms Algorithms used to transform clear text into coded, unintelligible text for secure storage or communication. Commonly used methods are DES, 3DES, and AES. 429

Enterprise 2.0 The application of Web 2.0 technologies, collaboration systems, social networking, and related technologies to facilitate the cooperative work of intellectual workers in organizations. 267

Enterprise application integration (EAI) The integration of existing systems by providing layers of software that connect applications and their data together. 234

Enterprise DBMS A software product that processes large organizational and workgroup databases. These products support many users, perhaps thousands, and many different database applications. Such DBMS products support 24/7 operations and can manage databases that span dozens of different magnetic disks with hundreds of gigabytes or more of data. IBM's DB2, Microsoft's SQL Server, and Oracle Database are examples of enterprise DBMS products. 155

Enterprise information system Information systems that support cross-functional processes and activities in multiple departments. 219

Enterprise resource planning (ERP) A suite of applications called modules, a database, and a set of inherent processes for consolidating business operations into a single, consistent, computing platform. 229

Enterprise resource planning (ERP) system An information system based upon ERP technology. 229

Entity In the E-R data model, a representation of some thing that users want to track. Some entities represent a physical object; others represent a logical construct or transaction. 156

Entity-relationship (E-R) data model Popular technique for creating a data model whereby developers define an abstraction of the things that will be stored in the database and identify the relationships among them. 156

Entity-relationship (E-R) diagrams A type of diagram used by database designers to document entities and their relationships to each other. 158

Ethernet Another name for the IEEE 802.3 protocol, Ethernet is a network protocol that operates at Layers 1 and 2 of the TCP/IP–OSI architecture. Ethernet, the world's most popular LAN protocol, is used on WANs as well. 181

Exabyte (EB) 1,024PB. 108

Experimentation A careful and reasoned analysis of an opportunity, envisioning potential products or solutions or applications of technology, and then developing those ideas that seem to have the most promise, consistent with the resources you have. 7

Expert system Knowledge-sharing system that is created by interviewing experts in a given business domain and codifying the rules used by those experts. 324

eXtensible Markup Language (XML) An important document standard that separates document content, structure, and presentation; eliminates problems in HTML. Used for Web Services and many other applications. 195

Fields Also called *columns*; groups of bytes in a database table. A database table has multiple columns that are used to represent the attributes of an entity. Examples are *PartNumber*, *EmployeeName*, and *SalesDate*. 144

File A group of similar rows or records. In a database, sometimes called a *table*. 144

File server A computer that stores files. 48

File Transfer Protocol (FTP) A Layer-5 TCP/IP protocol used to copy files from one computer to another. In interorganizational transaction processing, FTP enables users to exchange large files easily. 48

Firmware Computer software that is installed into devices such as printers, print services, and various types of communication devices. The software is coded just like other software, but it is installed into special, programmable memory of the printer or other device. 120

Five-component framework The five fundamental components of an information system—computer hardware, software, data, procedures, and people—that are present in every information system, from the simplest to the most complex. 8

Five forces model Model, proposed by Michael Porter, that assesses industry characteristics and profitability by means of five competitive forces—bargaining power of suppliers, threat of substitution, bargaining power of customers, rivalry among firms, and threat of new entrants. 77

Flash An add-on to browsers that was developed by Adobe and is useful for providing animation, movies, and other advanced graphics within a browser. 194

Folksonomy A structure of content that emerges from the activity and processing of many users. 267

Foreign keys A column or group of columns used to represent relationships. Values of the foreign key match values of the primary key in a different (foreign) table. 145

Form Data entry forms are used to read, insert, modify, and delete database data. 152

FTP (File Transfer Protocol) A Layer-5 protocol used to copy files from one computer to another over the Internet. 187

Gantt chart A chart that shows tasks, dates, dependencies, and possibly resources. 373

Gigabyte (GB) 1,024MB. 108

GNU A set of tools for creating and managing open source software. Originally created to develop an open source Unix-like operating system. 121

GNU General Public License (GPL) Agreement One of the standard license agreements for open source software. 121

Google Docs A free thin-client application for sharing documents, spreadsheets, presentations, drawings, and other types of data. Includes version tracking. 49

Gramm-Leach-Bliley (GLB) Act Passed by Congress in 1999, this act protects consumer financial data stored by financial institutions, which are defined as banks, securities firms, insurance companies, and organizations that provide financial advice, prepare tax returns, and provide similar financial services. 426

Green computing Environmentally conscious computing consisting of three major components: power management, virtualization, and e-waste management. 400

Hacking A form of computer crime in which a person gains unauthorized access to a computer system. Although some people hack for the sheer joy of doing it, other hackers invade systems for the malicious purpose of stealing or modifying data. 417

Hardening A term used to describe server operating systems that have been modified to make them especially difficult for them to be infiltrated by malware. 437

Hardware Electronic components and related gadgetry that input, process, output, store, and communicate data according to the instructions encoded in computer programs or software. One of the five fundamental components of an information system. 106

Health Insurance Portability and Accountability Act (HIPAA) The privacy provisions of this 1996 act give individuals the right to access health data created by doctors and other health-care providers. HIPAA also sets rules and limits on who can read and receive a person's health information. 426

Hives In social media, a group of people related by a common interest. 258

Horizontal-market application Software that provides capabilities common across all organizations and industries; examples include word processors, graphics programs, spreadsheets, and presentation programs. 118

Host operating system In virtualization, the operating system that hosts the virtual operating systems. 116

Hot site A utility company that can take over another company's processing with no forewarning. Hot sites are expensive; organizations pay $250,000 or more per month for such services. 441

Href In HTML, the attribute for a hyperlink. 194

HTTPS An indication that a Web browser is http supplement with the SSL/TLS protocol to ensure secure Web page communication. 187

Hyper-social organization An organization that uses social media to transform its interactions with customers, employees, and partners into mutually satisfying relationships with them and their communities. 273

Hyperlink In HTML, a pointer on a Web page to another Web page. A hyperlink contains the URL of the Web page to access when the user clicks the hyperlink. The URL can reference a page on the Web server that generated the page containing the hyperlink, or it can reference a page on another server. 193

Hypertext Markup Language (HTML) A language that defines the structure and layout of Web page content. An HTML tag is a notation used to define a data element for display or other purposes. 193

Hypertext Transfer Protocol (HTTP) A Layer-5 TCP/IP protocol used by browsers and Web servers to process Web pages. 186

Identification The process whereby an information system identifies a user by requiring the user to sign on with a user name and password. 428

Identifier An attribute (or group of attributes) whose value is associated with one and only one entity instance. 156

IEEE 802.3 protocol A standard for wired networks, also called *Ethernet*; it operates at Layers 1 and 2 of the TCP/IP–OSI architecture. Ethernet, the world's most popular LAN protocol, is used on WANs as well. 181

IEEE 802.11 protocol A wireless communications standard, widely used today, that enables access within a few hundred feet. The most popular version of this standard is *IEEE 802.11n*, which allows wireless transmissions of up to 600 Mbps. 181

If ... then ... Format for rules derived from a decision tree (data mining) or by interviewing a human expert (expert systems). 321

Indexing The most important content function of knowledge management applications, which uses keyword search to determine whether content exists and provides a link to its location. 323

Industry-specific solutions An ERP template that is designed to serve the needs of companies or organizations in specific industries. Such solutions save time and lower risk. The development of industry-specific solutions spurred ERP growth. 240

Information (1) Knowledge derived from data, where *data* is defined as recorded facts or figures; (2) data presented in a meaningful context; (3) data processed by summing, ordering, averaging, grouping, comparing, or other similar operations; (4) a difference that makes a difference. 14

Information silos A condition that exists when data are isolated in separated information systems. 222

Information system (IS) A group of hardware, software, data, procedure, and people components that interact to produce information. 8

Information technology (IT) The products, methods, inventions, and standards that are used for the purpose of producing information. 13

Infrastructure as a Service (IaaS) The cloud hosting of a bare server computer or disk drive. 201

Inherent processes The procedures that must be followed to effectively use licensed software. For example, the processes inherent in ERP systems assume that certain users will take specified actions in a particular order. In most cases, the organization must conform to the processes inherent in the software. 228

Input hardware Hardware devices that attach to a computer; includes keyboards, mouse, document scanners, and bar-code (Universal Product Code) scanners. 106

Internet When spelled with a small *i*, as in *internet*, a private network of networks. When spelled with a capital *I*, as in *Internet*, the public internet known as the Internet. 179

Internet Corporation for Assigned Names and Numbers (ICANN) The organization responsible for managing the assignment of public IP addresses and domain names for use on the Internet. Each public IP address is unique across all computers on the Internet. 188

Internet Protocol (IP) A Layer-3 TCP/IP protocol. As the name implies, IP is used on the Internet, but it is used on many other internets as well. The chief purpose of IP is to route packets across an internet. 187

Internet protocols and standards Additions to TCP/IP that enable cloud-hosting vendors to provide processing capabilities in flexible, yet standardized ways. 198

Intranet A private internet (note small *i*) used within a corporation or other organization. 179

Intrusion detection system (IDS) A computer program that senses when another computer is attempting to scan the disk or otherwise access a computer. 420

IP address A series of dotted decimals in a format like 192.168.2.28 that identifies a unique device on a network or internet. With the IPv4 standard, IP addresses have 32 bits. With the IPv6 standard, IP addresses have 128 bits. Today, IPv4 is more common, but IPv6 is gaining popularity. With IPv4, the decimal between the dots can never exceed 255. 188

IP spoofing A type of spoofing whereby an intruder uses another site's IP address as if it were that other site. 417

IPv4 The most commonly used Internet layer protocol; has a four-decimal dotted notation, such as 165.193.123.253. 189

IPv6 An Internet layer protocol that uses 128-bit addresses and is gradually replacing IPv4. 189

Islands of automation The structure that results when functional applications work independently in isolation from one another. Usually problematic because data are duplicated, integration is difficult, and results can be inconsistent. 222

Kerberos A system, developed at MIT, that authenticates users without sending their passwords across a computer network. It uses a complicated system of "tickets" to enable users to obtain services from networks and other servers. 429

Key (1) A column or group of columns that identifies a unique row in a table. (2) A number used to encrypt data. The encryption algorithm applies the key to the original message to produce the coded message. Decoding (decrypting) a message is similar; a key is applied to the coded message to recover the original text. Also referred to as Primary Key. 144

Key escrow A control procedure whereby a trusted party is given a copy of a key used to encrypt database data. 434

Key users Users trained to perform social media (SM) engagement and management tasks. 276

Kilobyte (K) 1,024 bytes. 108

Knowledge management (KM) The process of creating value from intellectual capital and sharing that knowledge with employees, managers, suppliers, customers, and others who need it. 322

LAN device A computing device that includes important networking components, including a switch, a router, a DHCP server, and other elements. 180

Library In version-control collaboration systems, a shared directory that allows access to various documents by means of permissions. 53

License A contract that stipulates how a program can be used. Most specify the number of computers on which the program can be installed, some specify the number of users that can connect to and use the program remotely. Such agreements also stipulate limitations on the liability of the software vendor for the consequences of errors in the software. 116

Lift In market-basket terminology, the ratio of confidence to the base probability of buying an item. Lift shows how much the base probability changes when other products are purchased. If the lift is greater than 1, the change is positive; if it is less than 1, the change is negative. 317

Linkages Process interactions across value chains. Linkages are important sources of efficiencies and are readily supported by information systems. 82

Local area network (LAN) A network that connects computers that reside in a single geographic location on the premises of the company that operates the LAN. The number of connected computers can range from two to several hundred. 178

Localizing software The process by which computer programs are modified to use different human languages and character sets. 455

Lost-update problem A problem that exists in database applications in which two users update the same data item, but only one of those changes is recorded in the data. Can be resolved using locking. 155

Machine code Code that has been compiled from source code and is ready to be processed by a computer. 123

Main memory A set of cells in which each cell holds a byte of data or instruction; each cell has an address, and the CPU uses the addresses to identify particular data items. 107

Maintenance In the context of information systems, (1) to fix the system to do what it was supposed to do in the first place or (2) to adapt the system to a change in requirements. 366

Malware Viruses, worms, Trojan horses, spyware, and adware. 431

Malware definitions Patterns that exist in malware code. Antimalware vendors update these definitions continuously and incorporate them into their products in order to better fight against malware. 433

Management information systems (MIS) The development and use of information systems that help organizations achieve their strategy. 8

Managerial decision A decision that concerns the allocation and use of resources. 37

Many-to-many (N:M) relationship A relationship involving two entity types in which an instance of one type can relate to many instances of the second type, and an instance of the second type can relate to many instances of the first. For example, the relationship between Student and Class is N:M. One student may enroll in many classes, and one class may have many students. Contrast with *one-to-many relationships*. 158

Margin [of a business process] The difference between the value of outputs in a business process and the cost of the process. 79

Market-basket analysis A data mining technique for determining sales patterns. A market-basket analysis shows the products that customers tend to buy together. 316

Mashup The combining of output from two or more Web sites into a single user experience. 279

Maximum cardinality The maximum number of entities that can be involved in a relationship. Common examples of maximum cardinality are 1:N, N:M, and 1:1. 159

Measure The data item of interest on an OLAP report. It is the item that is to be summed, averaged, or otherwise processed in the OLAP cube. Total sales, average sales, and average cost are examples of measures. 311

Megabyte (MB) 1,024KB. 108

Memory swapping The movement of programs and data into and out of memory. If a computer has insufficient memory for its workload, such swapping will degrade system performance. 109

Metadata Data that describe data. 146

Microsoft Exchange A Microsoft product that provides email services. Exchange provides the post office services and programs like Outlook and browsers serve as personal mail boxes. 60

Microsoft Lync A Microsoft product that supports collaboration communication including IM, voice, videoconferencing, screen sharing, and whiteboards. 55

Minimum cardinality The minimum number of entities that must be involved on one side of a relationship. 159

Modem Short for *modulator/demodulator*, a modem converts the computer's digital data into signals that can be transmitted over telephone or cable lines. 182

Modules A suite of applications in an ERP system. 229

Moore's Law A law, created by Gordon Moore, stating that the number of transistors per square inch on an integrated chip doubles every 18 months. Moore's prediction has proved generally accurate in the 40 years since it was made. Sometimes this law is stated that the performance of a computer doubles every 18 months. Although not strictly true, this version gives the gist of the idea. 4

Multi-user processing When multiple users process the database at the same time. 154

My Maps A browser-based mapping system provided by Google that enables users to mash up their content with content provided by others as well as with maps provided by Google. 279

MySQL A popular open source DBMS product that is license-free for most applications. 147

Narrowband Internet communication lines that have transmission speeds of 56 kbps or less. A dial-up modem provides narrowband access. 183

Network A collection of computers that communicate with one another over transmission lines. 178

Network interface card (NIC) A hardware component on each device on a network (computer, printer, etc.) that connects the device's circuitry to the communications line. The NIC works together with programs in each device to implement Layers 1 and 2 of the TCP/IP–OSI hybrid protocol. 180

Neural networks A popular supervised data mining technique used to predict values and make classifications, such as "good prospect" or "poor prospect." 316

Nonvolatile (memory) Memory that preserves data contents even when not powered (e.g., magnetic and optical disks). With such devices, you can turn the computer off and back on, and the contents will be unchanged. 110

Normal forms A classification of tables according to their characteristics and the kinds of problems to which they are subject. 161

Normalization The process of converting poorly structured tables into two or more better-structured tables. 159

Object Management Group (OMG) A software industry standards organization that created a standard set of terms and graphical notations for documenting business processes. 348

Off-the-shelf software Software that is used without making any changes. 120

Off-the-shelf with alterations software Software bought off-the-shelf but altered to fit an organization's specific needs. 120

Office 365 A suite of programs for collaboration. It consists of Lync, SharePoint Online, and hosted Exchange. 55

Office Web Apps License-free Web application versions of Word, Excel, PowerPoint, and OneNote available with Office 365 and with Microsoft SkyDrive. 50

OLAP See *Online analytical processing*. 311

OLAP cube A presentation of an OLAP measure with associated dimensions. The reason for this term is that some products show these displays using three axes, like a cube in geometry. Same as *OLAP report*. 311

Onboard NIC A built-in network interface card. 180

One-of-a-kind application Software that is developed for a specific, unique need, usually for a single company's requirements. 118

One-to-many (1:N) relationship Relationships involving two entity types in which an instance of one type can relate to many instances of the second type, but an instance of the second type can relate to at most one instance of the first. For example, the relationship between *Department* and *Employee* is 1:N. A department may relate to many employees, but an employee relates to at most one department. 158

Online analytical processing (OLAP) A dynamic type of reporting system that provides the ability to sum, count, average, and perform other simple arithmetic operations on groups of data. Such reports are dynamic because users can change the format of the reports while viewing them. 311

Operating system (OS) A computer program that controls the computer's resources. It manages the contents of main memory, processes keystrokes and mouse movements, sends signals to the display monitor, reads and writes disk files, and controls the processing of other programs. 109

Operational decisions Decisions that concern the day-to-day activities of an organization. 37

Optical fiber cable A type of cable used to connect the computers, printers, switches, and other devices on a LAN. The signals on such cables are light rays, and they are reflected inside the glass core of the optical fiber cable. The core is surrounded by a *cladding* to contain the light signals, and the cladding, in turn, is wrapped with an outer layer to protect it. 180

Oracle Database A popular, enterprise-class DBMS product from Oracle Corporation. 147

Organizational feasibility Whether an information system fits within an organization's customer, culture, and legal requirements. 360

Output hardware Hardware that displays the results of the computer's processing. Consists of video displays, printers, audio speakers, overhead projectors, and other special-purpose devices, such as large, flatbed plotters. 107

Outsourcing The process of hiring another organization to perform a service. Outsourcing is done to save costs, to gain expertise, and to free up management time. 393

Packet In a network, a small piece of an electronic message that has been divided into chunks that are sent separately and reassembled at their destination. Used most frequently with reference to the IP protocol in TCP/IP. 187

Parallel installation A type of system conversion in which the new system runs in parallel with the old one and the results of the two are reconciled for consistency. Parallel installation is expensive because the organization incurs the costs of running both systems, but it is the safest form of installation. 366

Partitioned database A distributed database that is divided into nonoverlapping segments and two or more segments are distributed into different geographic locations. 456

Payload The program codes of a virus that causes unwanted or hurtful actions, such as deleting programs or data, or even worse, modifying data in ways that are undetected by the user. 431

PC mules Business professionals who carry one or more personal computers wherever they go. 128

PC virtualization Synonym for *desktop virtualization*. 116

People As part of the five-component framework, one of the five fundamental components of an information system; includes those who operate and service the computers, those who maintain the data, those who support the networks, and those who use the system. 8

Personal DBMS DBMS products designed for personal and small workgroup database applications. Such products are typically used by fewer than 100 users, and normally fewer than 15. Today, Microsoft Access is the only prominent personal DBMS. 155

Personal identification number (PIN) A form of authentication whereby the user supplies a number that only he or she knows. 428

Petabyte (PB) 1,024TB 108

Phased installation A type of system conversion in which the new system is installed in pieces across the organization(s). Once a given piece works, then the organization installs and tests another piece of the system, until the entire system has been installed. 366

Phisher An individual or organization that spoofs legitimate companies in an attempt to illegally capture personal data, such as credit card numbers, email accounts, and driver's license numbers. 416

Phishing A technique for obtaining unauthorized data that uses pretexting via email. The *phisher* pretends to be a legitimate company and sends an email requesting confidential data, such as account numbers, Social Security numbers, account passwords, and so forth. 416

Pilot installation A type of system conversion in which the organization implements the entire system on a limited portion of the business. The advantage of pilot implementation is that if the system fails, the failure is contained within a limited boundary. This reduces exposure of the business and also protects the new system from developing a negative reputation throughout the organization(s). 366

Platform as a Service (Paas) Vendors provide hosted computers, an operating system, and possibly a DBMS. 201

Plunge installation A type of system conversion in which the organization shuts off the old system and starts the new system. If the new system fails, the organization is in trouble: Nothing can be done until either the new system is fixed or the old system is reinstalled. Because of the risk, organizations should avoid this conversion style if possible. Sometimes called *direct installation*. 366

Pooled The situation in which many different organizations use the same physical hardware. 198

Presence indicator In Office 365, an icon colored according to team members' availability. If it is green, it can be clicked to start a Lync conversation with that person. 61

Pretexting A technique for gathering unauthorized information in which someone pretends to be someone else. A common scam involves a telephone caller who pretends to be from a credit card company and claims to be checking the validity of credit card numbers. Phishing is also a form of pretexting. 416

Primary activities In Porter's value chain model, the fundamental activities that create value: inbound logistics, operations, outbound logistics, marketing/sales, and service. 79

Primary key A column in a relation whose values identify a unique row of that relation. 144

Privacy Act of 1974 Federal law that provides protections to individuals regarding records maintained by the U.S. government. 426

Private cloud In-house hosting, delivered via Web service standards, which can be dynamically configured. 200

Private IP address A type of IP address used within private networks and internets. Private IP addresses are assigned and managed by the company that operates the private network or internet. 188

Probable loss The "bottom line" of risk assessment; the likelihood of loss multiplied by the cost of the loss consequences (both tangible and intangible). 425

Problem A *perceived* difference between what is and what ought to be. 38

Procedures Instructions for humans. One of the five fundamental components of an information system. 8

Process blueprint In an ERP application, a comprehensive set of inherent processes for all organizational activities, each of which is documented with diagrams that use a set of standardized symbols. 236

Process effectiveness A measure of how well a process achieves organizational strategy. 220

Process efficiency A measure of the ratio of process outputs to inputs. 220

Project data Data that is part of a collaboration's work product. 43

Project metadata Data that is used to manage a project. Schedules, tasks, budgets, and other managerial data are examples. 43

Protected data Data about candidates' sex, race, religion, sexual orientation, and disabilities that is illegal to use for hiring decisions. 219

Protocol A standardized means for coordinating an activity between two or more entities. 179

Public IP address An IP address used on the Internet. Such IP addresses are assigned to major institutions in blocks by the Internet Corporation for Assigned Names and Numbers (ICANN). Each IP address is unique across all computers on the Internet. 188

Public key/private key A special version of asymmetric encryption that is popular on the Internet. With this method, each site has a public key for encoding messages and a private key for decoding them. 430

Publish results The process of delivering business intelligence to the knowledge workers who need it. 300

Pull publishing In business intelligence (BI) systems, the mode whereby users must request BI results. 300

Push publishing In business intelligence (BI) systems, the mode whereby the BI system delivers business intelligence to users without any request from the users, according to a schedule, or as a result of an event or particular data condition. 300

Quad processor A computer with four CPUs. 107

Query A request for data from a database. 153

Quick Launch A partial list of resources contained within a SharePoint site. 57

RAM (Random Access Memory) Main memory consisting of cells that hold data or instructions. Each cell has an address that the CPU uses to read or write data. Memory locations can be read or written in any order, hence the term *random access*. RAM memory is almost always volatile. 107

Real Simple Syndication (RSS) A standard for subscribing to content sources; similar to an email system for content. 323

Record Also called a *row*, a group of columns in a database table. 144

Regression analysis A type of supervised data mining that estimates the values of parameters in a linear equation. Used to determine the relative influence of variables on an outcome and also to predict future values of that outcome. 315

Relation The more formal name for a database table. 145

Relational database Database that stores data in the form of relations (tables with certain restrictions) and that represents record relationships using foreign keys. 145

Relationship An association among entities or entity instances in an E-R model or an association among rows of a table in a relational database. 157

Remote access system An information system that provides action at a distance, such as telesurgery or telelaw enforcement. 202

Replicated database Database that is stored and processed in two or more locations. Data are duplicated in all of the replications. 456

Report A presentation of data in a structured or meaningful context. 152

Reporting application A business intelligence application that produces information from data by applying reporting tools to that data. 309

Repository A collection of something; a database is a repository of data and a raw material repository is an inventory of raw materials. 84

Resources People or information system applications that are assigned to roles in business processes. 344

RFM analysis A technique for ranking customers according to the recency, frequency, and monetary value of their purchases. 310

Risk The likelihood of an adverse occurrence. 425

Roles Sets of activities in a business process; resources are assigned to roles. 344

Router A special-purpose computer that moves network traffic from one node on a network to another. 188

Row Also called *record*, a group of columns in a database table. 144

RSS See *Real Simple Syndication*. 323

RSS feed A data source that transmits using an RSS standard. The output of an RSS feed is consumed by an RSS reader. 323

RSS reader A program by which users can subscribe to magazines, blogs, Web sites, and other content sources; the reader will periodically check the sources, and, if there has been a change since the last check, it will place a summary of the change and a link to the new content in an inbox. 323

Safeguard Any action, device, procedure, technique, or other measure that reduces a system's vulnerability to a threat. 414

Schedule feasibility Whether an information system will be able to be developed on the timetable needed. 360

Screen-sharing applications Applications that offer users the ability to view the same whiteboard, application, or other display over a network. 46

SEAMS In social media, a process for transitioning organizational messaging from a structured to a dynamic process. 275

Secure Socket Layer (SSL) A protocol that uses both asymmetric and symmetric encryption. SSL is a protocol layer that works between Levels 4 (transport) and 5 (application) of the TCP–OSI protocol architecture. When SSL is in use, the browser address will begin with https://. The most recent version of SSL is called TLS. 430

Security policy Management's policy for computer security, consisting of a general statement of the organization's security program, issue-specific policy, and system-specific policy. 424

Seekers of the truth In social media, a community that shares to learn something, solve a problem, or make something happen. 264

Self-efficacy A person's belief that he or she can successfully perform the tasks required in his or her job. 242

Semantic security Concerns the unintended release of protected information through the release of a combination of reports or documents that are not protected independently. 330

Server(s) A computer that provides some type of service, such as hosting a database, running a blog, publishing a Web site, or selling goods. Server computers are faster, larger, and more powerful than client computers. 111

Server farm A large collection of server computers that is organized to share work and compensate for one another's failures. 111

Server tier In the three-tier architecture, the tier that consists of computers that run Web servers for generating Web pages and responding to requests from browsers. Web servers also process application programs. 191

Server virtualization The process of running two or more operating system instances on the same server. The host operating system runs virtual operating system instances as applications. 117

Service description A document that specifies how a service can be utilized. Web service providers publish the service descption using a standard language called Web Service Description Language (WSDL). 243

Service-oriented architecture (SOA) A design philosophy that specifies that work be organized into encapsulated services that can be accessed using standard protocols. Web services are an implementation of SOA. 242

SharePoint Online An industrial-strength product for content sharing that is hosted by Microsoft. It has rich features and can process massive amounts of data and hundreds of users. SharePoint sites consist of libraries, lists, wikis, surveys, discussion boards, blogs, subsites, and other features that groups use to manage and control group content. 57

Silverlight A browser add-on that was developed by Microsoft to enhance browser features to improve the user interface, to include movies, audio, and animation, and to provide greater programmer control of user activity. 194

Simple Mail Transfer Protocol (SMTP) A Layer-5 TCP/IP protocol used to send email. Normally used in conjunction with other Layer-5 protocols (POP3, IMAP) for receiving email. 187

Site license A license purchased by an organization to equip all the computers on a site with certain software. 116

SLATES Acronym developed by Andrew McAfee that summarizes key characteristics of Enterprise 2.0: search, links, author, tagged, extensions, signaled. 267

Small office/home office (SOHO) A business office with usually fewer than 10 employees often located in the business professional's home. 179

Smart card A plastic card similar to a credit card that has a microchip. The microchip, which holds much more data than a magnetic strip, is loaded with identifying data. Normally requires a PIN. 428

Sniffing A technique for intercepting computer communications. With wired networks, sniffing requires a physical connection to the network. With wireless networks, no such connection is required. 417

Social capital The investment in social relations with expectation of future returns in the marketplace. 268

Social CRM CRM that includes social networking elements and gives the customer much more power and control in the customer/vendor relationship. 265

Social media (SM) The use of information technology to support the sharing of content among networks of users. 258

Social media application providers Companies that operate social media sites. Facebook, Twitter, LinkedIn, and Google are all social media application providers. 261

Social media policy A statement that delineates employees' rights and responsibilities when generating social media content. 283

Social media sponsors Companies and other organizations that choose to support a presence on one or more social media sites. 261

Software Instructions for computers. One of the five fundamental components of an information system. 8

Software as a (free) Service (SaaS) (1) Business model whereby companies (such as Google, Amazon.com, and eBay) provide license-free services based on their software, rather than providing software as a product (by means of software-usage licenses). Software as a service is an example of Web 2.0. (2) Business model whereby companies (Microsoft, Oracle, Salesforce.com) provide services based on their software for a fee. Users need not install software on their computer, but rather pay a fee based on usage of software installed on the seller's servers, somewhere in the cloud. 201

Source code Computer code as written by humans and that is understandable by humans. Source code must be translated into machine code before it can be processed. 123

Spoofing When someone pretends to be someone else with the intent of obtaining unauthorized data. If you pretend to be your professor, you are spoofing your professor. 417

Spyware Programs installed on the user's computer without the user's knowledge or permission that reside in the background and, unknown to the user, observe the user's actions and keystrokes, modify computer activity, and report the user's activities to sponsoring organizations. Malicious spyware captures keystrokes to obtain user names, passwords, account numbers, and other sensitive information. Other spyware is used for marketing analyses, observing what users do, Web sites visited, products examined and purchased, and so forth. 431

SQL Server A popular enterprise-class DBMS product licensed by Microsoft. 147

Static reports Business intelligence documents that are fixed at the time of creation and do not change. 326

Steering committee A group of senior managers from a company's major business functions that works with the CIO to set the IS priorities and decide among major IS projects and alternatives. 393

Storage hardware Hardware that saves data and programs. Magnetic disk is by far the most common storage device, although optical disks, such as CDs and DVDs, also are popular. 107

Stored procedures A computer program stored in the database that is used to enforce business rules. 236

Strategic decision A decision that concerns broad-scope, organizational issues. 37

Strength of a relationship In social media, the likelihood that a person or other organization in a relationship will do something that will benefit the organization. 271

Strong password A password with the following characteristics: nine or more characters; does not contain the user's user name, real name, or company name; does not contain a complete dictionary word, in any language; is different from the user's previous passwords; and contains both upper- and lowercase letters, numbers, and special characters. 22

Structured decision A type of decision for which there is a formalized and accepted method for making the decision. 37

Structured enterprise processes Structured processes that span an organization and support activities in multiple departments. 219

Structured interenterprise information systems IS that support interenterprise processes. Such systems typically involve thousands of users, and solutions to problems require cooperation among different, usually independently owned, organizations. Problems are resolved by meeting, by contract, and sometimes by litigation. 219

Structured interenterprise processes Structured processes that span two or more independent organizations. 219

Structured processes Formally defined, standardized processes that involve day-to-day operations: accepting a return, placing an order and purchasing raw materials are common examples. 217

Structured Query Language (SQL) An international standard language for processing database data. 149

Subscriptions User requests for particular business intelligence results on a stated schedule or in response to particular events. 327

Supervised data mining A form of data mining in which analysts develop a model prior to the analysis and apply statistical techniques to data to estimate values of the parameters of the model. 315

Structured departmental process A structured process that exists to enable departmental employees to fulfill the charter, purpose, and goals of their organizational unit. 217

Supply chain A network of organizations and facilities that transforms raw materials into products delivered to customers. 458

Support In market-basket terminology, the probability that two items will be purchased together. 316

Support activities In Porter's value chain model, the activities that contribute indirectly to value creation: procurement, technology, human resources, and the firm's infrastructure. 79

Swim-lane layout A process diagram layout similar to swim lanes in a swimming pool; each role in the process is shown in its own horizontal rectangle, or lane. 348

Switch A special-purpose computer that receives and transmits data across a network. 180

Switching costs Business strategy of locking in customers by making it difficult or expensive to change to another product or supplier. 88

Symmetric encryption An encryption method whereby the same key is used to encode and to decode the message. 429

Synch The process of synchronizing the data on two or more computers. For example, if you work on your computer at home, when you get to work, you have to synchronize (or synch) your computer at work with any changes you've made on the computer at home. 129

Synchronous communication Information exchange that occurs when all members of a work team meet at the same time, such as face-to-face meetings or conference calls. 44

System A group of components that interact to achieve some purpose. 8

System conversion The process of converting business activity from the old system to the new. 366

Systems analysts IS professionals who understand both business and technology. They are active throughout the systems development process and play a key role in moving the project from conception to conversion and, ultimately, maintenance. Systems analysts integrate the work of the programmers, testers, and users. 360

Systems development The process of creating and maintaining information systems. It is sometimes called *systems analysis and design.* 357

Systems development life cycle (SDLC) The classical process used to develop information systems. The basic tasks of systems development are combined into the following phases: system definition, requirements analysis, component design, implementation, and system maintenance (fix or enhance). 357

Systems thinking The mental activity of making one or more models of the components of a system and connecting the inputs and outputs among those components into a sensible whole, one that explains the phenomenon observed. 7

Table Also called a *file*, a group of similar rows or records in a database. 144

Tag In markup languages such as HTML and XML, notation used to define a data element for display or other purposes. 193

Target The asset that is desired by a security threat. 415

TCP (Transmission Control Protocol) The most popular Layer-4 protocol in the TCP/IP protocol architecture. As a transport protocol, TCP has many functions. One is to break messages into pieces, called *segments*, and provide reliable transport for each segment. 187

TCP/IP–OSI (protocol) architecture A protocol architecture having five layers that evolved as a hybrid of the TCP/IP and the OSI architecture. This architecture is used on the Internet and on most internets. 186

Team survey A form of asynchronous communication in which one team member creates a list of questions and other team members respond. Microsoft SharePoint has built-in survey capability. 46

Technical feasibility Whether existing information technology will be able to meet the needs of a new information system. 360

Technical safeguard Security safeguard that involves the hardware and software components of an information system. 428

Telediagnosis A remote access system used by health care professionals to provide expertise in rural or remote areas. 202

Telelaw enforcement A remote access system that provides law enforcement capability. 202

Telesurgery A remote access system that links surgeons to robotic equipment and patients at a distance. 202

Terabyte (TB) 1,024GB. 108

Test plan Groups of action and usage sequences for validating the capability of new using software. 366

The Internet The internet that is publicly used throughout the world. 179

Thick client A software application that requires programs other than just the browser on a user's computer; that is, that requires code on both client and server computers. 118

Thin client A software application that requires nothing more than a browser and can be run on only the user's computer. 118

Threat A person or organization that seeks to obtain data or other assets illegally, without the owner's permission and often without the owner's knowledge. 414

Three-tier architecture Architecture used by most e-commerce server applications. The tiers refer to three different classes of computers. The user tier consists of users' computers that have browsers that request and process Web pages. The server tier consists of computers that run Web servers and in the process generate Web pages and other data in response to requests from browsers. Web servers also process application programs. The third tier is the database tier, which runs the DBMS that processes the database. 191

Trade-off In project management, a balancing of three critical factors: requirements, cost, and time. 374

Train the trainer Training sessions in which vendors train the organization's employees, called Super Users, to become in-house trainers in order to improve training quality and reduce training expenses. 237

Transport Layer Security (TLS) A protocol, using both asymmetric and symmetric encryption, that works between Levels 4 (transport) and 5 (application) of the TCP/OSI protocol architecture. TLS is the new name for a later version of SSL. 430

Tribe In social media, a group of people related by a common interest. 258

Trigger A computer program stored within the database that is executed when certain conditions arise. Primarily used to maintain database consistency. 236

Trojan horse Virus that masquerades as a useful program or file. A typical Trojan horse appears to be a computer game, an MP3 music file, or some other useful, innocuous program. 431

Tunnel A virtual, private pathway over a public or shared network from the VPN client to the VPN server. 190

Uncertainty Those things we do not know that we do not know. 425

Unified Modeling Language (UML) A series of diagramming techniques that facilitates OOP development. UML has dozens of different diagrams for all phases of system development. UML does not require or promote any particular development process. 156

Uniform resource locator (URL) A document's address on the Web. URLs begin on the right with a top-level domain, and, moving left, include a domain name and then are followed by optional data that locates a document within that domain. 189

Universal Serial Bus (USB) A standard for connecting computers and external devices such as printers, scanners, keyboards, and mice. A USB device is a peripheral device that conforms to the USB standard. 107

Unshielded twisted pair (UTP) cable A type of cable used to connect the computers, printers, switches, and other devices on a LAN. A UTP cable has four pairs of twisted wire. A device called an RJ-45 connector is used to connect the UTP cable into NIC devices. 180

Unstructured decision A type of decision for which there is no agreed-on decision-making method. 38

Unsupervised data mining A form of data mining whereby the analysts do not create a model or hypothesis before running the analysis. Instead, they apply the data mining technique to the data and observe the results. With this method, analysts create hypotheses after the analysis to explain the patterns found. 315

User-generated content (UGC) Content on an organization's social media presence that is contributed by nonemployee users. 284

User tier In the three-tier architecture, the tier that consists of computers that have browsers that request and process Web pages. 191

Usurpation Occurs when unauthorized programs invade a computer system and replace legitimate programs. Such unauthorized programs typically shut down the legitimate system and substitute their own processing. 417

Value According to Porter, the amount of money that a customer is willing to pay for a resource, product, or service. 79

Value chain A network of value-creating activities. 79

Value of social capital Value of social network that is determined by the number of relationships in a social network, by the strength of those relationships, and by the resources controlled by those related. 269

Version control (1) Use of software to control access to and configuration of documents, designs, and other electronic versions of products. (2) The process that occurs when the collaboration tool limits and sometimes even directs user activity. 51

Version management Tracking of changes to documents by means of features and functions that accommodate concurrent work. The means by which version management is done depend on the particular version-management system used; three such systems are wikis, Google Docs, and Windows Live SkyDrive. 49

Vertical-market application Software that serves the needs of a specific industry. Examples of such programs are those used by dental offices to schedule appointments and bill patients, those used by auto mechanics to keep track of customer data and customers' automobile repairs, and those used by parts warehouses to track inventory, purchases, and sales. 118

Videoconferencing Communication technology that enables online conferencing using video. 46

Viral hook An inducement that causes someone to share an ad, link, file, picture, movie, or other resource with friends and associates over the Internet. 260

Viral marketing A marketing method used in the Web 2.0 world in which *users* spread news about products and services to one another. 279

Virtual machines A computer program that presents the appearance of an independent operating system within a second host operating system. The host can support multiple virtual machines, possibly running different operating system programs (Windows, Linux), each of which is assigned assets such as disk space, devices, network connections, over which it has control. 116

Virtual meeting A meeting in which participants do not meet in the same place and possibly not at the same time. 45

Virtual private network (VPN) A WAN connection alternative that uses the Internet or a private internet to create the appearance of private point-to-point connections. In the IT world, the term *virtual* means something that appears to exist that does not exist in fact.

Here, a VPN uses the public Internet to create the appearance of a private connection. 189

Virtualization The process by which multiple operating systems share the same computer hardware, usually a server. 116

Virus A computer program that replicates itself. 431

Volatile (memory) Data that will be lost when the computer or device is not powered. 110

Vulnerability An opening or a weakness in a security system. Some vulnerabilities exist because there are no safeguards or because the existing safeguards are ineffective. 414

Wide area network (WAN) A network that connects computers at different geographic locations. 178

WAN wireless A communications system that provides wireless connectivity to a wide area network. 183

Web The Internet-based network of browsers and servers that process HTTP or HTTPS. 187

Web 2.0 A loose grouping of capabilities, technologies, business models, and philosophies that characterize new and emerging business uses of the Internet. 277

Web farm A facility that runs multiple Web servers. Work is distributed among the computers in a Web farm so as to maximize throughput. 193

Web page Document encoded in HTML that is created, transmitted, and consumed using the World Wide Web. 191

Web server programs that run on a server-tier computer and that manage HTTP traffic by sending and receiving Web pages to and from clients and by processing client requests. 192

Web service An encapsulated software service provided over the Internet using standard protocols. 243

Web Service Description Language (WSDL) A standardized language for publishing Web service descriptions. 243

Web service standards SOA standards that utilize HTTP and are used to specify how computers interoperate. 200

Webinar A virtual meeting in which attendees can view a common presentation and possibly each other on computer screens. 46

Wi-Fi Protected Access (WPA and WPA2) An improved wireless security standard developed by the IEEE 802.11 committee to fix the flaws of the Wired Equivalent Privacy (WEP) standard. Only newer wireless hardware uses this technique. 429

Windows Live SkyDrive A cloud-based file storage location supported by Microsoft that provides free file storage and Web-based versions of Word, Excel, PowerPoint, and OneNote. 50

Wired Equivalent Privacy (WEP) A wireless security standard developed by the IEEE 802.11 committee that was insufficiently tested before it was deployed in communications equipment. It has serious flaws. 429

Wireless NIC (WNIC) Devices that enable wireless networks by communicating with wireless access points. Such devices can be cards that slide into the PCMA slot or they can be built-in, onboard devices. WNICs operate according to the 802.11 protocol. 180

Work breakdown structure (WBS) A hierarchy of the tasks required to complete a project; for a large project, it might involve hundreds or thousands of tasks. 371

Workflow control Use of information systems to monitor the execution of a work team's processes; to ensure that actions are taken at appropriate times and to prohibit the skipping of steps or tasks. 54

Worm A virus that propagates itself using the Internet or some other computer network. Worm code is written specifically to infect another computer as quickly as possible. 431

WPA2 See *Wi-Fi Protected Access.* 429

XML See *eXtensible Markup Language.* 194

Index